SA Lit

SA Lit

Beyond 2000

Edited by

MICHAEL CHAPMAN

and

MARGARET LENTA

UNIVERSITY OF KwaZulu-Natal Press

Published in 2011 by University of KwaZulu-Natal Press
Private Bag X01
Scottsville, 3209
South Africa
Email: books@ukzn.ac.za
Website: www.ukznpress.co.za

© 2011 University of KwaZulu-Natal

All rights reserved. No part of this publication may be reproduced or transmitted in any form or by any means, electronic or mechanical, including photocopying, recording, or any information storage and retrieval system, without prior permission in writing from University of KwaZulu-Natal Press.

ISBN: 978-1-86914-212-4

Managing editor: Sally Hines
Editor: Alison Lockhart
Typesetter: Patricia Comrie
Proofreader: Juliet Haw
Indexer: Catherine Dubbeld
Cover design: MDesign
Cover photograph: Original photograph of Flatfoot Dance Company taken by Val Adamson

Printed and bound by Interpak Books, Pietermaritzburg

Contents

Preface . . . vii
Acknowledgements . . . ix

Introduction: SA Lit beyond 2000? . . . 1
    Michael Chapman

1. The End of 'South African' Literary History? Judging 'National' Fiction in a Transnational Era . . . 19
    Leon de Kock

2. Expanding 'South Africanness': Debut Novels . . . 50
    Margaret Lenta

3. On the Street with Vladislavić, Mhlongo, Moele and Others . . . 69
    Sally-Ann Murray

4. Breaking the Silence: Black and White Women's Writing . . . 97
    Eva Hunter and Siphokazi Jonas

5. Silenced by Freedom? Nadine Gordimer after Apartheid . . . 119
    Ileana Dimitriu

6. Reconciling Acts: Theatre beyond the Truth and Reconciliation Commission . . . 137
    Marcia Blumberg

7. The Road That Calls: From Poor Theatre to Theatres of Excess . . . 159
    Miki Flockemann

8. 'Sequestered from the winds of history': Poetry and Politics . . . 177
    Michael Chapman

9	Of 'Chisels' and 'Jack Hammers': Afrikaans Poetry 2000–2009 *Louise Viljoen*	203
10	Antjie Krog: Towards a Syncretic Identity *Helize van Vuuren*	224
11	Technauriture: Multimedia Research and Documentation of African Oral Performance *Russell H. Kaschula*	243
12	Family Albums and Statements from the Dock of History: Autobiographical Writing 1999–2009 *Annie Gagiano*	259
13	Healing the Wounds of History: South African Indian Writing *Devarakshanam Betty Govinden*	283
14	Zulu Literature: New Beginnings *Nhlanhla Mathonsi and Gugu Mazibuko*	299
15	Representing the African Diaspora: Coetzee, Breytenbach, Gordimer, Mda, Pinnock *J.U. Jacobs*	315
16	Postcolonial Pomosexuality: Queer/Alternative Fiction after *Disgrace* *Cheryl Stobie*	335
17	Literature and Ecology in Southern Africa *Dan Wylie*	353
Contributors		373
Index		377

Preface

This book offers new essays on the current literary scene in South Africa. The arrangement is broadly generic, with contributions on fiction, drama, poetry and autobiography preceded by Leon de Kock's essay which, as explored in the introduction, poses the challenging question of what beyond 2000 – rhetorically, beyond J.M. Coetzee's *Disgrace* (1999) – might constitute 'South African Literature'. Following the generic essays are contributions on thematic/conceptual topics such as the African diaspora, postcolonial 'pomosexuality', oral performance, and literature and ecology. To devote separate entries to South African Indian literature, Zulu literature, Afrikaans poetry and poetry in English could be interpreted as a return to pre-1990 race and language classifications. The reality is more complex: in the light of a history of division, many writers continue to draw on the experiences of group affiliation as a spur to their literary imaginings. The intention is to broaden interest and involvement.

Recurrent preoccupations or patterns identify relationships between the local and the global, or the national and the transnational. A specific community – say, the Indian community – is alert to both its 'settler' presence and its histories of migration. Given the differences between indentured (mainly Hindu) and passenger (mainly Muslim) Indians, however, is the conceptualisation of a singular community appropriate? Was it ever appropriate? Similarly, Afrikaans poetry reaches beyond any single 'class' of accent while previously silent, or silenced, minorities – for example, gay men and women, descendants of Malay slaves, street children and border-crossers, both legal and illegal from the rest of Africa – are given voices. An increasing number of women writers cover a spectrum of concerns, including those of a heterogeneous middle class. Older journeys from rural innocence to urban experience are erased as the AIDS pandemic travels its destructive path (see Chapters 3 and 14).

These are some of the critical surveys, a term that wishes to suggest reasonable coverage while avoiding claims of comprehensiveness. With writing in English enjoying most attention, there are lacunae: major Afrikaans novelists such as André Brink and Etienne van Heerden, to name only two, do not figure in the contents; African-language literature is not widely represented; the essays on poetry grant greater prominence to written forms than to the city-wise oral voices of slams and festivals.

The contraction of South African Literature to SA Lit plays, ironically, on the authority once lent to designations like Eng Lit. Here, categories are regarded as provisional (the lists of references at the end of each of the essays, nonetheless, point to the scope of the literary output in the period of focus). Commenting on an upsurge of 'writing crime' in South Africa, Anthony Egan at the *Mail & Guardian* Literary Festival (3–5 September 2010) asks, 'Is crime the new South African political literature?' The question awaits deliberation elsewhere. What is apparent, though, is that the 'political' is no longer easily separable from the civic, the ecological, or the spiritual dimension (Chapter 5 on Nadine Gordimer explores such interconnections in the Nobel laureate's more recent work). Generally, the state has retreated as antagonist, 'post-apartheid'.

The term 'post-apartheid' is of course problematic. A sociological analysis might question whether, in terms of economic consequences, apartheid has actually ended for many who, in a vastly unequal society, continue to live in poverty. However, in the subjective, experiential terrain, the terrain of literary expression, *then* is distinct from its counterpart *now*. Even the *now* requires its own gradations, not only after the unbannings of 1990 (signalling a 'new South Africa'), but also after the 1996 Truth and Reconciliation Commission (TRC). Perhaps surprisingly, it is theatre, the stage, which, beyond 2000, is the heir of the initial output of TRC writings; Antjie Krog's *Country of my Skull* (1998) remaining the exemplar (see Chapter 6 as well as Chapter 10 on Krog).

In this vein, a retrospective overview of the contributions gives rise to the observation that, as suggested in the introduction, a critical concern with difference in the 1990s has shifted to a concern with connection. If indeed this is so, it is appropriate that attention shifts from Coetzee's refusal to impose the Self on the Other (that is how several influential critics, initially responding to Coetzee in the 1990s, interpret his fiction) to Krog's pursuit of what Helize van Vuuren refers to in Chapter 10 as a 'syncretic identity'.

Such tentative turns point if not post-apartheid, or even post-post-apartheid, then at least beyond 2000.

Acknowledgements

The editors wish to thank all the authors whose work appears in this book. Several of the articles appeared in earlier forms in *Current Writing* 21 (1&2) (2009). Others are new and appear for the first time here. All have been independently peer-reviewed for this publication.

Michael Chapman thanks the National Research Foundation for its generous grant to him, which has been important in the production of this book. The opinions expressed within it, whether by individual authors or by the editors, are entirely their own.

Introduction
SA Lit beyond 2000?

MICHAEL CHAPMAN

The impulse to look beyond 2000 was provoked by Leon de Kock's article, 'Does South African Literature Still Exist?' (2005). It is a question that is applicable not only to the essays offered here, but also to several of the critical works and articles of the last decade to which I shall refer in this introduction. How do we delineate a field, 'South African Literature', in relation to descriptive and definitional terms that have begun to be used with some persistence: post-apartheid literature; South African literature in/after the transition, or after the 1996 Truth and Reconciliation Commission (TRC); South African literary culture *now* as distinct from *then*; South African literature in the transnational moment, 'transnational' denoting the nation caught in movement – possibly transformational movement – 'in-between' local and global demands. If post-apartheid usually means after the unbannings of 1990, or after the first democratic elections of 1994, or in/after the transition, then beyond 2000 begins to mark a quantitative and qualitative shift from the immediate 'post' years of the 1990s to another 'phase'.[1] It is a phase in which books tangential to heavy politics, or even to local interest, have begun to receive national recognition. An example is the 2009 double prize-winning novel, *The Rowing Lesson* (2008),[2] by Anne Landsman, in which a father-daughter relationship exceeds the shaping force of any local scene. There is also Michiel Heyns's award-winning *Bodies Politic* (2008),[3] a novel set in early twentieth-century suffragette England. It is a phase in which the dominant figure of the 1990s, J.M. Coetzee, in his quieter, suburban Australian novels (2005, 2007a) or even in his self-deprecating *Summertime* (2009), appears to have gone beyond his traumatised vision of his home country: that is, beyond *Disgrace* (1999). But if Landsman or Heyns inhabits a landscape outside of any apartheid/anti-apartheid narrative, the winning book in the 2009 Sunday Times-Alan Paton Prize category for non-fiction, Peter Harris's *In a Different Time* (2008), returns us to the trial of the Delmas Four: African National Congress (ANC) Umkhonto we Sizwe operatives who, in the late 1980s, militarily opposed the apartheid state. As the lawyer who defended the Four – at times in the face of their own reluctance to grant the charges or the court even a modicum of legitimacy – Harris's vivid 'translation' of legalities into human drama alerts us not only to a recurrent feature of literature from this country – its genre-crossing potential – but also to the fact that *then* and *now* retain a power of symbiotic memory. A similar symbiosis is characteristic of prize-winning novels in the 2010 round of literary awards. Imraan Coovadia's *High Low In-between* (2009) has its globe-trotting photographer curtailed by his Durban-based South African Indian family while Sally-Ann Murray's *Small Moving Parts* (2009) attaches its young protagonist's coming-of-age to her white working-class environment in old apartheid South Africa. Phases of chronology are ordering conveniences rather than neatly separable entities.

In posing the question, 'Does South African Literature still exist?' – the question supersedes its rhetorical provocation – De Kock reminds us that he himself is a key interpreter of the literature. His introduction to the special 2001 issue of *Poetics Today* (subsequently published in book form – see De Kock, Bethlehem and Laden 2004) developed the metaphor of the 'seam'. This is taken from Noël Mostert's monumental historical novel *Frontiers*, in which it is posited that 'if there is a hemispheric seam to the world between Occident and Orient, it must be along the eastern seaboard of Africa' (1992: xv). For De Kock the seam – a stitching instrument which seeks to suture the incommensurate – illustrates the problem of defining not only a South African national imaginary (the question of identity recurs in post-1990 fictional and critical response), but – more to the point here – a field of South African Literature. We inhabit a culture of largely 'unresolved difference'; of 'radical heterogeneity'; a site where 'difference and sameness are hitched together, always uneasily' (De Kock 2001: 272–6). Such a conundrum of interstitial identities, of 'identities caught between stasis and change' (Attwell and Harlow 2000: 3), of 'cultural bastardization' (Breytenbach 1998: 263), or 'creolisation' (Nuttall 2009: 21) – all typified as the creativity of our many differences – simultaneously suggests its own negation: the perverse difference of apartheid, its enforced separations. In contrast, sameness as the cohesion of multiple groups and languages in the single geographical space called South Africa (our 'bodies politic'?) may signal, again simultaneously, a negative corollary: the erasure of local distinctiveness, of difference. In the master narratives of Western provenance, the current is neo-liberal globalisation.

Introduction

A key pursuit since the 1990s has been how to cope with the concept and practice of 'difference'. It is a challenging puzzle at the heart of the 'post-' debate (post-apartheid, postcolonialism, postmodernism) not only in South Africa, but also in northern institutions of society and culture.[4] How does Western Europe, which still wishes to see itself as predominantly white and bourgeois, as does the US, cope with its own increasing and heterogeneous 'minorities'? Whereas De Kock's summarising metaphor is the seam, David Attwell adopts Fernando Ortiz's (1995) Cuban-inspired notion of transculturation, formulated in the late 1940s: 'multiple processes, a dialogue in both directions [centre to periphery, periphery to centre] and, most importantly, processes of cultural destruction followed by reconstruction on entirely new terms' (Attwell 2005: 17–19). In illustration, Attwell demonstrates that black modernity in South Africa has never constituted a linear path from oppression to liberation, whether cultural or political, but has poached from both the West and Africa to fashion its own temporal habitations. Isabel Hofmeyr – looking first at John Bunyan's *The Pilgrim's Progress* as a missionary text (2004), then at the Indian Ocean seam (2008) – unravels the binaries of centre/periphery and coloniser/colonised as she charts new transnational circuits of texts and identities. Michael Titlestad (2004) utilises jazz as a metaphor to disrupt fixed categories of sense-making and it is the notion of complicity which, in the light of TRC testimony, Mark Sanders (2002) uses to dislodge any simple alternatives of conviction and challenge. He explores, among other cases, that of the major Afrikaans poet N.P. van Wyk Louw whose commitment to Afrikaner identity led him at the same time to project an ethical commitment beyond the apartheid system in which he was complicit. 'Entanglement' is Sarah Nuttall's shorthand for a condition of the 'now': 'So often the story of post-apartheid has been told within the register of difference – frequently for good reasons, but often, too, ignoring the intricate overlaps that mark the present and, at times and in important ways, the past as well' (2009: 1). Like Sanders, Nuttall seeks 'human foldedness' (6).

What might such foldedness invoke? My own literary history, *Southern African Literatures* (2003 [1996]), provoked debate on whose story shapes our literature and identity.[5] My collection of essays, *Art Talk, Politics Talk* (2006), is subtitled 'A Consideration of Categories'. Attwell argues for 'rewriting modernity' and for a 'more heterogeneous and cosmopolitan dialogue' (2005: 14). Hofmeyr (2004), Loren Kruger (2002), Ronit Frenkel (2010), and others open outwards to Indian Ocean transculturation. Achille Mbembe (2002) turns his analytical lens on what he terms the two major historiographical traditions in decolonised Africa, of nationalist Marxism and nativism, neither of which he believes retains explanatory persuasion in the time-space compression of global circulation. It is by returning to and repositioning 'minor' stories that Kruger seeks human foldedness in the *now*. Achmat Dangor's protagonists, she argues, elude the grasp of the reader looking to identify with the certainties of anti-apartheid feeling: his protagonists, the bastardised progeny of Indian-Malay slaves at the Cape, of indigenised Cape Muslims, are not suitable anti-apartheid subjects; they are neither the victims of apartheid violence nor activists against it. Accordingly, Dangor's stories (1981, 1997) are neither anti-apartheid nor post-apartheid, but 'post-anti-apartheid' (Kruger 2002: 35). (The same appellation may be applied to Yvette Christiansë's collection of poetry, *Imprendehora*, 2009.)

Human foldedness, then, does not denote a comfort zone. Out of its sutured folds – in Titlestad's study (2004) – emerges the stranger who jolts our habitual awareness. Here Titlestad returns to a Levinasian ethical path: respect the radical Otherness of the other, which in the 1990s lent general direction to criticism on Coetzee.[6] In Titlestad, however, the stranger has shed its Levinasian ambiguity as either human or deity to become a more tangible character in the ordinary, but marginalised life of the South African city: a stranger because, as in Dangor's fiction, neglected in apartheid/liberation narratives. Out of human foldedness Ashraf Jamal (2005) plucks neither heroes nor victims; neither Njabulo S. Ndebele's (2006 [1991]) return to the ordinary nor Titlestad's stranger, but an ethical 'extraordinariness'. Recollecting Albie Sachs's (1990) desire for culture beyond the weapons of struggle, Jamal gathers together theorists of 'play' (Homi Bhabha, for one, is put to the service of his argument) in, some might say, a new romantic need to be free of all constraining categories. Citing Brett Bailey's theatre as a daring exploration of 'unresolved heterogeneity' (150) – De Kock is marshalled to Jamal's side – Jamal urges us all to revel in our category explosions. He wishes us to abolish vanity and self-possession, to break whatever the 'sage wisdom' that would be an excuse to keep the imagination in thrall and, in a psychic rupture of our systems, begin to love the South Africa that has too often been characterised as an unlovable place (159–62). Tying commitment to place with a greater measure of groundedness than Jamal, both Ari Sitas (2004) and Brenda Cooper (2008) energise the value of people's ordinary agency in African socio-scapes of difficult transition, while for Meg Samuelson (2008) our home beyond the threshold of transition may begin to lay the foundation of a new national culture, a signal being bold voices among young black women. In this vein and eschewing the demeaning categorisation of 'coconut' or 'cheese girl' (white inside), Asandi Phewa (2009) – whose play *A Face Like Mine* was first performed at the Grahamstown National Arts Festival in 2009 – agrees with Mbali Kgosidintsi of the theatre company Right 2

Introduction

Speak, a company that focuses its performances on the struggles of a new generation of South African women to redefine blackness:

> I know where I'm going but not what or who I am leaving behind and that is where the search for identity comes in. There is this trend for those of us living in Sandton to still go back to the township every Sunday to reconnect. But when you know who you are you don't have to hold onto anything (Kgosidintsi 2009: 27).

Beyond a politics of exclusion (Samuelson reminds us of the deathly face of xenophobia in the new South Africa), we hear voices that in the liberal-Marxist culture wars of the 1980s would have been ignored, voices that are not prominent either in international postcolonial criticism's fixation on big names (Soyinka, Rushdie, Coetzee, etc.). In elevating as 'national marker' not Athol Fugard's intricate moral explorations but Brett Bailey's spectacular disruptions (the Xhosa past, Shakespeare's *Macbeth*, whatever or whoever can be stirred into the witches' brew, or the *inyanga*'s muthi).[7] Jamal (2005: 161) has it that Ndebele – and the generation of mainly white academics who embraced his return to the ordinary – got it all wrong. Rather, South Africa is a country of chaotic intervention. Ndebele (2007), for his part, has limited truck with endless exhortations of difference, endless deferrals of mimetic consequence. Seeking instead 'fine lines from the box', he declares: '[T]he challenge of the future in South Africa is nation building: no more, no less. It is the massive task of creating one nation out of the institutional divisions that currently beset it' (24). Ndebele does not entertain the question as to whether South Africa has a national imaginary, or whether South African Literature still exists.

* * *

Ndebele notwithstanding, I wish to pursue a few recent studies which focus on the issues that I have somewhat brutally summarised so far. Similarly to Hofmeyr, Sanders and (in his meticulously sourced interpretative history of South African literary censorship) Peter D. McDonald (2009) and Andrew van der Vlies in *South African Textual Cultures: White, Black, Read All Over* (2007) turn to textual cultures or, as it is nowadays more commonly denoted, book history. Van der Vlies's by now familiar 'post'-inspired conclusion is that a singular delineation of South Africa or South African (see Chipkin 2007) is defeated by a history of radical heterogeneity (that is, De Kock's 'seam'). In the same way the category 'South African Literature' and, by extension, its equivalent national literature remains problematic in a country in which territorial borders were colonial conveniences and politics was inhospitable to fundamental requirements of converting groups into a nation. These include the pursuit of widespread, multiclass literacy in a common language and the example, or the pursuit, of a common, functioning society.

Most critics would concur with Van der Vlies's conclusion that in South Africa (in fact, in the colonies or postcolonies, wherever the particular periphery) the 'literary', as a category, has been authorised not entirely by the local response, but by 'complex, multipolar, fragmented, often inconsistent and at best self-interested Anglophone metropolitan (both British and North American) fields of publishers, reviewers and readers' (2007: 175). The character of a national cultural identity, whether in South Africa, Nigeria, Australia, etc., is, accordingly, ambivalent. 'Whose language, culture or story can be said to have authority in South Africa,' I asked in the preface to *Southern African Literatures*, 'when the end of apartheid has raised challenging questions as to what it is to be a South African, whether South Africa is a nation and, if so, what is its mythos?' (2003: xiv).

The value of Van der Vlies's study is not to be found in his introductory rehearsal of arguments as to whether or not it is possible satisfactorily to write literary history. Whether it is or is not, literary histories of different persuasions will continue to be written (see not only Chapman, but also Heywood [2004], Van Coller [2006] and Attridge and Attwell [forthcoming 2012]). Rather, the value of *South African Textual Cultures* is to be found in its contribution to book history. Whereas literary criticism is concerned primarily with the 'meaning' of the text, with its narrative, its poetic, its dramatic shape, book history explores how these meanings, these aesthetic configurations, are influenced by factors beyond the control of authors themselves: by publishing pressures, the ruling discourse of reviewing, censorship, educational institutionalisation, the literary-prize culture. In the case of South African Literature – as Van der Vlies argues in several case studies – South African writers have often had their achievement sanctioned in zones of reception between the metropole and the colony. How did British reviewers initially receive Olive Schreiner's *The Story of an African Farm* (1883)? Originally published in England, the book would have had to satisfy several nineteenth-century British expectations. As literature, *African Farm* was deemed by some to be second-rate. But, then again, by others in Britain *African Farm* was identified as what today we would call a proto-feminist text. More surprisingly (in anticipation of postcolonialism?), Schreiner's book was seen as typical of the colonies where margins produce not the central, but the hybrid subject (Van der Vlies 2007: 21–45).

Introduction

Turning to Coetzee's *In the Heart of the Country* (1976), we are reminded by Van der Vlies that there was a significant difference between the edition of this novel published in Johannesburg (by Ravan Press) and the editions published abroad. In the South African edition Magda's stream of consciousness is filtered into Afrikaans (her mother tongue); in the international editions, totally in English, the reader, if the claustrophobic Afrikaner Calvinist mental landscape is to be permitted its full effect, must make a linguistic leap from the English on the page to an imaginatively transliterated Afrikaans syntax and rhythm. Reception abroad emphasised the universality of a tortured soul; local reception spoke of religious and sexual trauma according to which Magda's anguish is partly provoked by the 'sin' of her father's fucking his 'non-white' servant. To accentuate the local in Coetzee in the 1970s helped English departments in South Africa wean syllabuses from the Leavisian Great Tradition. Ironically, English departments today, having to justify the study of literature within a so-called developmental state where literacy training is a prerogative, probably prefer the international Coetzee. Such shifts of reception in Van der Vlies's conclusion to his case study of Coetzee neatly summarise his own 'book history' purpose: Coetzee in the 1970s tacitly recognised (in his English and Afrikaans Ravan Press text) that he was contributing to a South African Literature, even as *In the Heart of the Country* contributed to his project of rendering such a category problematic (2007: 134–54).

Does such a project lead us to a situation – familiar to the postcolonies – in which the 'locality' is once again subsumed by a global imperative or, to revert to an older discourse, by an ongoing 'colonisation'? Are we to applaud the fact that books outside of or tangential to South African localities show a resurgence of prize-winning potential in South Africa? Or do we endorse what the Marxist-inclined commentator is likely to say: know the ideological predispositions of the adjudicators to know to what kind of book they will award a prize?

In the light of this, I return to De Kock's article 'Does South African Literature Still Exist?' and complete his title, 'South African Literature is Dead, Long Live Literature in South Africa'. To pursue such considerations, or rather reconsiderations, of category can be liberating. Tired of anti-apartheid literary realism, for instance, De Kock (2005: 80) wishes to read what appeals to him, whether it is politically correct or not, whether its references are South African or not. (The tarnishing of the 'rainbow nation' – Coetzee's *Disgrace* is metonymic – is severely felt in literary circles.) Hofmeyr utilises book history to suggest that Bunyan's *The Pilgrim's Progress* in its travels along the missionary circuits of Africa requires us to consider the space of empire, both intellectually and economically, as a difficult interrelationship, rather than a neat separation of 'metropole' and 'colonies'.

Should *The Pilgrim's Progress* – a 'classic' of English Literature, according to F.R. Leavis (1962 [1952]: 206) – be included in a classification, South African Literature, or Literature in South Africa?

As I have already suggested of De Kock's project, his question is not meant to be merely rhetorical.[8] There remains a historical need to anchor literatures, whether from South Africa, Africa, or any other peripheries of the North Atlantic circuit, somewhere in the world: somewhere shaped by the priorities of particular literary works. Whatever critics or reviewers in the metropole might have said about Schreiner or say about Coetzee, reception from the South African focal point cannot ignore the immediate context. There is in the literature of South Africa the shared experience of colonialism in its abrasive, economic form attendant on a strong and permanent 'settler' population. As a result, the racial theories, practices and values of Europe have featured prominently in the language and texts of literary response. Transitions from traditional to modern loyalties in aggressive, industrialising economies have led to swift, often desperate disjunctions in both literature and life. In these contexts the challenge of urbanisation has characterised forms of expression in several languages and in oral and written modes. The consequence is that any history of South African Literature, whatever the transnational allure, cannot confine its field to those works that adjust their local specificity to a generic (individual, liberal, middle-class, whatever) international 'horizon of expectation' (see Jauss 1982). This is not to deny Van der Vlies's conclusion that given South Africa's peculiar amalgamation of the West in Africa, its literary output will continue both to invite and to resist description in national terms (2007: 175). It is to be cautious, however, of Van der Vlies's attendant conclusion that an ever-growing body of the writing will be published both in South Africa and abroad. This will not be the case. Only those writers whose work meets an internationally acknowledged horizon of expectation – novelists in English, the novel being the most accessible travelling form – are likely to be read worldwide. If my argument has avoided reducing a passage of debate to a narrow lane of global travellers, then the category, South African Literature, continues to have value in its persistence.

It is a persistence not really at odds with De Kock's question as to whether South African Literature still exists. As we should have understood by now, his is a suitably qualified question that does not ask for any emphatic 'yes' or 'no'. Instead, it encourages an interrogation of the category that is the purpose of this introduction: an interrogation that is at the core also of two further recent studies, Shane Graham's *South African Literature after the Truth Commission* (2009) and Monica Popescu's *South African Literature beyond the Cold War* (2010). For both authors the key element is the mapping, or remapping, of the literary terrain. Utilising Gilles Deleuze and Félix Guattari's (1987) metaphor of the 'rhizome' Graham seeks an 'anti-cartographic map' of indeterminacy and flexibility as appropriate to what he identifies as the challenge facing writers after the TRC. South Africa after the TRC, he states, 'exhibits a collective sense of loss, mourning and elegy, as well as a sense of disorientation amid rapid changes in the physical and social landscape' (2009: 1). Such changes necessitate new forms of 'literal and figurative mapping, of space, place and memory' (1). The last is seen to be particularly crucial: how to position the TRC not as a final truth but as a 'well-stocked archive' (3) on which to draw sustenance in the process of ongoing transformation, both psychological and material. In short, how do we avoid freezing the 'liberation' moment into new sectional myths and new regimes of power? The writers whom Graham sees, at least in particular works, as most alert to the dangers of memorialisation, as most attuned to mapping as 'palimpsest' (14–18) showing not just fixed locations in space, but also trajectories through time-space are: Antjie Krog, Ingrid de Kok, Sindiwe Magona, Achmat Dangor, Ivan Vladislavić, Phaswane Mpe, K. Sello Duiker, Aziz Hassim, Anne Landsman, Zoë Wicomb and Zakes Mda.

Of the above names Wicomb and Vladislavić feature also in Popescu's mapping. Her study seeks creative interactions between two strands of postcolonial theory (colonial discourse analysis and Marxism) in order to turn the 'post-' gaze from what she sees as its own fixity: the West versus the rest, or the South always writing back to the North. Rather, drawing on her close understanding of the former Eastern Europe – she is a Romanian teaching in Canada – Popescu seeks a model of interpretation that, linking the postcolonial project to conditions of the Cold War, eschews 'vertical connections with tutelary Western societies' and focuses instead on '(bi-) lateral relations with largely overlooked cultures' (2010: 21). Her particular 'horizontal' mapping identifies reciprocal influences throughout the twentieth century between Eastern Europe and South Africa. The approach offers refreshing angles on, among others, the Nobel laureates Nadine Gordimer and J.M. Coetzee. An 'East European' trace – Popescu avers – is a recurring feature of Gordimer's work from the departure of East European Jewish immigrants in search of a new life in South Africa ('My Father Leaves Home', in *Jump*, 1991) to the story, 'Karma' (in *Loot*, 2003), which through spiritual refraction pursues the path of the vulnerable young woman, Elena, amid the economic chaos following the dissolution of the Soviet Union and Russia's embrace of a capitalist society. Coetzee's *The Master of Petersburg* (1994) is seen as formulating the anxieties of waiting in transition, the Dostoevsky analogy having pertinence, post-1989, to both Eastern Europe and South Africa. Unlike Alex La Guma's *A Soviet Journey* (1978) which idealised the Soviet model – Popescu is somewhat scathing of the naivety of early South African communists – Wicomb's *David's Story* (2001), Popescu argues, explores the moral confusion, the breakdown of teleological narratives, as a work of fiction that, again post-1989, resonates with changes in literary and scholarly debates over the aims and form of history writing. Similarly nuanced narratives are identified in Mandla Langa's *The Memory of Stones* (2000) and Vladislavić's *Propaganda by Monuments* (1996). In Vladislavić's case, 'the space-time condensation specific to the age of globalization' ensures that 'signifiers of historical moments happening thousands of miles away on a different continent can be instantaneously translated into objects which appeal to the South African population' (Popescu 2010: 23).

Graham in 'shout lines' on the cover of Popescu's book acknowledges her purpose as similar to his own: to recognise that 'South African literary studies in the 21st century are taking a transnational turn'. As I have suggested, the turn is not so decisive. One may argue, in fact, that South African literary studies have always found points of intersection with other literary cultures. A challenge of the 1970s in a climate of Leavisite adulation in English departments, paradoxically, was to lend not a transnational, but a local currency to writers such as Pringle, Schreiner, Campbell, Plomer and others, who had tended to be received in South Africa, if at all, as offshoots of British traditions. Despite this, one understands the spirit of Graham's observation: the world, post-1989, has entered a new comparative episteme. As in politics so in literature the paradigm is no longer that of two achievements in two Western European languages from two nation states; neither – despite the postcolonial vertical axis – is the paradigm that of decolonisation: the West versus the rest. Instead, we have a proliferation of new migrations: patterns at once creative and traumatic. Graham is alert to the complexity of this post-1989 comparative mapping when he quotes with trepidation Fredric Jameson's 'crisis of historicity' (1991: 6), that is, a forgetting of the past in a postmodern 'depthlessness' of global culture. Seeking to contribute to a non-parochial, wide-reaching South African 'national project' – in South Africa itself the phrase unfortunately flows too easily off the tongues of opportunistic politicians or starry-eyed World Cup football commentators – Graham almost admits to the idealism of his own task: '[Has] the window of opportunity already begun to close [under the pressures of global interchange] for the kind of radical transformation of spatial relationships that I have called for?' (2009: 180). Noting xenophobic outbursts and razor-wired townhouse complexes, Graham points to a widening gap between rich and poor; to a post-apartheid society which, in its consumer practices, reveals many of the

Introduction

negative features of the very transnational turn that literary critics, including to a degree Graham himself, would wish to invoke (169–73).[9] As Simon Gikandi puts it in pursuing the question of a global imaginary, local identities might borrow patterns and processes of self-definition from elsewhere, but they equally reflect local concerns and problems (2001: 632).

Where does such a perspective leave us, if not in perpetual paradox? Louise Bethlehem probably summarises the 'problem' in her two almost contradictory insights. She is concerned that a 'rhetoric of urgency' (the political imperative) has imposed a flat-earth 'trope-of-truth' on South African literature and criticism (2001: 368). Yet at the same time as she favours an opposing disruption of signifier from signified (life is not so much 'out there' as constructed in language), she notes with regret that the swing to textuality in the 1990s led to the large abstractions of continental philosophy being applied, too often without precision of adjustment, to the subjective experience of the particular author's texts. A consequence was that Coetzee began to function 'virtually by default, as a convenient point of reference through which to hone by-now predictable aspects of postcolonial [one might equally say, postmodern] theory in its metropolitan guises' (2000: 153; see also Bethlehem 2006). Coetzee's own critical essays, in contrast, respect the particularity of each text, whether he is reviewing novels from 'Europe's dark recent history' (the words are Derek Attridge's from his introduction to Coetzee's *Inner Workings* [2007: xi]) or whether he is posing to Nadine Gordimer a question that he has posed to himself: '[W]hat historical role is available to a writer . . . born into a late colonial community?' (Coetzee 2007b: 255). To label Coetzee or Gordimer a South African writer is constraining; not to label them South African writers is to ignore in their work the troubled 'late colonial community' in which they found their distinctive voices, the local accents of which probably played a decisive role in their Nobel recognition.

* * *

Ironically, what got reviewers in South Africa talking in 2009, at least in newspaper columns, was not so much the books that won the several literary awards but rather the first novel – actually a thinly disguised 'life story' – by Thando Mgqolozana, *A Man Who Is Not a Man* (2009). The author tackles the taboo subject of circumcision in the traditional Xhosa rite of manhood. By July of 2009 such practices in the veld had led to the deaths of 49 young men and the hospitalisation of 139 others, 13 of whom had to undergo an amputation of the penis. Mgqolozana's aim is to 'break the silence' (2009b: 3), an action which at the launch of his book at the

2009 Grahamstown National Arts Festival had an imposing man who described himself as a 'traditionalist' wanting to 'smack' the author because of his mentioning the unmentionable in front of women and the uninitiated. In his story of Lumkile, who after a botched circumcision ends up in hospital, Mgqolozana introduces several pressing contemporary issues in South Africa: tradition and modernity; patriarchy; gender; AIDS; and the ongoing, emotive question of race. A cynical response might be that *A Man Who Is Not a Man* excited the interest of the still predominantly white chattering classes because it seemed to confirm the prejudices and fears of a dark heart of Africa in the middle of a democratic state. In fact, none of the commentators to whom I refer revealed such prejudice, while there has been support for Mgqolozana's breaking the silence from several black South Africans.[10] As I suggested in my earlier reference to the theatre group Right 2 Speak, African society, indeed South African society, is not monolithic. The categories require new definition.

My point is that if the 1990s sought to cope with difference, the current priority might be how to connect in a society which at the same time is alert to the 'transnational' perspective of Landsman's *The Rowing Lesson* and the 'indigeneity' of Mgqolozana's *A Man Who Is Not a Man*. I am reminded here of Attwell's key insight: it is not simply that the post-apartheid society has heralded a 'civil turn'; it is rather that a civil turn has been with us all along and that what is different *now*, to *then*, is our 'capacity to recognise more intricately the complex picture' (2005: 9). It is a picture that reveals not only a civil, but also a literary turn to a more nuanced relationship between the text and its contexts of reception. To reiterate points made in the preface, there is a widening of the social/imaginative spectrum both 'nationally' and 'transnationally'. South Africa may not yet be categorised easily as a single nation, but the space begins to be populated by newer voices: for example, a 'born-free' generation of different colours, or an Indian presence occupying almost simultaneously its difficult location in-between its apartheid-enforced 'separate' communities and its diverse inheritance of diaspora and migration. At the same time, there is a variegated response to belonging to the middle class, in which the concept 'middle class' begins to reflect new and challenging race-class gradations.[11] With change signalling both threat and emancipation, there have been turns – as in the world at large – from quotidian conditions to metaphysical dimensions, the religious and spiritual as potent force in postcolonies.[12] These dimensions (both conservative and progressive) have been almost entirely ignored in a postcolonial discourse which arose out of secular metropolitan conflicts between liberalism and Marxism, or capitalism and socialism. Indeed, if postcolonial categorisation is to retain its purchase, then – as Robert J.C. Young (2001: 7–9), Attwell and others have noted – the postcolonial can no longer be regarded as 'the chimera of a [single] position', or even as a 'common theoretical explanation', but must denote a naming of 'those institutional spaces in which people from widely different backgrounds and situations can at least talk to one another' (Attwell 2005: 13).[13] Or as Craig MacKenzie puts it, *then* writers were urged to speak on behalf of the structures, of the people, of the new nation – he quotes Barbara Masekela ('Culture in the New South Africa', *Akal*, October 1990) – whereas *now* it is a book such as Coovadia's *High Low In-between* (2009) that probably best captures the new tenor: '[I]t is not on this side or that, speaking on behalf of this group or that, espousing this ideology or that. It is on the new high that is South African lit, it plumbs the lows; it is also elusively, unclassifiably in-between' (2010: 6). Hence our 'in-between' title, *SA Lit*. In such spaces we may begin to ask a question – the question is implicit in Sally-Ann Murray's Chapter 3 here – which in the political emergency of the 1980s and in the post-apartheid phase of the 1990s was rarely asked: is this work, whether story, play or poem, not only ethically but also aesthetically, a challenging contribution to, or indeed a challenge to, the category 'South African Literature'?

Notes

1. The following 'thematic' issues of journals have pertinence to this introduction: *Alternation* 15(2), 2008 (Literature, Language and Cultural Politics); *Current Writing* 15(2), 2003 (Region, Nation, Identity); *Current Writing* 16(2), 2004 (African Shores and Transatlantic Interlocutions); *Current Writing* 20(2), 2008 (Postcolonialism and Spirituality); *English Academy Review* 24(1), 2007 (Africa in Literature: Perspectives); *English Academy Review* 25(1), 2008 (The Local, Global and the Literary Imagination); *English Academy Review* 26(1), 2009 (Culture, Identity and Spirituality); *English in Africa* 33(2), 2006 (Postcolonialism: A South/African Perspective); *English in Africa* 35(1), 2008 (on book history); *Journal of Literary Studies* 18(1/2), 2002 and 19(3/4), 2002 (Alternative Modernities in African Literatures and Cultures); *Journal of Literary Studies* 19(3/4), 2003 and 20(1/2), 2004 (Aspects of South African Literary Studies); *Scrutiny2* 10(2), 2005 (Transnationalism and African Literature); *Kunapipi* XXIV(1&2), 2002 (South Africa Post-Apartheid); *Modern Fiction Studies* 46(1), 2000 (South African Fiction after Apartheid); and *The South Atlantic Quarterly* 103(4), 2004 (After the Thrill is Gone: A Post-apartheid South Africa).
2. Winner of the Sunday Times Prize for Fiction and the M-Net Literary Award.
3. Shortlisted for the Sunday Times Prize for Fiction, Heyns's novel won the 2009 Herman Charles Bosman Prize.
4. For the 'post- conundrum' – history as continuous 'story' or history as discrete 'stories' – see Chapman (2006: x–xxiii) and (2008: 1–15). In relation to 'women writing Africa' see Driver (2002). Driver refers to Daymond, Driver and Meintjes (2004).

5. See also Chapman (1998).
6. The Levinasian trope – utilised by Attridge with greater finesse than by several other commentators in the 1990s – is the structuring device of his study on Coetzee (Attridge 2005; see also Helgesson 2004). Such studies defend Coetzee against charges of his disengagement from racial issues. Attridge invokes Coetzee's principled refusal to subsume the marginal 'Other' in the dominant 'Same' (the Other and the Same being Levinasian concepts). The argument is that in Coetzee's fiction acts of reciprocity respect 'difference' (see also Chapman 2010).
7. See Greig (2002).
8. See also De Kock (2003, 2008).
9. On the influence on writers of the TRC see Poyner (2008).
10. See Isaacson, Brouard and Zvomuya (all 2009).
11. On identity see, among other pertinent references, Coullie et al. (2006), Distiller and Steyn (2004), Govinden (2008), Moran (2009) and Steyn (2001).
12. On the religious and spiritual see, among other pertinent references, Bennum (2004), Brown (2009), Green (2008), Gunner (2004), Mathuray (2009) and Wenzel (2009). See also relevant 'thematic' issues of journals listed in note 1, above.
13. Several recent studies invoke 'postcolonial tropes'. See, for example, Barnard (2007), Bell and Jacobs (2009), Chapman (2008), Coullie (2001), Coullie and Jacobs (2004), Daymond, Driver and Meintjes (2003), James Graham (2009), Kearney (2003), Potts and Unsworth (2008), Stiebel and Gunner (2005) and Viljoen and Van der Merwe (2004, 2007).

References

Attridge, Derek. 2005. *J.M. Coetzee and the Ethics of Reading*. Chicago: University of Chicago Press; Pietermaritzburg: University of KwaZulu-Natal Press.

———. 2007. 'Introduction' to J.M. Coetzee's *Inner Workings: Essays 2000–2005*. London: Harvill Secker: ix–xiv.

Attridge, Derek and David Attwell (eds). Forthcoming 2012. *The Cambridge History of South African Literature*. Cambridge: Cambridge University Press.

Attwell, David. 2005. *Rewriting Modernity: Studies in Black South African Literary History*. Pietermaritzburg: University of KwaZulu-Natal Press.

Attwell, David and Barbara Harlow. 2000. 'Introduction: South African Fiction after Apartheid'. *Modern Fiction Studies* 46(1): 1–9.

Barnard, Rita. 2007. *Apartheid and Beyond: South African Writers and the Politics of Place*. Oxford: Oxford University Press.

Bell, David and J.U. Jacobs (eds). 2009. *Ways of Writing: Critical Essays on Zakes Mda*. Pietermaritzburg: University of KwaZulu-Natal Press.

Bennum, Neil. 2004. *The Broken String: The Last Words of an Extinct People*. New York: Viking.

Bethlehem, Louise. 2000. 'In the Between: Time, Space, Text in Recent South African Literary Theory'. *English in Africa* 27(1): 140–58.

———. 2001. '"A Primary Need As Strong As Hunger": The Rhetoric of Urgency in South African Literary Culture under Apartheid'. *Poetics Today* 22(2): 365–89.

Introduction

———. 2006. *Skin Tight: Apartheid Literary Culture and Its Aftermath*. Pretoria: Unisa Press; Leiden: Koninklijke Brill.
Breytenbach, Breyten. 1998. *Dog Heart: A Travel Memoir*. Cape Town: Human & Rousseau.
Brouard, Pierre W. 2009. 'Becoming a Man'. *Mail & Guardian* ('Friday' supplement), 17–23 July: 2–3.
Brown, Duncan (ed.). 2009. *Religion and Spirituality in South Africa: New Perspectives*. Pietermaritzburg: University of KwaZulu-Natal Press.
Chapman, Michael. 1998. 'The Problem of Identity: South Africa, Storytelling and Literary History'. *New Literary History* 29(1): 85–99.
———. 2003 [1996]. *Southern African Literatures*. Pietermaritzburg: University of KwaZulu-Natal Press.
———. 2006. *Art Talk, Politics Talk*. Pietermaritzburg: University of KwaZulu-Natal Press.
———. 2008. 'Introduction: Postcolonialism: A Literary Turn'. In: *Postcolonialism: South/African Perspectives*, edited by M. Chapman. Newcastle: Cambridge Scholars Publishing: 1–15.
———. 2010. 'The Case of Coetzee: South African Literary Criticism, 1990 to Today'. *Journal of Literary Studies* 26(2): 103–17.
Chapman, Michael (ed.). 2008. *Postcolonialism: South/African Perspectives*. Newcastle: Cambridge Scholars Publishing.
Chipkin, Ivor. 2007. *Do South Africans Exist? Nationalism, Democracy and the Identity of 'The People'*. Johannesburg: Wits University Press.
Christiansë, Yvette. 2009. *Imprendehora*. Cape Town: Kwela Books.
Coetzee, J.M. 1976. *In the Heart of the Country*. Johannesburg: Ravan Press.
———. 1977a. *From the Heart of the Country: A Novel*. New York: Harper & Row.
———. 1977b. *In the Heart of the Country: A Novel*. London: Secker & Warburg.
———. 1994. *The Master of Petersburg*. New York: Viking.
———. 1999. *Disgrace*. London: Secker & Warburg.
———. 2005. *Slow Man*. London: Secker & Warburg.
———. 2007a. *Diary of a Bad Year*. London: Harvill Secker.
———. 2007b. 'Nadine Gordimer'. In: *Inner Workings: Essays 2000–2005*. London: Harvill Secker: 244–56.
———. 2009. *Summertime*. London: Harvill Secker.
Cooper, Brenda. 2008. *A New Generation of African Writers: Migration, Material Culture and Language*. Oxford: James Currey; Pietermaritzburg: University of KwaZulu-Natal Press.
Coovadia, Imraan. 2009. *High Low In-between*. Cape Town: Umuzi.
Coullie, Judith Lütge (ed.). 2001. *The Closest of Strangers: South African Women's Life Writing*. Johannesburg: Wits University Press.
Coullie, Judith Lütge and J.U. Jacobs (eds). 2004. *a.k.a. Breyten Breytenbach: Critical Approaches to his Writings and Paintings*. Amsterdam and New York: Rodopi.
Coullie, Judith Lütge, Stephan Meyer, Thengani H. Ngwenya and Thomas Olver (eds). 2006. *Selves in Question: Interviews on Southern African Auto/biography*. Honolulu: University of Hawaii Press.
Dangor, Achmat. 1981. *Waiting for Leila*. Johannesburg: Ravan Press.
———. 1997. *Kafka's Curse: A Novella and Three Stories*. Cape Town: Kwela Books.
Daymond, M.J., Dorothy Driver and Sheila Meintjes (eds). 2003. *Women Writing Africa: The Southern Region*. New York: The Feminist Press at the City University of New York.

De Kock, Leon. 2001. 'South Africa in the Global Imaginary: An Introduction'. *Poetics Today* 22(2): 263–98.
———. 2003. 'Splice of Life: Manipulations of the "Real" in South African English Literary Culture'. *Journal of Literary Studies* 19(1): 82–102.
———. 2005. 'Does South African Literature Still Exist? Or: South African Literature Is Dead, Long Live Literature in South Africa'. *English in Africa* 32(2): 69–83.
———. 2008. 'A History of Restlessness: And Now for the Rest'. *English Studies in Africa* 51(1): 109–22.
De Kock, Leon, Louise Bethlehem and Sonja Laden (eds). 2004. *South Africa in the Global Imaginary*. Pretoria: Unisa Press; Leiden: Koninklijke Brill.
Deleuze, Gilles and Félix Guattari. 1987. *A Thousand Plateaus: Capitalism and Schizophrenia*. Translated by B. Massumi. Minneapolis: University of Minneapolis Press.
Distiller, Natasha and Melissa Steyn (eds). 2004. *Under Construction: Race and Identity in South Africa Today*. Johannesburg: Heinemann.
Driver, Dorothy. 2002. 'Women Writing Africa: Southern Africa as a Post-apartheid Project'. *Kunapipi* XXIV(1&2): 155–72.
Frenkel, Ronit. 2010. *Reconsiderations: South African Indian Fiction and the Making of Race in Postcolonial Culture*. Pretoria: Unisa Press.
Gikandi, Simon. 2001. 'Globalization and the Claims of Postcoloniality'. *The South Atlantic Quarterly* 100(3): 627–58.
Gordimer, Nadine. 1991. *Jump and Other Stories*. Cape Town: David Philip.
———. 2003. *Loot and Other Stories*. Cape Town: David Philip.
Govinden, Devarakshanam Betty. 2008. *A Time of Memory: Reflections on Recent South African Writings*. Durban: Solo Collective.
Graham, James. 2009. *Land and Nationalism in Fictions from Southern Africa*. London: Routledge.
Graham, Shane. 2009. *South African Literature after the Truth Commission*. New York: Palgrave Macmillan.
Green, Michael Cawood. 2008. *For the Sake of Silence*. Cape Town: Umuzi.
Greig, Robert. 2002. 'Horrific and Funny Product of a Darker Vision: Brett Bailey's *Macbeth*'. *Sunday Independent*, 14 July: 10.
Gunner, Liz (ed.). 2004. *The Man of Heaven and the Beautiful Ones of God/Umuntu waseZulwini nabantu abahle bukaNkulunkulu. Isaiah Shembe and the Nazarite Church*. Pietermaritzburg: University of KwaZulu-Natal Press.
Harris, Peter. 2008. *In a Different Time*. Cape Town: Umuzi.
Helgesson, Stefan. 2004. *Writing in Crisis: Ethics and History in Gordimer, Ndebele and Coetzee*. Pietermaritzburg: University of KwaZulu-Natal Press.
Heyns, Michiel. 2008. *Bodies Politic*. Johannesburg: Jonathan Ball.
Heywood, Christopher. 2004. *A History of South African Literature*. Cambridge: Cambridge University Press.
Hofmeyr, Isabel. 2004. *The Portable Bunyan: A Transnational History of 'The Pilgrim's Progress'*. Princeton: Princeton University Press; Johannesburg: Wits University Press.
———. 2008. 'Indian Ocean Lives and Letters'. *English in Africa* 35(1): 11–25.
Isaacson, Maureen. 2009. 'An Initiate Claiming His Space as a Man'. *The Sunday Independent*, 28 June: 17.

Jamal, Ashraf. 2005. *Predicaments of Culture in South Africa*. Pretoria: Unisa Press.
Jameson, Fredric. 1991. *Postmodernism, or the Logic of Late Capitalism*. Durham, NC: Duke University Press.
Jauss, Hans Robert. 1982. *Toward an Aesthetic of Reception*. Translated by T. Bahti. New Jersey: Harvester.
Kearney, J.A. 2003. *Representing Dissension: Riot, Rebellion and Resistance in the South African English Novel*. Pretoria: Unisa Press.
Kgosidintsi, Mbali. 2009. 'The Great Black Hope'. Interview with Mary Corrigall. *Sunday Independent*, 9 August: 26–7.
Kruger, Loren. 2002. '"Black Atlantics", "White Indians", and "Jews": Locations, Locutions and Syncretic Identities in the Fiction of Achmat Dangor and Others'. *Scrutiny2* 7(2): 34–50.
La Guma, Alex. 1978. *A Soviet Journey*. Moscow: Progress.
Landsman, Anne. 2008. *The Rowing Lesson*. Cape Town: Kwela Books.
Langa, Mandla. 2000. *The Memory of Stones*. Boulder, CO: Lynne Rienner.
Leavis, F.R. 1962 [1952]. 'Bunyan through Modern Eyes'. In: *The Common Pursuit*. London: Penguin: 204–10.
MacKenzie, Craig. 2010. 'More Rebellious Than Ever'. *Mail & Guardian*, 27 August – 2 September, supplement on the M&G Literary Festival, Johannesburg, 3–5 September: 6.
Mathuray, Mark. 2009. *On the Sacred in African Literature: Old Gods and New Worlds*. Basingstoke: Palgrave Macmillan.
Mbembe, Achille. 2002. 'African Modes of Self-Writing: A Critique of Political Economy and Nationalism.' Translated by S. Randall. Paper presented at the Wits Institute for Economic and Social Research, University of the Witwatersrand (February). Quoted in Isabel Hofmeyr and Liz Gunner, 2005, 'Introduction'. Theme issue on Transnationalism and African Literature. *Scrutiny2* 10(2): 4.
McDonald, Peter D. 2009. *The Literature Police: Apartheid Censorship and Its Cultural Consequences*. Oxford: Oxford University Press.
Mgqolozana, Thando. 2009a. *A Man Who Is Not a Man*. Pietermaritzburg: University of KwaZulu-Natal Press.
———. 2009b. 'From the Mouth of the Author'. *Mail & Guardian*, 17–23 July: 3.
Moran, Shane. 2009. *Representing Bushmen: South Africa and the Origin of Language*. Rochester: University of Rochester Press.
Mostert, Noël. 1992. *Frontiers: The Epic of South Africa's Creation and the Tragedy of the Xhosa People*. London: Jonathan Cape.
Murray, Sally-Ann. 2009. *Small Moving Parts*. Cape Town: Kwela Books.
Ndebele, Njabulo S. 2006 [1991]. *Rediscovery of the Ordinary: Essays on South African Literature and Culture*. Pietermaritzburg: University of KwaZulu-Natal Press.
———. 2007. *Fine Lines from the Box: Further Thoughts about Our Country*. Cape Town: Umuzi.
Nuttall, Sarah. 2009. *Entanglement: Literary and Cultural Reflections on Post-apartheid*. Johannesburg: Wits University Press.
Ortiz, Fernando. 1995. *Cuban Counterpoint: Tobacco and Sugar*. Translated by H. de Onis. Durham, NC: Duke University Press.
Phewa, Asandi. 2009. 'The Great Black Hope'. Interview with Mary Corrigall. *Sunday Independent*, 9 August: 26–7.

Popescu, Monica. 2010. *South African Literature beyond the Cold War*. New York: Palgrave Macmillan.

Potts, Donna L. and Amy D. Unsworth (eds). 2008. *Region, Nation, Frontiers*. Newcastle: Cambridge Scholars Publishing.

Poyner, Jane. 2008. 'Writing under Pressure: A Post-apartheid Canon?' *Journal of Postcolonial Writing* 44(2): 103–14.

Sachs, Albie. 1990. 'Preparing Ourselves for Freedom'. In: *Spring Is Rebellious: Arguments about Cultural Freedom by Albie Sachs and Respondents*, edited by I. de Kok and K. Press. Cape Town: Buchu Books.

Samuelson, Meg. 2008. 'Walking through the Door and Inhabiting the House: South African Literary Culture and Criticism after the Transition'. *English Studies in Africa* 51(1): 130–7.

Sanders, Mark. 2002. *Complicities: The Intellectual and Apartheid*. Durham, NC: Duke University Press.

Schreiner, Olive. 1883. *The Story of an African Farm*. London: Chapman and Hall.

Sitas, Ari. 2004. *Voices That Reason: Theoretical Parables*. Pretoria: Unisa Press.

Steyn, Melissa. 2001. '*Whiteness just isn't what it used to be': White Identity in a Changing South Africa*. Albany: State University of New York.

Stiebel, Lindy and Liz Gunner (eds). 2005. *Still Beating the Drum: Critical Perspectives on Lewis Nkosi*. Amsterdam and New York: Rodopi.

Titlestad, Michael. 2004. *Making the Changes: Jazz in South African Literature and Reportage*. Pretoria: Unisa Press; Leiden: Koninklijke Brill.

Van Coller, H.P. (ed.). 2006. *Perspektief en profiel: 'n Afrikaanse literatuur-geskiedenis*. Pretoria: Van Schaik.

Van der Vlies, Andrew. 2007. *South African Textual Cultures: White, Black, Read All Over*. Manchester: Manchester University Press.

Viljoen, Hein and Chris N. van der Merwe (eds). 2004. *Storyscapes: South African Perspectives on Literature, Space and Identity*. New York: Peter Lang.

———. (eds). 2007. *Beyond the Threshold: Explorations of Liminality in Literature*. New York: Peter Lang.

Vladislavić, Ivan. 1996. *Propaganda by Monuments and Other Stories*. Cape Town: David Philip.

Wenzel, Jennifer. 2009. *Bulletproof: Afterlives and Anticolonial Prophecy in South Africa and Beyond*. Chicago: University of Chicago Press.

Wicomb, Zoë. 2001. *David's Story*. Cape Town: Kwela Books.

Young, Robert J.C. 2001. *Postcolonialism: An Historical Perspective*. Oxford: Blackwell.

Zvomuya, Percy. 2009. 'Tackling the Matter Head-On'. *Mail & Guardian* ('Friday' supplement), 17–23 July: 2–3.

1

The End of 'South African' Literary History?
Judging 'National' Fiction in a Transnational Era

LEON DE KOCK

A few years ago, I asked the question, 'Does [English] South African Literature Still Exist?' (2005a) in a keynote address for a Wits University colloquium dealing with the contested terrain we used to call South African literature (often eliding the important qualifier, English). Whether we can or should still talk about South African English Literature and whether it does or should continue to exist is partly the subject of this chapter. In the Wits address, I suggested that South African literature in English, in the 1960s 'Knuckles Fists Boots' mode (Dennis Brutus), or in the 1970s 'Looking on Darkness' moment (André Brink), was dead and that I was glad of it. In the same way that Es'kia Mphahlele (1959: 199) declaimed in the late 1950s against the kind of (South African) writing composed at 'white heat, everything full of vitriol', confessing to his exhaustion with it, my reading, then, was that a feeling of 'enough' with landlocked, 'vitriol' writing had become widespread, even among the adherents of SA Lit. In its wake, a phenomenon one might call (assuming 'English' as implicit) 'Literature out of South Africa' – writing emanating from the country and written after a decisive transnational rupture – had arisen in defiance of, or in a state of indifference to, the codes and conformities of the earlier historical-political emphases in the country's corpus of writing. This newer writing was no longer necessarily held within the seam of intercultural convergence, no longer always seeking to flatten out the ridge of that seam, yet leaving in its wake the mark of that suture.[1] A couple of years later I asked the rhetorical question whether many of us who had previously regarded ourselves as scholars of 'South African English Literature' had not now become, or wanted to become – in the wake of the poststructuralist turn and the death of the author as a revered figure – academic 'rock stars' in our own right, more interested in writing in our names on any number of sexy topics (cities, oceanic discourse, jazz, metropolitanisms, whiteness studies, ugly/beautiful aesthetics, self-styling, to name a few) than in the more modest tasks of assessing, describing and evaluating the writings of others demarcated as 'imaginative SA writers'. I warned, however, that a more broadly cultural imaginary, out of which the newer forms of critical writing necessarily emerged, depended on the continued existence of a literary-imaginative archive and that if we failed to record and assess the newer writers and their works, even the broader cultural imaginary could well become etiolated (2008a).

In that address, I named a selection of the newer South African writers, aiming to jolt the audience into a sense of unfamiliarity with their names. Then, the litany sounded as follows: Gabeba Baderoon (2005, 2006), Andrew Brown (2007), Russel Brownlee (2005), Imraan Coovadia (2006), Finuala Dowling (2005, 2007), Lisa Fugard (2005), Manu Herbstein (2001), Craig Higginson (2005), Shaun Johnson (2006), Aryan Kaganof (2002, 2006, 2007), Fred Khumalo (2006a, 2006b, 2008), Gerald Kraak (2006), Lebo Mashile (2005), Kopano Matlwa (2007), Niq Mhlongo (2004, 2007), Kirsten Miller (2007), Sarah Penny (2002), Henrietta Rose-Innes (2000, 2004), Angelina Sithebe (2007), Heinrich Troost (2007) and Rachel Zadok (2005). This list was already sharply abbreviated, excluding well-known names such as Mark Behr (1995, 2000), K. Sello Duiker (2000, 2001, 2006), Rayda Jacobs (1998, 2001, 2003, 2004, 2005, 2006), Ashraf Jamal (1996, 2002), Phaswane Mpe (2001), Mike Nicol (1994, 2006, 2008), Jo-Anne Richards (1996, 2008), Ivan Vladisavić (2001, 2004) and Zoë Wicomb (2001, 2006); it excluded Afrikaans and African-language writers, in whose ranks there were literally scores of new examplars of literary worth, and poets (apart from two exceptions), who, I added, had always outrun literary reckonings and still do, existing for the most part in a kind of nether-space of literary semi-visibility, unless they take to the stage and sing like troubadours for people's entertainment. Dramatists are equally marginal for reasons peculiar to the pedagogies of teaching literature in classrooms.

To the above list, still confined to English South African writers alone, I would now add at least another twenty-five names, including Sean Badal (2008), Lauren Beukes (2008), Kevin Bloom (2009), Edyth Bulbring (2008), Jacob Dlamini (2009), Tracey Farren (2008), Rosamund Kendal (2008), Lauren Liebenberg (2008), Rozena Maart (2008), Jassie Mackenzie (2008), Chris Marnewick (2008), Richard Mason (2008), Zinaid Meeran (2009), Kgebetli Moele (2009), Nthikeng Mohlele (2008), Sally-Ann Murray (2009), Futhi Ntshingila (2008), Hamish Hoosen Pillay (2008), Susan Rabie (2008), Diale Tlholwe (2008) and still more. The great majority of these works were published inside the country by South African publishers (Umuzi, Picador Africa, Kwela Books, Penguin SA, New Africa Books,

The End of 'South African' Literary History?

Modjaji Books, Shuter & Shooter, University of KwaZulu-Natal Press, Jacana Media, Human & Rousseau, Jonathan Ball, 30 Degrees South). As the list of references at the end of this chapter alone should show, the cumulative list since 2000 of fiction, poetry and autobiography becomes very long. And this list accounts mainly for works published inside the country, which pass through the publishers' own gatekeeping measures, themselves rigorous enough to ensure that only *one per cent* of submitted manuscripts makes it into print.[2] The point should be obvious: it has become almost impossible to 'keep up' with the newer literature emerging from a reconstituted, formally democratic state, let alone with the writing published by South Africans transnationally and in Afrikaans and African languages within the country. 'South African English literature' has exploded out of its 'special status' confines, in which it was nursed by committed local scholars in a regenerative flourish during the 1980s and 1990s. This critical nursing of the literature was largely done so that it could see off the neo-colonial metropolitan bias in university teaching hegemonies. As Derek Barker shows in his account of literary academic discourse in South Africa between 1958 and 2004, the fight for what we called in English 'South African Literature' was decisively won and the subject of South African writing came to dominate the space of peer-review journal articles in the English-speaking academy well into the 2000s (2007: 170–242; see also Barker's 76-page statistical appendix).

Barker's data synthesis on published academic articles also shows that a consensual English SA canon, in statistical terms (number of articles published in peer-review journals) accrued around the following authors: J.M. Coetzee, Nadine Gordimer, Olive Schreiner, Pauline Smith, Bessie Head and Alan Paton (Appendix: 75). Although his account stops at 2004, it is my impression that detailed stocktaking of the newer work has largely tailed off, despite work by scholars such as Michael Titlestad, Mike Kissack, Sarah Nuttall, Michael Chapman, Meg Samuelson, Dorothy Driver, Rita Barnard and others.[3] What was once a critical industry which prided itself on the recovery of 'lost' or neglected work, and which often resorted to large-scale and detailed histories, now tends to draw out themes and append individual works to such themes (cities, metropolitanisms and oceanic themes being particularly prevalent currently). The earlier imperative of a critical and empirical recapturing of literary artefacts which had been neglected, or which were emergent but invisible as a result of critical bias, appears to have waned significantly. In addition, the impetus to anthologise, record and publish the elements in the field, keeping up to date with emerging work, seems less marked now than before. Perhaps this falling off has something to do with the rise of 'theory' in the South African literary academy from the early 1980s onwards –

poststructuralist, postcolonial, postmodern, cultural studies (see Barker 2007: 34; 53–5) and now transnational theory – and perhaps it was generally felt that the territory had been secured. 'South African [English] Literature' as a field of study had been achieved: South African works were being taught at universities, both at home and abroad, and we would soon have not one but two Nobel prizewinners among our writers.

Theory and cultural studies, then, gradually began to assume a higher profile, sexier, no doubt, than cleaning up and annotating old manuscripts. In addition, what is now often referred to as the 'transnational turn' ushered in a much bigger world. Before this historical moment, progressive South African scholars, radically nationalist by persuasion (in contrast to Afrikaner Nationalists, they inclined towards a more inclusive, African National Congress-inspired nationalism), had tended strongly to resist metropolitan critical agendas, imposed from a hierarchical 'centre' upon an allegedly backwater 'periphery'. But now the world had begun to flatten out laterally; national boundaries suddenly became superfluous in the wake of economic and technological flows uniting people within global networks. The Berlin Wall had come down, 'East' and 'West' were old news, apartheid had collapsed and South Africa began to see beyond the cultural boycott. In literary-cultural pursuits the desire was to step beyond the enclosure of the 'national', the cultural-boycott hothouse, the 'struggle' terrain. That this new horizon was distinctly transnational, in many different ways and directions, was convincingly argued by Isabel Hofmeyr and Liz Gunner (2005: 1–8), among others, while Hofmeyr's work on the circulation of texts across borders and boundaries demonstrated the transnational turn in its historical manner of accounting for cultural change over time (2004). What we might now call the transnational rupture in both literary-critical and imaginative writing coming out of South Africa from the early 1990s onwards was both centrifugal and centripetal, both a category-implosion as well as an outwardly liberating thrust.

I do not mean to suggest that there is a linear development from 'national' to 'transnational', or a straight line of temporality from the one to the other. Clearly, what might now be termed 'transnational' or, more accurately, *metropolitan* influences were widely in circulation in the field of South African writing and culture from the start – from the colonial period, in various manifestations, through to the twentieth century, when many writers were variously influenced by modernism (William Plomer, Roy Campbell), the Harlem Renaissance and discourses of American jazz (various black writers, including the '*Drum* Generation'), European existentialism (the 'Sestigers'), postmodernism (the 'Tagtigers') and so on. The transnational 'turn', as a temporal marker, suggests a quantum leap in such cross-appropriations and a concomitantly enhanced fluidity in the technological (electronic communication) and political fields (weakening of national sovereignty) that was not present in quite such a marked way in earlier manifestations of transnational literary-cultural activity.

The space of the transnational

In her essay, 'Transnationalizing the Public Sphere', Nancy Fraser (2007 [2002]), reviewing public-sphere theory in the wake of Jürgen Habermas's contributions in this field, writes that developments which were gathering pace in the early 1990s 'problematize public sphere theory's presupposition of a national literature, which was supposed to constitute a medium for the formation of a solidary national identity' (11). She continues:

> Consider the increased salience of cultural hybridity and hybridization, including the rise of 'world literature'. Consider also the rise of global mass entertainment, whether straightforwardly American or merely American-like or American-izing. Consider finally the spectacular rise of visual culture, or better, of the enhanced salience of the visual within culture and the relative decline of print, the literary, etc. In all these ways, it is difficult to accord conceptual primacy to the sort of (national) literary cultural formation seen by Habermas (and by Benedict Anderson) as underpinning the subjective stance of public-sphere interlocutors. On the contrary, insofar as public spheres require the cultural support of a national identity, rooted in national literary culture, it is hard to see them functioning effectively today absent from such solidary bases (11–12).

Fraser makes the following useful conclusion:

> In general, then, public spheres are increasingly transnational or post-national with respect to each of the constitutive elements of public opinion. The who of communication, previously theorized as a Westphalian-national citizenry, is now a collection of dispersed subjects of communication. The what of communication, previously theorized as a Westphalian-national interest rooted in a Westphalian-national economy, now stretches across vast reaches of the globe, in a transnational community of fate and of risk, which is not however reflected in concomitantly expansive solidarities and identities. The where of communication, once theorized as the Westphalian-national territory, is now deterritorialized

cyberspace. The how of communication, once theorized as Westphalian-national print media, now encompasses a vast translinguistic nexus of disjoint and overlapping visual cultures. Finally, the addressee of communication, once theorized as Westphalian state power to be made answerable to public opinion, is now an amorphous mix of public and private transnational powers (suggestively named 'the nebuleuse' by Robert Cox), that is neither easily identifiable nor rendered accountable (13).

It was in such a globally dispersed and differently conceived public sphere that Antjie Krog's phenomenally successful book, *Country of my Skull* (1998), found its purchase as a story of affect and suffering under criminally oppressive national regimes, touching people who, across the globe, could relate to precisely such a condition within a postnational conception of 'fate and risk' across the globe. These conditions were palpable not only in South Africa, but also in many other national polities such as Israel, Iraq, Zimbabwe, Pakistan, China and elsewhere; in pockets of ugly nationalist enclosure where leaders were ignoring the newer world-ethical imperative to open up rather than close down spaces of human mobility and the freedom to choose from a postnational, rather than from a national menu of options for subjectivity and identity.

This transnationalising public sphere, Anthea Garman reminds us, relying on Michael Warner (2002), Shalini Randeria (2007) and Kate Nash (2007), consists of 'reflexive modern subjects', people who 'identify as fellow humans across national boundaries and who use transnational public spheres to crystallise the salience of events and issues with which to become involved' (2010: 192). In her work on Krog as a public intellectual, Garman identifies certain key factors that appear to have coalesced in the shaping of a new transnational reading subject within a global-local nexus, amounting to a reconstituted audience for a formerly hermetic Afrikaans poet:

> I am theorising that a particular confluence of a global issue (dealing with the past via truth commissions), a global publishing context and the work of a local writer with a record of literary work and political action enabled a fit which resulted in Krog coming to prominence on a world stage as having the capacity to speak about the country's transition in all its complexity (2010: 188).

This circumstantial and historical nexus made possible the public expression and globally reconfigured publics' hearing of Krog's voice as oracular, as representative, as witness, given to the expression of her own and others' *enunciatory* rights – according to Homi Bhabha (cited by Garman 2010: 190) 'not just a right to speak but also a right to proclaim and therefore make claims' in a world, for Bhabha, of 'jurisdictional unsettlement' – a scene, Garman adds in paraphrase, in which the settled ideas of nation and nationality are being rendered increasingly complex. This is a world, Bhabha suggests, in which the 'great social movements of our times – diasporic, refugee, migrant' – have brought about the 'right to narrate' (Garman 2010: 190); hence the worldwide appetite for life narratives, for memoirs and acts of witness, expressions of pain and suffering, resolve and survival, that cut across the narrower interests and manipulations of polities and nation states.

If this were true of a newer world order emerging decisively from the post-Cold War era, how much truer might it have been for a South African citizenry only just emerging from decades of pariah status, hungry for reconnection with global developments, global entertainment and the new, alluring mesh of global connectivity. As the ranks of the transnational, 'reflexive modern subjects' swelled and the world transformed from multinational to transnational, getting smaller and more connected in the process, so the special status of apartheid and South Africa as a political 'hotspot' diminished. For the newer generation of South Africans born in the 1980s, or for those born in the 1990s, 'apartheid' would increasingly now become a refrain in the mouths of their parents and the pages of their school history books. Into the 2000s, writers were emerging who had little recall of formal apartheid as a lived experience. When I interviewed the young novelist Henrietta Rose-Innes in 2005 about her novel, *The Rock Alphabet*, she stated that known South African 'history' was often inaccessible to her characters and, by implication, to people now growing up in South Africa. She added:

> It's a mysterious thing and they cannot decipher it. And it is often unrelated to their [own] stories that have happened on the same landscape ... The novel is partly about confronting the fact that history and what happened in the past does not necessarily have an explanation. It cannot be solved (De Kock 2005b).

In that piece, I wrote that Rose-Innes wanted to show it was possible to live outside the straitjackets of identity as historically conceived in South Africa and to feel freer in the choice of the language one speaks, literally and figuratively, than ever before. This movement is given ironic form by the resolution of Rose-Innes's novel. Whereas the new language of the ungovernable brothers in *The Rock Alphabet*'s story and the older languages of the past – such as contained in the museum collections evoked in the novel – are not exactly conjoined, the load of pre-given, already-known meaning is lightened and made ironic.

Such a 'lightening' effect, as well as the ironising dimensions, I would argue, are evident in what we might call, following Loren Kruger's useful phrase 'post-anti-apartheid' (2002: 35), South African writing in the transnational turn. And yet this writing – exemplified most prominently by fiction – awaits a sustained project of critical stocktaking, or even sustained and serious attention apart from occasional reviews, critical articles and encyclopaedic essays. The forthcoming *Cambridge History of South African Literature* (Attridge and Attwell 2012) may go some way towards redressing this state of affairs, but only some way, as it is organised along broad thematic lines, in over thirty thematic essays. (At a planning colloquium in preparation for the individual essays at Wits in 2008, the editors urged writers to imagine they were writing for an audience conceived of transnationally, with little prior knowledge of the field. Writers were urged to let go of the 'internal' or older national disagreements and controversies in South African criticism. These are market-driven considerations, which are revealing of the imperative to recast histories of literature in a transnational market rather than a national one.)

One might make the argument, accordingly, that in a global or transnational public sphere which disavows the 'national' as an entity for the purposes of self-identification, the newer, 'reflexive modern subjects' of this meta-national order have little use for reconfigured 'national' literary histories. Not only has the more recent writing decisively loosened itself from 'South African history' and the 'struggle', in all its manifestations, it has also hungrily embraced a larger membership of 'world' literature. In such a category of literature, surely the category 'South African Literature' has become redundant?

My own answer to this question would be 'yes and no'. Yes, for all the reasons set out above. No, because my sense is that the 'trans' in transnational creates a cusp between the national and what lies beyond it, not a severance. I would argue that, for example, in the two best novels of 2008 written by South African citizens in English – Anne Landsman's *The Rowing Lesson* and Michiel Heyns's *Bodies Politic* – it is precisely the transnational cusp, and the way this bi- or multi-directional conjunction plays out in their novels, that made them especially interesting (the same might be said for the best novel in 2008 in Afrikaans, Etienne van Heerden's *30 nagte in Amsterdam*).[4] The novel adjudged to be the best written in 2007 by a South African citizen (by the 2008 M-Net Literary Award for Fiction in English judges) was J.M. Coetzee's *Diary of a Bad Year* (2007).[5] At a public discussion at the 2008 Cape Town Book Fair on the morning following the award of the prize, I asked M-Net fiction-prize judge Michael Titlestad whether the award of the prize to a writer no longer living in South Africa and no longer (in the main) writing about

South Africa – in *Diary of a Bad Year*, at least – had not presented the judges with a conundrum. Titlestad said that the matter had indeed been deliberated at length by the judges, before the award of the prize and that a critical consensus had emerged.

The consensus (according to Titlestad) was that 'South African' writers, who in the past were often diasporic by virtue of living in forced exile, were now even more frequently disaporic in a migratory (rather than a politically exilic) sense; this was so much so that it no longer made sense to define the category 'South African' with primary reference to geographical territory as a fixed category, or in a dualistic home-exile conjunction. (Those who work as writers from abroad frequently return and then leave again, only to return again intermittently as – economic and other – circumstances permit, setting up cyclical migration paths perhaps; they tend to come for relatively short visits, or write in sessions, here and there, such as Eben Venter writing now in Prince Albert, Karoo, now in Melbourne, Australia.) So, apart from Coetzee, any number of South African writers either write from within a range of transnational sites – Anne Landsman (US), Marita van der Vyver (France), Breyten Breytenbach (France), Elleke Boehmer (UK), Athol Fugard (US), Justin Cartwright (UK), Joanne Fedler (Australia), Zakes Mda (US), to name a few, while Koos Kombuis does 'London Pub' tours to play to various constituencies of South Africans, both Afrikaners and others, in the UK 'diaspora' – and the M-Net competition rules helpfully demarcate the prize on the grounds of South African citizenship, not residence in the country.

My question to Titlestad was also about the subject matter of *Diary of a Bad Year*. Although Señor C, the Coetzee-lookalike author-persona in this novel, is a 72-year-old South African émigré writer living in Australia, he has relatively little to say about his former home country. Titlestad's answer was that migrant writing would necessarily yield migrant, or migrating themes. 'South Africa' could no longer be contained. Yes, I felt, this is the feel of so much of the 'new' writing. And yet the link is there in *Diary of a Bad Year*, as it is in many other transnational works: Señor C remains an émigré South African writer and this surely informs his points of view, despite now being triangulated by meta-national, multivectoral connections. Witness Señor C's opening essay on the unpalatable nature of 'democracy', how unfree its supposedly 'free' choice actually is, or feels. Such indirect comment 'on' South African post-anti-apartheid politics is present in Heyns's *Bodies Politic*, too, as well as in other, more recent works written in the wake of the transnational turn. Michael Cawood Green's *For the Sake of Silence* (2008), in its story of faith, contemplation and grace, links the Trappist enterprise in South Africa to its world reach. (Green's work of history-fiction won the 2010 Olive Schreiner Literary Award for best first novel.)

Yet, as I make such a 'transnational' observation, an immediate qualification is necessary: the two novels which in 2010's literary competitions consistently impressed the judges have an unmistakably 'local' flavour: Imraan Coovadia's *High Low In-between* (winner of the Sunday Times Fiction Prize and the UJ [University of Johannesburg] Literary Award, shortlisted for the M-Net Literary Award) traces the idiosyncrasies of a South African Indian family, while Sally-Ann Murray's *Small Moving Parts* (runner-up for the UJ Literary Award, shortlisted for the Sunday Times Fiction Prize, winner of both the M-Net Literary Award and the Herman Charles Bosman Prize) explores the coming-of-age of her young female protagonist whose formative years rubbed both harshly and poetically against the white working-class accents of apartheid South Africa in the 1960s and 1970s.[6]

So, consistent with my 'yes and no' earlier on, I would argue that the category 'South African' as a marker of a literary field remains important, even necessary for a sense of history and determination in what one might call a 'national imaginary', but that the space of the 'national' has irrevocably entered into the fluid waters of 'trans', the transitive cusp of crossing and recrossing, of absorbing the fictional self into (now easier, more fluid) spaces of related elsewheres and of absorbing the otherness of such elsewheres into the fictional self. To 'write up' such a transnational history is a yet more daunting task than was writing up the older 'national' literary history. Even that task was frequently acknowledged to be quixotic (see the essays in Smit, Wade and Van Wyk 1996). The need to limit one's brief to smaller stories, or larger patterns, within the acknowledged sense of a postnational configuration – indeed, now a transnational constellation – strikes me as more pressing under contemporary circumstances.

The pragmatic historiography of literary prizes

Such philosophical considerations do not prevent a more pragmatic form of historiography from occurring year in and year out in the workings of various major literary prizes.[7] I want to confine myself here – since I acted as one of three judges in both 2009 and 2010 – to the M-Net Literary Award, which is awarded for the best work of fiction published by a South African citizen (including dual citizenship) in the calendar years 2008 and 2009, respectively. In the absence of anything in the way of significant critical reception of new works of writing by South African authors in the popular South African media, and in the absence of up-to-date general literary stocktaking, prizes such as the M-Net Literary Award have come to occupy the space of critical reception in that they demarcate a field (here, a subfield, fiction) by citizenship, genre and year of publication: they compile a list of works submitted by publishers and generate critical description and evaluation of the works by engaging scholars to do this work. Although the list and the critical descriptions/evaluations so generated are seldom published, these literary-critical effects are circulated among judges and so a record is established. It says a great deal about the state of critical reception that, for a researcher of emerging writing, such lists and records are the most accessible way to delimit the field and to get a comprehensive list of the datum of what has been published (in this case, in the genre of fiction, although the UJ Literary Award includes poetry and non-fiction). For a researcher into current writing, one way of establishing greater comprehensiveness is to approach the prize conveners and ask for their list of entries.

So, in the absence of consistent work in the way of a regular programme of literary stocktaking by the academy, the labour of recording South African literature has fallen to the prize conveners, themselves directed by the media giants (Avusa Media, publisher of the *Sunday Times*, Multichoice, owner of M-Net); or directed by universities or cultural institutions, where the capital sources are possibly more mediated, but where marketing remains a prime motivation for having awards. There is nothing new about capital acting as patron to the arts, but it remains an irony, given the historical preoccupation of literary criticism in South Africa with the depredations of capitalism, the pernicious conjunctions of class and race and the critiques of self-deluding cultural states of innocence such as 'Butlerism' (see Kirkwood 1976): that is, the mistaken conception among the capital-rich English-speakers that they were innocently buffered between two nasty nationalisms, Boer versus Black. How things have changed! Certainly, the entrepreneurs and money-makers now continue to leverage the symbolic capital of 'culture' and 'literature' by front-ending their business with the finesse of literary appreciation, but it is ironic that the critics, the radical questioners and campaigners for cultural revolution, have left the field to what they would earlier have typified as the vultures of capital accumulation. For a critic or a reader trying to make sense of the country's writing in a way that is complete and thorough, the scholarly journals (whether of a radical persuasion or not) will not help all that much. Neither will the under- and postgraduate courses at universities, which to a great extent have ditched the demarcated field of 'South African' writing in favour of the much jazzier hold-alls of transnationalism, global contrapuntalism, diasporic literature, self-styling, public culture, the practice of everyday life, improvisational practice, the end of theory, the body (both dead and alive), cities, topographies, keywords – you name it.

The initial list compiled by convenors of prizes at least covers the field, year by year. The judges' shortlist – at least in the case of the M-Net Literary Award – is the result of lengthy deliberation among the judges, both via email and in session. The judges make concise notes on the shortlist, which they are required to write up and deliver. Researchers might ask for the brief commendation statements prepared for the announcement of the shortlisted works prior to the announcement of the overall winner and the citation read out when the winner is announced. These critical nuggets – derived from literary and cultural critics drawn from both the academy and the more general public sphere – are a starting point, something to take issue with or follow up. The judges, after all, have taken the trouble, over several months of sustained reading, to reflect on the value and stature of individual works within a grouping of related writing.

Such acts of public critical deliberation do not happen in any systematic way unless they are convened and the institutions convening a public consideration of literature in a year-by-year, exhaustive manner are mainly outside of the academy, though drawing in figures both from within the academy and without. This is being done in pursuit of an explicitly evaluative outcome: to decide which work is the *best* and which four (or two, in some cases) are to be deemed as runners-up. In a field of about forty works, all shortlisted works for the M-Net Literary Award, or for the UJ Literary Award, must be regarded as 'winners', distinguished from the rest as distinctly above the average. This raises questions of evaluation against critical description, canon-formation and selective reception, but since the prize culture and to some extent the 'festival' culture (also back-end supported by the capitalists for their own front-end purposes) are the most significant sites of comprehensive literary reckoning left, we may as well take what we can from the bonanza-version of literary appreciation.

Methodologies of judging

What are the methodologies of judging literary prizes? What standards inform the value judgements made in the course of determining a shortlist and an overall winner? What standards do the judges use to make their calls on which works are better, and which worse, than others? (I focus here on the judges' reflections in 2009; the time-frames of the 2010 literary competitions almost coincided with the finalisation of the present publication.) In some senses, the prize-culture creates the conditions for a refreshingly no-nonsense form of reckoning. In both the prizes in which I was involved in 2009, areas of consensus emerged in the initial shortlists. Almost every judge across both prizes shortlisted Damon Galgut's *The Impostor* and Michiel Heyns's *Bodies Politic* and there was implicit consensus about the literary value of works such as Anne Landsman's *The Rowing Lesson*, Chris Marnewick's *Shepherds and Butchers* and Peter Harris's *In a Different Time*. Equally, there was implicit consensus around the absence from both shortlists of works that might have been expected to feature, such as Mandla Langa's *The Lost Colours of the Chameleon* (which won the 2009 Commonwealth Writers' Prize) although Langa was excluded from the M-Net Literary Award reckoning because he was an executive within the Multichoice corporate structure. Michael Cawood Green's *For the Sake of Silence*, which might also have been expected to feature, was a surprising absence. Such areas of consensus among a diverse judging group would seem to suggest that literary reckoning – in the evaluative sense – is not quite so wayward as one might have expected; that there might well be underlying operative methodologies of evaluation.

Indeed, the responses that I solicited from the judges of both prizes (in the English category) to the question, 'What were your values and your implicit methodologies of judging the literary works submitted to you?' revealed a distinct trend. I asked several judges, via email, to provide, 'off the top of [their] heads', a 'brief summary of the implicit literary values and the implicit critical methodology [you] employ when making [your] calls for the [prize] shortlist'. I wanted 'top-of-head' reflex responses, since I believe these are the operative as opposed to the agreed literary criteria. I believe, nonetheless, that the judges who did respond would have retained their core criteria had they been given ten days and ten pages in which to respond.

Karen Scherzinger, professor and chair of English at the University of Johannesburg, replied with the opening statement that in judging the UJ Literary Award, she worked on the premise that

> award-winners should represent excellence in Literature with a capital 'L', as Fay Weldon unapologetically puts it, in *Letters to Alice on First Reading Jane Austen*. The questions I keep in mind when I am reading the submissions are: could I teach this novel (or poem, or memoir, or whatever else it might be) to my university-level students? Does it have the complexity, ambiguity and metaphorical originality and richness that could sustain a series of lectures? Is this the kind of text on which I might be inspired to write an academic article? So I suppose what I am looking for is that strange creature, a text of literary and academic merit – although it is almost impossible for me to articulate precisely what those terms mean, especially in the space of one paragraph. I'm not looking for a text that is 'popular' so much as one that is *challenging*. That said, the 'sjoe' factor is a real one – especially in the debut category, where we are given the opportunity simply to applaud energy, enthusiasm and courage, without dwelling too much on a submission's level of High Seriousness.[8]

Craig MacKenzie, professor and former chair of English at the University of Johannesburg, had the following to say:

> I have thought quite a lot about this (having had to read something like 250 texts in the last two and a half years for various literary prizes). I don't believe I have anything particularly in mind when approaching a batch of reading, but look out for readability; a compelling narrative thread; an unusual angle; humour; incisiveness; unpredictability; clean, accomplished language. The feeling I have when reading any text is: why should I go on reading? Is there not something better for me to read (given that only so many books can be read in a lifetime)? Things that put me off completely are shoddily written, predictable texts, or those that require a great deal from their reader without yielding any reward.

David Medalie, professor of English at the University of Pretoria and a writer of (South African) fiction himself, commented in these terms:

> The quality of the language: no matter what the subject matter, a winning entry would, for me, need to be linguistically impressive. I am drawn to works which are linguistically ambitious, but which do not reach too far or show signs of strain: there must also be delicacy, restraint and understatement to offset the richness of the language and to show that the writer is fully in control of his or her material.

Jane Rosenthal, novelist and critic, gave the following account:

> In previous years I had a little system in which I rated each book on a five-point scale in categories such as strength of characters, plot, themes, structure and quality of writing. This worked reasonably well to help get some sort of steadiness of assessment into the process, but it was rather tedious. This year I decided to just read headlong through each novel and see what I thought at the end of it. Some novels I abandoned after a few pages as they were conspicuously not going to make a short or even a long list. The criteria which would ensure that a book was actually read to the end would include one or all of these: originality (of ideas, language, character); complexity (the author's ability to embrace many strands and ideas); subtle grasp of character; a sustained emotional tone or tones; suspense (the reader should have some strong desire to know how the novel

turns out); high level of language sophistication in use of specific idiom, clever dialogue, metaphor, rhythm – a perfection of style (which could be dense and cluttered or simple and clear); seriousness of themes.

My own off the top of my head response (and the one I used in the 2009 M-Net judging deliberations) is the following:

In the judging, I singled out the following factors: 1) readability score; 2) moral, ethical and philosophical acuity or vision in the thematics of the work; and 3) the deeper intelligence of form in the work, or the implicit, second-order intelligence that resides not only in the work's thematic content, but also in its structuration. In valuing these categories, I took into consideration the extent to which the works were in keeping with what I regarded as the contemporary conditions of (South African) writing, best summed up as transnational as well as post-anti-apartheid, and the extent to which the work was polyphonic, or the multivocality of the work.[9]

I did not ask the judges to frame their responses within a consideration of the category 'South African fiction' or 'South African writing'. It is nevertheless striking that these responses – which I believe to be a mark of maturity in the South African academy in terms of their formal sophistication – seem almost uniformly to eschew, at the primary level of formulation, criteria that relate specifically to the 'national' question, or the 'political', or class and race factors. The quoted critics decidedly do have opinions on these matters and their off the top of their head responses were framed by a general and deliberately undifferentiated question. I find it to be valuable critical and historiographic data that the critics' first enunciations on literary value suggest a move towards what I tentatively call a more internationalist formalism, a preoccupation with the textures of textuality, in preference to earlier forms of 'engaged' or 'sociological' critical criteria in the academy. I am largely in agreement with the various strands of criteria given by the judges quoted above. I believe that such evaluative standards based on what I would call the *formal, operational dynamics of writing* are good, and necessary, for the formal judging and ranking of fiction. My bigger point is that South African exceptionalism (as Mahmood Mamdani [1996: 27] pointed out a while ago in relation to political history) has worn away to almost nothing. Surely it is revealing that in judging *South African* literary prizes in the year 2009 the judges' criteria seem largely indistinguishable in the final analysis from criteria used to judge the Man-Booker or any other world literary prize?

Whether this is a good or a bad thing is a different debate. For the moment the point I would like to make is that the geographical collocation of works under the moniker 'South African' appears to have become little more than incidental. Certainly, the sponsors of the prizes are likely (in some instances, perhaps not all) to market their validation of literature with money and honour under the mantle of a South African nationalism (largely idealistic in the rainbow-mould, calling on notions of national belonging), but for the judges, the works were judged as literature. Or, let us say, primarily as literature and only then as 'South African literature'. As Scherzinger puts it, literature 'with a capital L'. To this, many would say, 'Bravo!'. At last, 'we' have come of age. 'We' have joined the rest of the world. In a relentlessly transnationalising, globalised world, there is no other option. Not only has 'our' literature broken the bounds of national exceptionalism, but this is desirable and inevitable. The case for this argument is suggested by the pattern of validation in the very best Afrikaans writing: publication in Afrikaans within the country, followed by international publication in translation. For these Afrikaans authors, such as André Brink, Marlene van Niekerk, Eben Venter, Deon Meyer and Etienne van Heerden, writing is an expansionary thrust from committedly located identity into a transnational reading public. International publication in English is a vital second life of literature for them, an extension of their beings as writers, not to mention an extension of their reading publics and their potential sales.

Conclusion: Distant reading as a practice for 'South African' fiction?

Franco Moretti scandalised the literary academy in 2000 by proposing what he called 'distant reading', in defiance of the US tradition of 'close reading'. Moretti was looking for a way of doing what the comparatists call 'world literature' and he made a compelling point: the more texts you study, the greater the distance from the text. The 'trouble with close reading (in all of its incarnations, from the new criticism to deconstruction),' he wrote, is that

> it necessarily depends on an extremely small canon. This may have become an unconscious and invisible premiss by now, but it is an iron one nonetheless: you invest so much in individual texts *only* if you think that very few of them really matter. Otherwise, it doesn't make sense. And if you want to look beyond the canon (and, of course, world literature will do so: it would be absurd if it didn't!) close reading will not do it. It's not designed to do it, it's designed to do the opposite (2000: 57).

The End of 'South African' Literary History?

Close reading, Moretti argued, was really a 'theological exercise', what he describes as 'very solemn treatment of very few texts taken very seriously'. What was really needed, he wrote, was 'a little pact with the devil':

> [W]e know how to read texts, now let's learn how *not* to read them. Distant reading: where distance, let me repeat it, *is a condition of knowledge*: it allows you to focus on units that are much smaller or much larger than the text: devices, themes, tropes – or genres and systems. And if, between the very small and the very large, the text itself disappears, well, it is one of those cases when one can justifiably say, Less is more. If we want to understand the system in its entirety, we must accept losing something. We always pay a price for theoretical knowledge: reality is infinitely rich; concepts are abstract, are poor. But it's precisely this 'poverty' that makes it possible to handle them, and therefore to know. This is why less is actually more (57–8).

Moretti is arguing for a way of describing large units of 'literature' within the quixotic quest to write a 'world' literary history. World literature, he writes, 'is not an object, it's a *problem* and a problem that asks for a new critical method: and no one has ever found a method by just reading more texts' (2005: 55). Reading Moretti's controversial essay, the question arises: is what we call 'South African literature' massifying and transnationalising to such an extent, and so diversifying in theme and content, that it is a 'problem' rather than an object and it requires 'distant reading'? To some extent, this has always been the case – witness the fact that Stephen Gray's landmark *Southern African Literature: An Introduction* (1979) was itself an act of 'distant reading', a drawing out of what Moretti calls 'devices, themes, tropes' from a vast range of works. A similar argument might be made of Michael Chapman's *Southern African Literatures* (2003 [1996]) – indeed, the differential between inclusion and exclusion of individual works as against shapes and motifs in the literature as a whole was at the core of that book's contested critical reception.[10] If distant reading has been a precondition for writing South African literary history, might it not be true of current literary production, which appears to have outstripped the bounds of detailed critical stocktaking or, indeed, the category 'South African Literature'?

An example of practice, or a case in point, is this chapter itself. To take the instance of Michiel Heyns's *Bodies Politic* which won the Herman Charles Bosman Prize in 2009 and ended up on the shortlists of both the UJ and the M-Net Literary Awards, it requires a stretch of the imagination to call the novel 'South African' in any but an indirect sense. The story takes place in England and it deals with the suffragette movement in the early twentieth century, particularly with the lives of the Pankhurst family. Faced with this situation, a critic can argue for the relevance of themes in the supposedly 'non-South African' work for the 'South African' case (as I did in the M-Net deliberations, saying that the subordination of the personal body and the affective realm to the *body politic*, as occurs in Heyns's novel, is a potent theme in the era of Jacob Zuma); or argue that 'South African' content is a red herring: 'South African' authors are increasingly competing for readership in a world market, as well as within the general category of 'world literature'. One can argue for both: if one sees the first option as centripetal and the second as centrifugal, then surely both are apt? Surely both centripetal and centrifugal forces are characteristic of the transnational rupture? It is, however, only possible to take the inward-bound view via a practice of distant reading. Only through a distillation of themes and a cognitive process of analogy and pattern-recognition can one make the case for the relevance of Heyns's *Bodies Politic* to a 'South African' situation, polity or thematic field.[11] Close reading will not do it. At the same time, to return to my earlier qualification concerning the transnational, Imraan Coovadia's prize-winning *High Low In-between* deals with Mbeki-era AIDS denialism while, in its slightly satirical portrait of the Indian matriarch, it also captures a new kind of racial (and often racist) discourse that has emerged strongly in the not-quite-post-apartheid South Africa. And although Sally-Ann Murray's award-winning *Small Moving Parts* might be almost Joycean in its semantic storehouse of wordplay and 'global' in a structure that is alert to contemporary theories of the *Bildungsroman*, its subject remains the tangs, textures and experiences of growing up in Durban or, more precisely, the 'hood Umbilo, Durbs. Again, there is no neat separation of the categories transnational and South African Literature.

My larger point, however, remains: who, apart from the M-Net judges and the judges of the other big prizes, is conducting a critical audit of everything written by South African writers in every given year and rating/evaluating it as well as making notes on it? Those who are looking at recent work inevitably do it selectively, according to Moretti's devices, themes and tropes. Generally, the thinking of the various judges and their notes remain unpublished. For as long as I am a judge, I shall endeavour to write up the process for publication on a yearly basis.[12] But I could be replaced as a judge at the whim of the conveners. Does it matter? If, as Moretti argues, you want to look beyond the canon, close reading will not do the job. What we increasingly have, I would suggest, is a 'problem' rather than a 'literature' and that problem remains, how do we best read the writing by and among South Africans, wherever they are, in the context of, and in relation to, the much larger world to which we have become integral? Writers' nationality has now become of secondary interest. The local is of interest only in the way it infuses global concerns with a critically located inflection. There may well be a subsidiary 'South African' reading market, represented by South African publishers and readers, but the critics have, largely, jumped ship, to use a curiously apt idiom given the current (and growing) preoccupation with the category of the ocean and oceanic studies. So, if 'South African literature' is adrift, so to speak, then it may not necessarily be such a bad thing.

Notes

1. This argument is drawn from 'South Africa in the Global Imaginary: An Introduction' (De Kock 2001, 2004).
2. See 'How to Get into Bed with a Publisher', *Sunday Times Lifestyle* (De Kock 2008b), in which this figure is deduced from statistics given by South African publishers at a colloquium with publishers (Wits University, 2008).
3. See Nuttall's *Entanglement* (2009) and work by Rita Barnard as well as Titlestad (along with others) in the forthcoming *Cambridge History of South African Literature*, currently in preparation under the editorship of Derek Attridge and David Attwell. Samuelson's overview in *English Studies in Africa* (Samuelson 2008) is helpful and detailed. See also Chapman and others in this volume.
4. 'Best' as judged by the prestigious M-Net Literary Award for English fiction, of which I was one of three judges for the English category. Landsman's novel won the prize, while Heyns was a close second. (Van Heerden's *30 nagte in Amsterdam* won both the 2009 UJ Literary Award and the 2009 M-Net Literary Award for Afrikaans fiction.)
5. I did not sit on this panel of judges. The judges were Michael Titlestad, Imraan Coovadia and Jane Rosenthal.
6. See Appendix 1 for lists of 2009 and 2010 prize-winning and shortlisted works.
7. For example, the M-Net Literary Award for fiction, the UJ Literary Award, the Sunday Times Prize for Fiction, among others.
8. The judges' responses quoted here appear with the permission of their authors.
9. The condensed comments of my own and the other 2009 M-Net judges may be found in *Current Writing* 21(1&2), 2009: 51–6.
10. See, for example, Ampie Coetzee (1996); Helize van Vuuren (1997); Michael Green (1996); and Hennie van Coller (2008).
11. This was my argument at a 2006 gathering of global literary historiographers in Stockholm, which resulted in the book *Studying Transcultural History* (see De Kock 2006).
12. My judge's comments on the M-Net Literary Award for 2010 can be found in Appendix 2.

References

Attridge, Derek and David Attwell (eds). Forthcoming 2012. *The Cambridge History of South African Literature*. Cambridge: Cambridge University Press.
Badal, Sean. 2008. *The Fall of the Black-Eyed Night*. Cape Town: Umuzi. [novel]
Baderoon, Gabeba. 2005. *The Dream in the Next Body*. Cape Town: Kwela Books with Snailpress. [poetry]
———. 2006. *A Hundred Silences*. Cape Town: Kwela Books. [poetry]
Barker, Derek. 2007 [2006]. English Academic Literary Discourse in South Africa 1958–2004. Ph.D. thesis, University of South Africa, 2006. Published electronically by the University of Trier (Germany), 2007, http://ubt.opus.hbz-nrw.de/volltexte/2007/437/ (accessed 18 March 2011).
Behr, Mark. 1995. *The Smell of Apples*. London: Abacus. [novel]
———. 2000. *Embrace*. London: Little, Brown & Co. [novel]
———. 2009. *Kings of the Water*. Johannesburg: Penguin. [novel]
Beukes, Lauren. 2008. *Moxyland*. Johannesburg: Jacana Media. [novel]
Bloom, Kevin. 2009. *Ways of Staying*. Johannesburg: Picador Africa. [creative non-fiction]
Brown, Andrew. 2007. *Inyenzi: A Tale of Love and Genocide*. Cape Town: Zebra. [novel]
———. 2009. *Refuge*. Cape Town: Zebra. [novel]
Brownlee, Russel. 2005. *Garden of the Plagues*. Cape Town: Human & Rousseau. [novel]
Bulbring, Edyth. 2008. *The Club*. Johannesburg: Jonathan Ball. [novel]
Cartwright, Justin. 2009. *To Heaven by Water*. London: Bloomsbury. [novel]
Chapman, Michael. 2003 [1996]. *Southern African Literatures*. Pietermaritzburg: University of KwaZulu-Natal Press.
Coetzee, Ampie. 1996. 'Southern African Literatures'. *Alternation* 3(2): 231–7.
Coetzee, J.M. 2007. *Diary of a Bad Year*. London: Harvill Secker.
———. 2009. *Summertime*. London: Harvill Secker.
Coovadia, Imraan. 2006. *Green-Eyed Thieves*. Cape Town: Umuzi. [novel]
———. 2009. *High Low In-between*. Cape Town: Umuzi. [novel]
De Kock, Leon. 2001. 'South Africa in the Global Imaginary: An Introduction'. *Poetics Today* 22(2): 263–98. [Republished in De Kock, Leon, Louise Bethlehem and Sonja Laden (eds). 2004.]
———. 2005a. 'Does South African Literature Still Exist? Or: South African Literature Is Dead, Long Live Literature in South Africa'. *English in Africa* 32(2): 69–83.
———. 2005b. Interview with Henrietta Rose-Innes. *Sunday Times Lifestyle*, 6 March: 18.
———. 2006. 'Naming of Parts, or, How Things Shape up in Transcultural Literary History'. In: *Studying Transcultural Literary History*, edited by G. Lindberg-Wada, 12–22. Berlin: Walter de Gruyter.
———. 2008a. 'A History of Restlessness: And Now for the Rest'. *English Studies in Africa* 51(1): 109–22.
———. 2008b. 'How to Get into Bed with a Publisher'. *Sunday Times*, 8 June. http://www.thetimes.co.za/Books/Article.aspx?id=780495 (accessed 29 April 2009).
De Kock, Leon, Louise Bethlehem and Sonja Laden (eds). 2004. *South Africa in the Global Imaginary*. Pretoria: Unisa Press; Leiden: Koninklijke Brill.
Dlamini, Jacob. 2009. *Native Nostalgia*. Johannesburg: Jacana Media. [creative non-fiction]

Dowling, Finuala. 2005. *What Poets Need: A Novel*. Johannesburg: Penguin.
———. 2007. *Flyleaf*. Johannesburg: Penguin. [novel]
———. 2008. *Notes from the Dementia Ward: Poems*. Cape Town: Kwela Books.
Duiker, K. Sello. 2000. *Thirteen Cents*. Cape Town: David Philip. [novel]
———. 2001. *The Quiet Violence of Dreams*. Cape Town: Kwela Books. [novel]
———. 2006. *The Hidden Star*. Cape Town: Umuzi. [novel]
Emdon, Erica. 2009. *Jelly Dog Days*. Johannesburg: Penguin. [novel]
Farren, Tracy. 2008. *Whiplash*. Athlone: Modjaji Books. [novel]
Fedler, Joanne. 2008. *Things without a Name*. Sydney: Allen & Unwin. [novel]
Fraser, Nancy. 2007 [2002]. 'Transnationalizing the Public Sphere: On the Legitimacy and Efficacy of Public Opinion in a Post-Westphalian World'. *Theory, Culture & Society* 24(4): 7–30. [First delivered as a keynote address at the Graduate Center, City University of New York, at a conference on Public Space, February 2002.] Available online at http://www.yale-university.org/polisci/info/conferences/fraser1.doc (accessed 25 May 2009). Page numbers cited in this chapter refer to this version of the paper.
Fugard, Lisa. 2005. *Skinner's Drift*. Johannesburg: Picador Africa. [novel]
Galgut, Damon. 2008. *The Impostor*. Johannesburg: Penguin.
Garman, Anthea. 2010. 'Global Resonance, Local Amplification: Antjie Krog on a World Stage'. *Social Dynamics* 36(1): 187–200.
Gray, Stephen. 1979. *Southern African Literature: An Introduction*. Cape Town: David Philip.
Green, Michael. 1996. 'Southern African Literary History: Totality and/or Fragment'. Symposium: Institute for Cultural Studies, University of Essen (July).
Green, Michael Cawood. 2008. *For the Sake of Silence*. Cape Town: Umuzi.
Harris, Peter. 2008. *In a Different Time*. Cape Town: Umuzi.
Herbstein, Manu. 2001. *Ama: A Story of the Atlantic Slave Trade*. New York: E-Reads. [novel]
Heyns, Michiel. 2008. *Bodies Politic*. Johannesburg: Jonathan Ball. [novel]
———. 2009. Review of Sally-Ann Murray's *Small Moving Parts*. http://www.michielheyns.co.za/documents/Small%20Moving%20Parts.pdf (accessed 18 March 2011).
Higginson, Craig. 2005. *The Hill*. Johannesburg: Jacana Media. [novel]
Hofmeyr, Isabel. 2004. *The Portable Bunyan: A Transnational History of 'The Pilgrim's Progress'*. Princeton: Princeton University Press; Johannesburg: Wits University Press.
Hofmeyr, Isabel and Liz Gunner. 2005. 'Introduction: Transnationalism and African Literature'. *Scrutiny2* 10(2): 1–8. [Special issue on Transnationalism and African Literature, edited by Hofmeyr and Gunner.]
Jacobs, Rayda. 1998. *The Slave Book*. Cape Town: Kwela Books. [novel]
———. 2001. *Sachs Street*. Cape Town: Kwela Books. [novel]
———. 2003. *Confessions of a Gambler*. Cape Town: Kwela Books. [novel]
———. 2004. *Postcards from South Africa*. Cape Town: Double Storey. [short stories]
———. 2005. *The Mecca Diaries*. Cape Town: Double Storey. [memoir]
———. 2006. *My Father's Orchid*. Cape Town: Umuzi. [novel]
Jamal, Ashraf. 1996. *Love Themes for the Wilderness*. Cape Town: Kwela Books with Random House. [novel]
———. 2002. *The Shades*. Howick: Brevitas. [short stories]
Johnson, Shaun. 2006. *The Native Commissioner: A Novel*. Johannesburg: Penguin.

Kaganof, Aryan. 2002. *Hectic!* Johannesburg: Pine Slopes. [novel]
———. 2006. *Uselessly.* Johannesburg: Jacana Media. [novel]
———. 2007. *12shooters.* Johannesburg: Pine Slopes. [novel]
Kendal, Rosamund. 2008. *Karma Suture.* Johannesburg: Jacana Media. [novel]
Khumalo, Fred. 2006a. *Bitches' Brew.* Johannesburg: Jacana Media. [novel]
———. 2006b. *Touch My Blood: The Early Years.* Cape Town: Umuzu. [autobiography]
———. 2008. *Seven Steps to Heaven.* Johannesburg: Jacana Media. [novel]
Kirkwood, Mike. 1976. 'The Colonizer: A Critique of the English South African Culture Theory'. In: *Poetry South Africa: Selected Papers from Poetry '74*, edited by P. Wilhelm and J. Polley. Johannesburg: Ad. Donker: 102–33.
Kraak, Gerald. 2006. *Ice in the Lungs.* Johannesburg: Jacana Media. [novel]
Krog, Antjie. 1998. *Country of my Skull.* Johannesburg: Random House.
Kruger, Loren. 2002. ' "Black Atlantics", "White Indians", and "Jews": Locations, Locutions, and Syncretic Identities in the Fiction of Achmat Dangor and Others'. *Scrutiny2* 7(2): 34–50.
Landsman, Anne. 2008. *The Rowing Lesson.* Cape Town: Kwela Books.
Langa, Mandla. 2008. *The Lost Colours of the Chameleon.* Johannesburg: Picador Africa.
Liebenberg, Lauren. 2008. *The Voluptuous Delights of Peanut Butter and Jam.* London: Virago. [novel]
Lindberg-Wada, Gunilla. 2006. *Studying Transcultural Literary History.* Berlin: Walter de Gruyter.
Maart, Rozena. 2008. *The Writing Circle.* Pietermaritzburg: Shuter & Shooter. [novel]
Mackenzie, Jassie. 2008. *Random Violence.* Cape Town: Umuzi. [novel]
Mamdani, Mahmood. 1996. *Citizen and Subject: Contemporary Africa and the Legacy of Late Colonialism.* London: James Currey.
Marnewick, Chris. 2008. *Shepherds and Butchers.* Cape Town: Umuzi. [novel]
Mashile, Lebo. 2005. *In a Ribbon of Rhythm.* Johannesburg: Mutloatse Arts Heritage Trust & Oshun Books. [poetry]
Mason, Richard. 2008. *The Lighted Rooms.* London: Weidenfeld & Nicolson. [novel]
Matlwa, Kopano. 2007. *Coconut.* Johannesburg: Jacana Media. [novel]
Meeran, Zinaid. 2009. *Saracen at the Gates.* Johannesburg: Jacana Media. [novel]
Mhlongo, Niq. 2004. *Dog Eat Dog.* Cape Town: Kwela Books. [novel]
———. 2007. *After Tears.* Cape Town: Kwela Books. [novel]
Miller, Kirsten. 2007. *All is Fish: A Novel.* Johannesburg: Jacana Media.
Moele, Kgebetli. 2009. *The Book of the Dead.* Cape Town: Kwela Books. [novel]
Mohlele, Nthikeng. 2008. *The Scent of Bliss.* Johannesburg: Jacana Media. [novel]
Morgan, Alistair. 2009. *Sleeper's Wake.* Johannesburg: Penguin. [novel]
Moretti, Franco. 2000. 'Conjectures on World Literature'. *New Left Review* 1: 54–68.
Mpe, Phaswane. 2001. *Welcome to Our Hillbrow.* Pietermaritzburg: University of Natal Press. [novel]
Mphahlele, Es'kia (Ezekiel). 1959. *Down Second Avenue.* London: Faber and Faber.
Murray, Sally-Ann. 2009. *Small Moving Parts.* Cape Town: Kwela Books. [novel]
Nash, Kate. 2007. 'Transnationalising the Public Sphere: Critique and Critical Possibilities'. *Theory, Culture & Society* 24(4): 53–7.
Nicol, Mike. 1994. *Horseman.* London: Bloomsbury. [novel]

———. 2008. *Payback*. Cape Town: Umuzi. [novel]
Nicol, Mike (with Joanne Hichens). 2006. *Out to Score*. Cape Town: Umuzi. [novel]
Ntshingila, Futhi. 2008. *Shameless*. Pietermaritzburg: University of KwaZulu-Natal Press. [novel]
Nuttall, Sarah. 2009. *Entanglement: Literary and Cultural Reflections on Post-Apartheid*. Johannesburg: Wits University Press.
Pauw, Jacques. 2009. *Little Ice Cream Boy*. Johannesburg: Penguin. [novel]
Pillay, Hamish Hoosen. 2008. *The Rainbow Has No Pink*. Johannesburg: 30 Degrees South. [novel]
Penny, Sarah. 2002. *The Beneficiaries*. Johannesburg: Penguin. [novel]
Rabie, Susan. 2008. *Boston Snowplough*. Cape Town: Human & Rousseau. [novel]
Randeria, Shalini. 2007. 'De-Politicisation of Democracy and Judicialisation of Politics'. *Theory, Culture & Society* 24(4): 38–44.
Richards, Jo-Anne. 1996. *The Innocence of Roast Chicken*. London: Headline. [novel]
———. 2008. *My Brother's Book*. Johannesburg: Picador Africa. [novel]
Rose-Innes, Henrietta. 2000. *Sharks' Egg*. Cape Town: Kwela Books. [novel]
———. 2004. *The Rock Alphabet*. Cape Town: Kwela Books. [novel]
Sachs, Albie. 2009. *The Strange Alchemy of Life and Law*. Oxford: Oxford University Press.
Samuelson, Meg. 2008. 'Walking through the Door and Inhabiting the House: South African Literary Culture and Criticism after the Transition'. *English Studies in Africa* 51(1): 130–7.
Sithebe, Angelina S. 2007. *Holy Hill*. Cape Town: Umuzi. [novel]
Smit, Johannes, Jean-Philippe Wade and Johan van Wyk (eds). 2006. *Rethinking South African Literary History*. Durban: Y Press.
Steinberg, Jonny. 2008. *Three Letter Plague*. Johannesburg: Jonathan Ball.
Taylor, Jane. 2009. *The Transplant Men*. Johannesburg: Jacana Media. [novel]
Tlholwe, Diale. 2008. *Ancient Rites*. Cape Town: Kwela Books. [novel]
Troost, Heinrich. 2007. *Plot Loss*. Cape Town: Umuzi. [novel]
Van Coller, Hennie. 2008. 'Recently Published South African Literary Histories'. *English in Africa* 35(1): 151–75.
Van Heerden, Etienne. 2008. *30 nagte in Amsterdam*. Cape Town: Tafelberg.
Van Vuuren, Helize. 1997. 'Southern African Literatures'. *Journal of Literary Studies* 13(1): 190–209.
Vladisavić, Ivan. 2001. *The Restless Supermarket*. Cape Town: David Philip.
———. 2004. *The Exploded View*. Johannesburg: Random House.
Voysey-Braig, Megan. 2008. *Till We Can Keep an Animal*. Johannesburg: Jacana Media. [novel]
Wanner, Zukiswa. 2008. *Behind Every Successful Man*. Cape Town: Kwela Books. [novel]
Warner, Michael. 2002. *Publics and Counterpublics*. New York: Zone Books.
Wicomb, Zoë. 2001. *David's Story*. New York: Feminist Press at the City University of New York. [novel]
———. 2006. *Playing in the Light: A Novel*. New York: New Press.
———. 2008. *The One That Got Away*. Cape Town: Umuzi. [short stories]
Wilhelm, Peter and James A. Polley. 1976. *Poetry South Africa: Selected Papers from Poetry '74*. Johannesburg: Ad. Donker.
Zadok, Rachel. 2005. *Gem Squash Tokoloshe*. London: Pan. [novel]

Appendix 1
Winners and Shortlistings, 2009 and 2010

Winners and shortlistings (English sections) in several literary competitions in South Africa in 2009:

M-Net Literary Award
Winner: Anne Landsman, *The Rowing Lesson*
Shortlisted: Michiel Heyns, *Bodies Politic*; Damon Galgut, *The Impostor*; Zoë Wicomb, *The One That Got Away*; Chris Marnewick, *Shepherds and Butchers*

UJ Literary Award
Winner: Damon Galgut, *The Impostor*
Debut prize winner: Chris Marnewick, *Shepherds and Butchers*
Shortlisted: Michiel Heyns, *Bodies Politic*; Jonny Steinberg, *Three-Letter Plague*; Finuala Dowling, *Notes from the Dementia Ward*

Sunday Times Fiction Prize
Winner: Anne Landsman, *The Rowing Lesson*
Shortlisted: Tracey Farren, *Whiplash*; Damon Galgut, *The Impostor*; Michiel Heyns, *Bodies Politic*; Mandla Langa, *The Lost Colours of the Chameleon*
(Peter Harris's *In a Different Time* won the Sunday Times-Alan Paton Prize, the non-fiction category of the above-mentioned prize.)

Herman Charles Bosman Prize
Winner: Michiel Heyns, *Bodies Politic*

Olive Schreiner Literary Award: Finuala Dowling, *Notes from the Dementia Ward*

Winners and shortlistings (English sections) in several literary competitions in South Africa in 2010:

M-Net Literary Award
Winner: Sally-Ann Murray, *Small Moving Parts*
Shortlisted: Justin Cartwright, *To Heaven by Water*; J.M. Coetzee, *Summertime*; Imraan Coovadia, *High Low In-between*; Jacques Pauw, *Little Ice Cream Boy*

UJ Literary Award
Winner: Imraan Coovadia, *High Low In-between*
Debut prize winner: Jacob Dlamini, *Native Nostalgia*
Shortlisted: Sally-Ann Murray, *Small Moving Parts*; Mark Behr, *Kings of the Water*

Sunday Times Fiction Prize
Winner: Imraan Coovadia, *High Low In-between*
Shortlisted: Sally-Ann Murray, *Small Moving Parts*; J.M. Coetzee *Summertime*;
    Zinaid Meeran, *Saracen at the Gates*; Kgebetli Moele, *The Book of the Dead*
(Albie Sachs's *The Strange Alchemy of Life and Law* won the Sunday Times-Alan
    Paton Prize, the non-fiction category of the above-mentioned prize.)

Herman Charles Bosman Prize
Winner: Sally-Ann Murray, *Small Moving Parts*

Olive Schreiner Literary Award [for a debut novel]: Michael Cawood Green, *For the Sake of Silence*

Appendix 2
Leon de Kock's Judge's Comments on M-Net Literary Award for 2010

This year's entries were, in my opinion, less impressive than last year's, with fewer books of very high quality and a noticeable fall-off in quality from 2009. Nonetheless, quite apart from the shortlisted books discussed below, there were several other impressive and notable books, including Andrew Brown's *Refuge*, a strong treatment of issues of migrancy in contemporary South Africa; Erica Emdon's *Jelly Dog Days*, a similarly powerful story about social violence, marred somewhat by inconsistent and implausible use of narrative voice; [Alistair Morgan's] *Sleeper's Wake* and [Jane Taylor's] *The Transplant Men*, both vividly realised but not quite, for me, ultimate winners.

I want to make a case at this year's judging deliberations for the use of more defined criteria, so that the winner can be argued to have met certain key expectations that differentiate it from other works; and so that we don't end up having judging arguments in which one person's taste is up against another person's taste. Can we settle on criteria beyond mere literary taste? Arguments based on literary taste alone will surely lead us into a deep fog from which it is difficult to escape.

I would formulate my criteria thus: the winning work must perform a *significantly inventive and unique recreation of known elements* (language, form, memory, imagination and story) in ways that invite otherness into the world of the same; the winning work should *challenge the reader through transformed senses of possibility* within the elements of the familiar, but beckoning beyond the familiar;

and, finally, the winning work should contain a secondary level of meaning that speaks not only through its stated content, but through the *implicit intelligence of its use of form*. These factors should combine in a work that is likely to make a lasting impact on the body of literature and the society from which it arises.

After much reflection, consideration and reconsideration, I have come to the conclusion that *two* works are tied, neck-and-neck, for first place on the above criteria: *Small Moving Parts* and *Summertime*.

Small Moving Parts

Sally-Ann Murray's debut novel is lush in its textures of language and its minutely observed narration. This is a novel that does things with language that are demonstrably extraordinary and innovative. I would almost use the word 'Joycean' for the manner in which Murray delves into the semantic storehouses of wordplay, lyrical prose, unusual and rarely used terms and word combinations to evoke a correspondingly rich and somatically imagined childhood in Durban. Structurally, too, the novel is consistently innovative. I am not aware of any similar treatment by a South African writer of the *Bildungsroman* genre. Murray writes a series of subtitled fictional essays (no chapters) on many, minutely observed and detailed, phases of life and feeling, relationship and family event, in a style that represents a deep and concretely realised lyrical indwelling in the moment of experience. Taken as individual units of description, and read in a leisurely way, these narrative sections are richly evocative, reading almost with the kind of pleasure one gets from poetry. The novel's detailed historical recovery, in addition to its subjective experiential rendering, are such as to represent a landmark in South African fiction.

The most significant objection to Murray's novel is that it has proved to be a heavy-going reading experience for some readers. Such readers regard the novel's detail and wordplay as overdone, with several reporting that they were unable to complete the novel.

I would like to argue that this objection is valid as testimony of certain readers' experience of digesting the novel, but that it is not necessarily valid as a qualitative criticism of a complex work. Many people have said much the same about the works of James Joyce and Marcel Proust, let alone the works of postmodern novelists such as Donald Barthelme and John Barth. Difficulty may point to complexity of form of content as much as it may point to turgid writing.

I would like to argue that Murray's writing is indeed dense and complex, and therefore sometimes difficult to read from the point of view of an easy reading experience, but surely when one judges works for a literary prize one is doing something quite different from seeking an easy reading experience? On the contrary, my sense is that the outstanding qualities of Murray's writing lie precisely in the density and the complexity of her literary expression. In terms of the criteria stated above, Murray's novel:

1. Performs a *significantly inventive and unique recreation* of known elements (language, form, memory, imagination and story) in ways that invite otherness into the world of the same; I am not aware of any piece of South African writing that has rendered the *Bildungsroman* form with such lyrical beauty and complexity and which delivers an alchemy of memory and story in so minutely detailed and yet imaginatively transformative a form. That is, her novel combines both the imaginative and the real – for long two contending and often irreconcilable poles in SA writing – in ways that are unique and outstanding.
2. *Challenges the reader through transformed senses of possibility* within the elements of the familiar, but beckoning beyond the familiar. *Small Moving Parts* challenges the reader to understand the experience of white childhood in the 1960s in significantly more detailed, complex, contradictory and multilayered ways than any other similar work I am aware of in the corpus of English SA writing. In this sense, the work is recreating a sense of the past, in fact recreating the past as a narrative, and showing that this is in fact what it must always be; it does this in complex, unique and outstanding ways.
3. Contains a secondary level of meaning that speaks not only through its stated content, but through the *implicit intelligence of its use of form*. I believe this is the case in Murray's novel. The intelligence of the form is such that it implicitly renders the subjectivity of its characters, especially its main character, Halley, in a layered, *rhizomatic* form, thereby disproving and disavowing the tyranny of unitary representations of identity in racial, ethnic, cultural or other singular and restrictive categories, or in narrowly mimetic or realistic forms. This, to my mind, is a major achievement that the other shortlisted novels do not achieve in quite the same way.

Michiel Heyns, in his review of Murray's novel in the *Sunday Independent*, writes that Murray, as a prize-winning poet, 'knows that language can constitute reality as much as describe it'. He concludes as follows:

> If, here, the small moving parts are mainly an image of the precarious, puzzling nature of existence, in the novel as a whole they come to stand for its multifariousness, for the endlessly fascinating constituents of a world that repays magnificently the attention one bestows upon it. Murray's novel brings that world miraculously to life (Heyns 2009).

Heyns is a restrained critic who seldom uses words like 'magnificent' and 'miraculous'. Here, I feel, these terms are justified in describing a clear winner among this year's entries.

Summertime

As is the case with all Coetzee's oblique and referentially complex works, a whole phalanx of commentaries could be written about the intricacies of content and narrative rendering in *Summertime*. Coetzee adopts a stunningly smart conceit in this, his third (and final?) instalment of memoir-writing after *Boyhood* and *Youth*, in which he ultimately writes about himself by purporting *not* to write about himself. Instead, he employs a fictional biographer who, after Coetzee's 'death', is now conducting (fictional) interviews with several people who are supposed to have had interactions with Coetzee at various stages in his life. The playful narrative that ensues, funny and ironic, wistful and candid, takes on directly the many myths about Coetzee's social awkwardness, his gruff and strange manner with people and his obsessions. To this list Coetzee here adds his lack of sexual prowess or attractiveness. The effect of reading these 'accounts' of Coetzee (supposedly) by women while knowing that (ultimately) Coetzee himself has written such deeply unflattering descriptions, is strangely exhilarating, often quite hilarious and strongly compassion-inducing. Coetzee emerges as vulnerable and awkward, by his own account. He depicts himself as a person who is just as hobbled by his personality as other people are said to have been irritated by it, just as put off by his variously odd manners and mannerisms, as other people are said to have been, as so often reported in the media. This is a very rare and unusually moving piece of writing by this otherwise immensely distant author.

Summertime, however, does more than simply rearrange the perspectives held about Coetzee. It also asks fundamentally important questions about the narrativisation of identity and about the relation between documentation (a vital necessity) and narrativisation (a vortex of the distortion that necessarily follows *rearrangement*) – and therefore about the nature of truth in the representations of art as against other versions and formulations of truth.

Moreover, Coetzee's work also reopens unresolvable, but quintessential questions, and opposing versions, or narratives, or discourses, of and about *how to live* as a *white person in Africa* (in this work, the Karoo, the Cape), about melancholy for the land and its damaged people in the face of hard-nosed 'real-life' pragmatism and about lyrical sublimation of the land in the teeth of brutal power dynamics. He does this, ultimately, as author, from the point of view of one who has fled the country and yet still (by implication) is tortured by these unresolved conundrums of identity and belonging. His work shows that the intermeshing and irreconcilable versions of 'truth' around these questions render white subjects in Africa *fundamentally and remorselessly conflicted*.

In terms of the criteria stated above, Coetzee's novel:

1. Performs a *significantly inventive and unique recreation of known elements* (autobiographical form, memory and narrative rendering) in ways that invite otherness into the world of the same; Coetzee here turns the form of autobiography/memoir inside out by rendering himself through seemingly documented evidence, which is however re-narrativised by the imaginary biographer and ultimately re-renarrativised (made up?) by the author, Coetzee, in the last instance. This sets up a hall-of-mirrors effect which demonstrates powerfully, in its enactment as narrative art, that what one might call room for play is a key part of all narrativisation, whether documentary or 'made up'. In doing this, Summertime rejoins the debate about the distinctions between 'real' and 'imaginary', fiction and memoir, which are now so current in the age of what author David Shields calls 'Reality Hunger'. No small matter, indeed, in a world in which the question, 'what is real', and which form of truth has greater value ('documentary' or 'fictional') has become both vexing and of great importance to people and how they attribute value in the world.

2. *Challenges the reader through transformed senses of possibility* within the elements of the familiar, but beckoning beyond the familiar. Summertime challenges the reader to understand the experience of self-portraiture from the uniquely oblique angle of *othering*. That is, it presents the self through accounts of others and in ways in which the accounts of others necessarily *other* (used here as a verb) the subject being written about. This opens a vital philosophical question recalling the work of Emmanuel Levinas and the possibility or (more likely) the impossibility of *knowing the other*. Again, here Coetzee shows that the space between self and other might be conceived, not just as a tortuous space (as in Levinas), or a colonially exploitative space (as in much postcolonial theory), but also as a *space of play*, humour and half-truth. I mean 'half-truth' here not in a pejorative, but in a positive sense – if we cannot achieve truth entire and whole, as Coetzee also implies, then we might be able to achieve a playfully partial truth, so comically depicted in the representation of Coetzee through the eyes of Adriana, the Brazilian dance teacher, as a 'célibataire', 'disembodied' and a man 'who could not dance to save his life'; 'how can you be a great writer when you know nothing about love', she asks of Coetzee. We know, too, that this is Coetzee asking what is, in reality, a devastating question about himself, in a way that makes the reader laugh. Is this not a magnificent achievement of recombining?

3. Contains a secondary level of meaning that speaks not only through its stated content, but through the *implicit intelligence of its use of form*. Throughout *Summertime*, the implicit play of form, the tension between self-rendering and *being rendered by others* creates a formal intelligence which speaks volumes and which speaks resonantly in the silences, the margins, beyond the text. If there is one respect in which I feel Coetzee's text works better than Murray's, it is in this particular manipulation of perspective – of making the implicit, the unspoken irony contained in the form, speak so powerfully from the unspoken margins of the work. Just as Murray enlarges the perspective to capture the minutiae of the 'small, moving parts', so Coetzee *doubles* the perspective, and in the doubling, which he also minimises, the unspoken content of the form emerges. This is masterfully done.

High Low In-Between

Coovadia's third novel deals with the Mbeki era of AIDS denialism and the various morbid symptoms of power that played themselves out in that period, here with particular reference to the perversions of academic freedom committed in the name of such denialism at the University of KwaZulu-Natal under its controversial principal, Prof. Malegapuru William Makgoba (fictionally disguised here as a Zimbabwean academic). At the same time, Coovadia enters into the inner life of an established Indian family in Durban which contains both a politically heroic patriarch (the medical expert who went up against the denialist trend) and an older tradition of political activism which is also infected with a strong stain of mercantile corruption. Interestingly and ironically, the murder of the above-mentioned patriarch in the novel is committed for reasons related to financial corruption within the family rather than above-the-line political corruption. This is a very rich book in which many layers of social and intersubjective relations are depicted with a convincing and assured authorial hand. Especially amusing are the satirical portraits of the Indian matriarch and her odd relationship with her black servant, whom she treats dismissively and with annoyance, while elsewhere, in her life as a medical doctor, she is unimpeachable in her political ethics, although the problematic race relations between black and Indian she encounters at the hospital where she works are typical of a new kind of racial (and often racist) discourse that has emerged strongly in not-quite-post-apartheid South Africa.

To Heaven by Water

Justin Cartwright's novel is focalised via a cosmopolitan, retired UK media professional, David Cross, still famous for his television news-presenting personality and for his work as a foreign correspondent. Cross's narration is laced with observations and feelings about life and ageing in a world dominated by the surfaces of media and a mild obsession with evergreen health (the gym culture). Behind the taciturn surfaces of modern culture, as focalised by Cross, deeper feelings and fears, betrayals and turnarounds, play themselves out in contradistinction to the seemingly languid, seamless continuity of a genteel urban life. This novel has been written with a remarkably assured hand, imparting to the reader a sense of reassurance and community of feeling amid what is otherwise a bewildering tangle of social networking and multiple mediascapes. As a South African-born author, Cartwright remains at the top of his game and his books seldom fail to please and surprise.

Little Ice Cream Boy

Jacques Pauw's novelised life story of apartheid killer Ferdie Barnard, although far from a literary masterpiece, is an excellent read. Pauw has found that hotspot in South African writing, the place where truth is stranger, more thrilling and compelling, than fiction could ever be. Gideon Goosen is the novelistic reconstruction of Ferdie Barnard, the Civil Co-operation Bureau undercover operative who shot Wits academic David Webster in cold blood outside his Troyeville home on 1 May 1989. Pauw enters true-blue fictional territory by redrawing 'Barnard's' childhood and also by imagining the inside-prison, before-and-after frame of the story.

Pauw's writing often treads the line between keen satire and somewhat blotchy realistic description. It's as if the writing finds its mark in precisely this intersection, satirically overdrawn on the one hand, straining for realism on the other, and the tension is not always resolved. However, for the most part, Pauw's pyrotechnics of voice work well enough to carry the story, which in itself is enthralling. It is a story that reopens parts of a common heritage – white trash, chronic lawlessness, police criminality, culturally sanctioned patriarchal violence, the drug underworld, Jo'burg vice, mafia hits and manoeuvres – a dark heritage that needs solid fictional undercarriages. Pauw's hard-hitting first novel, even if crude in places, proves that there's a lot of dirt out there that we need to pick up in our otherwise genteel literary narratives.

2

Expanding 'South Africanness'
Debut Novels

MARGARET LENTA

I intend in this chapter to ask the question of how, in the post-apartheid, post-democratic-elections period in South Africa, specifically the years 1999–2010, obligations and interests have been reconsidered and the conclusions which have resulted have found their way into debut novels written and published in this country. After the pause in literary production which followed the fall of the apartheid regime, there has been a flowering of fiction by first-time novelists. South African debut novels which have appeared since 1999, although diverse in their nature and often related to the ethnic or language group of their authors, demonstrate a general awareness of new freedoms and new developments in South African society, as well as at times registering disappointment with the new regime.

The question has been asked by Derek Attridge and Rosemary Jolly about South African literature:

> How does writing by those who were classified as belonging to different racial groups under the apartheid system, by those who speak different languages, by those of different genders and sexualities, differently inflect the peculiar pressures and opportunities with which they were confronted during the past two and a half decades? (1998: 1)

I shall offer a multi-part answer to this question and will consider a different time span from that of Attridge and Jolly, whose *Writing South Africa: Literature, Apartheid, and Democracy 1970–1995* spans the period of mid- to late-apartheid and the early years of the post-apartheid era. Rita Barnard's *Apartheid and Beyond* (2007) goes so far as to consider works of the late 1990s, but follows the custom of most critical works published abroad in focusing on established authors whose works can be easily obtained outside this country.

Consideration of literary work of the apartheid era alongside post-apartheid work seems to become less appropriate as time goes on, though it cannot be denied, as Annie Gagiano has pointed out, that 'mourning the ugly and cruel past appropriately remains a feature of South African writing' (2006: 133). Even a novel in which the apartheid past is the major subject, Mtutulezi Nyoka's *I Speak to the Silent* (2004), deals with the sexual abuse of women cadres in the liberation movement: a matter that the solidarity of the struggle would have rendered inadmissible. None of the novels which I shall consider, or indeed any from the period 1999–2010 that I have encountered but have been forced by lack of space to omit, could have been written before the advent of democracy.

It is partly for this reason that a secondary and lesser intention of this chapter is to ask whether the entry into the literary scene – the debut – of so many writers is likely to have a lasting effect on the novel. Have writers such as Michiel Heyns, Imraan Coovadia, Kopano Matlwa, David Medalie and Zoë Wicomb, who have established themselves to the extent of producing further works of fiction after their debuts, changed the direction of literature produced in South Africa? Have they taken new directions? Have they, as Leon de Kock hopes in Chapter 1 of this volume, made novels published in this country less stiflingly South African, that is to say, confined in their subject matter to issues of social justice and, especially, relations between the different race groups?

More than forty years of apartheid government established the idea that serious literature should not merely be critical, but should enlighten readers as to the crimes of the government. Writers in the period nevertheless had to face the fact that some subjects were inadmissible, either because a book which focused on them was likely to be banned and therefore involve its publisher in financial loss, or because the consensus amongst oppositional people and parties was that they distracted from the great cause of bringing down the apartheid government.[1] 'Just as surely as certain sexual relationships were proscribed by apartheid, certain experiences or areas of knowledge were out of bounds to probing in words,' writes André P. Brink of the years of apartheid (Attridge and Jolly 1998: 15). He goes on to list topics, other than political opposition to the National Party government, which were forbidden: dates of black settlement in the sub-continent, the misuse of the Bible 'to instil an acceptance by the oppressed of their fate', 'the extent of miscegenation between Afrikaners and their slaves', 'the enslavement of indigenous peoples', 'strategies to ensure and perpetuate the marginalization of women in both black and white societies', all of which have become important subjects in the period 1999–2010.

The production of novels appears to have increased greatly since 1999 and debut novels have been particularly numerous. There has been a growth of publishing houses in South Africa and they have been willing to publish new authors. The theme which propels a writer into print for the first time, or into the writing of a first novel as opposed to work in other literary forms, stands a good chance of reflecting the issues which appear urgent to an author. The fact that a work is accepted for publication suggests the publisher believes that readers are likely to agree that these subjects are important – as well, of course, that the author has handled them well. Novels, in fact, at least collectively, offer a key to the era.

There is likely to be evidence of the novice status of the writer in debut works and some of the works which I shall discuss – K. Sello Duiker's *Thirteen Cents* (2000) is an example – have been followed by other, more mature novels.[2] I do not suggest that it is fair to pass any conclusive literary judgement on a debut novel, but rather that the subject matter and often the forms of these works are of considerable, if finally historical, significance. A first-person narrator is, not coincidentally, common. Although they differ in subject matter and form, these novels possess interests, I shall claim, which make them distinctively 'post-democracy', even though some of them are set in communities which seem not to interact with those outside of their own group.

I shall include in my consideration novels by authors who have had previous experience of writing for publication, but whose first novels appeared in this period. Yvette Christiansë, Heyns, Medalie, Phaswane Mpe, Njabulo S. Ndebele and Wicomb have all published in other literary forms: poetry, the short story, children's fiction and/or critical articles. All, not coincidentally, are or were academics. It is reasonable to assume, and in the case of Heyns, Medalie and Wicomb, as well as Aziz Hassim, it is actually the case, that these writers will continue to produce fiction for publication and that they may be part of the movement to extend the range of subject matter and treatments in South Africa. Though their work offers evidence that their literary and linguistic skills have been honed by past experience, my intention is not to award marks for literary merit but to distinguish the themes which have seemed sufficiently urgent to writer and publisher to motivate them to produce and publish long fiction.

I propose to confine myself to novels written in English, even though Afrikaans novels in the period have been of considerable interest and the movement, of which Antjie Krog, Marlene van Niekerk and Ingrid Winterbach are part, to allow their fiction and other literary forms to be translated from Afrikaans into English has been strong. None of these writers has produced a first novel between 1999 and 2010 and the decision to translate, and the process by which this occurs, in which author and translator are involved in a special, co-operative relationship, deserves a separate essay by a specialist in this area. Even in English, the volume of first novels which has appeared in South Africa in the period 1999–2010 is large and my selection of works, though not arbitrary, necessarily omits many which might be considered significant. The intention to represent rather than cover the novels of the period will motivate me, as well as, in some cases, personal preferences.

To categorise first novels in terms of subject matter is to do them partial justice, since most of the authors have included a complexity of interests and impulses. Responding to my own sense of what was politically suppressed or considered undesirable under apartheid, however, I shall look at the novels as responses to obligations which authors are now free to honour. The elements which I shall distinguish will be, first, the will to give voice to 'previously silent communities'; second will be 'sex and gender', which, given the proprieties of the apartheid era, often overlaps with the first; third, the mixture of languages now characteristic of novels by black authors; fourth, 'writing back', that is, responding to and taking issue with earlier works; fifth, the *roman à thèse*, implying a singleness of subject, to the extent that the work becomes fictionalised argument. The sixth element will be 'fusion', by which I mean that novels register the fact that people of different ethnic communities are now free to know each other outside of their work and to form what ties they wish.

A second meaning will be given to the term 'fusion': the exchange of values between communities can hardly be absent from present-day South African fiction. Postcolonial hybridity means that a work which appears to be confined within a single ethnic community will nevertheless bear marks of contact with others. With the partial exception of the *roman à thèse*, almost all the novels contain these elements and whilst drawing attention to a major element in each which could not have been dealt with in fiction, or at least not in the same way, in the apartheid era, I shall suggest the diversity of their interests.

* * *

An obligation, recognised in many debut novels, came with democracy, to tell from the inside the stories of previously silent minority communities. Zoë Wicomb's *David's Story* (2000) is concerned with the history and present-day significance of the Griqua people, as well as of women in the African National Congress (ANC) in exile. Imraan Coovadia's lively work, *The Wedding* (2001), takes as its subject a Muslim Indian husband and wife who leave India to settle in Durban. Coovadia has gone on to write two other novels about members of the Muslim community in

South Africa: a picaresque called *Green-Eyed Thieves* (2006) and *High Low In-between* (2009) which focuses on the violence that underlies the Durban medical scene at the present time. Aziz Hassim's *The Lotus People* (2002) is another first novel which tells the story of the Durban 'Indian' community and he has followed it with *The Revenge of Kali* (2009), in which part of the interest depends on the fact that it deals with indentured labour and the conditions under which such labourers worked. This is a subject in which the Indian community has become increasingly interested in the recent past. Yvette Christiansë's *Unconfessed* (2007), the narrative of a slave woman in the early nineteenth-century Cape, represents the same impulse to give voice to the silent. Three of these novels, *David's Story*, *The Wedding* and *Unconfessed*, are also strongly concerned with gender.

David's Story may well be the most ambitious as well as the finest novel which has appeared in the period. Its protagonist, David Dirkse, a former ANC cadre (the present of the novel is the post-1990 period), seeks to recover the history of his people, the Griquas, from the early period when the Koks and Le Fleurs taught national consciousness to a hybrid group of Khoi, Cape Dutch and slavery survivors, down to the present state of their descendants in Kokstad and Cape Town. It is a history of effort and determination, perpetually foiled by governments which believed that only whites should own land. The pursuit of respectability which becomes traditional for Coloured people is shown to originate in the Griqua wish to *deserve* a better destiny than they achieve.

A second thread of the novel deals with Dulcie, the dedicated woman cadre who is visited in the night by comrades who rape and torture her – 'fucking women was a way of preventing them from rising in the Movement' (2000: 179), these men believe. Dulcie's loyalty and dedication to the struggle prevent her from reporting the abuse she suffers and this suppression is the key to the parallel between her story and that of the Griquas, in whose origins – it was the Huguenot refugee Madame La Fleur who decided to bring her son with her to the Cape – and subsequent history women have been all-important but systematically obscured. This suppression is summarised for official history in the term 'steatopygous', used since the days of Saartjie Baartman to suggest that indigenous South African women have no characteristics other than the grotesque and physical.

David himself, the inheritor and collector of the history, says to the ironic and sceptical woman who is writing it down, '"There's surely no need for all the old women. Can't some of the oumas be turned into oupas? There's no harm in that, just turning the she's into he's"' (2000: 200). It is a process which has gone on for centuries and which he understands as natural. But when the recording woman suggests that Dulcie be turned into a man, his sense of her and what she has suffered will not allow it: '"No, no, that would not make sense at all. Dulcie is definitely a woman"' (2000: 200).

Wicomb's second full-length novel, *Playing in the Light* (2006), though it deals with the dilemma of a woman of colour, is not set in the Cape Coloured community as is *David's Story*.[3] Its protagonist is a woman who finds that her parents escaped from that community. For the sake of their child – and, of course, their own – they severed all ties of family and friendship and, as the cruel phrase has it, they 'played white'. It is another of the many situations now considered 'storyable' which under the previous regime were either ignored or criminalised.

Yvette Christiansë's *Unconfessed* deals with Cape slavery in the period between the abolition of the oceanic slave trade (1808) and the final abolition of slavery (1838). The title makes the point that the group to which its protagonist, who is the narrator for most of the work, belongs is that of women slaves, who are forced to be silent about their sufferings: Sila van den Kaap's very name is a falsehood to disguise the illegality of her enslavement. Robert C-H. Shell sets as the epigraph to his *Children of Bondage* (1994) the comment by W.W. Bird in 1822 that '[t]he acquisition of a male slave is a life interest; that of a female is considered to be a perpetual heritage' and *Unconfessed* reveals the stratagems of members of the slave-owning class to ensure that this remained the case.

A subset of this category of previously silent minority communities is the group of novels about homosexuals, which like *Unconfessed* belongs equally in the 'sex and gender' grouping. The new Constitution, finalised in 1996, which proclaimed the equality of the gender groups and legitimised all kinds of sexual orientation, has also allowed the production of novels in which homosexuals are major subjects. Heyns's *The Children's Day* (2002) is an example of such a work, as is, in its different way, Duiker's *Thirteen Cents* (2000).

The main theme of *The Children's Day* is the maturing of a boy, growing up in a Free State village, Verkeerdespruit, where homosexuality is unidentified in words, even by those whose sexuality is of that kind. The consequences – a suicide, a dreadful marriage and a life of concealment are amongst them – can only be hinted at. The boy, Simon, stands a little apart from the people of the village: he is the only child of the English-speaking magistrate; his mother is Afrikaans, but freethinking. The convention, made famous by Perceval Gibbon in *The Vrouw Grobelaar's Leading Cases* (1905), Herman Charles Bosman in *Mafeking Road* (1998 [1947]) and elsewhere, that people of such a village may be portrayed as comic caricatures, is present: Mr de Wet, Klasie the postmaster, Betty the Exchange and others are at times described in this way, but their vulnerable humanity is also revealed. Most important of the characters whom Simon must learn to understand is Fanie, a poor white, epileptic child whom his schoolfellows identify as a natural victim, but whom eventually Simon comes to understand and value.

Simon has various homosexual encounters as he grows up and it is clear at the end of the novel that he will soon understand his orientation better than he does, but the work's great merit is that it insists on the ordinariness of his life. The Free State village, as well as the conventionally snobbish boarding school to which he is sent, makes the point that homosexual people are and always have been part of the life of rural South Africa.

Heyns, in the years which have followed *The Children's Day*, has made major interventions on the South African literary scene as a critic and reviewer and a translator (his major work in this area is the English version of Van Niekerk's *Agaat* [2006]). His novels *The Typewriter's Tale* (2005) and *Bodies Politic* (2008) have attracted much attention and the fact that a South African novelist of distinction has gone outside this country for his subject matter has been seen as something of a turning point. *The Typewriter's Tale* is a fictionalisation of the life of Henry James and *Bodies Politic* deals with the lives of members of the Pankhurst family during the struggle for the enfranchisement of women in Britain.

Duiker's *Thirteen Cents* is narrated by a Coloured street child who tells the story of his life as a petty thief, an underling for adult criminals and a prostitute for affluent men. Like Sila van den Kaap, he belongs to a group which is exploited but required to be silent. His desperate, abused existence, facing starvation and assault every day, is movingly rendered, the more so because of his acceptance of it. The lyricism of the work and its single focus render it less of a novel than most of the works which I shall consider, but it shows great promise, which was to be fulfilled in Duiker's later works, *The Quiet Violence of Dreams* (2001) and *The Hidden Star* (2005).

Gender and the changing roles and relations between the genders are a major subject in black writing, both by women and men. Black women have felt freer than they did under apartheid to explore their position and aspirations: Matlwa's *Coconut* (2007) investigates a dilemma of our era, that of young middle-class black women, expected in the past and to an extent still to be guardians of tradition, but now puzzled as to which cultural position they should occupy. (Futhi Ntshingila's *Shameless* [2008] is a slighter work on a related theme.) *Coconut* consists of first-person narratives by two young women, Ofilwe Tlou, the daughter of a newly rich black family in Johannesburg and Fiki, who works as a waitress in the Silver Spoon, where the Tlous have Sunday breakfast. Ofilwe registers with pain the contradictions of her family and school life, the residual racism of children and teachers, her determinedly English-speaking home. She is ashamed that she does not speak sePedi well and tries to re-learn the language in order to take her place in her extended family. Her Africanist brother, Tshepo, rejects Christianity and efforts to Europeanise, but eventually quarrels with his father because he wants to be a writer, not an actuary. The different pressures on the brother and sister are strongly related to their genders.

Fikile is an orphaned township child who lives with 'Uncle', a failure and token affirmative action appointment in his firm. Until the last pages of the novel, she has no doubts about her wish for riches and Western culture. She is enchanted by the magazine version of well-to-do white life and though exploited at the Silver Spoon, accepts this as the cost of access to whiteness:

> 'Get on an apron and . . .' she waits for me to complete the sentence for her.
> 'Bake bread,' I say, humiliated.
> 'Yes,' she nods, 'bake bread!'
>
> I am mortified. I cannot believe I am being yelled at in this way in front of the kitchen staff. The bloody kitchen staff! Miss Becky would never degrade me in this manner. Miss Becky would never make me put on a plastic apron and a ridiculous hair net. It is her dumb daughter who has absolutely no understanding of how vital I am to the functioning of the Silver Spoon, that can go and disrespect me in that way in front of the kitchen staff. But I pull myself together.
>
> 'You heard her,' I say to the kitchen staff after Caroline has left the room. 'Stop standing around and bake bread!' (Matlwa 2007: 145)

A striking though minor feature of the novel, which it shares with Ntshingila's *Shameless*, is the treatment of sexual abuse by an uncle, which is seen as wrong, but by no means monstrous: cramped living quarters and damaged male egos are the cause.

Matlwa's second novel, *Spilt Milk*, not quite as well received as the first, appeared in 2010 and shows interests which are related but not similar to those of *Coconut*: it is concerned with the bitterness of a professionally successful black woman against a white man whom she believes exploited her sexually in her girlhood. Her attitude depends on her belief that he had choices which she did not have, though in fact he, too, was under unbearable pressure. What she discovers is the destructive nature of racial hatred.

Two novels by men, minor though interesting, in which gender relations are a secondary subject, are Mtutulezi Nyoka's *I Speak to the Silent* (2004) and Siphiwo Mahala's *When a Man Cries* (2007). In *I Speak to the Silent* the male protagonist beats up his wife when he is unhappy and though he comes to recognise that this is wrong, he does not go so far as to understand that his wife has suffered grief equal to his own. Sexual abuse of young women by powerful men is the major plot catalyst, but the book wanders through many other situations: dreary life in the impoverished Ciskei, the arrogance of rich white women (a favourite topic in works by black male authors – white men incur much less blame), the corruption of the police and the removal under apartheid of worthy community leaders.

Siphiwo Mahala's *When a Man Cries*, much of which was originally published as short stories, is also, though not to the same degree, multi-focused. Mahala's protagonist, Themba, a schoolmaster, comes to understand that sexual exploitation of his pupils is wrong, as is the sexual harassment of women colleagues. After a series of experiments in seduction and near-rape, which produce different kinds of disasters, he repents and is reunited with his wife. His growing understanding of the needs of the poor in his community is equally a subject.

Both of these male-authored novels portray male centrality and power in a way that seems to assume that they are unchangeable. In so far as they problematise wife abuse and marital infidelity, they may be an advance on male-authored black fiction of the past, which rarely admitted that such things occurred.[4] Women's novels, however, depict different attitudes: Matlwa's *Coconut* depicts the protagonist's father as casually unfaithful, and another debut novel, Angelina N. Sithebe's *Holy Hill* (2007), describes the violent jealousy of the female protagonist's fiancé. In both cases, the mothers of the offended women fail their daughters by condoning this facet of male behaviour – 'What can you expect?' is their response.

Sally-Ann Murray's *Small Moving Parts* (2009) tells the story of a family of South African whites who are poor and, as the narrator tells us, are struggling not to become 'poor whites'. Father deserts the family early and Murray's depiction of the mother's hard work and sacrifices (and the price that her children have to pay for those sacrifices) is always moving, even painful. White women family heads, especially if they were poor and struggling, were another group which the nation preferred in the past to ignore. Most striking in this novel is the depiction of a Durban childhood, the setting urban, but lush, green and fruitful in the most literal sense, yet dangerous and divided. *Small Moving Parts* is, as the 2010 M-Net Literary Award and Herman Charles Bosman Prize adjudicators have pointed out, innovative in that it is a female *Bildungsroman* with a protagonist who is born into the white working class.

Njabulo S. Ndebele's *The Cry of Winnie Mandela* (2003), which also contains elements of the 'previously silent' as well as of 'sex and gender', is a more serious questioning of gender roles. It draws on the myth of Penelope, who waited for years for her husband Ulysses to return from Troy, and therefore contains the 'fusion' elements common in postcolonial South African writing. Penelope is the archetype of a woman whose husband, after an absence of decades, assumes the right to a rapturous reception from his wife on his return; Winnie Mandela is the modern exemplar.

To an equal extent with authors such as Wicomb, Christiansë, Heyns and Duiker, Ndebele brings into the public arena the lives of people who have been required to be silent. He faces the fact that a marital relationship must change – perhaps fade – when a separation of great length occurs, for whatever reason. Male partners change and discard women with whom they no longer wish to be intimate or punish them for changing, on the assumption that women must remain constant. Ndebele's novel, however, focuses on women who have learnt to accept the changes in themselves. The passage in which Winnie Mandela reflects on what happened to her in Brandfort is full of insight into what may have changed the real woman:

> In Brandfort I stood out so much! I was too much for the benighted herrenvolk of Brandfort, the children of Hendrik Verwoerd. I brought Brandfort to the attention of the world. I brought it into the twentieth century. The fools in Pretoria! Instead of consigning me to Siberia, they sent me to Brandfort as an agent of revolution. In Brandfort I raged against everything in sight, until I had only myself to face. Then I raged against myself.
>
> Brandfort was my first real taste of power; something close to absolute power (2003: 102).

Ndebele's form, studies of the lives of four fictional black women whose menfolk have deserted them, as well as of a fictionalised Winnie Mandela, has led him to use terms from African languages. This 'multilingualism' is a prominent feature of most novels by black authors. Crucial to Ndebele's novel, for example, is the concept of the *ibandla*, the supportive group of women, who address their fellows as *zintombi*.

Ndebele's experience of growing up as an urban Zulu man, spending twenty years in exile in Lesotho and working in universities in that country and in South Africa has given him literary as well as spoken mastery of three of South Africa's major languages. The Constitution, which proclaims the official status of all eleven languages, offers an opportunity, he believes, for the writing of fiction which will be at least 'multilingual'. He is likely to be speaking for many black writers when he claims that 'there are aspects of my experience that I cannot imagine in English'; and that 'my history of using English as a medium for artistic expression is incomparably much longer than my use of Sesotho and isiZulu for that purpose' (2007: 151). This double-bind leads him to the following conclusion about the possibilities for 'multilingual' writing:

> First is the possibility of fiction woven together in at least three languages ... The average South African speaks any combination of at least two languages. The average black South African speaks any combination of at least three languages. In the Johannesburg area, the average rises to four or five languages ... This means that a multilingual fiction has a potentially large multilingual black readership, on condition that a speech community located at a multilingual intersection actually amounts to a reading community. Such a development cannot happen on its own. Readers of multilingual fiction have to transform speech habits into a reading discipline, making possible the growth of a dialogue between writers and readers (2007: 151–2).

Ndebele's essay does not go on to consider the problems of 'transforming speech habits into a written discipline', but they are briefly considered in Mpe's *Welcome to Our Hillbrow* (2001), where a black woman, Refilwe, has been made commissioning editor for books in sePedi in a publishing house:

> But she soon discovered the frustrations which went with her new and prestigious position. Although she knew what good books looked like, the company she worked for kept on reminding her that good books were only those that could get a school prescription. What frustrated her so much was the extent to which publishing was in many ways out of touch with the language and events of everyday life.
> It was a very different story with other creative forms; music for instance. In the music trade, unlike publishing, producers and public alike were receptive to work that broke new ground. To songs that spoke in the hard language that people used in their everyday lives ... a fairly open-minded Commissioning Editor in Sepedi had to be frustrated when she could not take a crop of newly-emerging, critical writers onto her list ... (2001: 94).

Refilwe's impulse is to facilitate the production of an adult literature in sePedi; her superiors insist that it must remain juvenile, in the sense decreed by the government-controlled educational authorities under apartheid. It might be argued that potential readers of sePedi literature are themselves conservative and resistant to works 'in the hard language' that people use in their everyday lives, but Refilwe (and Mpe) know that this is not consistently so.

Nevertheless, as Ndebele and other black South African writers are aware, the readership for novels written in the indigenous languages of this country, other than Afrikaans, is tiny. The decision taken by many, following Chinua Achebe's early example in *Things Fall Apart* (1958), is to include in English-language novels those proverbs and characteristic expressions from their mother tongues which, as Ndebele says, they cannot imagine in English. Examples of works in which this occurs are Mpe's *Welcome to Our Hillbrow*, Nape á Motana's *Fanie Fourie's Lobola* (2007) and Mahala's *When a Man Cries*, as well as, of course, *The Cry of Winnie Mandela*. A related phenomenon is the growing reluctance of publishers' editors to sanitise black English into the standard forms: Sandile Memela's *Flowers of the Nation* (2005) unselfconsciously uses what would be cliché and slang in standard English, as well as unexplained pieces of township vocabulary, to convey the experience of two black children.[5] Duiker's *Thirteen Cents* uses, as part of its strategy to make known a group which literate society has chosen to ignore, the dialect of Cape Town street people, which is a mixture of English, Afrikaans and isiXhosa.

Given the privileging of certain groups as the legitimate voices of South Africa in the past, it is to be expected that 'writing back' will be important. *The Cry of Winnie Mandela* writes back to *The Odyssey*, maintaining that the return of a husband after an absence of decades is at least problematic. *Unconfessed* can be see as a 'writing back' to fictions of slavery like Brink's *A Chain of Voices* (1982), in which women slaves, beaten and sexually exploited as they are, are nevertheless shown to accept their sufferings, without judging their oppressors.

Mpe's rhapsody of urbanisation, *Welcome to Our Hillbrow*, written in the second person, 'writes back' to another familiar South African form, the 'Jim comes to Jo'burg' of the past, in which a naive country boy is corrupted by city life: famous examples are Douglas Blackburn's *Leaven* (1991 [1908]), R.R.R. Dhlomo's *An African Tragedy* (1928) and Alan Paton's *Cry, the Beloved Country* (1948). Mpe's young people come to Johannesburg from the rural village of Tiralong and several of them die as a result of their urban experiences, but there is no sense such as exists in the earlier novels that the rural areas are productive of innocence which will be lost in the city. Tiralong is a place of malicious gossip, men throwing the bones and lying about responsibility for crimes and murders, including the 'necklacing' of witches. In Johannesburg, promising young people meet foreigners and profit from association with them. A dark shadow in this novel is the spread of HIV and AIDS and the last pages, in which the death of Refilwe is portrayed as a happy reunion with the ancestors, only carry conviction if the reader accepts the personal history of the author, which has caused him to offer a picture of a city which may be glamorous, squalid and fatal at the same time.[6]

The *roman à thèse*, as I have suggested, is an extreme case of response to different 'pressures and opportunities' in which a writer has cast into fictional form arguments related to a single moral preoccupation. Chris Marnewick's *Shepherds and Butchers* (2008), in which a discussion of state executions in the last years of apartheid is fictionalised, is perhaps the clearest example of a novel in this category. Any criticism of the prison services was strictly forbidden under the apartheid regime. Another novel which belongs here is Johan Steyn's *Father Michael's Lottery* (2005). Set in Botswana, though written by a South African and published in this country, it deals with the AIDS pandemic and the refusal of state medical services to spend funds on the treatment of the poor, a theme which has preoccupied South Africans for the last ten years at least.

The category of the *roman à thèse*, even less than the others, is by no means watertight: many of the novels which I discuss or allude to belong to an extent in this category, since they engage with moral issues considered inadmissible under apartheid. Jonny Steinberg's *The Number* (2004), though its back cover identifies it as a documentary based on a series of interviews with an offender in prison, has some of the licence of fiction in as much as Steinberg admits that he altered names and that some of the dates are approximate: 'prison gangsters are not wont to keep records, so fixing the date and time is at best an educated guess' (2004: xi). Its prime loyalty is to the truth of prison life, but Marnewick and Steyn would declare comparable loyalties to the facts. Another novel which is related to large-scale phenomena of the period as these is Jonathan Morgan's *Finding Mr Madini* (1999), which deals with xenophobia and the homeless – and Duiker's *Thirteen Cents* belongs here, as much as in the other categories I have identified.

The forward-looking features of many novels of this period – which I have called 'fusion' novels – have been recognised by Gagiano:

> [M]ost of the post-1999 texts included here do also register a life-current onward and several can be considered confident stake-claimers in their commemorative or affirmative recognition of a range of cultures – using the term (as used by writers such as Duiker) to refer not only to racial or linguistic units, but to many kinds of established alliances – regional (both rural and urban), political, historical, or exploratory and tentative (2006: 153–4).

These 'fusion' novels have, for the most part, a happy relationship to the new dispensation. Motana's *Fanie Fourie's Lobola* brings new subject matter to the novel. Set amongst working-class people (both white and black), its language, by the conventional standards of middle-class, highly literate whites, is at times inappropriate to a novel. There is much mention of women's biceps and a striking number of references to bodily functions. It tells in broadly comic mode the story of an Afrikaner's marriage to a Pedi woman, Dimatkatjo Machabaphala, whom he meets in a (black) doctor's surgery, where she is a nurse. Fanie's mother disapproves, but he is determined to marry Dimatkatjo, which, his black friend George explains, will entail paying lobola.

The rest of the novel is a farcical account of the lobola negotiations and the wedding. Dimatkatjo's unscrupulous brother and cousin try to increase the agreed-upon lobola; another cousin borrows Fanie's car and comes close to wrecking it. Eventually Malome, the uncle of the bride, intervenes and peaceful agreement is achieved. Motana's sense that African tradition must prevail, that Fanie must conform to it and the younger generation must not be allowed to corrupt it, is striking and in its way postcolonial. SePedi proverbs and maxims are crucial to the novel.

David Medalie's *The Shadow Follows* (2006), a very different 'fusion' novel, is Dickensian in its complexity and in the way that ties of kinship, adoption, sexuality and friendship are discovered and serve to unite people who might be thought unlikely ever to meet. It is set in the affluent, multiracial society of Johannesburg, where friendships, business associations and even families are re-forming themselves to render race irrelevant. Medalie has followed this novel with a collection of stories, *The Mistress's Dog* (2010).

Fusion, in the sense of the productive co-existence of people of different groups, is an element of Ishtiyaq Shukri's *The Silent Minaret* (2005), which also belongs in the 'previously silent minority' category, though it is a politicised work of the post-9/11 period. Like other novels of the period – Barbara Fölscher's thriller *Blind Faith* (2007) is another example – it allows its characters to have meaningful lives whilst in exile, facing the colonial and postcolonial fact that South Africans travel and interact with metropolitan cultures.

In an article entitled 'Does South African Literature Still Exist?' (2005), Leon de Kock recognises the fact that what homogenised South African texts under apartheid was political and that now 'our various acts of writing are no longer held in this clasp of denial and counter-statement' (70). He celebrates the 'death of South African literature as we used to know it' and the freedom of authors to draw inspiration from models other than South African. De Kock's example is *Agaat*

(2004), by Marlene van Niekerk, originally written in Afrikaans and later translated into English (2006). Another accomplished novel of this period, which departs, formally and in its subject matter, from apartheid expectations is Ceridwen Dovey's *Blood Kin* (2007). It is set, in a manner reminiscent of J.M. Coetzee's *Waiting for the Barbarians* (1980), in an undefined state, where an absolute ruler has just been toppled and three men who depend on his patronage (his chef, portraitist and barber) are imprisoned in his residence. Their womenfolk – daughter, wife and lover – feel themselves involved in the men's fate, but also freed by their fall. Power, insecurity, fear, sexual passion – these are the matters which Dovey has considered, as experienced by people whose behaviour and emotions are not tied to a particular, recognisable state. Though Coetzee's influence is evident, so is Kafka's and there can be no suggestion nowadays that Dovey will be reproached, as was Coetzee in the early 1980s, with neglect of subjects which ought to be irresistible or with the use of an elitist form.

* * *

De Kock claims that the category of 'South African literature' has become unimportant and, if it is understood as implying similarity of subject matter and attitudes, it is appropriate that this should now be the case. Most of the novels which I have discussed above are, however, sited in South Africa and would be recognised by South Africans and foreigners alike as South African in their subject matter. A few venture outside this country, making a quiet claim that South Africans too may concern themselves with the wider world.

It is nevertheless easy to detect an absence or perhaps a de-emphasis common to these novels: compared to the fictions of the apartheid era, the state is a remote presence. Whereas typically the plot of an apartheid novel would involve the individual's conflict with the state, this is no longer the case in the novels of 1999–2010. Even a non-realistic novel of the apartheid period, Coetzee's *Life & Times of Michael K* (1983), focuses on the resistance of an individual to the will of the state to control him. In the fictions of 1999–2010, this subject has declined in importance, even when the author is dealing with the apartheid period. In Coovadia's *The Wedding*, for example, which focuses on the pre-apartheid, segregationist period, moving into apartheid towards the end of its protagonists' lives, the state is a minor matter. And in Christiansë's *Unconfessed*, where the reader might expect unjust laws to be a major subject, it is the previously slave-owning class and its will to circumvent the law which is important. Duiker's *Thirteen Cents* reveals the lives of people who live unsupported by the state, as does

Morgan's *Finding Mr Madini*. Even Nyoka's *I Speak to the Silent*, where the focus is mainly on the apartheid period, has as its major subject an abuse within the liberation movement. Ndebele's *The Cry of Winnie Mandela*, which presents women whose unequal relationship to their husbands was a matter of law under apartheid and which, in the novel's present, is customary, may be said to span this shift. The result of this decline in interest in interventionism and control by the state has been a stronger emphasis in novels on the power of individuals and their negotiating abilities – politics, in fact, at the level of cultural criticism.

What these debut novels collectively, and at times individually, achieve is an expansion of the idea of 'South Africanness', which, they assert, is not confined to any kind of political orthodoxy, or to a language or ethnic group, or to a gender group or a class. Their diversity is not merely a recognition of the different traditions and interests of the various South African groups; equally importantly, it declares the authors' and publishers' confidence that members of other groups need and want to read about them. Writing of the pre-apartheid documents produced in or about South Africa, De Kock lists as examples

> the epic account of Portuguese seafaring around the Cape, the Dutch register of occupation, the English travel diary, the Xhosa praise song, the French pastoral narrative of Africa . . . the Scottish romantic ballad. These objects of culture have seldom been aware of each other, despite their geographical contiguity (2001: 264).

The major departure of the novels of the period 1999–2010 may be that while they are as diverse, culturally if not in national origins, as the documents named by De Kock, their intention is to extend awareness of their subject matter to as large as possible a section of the South African public. This is not equally the case in all: it is more evident in a minor work like Motana's *Fanie Fourie's Lobola* than in Dovey's *Blood Kin*, but in most of the works the impulse to exclude certain groups, or to include them only as 'comically uncultivated people' (De Kock 2001: 266) has passed. Heyns, for example, in *The Children's Day*, shows the people of Verkeerdespruit as possessed of the full range of human possibilities; Christiansë's *Unconfessed* demonstrates the falseness of the Robben Island overseer's verdict on the wretched women slaves, that they are merely animals.

The multilingualism advocated by Ndebele and others is a further move towards extending the South African readership of fiction beyond the white educated middle class.[7] It must be admitted, however, that the presence of untranslated (or perhaps even translated) phrases in indigenous languages in a novel may not make it easier to market it abroad. Both Brink (1998: 16–17) and De Kock (2001: 284) deplore the fact that few South African authors have been successful elsewhere.

Considering the diversity which I have demonstrated, can it be claimed that there is a 'South African literature' in the present day? It is of course easier to make this judgement retrospectively than in the present: in 40 years homogeneity in the novels of the early twenty-first century may be easier to detect. I would claim, however, that the debut novels of 1999–2010 have sufficient in common in the impulses of their authors, though not in their immediate subjects, to mark them as distinctively of their period. The fact that a substantial number of authors who made their debuts between 1999 and 2010 have now established themselves on the literary scene means that their will to innovate, their characteristic but once unorthodox preoccupations are also now a part of that scene.

Notes

1. Herman Wittenberg has written of the dilemma which confronted Ravan Press in the late 1970s when J.M. Coetzee's novel *In the Heart of the Country* seemed likely to be banned on publication, thus involving its publisher in considerable financial loss. Wittenberg explains the change in the attitudes and practice of the Board of Censorship:

    HOC was written during the years of the opaque and arbitrary censorship bureaucracy under Judge Lammie Snyman who chaired the Publications Control Board into the late 1970s. After the showdown between Afrikaans writers and intellectuals and the state in 1978 around the controversial banning of Etienne Leroux's novel *Magersfontein, O Magersfontein!*, a more moderate and reformist Publications Control Board, under the chairmanship of Professor J. van Rooyen, took control and sought to bring a measure of rational certainty and scientific rigour to the process.

    The earlier Publications Control Board had considered the probable reactions of 'the ordinary reader', whereas the new Board made judgements on the basis of the reactions of 'the likely reader'. In both cases, literary merit was, it was claimed, a criterion. *In the Heart of the Country*, first published by Secker & Warburg, was in fact 'embargoed by Customs on its arrival in Cape Town ... and referred to the censorship board for a decision' (Wittenberg 2008: 136–7).
2. K. Sello Duiker's later novels are *The Quiet Violence of Dreams* (2001) and *The Hidden Star* (2006).
3. Wicomb also published a volume of stories, *The One That Got Away*, in 2008.
4. An early and notable exception is Es'kia Mphahlele's *Down Second Avenue* (1959).
5. See Bregin (2007) for more on some of the issues involved in the process of editing black writers' books in English.
6. Phaswane Mpe died at the age of 34 of HIV-related causes in 2004.

7. It is interesting to note that this multilingualism, in a more extensive form made possible by subtitles, has spread to SABC programmes such as *Isidingo*, a few years ago entirely scripted in English.

References

Achebe, Chinua. 1958. *Things Fall Apart*. London: Heinemann.
Attridge, Derek and Rosemary Jolly (eds). 1998. *Writing South Africa: Literature, Apartheid, and Democracy, 1970–1995*. Cambridge: Cambridge University Press.
Barnard, Rita. 2007. *Apartheid and Beyond: South African Writers and the Politics of Place*. New York: Oxford University Press.
Blackburn, Douglas. 1991 [1908]. *Leaven: A Black and White Story*. Pietermaritzburg: University of Natal Press.
Bosman, Herman Charles. 1998 [1947]. *Mafeking Road and Other Stories*. Cape Town: Human & Rousseau.
Bregin, Elana. 2007. 'Making Space for New Voices: The Politics of Editing in South Africa'. *Current Writing* 19(1): 153–9.
Brink, André. 1982. *A Chain of Voices*. London: Faber & Faber.
Brink, André P. 1998. 'Interrogating Silence: New Possibilities Faced by South African Literature'. In: *Writing South Africa: Literature, Apartheid, and Democracy, 1970–1995*, edited by D. Attridge and R. Jolly. Cambridge: Cambridge University Press: 14–28.
Christiansë, Yvette. 2007. *Unconfessed*. Cape Town: Kwela Books.
Coetzee, J.M. 1980. *Waiting for the Barbarians*. Johannesburg: Ravan Press.
———. 1983. *Life & Times of Michael K*. Johannesburg: Ravan Press.
Coovadia. Imraan. 2001. *The Wedding*. New York: Picador.
———. 2006. *Green-Eyed Thieves*. Cape Town: Umuzi.
———. 2009. *High Low In-between*. Cape Town: Umuzi.
De Kock, Leon. 2001. 'South Africa in the Global Imaginary: An Introduction'. *Poetics Today* 22(2): 263–98.
———. 2005. 'Does South African Literature Still Exist? Or: South African Literature Is Dead, Long Live Literature in South Africa'. *English in Africa* 32(2): 69–83.
Dhlomo, R.R.R. 1928. *An African Tragedy*. Lovedale: Lovedale Institution Publishers.
Dovey, Ceridwen. 2007. *Blood Kin*. Johannesburg: Penguin.
Duiker, K. Sello. 2000. *Thirteen Cents*. Cape Town: David Philip.
———. 2001. *The Quiet Violence of Dreams*. Cape Town: Kwela Books.
———. 2006. *The Hidden Star*. Cape Town: Umuzi.
Fölscher, Barbara. 2007. *Blind Faith*. Cape Town: Human & Rousseau.
Gagiano, Annie. 2006. 'Moving beyond Compartmentality: South African English Writing from 1999–2005'. *IWU: Literatur in Wissenschaft und Unterricht* XXXIX(2/3): 133–55.
Gibbon, Perceval. 1905. *The Vrouw Grobelaar's Leading Cases*. Edinburgh: William Blackwood.
Hassim, Aziz. 2002. *The Lotus People*. Durban: Madiba Publishers.
———. 2009. *The Revenge of Kali*. Johannesburg: STE Publishers.
Heyns, Michiel. 2002. *The Children's Day*. Johannesburg: Jonathan Ball.

———. 2005. *The Typewriter's Tale*. Johannesburg: Jonathan Ball.
———. 2008. *Bodies Politic*. Johannesburg: Jonathan Ball.
Mahala, Siphiwo. 2007. *When a Man Cries*. Pietermaritzburg: University of KwaZulu-Natal Press.
Marnewick, Chris. 2008. *Shepherds and Butchers*. Cape Town: Umuzi.
Matlwa, Kopano. 2007. *Coconut*. Johannesburg: Jacana Media.
———. 2010. *Spilt Milk*. Johannesburg: Jacana Media.
Medalie, David. 2006. *The Shadow Follows*. Johannesburg: Picador Africa.
———. 2010. *The Mistress's Dog*. Johannesburg: PanMacmillan.
Memela, Sandile. 2005. *Flowers of the Nation*. Pietermaritzburg: University of KwaZulu-Natal Press.
Morgan, Jonathan and the Great African Spider Writers. 1999. *Finding Mr Madini*. Cape Town: David Philip.
Motana, Nape á. 2007. *Fanie Fourie's Lobola*. Pietermaritzburg: University of KwaZulu-Natal Press.
Mphahlele, Es'kia. 1959. *Down Second Avenue*. London: Faber & Faber.
Mpe, Phaswane. 2001. *Welcome to Our Hillbrow*. Pietermaritzburg: University of Natal Press.
Murray, Sally-Ann. 2009. *Small Moving Parts*. Cape Town: Kwela Books.
Ndebele, Njabulo S. 2003. *The Cry of Winnie Mandela*. Cape Town: David Philip.
———. 2007. *Fine Lines from the Box: Further Thoughts about Our Country*. Cape Town: Umuzi.
Ntshingila, Futhi. 2008. *Shameless*. Pietermaritzburg: University of KwaZulu-Natal Press.
Nyoka, Mtutulezi. 2004. *I Speak to the Silent*. Pietermaritzburg: University of KwaZulu-Natal Press.
Paton, Alan. 1948. *Cry, the Beloved Country*. New York: Charles Scribner's Sons.
Shell, Robert C-H. 1994. *Children of Bondage: A Social History of the Slave Society at the Cape of Good Hope, 1652–1838*. Johannesburg: Wits University Press.
Shukri, Ishtiyaq. 2005. *The Silent Minaret*. Johannesburg: Jacana Media.
Sithebe, Angelina N. 2007. *Holy Hill*. Cape Town: Umuzi.
Steinberg, Jonny. 2004. *The Number*. Johannesburg: Jonathan Ball.
Steyn, Johan. 2005. *Father Michael's Lottery*. Pietermaritzburg: University of KwaZulu-Natal Press.
Van Niekerk, Marlene. 2004. *Agaat*. Cape Town: Tafelberg. [Afrikaans edition]
———. 2006. *Agaat*. Translated by Michiel Heyns. Cape Town: Tafelberg/Jonathan Ball.
Wicomb, Zoë. 2000. *David's Story*. Cape Town: Kwela Books.
———. 2006. *Playing in the Light*. Cape Town: Umuzi.
———. 2008. *The One That Got Away*. Cape Town: Umuzi.
Wittenberg, Hermann. 2008. 'The Taint of the Censor: J.M. Coetzee and the Making of *In the Heart of the Country*'. *English in Africa* 35(2): 133–50.

3

On the Street with Vladislavić, Mhlongo, Moele and Others

SALLY-ANN MURRAY

Trailblazing

For over twenty years, I've been following Ivan Vladislavić around his changing cities, trailing the real as it is transmuted into the fictional. His early short story collections – *Missing Persons* (1989) and *Propaganda by Monuments* (1996) – led me into Pretoria and Johannesburg, only for him to veer mischievously from the familiar South African political madness into an incipient supra-realism that has since been praised as an exemplar of '[p]ost-apartheid post-modern writing at its best' (Kellas 2004; Popescu 2003, 2008). In retrospect, as a reader finding my way into this other world, I must have resembled the girl in *Portrait with Keys* (2006a) who is spotted breathing her way down the street in goggles and snorkel, unselfconsciously immersed in an utterly new experience of a once-familiar locality.

The quirkiness of Vladislavić's fiction has been said to signpost a 'South African "white writing" which ... parallels ... the new direction taken by our society', replete with all the 'ironies, the neuroses, [and] the ludicrous elements' while eschewing 'the queasy seriousness' traditionally characteristic of white South African fiction (Nicholls 1999: 159–60). Even his later work, where some discern a more realist frame of reference (Morphet 2006), subtly 'play[s] with the conventions of fiction' as it 'speak[s] about contemporary realities in South Africa today' (SouthAfrica.info 2008). The recent re-issue of Vladislavić's early stories as a single volume entitled *Flashback Hotel* (2010) further complicates the timelines of the imagined relevance and freshness which Elleke Boehmer and Deborah Gaitskell (2004) claim for this writer's work: the noisy 'now' forfeits some of its authoritative insistence and is wonderfully unsettled by the persistent linguistic vitality of these stories from 'the past'. The effect is to imply the blurred reach and stretch of Vladislavić's imagination, its ability to re-animate even ossified worlds, words and expectations.

Vladislavić is by now a well-established white South African writer,[1] a canonical heavyweight in whose prose critics have recognised the embattled 'world' figures, many of them white males, who populate current South African white writing in English (see, for instance, Helgesson 2004; Miller 2006.) In *Entanglement*, Sarah Nuttall points out that Vladislavić tends to be considered representative of (*the* representative of?) the 'new' and the 'now' in South African literature only 'because of a failure by researchers to register emergent writing 'by young and often black South Africans' (2009: 94; see also De Kock 2005). Vladislavić, it seems, 'stands in' for innovation even while he and his disgruntled or displaced characters cannot give a clear or impartial account of present-day South African realities. As Nuttall sees it, his writing is marked 'by aporias', a racial and 'generational aporia' (2009: 93), typical of 'a white man of a certain generation' (106). This has some purchase, but it also refuses to concede the continuing validity and unusualness of Vladislavić's form of 'white writing'. If Vladislavić's acerbic Tearle, for instance, finds the 'pace of change' in Johannesburg 'to be a source of deep anxiety and dismay' (Graham 2007: 81), his thwarted attempts to give order to his old-new city of increasingly inclement words and alarmingly porous meanings have also been widely acknowledged as an exceptionally original authorial imprint. Through Tearle, Vladislavić 'minoritises' the English language and Literature, effecting a metafictional democratisation 'of English from within' (Helgesson 2004: 778). Where else, in current South African English writing, is this happening? This experimental literariness and the imaginative lengths to which he takes the English language into an encounter with an unusually layered treatment of urban space give this writer a noteworthy, if equivocal position in local writing. Even after so many years, these traits continue to signal a degree of stylistic and linguistic innovation which sets his prose apart from that of a younger 'vexed generation' (Donadio 2006) of South African novelists.[2]

Where does that leave English South African literature? Divided, despite the common use of English, between old camps and hip clubs, ivory towers and black ghettos? Certainly, some commentators seem to think it's not worth waiting for South African literature to cross the borders of black and white. Laurice Taitz (2008), for instance, musing on SA Lit after a Sunday Times Prize dinner themed 'Writers in Troubled Times', 'can't help feeling disappointed in its "unAfricanness", its seeming dislocation from place and time'. For Jane Rosenthal, even innovative texts by young black writers are marred by a persistent blank: nowhere, she regrets, is there 'any sort of racial sharing of the new South Africa' (2008). Rachel Donadio remarks: 'Twelve years after apartheid the South African literary scene remains as fragmented as ever, with writers exploring their own ethnic experience' (2006). Nuttall, for her part, takes issue especially with Vladislavić, finding it 'surprising' that in *Portrait with Keys* there is a 'lack of cross-racial friendship in his social life in the city'. She goes on to ask whether one can 'write oneself in to Johannesburg, a city one feels to be receding from one's grasp, unless one inhabits at least the beginnings of a cross-racial world?' (2009: 93).

I don't know. 'One' is a terribly anxious, solitary figure. And I recall that even Vladislavić's bitterly displaced 'Tearle', as a colleague pointed out, is a telegrammatically hopeful anagram of 'relate'.

Interregnum
Back in 2005, after the exhilarating highs of Rainbow Nationism had given way to the ambiguities of the postcolony, Vladislavić described South Africa's situation as 'a second interregnum, a parenthetical era, in which a provisional country asserts itself, but drags its history behind it in brackets' (2005: 88). This is a disconcerting image. It gives life to a strange, half-formed creature reminiscent of Jane Alexander's sculpture 'The Butcher Boys'. The image is of an agency at once powerful and damaged; a shackle of frightening authority, an egotistical infant and determined walker. Vladislavić was likely conscious of writing his way into the gap of the present through layers of archived memory and, by using the memorable term 'interregnum', he brackets a reverberative conceptual space that recalls the title of Nadine Gordimer's 1982 James Lecture, 'Living in the Interregnum'. 'The old is dying, and the new cannot be born,' Gordimer declared and 'in this interregnum there arises a great diversity of morbid symptoms' (1988: 220). Here, quoting from Antonio Gramsci's *Prison Notebooks* of the early 1930s (Gramsci 1971), she characterises 1980s apartheid while also seeking to anticipate the eschatology to come. For white South Africans, the likelihood was a fearful state of contradictory consciousness and internal friction, an interregnum 'not only between two social orders but between two identities, one known and discarded, the other unknown and undetermined' (1988: 226). She envisaged tough times ahead for white writers – 'a minority within a minority' (227), part of an improvised South African intellectual life. 'Can the artist go through the torrent with his precious bit of talent tied up in a bundle on his head?' she asked, replying 'I don't know yet. I can only report'. And as an emissary of the future, girding her strength in preparation for necessary impress; a resourceful Marco Polo elaborating upon his wish to return unscathed from a remote, fabulous kingdom, she went on to report 'that the way to

begin entering history out of a dying white regime is through setbacks, encouragements and rebuffs from others, and frequent disappointments in oneself' (233).

The challenges for white writing since then have been many. No more confident linguistic certainty and, certainly, the strategic diminution of categories such as English Literature. The quest for relevance: what would come after the hard-hitting, ethically engaged stories that had found most favour (a morbid critical symptom, in Gordimer's view) as South Africa's red badge of courage? How to write – why write? – when the persistent noise of your privilege seemed to rebuke the cries, variously faint and strident, of topics, styles, human lives, previously stifled? Sitting down to write, after all. Listening for the small, persistent scratchings of the cockroach, the story in history, even as white writers, in 'this transitional period of South African history' (Horrell 2004: 775) were being taken to task for white writing, for 'still, uneasily, "thinking white"' (776), their ideas and identities 'snagged on the hooks and burrs, shaded with hues of guilt and anxiety' (766).

We're back, here, in the shackled brackets of Vladislavić's 'parenthetical era' (2005: 88), the old story trapped in 'a dog-eared field, collapsing from one attitude to another, dragging your ghosts through the dirty air' (Vladislavić 2006a: 182). However, is it only trite to remember that the all-too-obvious axiom of 'memory is forgetting', a casual or contrived or latently traumatic emptiness which would be as dangerous a trope, post-apartheid, as the supposedly empty landscape of white writing's early encounter? This may be one reason, as Shane Graham illustrates, that a 'recurring theme in all of Vladislavić's writing is . . . the disorientation and historical amnesia that characterise postapartheid life and culture' (2007: 73). This is a morbid symptom, perhaps, something dying to be born, yet as Vladislavić acknowledges through an epigraph from Michel de Certeau that he chooses for *Portrait with Keys*: 'Haunted places are the only ones people can live in'.

Just a footnote?

The judges of the 2007 Sunday Times-Alan Paton Prize for non-fiction praised *Portrait with Keys* (2006a) as 'a profound portrait of the post-apartheid landscape' (Donaldson, Jordaan and Jurgens 2007). Billed by Umuzi as a 'chain of lyrical texts [which] brings together memoir, history, snapshots, meditations, asides on the arts' (front flap), I find, like Fred de Vries, that the book cannot 'really be read for its narrative' (2007). This is in keeping with Vladislavić's comment that if a 'narrative thread is as reassuringly solid as a concrete path underfoot', other devices for organising ideas, a list, for instance, can be 'porous and soft', illustrating 'the provisional nature of the terrain in which we choose to express ourselves' (2005:

52). Reading *Portrait with Keys*, I need to keep this in mind, along with Maureen Whitebrook's reminder that

> the imposition of a sentimental, or false, narrative on the disparate and often random experience that constitutes the life of a city or a country means, necessarily, that much of what happens in that city or country will be rendered merely illustrative, a series of set pieces or performance opportunities' (2001: 2).

Any account of *Portrait with Keys* in relation to 'citiness', then, must acknowledge the text as a creative miscellany of the urban, a multipli*city* that 'includes vignettes, second-hand tales, episodic insertions, tidbits from diaries and memoirs, histories and newspapers, along with simple lists of items seen' (Kambrogi 2007). In this book, it is the close fit between form and subject which 'provide[s] the key' (De Vries 2007), with the 138 'seemingly disconnected pieces', written between 1998 and 2003, conveying 'Joburg's collapse and simultaneous regeneration', the fragments 'a style that reflects the byzantine process' of the city's changing contemporary spatiality. Vladislavić's city lives vividly – solely? – in the material of words, whether documentary record or 'the alibi of fiction' (Helgesson 2004: 784). This textuality is evident, for instance, in the writer's account of the day when he signed on in 1984 as social studies editor of the magazine *Staffrider*. The eager apprentice, he follows Chris van Wyk up a ladder and into an attic piled with teetering Ravan Press titles, a 'little high-rise Hillbrow made of books and magazines' (2008). As his understanding of the editorial environment grew, he could not deny the idealistic feeling that *Staffrider* 'held out a simple promise. Here was a South Africa in which Meadowlands and Morningside were on the same page, where Douglas Livingstone of Durban and Mango Tshabangu of Jabavu were side by side, with nothing between them but a stretch of paper and a 1-point rule'. In an imaginative correlative of the democratic charter which would years later be envisaged by the South African Constitution – and despite the vagaries and contingencies of a nationalising imperative – the magazine was felt by the young white writer to be a space which 'belongs to all who live in it'.

In drawing the *Portrait* of 'his' city – of himself in this city – Vladislavić cites and alludes to books, stories, papers and authors, variously familiar and obscure, ephemeral and enduring, regionally particular and more international. The references might be made merely in passing, as natural to his habitus as a close relation, or they might be developed as the focus of deliberate pause and extrapolation. In this, Vladislavić assumes readers' mutual interest, crediting their intelligence and imagination as implied interlocutors somehow conversant with his invisible city. He has written, indeed, as if through a wishful longing for an ideal reader, possibly a virtual double of his own education and 'Afro-European' intellectual curiosity. The book lover is not (yet) a tomason,[3] he seems to be implying and reading is not to be equated with abstracted bookishness. Similarly, as in the 'concluding' fragment of *Portrait with Keys*, during a security guards' strike in President Street, the Johannesburg Public Library can do odd double duty for all the people hoping to find refuge: the 'lobby looks and sounds like a marketplace. A hubbub as if every unread book had begun to speak at once' (2006a: 195) and while the reference section has been closed – for the safety of the books – the reading room, as ever, remains open to the public.

An instance of the expansive, layered textuality of citiness is also to be found in Vladislavić's 'Author's Note' to *Portrait with Keys*. Here, he expresses a debt to the astute, revealing anecdotes gleaned years back during an informal tour of Johannesburg with the social historian Tim Couzens, for instance, but also explains that he simultaneously felt as if he were entering 'one of Calvino's invisible cities', the 'unhappy city ignorant of the happy city at its heart', or 'the unjust and the just city, wrapped in one another like onion skins' (2006a: 209). Aptly, then, among Vladislavić's 'Itineraries' to his *Portrait*, alphabetised under 'W', is the 'Writers' book'. Here, he bookmarks authors to whom he has referred, offering a reader alternative access through the book, as he has written it, of his city. However, the list of names retains an incomplete, unfinished feel. As in several other places, the punctuation intentionally flouts convention; no end stop concludes the series of commas, for instance, and a quick check suggests that the range of textual influence and citation sprawls far beyond the clear inventory of thirteen named authors to include 'unregistered' appearances, elsewhere in the prose, by Italo Calvino, the film-maker Humphrey Jennings, Isobel Dixon, Tony Morphet and Mike Kirkwood . . . Indeed, in addition to the 'Itineraries', *Portrait* has extensive explanatory material following the text proper – 'Notes and Sources' and 'Author's Note' – an apparatus which not merely extends a reading experience, but also protracts it and renders it perplexing, further de-forming and destabilising the shape of the unusual book a reader has ostensibly just finished. The implication is that for a reader there is always more reading: the beckoning of the same book, to be read again, differently; of other books, a crisp passage through new titles and a shuffled rummaging through 'second-hand literature' and 'reforgotten' writers in libraries and bookshops (Sinclair 1997: 326–7).

In terms of the affective, open-plan logic through which Vladislavić imagines the touching, tender geography (Bruno 2002) of his Jo'burg neighbourhood, it could be argued that even books which do not explicitly feature in *Portrait with Keys* may be experienced by a reader as relevant to the text's prevailing structure of feeling. One such title is Denis Hirson's *White Scars* (2006) – runner-up to Vladislavić's prose 'what-what' in the 2007 Sunday Times-Alan Paton Prize. Hirson's book is a generically disruptive, experimental memoir of emotional-political exile as link and estrangement, constructed through the reading of four personally influential texts. Raymond Carver, Ambrose Reeves, Breyten Breytenbach and Georges Perec each wrote a book which was experienced by Hirson through its 'telling dissonance' (10) with the life he was living at a particular time. Like *Portrait with Keys* – like, indeed, Perec's *Species of Spaces and Other Pieces* (1997), a psycho-geographic exercise on life in Paris – Hirson's book works through fragments that shift perspective 'from the literary to the historical, from the linguistic to the intensely personal' (2006: 16), leaving deliberate gaps which can be but partially filled by the accompanying series of 'word keys' (pass, island, amnesia, nomad, corridor, border...) modelled after Raymond Williams's *Keywords*. As Vladislavić might read Hirson's account of reading his ways into and out of place, home and away, *White Scars* 'present[s] memory in intriguingly concrete terms'; the key texts chosen by Hirson comprise his 'double address, in the echo chambers of the head and street', the 'secret signs for those who come after us, whom we expect to speak the same language' (Vladislavić 2006a: 188). In this regard, it's not incomprehensible that Vladislavić's *Portrait*, X-rayed by cultural historians, might just show traces of his reading of Iain Sinclair's *Lights Out for the Territory: 9 Excursions in the Secret History of London* (1997). The book is described by Granta as one in which the author, taking 'long journeys on foot', compulsively 'walks the streets of London'. A little smugly, perhaps even narcissistically in the know, traits not shared by Vladislavić, Sinclair 'reads the hidden language of the city', making 'strange connections between people and places' – the artists, writers and film-makers of London at the edge of the century – all the while 'walk[ing] the reader into a deranged [urban] remapping' that has no regard for English niceties and national propriety (cover blurb).

In Vladislavić's spacious, conceptually 'hyperlinked' imagination, Hirson, Sinclair, Dale Carnegie and W.G. Sebald probably all have a place and Charles Dickens's *Sketches by Boz* (1996 [1836]) is potentially as valid a prompt to the thinking about contemporary Jo'burg citiness as the interdisciplinary, generically experimental material in *blank*, the 1998 volume subtitled *Architecture, Apartheid and After* which Vladislavić co-edited with Hilton Judin. It's not merely that Dickens wrote 'about' London, Vladislavić remarks; rather, his writing wrote this city into public imagination. In other words, we are given to understand, his creative representations helped to *make* it metropolitan in the sense that writers of

Johannesburg would give rise to what Nuttall calls 'the literary city' by taking 'the city as their constitutive subject' (2009: 33).

Vladislavić is aware, however, that even his expansive imagined community of print has its limitations. The broken-backed world of his text is scarred with traces of his sometimes cracked logic and frail hopes, the difficulties shown to derive not solely from the limits of South African society in which basic literacy is under threat, an apartheid legacy not well addressed by post-apartheid governments, but also from the lifelong reading habits and preferences which distinguish him as an author and a reader, setting him apart from millions of others. Consider but one of Vladislavić's takes on citiness, where Dickens, who 'couldn't work without the noisy rhythm of London outside his window', is invoked to illustrate his argument against going to live in a secure, gated complex. An intelligent observation, a reader might think. Snappily apt and, in keeping with the habitual flyting, or exchange of taunts, which characterises the relationship of the brothers Ivan and Branko in *Portrait with Keys*. But the observation is brusquely unhanded by Branko, who snorts, '"Dickens again. Christ, I wish you'd read some Mayhew instead. Better yet, some Auster or some DeLillo. We're already in the twenty-first century and you're still harking after charabancs and gaslight. Get with it, man. The clock's ticked over and you're *two* centuries behind the times"' (2006a: 145). Vladislavić's narrator flogs no direct reply to either his brother or a reader; the flindered quality of his piecemeal text is left to represent the obstinate reality: that the question of relevance, like so many other cultural debates, is unresolved by the larger social context, the case frustratingly – democratically? – undecided.

Sky writing

In his now famous observations in 'Walking in the City', which readers now find on the page but which were initially imagined by the writer from atop one of the towers of the World Trade Center, De Certeau envisaged the twinned buildings as 'the tallest letters in the world' (1984: 91), a dramatic form of 'sky writing'.

'I live,' observes Gordimer in her interregnum essay, 'at 6,000 feet' (1988: 22). This is comfortably above sea level; however long a writer may have spent identifying with material struggles and grassroots politics, there's no telling whether she has seen the writing on the reef, the word 'MSAWAWA' painted on the township roof. But flying over Chiawelo a light aircraft pilot might home in on the spot; winging high, even a bird, passing literate, could see the huge red letters. 'MSAWAWA'. Loud and clear.

To some, the word scripted upon the roof of Niq Mhlongo's house might seem obscure. Yet to the select group of streetwise insiders, neighbours who yet might never see the letters from the sky, this is a homely expression often used to describe Soweto, meaning 'here at home'. Mhlongo explains: 'I felt it would be the appropriate way to communicate the subculture of the place to whomever happened to see it, whether they were taking a chopper ride over the township, or exploring on Google Earth' (Msimango 2009: 5). He is the author of *Dog Eat Dog* (2004) and *After Tears* (2007), a talent who has been described in the *New York Times* (if rather glibly) as 'one of the most high-spirited and irreverent new voices of South Africa's post-apartheid literary scene' (Donadio 2006). Here is a writer versed in 'street lingo' (Ledwaba 2008) who is highly aware of the possibilities for shaping his identity as a literary 'performer'. He 'is not your typical man of letters,' observes Lucas Ledwaba, a label intended to mean 'rather dour, scholarly, uptight . . . If you didn't know he was a writer, you would easily mistake him for a township hustler'. Can Themba is the comparison drawn by Ledwaba, referring to writers who 'love[] a good party and a tipple'. That said, Mhlongo is involved in the Soweto Heritage Trust and he is a writer-researcher with an outfit called House of Memory; one of his pre-eminent literary influences is Es'kia Mphahlele, along with other writers in the Heinemann African Writers series that formed influential reading in the 'fast, furious, turbulent Soweto' of his youth. As it happens, he's also fluent in BlackBerry®, which should hardly be surprising as the media of *then* and *now* find new alignment.

In *Entanglement*, Nuttall praises Mhlongo for his student character Dingz, who is 'a sharp reader of the changing political landscape' (2009: 54). He is an astute observer who is adept at playing the race card, the tradition card – you name it, it's up his sleeve, anything to secure his precarious life in Jozi on the Wits campus. '[I]nciting, inducing, seducing, hustling' (55–6), these are but a few of the resourceful tactics through which Dingz, both victim and beneficiary, works to feel 'here at home' in the casual crookedness and strangling bureaucracy which have become part of a South Africa post-1994. The very title *Dog Eat Dog* conveys the ruthless expedience that has become necessary for survival – making 'the best out of a raw deal in a dog eat dog world' (Scott 2009) and in an aptly interrupted narrative which accommodates various stories and difficulties, the novel offers a stark new take on *ubuntu* and cultural respect. Yes, the narrative treatment is 'a long way from flawless,' concedes Lara Scott, 'but who cares, it should get a chance at going global as a riotous blast of reality. Maybe that is why it won't . . . It is far removed from the novels picked up by the now defunct Heinemann African Writers Series'; it's not romanticised, and could become 'a potential trendsetter and literary equivalent of some of South Africa's great semi-educational TV for teenagers' (2009). 'Remotewords', then, Mhlongo's fiction is not. Though published in English, it exploits the linguistic mixing of a streetwise 'Zutho' along with a pace that echoes a thumping kwaito beat to address a younger generation's battle with unemployment, poverty, AIDS and disillusionment.

In *After Tears*, Mhlongo's setting encompasses Cape Town and Bafana's 'beloved township Chi'. In this novel, the township is rendered increasingly uncomfortable through Bafana's persistent pretence that he has not flunked his law degree at the University of Cape Town. Instead, buying a degree and playing at success, 'Advo' becomes party to complicated subterfuges and is repeatedly called on to mediate in the troubles of his township relatives and friends as they aspire to sue this entity and that, hoping to realise the dream of getting rich (Raditlhalo 2008).

Mhlongo's fictions of the 'here at home' are clearly closely linked to his attempts to define a place of belonging. In an interview with Laura Arenschield (2008), for instance, he points out that before he dropped out of his law studies in Cape Town, 'fondly called "The mother city"', he found it

> not 'motherly' at all. For a Jo'burger like me, it was like I was outside South Africa where people behaved in a strange cultured way. It was difficult to adapt. Strangely, I missed the barking of the dogs at home during the night. I missed the drunken people from the seven shebeens along our street. I missed the township lingo/tsostitaal, I missed the kids playing diketo in the middle of the street, and so on. To escape from this loneliness and strangeness I decided to write (Arenschield 2008).

Feeling *not* 'at home' in Cape Town (or in law), impelled by recurrent longing and perhaps even displaced by alienation, Mhlongo retrospectively offers the interviewer a narrativised account in which he decided to write, an agency through which he elects to represent his identity, or even the more self-consciously studied persona of successfully authorised subjectivity. He is a writer, not a failed lawyer; and his writing has a particularly material relation to place. Most recently – and contentiously, for those who object to the continuing image of 'the township' as some fascinating dark/ie spectacle – Mhlongo wrote the introduction to photographer Jodi Bieber's book-length photo essay *Soweto* (2010). Mhlongo's spot, more specifically than the sweeping generic simplicity of 'Johannesburg' or 'Jozi', or even the conceptual sprawl of 'Soweto', 'the township once synonymous with the privations of apartheid' (Smith 2009: 12) is Chiawelo. This is variously referred to in sources as a *suburb* of Soweto and an *informal settlement*, categorisations which throw 'city' and 'township', 'belonging' and 'difference' sharply into question. As South Africans know, place – 'location' – means so many different things. Chiawelo may have begun as a series of basic site-and-service plots for Tsonga- and Venda-speaking black people under apartheid, but estate agents apparently now tout the place as one of the most metropolitan townships in South Africa, a trendsetter for style and politics. At the same time, though, Chiawelo has a parallel other life as 'the backdrop to *District 9*, the hit sci-fi blockbuster of the season'. The film was 'shot in the slums' of this township, where one side of the street is a 'blasted landscape', 'desolate' and 'post-apocalyptic', 'dotted with rubble, cesspools and ramshackle buildings of concrete or tin' and on 'the opposite side . . . are the brick houses and shops of modern Soweto' (Smith 2009: 12). Mhlongo's novels are pertinent in this regard. As Sam Raditlhalo remarks, for instance, what *After Tears* captures 'is the question of *dis-location* in these ostensible "locations" . . . Discussions range from HIV/AIDS, the now standard xenophobia, black economic empowerment, government plans for prepaid water and electricity and resistance to such plans, infidelity, philandering and attempts to get by' (2008). Chi is the particular setting, abbreviated into the familiar shorthand, in which Mhlongo is said to find his inspiration and yet for many readers – outsiders? – the intimate linguistic tag is quickly recast into the more iconically familiar 'township': in *Dog Eat Dog*, 'the odours of the township and trains plunge me down the underworld of Africa's most developed nation' as Mhlongo 'allows his characters . . . to toss us headlong in to the wild waters of change the country desires to ford . . . but is afraid to fully venture into' (Umez 2008).

Mhlongo's roof – a view on, or of, or into 'the township'?; a voyeuristic township vernacular for outsiders? – is an analogous page for Remotewords, a German-South African art migration collaboration which aims to paint pixellated 'messages on roofs across the planet' (Msimango 2009: 5), each 'text intervention' part of a goal to 'disseminate literary statements' across the world using 'Google Earth and other satellite mapping programmes' (Buys 2010: 11). Like his second novel, *After Tears*, which lets a reader in to 'the idiosyncrasies of a multi-ethnic, multi-generational community' (Khumalo 2007), Mhlongo's roof is emblematic of his township belonging writ large, a graffito screen that designs and announces his affiliation virtually as a quasi label of identity and attempts to shift received opinion by means of an aesthetic based on 'roaming urban land art' (Buys 2010: 11). Against disaffected takes on township life – the foraging jobless, 'rats crawl[ing] over piles of garbage', 'squalid shacks behind barbed wire' (Smith 2009: 12) – Mhlongo's novels affirm a perhaps idealising *msawawa*, endorsing homeliness over alienation. As Mhlongo shrugs to Maureen Isaacson, he was born in Midway-Chiawelo in Soweto in 1973 and still lives there today ('I would love to move out but as a writer, money is too tight to mention') (Isaacson 2008: 17). 'Tshiawelo', I find, 'is a Venda name meaning "a place of rest"' and '[w]hen u have it as Chiawelo it has no meaning' (Soweto uprisings.com 2007).

Written in major cities around the world, the Remotewords' rooftops turn middle-class interiority inside out and simultaneously invite monumentalist marketing machineries into more human housing. The rooftops, visually re-embedded, are partly metafictional name plaques in which the idea of the exceptional 'writer in residence', or even the aggrandising place of literature as elite discourse, are re-situated as part of an unexceptional ordinary. In a word, and whatever the writer's annoyance that in his mid-thirties he should be equated with a (still?) young black literature that scholars can trace back decades, *msawawa* is Mhlongo's 'location' and his signature locution as the 'voice of the kwaito generation' who 'wrote with verve and candour about the anxieties of his demographic' (Donadio 2006). *Msawawa* becomes his distinctive individual street address among the broader, implied collective positioning of township connectivity, part of an imaginative writer's 'e'ddress to his imagined publics. This 'virtual' link to his 'home page' materialises through a startlingly visual medium, a version of what Leon de Kock identifies in Gordimer's changing fictional foci: a 'remarkable move outwards, from closely observed turns' of South Africa's socio-historical fate to 'how issues of national identity are traversed by the surges of global and transnational flows, means and potentialities' (2005: 76).

Clearly, there are creative, quasi-Situationist views on language flagged by the Remotewords project and, as Anthea Buys remarks, it plays with the extent to which new technologies 'have given ordinary people access' to previously unimaginable views onto the world, 'visual simulacra' which, glancing past De Certeau, recall Renaissance painters' fictionalised aerial perspectives onto a world that they had experienced only 'on the ground' (2010: 11). Remotewords is a curious project. On the one hand, it is 'about destabilising the power of Google's totalising eye' by introjecting 'small, humanizing' specificities into 'the official story of a landscape'. But on the other hand, Remotewords is disquieting: it reminds me, a little, of the invasive mindset of photo reconnaissance, the sinister, disembodied reach of aerial scoping. Long-range missiles grid-locked from afar on a pre-determined target. Collateral damage. Cyber-empires. Remotewords makes me twitchy about the 'largely reduced' space allotted to the literary in contemporary culture, merely an artful sop to a word here and there, in keeping with the ADHD (attention deficit hyperactivity disorder) attention spans of corporate-driven new media technologies. Yet who, 'in connective South Africa', would wish to belong to that inconsequential category of 'erasure and absence ... revealingly known in cyberspeak as "PONA" . . . people of no account'? (Oguibe 1996). Not I, no Neo-Luddite. So perhaps – like De Certeau who has been criticised for romanticising the evasive possibilities of the urban as an insistently cursive, *handwritten* script (see Morris 1998 and Thrift 2004) – I'd best reconcile myself to new forms of authenticity in an age of electronic signatures.

Reading (about) Mhlongo's *msawawa*, I find myself wondering about the meanings of home as expediently flagged and fixed, 'home' as a brand. The Rainbow Nation. The African Renaissance. A World in One Country. *Mzansi fo'sho*. Host country 2010. The roof as a screen, at once concealing and revealing. In competitive internationalised economic hustings, hustling on the rooftops of the marketplace entails packaging and promoting a nation in terms of commodified global standards and might even have become an obligatory part of the contemporary artist's attention-getting deal. Just so, the *'nom d'artiste*, "S. Majara"', of Vladislavić's conceptual artist character Simeon Majara in the story 'Curiouser', 'is always written within' quotation marks (Helgesson 2006: 31) and Vladislavić makes the point that this artist, working as he does with commodified images, also has a 'knack for publicity' (2004: 115). 'I know many writers who share my ambivalence about the marketing machinery,' says Vladislavić, 'But as you know, everyone is now required to double as a performer and publicist' (Jooste 2006).

Which – a momentary madness after reading De Kock's provocative speculations on the existence or otherwise of a national literature (2005)? – suddenly prods me towards a tendentious idea: that it might be possible, through a virtual extension of Remotewords, to arrive at a single, babeled structural artifice symbolising 'South African Literature'. Or, using a teetering mixture of brick sizes, 'southern African literatures'. So, not just another national monument, or laagered journal of a wall. Under which watchword would a writer want to appear in this nation-building enterprise? Njabulo S. Ndebele as 'ordinary' and Marlene van Niekerk . . . would she demur at 'gaat'? Coetzee as 'magister' and Kopano Matlwa . . . would 'coconut' offend? And Ivan Vladislavić? He's notoriously difficult to place. In my alphabet of surplus people he might just agree to live under 'X marks the spot' (2006b), a suitably un-fixed signifier for his hidden hand as editor of numerous influential South African texts, his screened effacement of self in his writing (Helgesson 2004) and his controversially tangential representation of contemporary South African situations and subjectivities, projecting locality through an experimentalism that borrows from many elsewheres and brings 'the foreign' home.

All too soon, however, in the conceptual syntax of the folly I'm planning to house SAL/sAl, I encounter problems. The tower teeters. The doxa threaten to collapse into debris. Well, what did I expect, when I'm sceptical of nationalism generally, finding it tendentious? Why, then, would the construct(ion) of a national literature warrant special pleading? It, too, is a compromised formation.

Consider the place of Phaswane Mpe's *Welcome to Our Hillbrow* (2001). Mpe's novel, Michael Green argues, translates idealist and inclusivist assumptions about democratic nationhood into more problematic shape, even 'damning... the destructiveness of effusive nationalism' (2008: 335). Yet because of a focus on the typically post-apartheid concerns of AIDS, migrancy, sexual violence, identity, xenophobia and language – all of which are preferred 'canonical criteria' of new South African literature – the novel has earned Mpe 'a regular place in recent accounts of post-apartheid literature', where he is sometimes listed with Zakes Mda and K. Sello Duiker as a 'triumvirate forming the kernel of a new canon for the new nation' (334).

Which is not to say the book doesn't warrant attention; but it is to concede that literary nation-building, indeed the very idea of literariness, is part of a complex interplay of forces that occurs beyond the contained shape of 'the book' per se.

Mpe's book opens with a disturbing apostrophe, 'If you were still alive' (2001: 1), and the author's haunted, second-person address follows the travails of characters who have come to Jo'burg through a series of settings that expands and contracts to take in Hillbrow, Tiragalong and Oxford. Mpe's 'Hillbrow: The Map' is a shifting space, part suburb, part outskirts, uneven midtown and deep inner city of the heart and his descriptions emphasise the new South African difficulty, especially acute for black people who have historically been unwelcome participants in the white city's deceptive urbanity, of locating oneself in a space that presents as rapidly accelerated modernity while erratically invoking and respecting the rights of tradition. In *Welcome to Our Hillbrow*, the details of individual life and self are subsumed in the ambiguous anonymity of Hillbrow: the streets are 'our Heaven' (2001: 124), the emblem of a desired collective in an 'other world' of urban strangers; but at the same time the city street is shown to be a hostile new South African correlative of the unforgiving village, in terms of whose judgement a transgressing city woman 'deserved what she got. What had she hoped to gain by opening her thighs to every *Lekwerekwere* that came her way?' (54). In a brief 124 pages, the brevity a mark of living curtailed, *Welcome to Our Hillbrow* allows a reader to taste 'the sweet and bitter juices' (124) of Jo'burg city life, 'city of gold, milk, honey and bile' (56).

The impetus of *Welcome to Our Hillbrow*, it could be said, is the 'resolution... to pour all... grief and alienation into the world of storytelling' (55). Indeed, it seems expressly to be the *written* word that is desired as an affirmation, a record, of the modern, urban identities of Mpe's black characters. Like Mpe, his character

Refentše writes. Like Refentše, her diseased character writes. There is a short story about a village woman who comes to Jo'burg and works in the kitchens, slowly accumulating credits towards her BA with Unisa; a novel 'about Hillbrow, xenophobia and AIDS and the prejudices of rural lives' (55). Refentše, however, writes in sePedi which means, in the predominantly English South African publishing industry (see Green 2008), that her manuscript is about good as dead. (Mpe himself died, suddenly, of an unspecified illness in 2005 and I've had to look hard to find any who will say the word that names his death: 'probably of AIDS', ventures Donadio [2006]. How hopelessly naive, then, to imagine that there is some word – Hillbrow? Avalon? Heaven? Book? – in and under which Mpe could live. How does AIDS, asks Lizzy Attree's research into Mpe's fiction, 'overshadow visions of Johannesburg's future?' [Attree 2005a].)

And what of the afterlife of published books? In this country of nearly fifty million people, the general book-buying public is numbered between 800 000 and 1 000 000 (Tryhorn and Wray 2009; Morris 2008). This gives a poignant accuracy to Mpe's ingenuous comment that 'there's a big big big big audience that I'm not reaching and probably I'm never going to reach' (Attree 2005b: 143). Here, at home, while a tax on luxury vehicles is removed, VAT on books remains, since to lift this burden, the government believes, would benefit only the rich (Bell 2009: 17). In Hillbrow, home to over one hundred thousand people, there is but one library, with twenty seats (Gevisser 2008: 327). In South Africa, more than twenty million people, 60 per cent of the population, 'can barely read or write a few words' (Bell 2009: 17), rendering a voter's carefully considered 'X' almost surreal, a pointer posthumous before it properly lives. This, too, is the shape of the citiness that South African authors write, somewhere between 'statistics and ... subjective impressions', as Stefan Helgesson says of Vladislavić's work, an antinomial atrocity of '[k]nowledge and unknowability. Intimacy and anonymity. Separation and connection' (2006: 27–8). This, I fear, is a preposterocity of remotewords far more complex to figure than some extravagantly silly, pie-in-the-sky signwriting venture featuring all of South African literature at large.

'I live at 6, 000 feet,' said Gordimer, 'in a society whirling, stamping, swaying with the force of revolutionary change ... The city is Johannesburg, the country South Africa, and the time' – then, it was 'the last years of the colonial era in Africa' (1988: 22). Now, we are here. Here and now. Now is here. Is it too much to imagine that there might be a writer here, who can now do this justice? Who can do this *now* justice?

Sindiwe Magona makes a brave effort, offering an uncompromising view of contemporary black South African realities in *Beauty's Gift* (2008), her testing, taboo-breaking novel of HIV and AIDS and related denialisms. In these terrible, terrible times, her narrative insists, if women are to enjoy the gift of old age, they must be done with 'irresponsible men who sleep around and produce children all over the place. "It's not enough to sire them, guys. We need to father them"' she tells Margaret von Klemperer in an interview. The very phrasing, mediated through the patiently encouraging female voice, becomes a sign of the child-rearing burden that is transposed onto women – mothers, sisters, grandmothers . . . – by the absence of many men as fathers (Von Klemperer 2009). Also interesting on the emergent shapes of black South African identities are several thirty-something female writers, Zukiswa Wanner, for example, and first-time novelist Cynthia Jele. Wanner – with tangled Zambian, South African and Zimbabwean roots that give the lie to discrete nationalism – is the sassy, sharp-tongued author of *The Madams* (2006), *Behind Every Successful Man* (2008) and *Men of the South* (2010). In her punchy, conversational prose style, Zuki calls contemporary black life as she sees it and watch out the person, man or woman, who tries to tell her differently. If she wants to create a provocative 100 per cent Zulu Boy cosmopolitan gay guy – well, she's a black woman who writes what she likes, and if she likes, she'll damn well do it in trousers. In *Happiness is a Four-Letter Word* (2010), Jele, who won the 2008 BTA/Anglo-Platinum Short Story Competition, explores the loves and lives of several independent-minded young women in Jo'burg's fast lanes. The characters Nandi, Tumi, Princess and Zaza are distinctively drawn, whether the style is glam couture or frizzy chizkop. Even if we're not completely persuaded by Nuttall's claims for the hip, youthful 'Zone' of Rosebank, Jele's writing adds a necessary layer to local black fiction, reminding a reader that topics such as weddings and Casanova-ing are not mere fluff; that fashions in clothing and music and taste play important roles in the history of the postcolony. (Come to think of it, what I still recollect, from Duiker's *The Quiet Violence of Dreams* [2001], more even than the troubled gay masculinities, is his character's claim that it is the dance floor which is the contemporary social equaliser and designer labels the new Esperanto.) Writers such as Wanner and Jele surely have a large potential market in a country where more than half of the population is under 25 and where women, far more than men, are the reputed readers of fiction. 'Chick-lit', some may frown, but why quibble when there's no doubting that these women can turn a phrase?

So far, though, it seems to be the street – or more accurately, the *figure* of the street – that has dominated recent black South African fiction. However, this view may well be the result of my own predisposition to find the street in local black writing, even without the hidden agenda of wanting to keep black fiction where it putatively 'belongs'. Take Zachariah Rapola's *Beginnings of a Dream* (2007). This collection of short stories, winner of the 2007 Noma Award for Publishing in Africa, unflinchingly represents some of the battered lives which fall through the cracks of contemporary modernity on the Reef. (His characters might well be people whom Vladislavić sees on the street, hawking or pacing or car guarding, the white writer able to offer only a glimpse onto an otherwise unknown life as it crosses his path.) In Rapola's especially noteworthy story 'Street Features', the narrative is a labyrinthine phantasmagoria across ten years of social change, conjuring the street as a sinuous place bewitched by a voracious snake. Rapola is no urban romanticist; his imagination allows him no Toloki, Zakes Mda's optimistic, mid-1990s protagonist in *Ways of Dying* (1995) stepping out into the fabulous dream of urban freedom, where the beautifully tended flowerbeds and well-maintained streets of the author's geographically obscure city seem, in a reciprocal civic-minded bond, like a hopeful contract, a promise to love and obey, to tend and maintain, Toloki's uniquely modern individuality of living through dying. Instead, Rapola's narrator in 'Street Features' 'fumbles along the merciless street' (2007: 83) of the new city, recognising that even 'in the old days' of ' "woza weekend" ' (79) the street was 'never a piece of architectural genius' or 'inspired engineering' (78). It was simply one of many 'scrap-heaps' (80), frequently home to gangs of prostituting women, 'vulture-like' thieves and 'terrorising' vagrants (80).

As the story wraps, the frantic narrator fails to find his longed-for lover (both lost woman and city of his dreams). He hears all the 'familiar sounds: distant laughter, whistles ... hooters'. But there is no sound that would 'nurse her from her sick-bed or intensive care unit ... or awaken her from the grave' (Rapola 2007: 82). Instead, ' [i]n the end she merged with the other insignificant particles of that street – artlessly laid granite paving-stones, hurriedly levelled tar ... cigarette stubs ... urine odour. And here and there, orange and banana peels strewn around' (83).

Rapola's striking style, coupling the marks of mother-tongue interference with a somewhat formal English, could be considered emblematic of the tensions between innovation and accommodation in new South African writing and perhaps, also, of the push-pull between literacy and the literary, oral telling and written narrative. (Interestingly, he acknowledges Nadine Gordimer and Lionel Abrahams as among his creative mentors, a form of 'elective affiliation' [Harrison 2003: 104] which, as occurs in some detail in *Portrait with Keys*, implies the importance of antecedent writers as an influential 'medium' of a writer's imagined belonging.) Notably, too, Rapola's depictions of Johannesburg and Alexandra cut intriguing paths across a reader's constantly unsure perception of current South African citiness. His stories conceptually crisscross the claim that researchers incline towards a cynical 'Afropessimism' that envisages African citiness as inevitably 'made up of social black holes' (Nuttall and Mbembe 2005: 194) rather than the capacity for resourceful socio-cultural invention. Rapola's fiction acknowledges that the South African urban is now all-too-frequently manifest as 'the precarious city', a dysfunctional space experienced by middle-class people as inefficiency, inconvenience and intensifying metropolitan failure and by the unemployed as destitution and deepening despair. At the same time, though, his writing reaches after the truth that '[f]or the poor', in some tangled sense premised at once on the dregs of a fading dream and a final chance for future life, 'cities offer a last vestige of hope' (Machen and Hobbs 2008). In Rapola's stories, those who fail hopelessly to make their way in the metropolis have no choice but to reverse their journeys; they leave the city and return to the rural areas.

In the English-speaking suburbs of South Africa's city of literary words, critical interest in the last few years has been piqued especially by the tough realism, the 'harrowing reality' of 'novels that explore what young black men are doing with freedom, now that it is here' (Rosenthal 2008). In addition to Mhlongo's novels (his own impatience with the epithet 'young' aside), critics have noted the work of Kgebetli Moele. His *Room 207* (2006) was the winner of the 2007 UJ (University of Johannesburg) Literary Award in the debut category and joint-winner of the Herman Charles Bosman Prize in the same year. The novel charts the lives of aspirant musos, producers, word artists and other young black creatives – all dropouts from further education. Critics have been struck by the book's devil-may-care humour, its edgy combination of cynicism and idealism and 'real', blunt storytelling. Rosenthal describes the novel as 'a pacy, stylish and often heartbreaking sortie into the lives of six young guys who share a bachelor flat in Hillbrow. It is quite shocking in places, but so is the life of these men' (2007: 6). Michael Titlestad, however, in a deftly disorientated spatial metaphor, credits Moele's impulse to 'eschew the niceties of novelistic prose' so as 'to open a window on the underside' of Hillbrow's 'gritty post-apartheid reality' (2007), but admits to finding *Room 207* 'brutally misogynistic' and 'fundamentally unfinished'. ('Don't shoot the messenger,' Moele is alleged to have replied.)

Rough around the edges. Ragged to the core. These are maybe the predictable features of a young black literature in a country in which reading and writing, whatever the colour, occupy an extremely insecure place. And they also form a continuing mark of so many black people's lives under the elitist, self-serving variant of democracy that has come to dominate post-apartheid South Africa. Yet in this respect, too, as Raditlhalo points out, Moele's *Room 207* has been subjected to 'vituperative criticism' (2007) by the likes of 'Messrs Kopano Ratele and Solani Ngobeni' whose simplistic reading rebukes the text 'for not reflecting' the aspirational middle-class values of a black-economic-empowerment bourgeoisie. Instead, the style and subject matter are raw, 'show[ing] unbridled sexuality and apparent addictions to alcohol'. Which flaws necessarily mean, to these critics – and here Raditlhalo's scorn is palpable – that the novel 'is antithetical to the aspirations of the black middle class' (2007). Literature as reflection and projection. Talk about refusing to face the failings of your upwardly mobile class in the mirrored paintwork of your Hummer.

Granted, even in my sympathetic reading, Moele's *Room 207* is uneven; there are chunks and characters I'd like to smooth out (just as, perhaps, Moele might want to cut and rough some of my own novelistic lyricism). But it's not difficult to find his style intriguing, to understand that if the unevenness is partly attributable to the author's status as a novice writer who reputedly knocked off a punchy manuscript in extra quick time, it's also a style which is affected with some deliberation. His editor points out quite tersely, for instance, that far from the book being hurried and unfinished, Moele worked for over two years on the manuscript under editorial guidance (Woodhouse 2007). Certainly, there are evident motifs that hold the narrative together: boozing, for instance, which is paradoxically both a war against, and a discipleship of, the god of Isando, home to South African Breweries. Similarly, there are people precariously placed in the city – a man with 'four children with four different mothers' (Moele 2006: 40); Justice, a homeless man who brings the smell of the street to Room 207 when he comes by for a bath; Molamo's 'lawyer woman' who also has a swanky 'keep-company' man (43). In this environment, Moele shows, there is always another 'very long, sad black story' (48). Room 207 is in a building which used to be a hotel and is still crowded with people and cut across by movement and passage. The novel is shaped by the fact of citiness, people moving through time and place. When they make it, the narrator and his 'chanas' are planning 'the biggest party Hillbrow had ever seen' (65) and he intends one successful day to drive out of Jo'burg, waving goodbye to the poorman's minibus taxi. I am reminded, here, of the place of the car in the city, the street as a fundamental constituent of postpedestrian citiness, not side road or pavement, but high-speed highway, hostile to walkers. Moele's narrator does not want to be a lowly walker, or even to remain a passenger. He wants to drive. This is not an incidental desire; it is in keeping with the co-existent, plural spatialities of his life: the crowded present of Room 207 and the tactical social mobility of his intention to move up and out of Hillbrow. Driving his own car becomes the vehicle of his imaginary projections, a sign of his future agency and successful status. In a car, he knows, he will feel differently embodied from the way he does in the close jam-pack of the room in Hillbrow. As a driver, he will have made it. For now, though, he says, 'Let us take a walk to ... Well, we'll see where we end up' (157). There is an insistent movement in the narrative, envisaged horizons placed in tension against the fraught hospitality of this temporary, single-roomed, rented refuge, 'our locker room away from home' where the residents don't really live though they stay there, off and on, for eleven years (13). Longing for. Yet living in. The unstable temporality is both disquieting and utterly ordinary.

Each chapter of *Room 207* has a heading. Sometimes, these refer to activities, for example, 'Weekending'. More often, they name the character on whose life the immediate focus will fall – Matome. Molamo. Modishi. Zulu-boy, Ntombifuthi, Tebogo, D'nice ... Playing off Mpe's *Welcome to Our Hillbrow* (even the phrase 'milk and honey' [14] recurs), this technique serves as a form of introduction or homeboy initiation to the newcomer – the reader among them: 'Come, come in. Welcome to Room 207'. And yet the naming and the narration also have the effect of layering individual consciousnesses and identities in such a way that a reader – *this* reader, for one – is easily confused, led blindfolded away from her familiar certainties through having to meet and greet and place the many men – and those of 'the female species' (25) – whom the room houses, at the same time as she is recoiling from the clamour of their frequently crass language and degrading behaviour. The feelings of ambivalence and uncertainty are exacerbated by the conflicting takes which the different characters have on life in Jozi and in Room 207 as a social microcosm – you must make your way through outrageous xenophobia, misogyny and ethnic tension, alongside pathos, lacerating envy, dreams deferred ... That such a small room should be obliged to contain all this! While the entire action does not occur in the bachelor flat, this is a recurrent space, the 'home' to which the narrative repeatedly comes back, and it becomes an uneasy rather than simply '*ubuntu*' collective space, one in which individuals sit awkwardly within a group identity. This, in turn, works as a fictional constraint which forcefully claims a reader's attention even as she may have the impulse to leave and firmly to shut the book-door.

In a book packed with the chafing, restless lives of young black men, their desperate dreams and frail hopes, among which is one man's determined celibacy, I read through pages of casual, on-off sex and sometimes crude, jack-off language in which men are 'deadly at poking' women (38), who are invariably 'whores'. Against this, I wonder what to make of the *ukupanda* through which the hustlers 'make life' (Raditlhalo 2007) by getting away with various kinds of non-payment ... I'm placed, as a reader, in tricky ethical situations that point to the luxury of my remove from the variously casual and conflicted predicaments of the characters. By the end of *Room 207*, the narrator's hopes have fallen hard and he has lost friends to an abusive marriage, a sharp career and AIDS. In the final chapter, entitled 'Badbye', he is still left wanting and waiting to leave Johannesburg after his failed urban adventure. No good life. No car. Nothing. The future 'turns pitch-black so that I can't see anything, even my big nose' (Moele 2006: 235). Finally, for all its 'boyz in da hood' bravura, a mixture of posturing and authenticity, *Room 207* is an extremely melancholy read.

When the book is done, despite stylistic flaws and some flat-out soap-boxing, I'm still thinking about the narrator, though the name of this invisible man repeatedly escapes me. He seems terribly split, torn. He lives full of need, only occasionally acknowledging the voice inside with which he 'can engage in a very intellectual conversation and share a laugh' (71). In a move doubtless revealing of my own inclinations, I remember him most vividly in 'the central library', of all places, quietly 'doing harm to boredom . . . in a favourite corner by the big window that I have made my own' (71). As he reads, he hears 'this voice': '"Welcome" . . . Then I think that maybe I'm dreaming. I shake my head, and look down at the book that I'm carefully reading . . . "Don't let anything scare you, you are home now. Welcome"' (71).

But given the way the book ends, the welcome doesn't deliver. So maybe it is *I* who am dreaming, summoning up visions of libraries in order to balance out my distaste for the narrator's sexed-up kwaito interests, his testosterone-crowded men's room. What could we possibly have in common? Is there anywhere else we could meet? On the potholed pavement, perhaps, walking an uneasy passage? Or in writing and reading? After all, he and his friends have an imaginative life full of 'innumerable handwritten papers that are more valuable to us than our lives'(13).

Moele's latest work, *The Book of the Dead* (2009), takes up this imaginative scripting. Although the novel was short-listed for the 2010 Sunday Times Fiction Prize, Moele has said that he likes this book much less than *Room 207*. While he was reluctant to be drawn, he implied that he had struggled to develop the original idea of an issue-based novel into the sustained characterisation of engaging fiction. Once again, it is true, readers have had problems with the unevenness of the work. Yet both Karina Szczurek (2010) and Attree (2010) find the novel remarkable for its outspoken characterisation of AIDS and they signal the novel as a first in articulating a previously absent voice in South African fiction, that of the virus. As Attree writes, 'Moele cleverly depicts twinned narrative perspectives as two sides of an angel of death . . . united in the haunted body' of the vengeful HIV-positive protagonist Khutso. In the 'Book of the Living', we enter his unpromising life where there 'were always things in the way. Things to live up to: wants, needs, wishes' (Moele 2009: 6). In the second half of the narrative, given over to the 'Book of the

Dead', the virus comes into its own, claiming a voice in the first person where HIV is 'personified' as 'a cynical, determined omnipresence' (Szczurek 2010). This is a callously ordinary world, peopled with promiscuous players and streetwise material girls, lonely women and misguided men; here, while the virus, like Khutso, is the most hardworking of 'writers', the greatest book is not housed for borrowers in a public library or in the Great Institution of tertiary study. Instead, like a 'a serial killer' determined to keep his accounts (Moele 2009: 83), the scribe records the names of the conquests and potential victims in a 'great book' of 'golden page[s]', 'a leather-covered journal with five hundred unnumbered' leaves. The 'honour of being the first entry ... went to Khutso ... I wrote 03 October 2002: ... CD4 count: 650' (89). The blurring of narrative voices and identities is startling, as the virus takes to life, and gives voice, inside the body of Moele's protagonist. The prognosis for this close-coupled teamwork is terrifying, at once open-ended and bluntly inevitable: 'We are going to fuck 'em dead, I told him, and he smiled' (89).

Am I in denial of this awful prognosis when, however far I enter Moele's fictional world, I always find myself glad to leave? Am I giving myself special status here, or even imagined exemption from the sick story that Moele tells, merely by supposed virtue of my educated, literate, literary, middle-class, white South African identity? I'd better watch my step, for as Szczurek remarks, this killer 'does not discriminate in the choice of its victims' (2010).

Whatever the reasons, I keep returning to Ivan Vladislavić's *Portrait with Keys* (2006a) as one measure of my own (sub)urban South African life precisely because this is a text marked not only by citiness and a contemporary streetwise appeal, but by an allusive, intertextual reference to the subtle ways in which writing the present entails reading and writing through the past, wandering and wheeling in the words of old-time literary Johannesburgers such as Herman Charles Bosman and Lionel Abrahams. As Stephen Gray points out, in 'many instances the *only* survival we have of Bosman's Johannesburg is the records he kept – of a slick, fast-changing commercial mecca which, as he obsessively observes, flourished on vandalizing and extinguishing its own past' (1986: 11). There is the allure of the trace in Vladislavić's writing, as the old and the new come into awkward, even abrasive conjuncture. Of course I recognise that Vladislavić, while formally as innovative as ever, is not very Jo'burg *now*; that with his artful collection of pencil stubs and an interest in word and text that could be called old-fashioned, he is to some extent allied to former life-worlds, parts of which are better off lost. He is a 'keeper of the old school', staking a passionate claim against the lowly status of books and literature in the new Johannesburg. Rather in the manner of the miniature plastic figurine of the zookeeper that the narrator of *Portrait with Keys* finds forgotten among the detailing of a concrete wall, the creative writer has become, over time, 'a little chipped and faded' (2006a: 76), belittled by the speed and flash of the contemporary times.

Yet I will not refuse the invitation of this writer's imagination, as he offers a framing of the urban which reaches far beyond the 'little green island' of private study, personal memory and youthful loss in order to invite readers, against habituated white South African aversions, not merely to contemplate, but to venture into, other/ed versions of citiness.

Listen: how noisy it is downtown, though Vladislavić must represent urban polysemy through the medium of English and though the city sounds are smoothed to white noise in order to make Vladislavić's own slight, slightly uncanny voice more audible. This, perhaps, is how the living dead speak. How they haunt us, hunt us, Vlad burning the midnight oil over his volumes, impaling his torn papers on the spike. The very self-consciousness of his textual making carries Vladislavić's knowledge that the poetic sea surge into which he somewhat sentimentally transforms the sound of the traffic should also be re-heard: as the swell of striking workers, or the voluble conversations of traders. The mutterings of the unsettled young white man who paces to and fro or the persistent tap-tappings of the iconographic black cobbler.

What is this human traffic to me, his words ask? An emergent sociability? A sign of my continuing isolation?

Vladislavić's prose shows him listening and trying to decipher. Re-turning and trying to see while moving uneasily between intimacy and distance. Many critics, indeed, remark Vladislavić's restrained and detached narrative voice, an unusual feature in a writer's opening of himself to his familiar city (for example, Schreffler 2009; Volner 2009). For Ian Volner, Vladislavić's reserve is part of the point. The prose, 'deliberately aloof', creates a barrier between writer and reader analogous to the walls which are such a common feature of Johannesburg experience. Paradoxically, his 'technical accomplishment' foregrounds the city over the singular writerly self and enables Vladislavić to 'write a city that can be walked in any direction' (2009). Not all readers are of a like mind, however, and Vladislavić's attempts to imagine a new social space in relation to the small histories of personal experience are for some readers nothing but a flop: 'too many of Vladislavić's mini-chapters consist of pointless anecdotes: allusions to friends and lovers who show up once or twice and never appear again, mystifying descriptions of construction sites and storage bins, monotonous encounters with inebriated beggars, parking attendants and other hustlers' (Hammer 2009: BR26). Deji Olukotun is less perplexed by the strange coming and going of feet and finds examples of beautiful writing in *Portrait with Keys*. But despite 'these lovely passages,' he feels 'a gulf seems to remain between Ivan Vladislavić and the new Jo'burg. It feels like he has been born too late – or too different'. While 'he is involved', he 'doesn't convincingly imagine the city from the point of view of its "newer" inhabitants, nor does he offer the razor-sharp engagement of a writer such as Kgebetli Moele in . . . *Room 207*' (2010).

So there's that distance again. The fact of always having to mind the gap. White. Black. Old. New. The perceptual and experiential differences which, apparently, writers white and black, old and young, will probably be trying to breach for some time to come.

As I read it, white eyes or none, Vladislavić's writing of city Johannesburg is variously heartfelt and mindful, affective and analytical. Everywhere in this citiness – on street corners and in manholes, in art galleries and standing guard outside local supermarkets, surfacing suddenly from the messy depths of the heart's past – is a tumultuous urbanism that calls out to be written. It can be quiet. It can be loquacious, but it needs both poetic and prosaic forms of truth if it is to be effectively (*affectively*) written. It requires a writer's acknowledgement that the page is not quite a pavement or the Logos a leg and that any passage – life itself – is always but in passing.

Notes

1. The arbitrariness of any categorisation is unwittingly signalled in the structure of the British Council's official booklist for the South Africa Market Focus at the 2010 London Book Fair: the 'Modern Masters' are given as J.M. Coetzee, André Brink, Breyten Breytenbach, Antjie Krog, Zakes Mda and Gillian Slovo; Ivan Vladislavić appears under 'Prize Winning Voices' with Damon Galgut, Nadine Gordimer, Peter Harris, Mandla Langa, Deon Meyer and Jonny Steinberg.
2. There is no convenient label for this youthful literary talent. Nuttall's theorising around Y Culture, Loxion, and the self-styling of The Zone may be pertinent, an imagining which transgresses conventional borders such as township and city (2009).
3. Relieved at having discovered a conceptual category for the superseded oddities he happens on in his walks, Vladislavić borrows 'tomason' from artist Genpei Akasegawa 'to describe a purposeless object found on a city street'. Tomasons thrive 'in spaces that are constantly being remade . . . for other purposes, where the function of a thing that was useful and necessary may be swept away in a tide of change' (Vladislavić 2006a: 175–6).

References

Arenschield, Laura. 2008. 'An Interview with Niq Mhlongo'. http://interviews.amagazine.org/?p=94 (accessed 3 June 2009).

Attree, Lizzy. 2005a. 'AIDS, Space and the City in Phaswane Mpe's *Welcome to Our Hillbrow*' [workshop abstract]. http://www.soas.ac.uk/literatures/Projects/City/city4abs.doc (accessed 18 March 2011).

———. 2005b. 'Healing with Words: Phaswane Mpe Interviewed'. *The Journal of Commonwealth Literature* 40(3): 139–48.

———. 2010. 'HIV Finally Speaks for Itself'. http://www.ru.ac.za/modules/blog_include/blog_content.php?blog_id=985 (accessed 27 May 2010).

Balseiro, Isabel. 2007. 'Introduction' to Zachariah Rapola's *Beginnings of a Dream*. Johannesburg: Jacana Media: xi–xiv.

Bell, Terry. 2009. 'May the New Broom Sweep Away the Tax on Knowledge'. *The Sunday Independent*, 26 April: 17.

Bieber, Jodi. 2010. *Soweto*. Johannesburg: Jacana Media.

Boehmer, Elleke and Deborah Gaitskell. 2004. 'Editorial'. *Journal of Southern African Studies* 30(4): 725–9.

Bruno, Giuliana. 2002. *Atlas of Emotion: Journeys in Art, Architecture, and Film*. London: Verso.

Buys, Anthea. 2010. 'Words for the Birds'. *Mail & Guardian* ('Friday' supplement), 21–27 May: 11.

De Certeau, Michel. 1984. 'Walking in the City'. In: *The Practice of Everyday Life*. Vol.1. Berkeley: University of California Press: 91–110.

De Kock, Leon. 2005. 'Does South African Literature Still Exist? Or: South African Literature Is Dead, Long Live South African Literature'. *English in Africa* 32(2): 69–83.

De Vries, Fred. 2007. 'Strolling through Troyeville with Ivan Vladislavić'. http://freddevries.co.archive/2007/08/19 (accessed 14 February 2009).

Dickens, Charles. 1996 [1836]. *Sketches by Boz*. London: Penguin.

Donadio, Rachel. 2006. 'Post-Apartheid Fiction'. *New York Times*, 3 December. http://www.nytimes.com/2006/12/03/magazine/03novelists.html?_r=1 (accessed 3 January 2008).

Donaldson, Andrew, Bobby Jordaan and André Jurgens. 2007. '*Agaat*, Portrait Scoop Awards'. http://www.thetimes.co.za/SpecialReports/BookAwards (accessed 27 May 2009).

Duiker, K. Sello. 2001. *The Quiet Violence of Dreams*. Cape Town: Kwela Books.

Gevisser, Mark. 2008. 'From the Ruins'. In: *Johannesburg: The Elusive Metropolis*, edited by S. Nuttall and A. Mbembe. Johannesburg: Wits University Press: 317–36.

Gordimer, Nadine. 1988. *The Essential Gesture*. New York: Knopf.

Graham, Shane. 2007. 'Memory, Memorialization, and the Transformation of Johannesburg: Ivan Vladislavić's *The Restless Supermarket* and *Propaganda by Monuments*'. *Modern Fiction Studies* 53(1): 70–97.

Gramsci, Antonio. 1971. *Selections from Prison Notebooks*. Translated and edited by Quentin Hoare and Geoffrey Nowell Smith. New York: International Publishers.

Gray, Stephen (ed.).1986. *Bosman's Johannesburg*. Cape Town: Human & Rousseau.

Green, Michael. 2008. 'Translating the Nation: From Plaatje to Mpe'. *Journal of Southern African Studies* 34(2): 325–42.

Hammer, Joshua. 2009. 'Holiday Travel Books'. *New York Times Sunday Book Review*, 6 December: 26.

Harrison, Robert Pogue. 2003. *The Dominion of the Dead*. Chicago: Chicago University Press.

Helgesson, Stefan. 2004. '"Minor Disorders": Ivan Vladislavić and the Devolution of South African English'. *Journal of Southern African Studies* 30(4): 777–87.

———. 2006. 'A Postcolonial Reading of *The Exploded View* by Ivan Vladislavić'. *Scrutiny2* 11(2): 27–35.

Hirson, Denis. 2006. *White Scars: On Reading and Rites of Passage*. Johannesburg: Jacana Media.

Horrell, Georgina. 2004. 'A Whiter Shade of Pale: White Femininity as Guilty Masquerade in "New" (White) South African Women's Writing'. *Journal of Southern African Studies* 30(4): 765–76.

Isaacson, Maureen. 2008. 'Dog-Eat-Dog World of the Township is Fast-Paced Enough to be Theatre'. *The Sunday Independent*, 6 July: 17.

Jele, Cynthia. 2010. *Happiness is a Four-Letter Word*. Cape Town: Kwela Books.

Jooste, Pamela. 2006. 'In Conversation with Ivan Vladislavić'. http://www.litnet.co.za/ (accessed 11 July 2007).

Judin, Hilton and Ivan Vladislavić (eds). 1998. *blank___: Architecture, Apartheid and After*. Rotterdam: Netherlands Architecture Institute; Cape Town: David Philip.

Kambrogi. 2007. 'Member Review of *Portrait with Keys*'. http://www.librarything.com/work/2014095 (accessed 5 April 2009).

Kellas, Anne. 2004. 'The "White Quartet", and the New Generation of South African Writers?' http://northline.blogspot.com/2004_08_01_archive.html (accessed 15 April 2007).

Khumalo, Fred. 2007. 'Celebrating Life: Hola Niq Mhlongo, Hola!' http://blogs.thetimes.co.za (accessed 11 February 2008).

Ledwaba, Lucas. 2008. 'In the Niq of Time' [An interview with Niq Mhlongo]. *City Press*, 26 July. http://jv.news24.com//City_Press/Entertainment/0,,186-1698_2363628,00.html (accessed 18 August 2010).

Machen, Peter and Stephen Hobbs. 2008. *D'Urban* [exhibition catalogue, part of the KZNSA Contemporary Visual Culture series, 13 May – 8 June].

Magona, Sindiwe. 2008. *Beauty's Gift*. Cape Town: Kwela Books.

Mda, Zakes. 1995. *Ways of Dying*. Cape Town: Oxford University Press.

Mhlongo, Niq. 2004. *Dog Eat Dog*. Cape Town: Kwela Books.

———. 2007. *After Tears*. Cape Town: Kwela Books.

Moele, Kgebetli. 2006. *Room 207*. Cape Town: Kwela Books.

———. 2009. *The Book of the Dead*. Cape Town: Kwela Books.

Miller, Andie. 2006. 'Inside the Toolbox: Andie Miller in Conversation with Ivan Vladislavić'. *Scrutiny2* 11(2): 117–24.

Morphet, Tony. 2006. 'Words First: Ivan Vladislavić'. *Scrutiny2* 11(2): 85–90.

Morris, Meaghan. 1998. *Too Soon Too Late: History in Popular Culture*. Bloomington: Indiana University Press.

Morris, Terry. 2008. 'Local Books Boom'. http://www.mg.co.za/article/2008-06-13-local-books-boom (accessed 14 June 2008).

Mpe, Phaswane. 2001. *Welcome to Our Hillbrow*. Pietermaritzburg: University of Natal Press.

Msimango, Ziphezinhle 2009. 'Messages to Mars'. *Sunday Times Lifestyle*, 5 April: 5.

Nicholls, Brendan. 1999. 'Review of *Propaganda by Monuments and Other Stories*'. *Journal of Southern African Studies* 25(1): 158–60.

Nuttall, Sarah. 2009. *Entanglement: Literary and Cultural Reflections on Post-apartheid*. Johannesburg: Wits University Press.

Nuttall, Sarah and Achille Mbembe. 2005. 'A Blasé Attitude: A Response to Michael Watts'. *Public Culture* 17(1): 193–201.

Nuttall, Sarah and Achille Mbembe (eds). 2008. *Johannesburg: The Elusive Metropolis*. Johannesburg: Wits University Press.

Oguibe, Olu. 1996. 'Forsaken Geographies: Cyberspace and the New World "Other" '. http://eserver.org/internet/oguibe/ (accessed 29 May 2008).

Olukotun, Deji. 2010. 'Review of *Portrait with Keys: The City of Johannesburg Unlocked*'. *World Literature Today*, 1 March. http://www.highbeam.com/doc/1G1-221417307.html?key=01-42160D517E1A1668170B051C06694B2E224E324D3417295C30420B61651B617F137019731B7B1D6B39 (accessed 30 May 2010).

Perec, Georges. 1997. *Species of Spaces and Other Places*. Translated by J. Sturrock. London: Penguin.

Popescu, Monica. 2003. 'Translations: Lenin's Statues, Post-Communism, and Post-Apartheid'. *The Yale Journal of Criticism* 16(2): 406–23.

———. 2008. 'Ivan Vladislavić'. *The Literary Encyclopedia*. http://www.litencyc.com/php/speople.php?rec=true&UID=11887 (accessed 5 June 2009).

Raditlhalo, Sam. 2007. 'Notes from a Lazy Scholar'. http://www.litnet.co.za/cgi-bin/giga.cgi?cmd=cause_dir_news_item&news_id=21262 (accessed 20 May 2010).

———. 2008. '*After Tears*: A Brave Experimentation'. http://www.litnet.co.za/ (accessed 20 June 2008).

Rapola, Zachariah. 2007. *Beginnings of a Dream*. Johannesburg: Jacana Media.

Rosenthal, Jane. 2007. 'Best Reads of 2007'. *Mail & Guardian* ('Friday' supplement), 14–20 December: 6.

———. 2008: 'From the Centre to the Margin'. *Mail & Guardian* Online. http://www.mf.co.za/article/2008-10-09-from-the-centre-to-margin (accessed 21 April 2009).

Schreffler, Brian. 2009. 'Review of *Portrait with Keys*'. http://citypaper.net/blogs/criticalmass/2009/08/05/portrait-with-keys/ (accessed 3 March 2010).

Scott, Lara. 2009. 'Tell the Truth, Laughing'. http://africanreviewofbooks.com/Review.asp?offset=15&book_id=130 (accessed 18 November 2009).

Sinclair, Iain. 1997. *Lights Out for the Territory: 9 Excursions in the Secret History of London*. London: Granta.

Smith, David. 2009. 'The Real District 9'. *Mail & Guardian*, 4–10 September: 12.

SouthAfrica.info. 2008. 'Arts and Culture: After Apartheid'. http://www.safrica.info/about/arts/923838.htm (accessed 2 July 2010).

Soweto uprisings.com. 2007. 'The Vuwani Secondary School Route (Tshiawelo)'. http://sowetouprisings.com/site/blog/2007/07/vuwani-secondary-school-chiawelo.asp (accessed 6 June 2009).

Szczurek, Karina. 2010. '*The Book of the Dead*'. http://www.itch.co.za/?article=218 (accessed 20 May 2010).

Taitz, Laurice. 2008. 'Writers in Trouble, or Just Living in Troubled Times?' http://blogs.thetimes.co.za/somethingtodo/2008/08/03/ (accessed 21 April 2009).

Thrift, Nigel. 2004. 'Driving in the City'. *Theory, Culture & Society* 21 (4&5): 41–59.

Titlestad, Michael. 2007. 'The Pitfalls of the Literary Debut'. http://www.shaunjohnson.co.za (accessed 28 April 2009) [originally in the *Sunday Times*, 25 March 2007].

Tryhorn, Chris and Richard Wray. 2009. 'Fuelled from the Periphery'. *Mail & Guardian* ('Friday' supplement), 1–7 May: 6.

Umez, Uche Peter. 2008. 'Bubo on My Groin – A Review of Niq Mhlongo's *Dog Eat Dog*'. http://www.eclectica.org/v12n4/umez.html (accessed 25 January 2009).

Vladislavić, Ivan. 1989. *Missing Persons*. Cape Town: David Philip.

———. 1996. *Propaganda by Monuments and Other Stories*. Cape Town: David Philip.

———. 2004. *The Exploded View*. Johannesburg: Random House.

———. 2005. *Willem Boshoff*. Houghton: David Krut Publishing.

———. 2006a. *Portrait with Keys: Joburg & What-What*. Cape Town: Umuzi.

———. 2006b 'X Marks the Spot: An Essay'. *Scrutiny2* 11(2): 125–28.

———. 2008. '*Staffrider*: An Essay by Ivan Vladislavić'. *Chimurenga*, March. http://www.chimurengalibrary.co.za (accessed 20 July 2009).

———. 2010. *Flashback Hotel: Early Stories*. Johannesburg: Umuzi.

Volner, Ian. 2009. 'Review of *Portrait with Keys: The City of Johannesburg Unlocked*'. 9 June. http://www.bookforum.com/review/3907 (accessed 12 March 2010).

Von Klemperer, Margaret. 2009. 'Margaret von Klemperer Interviews *Beauty's Gift* Author Sindiwe Magona'. http://nb.book.co.za/blog (accessed 15 May 2009).

Wanner, Zukiswa. 2006. *The Madams*. Cape Town: Oshun Books.

———. 2008. *Behind Every Successful Man*. Cape Town: Kwela Books.

———. 2010. *Men of the South*. Cape Town: Kwela Books.

Woodhouse, James. 2007. 'Not Rushed'. http://www.timeslive.co.za/sundaytimes/article86238.ece (accessed 27 May 2010).

Whitebrook, Maureen. 2001. *Identity, Narrative and Politics*. London: Routledge.

4

Breaking the Silence
Black and White Women's Writing

EVA HUNTER AND SIPHOKAZI JONAS

An obligation, recognised in many debut novels, came with democracy, to tell from the inside the stories of previously silent groups.
— Margaret Lenta, 'Expanding "South Africanness": Debut Novels'

For women novelists, this is perhaps our most exciting, liberated time in history. Censorship is dead, diversity is embraced, and apartheid has faded enough for authors to move and simply write what they love. The result is a flowering of personal stories, infinitely varied and fascinating. We're seeing smaller stories, funny stories, sad and strange and true stories – the whole spectrum of human experience.
— Catriona Ross, quoted in Alex Smith, 'Confidence Within (Part 1)'

The post-apartheid period has brought new freedom for all of South Africa's women writers, but their published work reveals that black women either encounter different problems in their lives from those of white women, or when they do experience similar problems, they experience them differently. While both Margaret Lenta and Catriona Ross, quoted above, emphasise that women now enjoy more latitude ('previously silent', 'our most liberated time'), what this may entail for a black writer is exposing abuse not only at the hands of the former racist state but also by male activist partners. Writing 'from the inside' carries with it the burden of 'obligation'; in contrast, a white woman may feel free to voice the 'smaller stories' that would previously have been regarded as too frivolous for this country. In this chapter we examine recent prose by South African women, tracing defining characteristics of and differences between the work of black and white women writers in the post-apartheid period.[1]

The terms 'white' and 'black' are redolent of apartheid's categories, but they also acknowledge the fact that the divisions forged by apartheid linger – to the extent that segregation may still be found even in the physical areas in which the writers and their protagonists have their homes and their workplaces. Further, even when physical spaces are 'mixed', internalised racism may raise barriers. The dominance of English also creates difficulties for some, as does the fact that the form of the novel brings with it metropolitan standards.

Black women writers: Obstacles

Many of the recent texts produced by the expanding post-apartheid South African publishing industry have been written by white women. The majority of white women have more leisure time than most black women – to read as well as write – and have material benefits such as space (a room of one's own), electricity and childcare. They continue to enjoy many of the privileges that most white women enjoyed relative to the majority of the population (excepting white men) during the apartheid period. Black women, however, have been, and many remain, part of a triply oppressed group: 'the Other of man, the Other of the West, the Other of other (Western/non-Western) women' (Trinh Ti Minh-ha, quoted in Nfah-Abbenyi 1997: 31).

The reasons for the shortage of black women writers under apartheid are voiced by Joyce, a domestic servant in Sindiwe Magona's *Living, Loving, and Lying Awake at Night*:

> White women may grow; they may become distinguished writers, champion golfers, renowned fashion designers, executives, and anything else; it is the unappreciated black women, who slave for them for next to nothing, who give them time to indulge their fancies, follow their dreams, and live their fantasies to the fullest (1991: 45).

Magona is herself a welcome exception: her life has been a struggle to free herself and her three children from poverty and inadequate education. At the time of writing, Magona is 65 and her bibliography includes two autobiographical works, two collections of short stories and thirty-five children's books. In post-apartheid South Africa more black women than before have been able to improve their economic status, so acquiring the material conditions necessary to produce a book. Daunting obstacles remain, however.

Siphiwo Mahala says that from the 1970s to the 1990s three black women writers, Miriam Tlali, Ellen Kuzwayo and Lauretta Ngcobo, 'became the household names in South African literature alongside their male counterparts' (2008). Their numbers and the status of their work were, however, outweighed by those of their male counterparts. Since the 1990s at least eight new black women writers have appeared: Magona, Lesego Kagiso Molope, Zukiswa Wanner, Angela Makholwa, Angelina N. Sithebe, Lesego Malepe, Nokuthula Maziboko and Kopano Matlwa. But some of these have only debut novels to their names and have a long way to go before becoming as well known to readers as the more established black male writers. They comprise a small section of the South African literary scene.

Indicative of the role of education in equipping younger black women for life as writers is the fact that in the post-apartheid period these emerging writers have acquired, or are acquiring, a university education, a number of them outside Africa. Poor education is often inextricably linked to weak economic and social standing, as Mahala points out: 'One of the crucial aspects that the female writers of today have to address is the redefinition of women's role in a transforming society' (2008). The entrenchment of women's place in society as one of submission to masculine superiority – as opposed to being recognised as a transforming force – has been a factor in denying black women the chance to express themselves through writing. Writing is viewed as not a woman's 'thing', perhaps, partly, because 'gender has also been seen as a play of power relations that offers men's and women's activities as public and domestic respectively' (Nfah-Abbenyi 1997: 17). Writing and publishing are located in the public domain and may play an integral role in questioning and undermining the patriarchal practices that keep black women in the proverbial kitchen. The paucity of public female voices mirrors the oppression and privatisation of women's concerns.

Another hurdle facing black women writers is the fact that despite their country's having eleven official languages, English and Afrikaans dominate within the publishing and bookselling economies. Alex Smith, a writer of light fiction, visited and telephoned branches of Exclusive Books and Wordsworths, the two largest chains of retail booksellers in the country, to find that

> [a]side from a handful of . . . picture rich books for children still learning to read . . . I found no works of fiction for sale in any of South Africa's official languages other than English and Afrikaans . . . Even the Soweto branch of Exclusive Books stocked fiction only in English and a smattering in Afrikaans (2008).

Azila Talit Reisenberg, a poet, says: 'If we in SA are serious about nurturing the cultural richness of our land, we must ensure that all citizens with inclinations and talent to write are allowed to write in their own mother tongue ... If not, we are doomed to bring about cultural reductionism' (quoted in Smith 2008).

Connected to obstacles raised by poor education and the dominance of English is the potential contraction of opportunity of which Kelwyn Sole warns. The publishers promoting women's writing are white, middle-class women. As Sole says in his article 'The State of South African Writing': '[I]n publishing and reviewing "fresh hierarchies" may be created: If most of the people reviewing women's literature are educated and middle-class the focus will tend naturally to fall on those writers who bear viewpoints and nodes of emotion and expression most immediately comprehensible to this group' (2008).

Black women's writing: New directions

While some white women writers are ready to move on from recording white guilt to telling their stories of a newer, freer South African identity, black writers are eager to explore and define the effects of apartheid on their lives, in the past and in the present. The fight for freedom from racial oppression silenced women in matters concerning the oppression and violence inflicted on them by the government and their white (often female) employers, but also in matters concerning their own men. When writing of the novel *I Speak to the Silent* (2004), by Mtutuzeli Nyoka, Lenta says that women could not speak of the sexual abuse that they suffered from liberation fighters as it was 'a matter that the solidarity of the struggle would have rendered inadmissible' (2009: 60). Lopsided accountability was also obvious during the reconciliation process wrought by the Truth and Reconciliation Commission, whose hearings were held from 1996 to 1998. Rape was not included under the human rights violations brought to the commission. Thus the bodies set in place to midwife a new democracy made no real effort to provide a platform for the voices of violated women.

Novels of the post-apartheid era, however, are breaking the silence in various ways. They show the 'obligation' that Lenta notes, of writing, not *for* the minority but *from* or *as* the minority. But before examining how novelists are using fiction to speak 'from the inside', it is essential to remember, as Juliana Nfah-Abbenyi says:

> she [the historically silent woman] has always spoken, she has spoken in alternative ways that have challenged and continue to challenge not only imperialism and colonial discourse but us, the critics as well, who have been slow to or have refused to hear and acknowledge when and how these voices have spoken (1997: 31).

It would be presumptuous to believe that the written word is the first mode in which black women have found a way of speaking up and in many disadvantaged communities they continue to speak without the assistance of writing.

Post-apartheid novels by black women may be roughly divided into two categories: novels and short stories set during apartheid and those set in the post-1994 period yet registering the continuing effects of the past. Interestingly, Magona's *Living, Loving, and Lying Awake at Night* (1991), although written during and about the apartheid era, relegates apartheid to the background of its short stories, which are concerned with apartheid's effects on people's personal lives, particularly socio-economic effects. Magona, Molope in *Dancing in the Dust* (2002) and *The Mending Season* (2005) and Sithebe in *Holy Hill* (2007) have all written 'stories concerning the unspectacular, the daily, the details of family and working life, above all the details of the lives of women not directly involved in the political struggle but in the more pressing struggle for material survival' (Callahan 2004: 85). Such stories represent 'the ordinary' that, even during apartheid, Njabulo S. Ndebele (1984) called for in South African fiction; such stories convey the survival of the full humanity of those oppressed by apartheid, in contrast with fiction that records apartheid as the overwhelming, determining force in their lives.

Wanner, Matlwa and Molope, like Magona in her later works, focus on the persistent effects of apartheid and its cultural imperialism in post-apartheid South Africa. Matlwa's *Coconut* (2007) earned her the 2007 European Union Literary Award and a publishing contract. In her early twenties, she has had a relatively privileged start in life: she was educated in an elite private school. In *Coconut* her experimentation with form and style contrasts with that of Magona, whose simple style and use of an unadorned realism match her didactic intent. Matlwa's prose is often lyrical as she subtly traces the consciousness of her two protagonists and the serious purposes of her book are conveyed with wit and irony. *Coconut* juxtaposes the lives of two adolescents growing up in contemporary Johannesburg. Ofilwe lives in a gated, predominantly white suburb; Fikile lives in a squalid black township, is an orphan and school dropout. Placed at either end of the scale of privilege, both girls are haunted by their belief that white culture is superior; their own is inferior. They are both 'coconuts', 'white' inside. Ofilwe, who attends an elite, mostly white school, muses: '*We dare not eat with our naked fingertips, walk in generous groups, speak merrily in booming voices . . . They will scold us . . . with their eyes*' (2007: 31, italics in the original). Fikile despises all black people, whether they are poor, 'traditional', or newly rich.

Coconut depicts apartheid's greatest success, manifesting itself in the psychological damage suffered by black South Africans, and this remains the main thrust in Matlwa's second novel, *Spilt Milk* (2010). Matlwa's control of her material in this more ambitious work is less assured than in *Coconut*, especially in her depiction of her characters. But she broadens her scope to depict tensions in black and white interactions and the climactic last paragraph of the tale has the main character, Mohumagadi, hold 'a white man's hand' in front of the assembled pupils at the elite school she runs. The hand is that of a philandering white priest who deserted her fifteen years before. Her hatred for him has led to the death of her most promising pupil and she now knows 'that we had to stop hating at some point' (195).

Another novel that does not shrink from addressing racism in post-apartheid South Africa – through inverting apartheid practice – is Wanner's *The Madams* (2006). The protagonist, Thandi, decides that, as a 'social experiment', she will employ a white woman as a domestic worker:

> This is not so much because I do not believe in 'sister power', but because I have a short fuse. Should I bring my office personality home, I would feel less guilty lashing out at a white person. Racist, you want to call me. I probably am, but there is one in all of us (xiii).

Thandi's open admission of her racism contrasts with her (white) friend Lauren's reluctance to confront hers. On the other side of the socio-economic fence, though race separates Marita from the other domestic workers in the neighbourhood, their shared inferior social status leads them to befriend each other and gossip about 'the madams'. As in Matlwa's *Coconut*, in which Ofilwe and Fikile despise and mistrust each other, class differences may assert themselves, even over 'race' categories. This phenomenon is the subject of a newspaper article by Mcebisi Ndletyana, editor of *African Intellectuals in 19th and Early 20th Century South Africa* (2008). Distinguishing between 'whiteness' and being of European descent, he says: 'It is a certain behaviour or attitude that defines one as white, not skin colour'; so, he continues: 'If whites are ever attacked on account of their whiteness, they won't be the only ones. Blacks too will fall victim to such attacks. Nowadays the phenomenon of whiteness includes middle- to upper-income blacks' (2010: 13).

The post-apartheid flexing of literary muscles by black women may manifest itself in branching into a genre such as crime fiction. Makholwa, in her racy thriller *Red Ink* (2007), uses black economic empowerment (BEE), a by-product of apartheid, as context for her plot, but BEE forms the context rather than propelling the plot's main action. As in Magona's *Beauty's Gift* (2008), there are no white characters: the writer's critique focuses on what is occurring within black society.

The boldness of post-apartheid black women writers may also appear in a strongly feminist attack on male chauvinism that was impossible to imagine pre-

1990, such as the attack Magona launches in *Beauty's Gift*. A female character says: '"[T]he black man's penis . . . is a deadly weapon'" (2008: 73). It is also remarkable for a black woman to be as outspoken in her attacks on the African National Congress in government as Magona is in *Beauty's Gift*, where an older, respected woman says at the funeral of yet another teacher who has died of AIDS:

> [C]an you think what would have happened had this Aids pandemic come during apartheid? We would have cried 'Genocide!' had the apartheid government dragged its feet the way our democratically elected government is dragging its feet now – even as our people die in their thousands . . . So why are our lips sealed now? (43).

One of the effective techniques used by black women writers to tell their stories 'from the inside' is to create protagonists who are like themselves or like other women in their communities. The heroine is often flawed, or not a heroine at all, emerging from the 'social processes' in which she finds herself (Ndebele 2006 [1991]: 23). By no means a stereotyped version of the all-suffering black woman, she is at times strong-willed, independent and stubborn, as in Makholwa's *Red Ink*, or, weakened and haunted by the past, she remains resilient, as in Sithebe's *Holy Hill*. Resilient, too, are the protagonists of Molope's two novels, *Dancing in the Dust* (2002) and *The Mending Season* (2005). In the first novel Tihelo matures in the time of school boycotts and police brutality. She has suffered loss and physical and sexual abuse at the hands of the racist government and adding to her difficulties is the fact that her skin is lighter in colour than everyone else in her family. Nevertheless she persists in trying to forge a stable identity. *The Mending Season* is set roughly a decade later, in the early 1990s. Again a young girl, Tshidiso, fails to fit into her neighbourhood, this time due to the unconventional way in which her mother and aunts live: their home is called 'home of the witches' (2005: 9). Further isolation arises when the sisters decide to send Tshidiso to a previously all-white school. Here, too, she is an outsider, as her language and accent expose her as a township girl. A racist incident at the school precipitates unexpected outcomes, one of which is her slow integration into her own community.

Both Molope's stories are written in the first person, a narrative technique that grants the reader access to the protagonist's consciousness and the consciousness of black women, which has been under-represented. This technique offers the reader the illusion that the protagonist is telling her story without an intermediary. Ndebele notes that the absence of authorial intervention has distinct advantages since 'the entertainment value of the story is enhanced, and the emotional involvement of the reader is thus assured' (1984: 15).

Ndebele's focus on the entertainment value of a story differs from the demands of the anti-apartheid or 'protest' tradition of writing, which demanded an overtly political agenda in order for a writer to be accepted as useful. Post-apartheid, however, as Jane Poyner says, 'novelists and writers have been enabled to turn their gaze inwards to the private sphere, to reflection and self-questioning' (2008: 103). Yet internal reflection may also facilitate public change. Magona's *Beauty's Gift* is an example of how the internal, the private, interacts with the public. HIV and AIDS are both very private and public diseases. Beauty's 'gift' is her plea, made to her four close women friends on her deathbed, that they not allow their lives to be shortened as hers has been: her unfaithful husband has infected her with AIDS. The novel calls on black women to insist that sexual partners be tested and use condoms.

As the four women in *Beauty's Gift* begin to re-evaluate their lives the process is represented through conversations the women have among themselves and with those around them. Magona is acutely aware of the need to break the silence imposed by ignorance and tradition, to expose those matters that are regarded as requiring 'sorting out within the family'. And to the multiple conversations among the women, Magona adds the public speech of a community leader mentioned above: 'A hush fell as those present, some perhaps for the first time, contemplated the enormity of the catastrophe towards which they were hurtling headlong' (2008: 85).

Wanner is another writer who speaks out about taboo issues. In *The Madams* she is often frank about female sexuality. She introduces a homosexual relationship between a white woman and a black woman, which even in the more open, post-apartheid society is still something that is often not spoken about or else considered shameful. This exploration of women and their sexual desires is conveyed largely through the characters' conversations with their friends, a necessity since as Nfah-Abbenyi points out:

> [T]he woman's body as openly pleasurable to the *woman* is not often openly debated by either men or women. For some men, woman's pleasure is not spoken of or meant to be spoken about. In some cases, it can be spoken about as long as it gives credit to their virility... For others, women can affirm their pleasure so long as it is done in private with other women-friends; otherwise she is seen as a slut (1997: 25)!

Wanner transmits these conversations to an audience who may as a result not only read about, but also think about, discuss and no longer deny women's bodily pleasure. On the other hand, this exercise has limits because, books being beyond the means of those in the lower socio-economic bracket, many black women will not have access to Wanner's printed words.

Gender constraints are invoked in the name of culture and tradition not only by men but also by women, often older women. In *Mother to Mother* (1998) Magona writes a fictional letter to the mother of Amy Biehl, an American student who was (in real life) murdered during the interim period between apartheid and democracy. The letter is 'written' in the voice of the mother of one of the killers. As she writes, Mandisa seeks to unravel the social processes that have damaged many young black men, like her son Mxolisi, and that have restricted her own life.

When Mandisa falls pregnant with Mxolisi at a young age, she is made to marry the child's father against her will and so becomes locked into an unhappy marriage. The prevalent attitudes towards 'fallen' women are encapsulated in this warning to Mandisa by her mother, when Mandisa's brother impregnates his girlfriend Nono: '"Nono should have taken better care of herself," she said. "It is the girl's responsibility, as far as I'm concerned, to see that certain boundaries are not crossed"' (97).

When Mandisa wants to complete her schooling, she has to seek permission from her father-in-law, who agrees, then stalls until she can no longer go. The belief that 'men will be men' and women should tolerate their behaviour, even at their own expense, is also evident in Sithebe's *Holy Hill*. Nana finds herself in an extremely abusive relationship. Her mother chides her: '"*Bekezela* – tolerate and persevere ... That boy loves you too much, sometimes when men love they get irrational"' (2007: 122–3). Nana does finally find the strength to leave her husband. In both *The Madams* and *Beauty's Gift*, when the protagonists discover that their husbands have been unfaithful, their mothers or female in-laws encourage them to remain in their relationships.

Gugu Hlongwane writes that Magona's criticism of 'African cultures which find ways of punishing "fallen women" who become pregnant outside of marriage or find themselves husbandless is important for society's overall transformation' (2004: 47). The same culture that punishes women for sexual laxity has no effective way to punish men for promiscuousness. Payment of 'damages' may be demanded, but Magona exposes the inadequacy of this practice in her short story 'It was Easter Sunday the Day I Went to Netreg' (in *Living, Loving, and Lying Awake at Night*). A migrant labourer impregnates a young girl; then, fourteen years later, impregnates her daughter, who turns out to be his child. The man never accounted for his first act and his later behaviour results in a child who has to be aborted.

Patriarchal oppression, in the names of tradition and culture, systematically opposes women's taking responsibility for their own destinies. In *Beauty's Gift*, when the dead woman's friends respond to her entreaty to exert agency, by insisting, for instance, on their men using condoms, they are met with strong resistance – from women as well as men. Women may oppress each other when they unthinkingly adopt cultural norms and they may resent freedoms claimed by other women if they themselves do not enjoy them. Magona is clear: in the era of HIV and AIDS, this sort of pressure puts black women's lives at risk.

White women's writing: Guilt and alienation

In an article published in 2004, Georgina Horrell said that texts published between 2000 and 2002 by Gillian Slovo, Elleke Boehmer and Sarah Penny inscribed, in their representations of white women, 'discursive paths . . . of whiteness' that tell of 'guilt and alienation; of truth and reparation; of women's place in a space inscribed by shame, fear, power and desire' (2004: 765, 774). Since Horrell's article, however, as observed by Ross, quoted in one of the epigraphs at the opening of this chapter, there has been a marked shift in white women's writing; she says: '[A]partheid has faded enough for authors to move and simply write what they love. The result is a flowering of personal stories, infinitely varied and fascinating . . .'.[2]

Ross's 'authors' may include far fewer black women than white at this stage of the country's democratic growth – especially in the rural areas, where illiteracy remains common. Even if she does not here acknowledge that many of the prime concerns of black women as they write 'from the inside' remain deadly serious concerns, such as exposure to crime and to AIDS, nevertheless the proliferation of 'smaller' and 'funny' stories is a welcome sign of the release of creative energies that were previously damped down. Some white women writers, among them two of South Africa's finest writers, Antjie Krog and Marlene van Niekerk, continue – appropriately, in light of Ndebele's observation as early as 1984 that 'the death of apartheid is a social process not an event' (2006 [1991]: 93) – to resurrect and confront the ghosts of the apartheid past. Others are choosing to write in a variety of genres, including popular genres, and are showing cosmopolitanism in their choice of themes and styles. These writers, many of them in their twenties and thirties, no longer view themselves as constrained by their complicity as partners, willy-nilly, to white men in an indefensible socio-economic structure.

Both Krog and Van Niekerk have set 'large' texts alongside these 'smaller' stories; Krog's *A Change of Tongue* (2003) (her first book written in English) and Van Niekerk's *Agaat* (2004; English translation 2006) are both impressive in their thematic scope. These Afrikaans-speakers do not view themselves as free of the apartheid past, yet there are constant shifts in their work. In the largely autobiographical *Country of my Skull* (1998), Krog raised the difficulty – even, perhaps, the impossibility – for a white writer to claim to write from a position of authority and integrity in post-apartheid South Africa, due, as Horrell says, to the fact that she 'both acknowledges and is repulsed by her specifically Afrikaner heritage' (2004: 775). In her second autobiographical text, *A Change of Tongue*, Krog continues her struggle to find an artistic identity acceptable to herself and others, now as an 'African' poet. The result of her quest is inconclusive and her account of the journeys she makes through the continent with a group of African poets ends on an elegiac note, at her father's graveside, on the farm that was her childhood home: 'We stand here forlornly, your children, lost in a landscape in which we so often feel we no longer belong . . . You could not safeguard a place for us here. You leave us bereft, unfamiliar with sharing' (364).

The fact that Krog wrote *A Change of Tongue* in English may be viewed as signalling her awareness of the declining role of Afrikaans in South Africa's public life. A later text, *There Was This Goat: Investigating the Truth Commission Testimony of Notrose Nobomvu Konile* (2009), is the result of three years' collaboration with two academics, Nosisi Mpolweni and Kopano Ratele, in which she depends on their translating and research abilities as well as their perspectives that arise from their being isiXhosa-speakers and black. In this study Krog and her co-authors subject to scrutiny some of the barriers to communication and understanding in post-apartheid South Africa. Krog completed her autobiographical trilogy with *Begging to be Black* (2009), also written in English, in which she examines the theme of violence, in South Africa and in Nazi Germany. She has also, besides publishing her own poetry, since 2004 organised poetry festivals. In these festivals orality and translation are central to her endeavours to overcome the barriers raised by the neglect of indigenous languages and of elitism: 'Over the years I have become obsessed with translation and feel that it is a crucial element in a country where we have to hear one another in order to live in respect and care' (email communication to Hunter, 22 September 2008).

The note of anguished remorse on which Krog ends *A Change of Tongue* is a note that thoroughly infuses Van Niekerk's *Agaat*. Van Niekerk is arguably one of South Africa's finest living poets and novelists. *Agaat*, her second work of fiction, is the most achieved in its aesthetic accomplishment and the scope of its thematic concerns among the works mentioned in this chapter. The Akademie vir Wetenskap en Kuns awarded Van Niekerk the Hertzog Prize, the most prestigious in Afrikaans literature, in 2007. The novel also won the M-Net Literary Award, the W.A. Hofmeyr Prize and the University of Johannesburg (UJ) Literary Award.

Horrell's description of white women's writing as characterised, and distorted, by 'shame, fear, power and desire', fits Milla van Rensburg's narrative of her relations with Agaat Laurier, her domestic servant. It is Van Niekerk's achievement not merely to replicate but also to critique such distortions by means of postmodernist techniques, such as making Milla an unreliable narrator, fracturing the narrative, juxtaposing different versions of occurrences and moving to and fro in time. Van Niekerk breaks new ground as she deepens, profoundly, the examination of the entanglement of white Afrikaner women in the web of race, class and gender relations that infected the power structures of apartheid. Moving beyond mere critique, she also exhorts white Afrikaners to rid themselves of the rigid definitions they have of themselves as Afrikaners.

Milla and Agaat are bound to each other in a relationship infected in the smallest of intimacies by the inequalities of power but in which, as the story opens, the balance of power has shifted. Milla, dying of motor neuron disease, is able to move only her eyelids; Agaat has become her nurse, as well as her sole means of communication with the world. This reversal of roles allows Agaat to exact revenge for Milla's callous, exploitative treatment of her as a child. Despite Milla's growing remorse and despite her bequeathing the farm to Agaat (a drastic act, considering the centrality of land, especially farmland, to the ideology of the *volk*) there is no hint of reparation: Agaat, having learnt the pertinent lessons from her former oppressors, is likely, the text hints, to prove a harsher employer to the farm's labourers and domestic staff than her dying mistress.

Exposing the grotesqueness and misery of life on a farm ironically named Grootmoedersdrift (as she exposed it among working-class Afrikaners in *Triomf*, her first novel, published in 1994) Van Niekerk subverts the lineage of Afrikaans farm novels that idealised the Farm, with the *Volksmoeder* at its moral, nurturing centre. In the disastrous mothering that Milla offers to Agaat and then her son Jakkie and, in the enmeshment of traditional female skills such as embroidery with *volk* ideology, Van Niekerk points to the complicity of women with the belief system that supported and justified apartheid. And, as the novel focuses on the pathology inherent in white-Coloured relations on the farm, it invites contemplation of the consequences of this pathology – as yet not fully known – since Van Niekerk has assigned to her novel the name of the Coloured servant about whom she sustains an air of mystery.

Narrative techniques in *Agaat* point to the impossibility of ever knowing the complete truth, in contrast with the carved-in-stone certainties of apartheid ideology. They also convey the state of uncertainty, insecurity and incomplete knowledge in which many South Africans are living. Willie Burger says: 'Van Niekerk in *Agaat* (as she was with *Triomf*) . . . is above all [making] the plea that it is necessary for any (South)-Afrikaner/African – precisely through speech, through language, to discard the rigid imago and form a new identity' (2006: 192, my translation).³

Van Niekerk has called for white Afrikaans writers to produce 'works . . . that would help . . . to create a dynamic of eager communicative exchange with other cultures and experiences' (Pienaar 2007). Unlike Krog, she continues to write her prose in Afrikaans and, upholding her role as an *Afrikaner* artist in post-apartheid South Africa, tempers her criticism of her cultural inheritance by recording – even if through the perspectives of a frequently deluded, unreliable narrator and her son Jakkie – the capacity of Afrikaans, despite the recent embedding of the rhetoric of nationalism, racism and militarism, to convey a caress in the names her forebears gave to woods, rivers and mountains, even as they claimed them: Botrivier, Riviersonderend, Kleinkruisrivier, Duivenhoks, Maandagsoutrivier, Slangrivier, Buffeljagsrivier, Karringmelksrivier, Korenlandrivier . . .

Van Niekerk also inscribes the intimate knowledge of flora and fauna that comes of a combination of attentive observation and a sense of wonder, knowledge that has enriched the lives of some farming folk (such as Milla, Milla's father and Jakkie) – as well as the favourite dishes of the Afrikaner farm kitchen. Above all, however, her affinity for her cultural inheritance lies in the sheer vigour, playfulness and fine aesthetic sensibility with which she uses her home language.

Jo-Anne Richards, who has had considerable popular success, is a writer whose protagonists' lives are defined by white guilt and alienation. In *My Brother's Book* (2008), her fourth novel, Thomas (her first male protagonist) shoulders the culpability of his whiteness with courage and determination: as a result, the colour of his skin has dominated his whole life, leading to imprisonment for his activism and to a life that continues, after his release from prison, to be devoid of intimacy and of enjoyment. Richards's work may not profoundly extend the reader's intellectual and emotional horizons relative to white identity and culpability, as does Krog's and Van Niekerk's work, yet her writing does invite understanding of the workings of apartheid and its painful consequences.

White women's writing: New freedoms

Many recent works by white writers do not focus on white women's complicity; frequently they do not focus on the past, but on the present (at times, the future) – which is in flux and complex. Many of the works do not rely entirely on the conventions of realism, instead using those of crime, science fiction and fable. Settings are frequently urban, rather than rural or in a small town. Sole speaks of a 'glut of book-publishing' and warns that this is not an 'entirely, unambiguously positive sign' (2008). Yet neither is the fact that some white women are writing so as to entertain readers and earn a living an 'entirely, unambiguously' negative 'sign'. It is with exhilaration that they are telling their 'smaller' stories in genres sanctioned by the disappearance of formal apartheid. There is, too, a case to be made for the potential of popular forms to instil among South Africans some sense of shared experience across the rifts that continue to exist and to do so the more readily precisely because they *are* popular forms. Tony Bennett, editor of *Popular Fiction: Technology, Ideology, Production, Reading*, says:

> [P]opular fiction is now increasingly studied with regard to its role in the formation and regulation of the aptitudes, capacities and subjectivities of extended populations, a role which is conceived as being dependent on the particular ways in which popular fictional texts are deployed within the developed social apparatuses or cultural technologies of cinema, television or publishing (1990: xii).

In contrast with earlier 'Marxist assessments of cultural forms being determined by the economic and technological conditions of their existence – [they are now] assessed as being simultaneously economic, technological, social and ideological in their conditions and effects' (Bennett 1990: xiii). Popular forms may both contribute to shaping a sense of community and to foregrounding some of society's fracture lines: crime fiction, for instance, a burgeoning sector in South African writing, focuses on a plague that affects all South Africans and, simultaneously, may make its readers aware that crime is experienced differently in poor and more affluent communities.

Crime fiction

Margie Orford, formerly an educator and journalist, has written three crime novels that have sold well locally and internationally. She said in a recent interview that behind her choice of genre is the wish to understand the roots of local violence, to create a sense of order for herself and her readers and to represent current reality more fully than journalism allows (Hunter 2010: 33–4). In line with the seriousness of her intentions is *Fifteen Men* (2008), her compilation of autobiographical pieces written by inmates at the Groot Drakenstein Prison, which lies outside the wealthy, chic town of Franschoek. Orford ran a series of writing workshops at the prison and all proceeds of the book will go to community projects.

Orford follows certain contemporary trends in the genre: crime is urban, often impersonal, enacted in a harsh, brutal world. Like such crime writers as Ian Rankin (Scotland), Henning Mankell and Stieg Larssen (Sweden) and the South Africans

Mike Nicol and Deon Meyer, she places crime within the context of society's ills and frequently traces international or cross-border criminal links. In her first title, *Like Clockwork* (2006), the hunt for a serial murderer-rapist of women exposes sex-trafficking and the post-apartheid penetration of international gangs into South Africa, due to the country's weak policing and the relaxation of its borders after 1994. The novel's exploration of evil forces lying just beneath a glamorous veneer is the more effective for placing such forces in the country's favourite tourist destination, its 'Mother City', Cape Town. In *Blood Rose* (2007), her second novel, violence is rooted in South Africa's expansionist past: the murderer was brutalised during his service in apartheid's armed forces in Namibia.

Orford's novels end with resolution and some measure of justice and vengeance on behalf of the victims: these endings may be read as manifestations of the pressure exerted on writers by the high levels of crime in this country: they feel duty-bound to offer readers closure in the form of a more conventional ending instead of an open-ended one – this, despite the fact that much crime does remain unsolved, and unresolved, in South Africa. Orford's prose is less hard-edged (and less controlled) than that of Mike Nicol (*Out to Score*, 2006; *Payback*, 2008) and Deon Meyer, two writers highly skilled in their craft. Nicol's poet's ear, for instance, results in dialogue enriched by the slang usages of gangsters and of police, while his plotting is elegant.

Nicol's and Meyer's protagonists, cops and bodyguards, are often of the maverick male, morally-compromised-but-keen-to-reform variety; Orford's protagonist in all three of her novels is a woman. Highly intelligent, well toned in body and mind, driven, Clare Hart is a profiler who works with the police; she is courageous and successful in her work. Police profiling is a profession suggestive of attributes commonly seen as feminine, such as the skill closely to observe and understand human behaviour ('intuition'), while physical strength is less important.

Makholwa's *Red Ink* (2007) is South Africa's first crime novel by a black woman. Her protagonist is not a fighter of crime, but a public relations consultant (like her creator), a profession that offers insight into the world she depicts, that of Johannesburg's ('Jozi's') post-apartheid 'black diamonds': they earn and spend fast, living on the edge of (or within) the ambit of drugs and crime. Makholwa's fiction, like that of Orford, Nicol and Meyer, suggests that a spirit of crass materialism is rampant in contemporary South Africa.

Light fiction
Rosamund Kendal's *The Karma Suture* (2008) is amusing, its protagonist frequently hapless. Sue Carey's insecurity regarding 'relationships' is typical of romantic light

fiction directed at a predominantly young, female readership, but her tale raises sober questions regarding personal and public identity. Sue is a resident at Tygerberg Hospital, a public facility. Patients, adults and children, are dying of AIDS and they bring their family woes with them to their hospital beds. The hospital is understaffed; equipment is old and inadequate. Apartheid's traces are imprinted in the poverty, ignorance and sickness of many of Sue's patients. Skin colour is never mentioned and the guilt troubling Sue is rooted not in her whiteness, but about whether or not she made the correct decisions when treating a patient who has died. Eventually, she realises: 'Perhaps I will not be able to save every single patient and right every single wrong. But to recognise the humanity in every patient, to alleviate suffering wherever I can, to truly care; that, I can do' (292).

Kendal's protagonist is, instead of flagellating herself about her identity, engaged with the business of living, which for her means saving lives and demonstrating her love for friends and a romantic partner (she does, of course, find one). The novel describes, more accurately than media reports could, the day-to-day events in a South African hospital; as a result, a work like *Karma Suture* fulfils one of the functions of imaginative fiction, which is to induce in the reader, through pleasurable means, understanding of this milieu and those who inhabit it.

Fable and fantasy

Kendal is in her twenties and, like Ceridwen Dovey and Lauren Beukes, has just begun her career as a published writer. It is possible that these writers, who have reached adulthood in the post-apartheid era, do not experience the weight of white guilt and fear to the same extent as do writers of previous generations, although their work reveals that they are neither ignorant of nor insensitive to persistent social and economic ills.

Dovey and Beukes, unlike Orford and Kendal, do not follow the conventions of realism. Dovey's fable, *Blood Kin* (2007), is set in an unnamed country. As Meg Samuelson says, Dovey writes of 'the workings of power', which, as in *Agaat*, are 'shown to course through, animate and tie together all the characters and their multivalent desires' (2007). While *Agaat* is set in a specific farming area in the Western Cape, Dovey uses the fable form, with its non-specificity of place and time. As a result, even though her dystopia mirrors anxieties about the abuses of power in South Africa, where corruption and cronyism at all levels of officialdom appear to be beyond legal control and betrayal and dishonesty appear to be rife among the powerful, her fable resonates not merely nationally but also transnationally. Dovey's sure treatment of theme and style earned her the 2007 UJ Literary Award and the Sunday Times Fiction Prize for 2008, as well as critical praise internationally.

Moxyland (2008), by Lauren Beukes, is also a fable, of a futuristic, high-tech kind. The comedy is witty but dark. The story is set in Cape Town, in 2018 and, as with Dovey's tale, there are connections with present local conditions; these, driven to their extremes in the novel, portend a dystopian future. Using the kinds of English that fit a mechanistic, soulless world, Beukes depicts a capitalist, consumerist society that is rigidly hierarchical, with power invested in an amalgam of the corporate and political elite. Life's transactions are contained within urban, enclosed spaces; dissension is suppressed. Tendeka, an activist, dies after a group of protestors is deliberately infected with a virus. The irrelevance of skin colour, which is unmentioned, rings true in a tale that reflects a South Africa in which one elite has replaced another, to flaunt its power and wealth in grotesque fashion and callously ignore the sufferings of the poor.

Stories of family, childhood and place

Stories of family, childhood and place remain favourite choices for white women writers. And, even when events occur during the time of apartheid and resistance to it, these are not necessarily central to the representation of the protagonist or persona. One example is Anne Landsman's *The Rowing Lesson* (2007), a family memoir thinly disguised as a novel. Bessie Klein presents a finely written account, elliptical, dense with imagery, of her childhood and how it has shaped her. Although Landsman lives and works in New York, the 'flavour' of *The Rowing Lesson* is South African, in its descriptions of landscape, the peppering of its English with Afrikaans words and the accounts of small-town life and seaside holidays. Other examples of novels of childhood, family ties and domestic wars – as well, often, of the power of place – are: Kirsten Miller's *All is Fish* (2007); Willemien de Villiers's *Kitchen Casualties* (2003) and *The Virgin in the Treehouse* (2007), Joanne Fedler's *The Dreamcloth* (2005) and Bridget Hilton-Barber's *The Garden of my Ancestors* (2007). The degrees of nostalgia and grief for the loss of childhood dreams vary in intensity, while descriptions of landscape may lead to lush imagery.

A philosophically stimulating engagement with the South African landscape is to be found in Julia Martin's *A Millimetre of Dust* (2008), the memoir of her journey to the Northern Cape to visit some Stone Age archaeological sites. In Wonderwerk Cave she realises:

> [O]ur life is just one millimetre of dust . . . for a moment, I see that beyond the brief small breath of our particular dust, the hill continues to flow.

Months, years, lifetimes, hundreds of years, thousands of years, tens of hundreds of thousands of years, whatever it takes to heal, the tough joy waits to sprout and leaf and fresh and fur again – swallows calling, returning home (182).

This is thoughtful, aesthetically polished writing, the imagination behind it unconstrained by guilt and fear relating to historical specificities, instead inviting consideration of questions relating to the meaning, within the context of vast sweeps of time, of an individual life and the life of a nation.

Conclusion

White and black women writers are breaking silences, but in ways that expose the fissures that still run through post-apartheid South Africa. Black women remain eager to write about the effects of apartheid on their protagonists during the apartheid period and post-1994; so Matlwa's *Coconut* inflects the novel of education with the workings of the internalised racism that plagues young black women in post-apartheid South Africa. Black women have also become bolder, in relation to their own social mores, in condemning oppressive, even dangerous, patriarchal sanctions exercised in the name of culture or tradition. Magona's *Beauty's Gift* attacks practices that threaten women's lives in a period when the sanctions that previously protected girls and women have broken down.[4] *Coconut* also warns of the power of consumerist capitalism, as do all the crime novels mentioned above. The thread that runs through all the stories by black women, no matter what the setting, is of women negotiating the constraints of their environment and trying to survive, with varying degrees of success. There remain, however, many untold stories and the shortage of black women writers is enduring evidence of the long-term effects of deprivation due to apartheid, overlaid with patriarchal beliefs.

Among white women, Krog and Van Niekerk continue to produce works that are literary touchstones for the necessary understanding of the guilt and complicity of white women in apartheid. Krog subjects the role of the white Afrikaner, the artist in particular, in the post-apartheid period to rigorous scrutiny; Van Niekerk calls for white Afrikaners to reconstruct their identity within the new dispensation. But a new generation is breaking silences imposed, on the one hand by apartheid censors and, on the other hand, by an awareness that personal stories would offend while the country was in crisis: without ignoring society's profound problems, these writers are able to step beyond fear and guilt. Skin colour is not mentioned in Kendal's *Karma Suture* nor is it relevant in Beukes's *Moxyland*, where all citizens are threatened by the new forces in power. *Moxyland* and Dovey's excellent *Blood Kin*, both using non-realist forms, step beyond the limitations of apartheid's form of racism to address trans-historical and transnational abuses of power. Class is not foregrounded by white writers and, on the whole, the world inhabited by the writers and their protagonists is that of the middle classes. Among black women writers, Wanner's *The Madams*, Matlwa's *Coconut* and Makholwa's *Red Ink* all point to emerging class differences, predominantly among the black population.

In the case of white women's productions in the genres of crime, science fiction and fable, publishing connections are being forged that are transnational and international. It is necessary to add that female writers who have been published to local and international recognition include some who are neither 'white' nor 'black' as the terms are being deployed in this chapter. The list includes fiction writers Rayda Jacobs (2008) and Mary Watson (2004), poet Gabeba Baderoon (2006), playwright Nadia Davids (2006) and poet and novelist Yvette Christiansë (2007). There is a new porousness in South Africa's cultural borders. Magona is an established writer, internationally as well as nationally and Matlwa, with her debut novel *Coconut*, has also received international recognition. However, the voices of black women – who are more exposed to AIDS, crime and poverty and are less likely to have enjoyed an adequate education – remain starkly under-represented compared to their white counterparts.

Notes

1. The sections on white women writers appeared in Hunter (2009).
2. Mary West's *White Women Writing White: Identity and Representation in (Post-) Apartheid Literatures of South Africa* (2009), is a well-argued, scholarly and broad-ranging exploration, located within the context of postcolonial whiteness studies, of whiteness 'as a cultural construct in contemporary white women's writing' in South Africa.
3. 'Van Niekerk is met Agaat (soos sy dit was met Triomf) besig om sekere verstarde beelde van die Afrikaner te ontmasker . . . Hierdie roman word daarom 'n oproep om iets nuuts . . . Daar is egter ook boweal die pleidooi dat dit noodsaaklik is vir enige (Suid)-Afrikaner om juis deur gesprek, deur taal, al meer die verstarde imago af te lê en 'n nuwe identiteit te vorm.'
4. It is instructive to compare Thando Mgqolozana's *A Man Who Is Not a Man* (2009). Mgqolozana does not attack the rite of male circumcision itself, but the fact that the elders are failing to provide correct advice and supervision, resulting in some cases in infection and death. Previously effective support systems have disintegrated.

References

Baderoon, Gabeba. 2006. *A Hundred Silences*. Cape Town: Kwela Books.
Bennett, Tony (ed.). 1990. *Popular Fiction: Technology, Ideology, Production, Reading*. London: Routledge & Kegan Paul.
Beukes, Lauren. 2008. *Moxyland*. Johannesburg: Jacana Media.
Burger, Willie. 2006. 'Deur die spieel in 'n raaisel: kennis van die self en die ander in Agaat deur Marlene van Niekerk'. *Journal for Language Teaching* 4(1): 178–93.
Callahan, D. 2004. 'Closure and Survival in Sindiwe Magona's *Living, Loving, and Lying Awake at Night*'. In: *Sindiwe Magona: The First Decade*, edited by S. Koyana. Pietermaritzburg: University of KwaZulu-Natal Press: 83–103.
Christiansë, Yvette. 2007. *Unconfessed*. Cape Town: Kwela Books.
Davids, Nadia. 2006. *At Her Feet: A Play in One Act*. Cape Town: Oshun Books.
De Villiers, Willemien. 2003. *Kitchen Casualties*. Johannesburg: Jacana Media.
———. 2007. *The Virgin in the Treehouse*. Johannesburg: Jacana Media.
Dovey, Ceridwen. 2007. *Blood Kin*. Johannesburg: Penguin.
Fedler, Joanne. 2005. *The Dreamcloth*. Johannesburg: Jacana Media.
Hilton-Barber, Bridget. 2007. *The Garden of my Ancestors*. Johannesburg: Penguin.
Hlongwane, Gugu. 2004. 'Writing Apartheid for the Post-apartheid Era: Magona's Autobiographical Works'. In: *Sindiwe Magona: The First Decade*, edited by S. Koyana. Pietermaritzburg: University of KwaZulu-Natal Press: 35–49.
Horrell, Georgina. 2004. 'A Whiter Shade of Pale: White Femininity as Guilty Masquerade in "New" (White) South African Women's Writing'. *Journal of Southern African Studies* 30(4): 765–76.
Hunter, Eva. 2009. 'A Change of Thinking: White Women's Writing'. *Current Writing* 21(1&2): 78–96.
———. 2010. 'Crime is a Fantasy Genre' [interview with Margie Orford]. *Wordsetc*. (First Quarter): 32–34.
Jacobs, Rayda. 2008. *Masquerade*. Cape Town: Kwela Books.
Kendal, Rosamund. 2008. *Karma Suture*. Johannesburg: Jacana Media.
Koyana, Siphokazi. (ed.). 2004. *Sindiwe Magona: The First Decade*. Pietermaritzburg: University of KwaZulu-Natal Press.
Krog, Antjie. 1998. *Country of my Skull: Guilt, Sorrow and the Limits of Forgiveness in the New South Africa*. Johannesburg: Random House.
———. 2003. *A Change of Tongue*. Cape Town: Umuzi.
———. 2009. *Begging to be Black*. Cape Town: Random House Struik.
Krog, Antjie, Nosisi Mpolweni and Kopano Ratele. 2009. *There was This Goat: Investigating the Truth Commission Testimony of Notrose Nobomvu Konile*. Pietermaritzburg: University of KwaZulu-Natal Press.
Landsman, Anne. 2007. *The Rowing Lesson: A Novel*. Cape Town: Kwela Books.
Lenta, Margaret. 2009. 'Expanding "South Africanness": Debut Novels'. *Current Writing* 21(1&2): 59–74.
Magona, Sindiwe. 1991. *Living, Loving, and Lying Awake at Night*. Cape Town: David Philip.
———. 1998. *Mother to Mother*. Cape Town: David Philip.
———. 2008. *Beauty's Gift*. Cape Town: Kwela Books.

Mahala, Siphiwo. 2008. 'Black South African Woman Novelists'. http://siphiwomahala.book.co.za/blog/2008/08/05/black-south-african-women-novelists/ (accessed 18 March 2011).
Makholwa, Angela. 2007. *Red Ink*. Johannesburg: Picador Africa/PanMacmillan.
Martin, Julia. 2008. *A Millimetre of Dust: Visiting Ancestral Sites*. Cape Town: Kwela Books.
Matlwa, Kopano. 2007. *Coconut*. Johannesburg: Jacana Media.
———. 2010. *Spilt Milk*. Johannesburg: Jacana Media
Mgqolozana, Thando. 2009. *A Man Who Is Not a Man*. Pietermaritzburg: University of KwaZulu-Natal Press.
Miller, Kirsten. 2007. *All is Fish: A Novel*. Johannesburg: Jacana Media.
Molope, Lesego Kagiso. 2002. *Dancing in the Dust*. Cape Town: Oxford University Press.
———. 2005. *The Mending Season*. Cape Town: Oxford University Press.
Ndebele, Njabulo S. 1984. 'Turkish Tales and Some Thoughts on South African Fiction'. *Staffrider* 6(1): 11–36. [Republished in *Rediscovery of the Ordinary*; see below.]
———. 2006 [1991]. 'Actors and Interpreters: Popular Culture and Progressive Formalism'. In: *Rediscovery of the Ordinary: Essays on South African Literary Culture*. Pietermaritzburg: University of KwaZulu-Natal Press: 73–100.
Ndletyana, Mcebisi (ed.). 2008. *African Intellectuals in 19th and Early 20th Century South Africa*. Cape Town: HSRC Press.
———. 2010. 'Working Class Blacks Hate Whiteness, Not People of European Ancestry'. *The Sunday Independent*, 4 April: 13.
Nfah-Abbenyi, Juliana. 1997. *Gender in African Women's Writing: Identity, Sexuality, and Difference*. Bloomington: Indiana University Press.
Nicol, Mike. 2008. *Payback*. Cape Town: Umuzi.
Nicol, Mike (with Joanne Hichens). 2006. *Out to Score*. Cape Town: Umuzi.
Nyoka, Mtutuzeli. 2004. *I Speak to the Silent*. Pietermaritzburg: University of KwaZulu-Natal Press.
Orford, Margie. 2006. *Like Clockwork*. Cape Town: Oshun Books.
———. 2007. *Blood Rose*. Cape Town: Oshun Books.
Orford, Margie (ed.). 2008. *Fifteen Men*. Johannesburg: Jonathan Ball.
Pienaar, Hans. 2007. 'Marlene van Niekerk: "So it is a risk, this business of writing' [interview]. http://www.oulitnet.co.za/nosecret/van_niekerk_pienaar.asp (accessed 18 March 2011).
Poyner, Jane. 2008. 'Writing under Pressure: A Post-apartheid Canon?' *Journal of Postcolonial Writing* 44(2): 103–14.
Richards, Jo-Anne. 2008. *My Brother's Book*. Johannesburg: Picador Africa.
Samuelson, Meg. 2007. ' "They are all the same, these men, and it is best to nip them in the bud": Review of Ceridwen Dovey's *Blood Kin*'. http://www.litnet.co.za/cgi-bin/giga.cgi?cmd=cause_dir_news_item&news_id=26314&cause_id=1270 (accessed 18 March 2011).
Sithebe, Angelina N. 2007. *Holy Hill*. Cape Town: Umuzi.
Smith, Alex. 2008. 'Confidence Within (Part 1)'. http://alexsmith.book.co.za./blog/2008/01/18/confidence-within-part-1/ (accessed 18 March 2011).
Sole, Kelwyn. 2008. 'The State of South African Writing'. http://www.litnet.co.za/cgi-bin/giga.cgi?cmd=print_article&news_id=3932&cause_id=1270 (accessed 18 March 2011).
Van Niekerk, Marlene. 1994. *Triomf*. Cape Town: Queillerie. [Afrikaans edition]
———. 1999. *Triomf*. Translated by Leon de Kock. Cape Town: Jonathan Ball.

———. 2004. *Agaat*. Cape Town: Tafelberg. [Afrikaans edition]
———. 2006. *Agaat*. Translated by Michiel Heyns. Cape Town: Tafelberg/Jonathan Ball.
Wanner, Zukiswa. 2006. *The Madams*. Cape Town: Oshun Books.
Watson, Mary. 2004. *Moss*. Cape Town: Kwela Books.
West, Mary. 2009. *White Women Writing White: Identity and Representation in (Post-) Apartheid Literatures of South Africa*. Cape Town: David Philip.

5

Silenced by Freedom?
Nadine Gordimer after Apartheid

ILEANA DIMITRIU

Nadine Gordimer's reputation is closely linked to her conscience and to her principled opposition to apartheid. What value does her work have now, as her society seeks to move beyond the political struggle? The question is pertinent to this Nobel laureate's own comments in her lecture 'Living in the Interregnum' (1989 [1982]), in which she reflected not only on the role of the writer in politics, but also on a time when a 'civil imaginary' might again be possible as a major concern of the writer of fiction. Throughout her career, in fact, Gordimer has commented on the tension she feels between her responsibility to 'national' testimony, her 'necessary gesture' to the history of which she is part, and her responsibility to the integrity of the individual experience, her 'essential gesture' to novelistic truth (1989 [1984]).

Statements made early in her career – 'I am not a politically minded person by nature. I don't suppose if I had lived elsewhere, my writing would have reflected politics much. If at all.' (1965: 23) – are not negated by her remarks during the states of emergency in South Africa of the 1980s: 'I admit that I am, indeed, determined to find my place "in history"' (1989 [1984]: 278). Indeed, in the late 1990s, she raised the question to fellow African writers:

> Do we seek, need that status, the writer as politician, as statesperson? Is it not thrust upon us, as a patriotic duty outside the particular gifts we have to offer? ... We have yet to be recognised with a status commensurate with respect for the primacy of the well-earned role of *writer-as-writer* in the postcolonial era (1999: 22; for a reiteration of similar ideas, see also Gordimer 2010).

It is in the context of such comments that I begin by posing a question which has often been applied to Gordimer: are writers expected to be national spokespersons of their societies? The question leads me to a consideration of Gordimer's practice since the demise of apartheid and particularly to her more recent position 'beyond 2000', in which I draw attention to an aspect of her work that has been under-researched, perhaps even undervalued: her preoccupation with the complexities of private life.

First, however, let me turn to the issue of the writer as national spokesperson. Like other writers of fiction who, since 1990, have emerged from authoritarian regimes – for example, Václav Havel (Czech Republic) and Christa Wolf (the former East Germany) – during the struggle years Gordimer felt obliged to interweave the private with the public, to tie her 'essential gesture' to her 'necessary gesture'. Prior to the 1990s, she made anti-apartheid pronouncements from the public platform, as well as through her fiction, and inevitably became associated with the role of anti-apartheid public intellectual, which formed part of the justification for her receiving the Nobel Prize in 1991 (see Chapman 2009). Yet with the coming to power of the African National Congress (ANC) government, she has apparently ceased to be a public interrogator of core national issues. She would say, no doubt, that the abomination of racism has been defeated and that her 'necessary gesture' may be allowed to yield to her 'essential gesture'. Such a claim, however, has also been interpreted as her reneging on her responsibility to a changed socio-political terrain. The ANC government has its own shortcomings and contradictions: its Mbeki-era AIDS denialism; its reluctance to act against misconduct in its own ranks; its manipulation of the law (for example, in the controversies surrounding current president, Jacob Zuma) and its condoning of political hooliganism (the ANC Youth League leader Julius Malema's controversial behaviour). The ANC has avoided explicit condemnation of Mugabe's violations of democratic governance in Zimbabwe, has sabotaged high-profile international efforts to restrain dictators in the Sudan and Myanmar and has refused to grant a visa to the Dalai Lama, a recipient of the Nobel Peace Prize. On all of these issues, Gordimer has remained silent.

Unsurprisingly, there are those who are critical of such apparent silence on abuses of power. Ulrike Ernst-Auga, for example, is disturbed by Gordimer's abdication from the public platform. Drawing on Manuel Castells's (1997) categories of 'the resistance intellectual' versus 'the legitimising intellectual', Ernst-Auga argues that, in avoiding criticism of the post-liberation ANC, Gordimer is disavowing her role as public intellectual: 'Gordimer became the tame critic of post-apartheid South Africa . . . "the legitimising intellectual". Erstwhile resistance writer, Gordimer has become the "state writer" of the ANC' (2003: 11) and, by implication, a 'silent' praise-singer of the new order. Various writers interviewed by Ernst-Auga have also expressed concern over Gordimer's shift to public silence. Peter Horn, for example, considers that Gordimer is on the side of the victors: 'Now she takes the side of the established government, those people who now hold power ... I do not have the impression that she is particularly critical of the current government, in those instances in which criticism would be necessary' (2002: 49). Stephen Gray articulates harsher criticism: 'I don't agree with her current endorsement of ANC politics ... She should have stayed an independent writer' (2002: 73).

Gordimer, in fact, is one of many intellectuals who have chosen to remain silent on the new dispensation's tendency to equate criticism of itself with 'counter-revolutionary' behaviour. There are only a few writers/artists who confront the authoritarian streak in the ANC. Nise Malange states in an interview with Ernst-Auga (2002) that 'since 1994 [artists] have experienced self-censorship' (110) for fear that should they speak out, the ANC would 'start questioning [their] loyalty' (111); 'anything that is critical has to be sidelined' (114). More recently, James Matthews lamented a retreat into silence: 'Dissident poets of the apartheid period are on the whole now marginalised. They have become exiles within ... It disturbs me to come to the conclusion that the pervading silence could be a case of self-censorship' (2009: 55–6). There have recently been calls for Nelson Mandela, as an elder statesman, to speak out against a 'culture' in the former liberation movement of silencing its critics: 'Sadly, Madiba, by his inaction, inadvertently joined the ranks of the many in the ANC who were cowed into silence' (Mgwaba 2009: 22). One could apply this reference to Mandela to Gordimer's current public stance.

Asked whether, in post-apartheid times, it is important for writers to foreground specific themes, Gordimer responded: 'You mustn't ask writers to become direct agents of change in this way. That is not our purpose. You are asking then for propaganda ... [W]riters must write what they want to write about' (2002: 144). Such a stance on writerly freedom may well be in step with current South African literary practice. The decades after the unbannings of 1990 have witnessed an outward move beyond the 'grand narrative' of oppression and resistance, whether in Gordimer, J.M. Coetzee, André Brink, Athol Fugard, Ivan Vladislavić or Zakes Mda, to focus on prominent figures, all of whom were writing during the transition to a new dispensation. Some critics even raise the question as to whether South African literature still exists, given that

> there appears to be a shift from the vortex of a single obsession [to] a more liberating repertoire for the improvisation of individual identity. If we argue

that the seam of compulsive identity formation under conditions of referential fracture has been undone, then the lines of affiliation are free to go where they like (De Kock 2005: 76–7).

As Gordimer keeps reminding us: 'I take the freedom to write what I want' (Isaacson 2005: 17).

My concern here, as I have suggested, is with writing in more 'civil' times or, at least, in times when public events have not obscured the rhythms of people's daily lives. In his influential study, subtitled *History from the Inside* (1986), Stephen Clingman perceived Gordimer's writerly freedom in the years of struggle to be overdetermined by the social narrative. The approach was apposite for the 1970s and 1980s: behind Clingman's method lies the general movement from a New Critical discourse to structuralist Marxism, a hermeneutics of suspicion being a recurrent purpose. But as South Africa seeks to go beyond what Jacques Derrida referred to in 1985 as 'this concentration of world history' (1985: 297), the insights of Njabulo S. Ndebele retain their relevance: as racial issues become more tangential, literature may dwell less on 'obscene social exhibitionism' and 'the highly dramatic, highly demonstrative forms' of literary representation (1991: 37).

The shift in Gordimer's 'post-apartheid' novels to a primary consideration of individual choice and responsibility does not mean that the political dimension vanishes. The effects of apartheid are felt in *None to Accompany Me* (1994), for example, where Vera Stark, the protagonist, is involved in issues of land dispute and resettlement claims, and in *Get a Life* (2005) Gordimer discusses issues of ecology in relation to economic and political interests. There is a subtle difference, nonetheless, in *Get a Life* in comparison with the novels written in the 1990s: the social issues are not central to the politics of nationhood and the private life proceeds without dramatic irruptions beyond the 'family'. *Get a Life* will be the focus of this chapter, but, before I discuss this novel, let me offer an overview of Gordimer's practice in the 1990s. I do so with the question raised by Ernst-Auga and others in mind: that of the responsibility of the writer to the politics of the time.

There is a sense of existential homecoming in *None to Accompany Me*, which articulates freedom as a condition based on the transition from social rebellion to individual responsibility. The novel is unadorned in its style, suggesting the necessity of maintaining a distance from the demands of people and events; Vera Stark's first responsibility is to herself. This is not to imply that the novel lacks a public dimension, offering as it does insights into its protagonist's work for a foundation that supports land-restitution policies. Yet how effective is Gordimer's resort to the public event in relation to its private counterpart? The immediate response is that the two do not seem to be linked as dynamically as was the case in *Burger's Daughter* (1979), for example, in which Rosa Burger the person and Rosa Burger the activist occupied identical dimensions. Ironically, one of the advantages of the 1970s and 1980s was that there was no escape from the public/private dialectic. In *None to Accompany Me*, on the other hand, events often detach themselves from the intricacies of private life and it is tempting to consider the work as two ill-fitting novels in one. We are presented – the novel 'tells' us, rather than 'shows' us – various social realities in the build-up to the 1994 elections. The reader is subjected to discussions on economic or land policy, corruption in office, federalism, the education crisis and AIDS. Gordimer seems anxious not to disappoint those readers for whom she might still be the national spokesperson. Yet a private story operates within the public life and engages most of the author's attention: the inward journey of Vera Stark, a sixty-something lawyer, who is influential in a foundation that helps black people with land ownership. In a process of psychological housecleaning, Vera, while remaining committed to her public duties, begins to free herself from commitments to other people and embarks on a kind of secular retreat. As her surname suggests, she is the seeker of the stark truth, who can discard those stages of her life that have exhausted their significance. Gordimer summarises the theme: 'Perhaps the passing away of the old regime makes the abandonment of an old personal life also possible' (1994: 315).

Inner discovery links *None to Accompany Me* to *The House Gun* (1998), the latter novel seeming to offer an answer to Gordimer's preoccupation in the previous novel: what are we able to leave behind? What will we take with us as we try to move house as a nation? *The House Gun* offers one answer to the question: violence has accompanied us; the new house contains a gun. Violence becomes an ominous character in its own right: the house gun, casually available, presents an invitation to take the law into one's own hands. Authorial meditations on the violence of transitional times and the collective effort needed to replace the old order with a new moral system constitute the 'public forum' of *The House Gun*, but the real point of interest is Duncan Lindgard's killing of his lover's casual partner in a fit of jealousy. The storyline follows Duncan's distraught parents as they attempt to come to terms with their son's act. In their effort to understand his lifestyle, which includes a gay lover and a sexual triangle, they become acutely aware of 'the Other Side . . . of privilege': '[E]verything had come to them from the Other Side, the nakedness to the final disaster: powerlessness, helplessness, before the law . . . Neither whiteness . . . nor money that had kept them in safety – that other form of segregation – could change their status' (1998: 127). The parents' story powerfully connects private and public realms. The thrust of the novel, however, focuses on Duncan's rebellion against middle-class convention. Like *None to Accompany Me*, *The House Gun* presents a juxtaposition of two apparently ill-fitting stories: the parents' story and their son's story do not interact with any illumination.

The Pickup (2001) also represents a juxtaposition of separate stories. The public dimension is again reminiscent of pre-1990 novels (for example, *Burger's Daughter* and *My Son's Story*, the latter no doubt penned prior to the unbannings), in which the author explored the framework of the political underground. *The Pickup* offers a glimpse into another type of underground: that of post-1990 illegal black immigration to South Africa. Abdu, an 'illegal' from an Arab country in North Africa, seeks residence in South Africa. He 'picks up' Julie Summers, a young white woman of means, who falls in love with him. Gordimer does not pursue the social causes of immigration; instead, she pursues the human story of Julie's following her deported lover to his desert country. Like Vera's, hers is another rite of passage, in sharp contrast with Abdu's trajectory: 'There is a disjunction between Julie's privileged rejection of globalised culture and [Abdu's] thirst to embrace it' (Kossew 2003: 24–5). Expelled from South Africa, Abdu seeks another destination in the 'new world', whereas Julie finds contentment in the unnamed North African state. Is Gordimer's removal of the protagonists from the familiar South African setting an escape from engaging with impenetrable post-1990 scenarios in this country? Wherever we wish to place the emphasis, we encounter again a novel that tells two distinct stories: one 'public' (forced emigration), the other 'private' (discovery of self). It is the latter that in the end engrosses Gordimer's imagination. We enter a story of location or dislocation, a symbolic country of the soul, exile-as-home. Like Vera, who gives up social and personal dependencies, Julie gives up her material bonds, her new husband and finally her desire to journey to another place. She will not accompany her husband to the land of his next opportunity, the United States, but chooses to immerse herself in the silence of the desert, her reward being the enhancement of self-knowledge.

* * *

Similarly, Gordimer's latest novel, *Get a Life* (2005), marks a shift in her handling of the public/private dynamic. Unlike its three predecessors, this novel does not seem to be two almost-separate novels in one – the one of the public, the other of the private domain. *Get a Life* focuses steadily on the private, on the life of a man and his family against a backdrop of ecological concern. Backdrop aside, to allude to 'green' concerns, however ultimately important – in a time of AIDS, high unemployment, pervasive criminality, failed service-delivery, violence, corruption, mismanagement and arrogance in high office – might strike some readers as a diversion from the more immediate challenges of the new democracy. Yet would such a response do justice to *Get a Life*? To return to Ernst-Auga, is this novel 'silent'? Can the form of a writer's 'boldness' be decreed? I shall suggest not.

It is true that the public world is made subordinate to the story of Paul Bannerman. At the centre of the novel is the impact that thyroid cancer and the ensuing radiation treatment have on Paul's body and mind, as well as his enforced isolation from his wife and child. His temporary return to his parents' home allows him to ponder personal and ecological commitments. As noted by Anthony Vital, the novel 'writes ecology as only one thread in the full weave of life' (2008: 93), for the full weave includes Paul's own identity crisis, which involves his physical and emotional recuperation from a life-threatening disease. Although it is taken seriously, the public forum is treated here in laconic, open-ended, reportage style and granted less attention than issues of self-discovery and Paul's new understandings of his roles as husband, father and son. The novel 'tells' us about interventions by ecological conservationists against high-level political drives for economic modernisation. Gordimer offers information on ecological activism in South Africa, while suggesting that there are no simple solutions to conservation in an ecologically aware global consciousness. Such issues, however, do not occupy Paul's centre of consciousness and – unlike the themes of other post-apartheid novels as described above – do not jar against Paul's 'family' story (see also Dimitriu 2001, 2006).

It is precisely such a reversal of the public/private dichotomy that has led several critics (notably Vital) to bemoan that 'the politics of nationhood, which in Gordimer's earlier fiction added crucial layers of significance to personal choice, seem peripheral' (2008: 92).[1] Vital regrets that the novelist has limited the environmental issue – environment for Vital has few metaphorical connotations – to the consciousness of white, middle-class people and their 'subjective appropriation of ecology' (104). I agree that Gordimer, indeed, has offered subjective insights into issues of ecology, but do not share Vital's regrets.[2] Are not all acts of fiction inescapably acts of the subjective imagination?

I return to a key consideration: should we as critics, at the end of dictatorial times, be dictating to writers the terms of their fictional engagements? In this case, are we supposed to condemn Gordimer for her focus on a certain class? If so, do we not then risk becoming ideologically prescriptive? The times of sloganeering, in which 'culture [was] a weapon of struggle' (1990: 19), need to be superseded by other challenges, as Albie Sachs reminded us in the late 1980s. Is it not – 'beyond

2000', almost twenty years into our democracy – legitimate to permit writers the freedom of their fictional choices to depict what they know most intimately? In the light of this, I would pose a question that neither Vital nor Ernst-Auga wishes to contemplate: does South Africa in the new millennium not require from its artists new, perhaps unexpected kinds of boldness? Let me pursue such a line of possibility.

The first part of *Get a Life* immerses the reader in Paul's retreat, where he finds himself under radiotherapy treatment, away from his life, not only as an environmental researcher, but also as a husband and father. This is a new Gordimer trope: a young man forced to retreat from the world into illness and isolation. It is tempting to ask, with Siddhartha Deb (2005: 19), 'And what does Paul's illness signify, especially in the possible contamination he carries within him?' What is the symbolism of Gordimer's 'chosen' disease for Paul? The organ affected by disease is the thyroid gland, which is considered from a spiritual-symbolic point of view as 'the seed and fruit of the Tree of Knowledge [so that] he who opens up this fruit has access to the Word and Knowledge' (De Souzenelle 1999: 333; my translation). According to interpretations of the body symbolism by Eastern philosophies,[3] the throat-region/chakra is also considered to be the seat of creativity and communication, 'a point of entry to the innermost recesses of the spirit and self-knowledge' (Ozaniec 1995: 152; my translation). On several occasions, Gordimer mentions that something 'had Paul by the throat' (2005: 3, 16), or that his 'ability to communicate was stifled' (43). My assumption is that Gordimer's choice of 'disease' is not haphazard: its bodily location has a metaphoric value that needs to be placed in relation to the other literary conventions of symbols, themes and characters in the economy of the novel as a whole. Paul's constricted ability to communicate verbally with others, as well as the danger of his radioactivity, keeps him in physical and emotional isolation. When he is diagnosed with cancer, 'he stood there, alone' (7). His 'cutlery is kept apart' (14); 'he's learning to be alone in his new way' (33); even the family dog avoids him (48); '[t]he new leper, that's how he thinks of himself' (6). Throughout the first part of the novel, Gordimer makes use of leprosy as shorthand: Paul is a 'lit-up leper' (33), 'the emanation' (37), 'the leper himself' (60), 'an Untouchable' (42). She also highlights various 'states of being' associated with leprosy: a lack of purpose (20); a sense of entrapment (with Paul 'inside . . . the word for jail seems the right one' [82]).

Gordimer's insistence on her protagonist's symbolic status as 'the twenty-first century leper' (56) makes one wonder about the wider significance she attributes to Paul. Does the physical disease perhaps suggest unease in any dimension beyond his family circle? Is a young, white male in the new South Africa 'the new leper'? As Mamphela Ramphele has recently pointed out:

Silenced by Freedom?

> The legacy of authoritarian rule ... has conditioned South Africans to accept themselves as insignificant in relation to those in position of authority ... Insignificance frames relations of power at every level of our society: citizens and government; individual members and their political parties, etc. ... We need a serious conversation about our identity crisis, our sense of insignificance (2009: 4).

Ironic as it is – and some might see here historical justice – the young, white male is told by the 'newly empowered' to accept his new post-apartheid status as insignificant. Gordimer, for her part, does not obviously invoke such a political parallel. It is nevertheless worth investigating the social implications of this novel's symbolism. When she says that Paul's state is that of an 'untouchable' whose 'emanation irradiates the hidden or undiscovered' (2005: 55), is she inviting levels of inference? Is she pointing to current issues which she feels cannot be spoken from the public platform? She said in an interview that her 'characters don't always explain everything ... I am interested in fiction that is demanding, that says to me I cannot tell you everything – you have to intuit for yourself things that are not spelt out' (Isaacson 2005: 17). Is her oblique style a new kind of oppositional stance? We may recall her satirical depiction, in *The Pickup*, of a pretentious, upwardly mobile member of the new black elite. To have turned, in the new South Africa, to a white male protagonist, by contrast, represents an unfashionable cause. Yet, to reiterate, is Gordimer being wickedly subversive? She offers a brittle portrait of Paul's advertising executive wife, while guiding her readers' sympathy to Paul – the apparently insignificant, though well-meaning, young, middle-class white male.

Another unexpected novelistic device is the topos of the story's unfolding. Paul spends much of his physical recovery in the family garden, which nurtures his introspection. (In many ways, the garden for Paul has a similar function to that of other new symbolic spaces in Gordimer's post-apartheid novels: the desert for Julie Summers; the cottage in which Vera Stark lives as a tenant; the prison cell for Duncan Lindgard.) Occasionally referred to as 'No-Man's-Land' (Gordimer 2005: 30, 47), the garden is also hinted at in biblical terms: when Paul reflects on the possibility of separating from his wife, we are reminded that 'it was in the Garden that expulsion came, once there was Knowledge' (58). Gordimer has chosen here to deploy the garden in the parabolic mode, though in a review in the 1980s she criticised J.M. Coetzee's novel *Life & Times of Michael K*, claiming that for a writer to focus on 'the idea of gardening' in times of emergency was an avoidance of politics and an abdication of the social responsibility to bear witness (1984: 1–6).

How then to explain Gordimer's symbolic choices in her novel of 2005? Is it simply an irony that she is foregrounding the garden symbolism? In a post-emergency society, is the writer free to meditate on ecology and gardens? Conversely, does a preoccupation with gardens necessarily mean an escape from history? I suggest that there has been a shift in Gordimer's writing to what Coetzee, in his comments on her latest works, starting with *The Pickup*, has welcomed as 'a spiritual turn in her thought' (2007: 252). Commenting on Coetzee's insight, Derek Attridge holds that he is

> welcoming [Gordimer] into a domain he has inhabited, not always comfortably, for some time . . . For if there are gleams of transcendence in Coetzee's [and, I would add, in Gordimer's] novels . . . they are not only hints of a possible justice, but of justice animated, as well as tested, by a more obscure demand that the word 'spiritual' can only gesture towards (2007: xiv).

These comments are certainly at variance with what Vital has criticised as Paul's 'escape' from reality – his 'lack of imaginative interest in the "otherness" of people' (2008: 100). I suggest that forced by his dis-ease, both physical and psychological, Paul retreats into nature, but not in narcissistic adoration. He is accompanied by his own thoughts about his roles in family and society; the garden is the place to be oneself, to face up to insignificance, in both private and public life: 'The garden . . . is both the place banished to . . . and the place to be yourself, against orders' (Gordimer 2005: 49).

The concept and condition of insignificance begins to suggest not simply atrophy, but a time to pause, to reflect, a time – to use the gardening metaphor – to sprinkle water on the old self. It is a state of being that would never have confronted the consciousness of an earlier white male like Mehring, the protagonist of Gordimer's struggle novel, *The Conservationist* (1974). Mehring was full of his own unreflecting self, a latter-day colonial hunter and sexual predator. Paul Bannerman, in contrast, is a new kind of white male, neither boorish (as was Mehring), nor weak (as was Ben, Vera Stark's husband in *None to Accompany Me*). Rather, Paul is 'in confrontation with an unimaginable state of self . . . It's more than a physical and mental state; it's a disembodiment, a state of existence outside the continuity of life' (2005: 67). Paul (the biblical disciple's name might be significant) is in confrontation with an unprecedented state of self, which is more than a physical and mental state: he undergoes, I suggest, a spiritual reassessment of his life. His sense of disempowerment (his 'night of the soul') is at its most acute in the scene where a nightly intruder in the garden is confronted by his mother,

Lyndsay. The incident, a reminder of crime 'among present living conditions' in South Africa (53), makes Paul feel 'less than a man, less than himself, stoned out of his mind into impotence as an inability to take any action' (53). Throughout this first section of the novel, Gordimer suggests that Paul's 'impotence' is not simply physical, but affects him at a deep psychological level: helplessness is 'blinding the brain' (54). As he faces his deepest fears and insecurities, marital/sexual, professional and social, Paul distances himself from everyday understandings of 'ordinariness' (67), whether such understandings be about what constitutes a happy marriage or professional significance or, indeed, the 'banality' of crime. Through Lyndsay's maternal eyes, Paul appears as 'in confrontation with an unimaginable state of self. She sees it in his face . . . [in] his choice of words, of what there is that can be said among all that cannot' (67). His state, however, is not that of a victim: 'It's more than a physical and mental state of an individual; it's a disembodiment . . . a state of existence outside the continuity of life' (67). It is a spiritual assessment preparing the way for a new beginning. A new Gordimer trope?

The garden acts as a facilitator, therefore, of Paul's emotional housecleaning. It offers him the metaphorical vocabulary he needs for self-discovery, while mediating numerous internal dialogues: 'The garden is where . . . there is the wise presence that changes solitude of monologue into some kind of dialogue. A dialogue with questions; or answers never heard, in the elsewhere' (54). It is in the garden that Paul gives cogency to his long-suppressed intuition regarding an incompatibility between himself and his wife: an incompatibility between the ideals of environmental protection (Paul's) and the lifestyle of the advertising industry (Benni's). He wonders: 'How could he, whose work, reason-to-be is preserving life, live so long with an intimate, herself, who was successfully complicit in destroying it' (59). It is in the garden that Paul for the first time contemplates divorcing Benni. The garden intensifies Paul's preoccupation with his role as an environmentalist. It is the space where he receives his colleague, Thapelo, who reports to him on the latest news about developments in the ongoing tug-of-war between government and environmentalist pressure groups (59–60). At this stage in the novel, the conflict of interest between the power-holders and the ecologists seems insurmountable, with government paying only lip-service to the environmentalists' research findings, which are 'given token attention, oh yes, the enterprise projects doctored up a bit as a concession – and the disastrous proceeds' (25).

To invoke archetypal illumination, the hero of folktale, having gained insight, returns to the world. As he recovers from his identity crisis, Paul slowly reconnects to his social roles as husband, father and middle-class professional, but not before having fully come to terms with his disease or, outside of the symbolic realm, with the dis-ease of his marginalisation in the new South Africa. Accordingly, his earlier confinement to his childhood home – which to Vital appeared as a complacent retreat from the world (2008: 98–9) – acquires new dimensions, as a necessary exercise in self-discovery. Paul is neither the colonial hunter nor the anti-apartheid activist. He is nonetheless a valuable member of the new South African society, a society in transformation from revolutionary to civilian times. As I have suggested, he emerges as the average, decent, politically sensitive, if not politically committed, young white South African: a person whom Vital probably despises, but in whom Gordimer invests her authorial commitment. Is this the 'silence' that Ernst-Auga has in mind?

From inhabiting a 'state apart' – as signified in the frequent allusions to a leper colony – Paul comes gradually to understand that his significance is bound to his being able to integrate himself to the ordinary, but diverse, demands and rewards of work and home. His 'retreat' is shown to have been a necessary exercise in self-discovery, based on increased self-knowledge, acceptance and wisdom: neither a state of victimhood nor of romantic nature worship, but an act of psychological introspection, of courageously making visible and naming one's 'states of being', one's 'states of existence' (Gordimer makes insistent use of these phrases throughout the novel; see, for example, 30, 57, 68, 71, 76, 80, 127,139, 143, 161, 172).

The route back to health, to life beyond physical and psychological dis-ease, lies in the realisation that his 'integrated self' is that of many professionals: a responsibility to family and occupation which may not be the stuff of the public forum or the newspaper headline, but has its own 'undramatic' purpose. Simply, Paul prepares himself to go home to wife and son: 'he would leave *home* this second time to go *home* as an adult' (88). His quarantine in his parents' home acquires, from the vantage point of hindsight, the dimension of a *regressus ad uterum* (a spiritual womb to which the archetypal hero has to return, in order to grow into mature understandings). Once out of this retreat, in his new 'state of existence', Paul stops thinking of himself as a leper. Rather, he meditates on the idea of the co-existence of diverse forms of life, energy and matter, a flow that accommodates contradictions.

Inspired by his recent project for saving the ecological system of the Okavango Delta (89–93), Paul meditates on the 'integrated' significance of ecosystems, the delta and deserts combined: water bringing seeds from afar, alien seeds growing into trees; waters bringing sand from afar, sand leaching salt; the risk of salt contamination being managed by nature and clean water continuing to fertilise the land. He brings his ecological knowledge to bear on his life:

> [W]e don't know how the salt is managed. It *is* . . . we drink the water. This is what we should work on: how with the Okavango the balance between positive and negative is achieved . . . as a spider's web is the most fragile example of organisation, so a delta is the grandest (92, 94).

Paul suggests that individuals should find inspiration from 'this intelligence of matter [that] receives, contains, processes' (92). His insight helps him accept the doubts – 'this heresy is born of the garden, as Evil was' (94) – that have arisen for him while in quarantine:

> All the waterways and shifting sand islands of contradiction: a condition of living.
>   Always find the self calling on the terminology of the wilderness, so unjudgmental, to bring to circumstances the balm of calm acceptance. The inevitable grace, zest, in being a microcosm of the macrocosm's marvel. Doubt is part of it; the salt content (94).

In the last part of the novel (158–87), Gordimer elaborates on a 'life-enhancing' solution for the integration of Paul's various 'states apart'. Having removed him from the parental home, as well as from the wilderness of his working life, she has him spend time with his entire family (wife, son, mother and his mother's adopted black child) in a zone in-between: 'half botanical garden . . . half wildlife protection habitat' (160). This is a space symbolically allowing for the integration of diversity: of marital, professional, racial and generational interests. The eagle which Paul spots in this zone (162–3) embodies the ambiguous nature of freedom and imprisonment, suggesting that there is no absolute freedom either in nature or in society. Paul reminds himself that eagles, in order to survive as a species, must allow their chicks to fight for their lives while still in the nest. There is only one winner, the fittest chick, who is wittily labelled 'Cain' in ecologists' parlance: 'Romanticising what's too difficult to handle. Cain and Abel. The old Bible provides an object lesson here in the non-human, the creatures who according to evolutionary hierarchy go back too far to have developed a morality. Except that of survival' (168).

    On his return to wife and son, Paul is willing 'to move towards contact with others . . . to come to life [to get a life!] in the variety of friends and stimulating jostle of lively acquaintances' (103). Environmentalists and advertisers, black and white, now allow one another to find common ground in new social spaces. Husband and wife regain old intimacies.

It is at this stage in his re-evaluation of self that Paul learns from his wife that they are going to have another child. Conception becomes possible at the symbolic level as well: life goes on; another human being 'gets a life'. The novel ends with the birth and the continuity – the survival – of those able to overcome the alienation of their 'states apart', as in Paul's full recovery from dis-ease.

* * *

I have attempted to suggest in my analysis of *Get a Life* a subtle, yet significant shift from Gordimer's first three post-apartheid novels. In these three novels, to which I referred earlier on, the public domain still intrudes via 'spectacular' incidents: township crime and violence; middle-class parents dealing with their son's imprisonment; the traumas of immigration and emigration. These are core social issues which, while they receive a prominent place in the novels prior to *Get a Life*, are not integrated into the private ambitions of the characters. Rather, the public events remain the 'necessary gestures' of Gordimer's struggle credentials, gestures of goodwill and reconciliation in a divided society: Vera Stark lives as a tenant in the newly empowered black man's yard; her lesbian daughter adopts a black child; Duncan Lindgard, in a bisexual triangle, plans to adopt the child of the triangle; Julie Summers, the wealthy young woman, rejects her suburban privilege. The impositions of public life are dramatic and perhaps were meant to shock middle-class readers into an awareness of the need for drastic change in their attitudes. The trouble is that one is tempted to interpret one's 'real' response to these solutions in the allegorical mode. (We are reminded of the Smales family's 'spectacular' resolution: the transportation from their comfort zone to an African rural community in *July's People* [1981]).

In *Get a Life*, by contrast, Gordimer's resolutions may be less dramatic in literary depiction, but they are more authentic to the class of people that – if we cast our minds back – have always been the focus of her fiction. The middle class is shown to *have* a life and Gordimer is at last bold enough to be unapologetic about it. She may not be making the kind of daring public statements that would satisfy Ernst-Auga; she may not have chosen to write the South African saga as straddling all classes of the population (Vital's implicit expectation of a 'radical' Gordimer). Instead, she focuses on the class she knows best: her boldness embraces the small stories and hesitant spiritual pursuits of suburban people. It is a shift that, to an extent, had also been signalled in her two most recent collections of short stories, *Loot* (2003) and *Beethoven Was One-Sixteenth Black* (2007). Has the Nobel laureate been silenced by 'freedom'? The critic, I suggest, should be sufficiently generous to grant the author the value of her own impulsions, sufficiently generous to permit Nadine Gordimer, after apartheid, to 'get a life'.

Notes

1. Several critics have remarked on the fact that Gordimer's post-apartheid novels focus on the personal at the expense of society's 'grand narrative'. Anthony O'Brien (2001), for example, is resolutely 'against normalization' in Gordimer's recent fiction. In detecting a sense of 'postmodern melancholy' in the 'small histories' of Gordimer's post-1990 novels, Simon Lewis (1999) echoes Dominic Head's (1994) reservations about Gordimer's recent interest in explorations of postmodern multiplicity at the expense of focused social investigation. These critics share a sense of disappointment in Gordimer's lessened interest in 'the politics of nationhood' and her inability, or unwillingness, to point to new visions for the collective future.
2. Vital (2008) believes that 'Gordimer reflects a widespread inability to crystallize a sense of a better social future – apartheid is over, whither South Africa?' (95). Ernst-Auga attacks Gordimer's choice of a particular class of people as the purveyors of social concern. She takes issue with her 'normalizing of middle-class discourse both through its inviting a sense of intimacy with its central characters, and by writing its central characters' discourse into national governing structures' (2002: 99). Although appreciating Gordimer's subtle play of closeness and distance vis-á-vis her characters and her own questioning of 'what a middle-class professional world comes to accept as normal' (2008: 104), Vital insists on what he perceives to be omissions in her novel, all of which are linked to the particular class under scrutiny. He finds it problematic that the characters do not explicitly engage with the country's colonial past (100, 105); that they do not take responsibility for their patterns of consumption and are not directly involved in broadbased environmental work (109). Vital also insists on the subjective nature of Paul's 'ecological thinking as profoundly ideological' (102) and suggests that Gordimer should have held it up to radical critique. The end of the novel is seen to be disappointing, for it does not offer closure, 'no ideological resting place, no closing harmonies' (111). Briefly, Vital would have preferred Gordimer to produce a different novel, which, I suspect, would have promoted specific solutions to social and ecological problems. (See also Dan Wylie's references to Vital's work and *Get a Life* in Chapter 17 of this volume.)

    The reception of *Get a Life* has been controversial. Vital's ideological reservations are shared by Deb, who also finds that the relationship of the characters to 'the upheavals of society and nation is tangential and often evasive' (2005: 19). Others have focused on Gordimer's style, deploring the novel's sketchy character development and its telegraphic discourse (for example, Harrison 2005). Others have been appreciative of the book – for example, Jacqueline Rose (2006) and Isaacson (2005). I share Isaacson's appreciation of Gordimer's existentialist-inspired exploration of the characters' 'states of being' (17).
3. In her short-story sequence, 'Karma', from the collection *Loot* (2003), for example, Gordimer turns to Eastern mystical allusion.

References

Attridge, Derek. 2007. 'Introduction' to J.M. Coetzee's *Inner Workings: Essays 2000–2005*. London: Harvill Secker: ix–xiv.
Castells, Manuel. 1997. *The Information Age: Economy, Society and Culture*. Oxford: Blackwell.
Chapman, Michael. 2009. 'Coetzee, Gordimer and the Nobel Prize'. *Scrutiny2* 14(1): 57–65.
Clingman, Stephen. 1986. *The Novels of Nadine Gordimer: History from the Inside*. Johannesburg: Ravan Press.
Coetzee, J.M. 2007. 'Nadine Gordimer'. In: *Inner Workings: Essays 2000–2005*. London: Harvill Secker: 244–56.
De Kok, Ingrid and Karen Press (eds). 1990. *Spring is Rebellious: Arguments about Cultural Freedom by Albie Sachs and Respondents*. Cape Town: Buchu Books.
De Kock, Leon. 2005. 'Does South African Literature Still Exist? Or: South African Literature is Dead, Long Live Literature in South Africa'. *English in Africa* 32(2): 69–83.
De Souzenelle, Annick. 1999. *Simbolismul Corpului Uman* [The Symbolism of the Human Body]. Timişoara: Amarcord.
Deb, Siddhartha. 2005. 'A Life beyond Comfortable: Nadine Gordimer and the Possibility of Desire'. *Times Literary Supplement*, 11 November: 19.
Derrida, Jacques. 1985. 'Racism's Last Word'. *Critical Inquiry* 12: 290–9.
Dimitriu, Ileana. 2001. 'A New Sense of Social Space: Gordimer's Civil Imaginary'. In: *Spaces and Crossings: Essays on Literature and Culture in Africa and Beyond*, edited by R. Wilson and C. van Maltzan. New York: Peter Lang: 335–48.
———. 2006. 'Postcolonialising Gordimer: The Ethics of "Beyond" and Significant Peripheries in the Recent Fiction'. *English in Africa* 33(2): 159–80.
Ernst-Auga, Ulrike (ed.). 2002. *From Anti-Apartheid to African Renaissance: Interviews with South African Writers and Critics on Cultural Politics beyond the Cultural Struggle*. London: Lit Verlag.
———. 2003. 'Intellectuals between Resistance and Legitimation: The Case of Nadine Gordimer and Christa Wolf'. *Current Writing* 15(1): 1–16.
Gordimer, Nadine. 1965. 'A Writer in South Africa'. Interviewed by Alan Ross. *London Magazine* 5(2): 20–8.
———. 1974. *The Conservationist*. London: Jonathan Cape.
———. 1979. *Burger's Daughter*. London: Jonathan Cape.
———. 1981. *July's People*. London: Jonathan Cape.
———. 1984. 'The Idea of Gardening'. [Review of *Life & Times of Michael K*]. *New York Review of Books* 3(6): 1–6.
———. 1989 [1982]. 'Living in the Interregnum'. In: *The Essential Gesture: Writing, Politics and Places*. Harmondsworth: Penguin: 261–84.
———. 1989 [1984]. 'The Essential Gesture'. In: *The Essential Gesture: Writing, Politics and Places*. Harmondsworth: Penguin: 285–300.
———. 1991 [1990]. *My Son's Story*. Harmondsworth: Penguin.
———. 1994. *None to Accompany Me*. London: Bloomsbury.
———. 1998. *The House Gun*. Cape Town: David Philip.
———. 1999. 'The Status of the Writer in the World Today: Which World? Whose World?' In: *Living in Hope and History: Notes from Our Century*. Cape Town: David Philip: 16–29.

———. 2001. *The Pickup*. Cape Town: David Philip.
———. 2002. 'Writers Need Readers' [interview by Ulrike Ernst-Auga]. In: *From Anti-Apartheid to African Renaissance: Interviews with South African Writers and Critics on Cultural Politics beyond the Cultural Struggle*, edited by U. Ernst-Auga. London: Lit Verlag: 135–47.
———. 2003. *Loot*. Cape Town: David Philip.
———. 2005. *Get a Life*. Cape Town: David Philip.
———. 2007. *Beethoven Was One-Sixteenth Black*. Johannesburg: Penguin.
———. 2010. *Telling Times: Writing and Living, 1954–2008*. New York: W.W. Norton.
Gray, Stephen. 2002. 'History is Invented the Morning After'. In: *From Anti-Apartheid to African Renaissance: Interviews with South African Writers and Critics on Cultural Politics beyond the Cultural Struggle*, edited by U. Ernst-Auga. London: Lit Verlag: 66–77.
Gumede, William and Leslie Dikeni (eds). 2009. *The Poverty of Ideas: South African Democracy and the Retreat of Intellectuals*. Johannesburg: Jacana Media.
Harrison, Sophie. 2005. 'Metaphor as Illness: Review of *Get a Life*, by Nadine Gordimer'. *The New York Times Book Review*, 18 December. http://www.nytimes.com/2005/12/18/books/review/18harrison.html?_r=1 (accessed 24 August 2010).
Head, Dominic. 1994. *Nadine Gordimer*. New York: Cambridge University Press.
Horn, Peter. 2002. 'The Counter-Rotating Fate of Writers'. In: *From Anti-Apartheid to African Renaissance: Interviews with South African Writers and Critics on Cultural Politics beyond the Cultural Struggle*, edited by U. Ernst-Auga. London: Lit Verlag: 36–49.
Isaacson, Maureen. 2005. 'Love, Radiation and Other States of Being'. *The Sunday Independent*, 4 December: 17.
Lewis, Simon. 1999. 'Under the Sign of the Gun: Welcome to the Postmodern Melancholy of Gordimer's Post-Apartheid World'. *Critical Survey* 11(2): 64–76.
Kossew, Sue. 2003. 'Beyond the National: Exile and Belonging in Nadine Gordimer's *The Pickup*'. *Scrutiny2* 8(1): 21–6.
Malange, Nise. 2002. 'To Understand the Gumboot Dance'. In: *From Anti-Apartheid to African Renaissance: Interviews with South African Writers and Critics on Cultural Politics beyond the Cultural Struggle*, edited by U. Ernst-Auga. London: Lit Verlag: 108–33.
Matthews, James. 2009. 'Democracy, Dissidence and the Poet'. In: *The Poverty of Ideas: South African Democracy and the Retreat of Intellectuals*, edited by W. Gumede and L. Dikeni. Johannesburg: Jacana Media: 52–6.
Mgwaba, Philani. 2009. 'It's a Shame Madiba Chose the Quiet Life'. *The Sunday Tribune*, 12 July: 22.
Ndebele, Njabulo S. 1991. *Rediscovery of the Ordinary: Essays on South African Literature and Culture*. Johnnesburg: COSAW.
O'Brien, Anthony. 2001. *Against Normalization: Writing Radical Democracy in South Africa*. Durham: Duke University Press.
Ozaniec, Naomi. 1995. *Chakra*. Bucharest: RAO International Publishers.
Ramphele, Mamphela. 2009. 'Insignificance: SA's Barrier to Success'. *Sunday Tribune*, 12 July: 4.
Rose, Jaqueline. 2006. 'A Use for the Stones: Review of *Get a Life*'. *London Review of Books*, 28(8), 20 April. http://www.lrb.co.uk/v28/n08/jacqueline-rose/a-use-for-the-stones (accessed 13 April 2011).

Sachs, Albie. 1990. 'Preparing Ourselves for Freedom'. In: *Spring is Rebellious: Arguments about Cultural Freedom by Albie Sachs and Respondents*, edited by I. de Kok and K. Press. Cape Town: Buchu Books: 19–29.

Vital, Anthony. 2008. '"Another Kind of Combat in the Bush": *Get a Life* and Gordimer's Critique of Ecology in a Globalized World'. *English in Africa* 35(2): 89–118.

Wilson, Rita and Carlotta van Maltzan (eds). 2001. *Spaces and Crossings: Essays on Literature and Culture in Africa and Beyond*. New York: Peter Lang.

6

Reconciling Acts

Theatre beyond the Truth and Reconciliation Commission

MARCIA BLUMBERG

More than four decades of apartheid were dismantled from 1990 onwards, but the regime ended juridically when South Africa became a fully realised democracy in 1994. The promise of this revolutionary achievement has yielded to the challenges of dealing with apartheid legacies – not only in terms of political reconciliation, but scenarios that include spiralling crime and violence, unemployment, poverty, corruption and a multitude of social problems that appear to be compounded in the present. One vital element in the negotiated settlement was the formation of the Truth and Reconciliation Commission (TRC), which provided a forum for testimony about the causes, nature and extent of gross violations of human rights committed against *all* the people of South Africa between 1 March 1960 and 5 December 1993 (Maja-Pearce 1996: 51). While nothing can reverse the egregious acts revealed at the TRC sessions, the voicing of these injustices brought into the public domain the pain previously borne in relative silence and anonymity by victims and their families. Although the hearings made an impact on all spheres of South African life, the initial euphoria has dissipated and the numerous problems and limitations of the TRC have raised questions about the efficacy of what many considered a necessary process and whether its official slogan 'Truth: The Road to Reconciliation' will prove accurate.

Two forms of theatre are associated with the TRC – firstly, the national drama of the TRC itself (the way it was constituted, how it functioned and its ramifications) and the theatrical productions that take the TRC for their theme. These stagings at a crucial period in South African history emerge as vital constituents in the process of provoking new awareness and initiating a complex journey for many South Africans – from brutalisation, silence and mourning to eventual *potential* reconciliation. Both forms of theatre have affected the course of the fledgling democracy by intervening between speakers/storytellers, victims/perpetrators and listeners/spectators.

At the TRC hearings victims and perpetrators provided statements and answered questions posed by commissioners in front of an audience, comprised of individual spectators, with their differing ideological baggage. Both the people in the designated venues around the country and the audiences of national TV and radio experienced a disruption of 'business as usual' and were challenged to address the horrors of the past, the putative norms and their roles. The TRC can be contextualised as a drama of national proportions; from February 1996 public sessions were staged in many towns. Lesley Marx categorises the live event in theatrical terms:

> The Truth Commission offers theatre of a very specific kind, analogous in some ways to the Medieval Mystery Cycles. Like the Cycles, the actors in this drama move around the country re-enacting a Christian allegory of birth, pain, passion, death and hoped-for resurrection, to which the audience gives its heart and its faith (1998: 213).

Marx acknowledges the linkage between theatrical and Christian attributes within the commision, which was led by Archbishop Desmond Tutu, who instituted prayer rituals and ensured that the tone of the proceedings emphasised forgiveness and charity rather than vengeance. Yet the event was neither a court hearing nor a confessional.

Viewpoints on the TRC have been diverse. H. Russel Botman and Robin M. Petersen insist: 'Reconciliation replaces the culture of revenge, not the culture of justice' (1996: 11); they assume that reconciliation is a necessary outcome. Brandon Hamber and Hugo van der Merwe have categorised reconciliation in five ways: 'a non-racial ideology; an ideology based on intercommunal understanding; a religious ideology; a human rights approach; a form of community building concerned with individual relationships . . . these can co-exist but have also caused conflict between groups' (1998).

While many agree that the TRC constitutes a significant step towards the healing of deep wounds in the body politic, some fear that reconciliation may become synonymous with amnesia. Tutu's caveat is significant: 'To accept national amnesia . . . would in effect be to victimise the victims of apartheid a second time' (1999: 29). One problem concerns the focus upon gross human rights abuses that neglects the structures of apartheid; these placed all black South Africans (the large majority of the population) in a subordinate position to whites and thus inflicted oppressive and unjust strictures on them, resulting in the everyday dehumanisation of the majority of South Africans. Fourteen years beyond the TRC there has been trenchant criticism of the amnesty process and the minimal reparations paid to victims. In the final analysis, no process can adequately redress the massive injustices, no commission can fully solve the problems or provide sufficient compensation for the horrors. Yet the stagings of truth-telling at the TRC have contributed to what Judge Albie Sachs notes as significant moments in South Africa: 'Judges do not cry; Archbishop Tutu cried' (2009: 74).

Tutu's hopeful designation of South Africa as a 'rainbow nation' imagined a future built on coalition rather than fracture and divisiveness, yet what change has actually occurred? How has theatre represented, shaped and sometimes anticipated events and socio-political dynamics? How does it challenge a conspiracy of silence, expose a culture of violence and offer powerful enactments of new and old struggles beyond the TRC? South African theatre continues to serve as one of the world's pre-eminent examples of committed theatre. This theatre sustains an internal dialogue within a still polarised nation and raises awareness at local and international festivals and theatres. The plays have transformed the hearings and TV programmes into a different aesthetic that has provoked powerful responses. I will examine some of these issues in selected theatre projects beyond the TRC in order to explore the dynamic of various acts of reconciliation.[1]

Greg Homan categorises theatre in democratic South Africa into three periods: 'pre-post-apartheid (1990–1996)', 'early-post-apartheid (1996–2002)' and 'post-apartheid (2002–2008)' (2009a: 2, 7, 11). This schema differentiates between various periods that relate to important socio-political events. Since context is vital in theatre, I approach this time in another way that constitutes two phases: an initial period of euphoria, patience and hope, starting with the inauguration of Nelson Mandela as the first president of democratic South Africa; then, the past decade, which I have called a 'second interregnum'. Gramsci defines the term thus: 'The old is dying; the new cannot be born: in this interregnum there arises a great diversity of morbid symptoms' (1971: 276). Instead of the anticipated continuation of the optimism and seemingly limitless potential of the Mandela years, there has arisen 'a great diversity of morbid symptoms'. During the latter period, 2001–2010, the instability of conditions and the desperation to break silences have translated into important theatrical performances that develop provocative directions. Grant Farred deploys the categorisation of an 'idiosyncratic interregnum': 'It is on this volatile terrain, in the interregnum between reconciliation and disaffection, that ideological tensions regarding race and class abound. This is the theatre in which the potentially explosive incommensurability between the articulations of reconciliation and the dominant black experience of poverty is being staged' (1997: 65).

Some plays, as I shall show, demonstrate this dynamic and others work to stage successful acts of reconciliation. Yet while an exemplary Constitution can insist on the prohibition of discrimination with respect to race, class, gender, ethnicity, religion and sexual orientation, it cannot effect changes in the mindsets of individuals and the dynamics of communities. Reconciling acts beyond the TRC have engendered both individual and collective transformations in the new democracy, yet volatile socio-political dynamics have often overtaken the positive advancements. I will examine the trajectory of these moments in selected plays and theatrical stagings.

Marginalised voices form a vital part of the post-TRC theatrical fare; previously oppressed and elided minority voices call attention to their positions to reclaim and validate personal and/or communal identity. This cluster of plays can be categorised as 'flying solo' since one performer enacts multiple roles in each play. Many of them foreground gender issues in a patriarchal society. Sachs notes that one of the few profoundly non-racial institutions in South Africa is patriarchy: 'Patriarchy brutalises men and neutralises women across the colour line. At the same time, gender inequality [means that] . . . some are more unequal than others' (1990: 53). This scenario is dramatised and resisted in several plays that explore gender relations; I will therefore first focus on performances by women.

The award-winning *A Woman in Waiting* by Yael Farber and Thembi Mtshali (2008) premiered at the National Arts Festival in Grahamstown in 1999 and appeared at the Carthage Festival in Tunisia (1999), the Edinburgh Festival (2000) and in London (2001) and Toronto (2002, 2005). *A Woman in Waiting* is testimonial theatre that represents the birth and growth of Thembi Mtshali from childhood to adulthood, from poverty and oppression to empowerment and international recognition. It is unabashedly autobiographical and charts a trajectory that connects the individual story and the national drama from the perspective of black women and, in particular, Thembi and her matrilineal family. The play includes scenes from Thembi's life with a cappella singing and monologues of regret and apology delivered to her daughter. This doubled linear structure adds poignancy and is a benchmark for the price of her success on the stage.

The play begins with storytelling and employs simple but powerful staging effects. A huge box holds a curled-up Thembi for the birthing scene; the appearance of her mother is a stunning visual moment when a ten-foot-tall African-print dress drops down on a clothes hanger and apparently shrinks to a miniature size in the toilet as her mother is excoriated by her boss and diminished as a human being for allowing Thembi to use his toilet. 'Waiting' lies at the heart of *A Woman in Waiting* so the pace is deliberately slow. Terror is palpable during the police night raid. Shame is also the constant companion of 'non-whites' such as domestic workers. Thembi's triumph, international recognition as an actor and singer, means financial stability and gives her the self-respect that her mother was denied. The finale, which incorporates acts of reconciliation with her family and within herself, offers hope, especially in the times beyond the TRC.

Nadia Davids's *At Her Feet* premiered in Cape Town (2002), played in other South African venues (2003–2009), as well as Holland (2004), New York (2004) and London (2010). *At Her Feet* is a post-9/11 solo play mostly situated within a Muslim community in Cape Town, although it opens with an honour killing in Jordan. Davids examines competing conceptions of Muslim women's identity, marked both by patriarchal religious fundamentalism and by Western anti-Islamicism and, specifically, a South African woman's identity, reconfiguring itself within a changed national conversation about race, gender and religion. She challenges the erroneous belief in monolithic Muslim stereotypes. In an interview with her sister Leila, Davids comments: 'Why are Muslim women not given the space to air their doubts and beliefs?' (Leila Davids 2006: 73). The play uses direct address to offer diverse portrayals of Muslim women, rendering visible what is usually concealed. It breaks the culture of silence to offer a range of voices that speak to conflicts between the putatively eternal truths of Islam, secular liberalism, Western feminism and the dichotomy between generational attitudes evident in conservative and radical perspectives on these issues. Davids's solo show has always featured Quanita Adams, who plays six different Muslim women. She performs not only distinct subjectivities, but also enacts the possibilities of empathy, insight and reconciliation within a community. The gendered silences that abound in public discourse for a range of Muslim women in Cape Town are framed by the story of Azra al Jamal, who tells us she has just been killed. To the accompaniment of tabla music, Azra, in full hijab, dances her body's response to the stoning ritual and sinks to the ground:

> [b]ecause I spoke to a man who was not my father/brother/uncle/cousin, and now my father/brother/uncle/cousin has taken rocks and flung them ... made me scream and beg and say 'I didn't mean to', but I did mean to and my intention doesn't matter now because I have no honour. And I have no voice (2006a: 25–6).

The final scene is a physical representation of the hadith, 'Paradise lies at the feet of her mother'. This poignant enactment of the story of Azra shows a ritual, honour killing, which is practised in many countries. Yet critics remind us that honour killings are not legitimised in the Qur'an.

Gabeba Baderoon argues that 'the play's energy, its power, lie in the use of familiar themes associated with Islam – patriarchal men and veiled, suffering women – taken in unexpected directions' (2006: 10). The cast of characters ranges from the university-educated narrator/poet, to her cousin, a newly married Indian-Muslim woman, who chooses her faith over the demands of her employers, to a friend, who is an avowed Afro-Marxist feminist slam-poet, and finally Aunty Kariema, a bigoted, brassy woman. Breaks between monologues facilitate costume changes, while music and other cultural references indicate the timeframe. The play provides a vehicle where individuals debate their views on veiling, faith and the cultural aspects of being a Muslim. Spectators are invited to develop a greater sensitivity to difference, otherness, marginality and commonality. As Davids told Carol Kaplan:

> The thread that runs through the piece is really about a journey – seeking justice and a sense of equality. There is certainly a sense that these women's lives are circumscribed by archaic, gendered laws and that their beings and bodies are dictated to by an outdated and often violent patriarchy (Kaplan 2004–2005: 725).

Davids has spoken about theatre in South Africa as being more than entertainment and the roles of theatre-makers today as ones associated with 'ethical responsibility . . . [Theatre] is a genuine cultural vehicle in which history can be re-visited. It is part of a larger national project to unearth the untold stories, and insist, gently or forcibly, on a reckoning' (2006b: 60). *At Her Feet* powerfully fulfils these criteria as it lifts the veil, breaks the silences by addressing marginalisation and offers reconciling acts within the numerous differences amongst Muslim women.

Another new female voice is that of Phillippa Yaa de Villiers, a storyteller, poet, healer, performer and writer of plays and screenplays. Her solo show, *Original Skin*, is a a semi-autobiographical narrative written and first performed by De Villiers in 2007 and remounted at the National Arts Festival in 2009. At the age of twenty she learned that she had been adopted and that her biological parents were a white Australian mother and a black Ghanaian father. As a transracial adoptee born during the 1960s she grew up in South Africa during the height of apartheid and felt her dichotomous racial identity and the problems of inequity despite being the adopted daughter of white Afrikaner parents. De Villiers plays multiple roles and shares her personal discoveries and humiliations, often enacted in flashbacks. She has created a journey that takes spectators from childhood to the healing moments of the performance in the present. She explains the value of this confessional writing and performance and the personal reconciling act this represents:

> In a world of silences, I itemise the infinite variety of experience, in telling I give new names to the unspoken, and liberate my suffering from an inarticulate chaos. When I name sorrow, loss, exploitation, racism, fear, disgust . . . I am no longer subject to them; in fact, they become my subjects (2007).

Original Skin foregrounds the subject position and voice of a Coloured woman, who was a target of abuse by bus drivers, cinema operators and others, who expelled her from white-designated areas. Her positioning can be understood when we hear the words of the late Marike de Klerk, then wife of a cabinet minister, in a 1983 lecture: 'The definition of a "Coloured" in the population register is someone that is not black, and that is not white, and is also not Indian, in other words a non-person . . . they are the left-overs' (quoted in Braid 1998: 17). De Villiers performs her journey with poetic beauty, humour, compassion, excruciating pain and poignancy. Audience members are ashamed at the bigotry and prejudice that she and many others experience and feel admiration for her courage in sharing her experience through writing and performing. Hers is a new, spirited voice that represents an unspoken past; reminding us that even sixteen years after apartheid has vanished juridically there is still much to deal with in a country which often manifests mindsets riddled with racism. De Villiers's exploration of her newly discovered identity constitutes a personal reconciliation that will also have an impact on her community.

In *Ncamisa! The Women*, Peter Hayes directed and co-created with Pam Ngwabeni a powerful performance piece that premiered at the National Arts Festival, Grahamstown (2009), played at the Dublin International Gay Theatre Festival (2010) and returned to Grahamstown in 2010. Using English and isiXhosa, Ngwabeni shares her world and offers a voice that is seldom heard in theatre – that of a black lesbian soccer player. The play addresses 'corrective rape', in which butch lesbians are raped in the presence of their partners, who are forced to watch this allegedly heterosexual sex act in order to prove that butch lesbians are 'real' African women. Many acts of rape are followed by beatings and stabbings resulting in death.

This solo show has a three-part structure. The frame constitutes Ngwabeni's joys, desires and challenges. She is dressed in soccer gear and is a bright and beautiful young woman replete with cellphone, girlfriend and soccer stories. She begins by admitting ignorance of the word 'lesbian' and acknowledges that her mother is homophobic. She moves in with her partner's parents who treat her like a daughter. In the central scene she rolls back the astroturf and in a meta-theatrical routine wears top hat, fake moustache and coat-tails to lip-synch the Sodom and Gomorrah show. A change of tone brings the news of Zoliswa Nkonyana's funeral in Guguletu. Ngwabeni enacts the dire threats of a local minister: 'You are bringing back Sodom and Gomorrah! So you are being destroyed' (2009: 7). Zoliswa's father, also a minister, is proud of her: 'Only God can judge' (7). Her girlfriend sings about Zoliswa who was kicked, beaten and stabbed by nine men. Listing details of four other lesbians who have recently been killed, Ngwabeni undresses and washes herself while singing: 'Unlock my love / And set me free' (10–11). The song exposes the pain and anticipation of being free to live according to her lesbian desires.

In the final scene Ngwabeni puts the astroturf back on stage and dons an Afro-wig and hip-hop ballgown: 'I love to kiss the women' (13). Later in the scene, she wears soccer garb and addresses her absent lover in poetic phrases that speak of love, of lesbian desire and her joy in her position as a soccer player: ' [a]nd the way you look at me: you win my love . . . I will score and so will you. Score our pleasure. Your legs mine: the goal posts of this day . . . my goal, your goal, our goal, GOAAAALLLL!!!!!!!' (14).

In this period beyond the TRC, even the progressive Constitution that prohibits discrimination against gays and lesbians is no protection against homophobic attitudes and ingrained conservatism. Ngwabeni's new voice represents black lesbians who have come out and despite disapproval from their families, who deem them 'un-African', are determined to seize the day. Her empowerment speaks to individual identity issues, enacts personal reconciliation as well as that within her community and also honours her sisters who have been raped and killed.

Shifting from women's voices, Peter Hayes's *I Am Here* premiered at the National Arts Festival, Grahamstown, in 2010. This autobiographical solo performance enacts a voyage to self-reconciliation that is at once poignant, humorous and cutting edge. His direct address to the audience evokes laughter and tears and a deep awareness that his truth-telling is immensely brave. The play begins in 2004 and includes his pilgrimage to Spain, the El Camino de Santiago de Compostela, where he imagines dreams and confronts nightmares. On his return home Peter experiences the reality of an HIV-positive diagnosis; he abandons his greatest hope – to adopt a child – and plans his life anew. He narrates treasured moments from his 40-day pilgrimage which involves gruelling physical hardship in searing heat and concomitantly brings emotional and religious unburdening for this lapsed Catholic. His diagnosis and its ramifications are suffused with the memories of one night of unprotected sex and myriad examples of abiding love from friends and family. The title becomes a mantra: '"I am here"... is one of the gifts of walking the Camino. HIV Positive and I have walked 1 000 kilometres and I have a brand new love and respect for my amazing body' (2010: 18). In his gratitude for life, Hayes's play inspires spectators to value their own and also finds him continuing to play a vital role in his own communities. A yellow arrow that is seen throughout the Camino walk is utilised by Hayes as a transformative prop: a cross of iron, a Christmas tree, a fun-house mirror and other objects, until its last incarnation when it is raised as a trapeze on which he swings. In the final moments he jumps down from the trapeze onto the stage and says: 'I am here'.

In contrast to solo plays, theatrical representations of the TRC may eschew simplistic scenarios such as 'forgive and forget' and instead analyse the concepts and their viability through specific plays after 1996. In *The Story I'm about to Tell* (created by the activist Bobbie Rodwell, writer Lesego Rampolokeng and director Robert Coleman) three actors and three TRC participants, who were members of the Khulumani Support Group, combine to tell stories in a simple setting. Using the idea of a minibus (constructed from chairs) to drive them all to a hearing of the TRC, the actors debate the value of the Commission with actual participants who take turns to leave the 'taxi' and sit alone in the spot-lit centre to offer their moving testimony. Mam Catherine speaks about her son's assassination; Thandi Shezi was repeatedly raped by four white police officers. Finally, Duma Khumalo, a member of the Sharpeville Six, spent seven years in gaol, three on death row. Spectators were grateful that a talk-back was built into every performance so that they could ask questions in a moderated environment. The play toured South Africa for five years until the untimely death of Khumalo in 2001. Both this play and the reworking of *Ubu and the Truth Commission* that I will analyse next have travelled to local and international theatres but their differing methodologies were strikingly evident in June 1999 when they were staged at the Tricycle Theatre one week apart during the London International Festival of Theatre (LIFT). While *The Story I'm about to Tell* is a simple yet powerful production with a minimalist set, *Ubu and the Truth Commission* is a theatrical spectacle replete with a variety of handcarved puppets, film projections and actors playing the Ubus (see Blumberg 2000).

Ubu and the Truth Commission (Taylor 1998) premiered at the Kunstfest, Weimar, in 1997 and opened immediately after at the National Arts Festival in Grahamstown. The production toured internationally in Europe (1997–1999), as well as in New York, Washington DC, and Los Angeles (1998), before finally going to London (1999). This collaborative effort by William Kentridge, Jane Taylor and Handspring Trust puppeteers, Basil Jones and Adrian Kohler, created a multimedia theatrical production that revisioned Jarry's *Ubu Roi* to position Ubu as an Afrikaner 'foot soldier' who carries out brutal torture and killings in the name of patriotism and apartheid. Pa Ubu appears before the TRC to give an account that is obviously a tissue of lies and he and Ma Ubu sail off into the sunset, scot-free. This spectacle acknowledges and, at the same time, radically disrupts generic, cultural, political, artistic and historical categories. *Ubu and the Truth Commission* enacts Adrienne Rich's notion of 're-vision[ing]: the act of looking back, seeing with fresh eyes, of entering an old text from a new critical direction' (1979 [1971]: 35).

Throughout the production Ma and Pa Ubu engage in a fraught domestic relationship where verbal sparring and physical blows enacted in stylised sequences keep the Ubus' interactions true to their Jarryesque forebears. The play also exemplifies a crisis in masculinity and demonstrates sexist dynamics. Pa's nightly ablutions, enacted in the glass booth/shower stall, are rendered more sinister when images on a large screen incorporate body parts washed away after his nightly torture sessions. If the actual events of the TRC granted equal consideration to a range of violent acts so long as these acts claimed to be politically motivated, the play utilises conventions of the absurd to accentuate by contrast the 'reality' that many who applied for amnesty were – like Pa Ubu or the police torturers of the old regime – nothing more than sadistic killers.

REwind: A Cantata: for Voice, Tape, and Testimony originated in 2005 when Antjie Krog suggested to the composer Philip Miller that there should be a tenth anniversary commemoration of the TRC. He worked with the designer Gerhard Marx, who also directed the project. *REwind* premiered in 2006 at St George's Cathedral in Cape Town on 16 December, the Day of Reconciliation. Performances followed at Prospect Park, Brooklyn (2007), Williams College, Massachusetts (2007), the Market Theatre, Johannesburg (2008) and the South Bank Centre in London (2010).

The title and the form of the cantata were inspired by one of the first recorded testimonies Miller heard from 'a mother, Eunice Tsepiso Miya, whose son was killed by the security police':

> The reason why I am here again is because I saw my child on TV and nobody had come to tell me that Jabulani had passed away. First of all we were listening to the news – with my daughter. One of the children was shown on TV who had a gun on his chest. Only to find out that it was my son, Jabulani. I prayed. I said, oh no Lord! I wish the news could be rewind [sic] (Zvomuya and Momoniat 2010).

Anthea Buys considers *REwind* 'simply devastating. It is so powerfully and sensitively executed – musically and visually – that the only argument I can muster is that its run at the Market Theatre from April 26 to 30 was far, far too short' (2008). Perhaps the huge cast restricted the production runs, since they have been brief whenever the cantata has been produced. For Sam Dub: '*REwind* is a work with no real parallel: both an extraordinary piece of music and digital art and a historical document with tremendous topical relevance. Above all, it is a commemoration of the dignity of those victims who suffered under the regime' (2010). Miller describes the TRC in diverse ways but emphasises:

> Piece by piece the collective memory of South Africans was built. We learned that the country belonged to the voices that tell its stories. When people could no longer speak, they sang. When they could no longer sing, they prayed. When they could no longer pray, they started talking again (2007).

The cantata evokes multiple processes, from horror to empathy, from agitation and anger to calmness and acceptance. The ethical choices in the creation of this work involved mindfulness of the enormity of the TRC's reach, as well as the dilemma about which narratives to include, however briefly, and those to exclude because of time constraints. The question of reconciliation no doubt needs more intense effort; volatility beyond the TRC too often provides alternatives that favour self-interest and ignore essential reconciliatory dynamics.

New plays have continued to interrogate issues raised by the TRC. John Kani's *Nothing but the Truth* premiered at the Market Theatre and then appeared at the National Arts Festival (2002), New York (2003), Los Angeles (2004), Sydney (2005) and London (2007) and returned to the Market (2009). The play involves three members of a black family, who must bury the ashes of an uncle who died in exile in London. Many familial conflicts arise and form the cultural and political concerns of the play. Zakes Mda notes, 'We must never forget, but this does not mean that we must cling to the past . . . We only look back in the past in order to have a better understanding of our present' (2004: ix). Refusing the didactic protest mode of anti-apartheid theatre, this play explores dilemmas and complexities amongst a group of black characters who can be reconciled. Sipho has made peace with his late brother: 'If I can forgive the white people for what they did to us in this country, how can I not forgive my brother?' (Kani 2004: 56). This play argues powerfully for the significance of reconciliation.

Two plays, first performed in 2007, nine years after the formal conclusion of the TRC, examine how individuals still need to confront the pain of personal happenings instead of those that were dealt with in public forums. Lara Foot Newton's *Reach* premiered at the Theaterformen Festival in Hanover, opened in South Africa at the National Arts Festival, and played in Cape Town and Johannesburg, followed by a tour of Sweden (2007). Craig Higginson's *Dream of the Dog* premiered at the National Arts Festival (2007) before touring to Johannesburg and the Hilton Festival (2008). It opened in London (2010) with Janet Suzman in a highly acclaimed production that immediately transferred to the West End. Although *Reach* is set in the future and *Dream of the Dog* in the present, both plays examine memory and the volatile notion of truth. In both narratives a young black man intrudes on the lives of elderly whites – in *Reach*, a dying woman and in *Dream of the Dog*, an old couple, Patricia and Richard. Despite the need for reconciliation, this ongoing, complex process demands transformative thinking. Confrontation with the past begins a dialogue that involves pain, confessions and the one-on-one acknowledgement of wrongdoing so that new awareness is instigated. In *Reach*, the young man, Solomon, arrives at Marion's home and wants to tell her about her son's death in which he participated seven years ago. This confession, which is a necessary stage in his initiation into manhood and the acceptance of responsibility, gives Marion release from a paralysis related to lack of knowledge about her son's murder. Furthermore, it instigates a new bond, which develops into a kind of mother-son linkage. *Dream of the Dog* revisits a murder that occurred fifteen years before. Richard, unhappy about a turn in an illicit relationship with his domestic servant, Grace, releases his vicious dog that attacks and kills her. Though anxious about the event, her boyfriend Looksmart has sublimated his anger until he confronts Richard and Patricia in their home. While Richard retreats into amnesia, Patricia moves from denial to horror when she learns more about the incident. Looksmart's sense that he has discovered the truth is an unstable realisation, as spectators hear another version from the present domestic worker, Beauty.

Homan, who has included both of these plays in his anthology, *At this Stage: Plays from Post-Apartheid South Africa*, argues that 'while Higginson cautions us against forgetting the past he also reminds us that any narrative of that past is subjective. Truth telling is inconsistent and self-serving' (2009b: 24). David Peimer's new anthology, *Armed Response: Plays from South Africa* (2009), also includes *Reach*. He notes: 'It is deeply ironic that, after the Truth and Reconciliation Commission, both hope and abandonment should emerge as prevalent South African themes. *Reach* gets inside the very nerve of the tension inherent in these conflicting feelings' (xv). Both plays foreground the complex dynamics of individual reconciling acts.

Reconciling Acts

Two plays that offer watershed theatrical experiences explore different acts of reconciliation and exemplify 'restorative theatre', a term I coined drawing on the model of restorative justice integral to South Africa's transformation from apartheid to democracy. My purpose is to examine theatre that refuses to perpetuate modes of vengeance in a society scarred by violence. Whereas the criminal justice system exemplifies retributive justice and focuses upon deterrents and punishments, restorative justice foregrounds the needs of victims and the responsibility of offenders to repair harm.

Molora ('ash' in seSotho), Yael Farber's revisioning of Aeschylus' *Oresteia*, was inspired by the 9/11 attacks in New York when the skies rained ash. It premiered at the National Arts Festival (2003) and toured many South African theatres, went to Japan (2006), then for a four-month tour to London, Oxford, Germany, Holland and Athens, as well as the USA (2008) and to Canada (2009). Klytemnestra appears before the TRC to answer questions about her torture of her daughter, Elektra. Flashbacks provide graphic scenes of violence: Elektra's immersion in water until she cannot breathe, burning her with a lit cigarette and a demonstration of the wetbag technique so clearly evoked by security policeman Jeffrey Benzien during the TRC testimony. Farber's Greek Chorus is replaced by the Ngqoko Cultural Group from the rural Eastern Cape, a chorus of wise elderly women and a male translator. The Chorus's split-tone singing is characterised by sounds that are ancient and unearthly. They also play ancient African musical instruments such as mouth bows and harps, calabash bows and drinking drums and with their two spiritual diviners manifest a deep respect for ancestral culture in their songs, dance and the performance of rituals such as the lighting of the herb *mphepho*, which provides communication with the ancestors.

The re-enactment of the *Oresteia* narrative occurs in the space between the tables used for testifying at the TRC. This area also contains Agamemnon's grave, which is the meeting place of Elektra and her exiled brother, Orestes, who returns disguised as a stranger to deliver 'his ashes' to the family. He wants to fulfil his duty with respect to parricide. He kills and cuts out the heart of Klytemnestra's lover, represented by an oversize shirt hanging from the flies, yet he is unable to commit matricide. He drops the axe, declaring: 'I cannot shed more blood . . . I am tired of hating' (Farber 2008: 83, 84). Screaming for vengeance, Elektra picks up the axe but is surrounded by the Chorus who remove the weapon to break the cycle of vengeance. Eschewing Aeschylus' solution in the *Eumenides*, where the first court of justice rules on Orestes' act of matricide and Athena casts the telling vote that allows for his release, Farber insists that no gods intervened in South Africa's destiny. Rather she attributes the bloodless change of power and the creation of democracy to the patience and goodwill of many ordinary men and women. The play examines the possibility of a more creative response to injustice than hatred and represents a dynamic of reconciliation in a radically revisioned *Oresteia*.

Another watershed play is Lara Foot Newton's *Tshepang: The Third Testament* which premiered in Amsterdam and at the National Arts Festival (2003) and has played to great acclaim in London (2004), Brisbane and Dublin (2005) and Toronto and Montreal (2009). It focuses on a community dealing with the rape of a nine-month-old baby, who miraculously survives. The play represents one of more than twenty thousand child rapes occurring each year in South Africa. *Tshepang* is a two-hander that takes place three years after the rape of baby Siesie, who is later named Tshepang [Hope]. We learn about the village from Simon, the narrator, who employs direct address during the entire play, moving between the past and the present and between stories and enactments. He evokes the lives of diverse villagers and provides a context for the horrifying details of the baby rape. In contrast, Ruth, the mother of Tshepang, remains silent throughout the play except for the final word, the quiet utterance of her baby's name, which signifies hope on different levels. Strapped to Ruth's back is a small version of the big bed on which Tshepang was raped, suggesting the way that African women carry their babies and, in this instance, foregrounding the indelible memory of her baby and the burden she carries. Ruth's gestural communication is masterful: not only does she respond physically to Simon's stories, her facial expressions and postures convey her grief, regret and guilt. Throughout the play she sits on a pile of salt, which she rubs into animal hides in order to cure them. What the playwright describes as '*her manic and obsessive rubbing of the salt*' (2005: 23) produces an incessant scraping sound that reminds us how Ruth traumatically revisits the event.

Even as it evokes a context of poverty, unemployment and hopelessness in a village in the Cape, a place where 'nothing ever happens', *Tshepang* is a cultural expression of the ongoing work of restorative justice in South Africa. The terrible act of baby rape is not perpetrated by a monster but by a man, Alfred Sorrows, who was brutally beaten as a young boy by his father's *houvrou* (kept woman). Simon enacts the atrocious violence of the *houvrou* by beating the straw broom on the ground so hard that it breaks into pieces. Then he takes one of the pieces, signifying Alfred, to penetrate a loaf of bread. Kaplan notes the playwright's refusal to perpetuate the cycle of violence and to refuse the sensationalism demonstrated by the media:

> Newton rejects the easy route of resorting to our customary notions of crime, punishment and justice. There is no criminal, no prosecutor, no

cathartic act, and no trial, jury, or judgment... The implications of the crime flow well beyond the village itself. It is here that Newton achieves the play's purpose: turning responsibility and culpability for the crime into a collective experience (2004–2005: 730).

Simon's love for Ruth is also part of the restorative nature of the play. Khuthala Nandipha appreciates that the play features

> a male narrator [who] speaks from a male perspective presenting a new dimension in the struggle against child abuse... [M]en still need to address their own issues related to violent abuse. 'We need to converse man to man, and realise just how big a part of the problem we are' (2005: 25).

Simon directs his fury against the journalists who come to investigate this sensational story and call the place 'the town of shame'. He takes pages of newspapers and pushes them onto the branches of trees near the miniature village. Pairs of spectacles hang from each tree and remind us that if the journalists have faulty sight that requires corrective glasses to improve their vision, they also lack insight and hurl blame at the villagers. Simon says, 'Shame on you!'(40) to the journalist and points to the audience during this powerful speech: 'Take your cameras and get out!... this town was fucking gang-raped a long, long, long, long time ago! Shame on us? Shame on you, shame on all of us' (40–1). His words poignantly address the depth of damage to his world. Ruth is devastated by guilt and tries unsuccessfully to end her life. As Simon points to the audience, I feel complicit as a spectator, since although I had nothing to do with the rape I also did nothing to facilitate societal change. So the focus alters from killing the 'monster' to analysing the monstrous action and asking what kind of lives and opportunities the villagers can have in the future. This exemplifies the Ibsenesque villain shift, when society rather than an individual becomes the villain; in focusing upon apartheid societal structures, their legacies and the lack of substantial change for millions of people, the necessity for reconciliation within communities becomes apparent. Rape statistics are so huge that they become incomprehensible – awareness-raising is vital on many different levels. Critic Adrienne Sichel comments on the role of the audience: 'On leaving the theatre there is no way anyone can say, "We didn't know." *Tshepang* is part of that canon of conscientising drama' (2001: xv).

Finally, Athol Fugard's most recent play, *The Train Driver*, is a powerful two-hander, which harks back to his early plays. It premiered in February 2010, at the new Fugard Theatre in District Six, Cape Town, and travelled to London later that same year. Other productions took place in La Jolla (2010) and Long Wharf Theatre, Connecticut (2011). Fugard returned to South Africa from his home in La Jolla, California, in order to direct what can be considered his darkest play. In Celia Dugger's interview with the playwright, she notes: 'Everything he has written before was, according to Fugard, "a journey to the writing of this play"' (2010). For Marianne Thamm the play is 'a devastating critique of post-apartheid South Africa' (2010). Fugard's customary optimism is represented as a momentary possibility of reconciliation before circumstances obliterate that possibility and enshroud the play in gloom.

The Train Driver is set in a windswept cemetery in the black township of Shukuma, near Motherwell in the Eastern Cape, and alternates between scenes in the paupers' section of the graveyard, where unclaimed bodies and unnamed graves represent South African society's 'throw-aways', and a shack on the edge of the graveyard – which together form the locale which the gravedigger, Simon Hanabe, calls home. The raked stage emphasises the off-kilter world that the play exposes. It explores the intrusion by a white Afrikaans train driver, Roelf Visagie, into the world of the black gravedigger and the disastrous consequences that ensue. When a nameless black woman with her baby on her back stands on the track in the path of the oncoming train it crushes mother and baby to death.

Fugard read about a similar incident in 2000 concerning a mother and her three children and was haunted by her story; he was unable to comprehend her total desperation, born of poverty and hopelessness, and tried to write a play soon afterwards. He explains, 'I cannot fathom a darkness so deep that a human being can finally say, "There is no hope"' (quoted in Dugger 2010). Instead he waited many years and imagined another perspective, that of the train driver, who suffered post-traumatic distress after the incident. The title focuses upon the white train driver who enacts a paean of pain, trauma and guilt. Other than the prologue and epilogue which are spoken by Simon, but still foreground Roelf, moments of dialogue are overshadowed by Roelf's monologues, which are performances of anguish for the loss of his family and his known world. This is problematic, since the plight of the woman, whom he calls Red Doek (red scarf), is elided except for his ventriloquised evocation of her situation. Spectators, however, journey first and foremost with Roelf, the unwitting perpetrator of the deaths, and the woman remains embedded in silence. Even Simon, who tries to help Roelf in his quest for her grave, is marginalised in the overwhelming focus on Roelf's problems.

Roelf's journey reveals a trajectory from his explosive breakdown to his death; his wife shouts that he should 'swear at "his woman" from the bush' (Fugard 2010:

41) and that becomes Roelf's goal: to 'get her name and swear at her properly' (42). Roelf searches the graveyard despite Simon's warnings of danger from tsotsis (young criminals). He undergoes a change of heart when he realises: 'I didn't want to swear at her because I was thinking . . . she lived in one of those pondoks [shacks] in the bush, about the smell of shit . . . That is what Red Doek called home . . . That is fucking hopeless, man' (53). He understands that the unnamed pauper's grave represents her poverty and abjection; Red Doek fulfils Judith Butler's categorisation of lives that 'will not even qualify as grievable' (2004: 32). Roelf's moment of reconciliation arises from his troubled understanding of her position: 'Nobody Wants Her!' (Fugard 2010: 54). He desires to commune with her spirit and claim her. The acceptance of an actual victim by a traumatised casualty is the only faint flicker of light in a very dark play. The following morning Simon finds Roelf's body stabbed by the tsotsis.

Simon's blood-stained spade augurs the figurative death of the gravedigger since the police confiscate it as evidence and he is fired because of his complicity with the white man. The termination of his work signifies the potential impossibility of his survival. The shortlived personal reconciliation between white and black from Roelf's perspective is obliterated by his death. The play evokes a country plunged in darkness where events are spiralling into disaster. This evocation meshes with David Klatzow's 2010 article on the inevitable result of African National Congress (ANC) policies, which analyses failed and disastrous courses of action, post-Madiba, with respect to hospitals, healthcare, education, policing and the justice system: 'Stop the rot before it destroys our country'.

* * *

The happening that signified a wholly other form of staging in South Africa is the FIFA World Cup in 2010, which represented an apparent national reconciliation of an undreamed-of magnitude, a miraculous reconciliation writ large by the presence of local and international media. The launch on 10 June was accompanied by explosions, not of a threatening kind, but rather of joy, pride, hope and a sense of self-esteem that have not marked South African society since the election of Nelson Mandela as state president (1994) and South Africa's win at the Rugby World Cup in 1995, when Mandela, wearing a Springbok jersey, joined François Pienaar, captain of the Springbok team. They both held aloft the cup to unite spectators in previously unimaginable ways (see the Clint Eastwood-directed film *Invictus* [2009]). These national acts of reconciliation between blacks and whites, especially Afrikaners, occurred even before the hearings of the TRC. In a BBC interview with Lyse Doucet, Tutu reminded us that 'that victory [and Mandela's involvement] in terms of bringing us together did more for our country than my sermons for a whole year' (2010). Verashini Pillay reports on the opening ceremony of the World Cup which 'burst on to the Soccer City Stadium floor in a flurry of flags, fireworks, dancing and singing' (2010). Fans from across the nation joined in support of the South African team, Bafana Bafana (The Boys), and celebrated the timely completion of stadiums, transport and other services. Overseas visitors swelled the ranks of this over-the-top crowd. More than seventy-thousand fans blew vuvuzelas (a single-note plastic horn). Tinyiko Sam Maluleke's 'ode to the vuvuzela' names it 'our most potent weapon':

> It is an instrument of assertion . . . We blow it for an end to the marginalisation of Africa . . . OK, let us face it; the vuvuzela will not bring back the land, the cattle, the oil and the mines . . . Having succeeded in forcing the world to look Africawards – let us proceed to take inspiration from the vuvuzela so that we take it upon ourselves, to win back our dignity in two dozen other ways (2010).

Mark Gevisser analyses the value of the World Cup: 'The South African Government believes the benefit is intangible, and immeasurable – a "Mandela moment" all over again; a jab in the eye of Afro-pessimism; invaluable global coverage; the cementing of national pride and identity' (2010). Even at this euphoric moment there is another perspective that has been temporarily played down. Since in South Africa there exists one of the greatest gaps in the world between rich and poor, the post-World Cup Soccer months may result in a backlash when millions of have-nots, angry at the huge expenditure, realise the concomitant neglect of urgent basic needs such as health, education and housing. Gevisser also notes that the expenditure of between three and five billion euros could leave South Africa 'with a herd of white elephant stadiums that will sap the economy for decades to come'. These complex problems signify a precarious future, at odds with the apparent unity and national reconciliation at the soccer stadiums.

Shari Cohen wrote two articles, four days apart, that speak to the contagious effect of a South African staging of a world-class international event. She arrived in South Africa in early May and on 11 June offered a scathing critique of her month doing development work: 'A fraction of that money could have changed the lives of the hundreds of thousands of orphans struggling to survive across the nation' (2010b). On 15 June she foregrounded 'the global embrace that South Africans have offered to the world . . . I have learned the value of *Ubuntu* [humaneness], and that when found and offered in abundance, the world is indeed a better place to live in' (2010a). Other than the obvious hysteria about the World Cup, how does one reconcile the articles? Genuine pride in hosting the event by South Africa is accompanied by the short-term economic benefit of an influx of tourists. But the negatives, as briefly analysed, are legion and cannot be forgotten in the excitement of the moment. Cohen occupies a privileged position: she has a paid job and the ability to travel and to return to a home in the USA. Surely it is more difficult to engage in *ubuntu* when many people are poverty stricken, dying from AIDS-related causes and harassed by crime and corruption. Thus the issue of lasting reconciliation will have to wait to be assessed.

Referring to his cantata, Miller believes 'the testimonies made in 1996 should continue to be heard, especially since the nation has not fully reconciled (quoted in Zvomuya and Momoniat 2010). Sachs argues that 'ultimately we can only have full reconciliation when conditions have been created where the full dignity of all South Africans is respected and everyone has equal life chances' (2009: 85). How will theatre continue to deal with unstable conditions and treat various problems including those that hamper reconciliation? No matter how volatile the political scene, the arts apparently thrive by responding in creative ways to challenges and raising new awareness. In South Africa there are ongoing attempts to expose and challenge divisions and inequities and to continue the reconciling acts beyond the TRC. Theatrical stagings in all their variety have a significant role to play.

Note

1. Sincere thanks to Phillippa Yaa de Villiers and Peter Hayes for generously sending me unpublished texts. Much appreciation to Darren Gobert for his input into my work. Immeasurable gratitude to Henry Blumberg for his ongoing support for my work and for sharing many visits to the National Arts Festival, as well as other theatre festivals.

References

Baderoon, Gabeba. 2006. 'Foreword' to Nadia Davids's *At Her Feet*. Cape Town: Oshun Books: 9–13.

Blumberg, Marcia. 2000. 'Re-membering History, Staging Hybridity: *Ubu and the Truth Commission*'. In: *Multiculturalism and Hybridity in African Literatures*, edited by H. Wylie and B. Lindfors. Trenton, NJ: Africa World: 309–18.

Botman, H. Russel and Robin M. Petersen. 1996. 'Introduction' to *To Remember and to Heal: Theological and Psychological Reflections on Truth and Reconciliation*, edited by H. Russel Botman and Robin M. Petersen. Cape Town: Human & Rousseau: 9–14.

Botman, H. Russel and Robin M. Petersen (eds). 1996. *To Remember and to Heal: Theological and Psychological Reflections on Truth and Reconciliation*. Cape Town: Human & Rousseau.
Braid, Mary. 1998. 'Part of a Wider Split'. *The Independent* (UK), 18 February: 17.
Butler, Judith. 2004. *Precarious Life: The Powers of Mourning and Violence*. London: Verso.
Buys, Anthea. 2008. 'A Loaf of Bread, a Choir and the TRC'. *Mail & Guardian*, 2 May. http://www.thoughtleader.co.za/antheabuys/.../a-loaf-of-bread-a-choir-and-the-trc/ (accessed 21 June 2010).
Cohen, Shari. 2010a. 'South Africa Rolls out the Ubuntu in Abundance'. http://www.huffingtonpost.com/shari-cohen/south-africa-rolls-out-th_b_611802.html (accessed 12 April 2011).
———. 2010b. 'South Africa's World Cup: Is Anyone Really the Winner?' http://www.huffingtonpost.com/shari-cohen/south-africas-world-cup-i_b_609028.html (accessed 12 April 2011).
Davids, Leila. 2006. 'Interview with Nadia Davids'. In: *At Her Feet*, written by Nadia Davids. Cape Town: Oshun Books: 67–74.
Davids, Nadia. 2006a. *At Her Feet*. Cape Town: Oshun Books.
———. 2006b. 'Notes from Afar'. *UCT News*: 60.
De Villiers, Phillippa Yaa. 2007. 'Shine: It Ain't a Sin to be Black'. http://philyaa.book.co.za/blog/2007/12/09/shine-it-aint-a-sin-to-be-black/ (accessed 12 April 2011).
———. 2009. *Original Skin* [unpublished script].
Doucet, Lyse. 2010. 'Interview with the Elders'. BBC interview, 10 June. http://news.bbc.co.uk/2/hi/programmes/newsnight/8735235.stm (accessed 12 April 2011).
Dub, Sam. 2010. 'Rewind: A Cantata for Voice, Tape and Testimony', 29 April. http://classicalmusic.southbankcentre.co.uk/2010/04/29/rewind-a-cantata-for-voice-tape-and-testimony/ (accessed 21 June 2010).
Dugger, Celia W. 2010. 'His Next Act: Driving out Apartheid's Ghost'. *New York Times*, 12 March. http://www.nytimes.com/2010/03/13/theater/13fugard.html?_r=1 (accessed 12 April 2011).
Farber, Yael. 2008. *Molora*. London: Oberon Books.
Farber, Yael and Thembi Mtshali. 2008. *A Woman in Waiting*. In: *Theatre as Witness: Three Testimonial Plays from South Africa*, edited by Y. Farber, T. Mtshali and T. Chokwe. London: Oberon Books: 29–85.
Farber, Y., T. Mtshali and T. Chokwe (eds). 2008. *Theatre as Witness: Three Testimonial Plays from South Africa*. London: Oberon Books.
Farred, Grant. 1997. 'Bulletproof Settlers: The Politics of Offense in the New South Africa'. In: *Whiteness: A Critical Reader*, edited by M. Hill. New York: New York University Press: 63–78.
Foot Newton, Lara. 2005. *Tshepang: The Third Testament*. Johannesburg: Wits University Press.
———. 2009. *Reach*. In: *At This Stage: Plays from Post-Apartheid South Africa*, edited by G. Homan. Johannesburg: Wits University Press: 31–68.
Fugard, Athol. 2010. *The Train Driver*. Cape Town: Junkets Publisher.
Gevisser, Mark. 2010. 'South Africa's World Cup Moment'. *New York Times*, 7 June. http://www.nytimes.com/2010/06/08/opinion/08iht-edgevisser.html (accessed 12 April 2011).
Gramsci, Antonio. 1971. *Selections from Prison Notebooks*. Translated and edited by Quentin Hoare and Geoffrey Nowell Smith. New York: International Publishers.

Hamber, Brandon and Hugo van der Merwe. 1998. 'What is This Thing Called Reconciliation?' *Reconciliation in Review* 1(1). http://www.csvr.org.za/wits/articles/artrcbh.htm (accessed 14 July 2010).

Hayes, Peter (with Pam Ngwabeni). 2009. *Ncamisa! The Women* [unpublished script].

Hayes, Peter. 2010. *I Am Here* [unpublished script].

Higginson, Craig. 2009. *Dream of the Dog*. In: *At This Stage: Plays from Post-Apartheid South Africa*, edited by G. Homan. Johannesburg: Wits University Press: 141–77.

Hill, M. (ed.). 1997. *Whiteness: A Critical Reader*. New York: New York University Press.

Homan, Greg. 2009a. 'Preamble' to *At This Stage: Plays from Post-Apartheid South Africa*, edited by G. Homan. Johannesburg: Wits University Press: 1–16.

———. 2009b. 'Introduction' to *At This Stage: Plays from Post-Apartheid South Africa*, edited by G. Homan. Johannesburg: Wits University Press: 17–29.

Homan, Greg (ed.). 2009. *At This Stage: Plays from Post-Apartheid South Africa*. Johannesburg: Wits University Press.

Kani, John. 2004. *Nothing but the Truth*. Johannesburg: Wits University Press.

Kaplan, Carol. 2004–2005. 'Voices Rising: An Essay on Gender, Justice and Theater in South Africa'. *Seattle Journal of Social Justice* 3(2): 711–48.

Klatzow, David. 2010. 'Meltdown, the Inevitable Result of ANC Policies'. *Cape Times*, 16 February. Republished 23 February: http://southafrica-pig.blogspot.com/2010/02/where-hell-are-we-going.html (accessed 12 April 2011).

Maja-Pearce, Adewale. 1996. 'Binding the Wounds'. *Index on Censorship: Wounded Nations, Broken Lives: Truth Commissions and War Tribunals* 172: 48–53.

Marx, Lesley. 1998. 'Slouching towards Bethlehem: *Ubu and the Truth Commission*'. *African Studies* 57(2): 209–20.

Miller, Philip. 2007. 'Rewind Cantata'. http://www.philipmiller.info/rewind-cantata (accessed 21 June 2010).

Maluleke, Tinyiko Sam. 2010. 'An Ode to the Vuvuzela'. http://www.thoughtleader.co.za/tinyiko sammaluleke/2010/06/12/an-ode-to-the-vuvuzela-on-occasion-of-fifa-world-cup-2010-in-south-africa/ (accessed 13 June 2010).

Mda, Zakes. 2004. 'Introduction' to *Nothing but the Truth*, written by John Kani. Johannesburg: Wits University Press: v–ix.

Nandipha, Kuthala. 2005. 'Fighting Child Rape through Theatre'. *Drum*, 14 April: 25.

Peimer, David. 2009. 'Introduction' to *Armed Response: Plays from South Africa*, edited by D. Peimer. Calcutta: Seagull Books: vii–xvii.

Peimer, David (ed.). 2009. *Armed Response: Plays from South Africa*. Calcutta: Seagull Books.

Pillay, Verashini. 2010. 'South Africa Celebrates Start of the World Cup'. *Mail & Guardian*, 11 June. http://mg.co.za/article/2010-06-11-south-africa-celebrates-start-of-world-cup (accessed 12 April 2011).

Rich, Adrienne. 1979 [1971]. 'When We Dead Awaken: Writing as Re-vision'. In: *On Lies, Secrets and Silence: Selected Prose 1966–1978*. London: W.W. Norton: 33–49.

Rodwell, Bobbie (with Lesego Rampolokeng and Robert Coleman). 1996. *The Story I'm about to Tell* [unpublished script].

Sachs, Albie. 1990. *Protecting Human Rights in a New South Africa*. Cape Town: Oxford University Press.

———. 2009. *The Strange Alchemy of Life and Law*. Oxford: Oxford University Press.
Sichel, Adrienne. 2001. 'Foreword' to *Tshepang: The Third Testament*, written by Lara Foot Newton. Johannesburg: Wits University Press: xiii–xvi.
Taylor, Jane. 1998. *Ubu and the Truth Commission*. Cape Town: UCT Press.
Thamm, Marianne. 2010. 'On the Other Side of a Beaten Track'. *Sunday Times*, 4 April. http://www.timeslive.co.za/sundaytimes/article384483.ece/On-the-other-side-of-a-beaten-track (accessed 12 April 2011).
Tutu, Desmond. 1999. *No Future without Forgiveness*. New York: Doubleday.
Wylie, Hal and Bernth Lindfors (eds). 2000. *Multiculturalism and Hybridity in African Literatures*. Trenton, NJ: Africa World.
Zvomuya, Percy and Yunus Momoniat. 2010. 'The Reverb of Rewind'. *Mail & Guardian*, 18 April. http://mg.co.za/article/2008-04-18-the-reverb-of-rewind (accessed 12 April 2011).

7

The Road That Calls

From Poor Theatre to Theatres of Excess

MIKI FLOCKEMANN

> I think one discovers more than one invents, and that invention is really discovery or rediscovery.
> — Eugène Ionesco, quoted in James Roose-Evans, *Experimental Theatre: From Stanislavsky to Peter Brook*

> This road calls me, waving for me to come, it is overwhelming.
> — Mandla Mbothwe, *Ingcwaba lendoda lise cankwe ndlela*

In arriving at experimental work, claims James Roose-Evans, 'we cannot escape our debt to the past even when it is necessary to break with it' (1989: 75). This has a bearing on the replacement of the stock-in-trade multipurpose teaboxes and beercrates associated with minimalist theatre productions in South Africa during the 1970s and 1980s by a proliferation of suitcases, shoes and 'Universal Refugee' bags as both symbol and symptom of travel, exile, escape and the search for 'home'. Do these staging devices signify a tired recycling of the urgent and strident tropes of the apartheid past where stripped-down sets and the visceral emphasis on the performing body were integral to speaking the truth to an apparently invincible power? After all, these strategies were shaped by the ideas of the historical European avant-garde theatre movement – particularly Jerzy Grotowski's concept of 'poor theatre' (1968) – but they also served the purely practical need for mobility in the face of state harassment. At the same time, by incorporating local performance and storytelling traditions, a distinctively South African theatre signature has evolved.

This raises further questions about how aesthetic legacies have been translated and transformed in recent theatre productions in South Africa. For instance, it has been claimed that 'we are still stuck with the limitations of the one-person show; the poor man's theatre, practised not for aesthetic or artistic reasons, but by economic default' (Meersman 2009). However, this recycling of protest-style performance strategies may achieve its power because of the way it speaks about conditions after the ending of institutionalised apartheid from within. To illustrate, I will discuss a number of one-handers which offer diverse perspectives while drawing on similar performance techniques and legacies; this will prepare the ground for a brief overview of some distinctive current theatre trends.

Since Marcia Blumberg's chapter has already explored a number of the major productions and concerns of the last decade, I will include some less well-known works and concentrate on the diversity of performance styles and concerns that have emerged recently, with a focus on attempts to find alternative ways of speaking. These aesthetic trends are often generated by encounters between local traditions and 'imported' performance styles associated with minimalist productions, as well as 'theatre of excess'. This term is taken from Antonin Artaud's description of theatrical spectacle which generates an 'excessive' response, which can shift consciousness through sensory saturation (1936: 136). For the purposes of this discussion, however, the aim is to explore how aesthetic legacies have been translated and transformed and how these speak to the postmillennial context.

In order to provide some background to the aesthetic legacies identified here, I want to introduce the notion of theatre as a 'virtual public sphere'. These legacies include encounters with practitioners such as Grotowski, Artaud, Bertolt Brecht and Peter Brook and also local evolving and traditional forms. (Many avant-garde or experimental practitioners were in turn drawing on the performance traditions of India, other parts of Asia and Africa, via the modernist preoccupation with primitivism.) The working through of imported ideas in South African theatre generally resulted in an 'effect' rather than a replication. For instance, Grotowski's *Towards a Poor Theatre* (1968) focused on the direct, 'live' communication between actor and spectator to foreground the difference between theatre and film (Power 2004: 12). He claimed that 'the body is memory' and a pathway to understanding: 'One should unblock the body to unblock memory' (Osterloff and Milkowski 2010). Grotowski insisted that the performer is not only an interpreter of a text, but also a co-creator. These ideas strongly shaped performance styles of writer-directors such as Athol Fugard and Barney Simon in the 1970s and 1980s. However, the methods employed locally to achieve these effects (usually through collaborative workshopped productions drawing on vernacular anecdote) were often different from the programme of sustained and concentrated discipline required by Grotowski from his 'priesthood' of dedicated performers who used symbolism to react against the repressive legacy of Stalin in Poland during the 1960s and 1970s (Brown 2009). On the other hand, what I have termed 'theatre of excess' does not refer to Njabulo S. Ndebele's (1991) much-quoted application of Roland Barthes's 'spectacles of excess' (which replicate stereotypical oppositions), but to the theatres of cruelty and ecstasy advocated by Artaud and others as a means of altering consciousness through sensory saturation and shock aesthetics. Again, these strategies need to be seen as an expression of the political ideals of what is termed the historical avant-garde and its reaction to the crisis of language in postwar Europe. It is claimed that the advent of postmodernism has dissipated the relationship between aesthetics and politics in avant-garde art movements. However, this has been challenged by Hal Foster (1994), among others, and does not necessarily apply to South African theatre and performance, where young directors are increasingly experimenting with strategies that have much in common (either directly or implicitly) with the aesthetics of theatre of excess, as well as forms of total theatre which blur the boundaries between spectators and performers, ritual and theatre, using multimedia forms, theatrical tableaux and performance installations to achieve a 'total' event.

Mandla Mbothwe's *Ingcwaba lendoda lise cankwe ndlela* (The grave of the man is next to the road) (2009), for instance, uses the choreographed corporeality of an ensemble of performers combined with a poetic and incantatory form of 'deep' isiXhosa to explore the unspoken psychic trauma experienced by members of a family of labour migrants travelling along the N2 between the rural Eastern Cape and Cape Town. English subtitles are projected onto a screen superimposed on a grainy moving road, flickering like a dream. This creates a profoundly unsettling effect as the spectators are made to bear witness to the trauma of migrancy through an apparently arcane and 'unfamiliar' language, which is translated into opaque metaphors. Such a work might be seen as what Artaud hoped to achieve when he claimed that 'all true feeling is in reality untranslatable' and can only exist 'in the poetry of the senses' (quoted in Roose-Evans 1989: 75). However, one should be wary of reading backwards through this aesthetic prism since Mbothwe is at pains to develop a local, indigenous aesthetic drawing on Xhosa storytelling traditions and rituals in order to enable 'reconnection' to home and to community.[1] Kennedy Chinyola points out that in the context of African performance traditions, cultural 'play', including storytelling, can be defined as 'a mode of aesthetic being' (2007: 14).[2] This can be contrasted with Mpumelelo Paul Grootboom's use of aesthetic shock tactics in staging sex and violence to present a critique of debased values in modern South Africa in his controversial *Foreplay* (2009). Grootboom's work appears to have much in common with theatres of excess which are also aimed at shifting consciousness. Unlike Mbothwe's work which draws on a living archive of Xhosa ritual and oral performance in order to establish connection, Grootboom's plays are characterised by intertextual play (*Foreplay* is a reworking of a 1903 Austrian play, *Der Reigen*, by Arthur Schnitzler). As Mary Corrigall observes: 'The kind of theatre that Grootboom has devised not only takes audiences to the brink of their comfort zones, but tries to penetrate the deepest level of their consciousness' (2010: 27). It has been claimed that 'Shock is, par excellence, the evidence of (something) happening, rather than nothing, suspended privation' (Lyotard, quoted in Guthrie 1996: 307); the use of shock here can be seen as an attempt at getting audiences to 'perceive differently'.

This 'alternative' perception is made possible partly because, as a public art form, theatre can be seen to mediate between intimate and public spheres. As Loren Kruger puts it, theatre has the capacity 'to constitute as a virtual public sphere the rehearsal of a potential alternative rather than merely a substitute form of public life' (2002: 4). The function of theatrical 'presence' also comes into play here. In his critique of theories of presence in theatre, Cormac Power notes that 'presence' is a historically shifting term. Nevertheless, '[t]heatre at once affirms presence by taking place *before* an audience, while simultaneously putting this correspondence into question: a fictional "now" often coexists with a stage "now". We see the stage and imagine the fiction, and so the whole question as to what *is* present is opened up' (2004: 3–4, emphasis in the original). Theatre, by virtue of factors such as the performative 'presence', provides a useful framework for foregrounding aesthetic trends manifesting in other narrative forms. The shift that has occurred since the 1990s from witnessing, protesting against and resisting 'what *is* present', to works aimed at getting audiences to perceive differently, has become a clearly defined trend. This has produced a substantial and growing body of work – one thinks of directors such as Brett Bailey, Lara Foot Newton, Mark Fleishman, Grootboom and Mbothwe. However, this does not mean that the traditions of the previous era have become entirely moribund.

The use of bags signifying the baggage of the past carried into the present, as well as being both sign and symptom of migration, a search for home and sense of 'self', has become ubiquitous in South African theatre of the last decade. As mentioned earlier, this is especially evident in the plethora of one-handers employing minimalist sets and drawing on some of the stylistic strategies associated with poor and physical theatre. While I tend to agree with Brent Meersman's claim that this 'has become a hopelessly overtraded genre' (2009), it nevertheless still has viable currency in productions that 'work upon and within' the genre to speak to the present. This includes works as diverse as *Itsoseng* (Wake yourselves up) by Omphile Malusi (2008), set in a gutted shopping complex in North West Province, and *A Man and a Dog* by Nhlanhla Mavundla (2006) in which Mavundla explores his own intimate journey into manhood. On the other hand, *Johnny Boskak is Feeling Funny* by Greig Coetzee (2009) uses a mock elegy in rhyming couplets to recount the tale of a marginalised troopie on a quasi-chivalric car-chase quest. These works make an interesting comparison with a crop of performances by young women in which a common thread is the exploration, often staged in an intensely self-reflexive way, of what it means to be young, African and a woman in South Africa today.

Written and performed by Malusi, *Itsoseng* presents an indictment of what has been referred to – often in Fanonian terms – as South Africa's failed or incomplete revolution (see Mngxitama [2009]). During the period when the Bantustan homeland of Bophuthatswana 'flourished' under Lucas Mangope, the people of Itsoseng (Malusi's home town) enjoyed the perks of a puppet regime, but they now live forgotten in poverty and despair. This is aggravated by the fact that during 1994, as a way of ridding themselves of the signs of Mangope's regime, the community burnt down a showcase shopping complex which to this day has not been rebuilt. According to Malusi (who was awarded the Brett Goldin bursary to spend time working with the Royal Shakespeare Company in 2007), 'the new struggle of the township is the economy' (2008: 19). He claims: 'I do not like discussing politics, I only want to tell the stories of our lives' (18). In telling the stories of the community to testify to how 'many feel betrayed by the freedom they fought for', Malusi taps into a strong current of disillusionment; this has a bearing on the fact that xenophobic violence in South Africa has been read as a symptom of the stark divide between the very poor and the rest of society, exacerbated by vulnerability to HIV and AIDS. What saves the play from being merely a recycled protest play, however, is Malusi's storytelling gift as he gives voice to and inhabits a cross-section of locals to present a compelling composite portrayal of the desolation of Itsoseng, 'a dry little township outside Mafikeng', evoked through a forlorn, trash-littered stage. The play takes the form of a wake that is also a journey:

MAWILLA: (*He sighs deeply as he sits on the corner of the trunk.*) I don't know what to do. I woke up this morning. Instead of going to the funeral, I took my blue suit and went to the backyard of the house, packed everything in my trunk, dragged it out of the yard, to the park, got on the main road and travelled. I thought I would travel for ever. *(Makes a sound of a jet taking off.)* But I found myself here on this forsaken piece of space (2008: 21).

While the play seems unrelenting in its depiction of wasted lives (as enacted and described by a fast-talking Mawilla who leaves but – absurdly – goes nowhere), there are moments of transcendent tenderness as this is also a love story of sorts. In the final scene, when we realise whose funeral it is that Mawilla is en route to, his staged diatribe has a striking affinity with the rage articulated by young activists like S'bu Zikode (Durban-based chairperson of the Abahlali baseMjondolo [Shack Dwellers] Movement). In a piece titled 'We are the Third Force' Zikode warns of the apparently banal ordinariness of the time-bomb of poverty, not only in rural backwaters such as Itsoseng, but in urban centres much closer to home. Zikode claims: 'Those in power are blind to our suffering. This is because they have not seen what we see; they have not felt what we are feeling every second, every day' (2006).[3] Clearly nothing much has changed, given that Zikode wrote this in 2006, the year in which *Itsoseng* was first performed. In fact, Zikode's sentiments are chillingly similar to Mawilla's staged outburst and point to the xenophobic violence that erupted in 2008 as a consequence of economic apartheid, still entrenched in race-based inequities:

> I hate what this place has become. Nobody listens, nobody hears us. Irrespective of how big we try to shout to them up there, our voices just bang on their walls, they fall and they bury them. 'Nothing happened, everybody is happy; the whole country is smiling, alive with possibilities.' Sometimes I wish all the townships would be burned to the ground like this shopping complex so that we could start afresh . . . to live. We are still living in a curse (Malusi 2008: 52).

In using this direct form of address, Malusi's *Itsoseng* revives the witnessing strategies of the past. The deployment of techniques associated with protest theatre, as one reviewer puts it, 'turns up the volume on voices often unheard' (Hutchinson 2008) to expose the powder-keg of poverty in our midst. At the same time, the play illustrates how theatre constitutes a 'virtual public sphere' to speak back to an actual public sphere which is indifferent or in denial: '*Nothing happened, everybody is happy; the whole country is smiling, alive with possibilities*'. Malusi's play is thus one example of how a recycled tradition is employed to testify to a 'new struggle'.

While *Itsoseng* has received substantial media attention and won the Scotsman's Fringe First Award in Edinburgh, Mavundla's *A Man and a Dog* has not received the same coverage. This is surprising, given that Mavundla is a consummate exponent of physical theatre and his performances have been well received by audiences. *A Man and a Dog* is an autobiographical work and embodies not only Mavundla's own evolution from child to man, but the evolution of those he encounters (including three dogs) associated with significant rites of passage along his journey. The work also employs techniques associated with poor and physical theatre, but in this case these strategies are used to expose states of consciousness and provide an intimate insight into the dynamics of manhood for a Zulu boy growing up in a female-led but patriarchal society with an abusive stepfather. Like Malusi's *Itsoseng*, *A Man and a Dog* offers a language for speaking about or 'turning up the volume' on the experience of abandonment and the enduring effects of a lack of intimacy and care (especially from male family members), not often spoken about in the public sphere. This happens through the physical presence of the actor who literally becomes his own memory as he enacts his embodied past by metamorphosing into the people and events that have shaped him, including the dogs.

His stepfather gives him a small dog to look after and instructs him in the rituals that are necessary to make the dog 'his' and forever obedient – which include cutting the tongue of the dog, cleaning his plate in a certain way and exposing him to scorpions to sharpen his bite. The stepfather says: 'Everything is mine – but the dog is yours'. However, the boy also resents the dog as it seems to get better treatment from the stepfather than he does, placing a spin on the expression 'treat him like a dog'. The dog becomes a site of struggle between the boy and the 'dog-obsessed' stepfather: when the boy later encounters the stepfather's own large and aggressive dog, he sees in the dog a mirror of his own fear of violence. Following a grotesque logic, the boy, who is savagely beaten by the stepfather, equally savagely beats the dog and then hangs the dog from a tree in order to free himself from his stepfather. The question running through the play is: 'Who am I in this family?' and the power of the work lies in the ways the performer stages his inner life: in Grotowskian terms, the body is memory. One of the props used is a bag of flour which at times represents the boy himself, as in the scene where he is 'taught a lesson' by the stepfather. The boy-bag lies on the floor lit by a spotlight that isolates the bag and the brutal, sjambok-wielding man – each time the sjambok thwacks down, motes of flour-dust rise, caught in the light and magnified, circling the imagined abject boy and suggestive of the way this event permeates his memory.

There are parallels here with Thando Mgqolozana's controversial novel, *A Man Who is Not a Man* (2009), which also deals with intimate 'secrets' of masculinity within black family contexts. Mgqolozana's account deals with the psychic and social fallout following a botched circumcision resulting from the failure of care from the men closest to him. It also describes an empathetic and complex relationship between the Xhosa initiate's own dog and the prized dog from the 'welcoming party' of men that he attacks with his knobkerrie (a symbol of newly acquired manhood). It seems fortuitous that *A Man and a Dog* was first performed in the same year that Ndebele published his essay 'The Year of the Dog', in which he claims: 'You can see why the word "dog" is never far away in the imagining of violence and abuse in our country . . . "Dog" is a pervasive metaphor regularly used to justify righteous brutality' (2007: 253). After a performance at Artscape in September 2006, Mavundla told the audience that for years he had battled with depression following his childhood trauma: 'I used to say: I am nothing, I can't do things because of poverty'. At one level, then, it is in performance that he achieves and affirms his own 'presence' by staging his personal history.

Quite a different tone is struck with another one-man play, Coetzee's *Johnny Boskak is Feeling Funny*. This work provides a glimpse into the lives of another marginalised group, in this case the white working class, in the person of a former troopie who has lost his sense of belonging and direction. Writer-performers such as Coetzee who employ a comedic framework to play with and destabilise familiar South African 'types' (in his case, an underclass of social misfits, misguided romantics as well as self-pitying former members of the South African Defence Force) have achieved immense popularity in a climate where the anxiety of identity negotiation is strongly present.

In similar comic vein Geraldine Naidoo, as writer-director, and partner and performer Matthew Ribnick, have produced sell-out successes with repeat performances of *Chilli Boy* (2004) and *Hoot* (2005). Here Naidoo explores the transformation of a slick businessman, Harold Potgieter, who loses everything: his wife, his house, his car; he is forced to board with an assortment of strangers and ends up becoming a driver of a minibus taxi. Ribnick gives a very funny but intelligently nuanced performance using only his body, voice, verbal and physical tics and an assortment of caps to morph into a motley cross-section of South Africans. Initially, because of the foreshortening involved in switching between roles, this feels uncomfortably like replicating stereotypes, but from the moment an old Indian woman (a fellow-lodger in the teeming boarding house where Harold shares a room) shows him how to do his washing, the characters come to life as individuals. *Hoot* presents an unlikely scenario: a white ex-businessman working as a minibus driver for a black taxi boss in Jo'burg, but the performance makes this believable and even inevitable in the logic of the play, in view of the enduring relationships Harold develops with his new family of friends and co-workers. By imagining what might be possible and giving it presence, even in such a hyperbolic comic form, this work provides another example of how theatre, by constituting a virtual public sphere, offers scope for rehearsing or testing out potential or alternative forms of public life (Kruger 2002: 4).

Evoking the suffering but simultaneously resilient black body as a sign of apartheid abuses and potential resistance was characteristic of poor-theatre-styled productions such as *Woza Albert!* during the states of emergency in the 1980s. In addition, linguistic code-switching was often employed to emphasise the difference between the totalising categories of 'oppressor and oppressed'. Strains of these oppositional discourses have hardened into current discourses of indigeneity and exceptionalism and underlie the targeting of foreign Africans as 'enemy aliens' (see Hassim, Kupe and Worby [2009]). Works such as *Hoot*, however, by imagining physically embodied social transformations through comedy, serve to 'interrupt' and even subvert racialised discourses of indigeneity and difference. This insistence on what Kwame Anthony Appiah calls 'commonality despite difference' (2006: xvii) presents a radical departure from the oppositions characterising poor theatre of the apartheid era, despite the overlap of form.

Another departure is the emergence of young women theatre practitioners. Two to three decades ago Gcina Mhlophe and others of her generation noted the difficulties experienced by black women working in theatre: these were primarily a consequence of socially assigned roles and a perception of women's 'objectified' subjectivity. The situation has certainly changed dramatically with the emergence of an ever-growing group of play-makers, many of whom are performers as well as writers, directors and academics. This could explain why much of the work is often intensely self-reflexive and influenced (sometimes awkwardly) by theories of subjectivity in postcolonial contexts. While the anxieties and contradictions of politically and socially marginalised identities have been explored in works dealing with Coloured, Islamic and Indian identities,[4] there has been a shift from a focus on the trauma of conflicted identities to claiming these as a way of being, or a means of self-identification – though obviously this, too, carries its own sets of internal contradictions.

There is often a common thread winding through these works, namely, a sense of being 'in-between' historical categories of South African identities by virtue of social class and education. An example is Mwenya Kabwe, whose nomadic lifestyle spans continents.[5] As a consequence, says Kabwe: 'My theatre-making impulse is drawn largely from this desire to self-represent' (2007: 50). This is an ongoing process which she describes as 'a daily task . . . to forge a sense of self from disparate sources and either overcome, mask or "play with" the self-consciousness of being so "in-between"' (51). A good example of theatre-making as self-representation is

Asanda Phewa's *A Face like Mine*, a work-in-progress performed at the 2009 Grahamstown National Arts Festival. Phewa exposes the co-existing selves which inhabit the body of a young black woman as she juggles between given, desired and acquired identities. The work is fresh and angry as Phewa performs the 'sources' informing a fragmented sense of self through a series of staged images. The images are informed by familiar discourses about black womanhood, from the historical to the popular, and expose the 'unspoken', pervasive but apparently invisible discourse of whiteness. (The two young white men on stage are mainly there as 'props' of a sort.) At the same time, the burden of traditional expectations hovers over her throughout, embodied in the ever-present mother perched aloft on a platform. Each scene image exposes – by putting on and stripping off – the various masks adopted to resist and respond to these discourses. In one scene this exposure is literal as she counters the gazes of others (including the audience) by taking ownership of the gaze by gazing at her own naked body. These stage images establish a conversation with one another. In Image 3: 'Attack of the bed', Girl describes her sense of inner dissolution: 'I feel myself coming out of my body. This is ridiculous. Parts of me, my feelings are seeping from my hands and thighs. When I walk, parts of me, my thoughts drip from behind my calves behind my knees.' This is juxtaposed against the belligerent voice she adopts in Image 4: 'Moisturizing my face':

> I am not the loud and jolly round-faced sisi from next door. My being is not defined by poverty and struggle . . . Calling me a coconut would suggest I had agency in that matter. I did not. I do however bear the brunt of that decision because I neither dream nor think in Zulu. Or Xhosa, my third language. Calling me a coconut would suggest I have secret longings or want in earnest to be white. I do not. I am not. I long for, I do miss, I desire a core inner filling . . . I feel the loss of self because neither reality, 'black' nor 'white', allows me the space to be myself . . . I'm not suicidal! Just angry![6]

In the final scene she provocatively puts on a domestic worker's uniform, as if to reject everything the mother had hoped for by sending her to 'good [English-speaking] schools'. By claiming the invisibility of the 'maid' she challenges the unsatisfactory masks she has constantly to negotiate: 'This dress gives me an identity. Definite rules laid out for me to follow.' Here she 'could deal with people not wanting to look at me or despise me because of the guilt I remind them of'. The play ends with a final retort to the protesting mother: 'This is your dream. This is what you fought for. But you never thought your dream would have a face like mine.' The discourses are made visible by being named, spoken and embodied, but simultaneously the self-reflexivity with which these discourses are played off against one another unsettles and undercuts their power over her – while not denying their effects. Girl's parting shot, 'a face like mine', offers a challenge in claiming this staged presence as 'mine' and refusing the fragmentations of being seen as 'a collection of not enoughs' projected upon her by others. The stage images in effect make a 'spectacle' of the debilitating discourses of whiteness and blackness. This offers a refreshingly iconoclastic approach to a topical concern – particularly if one compares Phewa's play to conventional approaches to the situation of the 'coconut' – as in *Tseleng: The Baggage of Bags*, a one-hander performed by Mbali Kgosidintsi (2010).[7]

In addition to the forced exile or migrancy described in works such as Mbothwe's *Ingcwaba lendoda lise cankwe ndlela*, there are explorations featuring a different kind of traveller, described by Kabwe as a 'tribe of wanderers'. Kabwe describes herself as an 'Afropolitan' and notes that this nomadic sub-group can be seen as a 'virtual community'. She notes that 'despite the vast differences in the details of each of our fragmentations, there are in fact ties that bind' (2007: 48). Kabwe's *Do Not Leave Your Baggage Unattended* invites 'a conversation around who black Africans are to each other, particularly when they migrate to other African countries'. This points to another shift: from looking at interactions between indigenous, often hostile, 'hosts' and migrant 'strangers' from elsewhere, to examining relationships between Africans in South Africa, as in Magnet Theatre's *Every Day, Every Year I Am Walking*, performed by Jennie Reznek and Fanisa Yiswa. Kabwe's *Do Not Leave Your Baggage Unattended*, a site-specific work, was performed in 2006 in Johannesburg's historic Drill Hall courtyard next to a busy taxi rank and involved interactions with the audience to create a collectively produced work. Kabwe claims: 'The re-enactment of a journey is what becomes central to the task of theatrically representing Afropolitan narratives.' The core impulse here is, 'the reflective opportunities as well as the desire to be witnessed in that journey' (2007: 62). Witnessing becomes a self-reflexive project, rather than witnessing to 'what is', as in Malusi's *Itsoseng*.

Elsewhere I have suggested that South African theatre can currently be seen as falling into three broad but overlapping traditions, loosely described as 'Reflective', 'Hard' and 'Thick' (see Flockemann 2009). 'Reflective art' has been opposed to 'visceral art' which aims for instant effects – such as those associated with theatres of ecstasy and excess. Reflective theatre is generally script-centred: it both reflects upon and re-presents aspects of the post-apartheid condition from diverse (though often conventionally staged) perspectives. Examples here include the later works of

Athol Fugard, including his most recent play, *The Train Driver* (2010), which revives some of the Fugardian dramaturgy of the past. Other examples are Nadia Davids's *Cissie* (2008) and Foot Newton's *Reach* (2008). 'Hard theatre' refers to more strongly issue-driven works which pose 'hard questions' about corruption, continuing social inequality and the plague of HIV and AIDS (Van Graan 2009: 9). This is aimed at provoking responses and is often refracted through comic or satirical modes, exemplified by the unapologetically political impetus of works such as Mike van Graan's *Iago's Last Dance* (2010) and Zakes Mda's 'The Bells of Amersfoort' (2002). On the other hand, 'thick' theatre (to borrow from Clifford Geertz's term 'thick description') gives physical expression to unspoken and half-recognised experiences. Drawing on local histories and vernacular traditions, it incorporates performance styles that unsettle surface realities and 'given' knowledge. 'Thick' theatre thus exhibits some of the features associated with the aesthetic legacies of the historical avant-garde, though it also needs to be seen in terms of a developing local aesthetic which deliberately draws on vernacular storytelling traditions and, in the case of Mbothwe, rehabilitates local languages as a medium of expression. This comprises work with diverse aesthetic signatures which have become associated with individual directors and companies. These include Foot Newton and her Masambe company, Bailey and Third World Bunfight, Mark Fleishman and Mbothwe of Magnet Theatre, as well as Grootboom, Yael Farber and Jay Pather, to mention some of the more significant players.

The danger here is that in some cases there is a straining after-effect or that the research may overlay the work, especially in collaborative productions. At their best, these productions transport the spectator through the power of story as performance, as in Bailey's *Orfeus* (2007) and Foot-Newton's *Karoo Moose* (2009). Bailey's lyrical retelling of the story of Orpheus uses site-specific installations which extend rather than fix the narrative through constantly unlocating and relocating it. In the process, claims Bailey in the programme author's note: 'I have twisted the thread of Greek myth through an African landscape, weaving it together with African stories and themes, following wherever it led me' (2007). The original myth recounts that a stranger poet-musician introduces the Greeks to an unfamiliar art form that offers social harmony. Bailey explains that his choice of Congolese musician Bebe for the role of Orfeus was not only for the haunting beauty of his voice, but also to speak to these restless times, 'blighted by violent xenophobia', in order 'to acknowledge the enrichment that foreign Africans bring into society' (Bailey 2009) (it should be remembered that Orpheus is killed by a mob). Recently, Bailey has shifted to performance installations and theatrical tableaux, moving beyond conventional theatre venues to inhabit and ambush audiences in ordinary urban or unexpected spaces. He acknowledges the variety of aesthetic traditions and conceptual frameworks that have shaped his vision: the strength of his work is that it is constantly shape-shifting, even though the core influences are African performance traditions and ritual, shamanism, Jung, Brecht and Artaud,[8] as well as ancient myths and stories 'that travel to us like the light of stars thousands of light years away' (2009). Yet especially in his recent work, these influences are so worked upon that they feel like something 'different' and 'new' in speaking to these present 'restless times'.

Foot Newton says in *Karoo Moose* that she worked mainly in terms of African storytelling traditions and the magical realist impulses generated by these. Nevertheless, reviewers, especially those situated outside South Africa, tend to read *Karoo Moose* as a combination of revenge tragedy combined with African storytelling (Fisher 2009). This highlights the nexus of aesthetic legacies informing (consciously or not) play-makers, spectators and reviewers. Originally *Karoo Moose* was envisioned as a film, based on an anecdote about a strange wild moose reported to have roamed the dry Karoo landscape. The play explores how fifteen-year-old Thozama, living in a no-hope, impoverished Karoo town, transcends her brutalising rape and despair through an encounter with and killing of the wondrous moose. The moose is embodied with elegant but comic pathos by a dancer-actor holding huge dry thorntree branches as antlers. Like the rest of the cast (apart from Chuma Sepotela as Thozama), the dancer-moose switches between roles, crossing generations and genders, in the process 'debunking patriarchal constructions of black masculinity' (Meersman 2007). As in Mavundla's *A Man and a Dog* and Mgqolozana's *A Man Who Is Not a Man*, the relationship between Thozama and the 'beast' is ambiguous. At one level it is an empathetic relation-ship: like her, the animal is hounded and reviled by the community; yet, in killing the moose (by mercifully slitting its throat), she achieves her own release (as does Mavundla's boy in killing the stepfather's dog). Meersman observes: 'The collective experience of theatre such as this functions in a similar way as Thozama's courageous act, when the escaped moose terrorising the imaginations of this small town is killed by her – a magical feat that releases her own power ...' (2007). This suggests that the terror is imagined, but at the same time that imagination is a source of terror.

In the work of both Bailey and Foot Newton there is a self-conscious awareness of the story as constructed by them as writers and yet apparently having a life of its own that lives itself out through performance. For instance, in Bailey's first production, *Ipi Zombi* (based on 'witch' killings in the Eastern Cape shortly after the 1994 election), the narrator announces: 'This is a story of this country... These are hungry times: the rich are eating the poor' (2003: 44). This then becomes a refrain: 'This is a hungry story' (74). At the end of the play, we are reminded that this is 'a true story'. At the same time the interchangeable agency of teller and tale is evoked: 'We are telling you this story, do you see how we die like flies, do you see how it eats us alive'; here 'it' suggests, amongst other things, the very story they are telling. This is reiterated in *Orfeus* where, as noted earlier, Bailey claims to follow wherever the story led him. In *Karoo Moose*, the story is seen almost as a character itself: 'stories are funny things,' we are told at the outset and a series of different narrators emphasise this; moreover, the story appears to have its own ideas about how it will end: the story itself is 'contemplating its outcome'. In fact, the play ends on a hopeful note as the young girl prepares to leave the dead-end town. Foot Newton says that because so many children like Thozama are denied a childhood, 'something magical was needed to break the cycle of violence' (Media Update 2010). However, Chris Thurman (2008) suggests that both the self-reflexivity of storytelling and the apparently optimistic ending have elicited criticism. For a number of reviewers the redemptive and optimistic ending is problematic in that it mystifies the real circumstances of child rape as experienced by young women like Thozama. On the other hand, it can be argued that the very self-consciousness of the storytelling is an attempt (successful or not) to interrupt hegemonic discourses by suggesting alternative ways of being – even if only imagined.

The power of these performed stories can be attributed not only to the theatre as constituting a virtual public sphere, but also to the way the disruption of time serves as a subversive intervention, associated with 'perceiving differently'. Drawing on Walter Benjamin's concept of *Jetztzeit*, or 'now time', Anna Schober refers to the effects generated when a specific past collides with an equally specific present to produce events 'filled with the presence of the now' (2009). This can introduce 'a momentous change in how we perceive the world', which interrupts 'the flow of hegemonic culture'. Furthermore, unlike fictional narratives such as the novel, which undergo a lengthy editing process before final publication, theatre and performance allows for work-in-progress to be seen publicly and then refashioned over time. This provides scope for aspirant young writers-director-performers such as Phewa to experiment by presenting work in various stages of play-making, especially at arts festivals. In addition, because of the contingencies of venues and staging arrangements, the work of some directors (Bailey is a good example) is revisioned and perceived differently at each new location.[9] When Mbothwe's *Ingcwaba lendoda lise cankwe ndlela* was performed in the Blue Hall in Khayelitsha – this time without English subtitles – I was struck by the enraptured and unusually silent audience, which included some elderly and some very young. This could be the effect of the incantatory 'deep' isiXhosa which serves as a form of aesthetic distancing, while at the same time there is the recognition of emotions and situations which are part of a common archive. But this archive may be different for different audiences. In this case, as we file into the hall, a woman (an incandescent performance by Faniswa Yisa) is already sitting there, waiting, but not for us. Next to her is an empty open suitcase; inside it, a single, lit candle. From time to time she gets up to look through us, as if searching the road (which we follow on the screen behind her), waiting for the owner of the suitcase to return. While this is a painfully familiar scene for the audience, most of whom are themselves migrants from the Eastern Cape, I was also struck by the image of that archetypal, patient, long-ago wife, Penelope, evoked in Ndebele's *The Cry of Winnie Mandela* (2003) – suggesting that texts can speak to one another, even if not directly.

Journeys and travel have featured strongly in the works discussed here, both as trope, subject and, as Kabwe points out, as a way of witnessing, self-reflexively, to the journey itself. It could be claimed, however, that in works by directors such as Bailey, Foot Newton and Mbothwe, 'the travelling is being done in the audience's mind' (Jenny Kemp, quoted in Guthrie 1996: 305) and is integral to getting audiences to 'perceive differently'. South African theatre in the new millennium in fact encompasses a healthy diversity of aesthetic legacies and future directions. This ranges from the redeployment of theatre traditions associated with the apartheid era to witness to a 'new struggle' (in one-handers such as *Itsoseng*), to telling 'the other side of the story' of migrant labour. The appeal of this evolving tradition lies in the associative thinking generated by some of the 'untranslatable' enigmas posed in a work such as Mbothwe's:

> Life is a riddle and the only one who can interpret is the great one
> They were visible in dreams but in the morning they vanished
> The fruit went ripe till it rotted
> Till when will I grow old on this road (2009).

There is, on the one hand, the poignant question: 'Till when will I grow old on this road'; on the other hand, there is the acknowledgement: 'This road calls me, waving for me to come, it is overwhelming'.

Notes

1. In an interview with Hazel Barnes, Mbothwe describes his theatre-making as an attempt to rediscover spiritual interconnectedness through theatre. He sees the colonial legacy as one of the reasons for a lack of connection, even with language – in this case isiXhosa:

    The wounds are so wet that people actually stop feeling the pain of the wound. The wound becomes them so much that it's their identity. It's the wound of making theatre using English, and the wound of only using their native language when they want to make a joke, or do comic relief in their play (unpublished interview 2009).

    A spiritual dimension is, as Brook notes, also at the heart of the work of practitioners such as Grotowski (Brown 2009).
2. Quoting play theorists such as Hans-Georg Gadamer and Inge Bretherton, Chinyola notes that 'the ability to create symbolic alternatives to reality is as deeply part of human experiences as the ability to construct adapted models of that reality' (2007: 15). He claims that 'the make-believe play frame aims to dissolve an order experienced as lacking or oppressive' (19).
3. Zikode's comments also have striking affinities with the 'everyday' experience of those at the receiving end of xenophobia (see Flockemann et al. 2010).
4. See, for instance, Malika Ndlovu's *A Coloured Place* (1999), Nadia Davids's *At Her Feet* (2006), and Rajesh Gopie's *Out of Bounds* (2008).
5. Kabwe is originally from Zambia, went to school in England and is currently on the staff of the Drama Department, University of Cape Town.
6. Unpublished script by kind permission of the author.
7. *The Baggage of Bags* is staged around a suitcase surrounded by a circle of large, colourful China bags. The suitcase serves as a sort of Pandora's Box of memories, while the China bags carry the props associated with the young woman's different masks or selves at stages of her life, articulated through the different voices she uses and manipulates.
8. Bailey's trilogy, *The Plays of Miracle and Wonder* is prefaced by a quotation from Artaud's *Theatre and the Plague* (2003: 9).
9. The first performances of *Orfeus* took place during a late-summer sunset on the Spier Wine Estate (Stellenbosch). The guide led us along a path through farmland to a dam (which mirrored the dramatic skyline) where the story began to unfold. From there we were led through a fantastical doorway that served as a threshold into the grotesque expanse of the now star-lit underworld. This clearly created an effect very different from the stark and confined quarry setting during mid-winter at the Grahamstown festival.

References

Appiah, Kwame Anthony. 2006. *Cosmopolitanism: Ethics in a World of Strangers*. London: Penguin.

Artaud, Antonin. 1936. *The Theatre and Its Double*. Translated by M.C. Richards. New York: Grove Press.

Bailey, Brett. 2003. *The Plays of Miracle and Wonder*. Cape Town: Double Storey.

———. 2009. 'Arts and the Hell of the African Underworld at the Holland Festival: Interview with Brett Bailey'. *Africaserver Magazine – Het leuke van Africa*, 26 May. http://www.africaserver.nl/magazine.html?taal = nl&art=a20090523142831095 (accessed 10 May 2010).

Brown, Mark. 2009. 'Grotowski in the 21st Century: Teatr Piesn Kozla (Song of the Goat Theatre). Wroclaw, Poland'. *Critical Stages: The IACT Webjournal*. Special issue: Theatre Legacy/Reclaiming the Legacy of Jerzy Grotowski. http://www.criticalstages.org/criticalstages/146 (accessed 18 March 2011).

Chinyola, Kennedy, C. 2007. 'Towards an Aesthetic Theory for African Popular Theatre'. *South African Theatre Journal* (21): 13–30.

Coetzee, Greig. 2009. *Johnny Boskak is Feeling Funny and Other Plays*. Pietermaritzburg: University of KwaZulu-Natal Press.

Corrigall, Mary. 2010. 'The Iconoclast'. *The Sunday Independent*, 24 January: 27.

Davids, Nadia. 2006. *At Her Feet*. Johannesburg: Oshun Books.

———. 2008. *Cissie*. Cape Town: Junkets Publisher.

Fisher, Philip. 2009. 'Karoo Moose'. *The British Theatre Guide*. http://www.british theatreguide.info/reviews/karoo-rev.htm (accessed 10 May 2010).

Flockemann, M. 2009. 'Facing the Stranger in the Mirror: Staged Complicities in Recent South African Performances' [unpublished paper].

Flockemann, M., K. Ngara, K. Roberts and W. Castle. 2010. 'The Everyday Experience of Xenophobia: Performing *The Crossing* from Zimbabwe to South Africa'. *Critical Arts* 24(2): 245–59.

Foot Newton, Lara. 2008. *Reach*. Johannesbug: Wits University Press.

———. 2009. *Karoo Moose*. London: Oberon Books.

Foster, Hal. 1994. *The Return of the Real: Art and Theory at the End of the Century*. Cambridge: Cambridge University Press.

Fugard, Athol. 2010. *The Train Driver*. Cape Town: Junkets Publisher.

Gopie, Rajesh. 2008. *Out of Bounds*. Cape Town: Junkets Publisher.

Grootboom, Mpumelelo Paul. 2009. *Foreplay* [unpublished script].

Grotowski, Jerzy. 1968. *Towards a Poor Theatre*. New York: Simon & Schuster.

Guthrie, Adrian John. 1996. 'When the Way Out Was In: Avant-Garde Theatre in Australia'. Ph.D. dissertation. New South Wales: University of Wollongong.

Hassim, Shireen, Tawana Kupe and Eric Worby (eds). 2009. *Go Home or Die Here: Violence, Xenophobia and the Reinvention of Difference*. Johannesburg: Wits University Press.

Hutchinson, Shaun. 2008. 'Review: *Itsoseng*'. *The New Black Magazine*, 16 September. http://www.thenewblackmagazine.com/view.aspx?index=1585 (accessed 18 March 2011).

Kabwe, Mwenya B. 2007. 'Transgressing Boundaries: Making Theatre from an Afropolitan Perspective'. *South African Theatre Journal* 21: 46–62.

Kgosidintsi, Mbali. 2009. *Tseleng: The Baggage of Bags* [unpublished script].

Kruger, Loren. 2002. *Post-Imperial Brecht: Politics and Performance, East and South*. Cambridge: Cambridge University Press.

Malusi, Omphile. 2008. *Itsoseng* and *For the Right Reasons*. Cape Town: Junkets Publisher.

Mavundla, Nhlanhla. 2006. *A Man and a Dog* [unpublished script].

Mbothwe, Mandla. 2009. *Ingcwaba lendoda lise cankwe ndlela* [unpublished script].

Mda, Zakes. 2002. 'The Bells of Amersfoort'. In: *Fools, Bell and the Habit of Eating: Three Satires*. Johannesburg: Wits University Press: 111–61.

Meersman, Brent. 2007. 'The Real Review: *Karoo Moose*'. *Mail & Guardian*, 14 October. http://realreview.co.za/tag/lara-foot-newton/ (accessed 10 May 2010).

———. 2009. 'New Audiences, New Fans'. *Mail & Guardian*, 24 December. http://www.mg.co.za/arricle/2009-12-24-new-audiences-fans (accessed 5 April 2010).

Mgqolozana, Thando. 2009. *A Man Who Is Not a Man*. Pietermaritzburg: University of KwaZulu-Natal Press.

Mngxitama, Andile. 2009. 'We Are Not All Like That: The Monster Bares Its Fangs'. In: *Go Home or Die Here: Violence, Xenophobia and the Reinvention of Difference*, edited by S. Hassim, T. Kupe and E. Worby. Johannesburg: Wits University Press: 197–8.

Media Update. 2010. 'Karoo Moose Returns to the Baxter'. http://www.mediaupdate.co.za/?ID story=27976 (accessed 12 April 2011).

Naidoo, Geraldine. 2004. *Chilli Boy* [unpublished script].

———. 2005. *Hoot* [unpublished script].

Ndebele, Njabulo S. 1991. 'The Redisovery of the Ordinary: Some New Writings in South Africa'. In: *The Rediscovery of the Ordinary: Essays on South African Literature and Culture*. Johannesburg: COSAS: 37–58.

———. 2003. *The Cry of Winnie Mandela: A Novel*. Cape Town: David Philip.

———. 2007. 'The Year of the Dog'. In: *Fine Lines from the Box: Further Thoughts about Our Country*. Cape Town: Umuzi: 251–6.

Ndlovu, Malika. 1999. *A Coloured Place*. Cape Town: University of Cape Town Press.

Osterloff, Barbara and Tomasz Milkowski. 2010. 'Working with Grotowski and After: Maja Komoroska'. *Critical Stages: The IATC Webjournal*. Special issue: Theatre Legacy/Reclaiming the Legacy of Jerzy Grotowski. http://www.criticalstages.org/critical stages/121?category=10 (accessed 16 April 2010).

Phewa, Asanda. 2009. *A Face like Mine* [unpublished script].

Power, Cormac. 2004. *Presence in Play: A Critique of Theories of Presence in Theatre*. Amsterdam and New York: Rodopi.

Roose-Evans, James. 1989. *Experimental Theatre: From Stanislavsky to Peter Brook*. London: Routledge.

Schober, Anna. 2009. 'Irony, Montage, Alienation: Political Tactics and the Invention of an Avant Garde Tradition'. *Afterimage*, November. http://www.allbusiness.com/trends-events/exhibitions/1387286-1.html (accessed 2 April 2010).

Thurman, Chris. 2008. 'Review: *Karoo Moose* (Lara Foot Newton)'. *Business Day*, 3 May. http://christhurman.net/reviews-interviews/review-karoo-moose-lara-foot-newton-html (accessed 10 May 2010).

Van Graan, Mike. 2009. 'The Arts of Democracy'. *Cape Times*, 9 March: 9.

———. 2010. *Iago's Last Dance*. Cape Town: Junkets Publisher.

Zikode, S'bu. 2006. 'We Are the Third Force'. htttp://www.abahlali.org/node/17 (accessed 10 March 2009).

8

'Sequestered from the winds of history'
Poetry and Politics

MICHAEL CHAPMAN

At the end of his book, *How to Read a Poem*, Terry Eagleton notes that of all the literary genres, 'poetry would seem the one most stubbornly resistant to political criticism, most sequestered from the winds of history' (2007: 164). A critic of Marxist persuasion, Eagleton says this not as negative judgement, but as recognition that poetry works in its own way, has its own 'thickness and density, which are not to be summarily reduced to symptoms of something else'. In almost the next sentence he might seem to refute his own statement when he asks: 'What kind of society is it in which poetry feels it has to turn its back? What has happened to the content of social experience when the poem feels compelled to take its own forms as its content, rather than draw from a common fund of meaning?' The questions, however, are rhetorical. Eagleton has provided his own context for recognising the uneasy relationship between poetry and politics. He paraphrases Roland Barthes's observation that a little form in poetry is a dangerous thing (i.e., a superficial splitting of form and content, a neglect of what is said for how it is said) while a large amount of form could be salutary (i.e., a more comprehensive grasp of form is like grasping the history of the political culture itself). To illustrate, Eagleton turns to Pope's heroic couplets: the balances, inversions and antitheses, disciplined within the paired pentameters as embodying the social ideology – order, harmony – of the eighteenth-century patrician class, or to Yeats's tone – his mournful resignation or defiant exaltation – as a register of the wider historical context: the decline of the Anglo-Irish governing class of which Yeats was a self-appointed representative (161–2). The politics of both Pope and Yeats are no doubt anathema to Eagleton's continuing Marxist commitment, yet he is able to appreciate the poetry.

Notwithstanding the distance of these two poets from the current state of British society, it is simpler in contemporary Europe or North America than in the politically overdetermined postcolonies of the world to appreciate the poetic medium even when its message is politically unpalatable. The relative value of form and content is an old story in South African literature, according to which we may chart the cultural wars of the 1970s and 1980s: Lionel Abrahams's (1987) individual vulnerability versus Jeremy Cronin's (1987) worker nobility; Stephen Watson's (1990 [1985]) denunciation of the politicisation of poetry; Michael Chapman's (1988) warning of constraints to the possibilities of imagination in a state of emergency, etc., etc. Closer to today, Kelwyn Sole (2005) grants 'content'-value not to most of the poets who are the subject of this chapter (in the spirit of 'class suicide' not even to the formal range of his own poetry, perhaps?), but to what have been described as the 'anti-mainstream', 'counterpublic' voices of literature collectives, such as the Botsotso Jesters, WEAVE and the Timbila Poetry Project.[1] The question is: has 'postliberation' in South Africa heralded a significant change in the uneasy relationship between poetry and politics? And, pertinent to the current enquiry, is there a content and a form to the descriptor, 'beyond 2000'?[2]

To such questions there are no neat answers. The unbannings of 2 February 1990 came as a jolt. The morally bankrupt National Party government, which had made a tactic of adjusting to crises, had evidently reached its end game. F.W. de Klerk's unbanning announcement engendered the catchphrase 'the new South Africa'. Art circles reacted with a sense of new challenges. What to write about after apartheid? Could colours, rhythms, rhyming and the private experience all replace the dour 'inartistic' speechscapes of political commitment? To those of political commitment, such questions confirmed the bad faith, the trivial moral sensibilities of many in the South African art world. The language of mutual antagonism produced its own reductiveness: bourgeoisie, Eurocentric, Africanism, the private Western lyric, the African oral voice, white aesthetics, black aesthetics. Peter Horn captured the leftist political response, a nightmare to the so-called bourgeoisie, when in taking issue with the 'dominant South African "canon" of reviewing', he stated that 'the debate about what would constitute an aesthetic of a new, democratic, non-racial, non-sexist, non-elitist South Africa has not yet even started in earnest' (1992: 5). To which Joan Metelerkamp, in a review of several volumes of poetry, replied: 'If one is going to talk of "an" aesthetic at all it cannot be a narrow one: different kinds of poetry appeal to different people and are useful for different ends (surely this is one of the criteria of democracy and fundamental human rights)' (1993: 119). And as if to show that she, who lives 'in the suburbs, in the white suburbs. I am. Ja, I accept it. Mothering in the white suburbs' (Berold

2003: 14), has remained alert to different kinds of poetry, Metelerkamp praises quite fulsomely Mongane Serote's lengthy, 'un-suburban' *Third World Express*:

> ... *this* is a *real* poem! ... The complexity of a long poem ... Serote grappling with the meanings of violence which lacks the allure of heroism ... the movement of the lines echoes the development of simplicity to complexity ... a symbol of process itself: there is nothing apocalyptic about it, even if it is powerful and noisy (1993: 120).

One might choose to find behind this literary appreciation a certain domestic anxiety, a relief, almost, that Serote does not advocate a takeover of the white suburbs. It is complexity – we are to understand – that lends *Third World Express* its value; it is a lack of complexity that, in contrast, condemns Sandile Dikeni's *Guava Juice* (1992) in its unalloyed exhortation to violence. 'Surely,' says Metelerkamp, with just a little condescension towards expression that 'eschews the questioning exploring "I"', this may be rousing at a political rally but it offers nothing new 'on the complexity of human experience in the eighties in the Cape ... surely, I was not the audience he [Dikeni] had in mind for the poems (a white woman, reading alone in her room in the suburbs)' (1993: 121). Unlike Dikeni – Metelerkamp concludes – Serote challenges Horn's 'parochial aesthetic, formally and thematically, by linking an immediate South African experience to the rest of the world' (120–1).

Whether Horn felt sufficiently chastised to change his 'parochial' tune or whether what he said was in the context of 'people's literature' (his words were published in *Staffrider*), his responses to questions put to him in 1995 deny any parochialism: 'I think there are ... three things really – that make great poetry ... having something to say ... a very individualised voice ... [and] we must break loose from preconceptions of what form is' (Berold 2003: 58). By way of illustration, Horn points to the content load of struggle poetry, to the distinctive voice of his own European inheritance and to a poetics sufficiently flexible to be adapted to the haiku, the lyric and oral praises. Of Serote, Horn says: '[H]e became weak in *Third World Express* ... too influenced by attempting to go back to his African roots', whereas in his earlier work there was a 'tension' between his political content and his 'speaking to a European [white South African?] audience' (60). Refuting any idea that because of his own commitment to the struggle he is a party ideologue, Horn makes clear that he will not defend the African National Congress (ANC) 'when it is indefensible' (62) and that any South African aesthetic is likely to invoke 'hybrids' of European and African 'ways of thinking and experiencing' (60).

The comments of both Metelerkamp and Horn are instructive. Despite each having particular preferences, neither endorses any reduction of poetry to a prescription. (Metelerkamp is at times narrower than Horn in that any poets who present women in ways which she regards as demeaning receive short shrift.) Neither ties categories such as Europe and Africa to rigid expectations of individualism or communalism, or closed (Western) lyrical forms or oral (African) expressiveness. Whatever the political talk (poets are citizens, who think and speak not only in the world of poetry), South African poetry talk, to its advantage, has always been and continues to be uneasy about its own threatened politicisation. Here are a few comments from South African poets on the subject:

> TATAMKHULU AFRIKA: 'After February 1990, it is still necessary to write a political poetry [as] a protest, not against political dominance but against dominance of wealth of privilege, residual class barriers, which are very much there... But we must write poetry which is poetry. It mustn't be sloganeering any more' (Berold 2003: 6–7).
> LESEGO RAMPOLOKENG: 'I've always tried to tread the midline between the word in motion, the word free – I mean without bounds – and the WRITTEN word... poetry that would leave a smudge on the page as it would on the stage' (Berold 2003: 32).
> KELWYN SOLE: '[W]e'll need a political poetry in the future: but not of the kind that mouths platitudes of praise, or is satisfied supporting politicians or institutionalised positions' (Berold 2003: 40–1).

It is partisanship that might well describe Serote's *History Is the Home Address* (2004), another of his 'epics', but without the experiential load, the complexity, which Metelerkamp found in the earlier *Third World Express*. In *History*, Serote displays his ANC colours in his resentment of those who attack then President Mbeki's AIDS-denialism: 'They don't understand the man,' we are told. 'Told' is the operative word: there is little rhythmical justification for the line breaks, cliché abounds and we are given roll-calls of heroes which, it is taken for granted, we will all endorse.

By the time of *History*, however, the social landscape had registered significant changes, changes even from the first years of freedom in the early 1990s. Disabusing South Africa of any exceptionalism, Alec Russell observes:

> The history of countries throwing off tyrannical regimes tends to follow a pattern. In the immediate aftermath there is euphoria, accompanied by utopian pledges for the future. Then the new rulers find the business of governing more difficult and messier than they could ever have imagined.

They also find that it is harder to overcome their own past than they had appreciated as they plotted their takeover in prison or in exile. It is in this second stage that the true meaning and trajectory of a revolution unfolds (2009: xiii).

Or, as Serote's one-time Black Consciousness Movement colleague Mamphela Ramphele puts it in the context of the withdrawal on technicalities by the National Prosecuting Authority of corruption charges against then ANC, now South African, president, Jacob Zuma: 'The conflation of the ruling party with the government and the state is fuelled by the myth of the ruling party as the liberator of a passive citizenry' (2009: 8). To turn the comment to poetry, Sole (possibly with Serote, now government apparatchik, in mind) says: 'When some of our older writers start getting comfy jobs as university professors, as members of parliament, at cultural desks, it's time for younger writers to get into the streets and hidden corners and find out how people are really living' (Berold 2003: 41). As Cronin in relation to Sole cannot be classified as an 'older writer', I must assume that Cronin is not being castigated here for having turned poetry into platitudes. That would be an unfair reflection on Cronin's achievement, which bears out in practice, I think, his reply to the question, 'so how do you find an aesthetics which will satisfy the lyric poet in you, while you are working in a political milieu?' (A leading figure in the South African Communist Party [SACP] and, therefore, a member of the 'tripartite alliance' of the ANC, SACP and the Congress of South African Trade Unions [Cosatu], Cronin is currently deputy minister of transport.) To the questioner, Cronin replies:

I suppose aesthetically I want the poems that I write to emerge from that full blast, from the conversation that is going on around all of us, in many registers, whether it be other poems, political debates, literacy classes, soap operas, the Truth and Reconciliation Commission evidence, or the monologic voice of CNN. Poetry has got to take its chances in the midst of all of that; it must emerge from public conversation and return to it. I would like poetry to be a fully fledged citizen in the midst of our complicated reality (Berold 2003: 129).

Language and form are to be eclectic; content, however, is to be directed to the intellectual challenge of our times which, according to Cronin, is 'to take on the deadening dogma of market totalitarianism, neo-liberalism' (129). Such a challenge, ironically, may not do justice to the range of Cronin's own poetry, in which he quarrels with the 'fatalistic assumptions of much lyrical writing' – poetry should be about the 'possibility', not the 'impossibility', of 'love and marriage, love and rearing kids, love and shopping' (128). Yet, a reference to family aside, the public sphere retains its primary purchase. It is a public sphere, at least, without Breyten Breytenbach's solipsistic despair (Cronin: 'Breyten ends up by declaring the whole post-1994 situation a sell-out' [133]) or Serote's denialisms (Cronin: 'Faced with the shortfall between reality and aspiration Serote incants the aspirational, over and over: "ah / where / where are those moments which can be magic".' [133]). What is required of South African poetry, rather, is that it 'force the actual and the desirable into continuous dialogue' (134). Or, as Afrika says: '[I]t's between the classicists and the new guys. I'm halfway between the two' (Berold 2003: 7) or, as Karen Press puts it, writing poetry is always 'being on the edge of falling off the world . . . Needing love, needing a kind of home that the universe doesn't offer you – there's all that mysterious human pain that goes beyond just being "an oppressed member of your class"' (Berold 2003: 19–20).

The aesthetic, then, has its various impulsions;[3] there are, however, recurrent features, summed up by Cronin as poetry trying to connect different discursive practices ('trying to be a fully fledged citizen in the midst of our complicated reality' [Berold 2003: 129]). It is what I have described elsewhere as poetry of the low mimetic (Chapman 2003[1996]: 414). Such an aesthetic (a post-apartheid aesthetic?) may be identified in distinction – and I am generalising for the sake of mapping a field – from a poetry of the high mimetic, such as we encounter in the work of Douglas Livingstone or Breyten Breytenbach or Patrick Cullinan or Wilma Stockenström, to name but four of several representatives of modernist predisposition. Theirs is a poetry that, in its abrupt juxtapositions of self-conscious form and elemental observation (sometimes occurring within a single poem), may be set aside somewhat from a low mimetic subscription to the language, rhythms and routines of ordinary living. Paradoxically, and in a different way, the high mimetic characterised also the Soweto poetry of the pre-1990 years, summarised – again, in a handy generalisation – by Njabulo S. Ndebele's (2006 [1991]) distinction between the 'spectacular' and the 'ordinary'. In its Fanonist psychodrama (a new language as constituent of a new social self) Soweto poetry is a poetry of 'high' confrontation: 'But what's good, is, I said it in his face, / A thing my father wouldn't dare do. / That's what's in this black "shit"' (Serote 1972: 8). When women appear in the universe of the high mimetic – to turn again to Metelerkamp's preoccupation (Berold 2003: 8–14) – their representation is likely to be iconic: Mary or Magdalen; Mother Afrika; sister of the [male] revolutionary hero, etc. The high mimetic is the inheritance also of Don Maclennan's considerable output of philosophical minimalism, in which the objective correlative, whether the bread and wine of existence or the anima-figure of sexual temptation, obeys the imagist tenet of the exact word as the adequate symbol. In short, Nick Meihuizen – one of the more astute commentators of the contemporary poetry scene – would not find it appropriate to apply to Livingstone, or even Maclennan, the critical register that he finds appropriate to the work of Chris Mann:

> *Heartlands* [2002] ... makes it that much easier to live in contemporary South Africa. Reading it is something of a lesson in living, loving, acknowledging, appreciating ... Consider the following from 'Carpark Oyster-sellers', where the poor and the downtrodden of the earth are a discomfiting, uncomfortable, haunting presence ...
>
> 'Please, my bossie,' she says. 'Me and my family is hungry.'
> You hate the blank-faced demeanour you use to distance her.
> You wince at the obsequious charade she starts to perform [25].
>
> Each poem is so well crafted, thought out, and so purely modest in its pretensions that it appears to be eternal, central, complete, even as it deals with transitory moments in changing history in a backward country on the edge of the world (2003: 75–7).

Not that poets of the high or the low mimetic have necessarily wished to acknowledge their poet-peers who live in this backward country on the edge of the world. Asked which poets have inspired them, which poets they admire, rarely do they acknowledge fellow South Africans. Despite a steady output of slim volumes in the 1990s and 2000s, the local poetry scene is small, somewhat incestuous, certainly not without its jealousies,[4] and the publishing opportunities are beholden to very few outlets.[5] In short, poetry is a minority genre, which does not feature prominently in university literature syllabuses, or in book-prize recognition. (Performance and slam sessions attract enthusiastic, younger audiences.)[6] Most reviewers are themselves practising poets and, as in South African literature since its inception, at least in English expression, the gaze across the waters signals a continuing colonial cringe. Meihuizen, whom I have just quoted – one of the few critics who is not also a publishing poet – usually intersperses his responses to the local scene with little pointers to wider (greater?) traditions. Gail Dendy's associative imagery, we are reminded (Meihuizen 2008: 42), has its antecedents in Hartley's influence on Coleridge's theories of the organic imagination and so on.

Refreshingly, black poets are not so predictably 'Eurocentric'. Unfortunately, however, outside of US/Third World rappers, the poet credited as formative (Ingoapele Madingoane) by both Rampolokeng and Vonani Bila had limited skill in the linguistic and structural demands of the printed page: like Madingoane before his death, Rampolokeng and Bila are adept at filling the theatre with sound. On the page, again like Madingoane, their lines veer from fire-power attacks on oppressive systems to repetitive, in their case, global cliché (like, 'Fuck the IMF, fuck the World Bank!'). It is with some justification that, in referring to Rampolokeng, Sarah Johnson coins the phrase, 'dirty aesthetics . . . of the gangsta rapper' (2003: 70).

To return to Barthes's observation on a large amount of form, what might an aesthetic of the post-1990s – an aesthetic which is the opposite of Romantic-symbolist modernism – suggest about the political culture? It may be that whereas the poets of the high mimetic felt compelled to pit the exceptional image or voice against the rigidity of big systems of authority – apartheid, the Cold War – poets of the 1990s, whether in South Africa or, let us say, in the former Eastern bloc, have experienced the new gradations of a civil space. Or, perhaps in the aftermath of the big systems there has been hesitancy about what to pursue, what to reject. Botsotso 'collective' pronouncements (if not always the voices of the individual poets), for example, see as the target a 'new mainstream' in the new South Africa (government-bourgeois collusion with the Washington consensus) even as they accept the cash offered by the new government's wish – through its National Arts Council – to promote diversity of the cultural voice. At the same time as they insult what they identify as an expanded middle class – a majority of whites, increasing numbers of upwardly mobile blacks, a consumer-conscious youth of all colours – Botsotso and the Timbila Poetry Project are not averse to courting the publishing houses of the mainstream that they profess to abhor (see note 1 on 'counterpublic' publishing).

One turns here to Ingrid de Kok to gain perspective on the challenges of a civil milieu. The times, she believes, call for 'historical decorum': 'Black people have gone through massive suffering and humiliation and appropriation. It behoves white people to be a little restrained, respectful, suspicious of themselves, as knowers of reality' (Berold 2003: 116). If 'decorum' to Botsotso can be a bourgeois swearword, so it is also to the white rapper Ewok, whose undoubted verbal punch has no ear for what might be historical decorum, no ear for moral distinctions between a class that has already risen and a class that now struggles to rise. Referring to businessman Schabir Shaik, convicted of a financially fraudulent relationship with then Deputy-President Zuma, and Zuma's comment to the judge at his rape trial that after unprotected sex he took a 'protective' shower, Ewok says:

'I'm sorry they had to Shaik you awake Mr Zuma . . . / I'm sorry they don make showers like they used ta Mr Zuma' ('Yo Mister' [2007: 74]). Whereas the trajectory in the era of struggle, De Kok continues, 'used to be forwards from suffering to a future utopia . . . now there's a reflection on history, the past, whether personal and national, and then individual and national compromise' (Berold 2003: 117). Without ignoring intimate joy and pain in her subtle lyrics – 'And grief is one thing nearly personal, / a hairline fracture in an individual skull' ('What Everyone Should Know about Grief' [2006: 58]) – De Kok is able to subject contemporary political enthusiasm for rewriting history (new names for towns, streets and buildings) to ironic contemplation:

> Let's put Verwoerd back
> on a public corner like a blister on the lips;
> let's walk past him and his moulded hat,
> direct traffic through his legs,
> and the legs of his cronies of steel and stone ('Bring Back the Statues' [2006: 124]).

We are all, whether poets or citizens, De Kok concludes, in need of some 'psychic reckoning, and that's a slow and arduous process' (Berold 2003: 117).

* * *

If the relationship between poetry and politics in the 1990s had its postliberation unease, then the terrain a decade on, in 2010, witnesses its own configurations of normalising experience punctuated by events of hyperbolic display, as in ANC Youth League/Women's League street anger at corruption allegations and rape charges against Zuma. The Zuma debacle – we can grant Ewok the singular 'truth' of his assaults on populism – impinged upon a democratic separation of powers. But perhaps not: voices of conscience, civil institutions, peaceful 2009 elections, the satirist's goading of the powerful, are proving to be resilient. (Cartoonist Zapiro was not cowed by Zuma's threats of libel action; in fact, whatever Zuma's shortcomings, he is not vengeful.) Were I to draw a parallel between the low mimetic and Sole's conception of 'quotidian experience . . . in postliberation South Africa' (2005: 182) I would grant the quotidian greater superstructural fluidity than is countenanced by Sole's political-economic base. Life for many flows in-between what Sole identifies as the co-existence in people's experience of 'utopian expectation and grim reality' (192). As I have outlined it, nonetheless, the poetry-politics question, in various ramifications, remains foregrounded in the commentary of poets who made their mark in the 1990s, and who since have been granted the authority of their pronouncements: among them, Afrika, Metelerkamp, Press, Ari Sitas, Watson, De Kok, Cronin, Sole, Rampolokeng, Mann. All continue to be active beyond 2000; all – Mann's recent turn to spiritual contemplation may be an exception (Levey and Mann 2007, Mann 2008) – continue to develop broadly within a low mimetic. Cronin's third collection, *More than a Casual Contact* (2006), for example, shows adeptness at connecting his lyrical voice to his project of 'normalising' the society:

> It's my friend, on TV, the minister,
> *'Now communities must learn*
> *To package themselves and their cultures.'*
>
> I think of poetry – when
> There's a sudden flouncing, knock-kneed
> Holding up of skirts that's neither
> Exotic nor packaged
> As the heron bolts off in pursuit of minnow ('Heron's place' [47–8]).

Almost rejecting the lyrical voice, Press in *The Little Museum of Working Life* (2004) pursues her poetic register to its 'literal' limit as she seeks a language – sometimes in the found poem – that does not detract from, but in its precision of observation accentuates, the burden of most people's daily lives:

> Monday is sausages
> Tuesday is chops
> Wednesday is rissoles
> . . . .
> go to bed, you've got school tomorrow
> . . . .
> we never went hungry, not one day in twenty years ('She came home every night and went straight into the kitchen' [46]).

Distinctions between the poetic and the prosaic are explored, too, in Sole's collection of prose poems *Land Dreaming* (2006). This is a series of finely judged, ironically foreshortened perspectives on a postliberation South Africa, in which 'liberation' has resulted too often in sardonic replays of entrenched racial positions: '[W]e also use leaves and twigs for coughs [. . .] My uncle said [. . .] / – no, Dick

[Mkhomazi Dindi], not actually. Your uncle was thinking of *Helichrysum nudifolium*' ('Gardening tips' [79]). Or, indeed, does liberation promise only greater freedom to be a charlatan?

> [. . .] My friend it's a miracle today that you
> receive this letter and you have to count yourself lucky.
> x Asthma, cancer, blood pressure, diabetes, body pains, x
> x epileptic fits, all skin diseases, AIDS symptoms gone! x
> [. . .] though if you want to speak to my spirits, that's a special arrangement
> ('This is not a chain letter' [81]).

In Sole's several collections, poems of personal or intimate relationship permit the 'rough edges of the real world out there to jag against [him]' (Berold 2003: 36); satires on what he sees as the white, elite South African literary tradition are mildly amusing; at times, a strenuous attention to postliberation failure carries the reader to the bedrock of the poet's economic quotidian; at other times, political conviction overrides verbal and rhythmical adroitness, threatening to shut down the potential of the poem.

For Bila the political *is* his poetry: in an interview with Robert Berold in 2000 it is as though his poetry is simply an adjunct to his political agenda (Berold 2003: 152–9), and there is a tendency in his Timbila Poetry Project, as in Botsotso manifestos, to elevate the message stridently over the medium. Considerations of aesthetic value are subsumed by assertions of a correct ideology, condemnatory of corporate culture and neo-liberal economics. This is a kind of social movement programme, in which the 'new mainstream' might be thought of as the bedfellows of the G20 club.[7] All this is in sharp contrast to De Kok's introspection on the responsibilities of tackling big issues. Commenting on her poem, 'At the Commission',

> Would it matter to know
> the detail called truth
> since, fast forwarded,
> the ending is the same,
> over and over? (2006: 63)

De Kok says:

> I think problems arise no matter how you write about the Truth Commission. The appropriating voice that 'shares' unbearable pain and loss is problematic. The omniscient narrator is problematic [but] I don't know

how you can write in South Africa and not reference this major revelatory complex mixture of truth and lying in some way. Yet it also seems impossible, invasive, to do so. The only way I can is to acknowledge the moral torment (Berold 2003: 115).

If 'collective' poets are often too certain of the truth of their own agenda to reflect moral torment, neither is 'moral torment' a phrase I would associate with the several voices which I want to separate from the 1990s in a category beyond 2000: at least, not moral torment fixed upon the big public-political issues; at times moral torment might invade private states, or be experienced in metaphysical dilemma. Yet even here, the term 'moral torment' has too heavy a notation. What distinguishes voices beyond 2000 is a tangential shift from art-politics interrogations towards forms of family habitation. An aesthetic of the low mimetic remains apt for ventures into a new content: a content that, under the banners of struggle, would have been derided too easily as 'bourgeois'. Whether Cronin's colleagues would wish to attach 'middle-class' intonations to his project of 'normalising our society' is debatable (see Berold 2003: 128). Nevertheless, the society of which Cronin's own family life is part can no longer be harnessed in its entirety to the demands of the political rally, but has to function increasingly in the routines of the everyday. The priority is no longer the toppling of the state, but the cultivating of myriad interactions between the private and the public domain. The desire for a home, a job, a safe environment for children, obviously has political ramifications, but such desires impinge, simultaneously, upon a need in all people for human flourishing, for an enriching emotional, imaginative and spiritual life. It is in such intimations that poetry may find a particular and distinctive signature.

Whose voices beyond 2000, accordingly, are contributing to a distinctive style of poetry-making? I confine my discussion to poets writing in English. I hardly know anything of the contemporary African-language poetry scene and am insufficiently abreast of contemporary Afrikaans poetry to do it justice (see Chapter 9 in this volume). I do not confine myself to poets of first collections, but look at those who to date have not enjoyed the same levels of publication or critical exposure as the poets to whom I have so far referred. The exception, as in the case of Antjie Krog, is when a significantly new development strikes me as characterising a poet's recent work. That the poets who have impressed me are mostly women is not reducible, I trust, to any '(male) public/(female) private' dichotomy. Rather, I would wish to apply, generally, Sole's observation on Metelerkamp's poetry: in citing Adrienne Rich and her desire to move 'out of the realm of men . . . [but] also to move into the realm of the brilliance of men, but on my own terms' (Cousins 1992: 24, 28), Metelerkamp associates her poetics, Sole says, with attention to 'detail and domesticity, but also to intellectual and creative work (spheres traditionally designated male)' (2005: 195).

So, in no particular order, I turn first to the enlivening language, the rhythms accentuated by judicious rhymes, that propel me into Phillippa Yaa de Villiers's (2006) world of tough love with responsibility, in which the flatlands of Jo'burg stretch any single conception of the middle-class life: '[I] set free / all the caged birds of my inner city' ('Connection' [37]). Rustum Kozain's (2005) wryly ironic portrait of his Coloured family is offset against his own struggles of identity and location: '*Kaalvoet*, we'd say, as an *armboer* [. . .] / Slavetongue become *witmanstaal*' ('Winter 2003' [109]). Whereas Mzi Mahola in 'In Memoriam Sizwe Kondile' (2006: 12–13) fails to transform the news story to poetic advantage, he succeeds, in a poem written in 1994 called 'Being Human', in evoking resonances of thought and feeling that reverberate beyond the simplicity of his actual words:

> Raising young ones is lovelier
> And tougher by far.
> Their easy laughter
> Puts a spark in my life,
> But each time they break
> It kills a part of me (2000: 11).

Mxolisi Nyezwa's (2008) is a similar talent to Mahola's, both poets so different in subtle self-interrogation from public exhortation: 'for days I looked for my poems in the streets [. . .] and children went for days / without food' ('for days I looked for my poems' [55]). Yet the public voice need not follow any manifesto, or be typified by Zuma's *Umshini Wami*, his machine-gun song and dance routine (Ewok: 'Lend me that machine gun when ye done, Mr Zuma!' [2007: 74]). Lebogang Mashile's (2005) oral rhythms, in contrast, sustain argument and self-reflection on home and exile; on the resources required to be a black woman in macho Jo'burg; on what, without narcissism, it is to love one's self:

> I smoked a spliff with Jesus Christ last night
> . . . .
> But he was Jesus
> And I'm a sister and I've been through more shit
> Because I'm black
> And life is hard in Jozi when you've got tits
> . . . .

> He saw me as a spirit lover sister mother
> Friend in arms like no other
> . . . .
> And how two spirits got real open
> When the herb was tight ('I smoked a spliff' [39–41]).

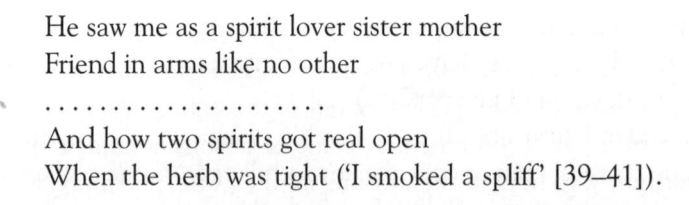

The value of the self devoid of selfishness, the challenges of relatedness in the family, recur in imaginative forms in several poets, including Megan Hall (2007) (disillusioned love disciplined to startling images), Colleen Higgs (2004) (surviving one's broken, lower middle-class white family), Liesl Jobson (2008) (wry observations on adult frailties), Helen Moffett (2010) (resilience against the disappointment of infertility), Fiona Zerbst (2010) (lyrical searches for tentative affirmation amidst loss) and, particularly impressive, Makhosazana Xaba's (2005, 2008) range from intimate portraits behind the public profile – 'I wish to write an epic poem about uMakabayi kaJama Zulu, / one that will be silent on her nephew, Shaka' ('Tongues of their Mothers' [2008: 25]) – to unusual juxtapositions in poems of personal relationship:

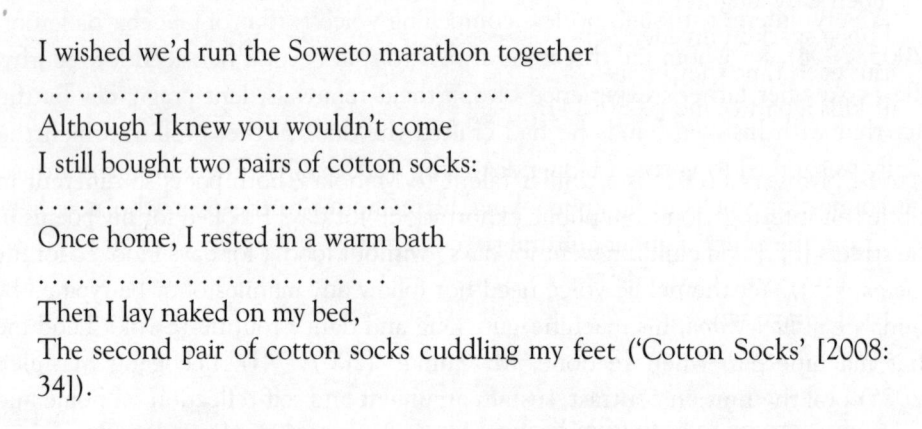

> I wished we'd run the Soweto marathon together
> . . . .
> Although I knew you wouldn't come
> I still bought two pairs of cotton socks:
> . . . .
> Once home, I rested in a warm bath
> . . . .
> Then I lay naked on my bed,
> The second pair of cotton socks cuddling my feet ('Cotton Socks' [2008: 34]).

We are reminded in Xaba's poetry that the middle class is no longer the preserve of white South Africa. It is in the light of such a reminder that Horn, a poet on the barricades in the 1970s and 1980s, continues to surprise us with his flexibility of response to the memorable voice. He writes appreciatively of Xaba's 'exact rendering of the everyday' and of the 'tenderness of real love poems' (2006: 118, 119).

A newspaper critic once remarked that, as Douglas Livingstone could make poetry out of the drabness of Durban, he must surely have talent. Sally-Ann Murray (2006), in acknowledging Livingstone ('After Douglas' [1]), shows that she can make poetry not only out of Durban, but out of almost anything: out of the detritus of the Mbilo River – 'The lower reaches float belly-up, / sluggish current slack against silt / *sif* with algal bloom' ('Mbilo' [72]) – or out of the killing of household rodents, or even pets that multiply beyond their welcome, as lessons not only to her children but, more significantly, to herself, the working mother, wife, and individual person living in the helter-skelter of domesticity:

> Come here then while I hold you tight. Listen:
> Stay away young ones from your mother who
> is exhausted; stay away from her she loves you
> too much so much you must leave her alone ('Vigour Mortis: an interminable domestic epic of life & death' [83]).

Sometimes, says Roy Robins, Murray 'isn't afraid to risk a poem over a gag – I am not sure this is a good thing' (2006: 53). But that is her daring. It is what gives us poems that, to quote Peter Strauss, 'are observant, witty, companionable (but not comfy)' (2007: 232).

A very different, though no less compelling voice is that of Gabeba Baderoon (2005, 2006), for whom life threatens always to spill beyond her need for security. She evokes her father's experience of apartheid removals, lent poignancy by the fact that with his own hands he had crafted the door of the dwelling which the family was forced to vacate ('How not to stop' [2006: 20]). There are, in contrast, the comforting smells of family cooking, as memories to the poet who now lives away from the country of her cultural ties:

> [. . .] I have slow,
> apricot memories
> . . . .
> A girl learning to keep from crying
> when she slices an onion, when
> she remembers the country she has left.
> All day I watch to keep from crying ('Hunger' [2005: 24]).

Baderoon brings normality to the experience of global citizenry: an experience of 'homelessness' enforced not by politics but, ironically, by the circumstances (love, marriage) of her own fulfilling life.

If delicacy of tone describes Baderoon, then humour, lightness and wit turned to the telling insight captures the flavour of Finuala Dowling's collections (2002,

2006, 2008): family triumphs in wicked juxtaposition to officialdom ('Census Man' [2002: 8–9]); detoxing connected, unexpectedly, to the sickness of the old apartheid state ('Detoxing' [2008: 26]); by wacky inversion, worms scoring higher in the polls than teenagers, or politicians:

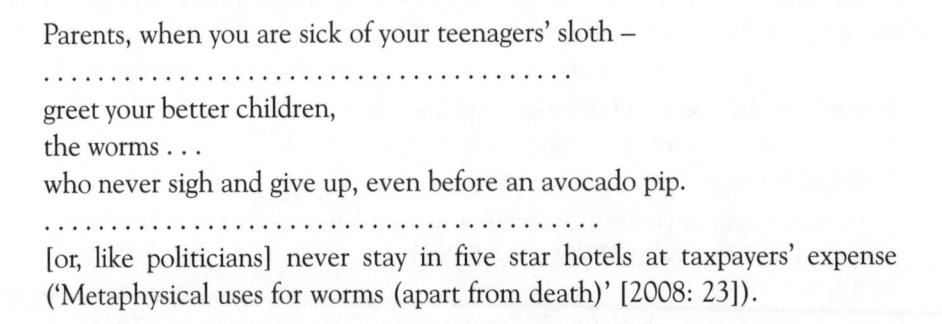

> Parents, when you are sick of your teenagers' sloth –
> ....
> greet your better children,
> the worms . . .
> who never sigh and give up, even before an avocado pip.
> ....
> [or, like politicians] never stay in five star hotels at taxpayers' expense ('Metaphysical uses for worms (apart from death)' [2008: 23]).

T.S. Eliot had it that modern poetry should be about both reading Spinoza and cooking: Dowling's suburbia manages to devour both its poetry and its lasagne, for '[t]here is an art to making lasagne while simultaneously / composing a poem. Lasagnes are quite complicated / and deep' ('Talk, share and listen' [2006: 77]).

Images of association – as Meihuizen (2008: 42) has pointed out – characterise Gail Dendy's strange, puzzling (the reader is sometimes left grasping for the connection), always challenging shifts from the mundane to the sublime. In 'Nipper' (2007: 43–4), the title referring to the name of the dog portrayed on old 'His Master's Voice' record labels, Dendy moves beyond the 'old vinyl's familiar scratch and hiss [. . . beyond, also] CDs and Dolby surround sound', to end with 'Dogstar [. . .] Pluto', in planetary transport 'fizzing like the future from out of the dark' (not so much Coleridgean association in this particular poem as an echo of the seventeenth-century Metaphysicals). Transportations between physical and metaphysical experience feature also in Wendy Woodward's (2008) struggles to expand the consciousness of our relatedness (human and animal) against the incursions of family life. In a climate of eco-awareness, the not-so-banal desire for a rodent-free home tests the purchase of this poet's humanist and intellectual ideals:

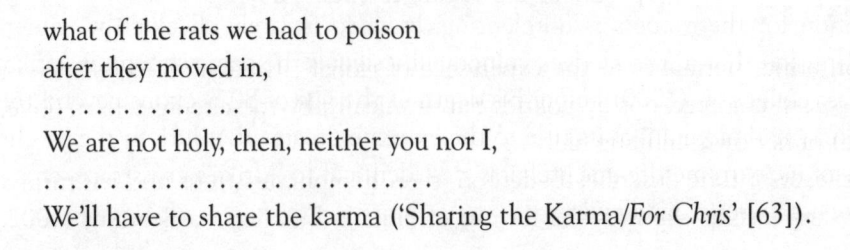

> what of the rats we had to poison
> after they moved in,
> ....
> We are not holy, then, neither you nor I,
> ....
> We'll have to share the karma ('Sharing the Karma/*For Chris*' [63]).

Both Mann and Shabbir Banoobhai – poets whose first work appeared in the 1970s – have sought in the last few years to introduce a spiritual resonance to their daily tasks and in their work. Mann's conflation of science and Heraclitan philosophy is shaped within poetic contemplation that is never far removed from the reality check of living in South Africa today (see, for example, 'Heraclitan Heresies' in *Heartlands* [2002: 16]). Banoobhai, who has begun to disseminate his poetry to an online readership, subjects the teasing paradoxes of ancient Islamic teaching to contemporary currents of thought and feeling:

> being who we are
> . . . .
> absorbed in ourselves we become a shadow
> of light; absorbed in peace we become
> light created from a shadow ('song of peace' [2004: 13]).

His lyrics remind us that, despite George W. Bush ('we'll smoke 'em out of their caves!'), the global interactiveness of the twenty-first century is inescapably about 'translated' selves: 'commit us to the suicide of our egos / fill the caves of our minds with emptiness / except for the light of your presence' ('Prayer' [2002: 9]).

In contrast to the sublime, Ike Mboni Muila (2004) asserts hard-living identities in the mingling of English and *isicamtho*, or tsotsi-taal, while Aryan Kaganof (2004) – 'up yours' to the 'Previously Dissed'!: 'You still getting dissed [. . .] Except for window dressing' (21) – revels in pushing the politically incorrect intrusion into whatever orifice presents itself: 'I apply my morning erection to her cinnamon passage' ('Vileness' [85]). As these poets rely on rapid-fire energy of words, it is not surprising that there are flaggings to even the most vitriolic (Muila) or deliberately shocking (Kaganoff) lines. Lisa Combrinck (2005), too, has difficulty, paradoxically to the benefit of her poetry, in sustaining a language, in her case, of sex shock as the route (or the root) to a liberation of the mind through the body: 'Masturbation is the obsession [. . .] Masturbation is a single candle, / [. . .] Above all, masturbation is a monologue, / a soliloquy to the self' ('Masturbation' [48]). Is this a 'diss' to South Africa's Afrikaner-Calvinist past? Whatever the case, provocation for these poets is unrelenting; bravado is rarely checked by vulnerability. Bravado that acknowledges vulnerability signals the achievement of Afrika, whose last collection (2000) before his death at the age of 80 beckons beyond the (Yeatsian?) 'mad old man' of its title to the extreme dreams that lurk in the psyche of many of us, extreme dreams probably not identical to Afrika's cross-race, cross-religious, homoerotic daredevilry:[8]

> Then we again mount [the motorcycle],
> slotting in our balls.
> But going where? – I
> but this old man dribbling his piss
> into midnight's sad bowl,
> shedding his as slow tears ('Pillion' [61]).

A no less shocking investigation of taboo experience places Krog almost as a new presence on the contemporary literary scene. Having expanded her reputation beyond that of a distinguished Afrikaans poet in her Truth and Reconciliation Commission-inspired 'autobiog/documentary', *Country of my Skull* (1998), Krog has regarded it as her project for the new millennium to seek connections across language and race divisions: a selection of her poems has appeared in English translation (2000); she has overseen the translation of African-language poems into Afrikaans (2002); like Stephen Watson (1991), Alan James (2001) and others, she has made available to contemporary readers 're-creations' from the Bleek and Lloyd collection of San/Bushman oral expression (2004a, 2004b); and, in both Afrikaans (*Verweerskrif*, 2006b) and English (*Body Bereft*, 2006a), she has approached, with uncomfortable honesty, the subject of ageing. The impact of these 'ageing' poems lies not in abstractable content, but in unflinching linguistic observation: more unflinching in Afrikaans than in the English equivalent.[9] We encounter a language of 'viscera' reaction: ' [M]eanwhile [if] terror lies exactly in how / one lives with the disintegrating body / [. . .] in how one resigns to vaginal atrophy and incontinence' ('God, Death, Love' [2006a: 20]), there are, at least for this poet, female compensations ('you no longer / use sex for yourself but for me [. . .] into the luxury of experience I stretch myself out') when

> at times it seems easier to rage
> against the dying of the light
> than to eke out
> the vocabulary of old age ('how do you say this' [2006a: 28–9]).

You might say, it is a case of a 'Dylan Thomas' grandiloquence punctured by 'bedpans [. . .] and something / that looked like a potato peeler' ('it is true' [2006a: 12]).

Not as uncompromising as Krog, but lending substance to any revaluation of the category 'middle class', or 'bourgeois', or 'suburban', we have Isobel Dixon's (2007) moving poems on her father's death (hospitals, wherever located, smell of the unromantic). There is Leon de Kock's (2006) unsparing sequence on the death of a marriage – 'so, the gloves are off, now / [. . .] a bicycle-spoke between the ribs' ('so, the gloves are off, now' [13]) – brief poems of emotional intensity which were followed in 2010 by poems of startling juxtaposition between the states of body and mind in which 'bodyhood', paradoxically of course, retains its fullness only through our mindscapes, in the 'impossibly difficult texts of each of us' ('Sorry for what, she asked' [15]). Kobus Moolman shifts tentatively from his earlier 're-arrangements' of the elements of our observations (2000) to poems in which he boldly confronts his own physical disability (2010): the world perceived through the disjointed anatomy of a hand separated from a foot, or feet, one good, one lame. And Malika Ndlovu (2010) journeys through the grief occasioned by the loss of her stillborn child, her voice giving way at intervals to medical and social perspectives on stillbirth and its effect on the bereaved woman: a 'genre-crossing' not as art choice, but as life necessity. Not even suburban living is as balanced as any would wish it to be.

* * *

To turn to suburbia – I use the term as a metaphor – is not fashionable. The objections of the politically and ethically engaged will remind us that in this country the suburb remains the preserve of a leafy few, who are still mainly white (as Kaganof says to the 'previously dissed', 'you still getting dissed' [2004: 21]). From suburbia, some among the leafy few might wish to divert their commitments to other communities (it is never comfortable to scrutinise oneself). Perhaps to divert attention to the homeless, as in this extract – chopped up here by me into a found poem – by the columnist Helen Walne:

> The couple arrived six months ago,
> his face framed by a grey beard;
> hers exposed beneath cropped hair.
> They sit on the bench with their belongings around them
> . . . .
> I wanted to know their story –
> how they had ended up there,
> huddling against a concrete wall at night,
> a patch of grass their mattress
> . . . .
> one day, he arrived for work
> and they had closed down and gone
> . . . .

> He thanked me when I handed him R20.
> And then I walked away, feeling like a fraud
> towards my house,
> with its backdoor and kettle
> and an oven
> which will blister red peppers for dinner.
> The two-ply toilet paper,
> the bath surrounded by bottles of stuff
> . . . .
> My home.
> My inside.
> I didn't even ask his name (2009: 11).

Yes, some in suburbia do live like this; many do not. Some may be classified as the 'privileged white upper-middle class' and, like this columnist, feel the need to let their guilt hang out; most, whether white, Indian, Coloured or African, live more humbly. Some whites, like Sole (he introduces the fact), grew up in 'lower middle-class . . . families' (Berold 2003: 34). Old-age pensioner, Afrika, always the 'other', lived both by choice and need in an outhouse in decidedly 'unleafy' surrounds. Despite Es'kia Mphahlele's (1981 [1967]) much-anthologised long story, 'Mrs Plum', the pampered white madam languishing in bed at ten in the morning is the stuff of caricature. So, I imagine, is the Mrs Plum who, as in Mphahlele's story, is dependent for sexual gratification on her pet pooch! My point is that the challenge, after apartheid, is to rehabilitate a more nuanced society; the challenge for the person of words is to break out of caricature, stereotype, simplification. Ja, Joan Metelerkamp, you are entitled to find fulfilment, or frustration, or whatever emotions move you to write poetry while 'mothering in the white suburbs'. It is not your fault that, in 2011, the suburbs can still be categorised as white or Indian or Coloured, or that townships are still poor and black. What Metelerkamp, like any other poet, needs to avoid in her poetry is an absorption in an experience that is either too domestically claustrophobic (2010) or too painful (2003) to open itself to the reader's own field of emotional empathy. The latter is the difficulty with the volume *Requiem*, provoked by her mother's self-inflicted death. What, to a degree, redeems *Requiem* is that it is not about blame.

Not only is there a kind of liberation in going beyond blame, but in the poetry I have discussed here there is also a pointer as to why Eagleton, whom I quoted at the beginning of this chapter, is able to identify poetry as the literary genre most resistant to political criticism. It is because the verbal invention most of us

'Sequestered from the winds of history'

associate with a poem, whether in shorter or longer form, leans towards lyricism. And lyricism, even of the low mimetic, favours the personal, expressive register, what Charles Altieri calls 'an excess beyond denotation' (2002: 24). (This holds good even for the deliberately flattened anti-poem, its short-line shape signalling its status as 'poem' in contrast to the lyric.) The poem does not ask the reader, immediately, for ethical consideration, but for imaginative participation. The difference between the oral expressiveness of Dikeni and the oral expressiveness of Mashile, for example, is that the former too often parades prescriptions for our endorsement while the latter pulls us into the poet's state of mind, persuading us to extend our sympathetic understanding. To turn again to Altieri (2002: 41–3), such states of mind touch our affective lives and, in consequence, we may (or, indeed, may not) be compelled by our participation to adapt or modify our ethical stance. If we are so compelled, it is because, to paraphrase Wittgenstein's dictum, there are dimensions to experience in which ethics and aesthetics are not necessarily mutually exclusive. It is to the value of such experience that, in a politically demanding society, poetry – the minority genre most 'sequestered from the winds of history' – may help to delineate the potential of everyday life. That such potential, if it is to be realised for the majority of South Africans, requires more than poetry is a fact that poets would be among the first to acknowledge.

Notes

1. The Botsotso Jesters – a multilingual performance poetry collective – was formed in 1994. Several of its early members were practising poets, including Allan Kolski Horwitz, Anna Varney, Siphiwe ka Ngwenya, Ike Muila, the late Isabella Motadinyane and Roy Blumenthal. The name 'Botsotso' – it refers to a style of jeans popular in the townships in the 1950s – was given also to a magazine on contemporary culture (Number 1, 1994). Besides the magazine, the collective has published several books of poetry, including the A-4 format of their 'collective' poems, *we jive like this* (1996); the first book bearing the Botsotso imprint, *No Free Sleeping* (1998), featuring Donald Parenzee, Vonani Bila and Alan Finlay; and edited by Michael Gardiner, *Throbbing Ink: Six South African Poets: Lilinda ka Ndlovu, Wisani Nghalaluma, Vonani wa ka Bila, Mbongeni Khumalo, Phomelelo Machika, Allan Kolski Horwitz* (2003). See the interview, 'Botsotso Jesters' (1998), with Robert Berold (2003: 118–26).

    Vonani Bila's Timbila Poetry Project – based at Elim in the Limpopo province – has published, among other collections, *Timbila 2001: A Journal of Onion Skin Poetry* (2001) and *Insight: Nosipho Kota, Alex Mohlabeng, Myesha Jenkins, Ayanda Billie, Themba ka Mathe, Righteous Common Man* (2003), edited by Alan Finlay and Siphiwe ka Ngwenya. A selection of Bila's poetry (*Handsome Jita*) was published in 2007 by University of KwaZulu-Natal Press, which also published Makhosazana Xaba's second book (2008), her first collection having appeared under the Timbila imprint in 2005.

The WEAVE Collective in Cape Town published *ink@boilingpoint: A Selection of 21st Century Black Women's Writing from the Tip of Africa* (2000), edited by Malika Ndlovu, Shelley Barry and Deela Khan. Joanna Helmsley and Roy Blumenthal edited for the South African NGO Coalition/Homeless Talk, *Of Money, Mandarins, and Peasants: A Collection of South African Poems about Poverty* (2000). Ari Sitas's *The RDP Poems* (2004) was published by the Durban-based Injula Co-operative. For information on 'counterpublic' publishing activities, see the unpublished Master's thesis by Alan Finlay (2009).

2. In addition to the works listed in the notes and references in this chapter, a list of poetry volumes and anthologies which were consulted in the writing of this chapter may be found in *Current Writing* 21(1&2), 2009: 192.
3. Referring to poems of the 1970s and 1980s, Denis Hirson, editor of the anthology of South African poetry, *The Lava of This Land* (1997), suggests that what runs through the poetry 'is that South Africans carry on singing through everything . . . if one begins to talk of a South African aesthetic, that quality of a transcendent song must be a key part of it' (Berold 2003: 81). While this is an interesting observation, it is too generalised to help us understand the range of the poetry, whether of the previous two or three decades, or of the contemporary scene.
4. As a single 'high profile' poetry squabble we had Stephen Watson (2005) accusing Antjie Krog (2006c) of plagiarism. Both had followed a South African 'tradition' of offering to contemporary readers versions of Bleek and Lloyd's nineteenth-century transcriptions and translations of San/Bushman oral expression.
5. The level of funding from abroad which, in the 1970s and 1980s, subsidised 'anti-apartheid' literary publishing diminished after the first democratic elections. Poetry publishing in the 1990s and 2000s has relied upon 'home industry' operations, such as Gus Ferguson's Snailpress and Robert Berold's Deep South, sometimes in association with new post-apartheid publishers such as Kwela Books and Umuzi (the latter a local imprint of Random House). Both Ferguson and Berold have encouraged a generous, wide-ranging view of poetry's potential. Poetry collectives have a more restricted focus on what they deem to be 'use' value (see note 1). Funds from the state National Arts Council and the National Lottery seek to enhance local cultural diversity with the priority on 'redress', particularly in the case of African-language publications. When the University of KwaZulu-Natal Press ventured into poetry, it was inundated with manuscripts and has now suspended its poetry publishing programme. In an age of desktop publishing, several poets have simply published their own work.
6. The annual Poetry Africa Festival (Centre for Creative Arts, University of KwaZulu-Natal), for example, has moved increasingly to performance poetry. Performance also defined the 2009 Cape Town-based Badilisha Poetry X-Change (Africa Centre, 22–25 May). Among the local participants were Emile Jansen of Black Noise, Megan Hall, Loftus Marais, the duo of Kai Lossgott and Mbali Vilakazi, Phillippa Yaa de Villiers, Eric Minyeni, iBushwomen (the sister collective of Tereska Muishond and Lavene da Silva), Jessica Mbangeni, and the father

and daughter collaboration of Ntokozo and Bhekimpi Madlala. On the programme were also poet-performers from Zimbabwe, the Democratice Republic of Congo, the UK and the US.
7. Yet, in apparent contradistinction to 'manifesto talk', editor of the journal *Botsotso*, Allan Kolski Horwitz, says: 'The political and aesthetic openness we practise enables diverse writers and artists to work under our umbrella' (Horwitz and Accone 2008).
8. Of unusually pale-skin pigmentation, Afrika, under apartheid legislation, had himself reclassified to his own social disadvantage as a 'non-white'; his bi-/homosexual predilections were in conflict with his turning to the Muslim faith (see Stobie 2007).
9. Although her argument is not focused on *Body Bereft*, see Christine Marshall (2007) for illuminating comparisons of Krog's Afrikaans and English poetic language. See also Chapter 10 in this volume.

References

Abrahams, Lionel. 1987. 'Reply to Cronin's "Poetry: An Elite Pastime Finds Mass Roots"'. *Weekly Mail*, 3–9 April: 24.
Afrika, Tatamkhulu. 2000. *Mad Old Man under the Morning Star*. Cape Town: Snailpress.
Altieri, Charles. 2002. 'The Literary and the Ethical: Difference as Definition'. In: *The Question of Literature*, edited by E.B. Bissell. Manchester: Manchester University Press: 19–43.
Baderoon, Gabeba. 2005. *The Dream in the Next Body: Poems*. Cape Town: Kwela Books (in association with Snailpress).
———. 2006. *A Hundred Silences*. Cape Town: Kwela Books (in association with Snailpress).
Banoobhai, Shabbir. 2002. *inward moon, outward sun*. Pietermaritzburg: University of Natal Press.
Banoobhai, Shabbir (with photographs by John Cleare). 2004. *book of songs*. Johannesburg: Wits University Press.
Berold, Robert (ed.). 2003. *South African Poets on Poetry: Interviews from New Coin 1992–2001*. Pietermaritzburg: University of KwaZulu-Natal Press.
Bila, Vonani. 2007. *Handsome Jita: Selected Poems*. Pietermaritzburg: University of KwaZulu-Natal Press.
Bila, Vonani (ed.). 2001. *Timbila 2001: A Journal of Onion Skin Poetry*. Elim: Timbila Poetry Project.
Bissell, Elizabeth Beaumont. 2002. *The Question of Literature*. Manchester: Manchester University Press.
Botsotso Jesters. 1996. *we jive like this*. Johannesburg: Botsotso Publishing.
Chapman, Michael. 1988. 'The Liberated Zone: The Possibilities of Imaginative Expression in a State of Emergency'. *English Academy Review* 5: 23–53.
———. 2003 [1996]. *Southern African Literatures*. Pietermaritzburg: University of KwaZulu-Natal Press.
Combrinck, Lisa. 2005. *An Infinite Longing for Love*. Pretoria: Skotaville Media Publications.
Cousins, Colleen Crawford. 1992. 'Interview: Joan Metelerkamp'. *New Coin* 28(2): 24–8.
Cronin, Jeremy. 1987. 'Poetry: An Elitist Pastime Finds Mass Roots'. *Weekly Mail*, 13–19 March: 22.

———. 2006. *More than a Casual Contact*. Cape Town: Umuzi.
De Kock, Leon. 2006. *gone to the edges*. Pretoria: Protea Book House.
———. 2010. *Bodyhood*. Cape Town: Umuzi.
De Kok, Ingrid. 2006. *Seasonal Fires: New and Selected Poems*. Cape Town: Umuzi.
Dendy, Gail. 2007. *The Lady Missionary: Poetry*. Cape Town: Kwela Books (in association with Snailpress).
De Villiers, Phillippa Yaa. 2006. *Taller than Buildings*. Johannesburg: Phillippa de Villiers.
Dikeni, Sandile. 1992. *Guava Juice*. Cape Town: Mayibuye Books.
Dixon, Isobel. 2007. *A Fold in the Map*. Johannesburg: Jacana Media.
Dowling, Finuala. 2002. *I Flying*. Cape Town: Carapace.
———. 2006. *Doo-Wop Girls of the Universe: A Collection of Poems*. Johannesburg: Penguin.
———. 2008. *Notes from the Dementia Ward*. Cape Town: Kwela Books.
Eagleton, Terry. 2007. *How to Read a Poem*. Oxford: Blackwell Publishers.
Ewok (Iain Gregory Robinson). 2007. *Word: Customized Hype*. Empangeni: Echoing Green Press.
Finlay, Alan W. 2009. 'Making Space: The Counterpublics of Post-Apartheid Independent Publishing Activities (1994–2004)'. Master's thesis. Johannesburg: University of the Witwatersrand.
Finlay, Alan and Siphiwe ka Ngwenya (eds). 2003. *Insight: Nosipho Kota, Alex Mohlabeng, Myesha Jenkins, Ayanda Billie, Themba ka Mathe, Righteous Common Man*. Elim: Timbila Poetry Project.
Gardiner, Michael (ed.). 2003. *Throbbing Ink: Six South African Poets: Lilinda ka Ndlovu, Wisani Nghalaluma, Vonani wa ka Bila, Mbongeni Khumalo, Phomelelo Machika, Allan Kolski Horwitz*. Johannesburg: Botsotso Publishing.
Hall, Megan. 2007. *Fourth Child*. Athlone: Modjaji Books.
Helmsley, Joanna and Roy Blumenthal (eds). 2000. *Of Money, Mandarins, and Peasants: A Collection of South African Poems about Poverty*. Cape Town: South African NGO Coalition/ Homeless Talk.
Higgs, Colleen. 2004. *Halfborn Women*. Cape Town: Hands-On Books.
Hirson, Denis (ed.). 1996. *The Lava of This Land: South African Poetry 1960–1996*. Evanston: TriQuarterly Books, Northwestern University Press.
Horn, Peter. 1992. 'Comment'. *Staffrider* 10(3): 5.
———. 2006. 'Review: Makhosazana Xaba'. *New Contrast* 34 (1&2):116–19.
Horwitz, Allan Kolski and Darryl Accone. 2008. 'Innovative Platforms for Local Literature'. *Mail & Guardian*, 20 August. http://mg.co.za/article/2008-08-20-innovative-platforms-for-local-literature (accessed 12 April 2011).
James, Alan. 2001. *The First Bushman's Path: Stories, Songs and Testimonies of the Xam of the Northern Cape*. Pietermaritzburg: University of Natal Press.
Jobson, Liesel. 2008. *View from an Escalator*. Johannesburg: Botsotso Publishing.
Johnson, Sarah. 2003. 'Review: It All Begins: Poems from Postliberation South Africa'. *New Contrast* 31(3): 68–73.
Kaganof, Aryan. 2004. *Post Mortemist Poems*. Johannesburg: Pine Slope Publications.
Kozain, Rustum. 2005. *This Carting Life*. Cape Town: Kwela Books (in association with Snailpress).
Krog, Antjie. 1998. *Country of my Skull*. Johannesburg: Random House.

———. 2000. *Down to my Last Skin*. Johannesburg: Random House.
———. 2002. *Met woorde soos met kerse: Inheemse verse uitgesoek en vertaal deur Antjie Krog en ander*. Cape Town: Kwela Books.
———. 2004a. *die sterre sê 'tsau': /Xam Gedigte van Diä!kwain, Kweiten-ta-//ken, /A!Kúnta, / Han?kass'o and //Kabbo*. Cape Town: Kwela Books.
———. 2004b. *the stars say 'tsau': /Xam Poetry of Diä!kwain, Kweiten-ta-//ken, /A!Kúnta, / Han?kass'o and //Kabbo*. Cape Town: Kwela Books.
———. 2006a. *Body Bereft*. Cape Town: Umuzi.
———. 2006b. *Verweerskrif*. Cape Town: Umuzi.
———. 2006c. 'Stephen Watson and the Annals of Plagiarism'. *New Contrast* 34(5): 72–7.
Levey, David and Chris Mann. 2007. 'Environmentally Aware Art, Poetry, Music and Spirituality'. *Alternation* 14(2): 218–37.
Loomba, Ania, Suvir Kaul, Matti Bunzl, Antoinette Burton and Jed Esty (eds). 2005. *Postcolonial Studies and Beyond*. Durham: Duke University Press.
Mahola, Mzi. 2000. *When Rains Come*. Cape Town: Carapace.
———. 2006. *Dancing in the Rain*. Pietermaritzburg: University of KwaZulu-Natal Press.
Mann, Chris. 2002. *Heartlands*. Pietermaritzburg: University of Natal Press.
———. 2008. 'Seeing the Cosmos in a Grain of Sand'. *Current Writing* 20(2): 108–26.
Marshall, Christine. 2007. 'A Change of Tongue: Antjie Krog's Poetry in English'. *Scrutiny2* 12(1): 72–92.
Mashile, Lebogang. 2005. *In a Ribbon of Rhythm*. Johannesburg: Mutloatse Arts Heritage Trust and Oshun Books.
Meihuizen, Nick. 2003. 'Review'. *Scrutiny2* 8(1): 75–8.
———. 2008. 'Review: Gail Dendy'. *New Contrast* 36(4): 41–5.
Metelerkamp, Joan. 1993. 'Review'. *Current Writing* 5(1): 119–27.
———. 2003. *Requiem*. Grahamstown: Deep South.
———. 2010. *Burnt Offering*. Athlone: Modjaji Books.
Moffett, Helen. 2010. *Strange Fruit*. Athlone: Modjaji Books.
Moolman, Kobus. 2000. *Time Like Stone*. Pietermaritzburg: University of Natal Press.
———. 2010. *Light and After*. Grahamstown: Deep South.
Mphahlele, Es'kia. 1981 [1967]. 'Mrs Plum'. In: *The Unbroken Song: Selected Writings*. Johannesburg: Ravan Press: 216–61.
Muila, Ike Mboni. 2004. *Gova*. Johannesburg: Botsotso Publishing.
Murray, Sally-Ann. 2006. *Open Season: Poems*. Durban: HardPressed.
Ndebele, Njabulo S. 2006 [1991]. 'The Rediscovery of the Ordinary: Some New Writings in South Africa'. In: *Rediscovery of the Ordinary: Essays on South African Literature and Culture*. Pietermaritzburg: University of KwaZulu-Natal Press: 31–54.
Ndlovu, Malika. 2010. *Invisible Earthquake: A Woman's Journey through Stillbirth*. Athlone: Modjaji Books.
Ndlovu, Malika, Shelley Barry and Deela Khan (eds). 2000. *ink@boilingpoint: A Selection of 21st Century Black Women's Writing from the Tip of Africa*. Cape Town: The WEAVE Collective.
Nyezwa, Mxolisi. 2008. *New Country*. Pietermaritzburg: University of KwaZulu-Natal Press.
Parenzee, Donald, Vonani Bila and Alan Finlay. 1998. *No Free Sleeping*. Johannesburg: Botsotso Publishing.

Press, Karen. 2004. *The Little Museum of Working Life*. Pietermaritzburg: University of KwaZulu-Natal Press.
Ramphele, Mamphela. 2009. 'Comment'. *Mail & Guardian*, 9–16 April: 8.
Robins, Roy. 2006. 'Review: Sally-Ann Murray'. *New Contrast* 34(4): 51–3.
Russell, Alec. 2009. *After Mandela: The Battle for the Soul of South Africa*. London: Hutchinson.
Serote, Mongane Wally. 1972. *Yakhal'inkomo*. Johannesburg: Ad. Donker.
———. 1992. *Third World Express*. Cape Town: David Philip.
———. 2004. *History Is the Home Address: A Poem*. Cape Town: Kwela Books.
Sitas, Ari. 2004. *The RDP Poems*. Durban: Injula Co-operative.
Sole, Kelwyn. 2005. 'The Deep Thoughts the One in Need Falls Into: Quotidian Experience and the Perspective of Poetry in Postliberation South Africa'. In: *Postcolonial Studies and Beyond*, edited by A. Loomba et al. Durham: Duke University Press: 182–205.
———. 2006. *Land Dreaming: Prose Poems*. Pietermaritzburg: University of KwaZulu-Natal Press.
Strauss, Peter. 2007. 'Review: Sally-Ann Murray'. *Current Writing* 19(2): 231–2.
Stobie, Cheryl. 2007. 'Shedding Skins: Metaphors of Race and Sexuality in the Writing of Tatamkhulu Afrika'. *Journal of Literary Studies* 23(2): 148–65.
Walne, Helen. 2009. 'Human League'. *Cape Argus*, 14 April: 11.
Watson, Stephen. 1990 [1985]. 'Poetry and Politicisation'. In: *Selected Essays 1980–1990*. Cape Town: The Carrefour Press: 9–20.
———. 1991. *The Return of the Moon: Versions from the /Xam*. Cape Town: The Carrefour Press.
———. 2005. 'Annals of Plagiarism: Antjie Krog and the Bleek and Lloyd Collection'. *New Contrast* 32(2): 48–61.
Woodward, Wendy. 2008. *Love, Hades and Other Animals*. Pretoria: Protea Book House.
Xaba, Makhosazana. 2005. *These Hands*. Elim: Timbila Poetry Project.
———. 2008. *Tongues of their Mothers*. Pietermaritzburg: University of KwaZulu-Natal Press.
Zerbst, Fiona. 2010. *Oleander*. Athlone: Modjaji Books.

9

Of 'Chisels' and 'Jack Hammers'
Afrikaans Poetry 2000–2009

LOUISE VILJOEN

Afrikaans poetry 2000–2009: Devices, themes, tropes

The years around the millennium change were marked by pessimism about the continued existence and viability of Afrikaans poetry. This was the result of several factors: a general *fin de millénaire* unease about the state and sustainablility of (Afrikaans) culture in the twenty-first century, uncertainty about the way in which South African politics would develop after the end of the Mandela presidency in 1999, developments in the (Afrikaans) publishing industry and a fear that an elitist genre such as poetry would have difficulty in surviving in an era that favours the novel (see Adendorff 2003 and Odendaal 2006). By the end of the first decade of the millennium critics were able to paint a more favourable picture, referring to renewed interest and productivity (see Kleyn 2008) as well as a significant increase in the publication of important debut volumes (Visagie 2009). The index of volumes published between 2000 and 2009 provided by the *Versindaba* (Poetry Indaba) website, set up to give coverage to Afrikaans poetry, bears out the renewed confidence in the genre. It records a total of 190 publications (including reprints, selections, translations and anthologies) for this period. The breakdown into number of publications per year indicates an increase from the number of volumes published in the first half of the decade (78 publications from 2000–2004) to the second half (112 publications from 2005–2009).

Although my present project is a more modest one than Franco Moretti's attempt to understand trends in world literature, this chapter follows him in employing a 'distant reading', which allows me to focus on 'units that are much smaller or much larger than the text: devices, themes, tropes – or genres and systems' (Moretti 2000: 57). In surveying Afrikaans poetry written between 1960 and 1997, Helize van Vuuren suggests that thematic changes in literary texts are usually triggered by socio-political contexts whereas formal or aesthetic changes can be related to the tension between tradition and renewal as well as the influences of other cultures (1999: 245). To a certain extent this is also true of Afrikaans poetry published in the period 2000–2009. Several of the most prominent themes and accompanying tropes (identity, language, socio-political commentary, the use of indigenous cultural materials) can be traced to the socio-political context in which the poetry was produced, whereas other themes reflect universal concerns (the body, the environment, death, family matters, intertextual connections). The formal changes or new devices (most notably, the move towards a more accessible style of poetry making use of narrative elements) emerging in this period can be related to renewed pressure on cultural forms perceived as elitist and inaccessible, as well as internal reactions and counter-reactions in the Afrikaans literary system.

In this chapter I address the most prominent formal change in the Afrikaans poetry of the past decade and then focus on certain important thematic trends. It is in the nature of an overview such as this that it can only draw bold lines and, of necessity, has to ignore finer distinctions. It is also not possible to include references to all of the volumes published in the decade under discussion, so that certain gaps and omissions are inevitable. My reading is highly selective, focusing on certain features of a volume and ignoring others for the sake of the argument.

Formal changes: The 'narrative turn'

Although narrative poetry has always been an integral part of the Afrikaans literary tradition, it has gained renewed prominence in the past decade after the publication of strong debut volumes by Danie Marais (2006), Carina Stander (2006), Bernard Odendaal (2007), Ronelda Kamfer (2008) and Loftus Marais (2008), all characterised to some degree by narrative features, anecdotal elements and a *parlando* style (approximating ordinary speech). In the ensuing discussions the opposition between narrative and lyrical poetry was soon equated with, or at least compared to, the opposition between accessible and hermetic poetry. This inevitably led to debates about what would constitute real poetry (as opposed to fake poetry) and good or interesting poetry (as opposed to bad or uninteresting poetry). Lina Spies (2004) and Marlene van Niekerk (2009) have both expressed their dismay at the seemingly effortless production of reams of anecdotal, narrative poetry that show little prosodic discipline, inner tension or complexity. In reaction to this, poets Marais (2009) and Charl-Pierre Naudé (2009) defended their own use of narrative elements in lyrical poems.

Marais's debut volume *In die buitenste ruimte* (In outer space) (2006) contains a number of long poems but also functions as a narrative whole that charts the breakup of its protagonist's marriage to his German wife, his feelings of alienation in Germany (as strong as if he were in outer space) and his (not uncritical) nostalgia for South Africa and Afrikaans.[1] The fact that the narrating voice in this volume coincides with that of the author reinforces the impression that Afrikaans narrative poetry tends to be autobiographical.

Naudé's second volume, *In die geheim van die dag* (In the secret of the day) (2004), also includes several long poems (often consisting of more than eighty lines) which narrate a specific incident and are written in long prose-like lines. These poems illustrate Naudé's point that the narrative itself eventually becomes a symbol. The subtitle of the lengthy poem 'Hoe ek my naam gekry het (of: 'n Beknopte relaas van kolonisasie)' (How I got my name [or: A brief account of colonisation]) gives an indication of what the narration it contains might symbolise. Naudé's poetry undermines established notions about the lyric poem's structuring of sound, rhythm, image, style and its multiplication of meanings through the intensive play on words. He refers to the carefully wrought 'illusion of the absence of poetic craft or style' in his own and other Afrikaans poets' narrative poems, pointing out that the craft lies in the deliberate concealment of style and the re-creation of an everyday narrative voice in order to foreground the narrative, which then attains its symbolic meaning (2009).

The same holds true for the deceptively simple poetic style of Kamfer's debut volume *Noudat slapende honde* (Now that sleeping dogs) (2008), which includes a number of narrative poems, mostly about life on the Cape Flats. Kamfer uses a laconic, almost deadpan poetic voice to relate her stories, amongst which are those about a young boy who became the victim of a bullet fired in a gang fight ('*Klein Cardo*' [Little Cardo]) and the woman who killed her husband and children ('*die huisvrou*' [the housewife]).

Although the 'narrative turn' is a strong trend in the work of recent debut poets, there are poets who uphold the tradition of hermetic poetry in Afrikaans, perhaps best exemplified by Breyten Breytenbach's complex, even obscure prison poetry published in the 1980s. This was continued in the past decade by Gilbert Gibson who made his debut in 2005 and published three volumes in quick succession: *Boomplaats* (2005), *Kaplyn* (Cleared borderline) (2007) and *Oogensiklopedie* (Encyclopedia of the eye) (2009). These volumes are characterised by dense imagery, extensive fields of reference, innovative structures (the poems in his volume *Oogensiklopedie* are arranged alphabetically rather than thematically), a wide range of intertextual references and complicated word games, with the result that individual poems are often difficult to decipher.

Themes evoked by the socio-political context

The profound political and social changes South Africa experienced in the 1990s led to the foregrounding of certain themes in Afrikaans literature, some of which were still pursued in poetry written after 2000. Amongst these were concerns with identity, language, the socio-political situation in the country and indigenous cultural materials. These themes often overlap and interact with each other, so that there will be some blurring of boundaries between the categories.

Identity

As suggested above, the transformation of South African society, the proceedings of the Truth and Reconciliation Commission (TRC) and the growing impact of globalisation in the 1990s led to Afrikaans writers' renewed engagement with the notion of identity. This trend was continued in the poetry written in the first decade of the new century, with new accents and nuances emerging under the pressure of unfolding events. To give an idea of the range of views and approaches to this theme, I will contrast Antjie Krog's work with that of Breytenbach, Diana Ferrus's work with that of Kamfer and Odendaal's work with that of Andries Bezuidenhout.

Krog and Breytenbach, two of the strongest poets currently writing in Afrikaans, both engage with the theme of identity in the volumes they published in the past decade. Although Krog (2000a: 47) refers to her distaste for the devious dealings at the 'barcounter of identities' in *Kleur kom nooit alleen nie* (Colour never comes on its own), the volume nevertheless concentrates on her attempts at redefining her own identity in a changed South Africa. The cycle *'land van genade en verdriet'* (translated as 'country of grief and grace' in *Down to my Last Skin* [2000b]) tries to deal with the feelings of Afrikaner guilt caused by revelations at the TRC and to transcend the category of race as the most important determinant of a South African identity. Another cycle of poems, *'van litteken tot stad'* (from scar to city), describes Krog's attempts to define herself as an African during a journey through West Africa to a poetry festival in Timbuktu. Her sense of an identity grounded in being an Afrikaner, a South African as well as an African, can be compared to the way in which Breytenbach continues his ongoing reflection on identity in the volumes he published in the past decade, *Die windvanger* (The wind-catcher) (2007) and *Oorblyfsel / Voice Over* (2009). Breytenbach prefers to define his identity as that of an 'uncitizen' of the 'Middle World', which he recently described as the space of those who have left home for good while carrying it with them, and of those who feel at ease on foreign shores without ever being at home (2010: 143). The poems in *Die windvanger* reflect the experience of just such a liminal figure, travelling between France, Spain, New York, Goreé, off the coast of Senegal, and his homeland, South Africa. This figure comments on world politics and global events, but there are also references to his own country from which he has had to flee because its people do not like his bitter criticism of what he sees as its degeneration into chaos and destruction. The volume *Oorblyfsel / Voice Over* is conceptualised as a conversation with the Palestinian poet Mahmoud Darwish, which then leads to the imagining of links between Afrikaner and Palestinian identity. Because of Breytenbach's famously ambivalent relationship with the Afrikaner nation as well as the political rulers of South Africa, these lines send a complex message about the way in which he conceives of Afrikaner and South African identity.

The narrator in black Afrikaans poet Ferrus's volume *Ons komvandaan* (Where we come from) (2005) embraces and celebrates her descent from South Africa's indigenous peoples and the slaves brought to the country.[2] The poem '*Na tien jaar*' (After ten years) shows that she accepts the possibility of a unified South African identity after ten years of democracy and that she wholeheartedly conceives of herself as a South African: the country is seen as a house in which all South Africans have come together under one big '*karos*'. In contrast with Ferrus, the younger poet Kamfer gives a much more uncompromising view of her own identity in *Noudat slapende honde* (2008). In the poem '*vergewe my maar ek is Afrikaans*' (forgive me but I am Afrikaans) she contemptuously reclaims her identity and the language Afrikaans from the white Afrikaner men who were the 'Boogie Men' of her dreams as a Coloured child.

Yet another take on South African identity is presented in Odendaal's debut volume *Onbedoelde land* (Unintended/Unpromised land) (2007). It gives a rueful reflection on an identity which the poet-narrator feels is reviled and misunderstood in post-apartheid South Africa, namely that of the Afrikaner male who knows that he has lost his power but still remains passionately attached to the (farm-)land and a store of memories which he cannot deny. The poem '*Gesog*' (Sought after) paints an ironical self-portrait of the white male responding to his victimisation in the discourses of postmodernism and postcolonialism:

die ganse postkoloniale
postmoderne projek
sou van stapel kwalik loop
sonder die stukrag van my haatlikheid
[the entire postcolonial
postmodern project
would hardly have gotten off the ground
without the impetus provided by my hatefulness] (2007: 55).

Whereas Odendaal's sense of identity is embedded in a rural past, Bezuidenhout's debut volume *Retoer* (Return) (2007) presents an identity rooted in Afrikaner urbanisation. When there is a reference to a family farm it is to one that the poet-narrator has never seen (*'Ons ry iewers naby Ottersfontein verby'* [We are driving past somewhere close to Ottersfontein]). Although Bezuidenhout's volume evokes Afrikaner history, he distances himself from Afrikaner nostalgia for the past as well as from an overt optimism about the future of South Africa in the poem 'Ons' (We).

Language: The focus on Afrikaans

Reflections on the making of poetry, on the possibilities of language as a medium and on the characteristics of the genre have been unfailing themes in Afrikaans poetry. Almost every poet who has published in the past decade has reflected in one way or another on the art of writing poetry. However, Afrikaans poets of the past decade have also used their poetry to engage with the history of their language, its present and its future. In the past, Afrikaans was both the language of the oppressor and the oppressed. After 1994 the language lost its privileged status as one of only two official languages in South Africa to become one of eleven official languages, so that many have doubts about the sustainability of Afrikaans in the face of English becoming both the most favoured language and the lingua franca of the country.

Afrikaans poets of the past decade have commented on the history and status of Afrikaans from a variety of perspectives. It is clear that the position of Afrikaans elicits a range of complex emotions from its poets. These include elation about the fact that the language has been liberated from its privileged past, guilt about its implication in past injustices, pleas for its continued existence and anger about its expected demise. At the beginning of the decade Krog stated that she experienced a great sense of freedom and pleasure as a poet from the fact that Afrikaans found itself vulnerable after being cut off from state power (Christiansë 2000: 16). Krog's optimism is shared by Ferrus who speaks from the perspective of the previously oppressed. Her volume *Ons komvandaan* sees Afrikaans as a language of reconciliation, stressing the fact that it originated from '*die buik van Afrika*' (the belly of Africa) and that it sings in a thousand voices despite the view that it was once the language of the oppressor (2005: 18). Daniel Hugo also describes Afrikaans as an indigenous language, a '*minerale taal*' (mineral language), originating in and purified from the ore of South Africa (2009: 8).

Other poets have been less inclined to see the positive side of the language's diminished status and its declining social capital. Amongst those who have poetically voiced anxieties about the continued existence of the tongue in which they write are Breytenbach, Spies, T.T. Cloete and Clinton V. du Plessis. In earlier years

Breytenbach often reacted with bitterness against Afrikaans in its official and political incarnations and more than once announced his intention to stop writing in his mother tongue, but recently he has become a staunch defender of Afrikaans language rights. Although his dark prediction that Afrikaans will become extinct in his lifetime was regarded by many as too pessimistic,[3] it is consistent with his volume *Die windvanger*'s metaphoric references to the poet's mother tongue as a '*verworde taal*' (degenerate language) and a '*dooie taal*' (dead language) (2007: 128, 137). T.T. Cloete's appeal to the hangmen of the *shoa* (Hebrew for destruction, catastrophe) to take into account the accomplishments of Afrikaans before they execute their sentence in his volume *Heilige nuuskierigheid* (Sacred curiosity) also suggests an apocalyptic view of the fate of Afrikaans (2007: 141). Taking another line of argument, Spies suggests in *Duskant die einders* (This side of the horizons) (2004) that Afrikaans is endangered by the cultural and moral laxity of its own speakers as much as by external factors. Black Afrikaans poet Du Plessis, who publishes his own work in pamphlet form, also foresees the death of Afrikaans in his poem '*die taal*' (the language) in his volume *gedigte, talk show hosts & reality shows* (poems, talk show hosts & reality shows) (2009).

Younger poets who made their debut in the past decade have also contributed to this theme. Marius Crous's volume *Brief uit die kolonies* (Letter from the colonies) (2003) reminds readers of the language's colonial past and asks forgiveness for the fact that it was part of the execution of inhuman policies in the poem '*Vergifnis*' (Forgiveness). The poem predicts that the language will become extinct like a prehistoric animal because it is unsuited for Africa. In contrast with this, Marais sees the language Afrikaans as wonderfully wild, untamed and dangerous (the killer whale in his bathtub, the anaconda in his living room) when he has to face life in a depressingly over-regulated Germany in *In die buitenste ruimte* (2006: 44).

Afrikaans is also a theme in the work of poets who use non-standard varieties of Afrikaans in their poetry. Peter Snyders rejects the criticism that the non-standard variety 'Kaaps' stereotypes Coloured people in the poem '*Ek is siëker Die Bruinmense*' (I must be The Brown People) in the volume *Tekens van die tye* (Signs of the times) (2002), insisting on using his own variety of Afrikaans which he calls '*die moedertaal se basterkind*' (the mother tongue's bastard child). Loit Sôls continues to use 'Goema', a vernacular mix of Afrikaans and English, as an instrument of poetic expression in his second volume *Die faraway klanke vanne hadeda* (The faraway sounds of a hadeda) (2006). The poem 'Goema II' (16) makes an argument for languages that are not fixed and will accommodate connection with other language groups. In contrast with poets like Snyders and Sôls, Kamfer, who also writes about the working class living on the Cape Flats in *Noudat slapende honde* (2008), does not make use of a non-standard variety of Afrikaans. As mentioned earlier, she defiantly takes back Afrikaans from the white patriarchs who regarded it as their exclusive property in the poem *'vergewe my maar ek is Afrikaans'*.

Socio-political commentary

Unlike Crous who writes that 'in the late 1980s most Afrikaans poets chose not to include the discursive elements associated with political oppression in their work' (2009: 200), I believe that political oppression and the fight for liberation were significant themes in Afrikaans poetry throughout the 1980s (especially in the struggle poetry produced by black Afrikaans poets like Snyders, Du Plessis, Hein Willemse, Patrick Petersen and Marius Titus as well as in the work of white poets Breytenbach, Krog, Barend Toerien and Fanie Olivier). An overview of the poetry written in the past decade shows that the trend to reflect socio-political issues continues, albeit with new emphases and nuances.

Two volumes which voiced opposing ideological positions were published in 2000: the anthology *Nuwe verset* (New resistance) and Krog's *Kleur kom nooit alleen nie*. The poems in *Nuwe verset* (edited by Daniel Hugo, Leon Rousseau and Phil du Plessis) were contributed by poets of different races and paint a largely dystopic view of the new dispensation, focusing on reverse racism, renewed racial exclusion, moral degeneration, crime (especially farm murders), corruption, unemployment, poverty, gangsterism, the position of Afrikaans, AIDS, urban degeneration and environmental issues. In contrast, Krog's *Kleur kom nooit alleen nie* directs its attention at the necessity of making amends for the apartheid past and pursuing the transformation of South African society.

Looking back on Afrikaans poetry written in the past decade, it appears as if the anthology *Nuwe verset*, rather than Krog's volume, has set the agenda for the way in which Afrikaans poets engage with socio-political issues beyond 2000. Political verse in this decade deals mainly with the subjects listed above. One of the more comprehensive attempts at dealing with socio-political problems in post-apartheid South Africa can be found in Louis Esterhuizen's *Liefland* (Beloved land) (2004). The fourteen poems in the volume's second section deal with topics such as the poverty which leads to drug abuse and prostitution, rape, gangsterism, murder (in townships, suburbs and on farms), homelessness and vagrancy. Also included in the volume is the cycle *'Elegie vir 'n vaderland'* (Elegy for a fatherland), a lyrical lament which addresses the fatherland of all victims, whatever their race may be, and expresses a profound pessimism. Odendaal's *Onbedoelde land* (2007) also addresses corruption and crime in post-apartheid South Africa, whereas several poems in Johannes Prins's *Een hart* (One heart) (2009) comment on the detached way in which journalists and poets deal with the phenomenon of violent crime. Toerien (2001) and Hennie Aucamp (2002) write about the decaying social fabric of Cape Town, whereas Breytenbach (2007, 2009) places the socio-political ills of post-apartheid South Africa in a global context.

Marais (2010: 6–7) has recently commented on the incapacity or unwillingness of Afrikaans poets to deal with the fears and prejudices surrounding race after 1994 in the way that Afrikaans novels such as Marlene van Niekerk's *Agaat* (2004) and Eben Venter's *Horrelpoot* (Trencherman) (2006) do. Marais mentions a few names, but does not really give credit to the way in which black Afrikaans poets such as Snyders, Julian de Wette, Sôls and Du Plessis have engaged with the issue of race in the past decade. Snyders includes several poems on the marginalisation of certain racial groups in the 'monochrome rainbow nation' of post-apartheid South Africa in *Tekens van die tye* (2002: 48). De Wette writes about the position of South Africans of mixed racial descent in *Tussen duine gebore* (Born amongst dunes) (2002) and P.J. Philander delves into South Africa's painful history of racism in *Trialoog* (Trialogue) (2002). Sôls writes about the irony of whites' sudden desire to co-opt and include him in the racism they direct at black people by using the word '*ons*' (we) (2006: 62). These examples show that black Afrikaans poets have not side-stepped the problem of race in their poetry.

The use of indigenous cultural material

A literary strategy that can be partly related to socio-political developments in the past two decades is the publication of poetic reworkings of indigenous material. Revisiting the history and cultures of South Africa's indigenous peoples became a general trend in South African literature and academic studies in the 1990s. Afrikaans poetry of the past decade formed part of this interest shown by other literatures in South Africa. Poets Hans du Plessis and Thomas Deacon published the first volumes in which they use Griqua Afrikaans and Griqua themes in the 1980s and 1990s and continued to do so after 2000. Du Plessis published three volumes in the past decade in which he transposed biblical material into Griqua Afrikaans: *Innie skylte vannie Jirre* (In the Lord's shelter) (2001), *Boegoe vannie liefde* (Buchu of love) (2002) and *Hie neffens my* (Here next to me) (2003). These volumes were best-sellers, possibly because they are reworkings of the Bible's most poetic and best-loved passages (Psalms, Song of Songs, 1 Corinthians:13) and evoke the image of the Griqua people as devoutly, almost naively, religious. Although Du Plessis is a skilled poet, a serious reader misses an element of self-reflection in these volumes. The poet does not give any indication that he is conscious of the implications of using or appropriating the voices of previously disadvantaged peoples and of portraying them in a one-dimensional way.[4] Although it has been said that Deacon is a less skilful poet than Du Plessis (Odendaal 2006: 114), his use of Griqua material in *Maagmeisie. Griekwastemme* (Virgin girl. Griqua voices) (2003) is less troubling than Du Plessis's transpositions. Deacon presents his volume as a representation of Griqua voices and attributes the different parts of the volume to different Griqua speakers. The inclusion of explanatory notes helps to contextualise the poems, placing the poet in the position of an outsider sharing information with the reader, rather than posing as an insider.

Krog is faced with the same problems in *Kleur kom nooit alleen nie* (2000a), in which she includes the voices of the indigenous inhabitants of the Richtersveld in the section '*ses narratiewe uit die Richtersveld*' (six narratives from the Richtersveld). Although Krog may be appropriating the voices of others for her own poetic purposes in this cycle, 'ownership' of the voices is clearly indicated through the use of the names of those quoted in her poetry. Her use of indigenous material also extended to the reworking of the /Xam material collected by Bleek and Lloyd in the nineteenth century. Her first engagement with this material formed part of a larger project to translate verse from the indigenous languages of South Africa into Afrikaans in *Met woorde soos met kerse* (With words as with candles) (2002). In 2004, Krog published further reworkings of /Xam material, both in Afrikaans (*die sterre sê 'tsau'*) and English (*the stars say 'tsau'*). This proved highly controversial: poet-academic Stephen Watson (2005) accused Krog of plagiarising his own reworking of the same material in *Return of the Moon* (1991) and for having 'a tin ear' when it came to reworking the /Xam poetry into English. Krog's two publications acknowledge the fact that the material was originally produced by five /Xam individuals, that it was only 'selected and adapted' by Krog and that Krog's reworkings form part of a long tradition dating from the 1920s of which Watson himself forms part, but it is clear that the use of the cultural material provided by indigenous and formerly oppressed peoples remains problematic. Some argue that it constitutes an unfair appropriation of previously disadvantaged people's cultural goods whereas others feel that these reworkings circulate cultural material that would otherwise have become lost.

Universal themes

During the past decade Afrikaans poets did not only react to the immediate sociopolitical environment in which they produced their poetry. Their poetic production was also driven by a wide range of universal concerns of which the following were thematically the most significant: the body, the environment, death and mortality, family matters, and intertextual connections. There is an element of arbitrariness in this choice of themes for discussion because a variety of other themes and issues, such as gender, history, religion, travel and migration, also feature in the poetry of the past decade.

The body: Wounded, violated, erotic, ageing, dead

Although it is by no means a new theme in Afrikaans literature, the poetry written in the past decade shows an ever more candid focus on the body, whether it be the wounded, violated, erotic, ageing or dead body. Krog's *Kleur kom nooit alleen nie* (2000a) uses various images of the wounded and scarred body to give physical embodiment to the trauma experienced in the course of South African history. Images of the Richtersveld landscape as a wounded body segues into the second section of the volume, titled '*Wondweefsel*' (Wound tissue), which focuses on the pain suffered during the Anglo-Boer War as well as the apartheid era. Stander focuses on the body wounded by violent crime in her debut volume *Die vloedbos sal weer vlieg* (The mangrove will fly again) (2006). She uses a series of vivid images for bodies violated by sexual crimes such as rape and the abuse that often goes with prostitution in the section with the evocative title '*Karkaskaal*' (As naked as a carcass).

A significant section of the love poetry in the period 2000–2009 focuses on the erotic body. Important here is the work of poets such as Breytenbach, Krog, Marlise Joubert and Stander. Both Breytenbach and Krog have long had the reputation of being the foremost poets on erotic love in Afrikaans. Thus it comes as no surprise that Breytenbach's *Die windvanger* includes a section of erotic poems, '*Die hart se dinge*' (Things of the heart), in which a surrealist and dreamlike atmosphere is combined with an emphasis on concrete bodily detail. Krog's *Kleur kom nooit alleen nie* also includes a section of poems based on paintings by Marlene Dumas, Walter Battiss and Picasso in which the erotic body is evoked to explore power relationships between men and women, between artists and their models, between writers and the written; the erotic body is honoured in a series of 'marital songs' published in both Afrikaans and English as *Verweerskrif* and *Body Bereft* (2006b, 2006a). Joubert's volume, *Lyfsange* (Body songs) (2001) is a celebration of the body in the erotic interplay between man and woman (see, for example, 'Lapis lazuli'). The emphasis is on the female body, admired and desired by the male, as in the poems '*bedding*' ([flower] bed) and the poem '*oorsprong*' (origin) which appropriates Gustave Courbet's famous painting *L'origine du monde* to describe the lover's gaze. Stander's above-mentioned volume *Die vloedbos sal weer vlieg* also focuses on the erotic body in the lushly worded love poems in the section '*Ewenaar*' [Equator].

The homoerotic poetry written by Aucamp, Crous, Marais and Johann de Lange also celebrates the (male) body. Several of the Shakespearean sonnets in Aucamp's volume *Hittegolf* (Heat wave) (2002), subtitled '*Wulpse sonnette*' (Lewd sonnets), describe the male nude in such explicit detail that they become the verbal equivalent of nude paintings or photographs. The body is also a prime focus in the love poems in Marais's debut volume *Staan in die algemeen nader aan vensters* (Generally stand closer to windows) (2008), although it seems as if Marais responds to Aucamp's explicit rendering of the male body by deliberately *not* describing the private parts of the lover's body, otherwise rendered in great detail in the poem 'Die anatomie van M' (The anatomy of M). De Lange's volume *Die algebra van nood* (The algebra of distress) (2009) focuses on the detail of bodily experience in situations such as taking drugs, cruising, having sex in the midst of the AIDS epidemic, and witnessing a corpse. The almost obsessive contemplation of the dead body was worked out a few years earlier in Crous's second volume *Aan 'n beentjie sit en kluif* (To sit and pick at a bone) (2006), which deals with the trauma of the beloved's death by exploring the relationship between erotic desire and feelings of revulsion for his corpse (see the poems 'Bed 1' and 'Bed 2').

The poets of the past decade also turned their gaze on the ageing body. De Lange evokes the body weathered by age in the poem 'Wabi-sabi' (a reference to the Japanese aesthetic which finds beauty in imperfection, impermanence and incompleteness) and finds beauty in the approachability of the imperfect body (2009: 110). Krog's volume *Verweerskrif* (2006b) also takes up the 'aesthetic of the imperfect body' in poems focusing on the ageing and menopausal female body. The daring use of a David Goldblatt photograph of the torso of a naked and aged female body on its cover and its explicit versification of bodily experience sparked controversy amongst Afrikaans- and English-speaking readers.[5] In *Afstande* (Distances), Lucas Malan paints mocking self-portraits in which he details the bodily deterioration that age brings in poems such as 'Genepoel' (Genetic pool) (2002: 17) and 'Bestek: 2009' (Reckoning: 2009) (see Nieuwoudt 2010: 13). I.L. de Villiers's volumes *Jerusalem tot Johannesburg* (Jerusalem to Johannesburg) (2005) and *Vervreemdeling* (Estrangement/Stranger) (2008) also describe the poet's aged body in concrete detail, viewing it with disbelief and distaste as if it were that of a stranger in ' 'n Ou man klim uit die bad' (An old man climbs out the bath) (2008: 65).

The environment, earth, landscape

Apart from the poems in which an explicitly political content is given to the concept 'land' (such as Krog's poems about land-ownership in *Kleur kom nooit alleen nie* and Odendaal's poetry about the Afrikaner's relationship to the land in *Onbedoelde land*), the environment, the earth and the landscape are also themes dealt with by Afrikaans poets in the past decade. The concern for environmental matters first gained prominence in Afrikaans poetry in the 1990s and has continued beyond 2000, most notably in the work of Johann Lodewyk Marais, Malan and Martjie Bosman. Marais became one of the foremost proponents of the environmental thematic in Afrikaans poetry, continuing his own work from the 1990s in the volumes *Aves* (2002) and

Plaaslike kennis (Farm/rural/local knowledge) (2004). The largest part of *Aves* is devoted to a kind of 'poetic encyclopedia' on birds, whereas a number of poems in the second volume reflect on the problems of rural development. Several poems in Malan's *Afstande* (2002) anticipate an ecological disaster of apocalyptic proportions. The poem '*Kuslangs: groen gedagtes*' (Along the coast: green thoughts) takes disfiguring developments that grow like fungus against coastal slopes as a point of departure for imagining a future in which Gaia will split open to destroy all that humankind has so perversely created during the course of its evolution. Bosman's volume *Landelik* (Rural) (2002) shows the same concern with humankind's impact on the planet. In contrast with Malan, however, she imagines Gaia playfully slipping away from underneath the markings on Mercator's map of the earth in the poem '*Kartografie*' (Cartography), thus escaping humankind's efforts to dominate, regulate and categorise her.

Rather than being explicitly concerned with environmental matters, Ilse van Staden's poetry has an elemental quality in the sense that she built the two volumes she has published thus far around three of the natural elements, namely water, earth and air. Her debut volume *Watervlerk* (Water wing) (2003) describes the human being as bound to the earth, but longing to be able to function in the mediums of water and air (hence the reference to wings of water). Her second volume *Fluisterklip* (Whispering stone) (2008) places the emphasis on the medium of earth or stone, building up to the conclusion that it is becoming increasingly difficult to hear what the earth is whispering because of the strained breathing and incoherent speech caused by environmental pressure (2008: 50). Heilna du Plooy explores the relationship between body and landscape in her volume *In die landskap ingelyf* (Embodied in the landscape) (2003). The poet-narrator in the cycle of poems '*Landskapsiklus*' (Landscape cycle) tries to enter the landscape in order to paint it, realising that it involves becoming an embodied part of the landscape as well as of the country South Africa as political and historical entity.

Ageing, mortality and death

Apart from poems that take the subject of death and dying into the political domain (as in the poems that comment on violent crime), there is also a substantial body of poetry in which death is dealt with as a private matter. The term 'gerontological poetry' has been coined by critics with reference not only to the poetry produced by poets advanced in age, but also to their thematic concerns of ageing, mortality and death. A significant number of poets in their seventies or eighties were still productive in the first decade of the twenty-first century. The grande dame of Afrikaans poetry, Elisabeth Eybers, published her last volume *Valreep / Stirrup-cup* (Afrikaans poems with English translations by the poet) in 2005 at the age of 90. Eybers turns her characteristically ironic gaze on approaching death in this volume, unmoved by what lies ahead: 'You're leaving all behind / and facing firm, emphatic emptiness', she says in the poem 'Résumé'. Other poets that belong to this group are Toerien (2001), Cloete (2007), Pirow Bekker (2002, 2008), Dolf van Niekerk (2006), Philander (2002), M.M. Walters (2004) and De Villiers (2005, 2008).

Breytenbach continues his almost obsessive concern with the theme of death from his debut volume onwards in *Die windvanger*, merging it with the themes of erotic love and the writing of poetry as before. Although younger than the 'gerontological' poets and more transgressive in her approach, Krog builds on the work of her predecessor Eybers in her poems on ageing and mortality in *Verweerskrif*. A young poet who also takes mortality and death as a dominant theme is Sarina Dönges. The title of her debut volume *In die tyd van die uile* (In the time of the owls) (2004) announces its preoccupation with the dream-like atmosphere of the night as well as premonitions of death. Dönges's poems also explore the links between eroticism and death (as in the poem '*Die dood as minnaar*' [Death as lover]) as well as the grim reality of death in poems about friends who have died.

Also popular in Afrikaans poetry of the past decade is the funerary poem, in which the deceased person is addressed, praised and lamented. Joan Hambidge's *Lykdigte* (Funerary/obituary poems) (2000) consciously employs the structures of classical funerary poetry, with its use of elements such as praise (*laus*), mourning (*luctus*) and consolation (*consolatio*), to reflect on the death of personal friends, poets and global celebrities.

Malan also devotes sections of his volumes *Afstande* (2001) and *Vermaning* (Exhortation) (2008) to funerary portraits of deceased writers, friends, family members and even pets. Other volumes that deal with this theme describe the death of a beloved in an attempt to come to terms with the trauma of the experience. Petra Müller's *Die aandag van jou oë* (The attention of your eyes) (2002) is built in its entirety around the death of the poet-narrator's husband, using poetry as a means of healing. Henning Pieterse sets up a dense symbolic construction based on the myth of Bluebeard's castle as well as Bartok's opera based on the same material to engage with the trauma of his wife's suicide in the volume *Die burg van Hertog Bloubaard* (Bluebeard's castle) (2000). Other examples of volumes constructed around the death of someone close are Trienke Laurie's *Uitroep* (Cry/outcry) (2001) and Crous's *Aan 'n beentjie sit en kluif* (2006).

Family matters
Family relationships have always been an important theme in Afrikaans literature. Most prominent in literary excavations of the Freudian family romance is undoubtedly

the relationship with the father, because of the different father figures present in the strongly patriarchal South African society. Afrikaans poets of the past decade have not given up pursuing family relationships as thematic resources, with the father again featuring prominently in their work.

Toerien's *Die huisapteek* (The medicine chest), published in 2001 when the poet was 80 years old, shows that old age does not necessarily resolve painful family relationships. Several poems recall the poet-narrator's difficult relationship with his father (using descriptions such as '*die nors een*' [the surly one] and '*die kwaai man*' [the bad-tempered man]) as well as a child's guilty dreams about murdering his father. The poet-narrator's reminiscences also picture the father's confidence as chairman of the Party in the midst of '*die ooms*' (an Afrikaans word that can refer to adult men as well as to uncles), thus linking the father with the patriarchs of early Afrikaner nationalism in poems such as '*Die egodokument*' (The ego document) and '*Tafereel, met kersieboord*' (Tableau, with cherry orchard). Zandra Bezuidenhout's poem '*Die middag van die ooms*' (The afternoon of the uncles) in *Dansmusieke* (Dance musics) portrays the confidence of farmers and the sons who will inherit their farms on their Sunday afternoon visits from the perspective of shy adolescent girls, hinting at the social arrangements and sexual tensions inherent in a patriarchal society (2000: 62–3). In contrast with Toerien's volume, the Afrikaner father, framed by the farm, is lovingly remembered in Odendaal's *Onbedoelde land* (2007) as well as Gibson's *Boomplaats* (2005) and *Kaplyn* (2007).

The cycle of poems '*Langnagvure*' (Long night fires) in Esterhuizen's *Sloper* (Demolisher) (2007) uses mining metaphors to tell the story of the protagonist Egbert's tempestuous relationship with his miner father and his struggle to forgive him for continuing the cycle of family violence. The complex relationship between father and son (shot through with ambivalent feelings of reproach, longing and regret) is also a constant in De Lange's poetry. He again takes up this theme in his 2009 volume *Die algebra van nood* with the poem '*Pa*' [Dad] and '*Petidiendroom*' [Pethydine dream] in which he dreams that his father offers him drugs in an attempt at reconciliation, but that he cannot find a place to use them. Kamfer evokes a variety of abject father figures (unemployed, gaoled, homeless, abusive, drunk, unresponsive) in her poem '*Pick 'n Pa*' [Pick a Dad] in *Noudat slapende honde* (2008), concluding with an ambiguous reference to the father she has never seen. In contrast with Kamfer's dispassionate and laconic style, Jeanne Goosen's poems about her family take on an almost surrealist atmosphere. Goosen's volume *Elders aan diens* (On duty elsewhere) represents a poet-narrator hovering on the edge of psychological breakdown and paints a series of well-loved but dysfunctional family figures, amongst them a father who smells of gas in heaven because he committed suicide (2007: 35) and a sister who has eggbeaters for hands (15). Other poets who try to unravel the complexities of the Freudian family romance in their poetry are Hambidge, Danie Marais and Loftus Marais.

Intertextual connections, conversations and rivalries

The tendency of poets to establish intertextual connections and engage in intertextual conversations and rivalries is by no means new or limited to specific literatures. Thus Afrikaans poets of the past decade, like poets everywhere, have felt the need to establish connections with other poets to foster poetic solidarity, to stimulate their growth and bolster the substance of their own work. They also rewrite the work of other poets in order to establish their own poetic identities and to assert themselves as rivals of poets and trends that they perceive as outdated. The following examples constitute but a small sampling of this trend in the poetry published between 2000 and 2009.

The trend is especially marked in the work of poets who made their debut in the past decade. Gibson, who published his first volume in 2005, conducts intricate intertextual conversations with a range of Afrikaans poets, most notably N.P. van Wyk Louw, D.J. Opperman and Breytenbach, in his second and third volumes *Kaplyn* (2007) and *Oogensiklopedie* (2009). He also establishes connections between his own work and that of a wide variety of writers from other literatures, such as Allen Ginsberg, e.e. cummings, Emily Dickinson, James Joyce, Seamus Heaney, Pablo Neruda and Jorge Luis Borges. Danie Marais is another member of the generation of debut poets of the past decade whose work makes use of a substantial number of references to local and international poetry, to popular (especially rock) music and to a variety of films. Neither Gibson nor Marais creates the impression that he wants to do battle with predecessors or fellow poets. The intertextual references in their work have the function of making them part of a larger community of writers on whom they can rely for inspiration; they also demonstrate their knowledge of a writerly tradition larger than only that of Afrikaans.

In contrast with Gibson and Danie Marais, debut poet Loftus Marais creates the impression that he wants to challenge poetic predecessors such as Van Wyk Louw and Opperman in *Staan in die algemeen nader aan vensters* (2008). In '*Die digter as rockstar*' (The poet as rockstar) he subverts the example set by Van Wyk Louw: instead of the chisel that Van Wyk Louw used as symbol for the poetic word in his classic poem '*Die beiteltjie*' (The little chisel), Marais wants to wield a '*fokken lugdrukboor*' (fucking jackhammer) in his poetry. In the poem ' '*n Pleidooi vir vinniger kuns*' (A plea for quicker art) Marais takes issue with Opperman's well-known poem '*Digter*' (Poet) in which he uses the image of an exile who painstakingly builds a ship in a bottle. Marais's poem argues for a rapid form of art that will contradict the careful craftsmanship suggested by Opperman's image and concludes with the poet converting the ship-in-a-bottle into a petrol bomb which he hurls at the reader.

A poet who often works in the intertextual and citational mode is Hambidge, who published four volumes in the past decade. By way of example one can cite her most recent volume *Vuurwiel* (Firewheel) (2009), which includes a section titled 'Toespelings' (Allusions) in which she rewrites, questions or parodies well-known Afrikaans poems as well as texts from other literatures. Rivalry lies on the level of content rather than form: she fills pre-existing forms with unexpected content (Van Wyk Louw's poems about a heterosexual love affair become lesbian love poems in Hambidge's rewriting) and her parodies honour the work of her predecessors as much as they mock or debunk it.

The diversity of Afrikaans poetry

In his preface to the anthology *Groot verseboek*, André P. Brink claims that the variety of voices, perspectives and themes in Afrikaans poetry written after 1990 make it difficult to generalise or identify one or two general trends. Diversity has become *the* characteristic of Afrikaans poetry, he writes (2008: xvii). His view is largely confirmed by the Afrikaans poetry published in the first decade of the new century. Looking back over the period 2000–2009, there seems to be little need for pessimism about the genre. Afrikaans poets have abundant opportunities to publish their work and can still rely on a relatively robust literary system in which their work will be reviewed, discussed, awarded, canonised and introduced into school and university syllabuses. Despite fears to the contrary, younger poets regularly publish volumes, although the hope that the writers of lyrics will become part of the system of Afrikaans poetry has not been realised. The most promising and provocative lyrics (for instance, those written by the group Fokofpolisiekar) have so far not been published in a form that bridges the gap between the so-called elitist sphere of poetry and popular culture. The diversity of the system is also maintained by the fact that the move towards writing more accessible poetry has not precluded the publication of more complex varieties.

Despite this largely positive view of the current state of Afrikaans poetry, it remains relatively insular. Afrikaans literature's move towards participation in the larger national and international contexts seems more difficult to realise in the case of poetry than in the case of the novel. Although some Afrikaans poets have gained exposure in the Dutch literary world because of the close connection between the two languages, fewer poets than novelists are translated from Afrikaans into English and other international languages. Poets themselves try to bridge the gap between the local (the Afrikaans literary system) and the global by building intertextual connections with other literatures in South Africa and the larger world. These provisos notwithstanding, the Afrikaans poetry produced in the first decade of the new century constitutes a remarkably diverse and vibrant body of work.

Notes

1. Keller describes the 'long poem' as a 'generic hybrid' and gives a partial list of the formal varieties that may be included within the ambit of the term: '[n]arrative poems, verse novels, sonnet sequences, irregular lyric medleys or cycles, collage long poems, meditative sequences, extended dramatic monologues, prose long poems, serial poems, heroic epics' (1997: 2–3).
2. Many Afrikaans writers of mixed racial descent find the use of the term Coloured (*kleurling*) racist and offensive because of its association with the history of oppression in South Africa. They therefore made a deliberate ideological choice in the 1980s to refer to themselves as black Afrikaans writers, thereby placing themselves and their writing in the political arena. The use of the term and the debates around it still persist.
3. An Afrikaans newspaper reported on 24 March 2010 that 70-year-old Breytenbach, in an interview on Talk Radio 702, predicted that Afrikaans will become extinct in his lifetime (Fourie 2010: 1).
4. For further reflection on this practice, see Britz (2001: 17), Van Zyl (2001: 9) and Viljoen (2003).
5. Spies (2006: 9), an Afrikaans reader, found the cover repulsive and the poetry unbearably explicit; Gray (2006), an English-speaking reader, found the English version of the volume lacking in sophistication and poetic quality.

References

Adendorff, Elbie. 2003. '*Digdebute teen die millenniumwending: 'n Polisistemiese ondersoek*'. Master's thesis. Stellenbosch: University of Stellenbosch.
Aucamp, Hennie. 2002. *Hittegolf*. Cape Town: Homeros.
Bekker, Pirow. 2002. *Stillerlewe*. Pretoria: Protea Boekhuis.
———. 2008. *Van roes en amarant*. Pretoria: Protea Boekhuis.
Bezuidenhout, Andries. 2007. *Retoer*. Pretoria: Protea Boekhuis.
Bezuidenhout, Zandra. 2000. *Dansmusieke*. Stellenbosch: Suider Kollege Uitgewers.
Bosman, Martjie. 2002. *Landelik*. Pretoria: Protea Boekhuis.
Breytenbach, Breyten. 2007. *Die windvanger*. Cape Town: Human & Rousseau.
———. 2009. *Oorblyfsel / Voice Over*. Cape Town: Human & Rousseau.
———. 2010. *Notes from the Middle World*. Chicago: Haymarket Press.
Brink, André P. 2008. *Groot verseboek. Deel 3*. Cape Town: Tafelberg.
Britz, Etienne. 2001. '*Psalms wat wil ontroer uit die hart van Griekwaland*'. *Rapport*, 24 June: 17.

Christiansë, Yvette. 2000. '"Down to my Last Skin": A Conversation with Antjie Krog'. *Connect: Art, Politics, Theory, Practice*, Fall: 11–20.
Cloete, T.T. 2007. *Heilige nuuskierigheid*. Cape Town: Tafelberg.
Crous, Marius. 2003. *Brief uit die kolonies*. Pretoria: Protea Boekhuis.
———. 2006. *Aan 'n beentjie sit en kluif*. Pretoria: Protea Boekhuis.
———. 2009. 'Afrikaans Poetry: New Voices'. *Current Writing* 21(1&2): 200–17.
Deacon, Thomas. 2003. *Maagmeisie. Griekwa-stemme*. Pretoria: Protea Boekhuis.
De Lange, Johann. 2009. *Die algebra van nood*. Cape Town: Human & Rousseau.
De Villiers, I.L. 2005. *Jerusalem tot Johannesburg*. Cape Town: Tafelberg.
———. 2008. *Vervreemdeling*. Cape Town: Tafelberg.
De Wette, Julian. 2002. *Tussen duine gebore*. Pretoria: Protea Boekhuis.
Dönges, Sarina. 2004. *In die tyd van die uile*. Pretoria: Protea Boekhuis.
Du Plessis, Clinton V. 2009. *gedigte, talk show hosts & reality shows*. Cradock: Ama-Coloured Slowguns.
Du Plessis, Hans. 2001. *Innie skylte vannie Jirre*. Pretoria: LAPA.
———. 2002. *Boegoe vannie liefde. Griekwahooglied*. Pretoria: LAPA.
———. 2003. *Hie neffens my*. Pretoria: LAPA.
Du Plooy, Heilna. 2003. *In die landskap ingelyf*. Pretoria: Protea Boekhuis.
Esterhuizen, Louis. 2004. *Liefland*. Pretoria: Protea Boekhuis.
———. 2007. *Sloper*. Pretoria: Protea Boekhuis.
Eybers, Elisabeth. 2005. *Valreep / Stirrup-cup*. Cape Town: Human & Rousseau.
Ferrus, Diana. 2005. *Ons komvandaan*. Cape Town: Diana Ferrus Uitgewery.
Fourie, Magdel. 2010. 'Afrikaans sterf, sê Breyten'. *Die Burger*, 24 March: 1.
Gibson, Gilbert. 2005. *Boomplaats*. Cape Town: Tafelberg.
———. 2007. *Kaplyn*. Cape Town: Tafelberg.
———. 2009. *Oogensiklopedie*. Cape Town: Tafelberg.
Goosen, Jeanne. 2007. *Elders aan diens*. Parklands: Genugtig! Uitgewers.
Gray, Stephen. 2006. 'Letting it (all) Hang Out'. *Mail & Guardian*, 17–23 March: 4–5.
Hambidge, Joan. 2000. *Lykdigte*. Cape Town: Tafelberg.
———. 2009. *Vuurwiel*. Cape Town: Human & Rousseau.
Hugo, Daniel. 2009. *Die panorama in my truspieël*. Pretoria: Protea Boekhuis.
Hugo, Daniel, Leon Rousseau and Phil du Plessis. 2000. *Nuwe verset*. Pretoria: Protea Boekhuis.
Joubert, Marlise. 2001. *Lyfsange*. Pretoria: Protea Boekhuis.
Kamfer, Ronelda. 2008. *Noudat slapende honde*. Cape Town: Kwela Books.
Keller, Lynn. 1997. *Forms of Expansion: Recent Long Poems by Women*. Chicago: University of Chicago Press.
Kleyn, Leti. 2008. ' 'n Ander bestekopname van die Afrikaanse poësie 2004–2007'. *LitNet Akademies* 5(1): 100–34.
Krog, Antjie. 2000a. *Kleur kom nooit alleen nie*. Cape Town: Kwela Books.
———. 2000b. *Down to my Last Skin*. Johannesburg: Random House.
———. 2002. *Met woorde soos met kerse*. Cape Town: Kwela Books.
———. 2004a. *die sterre sê 'tsau': /Xam Gedigte van Diä!kwain, Kweiten-ta-//ken, /A!Kúnta, /Han?kass'o and //Kabbo*. Cape Town: Kwela Books.
———. 2004b. *the stars say 'tsau': /Xam Poetry of Diä!kwain, Kweiten-ta-//ken, /A!Kúnta, /Han?kass'o and //Kabbo*. Cape Town: Kwela Books.

———. 2006a. *Body Bereft*. Cape Town: Umuzi.
———. 2006b. *Verweerskrif*. Cape Town: Umuzi.
Laurie, Trienke. 2001. *Uitroep*. Cape Town: Tafelberg.
Malan, Lucas. 2002. *Afstande*. Pretoria: Protea Boekhuis.
———. 2008. *Vermaning*. Pretoria: Protea Boekhuis.
Marais, Danie. 2006. *In die buitenste ruimte*. Cape Town: Tafelberg.
———. 2009. 'Die verhalende vers. Effe onmusikale worshonde, oftewel die poësie in die raamwerk van die verhalende vers'. http://versindaba.co.za/2009/07/14/die-verhalende-vers (accessed 6 July 2010).
Marais, Danie. 2010. 'Stilte in die hof!' *Rapport*, 4 April: 6–7.
Marais, Johann Lodewyk. 2002. *Aves*. Pretoria: Protea Boekhuis.
———. 2004. *Plaaslike kennis*. Pretoria: Protea Boekhuis.
Marais, Loftus. 2008. *Staan in die algemeen nader aan vensters*. Cape Town: Tafelberg.
Moretti, Franco. 2000. 'Conjectures on World Literature'. *New Left Review* 1: 54–68.
Müller, Petra. 2002. *Die aandag van jou oë*. Cape Town: Tafelberg.
Naudé, Charl-Pierre. 2004. *In die geheim van die dag*. Pretoria: Protea Boekhuis.
———. 2009. 'Die verhaal-element in liriese verse'. http://versindaba.co.za/2009/07/05/die-funksie-van-die-verhaal-element-in-die-liriese-vers (accessed 6 July 2010).
Nieuwoudt, Stephanie. 2010. ' 'n Digter wat uit sy murg kon dig'. *Rapport Boeke*, 2 May: 13.
Odendaal, Bernard. 2007. *Onbedoelde land*. Cape Town: Tafelberg.
Odendaal, B.J. 2006. 'Tendense in die Afrikaanse poësie in die tydperk 1998–2003'. In: *Perspektief en profiel: 'n Afrikaanse literatuur-geskiedenis. Deel 3*, edited by H.P. van Coller. Pretoria: Van Schaik: 105–48.
Philander, P.J. 2002. *Trialoog*. Pretoria: Protea Boekhuis.
Pieterse, Henning. 2000. *Die burg van Hertog Bloubaard*. Cape Town: Tafelberg.
Prins, Johannes. 2009. *Een hart*. Pretoria: LAPA.
Snyders, Peter. 2002. *Tekens van die tye*. Pretoria: Protea Boekhuis.
Sôls, Loit. 2006. *Die faraway klanke vanne hadeda*. Cape Town: Kwela Books.
Spies, Lina. 2004. *Duskant die einders*. Cape Town: Human & Rousseau.
———. 2006. 'Ongebluste kole van wellus en geluk'. *Die Burger (By)*, 15 July: 9.
Stander, Carina. 2006. *Die vloedbos sal weer vlieg*. Cape Town: Tafelberg.
Toerien, Barend. 2001. *Die huisapteek*. Pretoria: Protea Boekhuis.
Van Coller, H.P. (ed.). 2006. *Perspektief en profiel: 'n Afrikaanse literatuur-geskiedenis*. Pretoria: Van Schaik.
Van Niekerk, Dolf. 2006. *Nag op 'n kaal plein*. Cape Town: Human & Rousseau.
Van Niekerk, Marlene. 2004. *Agaat*. Cape Town: Tafelberg.
———. 2009. 'Met buskruit en salpeter. Marlene van Niekerk in gesprek met Louis Esterhuizen'. http://versindaba.co.za/2009/07/04/onderhoud-marlene-van-niekerk (accessed 6 July 2010).
Van Staden, Ilse. 2003. *Watervlerk*. Cape Town: Tafelberg.
———. 2008. *Fluisterklip*. Pretoria: LAPA.
Van Vuuren, Helize. 1999. 'Perspektief op die Afrikaanse poësie (1960–1997)'. In: *Perspektief en profiel: 'n Afrikaanse literatuur-geskiedenis. Deel 2*, edited by H.P. Van Coller. Pretoria: Van Schaik: 244–304.
Van Zyl, Wium. 2001. 'Streektaal weer ontgin'. *Die Burger*, 16 July: 9.

Venter, Eben. 2006. *Horrelpoot*. Cape Town: Tafelberg.
Viljoen, Louise. 2003. 'Nog 'n omdigting van Bybelse onthougoed'. *Literator* 24(3): 168–71.
Visagie, Andries. 2009. 'Van opstopper-gedigte tot muurpapierverse. Andries Visagie in gesprek met Louis Esterhuizen'. http://versindaba.co.za/2009/11/16/onderhoud-andries-visagie (accessed 6 July 2010).
Walters, M.M. 2004. *Satan ter sprake*. Pretoria: Protea Boekhuis.
Watson, Stephen. 1991. *Return of the Moon: Versions from the /Xam*. Cape Town: The Carrefour Press.
———. 2005. 'Annals of Plagiarism: Antjie Krog and the Bleek and Lloyd Collection'. *New Contrast* 33(2): 48–61.

10

Antjie Krog
Towards a Syncretic Identity

HELIZE VAN VUUREN

De Zuid-Afrikaanse literatuur houdt zich nog steeds bezig met het verleden. Poëzie begint wat mij betreft met ongehoorzaamheid, met verzet [South African literature is still preoccupied with the past. Poetry starts for me with disobedience, with resistance].
— Antjie Krog, quoted in Jan Kees van de Werk, *Karavaan van de verbeelding: Van Gorée naar Timboektoe* (my translation)

For people to be able to live together, to start singing from the same fold of skin . . . there is a need for unchangeable truths. We need common ground to grow a common humanity.
— Antjie Krog, *A Change of Tongue*

In June 1999 Antjie Krog took two months' leave at the end of the general election,

to see what remains inside her of the being of a poet . . . after so many years of testimony at the Truth Commission and political rhetoric in parliament . . . will she still be able to work in her mother tongue? . . . Her literary output seems to be divided in two. All her life, her poetry has been Afrikaans. Her professional journalism has been English. Her greatest literary achievement has been in English prose, and the money she earned from that has now allowed her to take unpaid leave to see if she can still write an Afrikaans poem. *Split by languages into genre and theme* (2003: 249, emphasis added).

Poet of eight collections between 1970 and 1995, Krog had achieved considerable status in the Afrikaans literary canon at the end of the twentieth century as a leading Afrikaans poet, alongside Breyten Breytenbach. The English-speaking world was more or less unconscious of her literary stature as poet, until the publication of *Down to my Last Skin* (2000a). This book only appeared after the considerable success of *Country of my Skull* (1998), her first book on the activities of the Truth and Reconciliation Commission (TRC). The TRC became the intense focus of national as well as international attention in the first years of the fledgling new democracy as South Africans struggled to work through apartheid history. This kind of reworking of the past, which Theodor W. Adorno called '*Aufarbeitung der Vergangenheit*' (literally, 'the work of coming to grips with the past'), is reflected in its South African version in Krog's *Country of my Skull*: a compilation of journalistic reports, testimonies by victims and perpetrators, poetical meditations, semi-autobiography and more. Extensively translated into most of the world's languages, the book earned Krog the Hiroshima Foundation Award for Peace and Culture in 2000, as well as numerous other national and international prizes. Overnight, with one English publication, the Afrikaans poet (hardly known outside the confines of the language) shot to fame and became an internationally recognised journalist, political commentator and writer. Admittedly the book encapsulates the essence of the apartheid experience, one that struck at the heart of the South African nation, and appeared when the whole world's attention was focused on the developments in the country. *Country of my Skull* captured and brought alive in graphic detail, interspersed with poetic language, a dense mosaic of microcosmic life stories in the form of first-person narration, meditation and psychological, political and philosophical discourse against the background of the life story of the journalist-poet narrator. (The film, *In My Country*, with Juliette Binoche and Samuel L. Jackson, followed in 2004.)

The key to Krog's stature as a poet is to be found in the effect of this powerful text: an ability to grip the reader with immediate involvement, a directness and immediacy through the high emotional intensity of the writing and a fearless daring in transgression of taboo subjects. Also striking in Krog's style is a singularly sure hand at a combination of the referential and the metonymic: a strong basis in contemporary events, combined with a sharp sense of the poetic.

In the immediate aftermath of the intense events of the TRC (at second hand also traumatising to personnel and journalists involved) Krog was faced with self-doubt and a creative dilemma: doubt about her ability as a poet and, above all, doubt about writing again in Afrikaans, the language for which she had asked forgiveness from victims in *Country of my Skull* (dedicated to 'every victim who had an Afrikaner surname on her lips'). Collective guilt weighed heavily on her (she later became the director of the Institute of Justice and Reconciliation), as did self-questioning about her creative career in Afrikaans and as a poet, after many years of working in journalism and writing prose, mainly in English. Krog's stature in Afrikaans literature at that stage was based on her eight collections of Afrikaans poetry (subsequently she published two new collections and translated into Afrikaans one collection of indigenous verse and one collection of /Xam narratives reworked into poems). Her stature was reflected in the many literary awards she had won for her poetry (the Eugène Marais Prize and the Dutch Reina Prinsen-Geerlings Prize for most promising young writer, the Rapport, RAU and Hertzog prizes). The literary and financial success of *Country of my Skull* alerted Krog to the fact that

> [i]n South African literature, English is the language in which writers reach each other, meet each other, get into conversation or debate. And, in the way of a mighty language, English does not care two hoots whether there are brilliant writers in Afrikaans or Xhosa or Sepedi: if a writer does not write in English, he or she does not really exist. *She realizes that translation is therefore one of the key strategies for survival* (2003: 270, emphasis added).

There followed intense reflection on translation as a creative practice, which for Krog coincided with reflection on transformation as a force necessary to change South African society. A 'change of tongue' (the title of her 2003 book) therefore does not only refer to the medium of another language in which to write, but also to a new way in which to speak and a different key in which to dream a new society. Translation is inextricably bound up with transformation – of the perceived identity of the self and of South African society. The need to remove barriers, break down the boundaries between black and white culture, between Afro- and Eurocentricism are especially the focus of *A Change of Tongue* (2003), *There Was This Goat* (2009) and *Begging to be Black* (2009). There is also a noticeable striving towards a new syncretic South African identity, a common humanity in which the best of black and white culture may be combined. This striving first becomes clear in the poetry collection *Kleur kom nooit alleen nie* (Colour never comes alone) (2000b) on the poetical level, where the poet attempts to shake off the complexity and rules of a Western writerly tradition in exchange for the greater accessibility and perceived contact with the community through the use of oral tradition. This process began in 1999 while Krog was on a poetry caravan with seven African poets travelling from Gorée to Timbuktu and was exposed to the tradition of the African griots (traditional oral poets). The journey resulted in a collection of poems in 2000, her first in five years, of which I offer a short overview to faciliate greater understanding of the phenomenon at play.

Colour never comes alone: *Kleur kom nooit alleen nie*

Krog's poetical oeuvre (1970–2006) can be divided into three phases. Phase one comprises juvenile and early adult poetry, with a small percentage of poems in the oral tradition, often from seSotho (the African language spoken in the Free State and the oral tradition best known to her when she was growing up). The collections in this early development phase are *Dogter van Jefta* (Daughter of Jephta) (1970); *Januarie-suite* (January suite) (1972); *Beminde Antarktika* (Beloved Antarctica) and *Mannin* (Virago), the last two from 1975. Phase two consists of *Otters in bronslaai* (Otters in watercress) (1981) and *Jerusalemgangers* (Jerusalem pilgrims) (1985), and culminates in the highpoint of her poetry in the Western 'writerly' tradition, *Lady Anne* (1989). The subsequent collection, published in 1995 and simply entitled *Gedigte 1989–1995* (Poems 1989–1995) marks a transitional phase in her work, with its radical political stance and extreme feminist and scatological poems. This collection seemed to be a cul-de-sac of sorts, as one could hardly envisage further growth-points from the intense anger at patriarchy and at apartheid oppression expressed in this volume. All boundaries of decorum, form and taboo are pushed to the limits in this challenging collection that hammers the reader relentlessly with shock tactics, anger and violence on a linguistic as well as a thematic level.

Indeed it took five years and the slow rebirth of a new South Africa before Krog published her next volume of poetry. The poems in *Kleur kom nooit alleen nie* (2000b) alert the reader via a medical motto ('the healing of wounds is the healing of the integrity of damaged tissue') that the process suggested in the poetry is the healing of a fragmented, wounded psyche, of an individual, but by implication also of a nation. A psychological process towards eventual healing is described via physical journeys (first to the Richtersveld and then through West Africa), a focus on the stoniness of the land, on rivers (first the Orange or 'Great Gariep' and later the Niger), living 'above' and 'below' ground (the poet as wife versus the poet as a writer). In the six 'narratives' from the Richtersveld, the poet struggles with an inability to translate the landscape into language: '*gee my taal vir klip pleit ek . . . ek soek taal*' (give me words for stone I plead . . . I search for words/language).

Resounding intertexts here are N.P. van Wyk Louw's '*Die beiteltjie*' (The little chisel) (1974 [1954]:186), '*Klipwerk*' (Stonework) (1974 [1954]: 189–216) and '*Groot ode*' (Great ode) (1970 [1962]: 322–32), all three poems on the struggle with African stone and articulation of the person's place in the landscape. As Louw recorded the collective orality of farm labourers and farmers in the rurally based oral poetry of '*Klipwerk*', so Krog finds in the stony landscape and the sociolect of the Coloured pastoral people of the Richtersveld (with their particularly concrete, biblical use of

'Orange River' Afrikaans) a poetical source of renewal for her mother tongue. She uses these 'narratives' of the Richtersveld as a conduit for the voices of various characters: '[A]s my oë kyk, kyk my oë klip' (when my eyes look they see stone), says Jan Links from Kommagas in 'Narrative of the diamond sorter' (Weinberg 2000: 62). The collection ends with a creative reworking in modern form of Boerneef's love poem 'Die berggans het 'n veer laat val' (The mountain goose has dropped a feather), in Krog's 'Niks by te voeg' (Nothing to add). This illustrates how close this collection moves to the oral tradition characteristic of Africa and older Afrikaans.

In the first section of *Kleur kom nooit alleen nie* 'colour' has to do with the spectrum of colours in the sunsets of the Richtersveld and the colour of stone. In section two the reader is confronted with the complexity of political violence and the 'baggage' of skin colour. In '*dagboeke uit die laaste deel van die twintigste eeu*' (diaries from the end of the twentieth century) the world of *Country of my Skull* is present in what can be called a catalogue of violence between people. Section three offers a disillusioning inside view of marriage and sexuality, with reference to a diversity of paintings. The last section contains poems dealing with the poet's trip through Africa. Krog re-creates the terror of the Rwandan genocide in graphic detail in '*klaaglied*' (lament):

> soundlessly death jogs through the dark
> jogs death panga-chopping, digging death
> (there's yesterday and tomorrow, but now is unbearable)
> through footsole and cartilage drones death through the dark
> it's the golden dark heart of Rwanda
> on a godless night in April (my translation from Krog 2000b: 77).

Healing of the psyche comes on a boat trip down the Niger in the poem '*afskeid*' (departure):

> dare skin say so much
> in the identity of words
>
> skin has many colours in Africa
> the heart many shapes
>
> not the colour of skin
> but the colour of heart (my translation from Krog 2000b: 100).

and in '*aankoms*' (arrival):

> with the scar of tongue
> do we write the soil under our feet
> do we write the space in which we breathe
> in your word one smells humanity one tastes African
> to write
> is to belong
> with you
> my voice is free for the first time (my translation from Krog 2000b: 103).

It is through association and alignment with the West African griots that Krog finds the strongest inspiration for her renewed creativity, expressed so vividly in the last five lines above.

The paradigm switch in her ars poetica (away from the Western writerly tradition and the modernist poetry of complexity and high art) is described in A *Change of Tongue*: 'How can I talk to you? You with your surface as warm as skin and your icy undertones? *Do I need a special language? A new tongue? How?*' (2003: 282, emphasis added). In a moment of introspection into the nature of her own work that she took with her on the poetry caravan, Krog wonders '*what* will work here?' and describes her view of the 'three tiers of poetry' as elitist (first world), middle class (dealing with 'love, lineage and lime tree') and an oral, working-class poetry (on struggle and liberation) (2003: 291). She wonders whether one type can 'talk to the other', but then concedes that 'such questions are immaterial here, and that is the real nightmare. Whatever she has to say will be inaudible, because her language does not exist here. Only her body and her colour'. Confronted with the performing griots she asks herself how poetry functions in that context of audience interaction and performance. During the journey she is informed about the role of griots in society:

> Griots are a caste. You are born into it . . . The griots have tasks they have to perform during festive occasions, births, weddings, funerals . . . The griot must be able to use his language skills *to transform points of contention and conflict* into enriching insight and ultimate peace (2003: 298, emphasis added).

Krog observes the power of repetition, dramatic microphone technique and audience participation in the performances by fellow African poets. Midway through the journey, 'it's as if she finds herself in a pool of poetic awareness' and she sets to work, writing a new piece, working out 'sound possibilities for the existing poems, how to use various parts and levels of her voice, rhythms and intonations, and she rewrites them accordingly' (2003: 303–4).

These insights, brought about by interaction with and exposure to the practice of the performing African griots, led to a moment of epiphany for Krog as a poet and a radical change in her own practice. The shift is reflected clearly in the change of tone, form and content between the first phase of her oeuvre and *Kleur kom nooit alleen nie*. This orally orientated collection forms a high point in her work and contrasts as a collection with the 'writerly' climax of the first phase, *Lady Anne*, described by the poet Barend Toerien as 'a novel in verse of epic proportions' (1990: 54). From behind the adopted white persona of the eighteenth-century society lady and artist, Lady Anne Barnard, the poet angrily questions the function of poetry in a world beset with socio-political problems. Between these two collections Krog's poetical assumptions shifted drastically: in the largely oral-based poetics of *Kleur kom nooit alleen nie* the orientation is that of an esssentially African poet functioning in, and for, a larger collective community (Richtersveld, South Africa, and as part of the larger African continent with its age-old imagined community of poets, griots, shamans and *izimbongi* or praise-singers). Admittedly this shift towards the oral was signalled much earlier in her work. In *Jerusalemgangers* (1985: 9–15) she experimented with the seSotho oral tradition in four orally based poems, most notably in 'lied van Peter Labase' (song of Peter Labase) (see Van Vuuren 1988: 163–71). Krog, as white Afrikaans poet, is grounded in the Afrikaans and Western writerly poetical tradition, yet here her orientation has changed to one where the poetry is much more accessible and open, the tone one of compassion for the collective. The anger of the transitional phase in *Gedigte 1989–1995* only reappears again in *Verweerskrif* (*Body Bereft*) six years later, although aimed not at political incapacitation and male chauvinism, but at the defenceless corporeality of the ageing female body and the finite nature of human life.

Flaunting the female body: *Verweerskrif/Body Bereft*

Dating back to her debut in 1970 with *Dogter van Jefta*, Krog has portrayed women at various stages of their lives. The collections follow Krog's own biological development. The genres of poetry and autobiography often seem to merge and overlap: a young adolescent in *Dogter van Jefta* and *Januarie-suite* (1972), bride and young woman in *Mannin* and *Beminde Antarktika* (both 1975), domestic drudge, as mother-and-wife behind the sink in *Otters in bronslaai* (1981), up to the 'writerly' high point in the Cape society lady and painter/writer in *Lady Anne* (1989). During this first phase Krog was still very much a 'writerly' poet, in the tradition of D.J. Opperman and the modernists. In 1995 this 'lady' of the Cape makes way in the transitional *Gedigte*

1989–1995 for her profile as political activist and feminist. This collection is stark and harsh, filled as it is with anger. In 2000, with *Kleur kom nooit alleen nie*, comes a new phase, orally orientated, more accessible, less writerly in many ways. The poetry has lost most of its modernist characteristics. The anger has made way for compassion for suffering humanity and a striving towards healing and communality. The ground tone is softer, gentler.

In *Verweerskrif* (entitled *Body Bereft* in its English version) the public sphere and functions are minimised and replaced almost completely with the private, physical space of the ageing, menopausal woman, her family (husband, children, grandchildren) and her home in Cape Town, near Table Mountain. The central theme of the collection is the degeneration and mortality of the human body, contrasted with the timelessness of the mountain in the background: 'finite human time' against 'eternity'. The Afrikaans title refers ambiguously to a text on degeneration, but can also mean a 'defence against a charge'. In this latter connotation, one might read an implied response to Stephen Watson's plagiarism charge against Krog in 2005 for both the publication of *die sterre sê 'tsau'/the stars say 'tsau'* (2004) and *Country of my Skull*. Krog's – the poet's – defence against the charge of plagiarism was to publish another collection of verse: to establish her stature as a strong and original voice. How many collections of poetry deal with menopause? And if such collections exist, which poets use such colloquial anatomical language to describe this female rite of passage? For originality of content and form, Krog cannot be faulted here, even if one grants her less stature, as Stephen Gray (2006) does, for her poeticism and/or her command of the English language. How many charges of plagiarism are answered in such a consciously 'in your face' form?

The theme of degeneration is announced on the cover page with a photograph by David Goldblatt of the nude torso of an ageing woman's breasts, arms and weathered hands. This cover debunks the cult of beauty associated with women's magazines. It suggests the taboo and transgression which materialises in the rest of the collection (menopausal symptoms, physical decay of the ageing female body) as well as a particularly direct, at times brutal, vocabulary of sex. This shock tactic has been present in Krog's oeuvre since parts of the 'township toilet' poem in *Gedigte 1989–1995* and again in the second and last sections of *Kleur kom nooit alleen nie*. However, in *Verweerskrif/Body Bereft* the language is taken to extremes, to such an extent that it becomes a barrier to some readers' appreciation of the poetry (see Gray 2006: 4–5). Gray's negative reaction started a debate on the functionality of the cover picture and the use of obscene language in poetical form.

Auguste Rodin used the erstwhile beauty who was the model for his famous sculpture, *The Kiss*, many decades afterwards in 1885 for a sculpture entitled, *She who once was the helmet-maker's beautiful wife* (also the title of a François Villon poem). In reaction to the perceived decadence and darkness of this art work, Rainer Maria Rilke remarked: 'When an artist . . . softens the grimace of pain, the shapelessness of age, the hideousness of perversion, when he arranges nature – veiling, disguising, tempering it to please the ignorant public – then he is creating ugliness because he fears the truth' (quoted in Elsen 1963: 64). Rilke accentuates the 'truth' of the abject in contrast with the dishonesty of romanticising, softening, sepia-coloured art. The similarity between the themes of Rodin and Krog is remarkable in the portrayal of the 'shapelessness of age'. In 'God, Death, Love' Krog spells out that she is conscious of breaking poetical taboos:

God, Death, Love, Loneliness, Man
are Important Themes in Literature
menstruation, childbirth, menopause, puberty
marriage are not

meanwhile terror lies exactly in how
one lives with the disintegrating body (2006a: 20).

Verweerskrif/Body Bereft deals with decay and physical disintegration, as well as increasing consciousness of the limits of human life. But in the final long poem on Table Mountain (2006b: 85–111) the mountain grows into a symbol of eternity: already passively there for 40 million years and still to be there long after the extinction of *Homo sapiens*. In this way 'important themes' are interwoven closely with the perceived 'non-important themes' such as menopause, birth and marriage: eternity is juxtaposed with '*mense-tyd*' (human time) as it is called in the final poem. In this way the collection attains a complexity which rises above the 'crude' language and the explicit physicality of the ageing woman with her experiences of a stroke, fear of breast cancer and the like.

The body in *Verweerskrif/Body Bereft* is a constant reminder of mortality. The dilemma, in this final poem, is a struggle with the concept of eternity and an intense denial of eternity because it is 'now that I want to live' (2006a: 93). Consolation for human mortality comes gradually and only partially through unwavering concentration on the lastingness of the landscape, the endurance of the mountain. But the fundamental emotion in the collection is anger against the speaker's lot as '*onthemelde*' (banned from heaven): 'I am blind with anger that I only / live once' (my translation from 2006b: 93).

This most recent poetry collection from Krog is thematically and technically innovative and of great complexity. Clearly it is also a collection which challenges and shocks the reader, as was evident in the literary debate that followed from the first reviews.

'Revolutionising the language' and transgressing taboos

Descriptions of violence and the scatological are typical of the later Krog, first obvious in the transitional collection, *Gedigte 1989–1995*. The register of poetic language is pushed further than ever before in Afrikaans poetry through: (a) the inclusion of sexual epithets, crude colloquial and sexually tinged language; (b) expletives; and (c) a mish-mash of Afrikaans and English as spoken increasingly in colloquial usage. Thematically Krog addresses topics 'about which one would never write a poem' ('toilet poem', 2000a: 54): (a) the details of excretory functions in a broken-down, over-used township toilet ('*verskrikking*'/'terror' continues this theme, complete with the poet's wiping her anus with her hand without toilet paper, 2000b: 93–6); (b) descriptions of genitalia and sex; and (c) detailed descriptions of the effect of brutal violence on human bodies in South and West Africa (2000b: 32–36, 77).

Although these descriptions are linked to political struggles in the various regions, the effect amounts to a relentless catalogue of horrors. These explicit depictions elicit questions as to their function. How many of Krog's shock tactics are purposely used to provoke response? Relevant here is a remark Krog made about the effect of the fame which *Country of my Skull* thrust upon her:

> And then you start becoming worried when that for which you stand and that in which you believe has become so acceptable. And *you have to move carefully so that you do not change the principle of your outputs just because you want to be controversial*. In other words, *you don't always want to elicit anger* (in Brümmer 2006: 13, my translation, emphasis added).

These remarks show that Krog is conscious of the controversy around much of her later work and that she has sometimes consciously sought to elicit angry reaction. If so, is this not a cheap trick? In what way do these graphic images of perpetrated violence differ from our nightly portion of horror on the SABC television news and in the daily media? Why are they utilised at all? In a poet with such proven poetic ability, why resort to shock tactics? One reason might be found in her ars poetica, driven as she is to 'revolutionize' her mother tongue. A comment in *A Change of Tongue* reads: 'I actually think you can only revolutionize a language if you have grown up in it' (2003: 271). To 'revolutionize' implies to renew, to overturn, to change drastically whatever exists and to replace it with something new. Applied to the literary sphere this implies a continuous striving for total renewal, based on originality.

Clearly, after *Country of my Skull* and the TRC period, Krog was uncomfortable with her mother tongue, at least in its standard version spoken by upright citizens, called by the elite *'algemeen beskaafde Afrikaans'* (general civilised Afrikaans) in linguistic circles until a decade or so ago. One way she found in her poetry to counteract this perceived elite and 'pure' (i.e., withstanding 'contamination' through Anglicisation) *'algemeen beskaafde Afrikaans'* was presumably to resort to using the 'mixed' colloquial lingua franca (with much English in-between the Afrikaans words) plus the language of the gutter, of 'bergies', of the underdog and of subcultures – to great effect, too.

Krog's poetical oeuvre always surprises, continually changes, is impressive, even brilliant in many instances, and is characterised by her ability to invoke intense emotional reactions from readers. Some readers object that the coarse street language 'deafens' them so that they cannot 'hear' Krog's poetical voice. This was said specifically of *Verweerskrif/Body Bereft*. Certainly Gray took exception to meeting Krog in the English version, as 'undressed and ever so candid, now with her loose pelvic floor' and to such 'obscenities [as] exited with the Beats' as 'drybaked cunt' (2006: 4–5). Yet the Afrikaans critic Louise Viljoen reads all these 'obscenities' from a feminist theoretical perspective and along Rabelaisian lines in a careful, detailed study of the '[g]rotesque, monstrous and abject bodies' in Krog's poetry (2009). To Viljoen the introduction of the abject and grotesque female body in Krog's oeuvre is to be read as reaffirming:

> Krog's position as someone who is constantly shifting the boundaries of her chosen genre by choosing impermissible themes and treating them in a transgressive way. In this regard she *practises a 'politics of the body' which rebels against the restrictions on the representation of the (female) body imposed by society as well as aesthetic traditions* (emphasis added).

Viljoen concedes that Krog's transgression of taboos goes against 'aesthetic traditions' but sees value in the conscious flaunting of the transgressive as a technique practised in the name of feminism, as it reclaims space for the female body and thus for female subjectivity. Gray, as male critic, denies Krog both the aesthetic space for this and the validity of the undertaking (how much of his irritation is founded in the perceived lack of quality in the translation is difficult to judge). In the debate that ensued after Gray's review, the poet Johann de Lange came to Krog's defence, praising her for her 'ability for self-renewal, to dare in new directions without fear, to never write in a way that ... is safe or acceptable to everyone, which makes her one of the most exciting contemporary poets and one of Afrikaans literature's most important voices' (my translation from De Lange 2006: 4).

Nic Dawes offers a different perspective with his view of Krog's translated collection *Body Bereft* as yet another stepping-stone in the translation programme she embarked upon in 2000 (expounded upon at length in *A Change of Tongue*) as an attempt towards creating a common humanity: '"I believe in translation for us to be able to live together", as Nelson Mandela told Krog when asking her to translate his autobiography, *Long Walk to Freedom*, into Afrikaans' (Dawes 2006).

These critics (Viljoen and De Lange on the one side and Gray and Dawes on the other side) are of course commenting on different texts, the first group on the Afrikaans original, the latter on English translations. In a note at the end of *Body Bereft*, Krog remarks on the translation process:

> The English text sometimes differs from the original Afrikaans in content and/or form. This is the case where the translation process required creative solutions, which in their turn opened up possibilities in the poems. *All translations were done by me*, except for 'manifesto of a grandma' and 'Four seasonal observations of Table Mountain', done by Andries Wessels, and 'it might have been a jellytot', done by Gus Ferguson (2006: 112, emphasis added).

Gray's vituperative reaction to what he perceived as the weakness of the English versions functions as a timely reminder that poetry translation is not an easy task and perhaps that poetry is in essence untranslatable.

Perhaps a question worth considering is whether there might be a distinction in the shock effect of the use of taboo language (e.g., expletives, coarse sexual terminology) and of taboo content matter (such as menopause) if one looks specifically at the reception of Krog's *Verweerskrif/Body Bereft*. Judging from the techniques used by that other accomplished stylist in taboo and transgression in Afrikaans literature, Marlene van Niekerk, in *Triomf* (1994), it was rather the relentless shock effect of the linguistic onslaught (racial pejoratives, sexual expletives) than the content/subject matter of incest which critics found beyond the pale in the reception of the novel. Michel Foucault, in another context, commented on this under-researched area of taboo words and their effect:

> humanity does not start out from freedom but from limitation and the line not to be crossed. We know the systems of rules with which forbidden acts are to comply; we have been able to discern the rules of the incest taboo in every culture. *But we still do not know much about the organisation of the prohibitions in language . . . the rule forbidding the utterance of certain words or*

expressions (the entire religious, sexual, magical series of blasphemous words) (1995: 293–4, emphasis added).

Possibly most illuminating for the use of explicit sexuality and expletives in Krog's work is the influence of Erica Jong (Viljoen 2007: 18). In a 1984 *Fair Lady* interview Krog stated: 'Erica Jong freed me from the Elisabeth Eybers image: the poet as regal woman. Her ideas rid me of a lot of complexes. I felt free to be a housewife, to be frustrated, to be myself' (quoted in Viljoen 2007: 18). Like Jong, Krog may be said to 'write from the female point of view with as much verve (and nerve) as Roth and Updike had written from the male' (Jong 1993: 15). Jong quotes Henry Miller on obscenity: 'When obscenity crops up in art, in literature more particularly, it usually functions as a technical device . . . *its purpose is to awaken, to usher in a sense of reality*' (9, emphasis added).

Translation and transformation: In search of a common humanity

In the Richtersveld in 1999 Krog experienced the 'healing (of) her mother tongue' (2003: 252) as she listened to the Nama pastoralists, 'the people of the stone desert speak'. Listening to their poetic, half-oral, half-biblical sociolect and the realisation that the community of Afrikaans-speakers was much wider than the white population on whose behalf she had suffered collective guilt enabled her to write poetry in Afrikaans again. The six 'narratives' of the Richtersveld, published in translation in Paul Weinberg's book under the title 'It takes a lot of God to survive here' (2000: 53–73), signal the end of her writer's block as Afrikaans poet. With the healing of the mother tongue came a realisation of the fragmented nature of South African society into race, class, multilingual communities and many cultures. This realisation, coupled with Mandela's request that Krog translate his autobiography into Afrikaans, spurred her on to a large translation project spanning a couple of years (see Mandela 2001), which also resulted in an anthology of indigenous verse from ten indigenous languages, *Met woorde soos met kerse* (With words as with candles) (2002), the reworking into verse of /Xam narratives and myths collected by W.H.I. Bleek and Lucy C. Lloyd, *die sterre sê 'tsau'/the stars say 'tsau'* (both published in 2004) and translations from Dutch, *Domein van glas* (Van Woerden 1998) and *Mamma Medea* (Lanoye 2002).

In 2005, Watson claimed that Krog's reworkings into Afrikaans verse of Bleek and Lloyd material (1968 [1911] and Bleek 1924, 1931) in *the stars say 'tsau'* constituted plagiarism. Surprisingly enough he had followed the same procedure in 1991 with his *Return of the Moon* (although admittedly his method was less nonchalant around the historical facts regarding the /Xam)! In Krog's creative reworking she is following an established tradition of increasing use of the /Xam culture by poets and writers such as Arthur Markowitz, Uys Krige, Laurens van der Post, Alan James, Watson and many others (for a more complete overview see Van Vuuren 2003: 1–27).

George Steiner argues that the act of translation is also an act of restitution: 'Some translations edge us away from the canvas, others bring us close' (2000: 189–90). Rewriting and versification of /Xam narratives may be seen as enlargement of the stature of the 'original', whether these new versions pull readers in or push them away. The 'original' in the case of /Xam oral narratives is unreachable, lost in the mists of time, no longer exists. All that remains are records and verbal notes of fragmented versions. In Markowitz's collection, *With Uplifted Tongue*, he talks about the transposition of the material: 'After many experiments I struck what I believe to be a tolerable compromise in making the stories easily understood without yet sacrificing too much of their elliptical style' (1956: n.p.). It is this 'elliptical style' plus the metaphoric, poetical quality of texts such as 'The Broken String', which inevitably draws poets to the material.

Two viewpoints remain: either one can state that respect is lacking for the cultural goods of the extinct /Xam culture where their narratives are reshaped and reworked to suit the later writer's purpose or one can choose Steiner's more tolerant perspective: all translation is an act of restitution, of homage to the poetical vitality embedded in the material. It is clear from the respective practices of Eugène Marais, Watson and Krog that using material from that vital source paradoxically enhances the stature of the later poet. The reason is that readers unfamiliar with the rather obscure Bleek and Lloyd sources inevitably attribute the new 'poems' or short stories (Marais) to the talent of the later poet or writer, as the reception of Marais's *Dwaalstories* (1985 [1927]) has clearly shown.

Translation is also pivotal to *There Was This Goat: Investigating the Truth Commission Testimony of Notrose Nobomvu Konile* (2009), co-authored with Nosisi Mpolweni and Kopano Ratele. The text is built around the thorough retranslation and reinterpretation of a little-understood testimony given in isiXhosa at the TRC hearings. Much attention is given specifically to the simultaneous translations done by interpreters at the TRC. Incorrect translation had led in Mrs Konile's case to incomprehension of this illiterate, uneducated and practically destitute rural Xhosa woman's testimony, her feelings and thoughts. This gives rise to questions about multilingualism and intercultural communication: 'How do we hear one another in a country where the past is still so present amongst us?' (Krog, Mpolweni and Ratele 2009: 42):

> In a country emerging from a divisive past, some narratives, such as that of Mrs Konile, are likely to reproduce old cultural, racial and geographical

divisions. To overcome that, as well as inevitable interpretation and transcription mistakes, there is almost no other way to proceed than by *collaboratively* working within a communally-orientated, human-centred methodology . . .

[E]very narrative is rooted. In order to really 'hear' a story we have to take its rootedness into account – especially in the light of a divisive past (46).

Krog's co-authors are specialists in isiXhosa (Mpolweni) and African psychology (Ratele). As Mrs Konile's narrative 'defied all the elements that render narratives "audible"', these three worked together successfully to 're-code' Mrs Konile's testimony from the 'incomprehensible' to the comprehensible. Before she died they traced her to Indwe (near Queenstown in the Eastern Cape), observed 'markers of healing' in her coping, forgetting, integrating and progressing, and were able to interview her once more before she died a year later.

The central questions for Krog in her large translation project are: 'How much of what we hear can we translate into finding ways of living together? How do we overcome a divided past in such way that the "Other" becomes "us"?' (Krog, Mpolweni and Ratele 2009: 42–3). Translation is understood as an intimate gesture of cultural interaction towards understanding and empathy, as transformation of the self and the other into a syncretic, collective 'us'. The implied ideological basis of this large translation project lies in a striving towards transformation of South African society into one where racial, cultural, linguistic and class barriers might be broken down, where a new communal identity might emerge, with the best of African culture and the best of Western culture combined in one syncretic whole. This can only come about through understanding, by translation of the different languages, the texts in the different languages, the dialogue of the 'other' self (as at the TRC hearings with its multiple translator-interpreters).

In her own practice of increasingly translating her poetry collections into English, this has not had ideal results, with André P. Brink especially (in a 2004 review of *the stars say 'tsau'*) and Gray (in his 2006 review of *Body Bereft*) both severely critical of the quality of the translations. With the prose works, *Country of my Skull* and *A Change of Tongue*, the attention was on the content, which tended to override close attention to the quality of the English. The reason probably lies in the expectations of the genre: prose is patient (the linguistic 'vehicle' is larger), but poetry is a more fragile, finer medium, where the aesthetic quality of each construct and turn of phrase is open to almost immediate scrutiny. Despite the flexibility of modern translation theory concerning the relationship of project purpose to appropriate method, source-text/target-text equivalence remains the widespread assumption (it is the assumption of both Brink and Gray). Accordingly, poetry translation is deemed to be notoriously difficult, if not impossible.

Conclusion

Krog's striving towards a new syncretic South African identity develops in her later oeuvre on two fronts: thematically in terms of content and, in relation to form, in terms of the increasing use of an African-based orally orientated poetics. Yet in her adoption of elements from the African oral tradition lie unresolved tensions in her work. The oral tradition is essentially pre-modern, with clearly described ground rules of communal orientation and the voicing of collective concerns. However, arguably, there is space for modernisation and renewal, as there is in all traditions. Michael Somniso (2008) illustrates how the genre of praise-singing has been adopted for contemporary socio-political use in the struggle against HIV and AIDS. At a public performance in Port Elizabeth the poet Mtshwane performed a very effective praise-poem called '*Isingxobo*' (Condom), which ends thus:

> Return your spear into your bag,
> This is no love war it's a life war,
> Return your thing to the bag,
> Condom – fellow brothers – Condom (Somniso 2008: 149–50).

Here we have praise-singing renewed as a reaction to socio-cultural pressures – the message in the struggle against HIV and AIDS is to 'condomise'. The praise-song has a humorous effect, but serious intent, and fairly explicit sexual content, although reference to the male sexual organ relies upon euphemism. In contrast, Krog proceeds by explicit naming.

When Krog adopts the oral mode in the poem about the Rwandan genocide, '*klaaglied*' (lament) – 'soundlessly death jogs through the dark / jogs death panga-chopping, digging death' (my translation from Krog 2000b: 77) – it becomes a haunting, lyrical poem on death, based on an oral poetics (utilising repetition, parallelism, concrete images, mnemonic devices). Yet it comes dangerously close to elevating death (and violence, in other poems set in an apartheid South African context) to the African status quo. Between the form of the elegy emanating from the Western literary tradition and the oral form from the African oral tradition, somehow there is no saving or healing perspective offered for the future. There exist unresolved tensions, therefore, in the implied ideological project of the later Krog oeuvre with the incorporation of the increasing orally orientated poetics which she has adopted. This striving towards healing of the communal and individual psyche in *Kleur kom noooit alleen nie* is largely sacrificed in *Verweerskrif/Body Bereft*, where it makes way for the intensely private and physical concerns of the ageing menopausal woman. It might be argued that the 'ageing' collection represents the silent audience of the poet's own age and gender profile or that death is a universal human concern. Whatever the view, the ideological perspective which has carried much of Krog's later work up to this point is less evident. The striving towards a common humanity is resumed in the moving narrative of Mrs Konile from Indwe in the co-authored *There Was This Goat*. And certainly, whatever the debates about the efficacy of translation, this extraordinarily moving text illustrates the strengths and profits of intellectual and creative collaboration on an intercultural basis. A similar commitment to connection amid divisiveness characterises Krog's 'creative-nonfictional' *Begging to be Black* (2009).

On the whole, Krog as a Western poet is an individualist, but with an ideological striving towards a new South African identity, according to which she utilises (incorporates syncretically) in her later oeuvre the communally based, collective traditions of African orality. This may bring with it unresolved tensions of modern and pre-modern systems in apparently paradoxical juxtapositions. Yet these same tensions may be identified as the source of the creativity out of which Krog's literary oeuvre continues to develop in challenging directions.

References

Bleek, D.F. (ed.). 1924. *The Mantis and his Friends: Bushman Folklore*. Cape Town: Maskew Miller.
———. 1931–1936. 'Customs and Beliefs of the /Xam Bushmen'. *Bantu Studies*, Vols. 1–10.
Bleek, W.H.I. and Lucy C. Lloyd (eds). 1968 [1911]. *Specimens of Bushman Folklore*. Cape Town: Struik.
Boorman, John. 2004. *In My Country* [film version of *Country of my Skull*].
Brink, André P. 2004. 'Ryp, deurwinterde bundel'. *Rapport*, 27 June: 24.
Brümmer, Willemien. 2006. 'Krog: "Met hierdie liggaam is ek"'. *Die Burger*, 2 June: 15.
Coetzee, Ampie, Ena Jansen, J.C. Kannemeyer, Gerrit Olivier and Edith Raidt (eds). 1988. *Woorde open die beskouing*. Durban: Butterworth.
Dawes, Nic. 2006. 'Fear and Loathing'. *Mail & Guardian Online*. http:// www.chico.mweb.co.za/art/2006/2006mar/060330-krog. html (accessed on 18 February 2008).
De Lange, Johann. 2006. 'Krog se nuutste verweer van bloed en ink'. *Rapport* (*Perspektief*), 16 April: 4.
Elsen, Albert E. 1963. *Rodin*. New York: Doubleday.
Foucault, Michel. 1995. 'Madness, the Absence of Work'. Translated by Peter Stasny and Deniz Sengel. *Critical Inquiry* 21: 291–8.

Gray, Stephen. 2006. 'Letting it (all) Hang Out'. *Mail & Guardian*, 17–23 March: 4–5.
Jong, Erica. 1993. *The Devil at Large: Erica Jong on Henry Miller*. London: Chatto & Windus.
Krog, Antjie. 1970. *Dogter van Jefta*. Cape Town: Human & Rousseau.
———. 1972. *Januarie-suite*. Cape Town: Human & Rousseau.
———. 1975a. *Beminde Antarktika*. Cape Town: Human & Rousseau.
———. 1975b. *Mannin*. Cape Town: Human & Rousseau.
———. 1981. *Otters in bronslaai*. Cape Town: Human & Rousseau.
———. 1985. *Jerusalemgangers*. Cape Town: Human & Rousseau.
———. 1989. *Lady Anne*. Johannesburg: Taurus.
———. 1995. *Gedigte 1989–1995*. Johannesburg: Hond.
———. 1998. *Country of my Skull*. Johannesburg: Random House.
———. 2000a. *Down to my Last Skin*. Johannesburg: Random House.
———. 2000b. *Kleur kom nooit alleen nie*. Cape Town: Kwela Books.
———. 2002. *Met woorde soos met kerse. Inheemse verse uitgesoek en vertaal deur Antjie Krog en ander*. Cape Town: Kwela Books.
———. 2003. *A Change of Tongue*. Johannesburg: Random House.
———. 2004a. *die sterre sê 'tsau': /Xam Gedigte van Diä!kwain, Kweiten-ta-//ken, /A!Kúnta, /Han?kass'o and //Kabbo*. Cape Town: Kwela Books.
———. 2004b. *the stars say 'tsau': /Xam Poetry of Diä!kwain, Kweiten-ta-//ken, /A!Kúnta, /Han?kass'o and //Kabbo*. Cape Town: Kwela Books.
———. 2006a. *Body Bereft*. Cape Town: Umuzi.
———. 2006b. *Verweerskrif*. Cape Town: Umuzi.
———. 2009. *Begging to be Black*. Cape Town: Random House Struik.
Krog, Antjie, Nosisi Mpolweni and Kopano Ratele. 2009. *There Was This Goat. Investigating the Truth Commission Testimony of Notrose Nobomvu Konile*. Pietermaritzburg: University of KwaZulu-Natal Press.
Lanoye, Tom. 2002. *Mamma Medea: na Apollonios van Rhodos en Euripides* [From the Dutch play *Mamma Medea*]. Translated by Antjie Krog. Cape Town: Queillerie.
Mandela, Nelson. 2001. *Lang pad na vryheid*. Translated by Antjie Krog. Johannesburg: Vivlia.
Marais, Eugène. 1985 [1927]. *Dwaalstories en ander vertellinge*. Cape Town: Human & Rousseau.
Markowitz, Arthur. 1956. *With Uplifted Tongue: Stories, Myths and Fables of the South African Bushmen Told in Their Manner*. Parow: Central News Agency.
Somniso, Michael. 2008. 'Intertextuality Shapes the Poetry of Xhosa Poets'. *Literator* 29(3): 139–56.
Steiner, George. 2000. 'The Hermeneutic Notion'. In: *The Translation Studies Reader*, edited by L. Venuti. London: Routledge: 187–99.
Toerien, Barend J. 1990. 'Antjie Krog: *Lady Anne*'. *World Literature Today* 64(1): 54.
———. 2000. 'Antjie Krog: *Kleur kom nooit alleen nie*'. *World Literature Today* 75(3/4): 124-5.
Van de Werk, Jan Kees. 2000. '*Karavaan van de verbeelding: Van Gorée naar Timboektoe*'. Amsterdam: Kit and Den Haag: Hivos.
Van Niekerk, Marlene. 1994. *Triomf*. Cape Town: Queillerie.
Van Vuuren, Helize. 1988. 'As jy gesien het, het jy vir altyd gesien . . . '. In: *Woorde open die beskouing*, edited by A. Coetzee et al. Durban: Butterworth: 163–72.

———. 2003. '"Die boesman in ons bewussyn": 'n histories-literêre oorsig van die Afrikaanse poësie'. *Stilet* XIV(2): 1–27.

Van Woerden, Henk. 1998. *Domein van glas* [From the Dutch *Een mond vol glas*]. Translated by Antjie Krog. Amsterdam: Podium.

Van Wyk Louw, N.P. 1970 [1962]. *Tristia en ander verse voorspele en vlugte 1950–1957*. Cape Town: Human & Rousseau.

———. 1974 [1954]. *Nuwe verse*. Cape Town: Tafelberg.

Venuti, Lawrence (ed.). 2000. *The Translation Studies Reader*. London: Routledge.

Viljoen, Louise. 2007. 'Antjie Krog en haar literêre moeders: die werking van 'n vroulike tradisie in die Afrikaanse poësie'. *Tydskrif vir letterkunde* 44(2): 5–28.

———. 2009. '"I have a body, therefore I am": Grotesque, Monstrous and Abject Bodies in Antjie Krog's Poetry'. Paper delivered at Triennial Conference of EACLALS (European Association of Commonwealth Language and Literature Studies), Venice, Italy (25–29 March).

Watson, Stephen. 1991. *Return of the Moon: Versions from the /Xam*. Cape Town: The Carrefour Press.

———. 2005. 'Annals of Plagiarism: Antjie Krog and the Bleek and Lloyd Collection'. *New Contrast* 33(2): 48–61.

Weinberg, Paul. 2000. *Once We Were Hunters: A Journey with Africa's Indigenous People*. Amsterdam: Mets & Schilt; Cape Town: David Philip.

11

Technauriture

Multimedia Research and Documentation of African Oral Performance

RUSSELL H. KASCHULA

African oral performance genres are presently reacting to factors such as technology and political events, as well as historical shifts towards more democratic regimes, which are accompanied by continued divisions between rich and poor. This is reflected in contemporary open-mike, spoken-word and slam poetry produced by artists ranging from the Zimbabwean Comrade Fatso to the South African Lebo Mashile, as well as to contemporary *izimbongi* or oral poets, such as Zolani Mkiva and storytellers such as Gcina Mhlophe.

Through the use of web networks and platforms, these performers are becoming more visible globally and are more able to market their literary talents. Sites that discuss, analyse and preserve material electronically are also emerging, the most recent being http://www.oralliterature.org, a site based in the United Kingdom.[1] This website is run by Mark Turin, under the auspices of the World Oral Literature Project, which was established at the University of Cambridge in 2009. The project aims to publish a library of oral texts and occasional papers and to make collections available through new media platforms. The first phase of the project is to provide grants to enable the collection of oral literary forms and the aim is for the site to become a permanent centre for the preservation and appreciation of oral forms by providing online access to digitised material. This and other websites are contributing to a new critical discourse which falls within what I term 'technauriture' (Kaschula 2004a, 2004 b).

This term includes technology, auriture and literature and involves both the oral and the aural. This seems appropriate when discussing both the production of oral literature and its reception through hearing and understanding, i.e., the aural aspects. David Coplan makes the point that '[m]any authors . . . pay lip service to the expressive inseparability of verbal, sonic, and visual media in constituting meaning in African genres, but do not address this unity in their analysis' (1994: 9). He thus makes use of the term 'auriture', 'for these performances act as a caution against the application of Western categories of literary analysis to African performance' (8). Auriture implies the use of a range of senses in one's appreciation of the oral word: hearing, speaking and the more abstract aesthetic analysis of the word – hence this word has been chosen to form part of the term 'technauriture'.

In the area of storytelling, the Iziko Museum in Cape Town and the International Museums Study Programme at the University of Bergen, Norway, have started an innovative web-based project as part of a communication initiative network. According to Katherine J. Goodnow and Yngvar Natland these museums 'have jointly developed a web-based concept that combines oral storytelling with new technology to connect schools in the South and the North' (2002: 122). Stories were collected from children and adults with the use of digital video and disseminated through handheld devices (personal digital assistants or PDAs) as well as through the Web to participating schools, museums and community groups. Information and Communication Technology (ICT) was used to incorporate storytelling into the museum environment and to relay it to a wider audience. Workshops are also used to encourage storytelling by children and adults from different backgrounds. The project explores the multiple forms of expression associated with storytelling, such as mime and dance, and how these can be captured and it shows how the Internet can be used in order to support and enhance forms of storytelling.[2]

Literature has been transformed by the spread of digital media over the last two or three decades. Contemporary orality can be captured, stored, disseminated and aesthetically appreciated in new ways. The face of the cellular phone now represents the contemporary page, with its own forms of indigenous language writing, especially in southern Africa, where there has been a proliferation of cellular phone usage, even amongst the poor. The pay-as-you-go communicative environment is impacting on general rules of politeness and producing new rules for communication. These rules conflict with traditional notions of *ubuntu* (sharing in the oral community) and the type of information generally associated with culturally acceptable communication skills in African languages, for example, isiXhosa. Nevertheless, the cellular phone allows for oral performance to be captured and disseminated. Globalisation and the emergence of new media, together with societal change, have fuelled a literary revolution in Africa, which, I believe, is best encapsulated in the term 'technauriture'.

This term provides a paradigm and a methodology that may allow researchers to find new ways of interpreting and analysing the changing oral literary scene. It is presently being explored in a Rhodes University Master's thesis by my student André Mostert, who is analysing the term in order to find suitable models for capturing, preserving and disseminating oral literature. What may be required more than ever before is a cross-disciplinary approach, which includes ICT and contemporary communication forums such as websites, blogs, Facebook, Myspace and YouTube. These forums provide a voice to the previously voiceless, though it must be stressed that access (and therefore 'literariness') is still characterised by class distinctions in Africa, with the wealthy having ready access to ICT, which the majority of the poor – despite their increasing use of cellular technology – still do not have the skills or resources to access. Yet technology now reaches everyone in some form or another. Increasing access through education and other means can narrow the gap between rich and poor. This belief is contrary to that of scholars who talk of the 'deepening divide' and inequality in the information age (for example, Van Dijk 2005). Increasingly in South Africa, the digital age is reaching the poor and the rural areas. The Siyakhula Living Lab computer facilities are being established in Dwesa in the coastal region of the former Transkei, with assistance from Rhodes University Computer Science Department and the Telkom Centre for Excellence (Van Wynegaard 2009). It is the cellular phone and ICT technology that are allowing orality to recover its importance alongside the word and the book (Landzelius 2006).

Many young people belong to writers' groups and also take part in performance poetry and even scriptwriting and film production through the use of cheap contemporary digital media. Questions that need to be researched are: how is this 'new' genre-mixed literature produced; how is it circulated and received; and how do scholars propose to disseminate, document and analyse this literature without violating artists' copyright? All these questions need to be answered in a single theoretical paradigm influenced by various disciplines, including ICT, ethnography, literary analysis and anthropology, as well as forms of critical theory, such as eco-literature, narratology, structuralism and postcolonial theories. By having the oral material digitised and made available in the mother tongues of the speakers as well as in English, thus allowing access to the source language, it is possible that counter-narratives may emerge that will challenge Western paradigms: new approaches might be provided for the understanding and re-interpretation of African history and literature.

The old Hymsean ethnographic research (see Kaschula and Anthonissen 1995) and Proppian structural literary analyses (Propp 1968) are no longer sufficient as theoretical paradigms in order to understand what is happening in the contemporary literary/historical arena in Africa. There are modern, multitalented cultural practitioners such as the Fingo Revolutionaries and the Botsotso Jesters in South Africa. In Zimbabwe the Book Café in Harare hosts spoken-word performances where political dissent is expressed. Comrade Fatso is one of the performers here. These Zimbabwean cultural activists operate under the Pamberi Trust and have further intellectualised their work through a relationship with contemporary literary and academic journals such as *Chimurenga* in South Africa and *Kwani?* in Kenya.[3] The online journal *LitNet* (http://www.litnet.co.za) operates in a number of languages in South Africa and offers literary artists and academics a platform to explore and showcase their work. Many spoken-word artists take part in poetry projects such as the Timbila Poetry Project in Newtown, Johannesburg, as well as the annual Poetry Africa Festival in Durban. The annual National Arts Festival in Grahamstown is a contemporary example of where the digital, the literary, the spoken word and visual art all come together. Wordfest, which is part of this festival, is an example of a meeting place for writers and performers in indigenous languages as well as in English. Book launches are held for books written in all the South African languages and seminars are also presented in various languages. Festivals such as these rely on the Web for publicity and most artists who visit these festivals have their own websites.

Southern African oral literature has generally been grouped into three primary genres: oral poetry (praise-poems and songs), narrative material (folktales, myths, legends, fables) and wisdom-lore (idioms, riddles and proverbs). What is now required is a paradigm to understand this mixing of genres and technologies in order to build on the seminal works of Walter J. Ong (1982), Ruth Finnegan (1988), B.V. Street (1995) and others. (An analysis of these genres and how they relate to aspects of modern-day African existence such as music, gender, medicine, theatre, cinema, religion, politics and history can be found in Kaschula 2001.)

Presenting a somewhat revolutionary approach as early as 1939, H.I.E. Dhlomo (1993) sought to explore the relationship between oral poetry and drama. By providing various examples of dramatic presentations, he attempted to prove that many *izibongo* were dramatic and produced for the purposes of entertainment. This argument speaks to the question of the mixing of genres, discourses and styles, suggesting that oral literature does not necessarily fall into clearly definable genres.

There is no performer in southern Africa who has not been touched by the influence of secondary orality and technology. In the following section, I turn to a Xhosa *imbongi* in order to see how this tradition adapts to new circumstances. These dynamics are evident in the work of southern African oral poets and literary voice-artists and have particular reference in the life and work of the late Bongani Sitole, a Xhosa *imbongi*.

Defining the Xhosa *imbongi*

The tradition of the *imbongi* or oral poet has never been static. As Jeff Opland puts it: 'The dynamic element is necessary in our approach since the tradition of Xhosa oral poetry has clearly changed and is continuing to change with changes in Cape Nguni society. Tradition is not a lifeless thing; it alters and adapts to new social circumstances' (1983: 236). Many traditional elements have been dropped or adapted, but the concept of singing praises still retains an identifiable character based on tradition. The *imbongi*'s relationship with the audience and the role which his *izibongo* (poetry) plays within that particular society are of utmost importance. Any analysis of the tradition will therefore have to take into account the context of the performance, the audience and the function and role of the *imbongi* in a society subjected to constant socio-cultural, political and technological pressure. Opland argues that the poet's role 'is to break down barriers between people; he is . . . a matchmaker, gathering people together who differ' (2005: 387). In relation to the well-known *imbongi* D.L.P. Yali-Manisi, Opland says:

> In performance he came alive, he was freed of the constraints of social intercourse, he broke free of the pains of his body, he could say what he wanted as he wanted. And what he said and the way he said it demanded attention and marked him as a man of stature, a true son of the soil of Africa, and one of its greatest poets (387).

Sitole's work shows how the tradition has adapted to a technologised, globalised world where orality, literacy and technology constantly interact. Coplan's research, which analyses changes in performance creativity and culture in South Africa over the years, provides concrete evidence of the adaptability of tradition. He argues: '[T]he production and reproduction of performances must be located within the set of political, economic, social and cultural, relations between performers and the total context in which they perform' (1994: 242). The contextualisation of Sitole's performances will provide a more holistic impression of the *imbongi* as well as the factors that have contributed to change in the tradition within the reality of globalisation and increasing reliance on 'technauriture'.

It might be necessary to build on the most recent definition of this term (Kaschula 2002: 47), since definitions require constant revision as their contexts change. In this definition it is suggested that the contemporary *imbongi* is a person involved in the oral production of poetry using traditional styles and techniques in any given context where he is recognised as mediator, praiser, critic and educator and accepted by the audience as such. There is, however, no mention of technology as a necessary part of a contemporary definition, although the discourse used by *izimbongi* is moulded within both the physical and technological contexts in which they find themselves.

New media forms and the work of Sitole

In *Qhiwu-u-u-la!! Return to the Fold!!* (Kaschula, Matyumza and Sitole 2006 [1996]) the technologising and digitising of Sitole's poetry was an essential part of the production of his work and the contemporary development of the oral word was found to be a five-fold process: capturing the oral word through technology and transcribing it into written isiXhosa; translating the written isiXhosa into English; the publication of both the isiXhosa and the English translation in book form; the digitising of some of the material and making it available on a website for downloading; and the oral and live performance of some of the poetry by innovative township youth groups.

How was the poetry collected? Where was it published? How did it reach book form? How has it come to appear on a website? What were the processes involved? What are the copyright issues involved in the further commercialisation of this oral art? To what extent does the technologising of the oral word, through the digitisation of the transcribed and translated word, bring it back to orality? Building on the work of Ong (1982), Finnegan (1988) and others, where the link between orality, literacy and technology is explored, I shall show that these three forms comfortably co-exist, as indicated in Finnegan's work. However, Ong's theoretical stance, which saw orality and literacy as separate modes of thought, can be misleading in the context of Sitole's work. Street sums this up as follows:

> Ong's thesis, then, appears to have little value in the investigation of the relationships between orality and literacy. We would do better to look for more specific relationships between literacy events and literacy practices on the one hand, and oral conventions on the other. In the project of investigating these relationships on a cross-cultural basis and in such a way as to yield fruitful generalizations, Ong's thesis does not provide much help and is, indeed, likely to mislead the unwary researcher (1995: 158–9).

Parts of Sitole's work are soon to be available online, together with an accompanying teacher/student guide. This completes the orality-literacy continuum and brings it full circle. Exercises accompany each of the poems in the book.[4]

Sitole's poetry was fuelled by events immediately prior to 1994 and contains historical perspectives regarding the struggle against apartheid. Again, the adaptation of themes reflects change in 'textual elements', those features which, according to Opland, are reflected in a transcribed text (1983: 241). The themes changed because the political and social environment on which the poetry is a commentary changed. Changes in themes are linked directly to changes in what Opland terms 'contextual elements' (253). The context in which the poetry is performed is no longer limited to an assembly in which the chief is the principal figure. The use of political rallies and meetings as well as contemporary open-mike sessions as a platform for the performance of *izibongo* has encouraged a change in the thematic repertoire of poets such as Sitole and the more recently acknowledged 'President's Poet', Mkiva, who has performed in honour of Nelson Mandela and Thabo Mbeki (see Kaschula 1999: 64–5). The repertoire now often reflects the new power bases that were legitimised with the emergence of a democratic South African society.

In terms of what Opland refers to as 'contextual elements' (those features which an audience can see and hear, but which are not reflected in a transcribed text) some changes have taken place. Individual poets have reacted differently to these contextual elements. Some, such as Sitole, have adapted their dress in order to suit their particular power bases. The poetry in Sitole's book was initially recorded on tape and video, with more than one hundred recordings made, reflecting the volatile pre-election period from 1990 to 1994. The poetry was then transcribed into isiXhosa by the performer. Sitole, together with the co-author of the book, Mandla Matyumza, and I then worked to translate the material into English. The book, *Qhiwu-u-u-la!! Return to the Fold!!*, containing fifteen selected poems in both languages, was published by Nasou Via Afrika in 1996 and re-issued in 2006.

Sitole's poems provide valuable insights into the socio-political issues facing South Africans immediately prior to the first democratic elections. They represent a 'slice of life' at a time when South Africa found itself at a turning point in its history. The following extract was produced at the re-burial of Chief Sabata Dalindyebo, an opponent of the independent homeland system and paramount chief of the Thembu clan. He was deposed by K.D. Matanzima, who became the first prime minister of the so-called independent homeland of the Transkei in 1976, in terms of the apartheid government's 'divide-and-rule' policy. Chief Sabata died in exile in 1986 in Zambia. When his body was brought back to Umtata (now Mthatha), it was forcibly removed from the funeral parlour by Matanzima's bodyguards and buried in a women's graveyard as a final insult. Matanzima was ousted in 1989 by Bantu Holomisa (now a parliamentarian and leader of the United Democratic Movement in the new South African democracy). With the blessing of Holomisa, who had by then become the new military leader and was pro-ANC (African National Congress), the immediate exhumation of Chief Sabata's remains was permitted and his remains were reburied at Bumbane Great Place. Here is an extract from Sitole:

Amandla!
Uza kuphakam' umzukulwana kaXobololo,
UXobololo uza kuxobul' ixolow' emthini kuvel' intlaka,
UXobololo uyaxoboloza,

UXobolol' unesifo sombefu,
Uxweb' impundu ngokuhlal' estoksini ngenxa kaDaliwonga

Power!
The grandchild of Xobololo is going to stand up,
Xobololo's going to peel the tree bark until gum appears,
Xobololo's trying,

Xobololo's suffering from asthma,
His buttocks are chaffed due to being jailed because of Daliwonga [Matanzima] (Kaschula, Matyumza and Sitole 2006 [1996]: 64).

The *imbongi* introduces the poem by making use of the word used to accompany the power salute during the struggle for freedom in South Africa: '*Amandla*' (power). This was common in the performance of *izimbongi* during this time. The audience would normally respond with a suitable reply, usually '*Awethu*' (literally, 'to us', meaning 'to the people'). This serves to integrate the audience with the occasion, the performer and the subject of the performance and creates a sense of unity and power. Sitole is critical of Matanzima, who is blamed for hardships experienced by the ANC in this region. By condemning his actions, the *imbongi* is emphasising the power base of the ANC. This is especially forceful if one bears in mind that Matanzima aligned himself with the apartheid regime.

The composition/performance described above, together with the poet's stylistic techniques, has now been transported into the realm of technology. This represents another leap in the revitalisation of oral tradition. The tradition was initially liberated in the 1990s, with political liberation, and it is now being allowed to reinvent itself within the realms of technology.

The technologising of Sitole's work: Towards technauriture

In late 2004, with a project team from elearning4Africa, a vision to collect, collate and digitise oral literature and tradition, beginning with Sitole's oral poetry, was adopted and began to be transmitted to local, national and international linkages. An open-source platform would make the Sitole material accessible to the widest possible audience, from learners in schools across South Africa to graduate students collecting oral traditions and writing teaching resources for postgraduate certificates and degrees, through to tourists learning about the 'real' history of the places they were to visit.

Through this open-source structure, contributions could be made in the following areas: cultural identity; indigenous knowledge systems; development of African language and history for postgraduate study routes; creation of a platform to support cultural tourism (initially in the Eastern Cape); expansion of open-source digitisation options across partner organisations; creation of community-based initiatives to promote the development and sustainability of the platform (initially with http://www.technowledgeable.com/fingo/); and the establishment of an international model for harnessing indigenous knowledge systems for the classroom and for the distribution of learning material.

The digitisation project, christened OLP (Oral Literature Project), and still in its early stages, is now being driven by the School of Languages and particularly the African Language Studies Section at Rhodes University in order to ensure that all aspects of the platform's potential are built within an institutional framework to support replication and sustainability. One of the first development areas has been supported by the Foundation for Human Rights, namely the technologising and digitisation of the Sitole material.

It is access to technology that creates and encourages a global culture of access to information. Orality, literacy and technology are developing a special relationship: the idea of computers as machines is being replaced by the concept of computers as companions, facilitating the ability to speak, interact and even translate from one language to another, thereby enabling communication to take place and, in many cases, facilitating community development.

The interaction between orality and literacy is now complex, as it involves technology. It is dependent on individual performers and their position on the oral-literacy-technology continuum, as well as on the extent to which they choose to allow orality and literacy to interact with modern technology. Isabel Hofmeyr (1993) rightly pointed out that there is an 'appropriation' of the oral into the literate and that the extent of this process depends on the individual performer. This appropriation is now often taken a step further into the arena of technology.

Those extra-linguistic elements, which are often lost in the transmission of orality into literacy, can be recaptured through technology, where sound-bites or video-clips are uploaded. The reaction of the audience, the performer's intonation, voice quality and emphasis, the effects of rhythm, context and speed of performance are lost in the written version, but can come alive in the technologised version. This allows fidelity to performances of differing impact and intensity. Accordingly, the differences between individual poets and performers complicate the debate surrounding appropriate literary criticism of transcribed oral texts (Yai 1989: 62–3). Added to this would be a literary criticism that incorporates aspects of technology. The dialectic between print, popular performance, technology and primary orality differs in terms of both individual performers and the culture-specific community of, for example, Sitole's world as described here.

The OLP Sitole project aimed to deliver the following: development of learning materials; the uploading of resources to the OLP platform; and the donation of books to pilot schools (in Qunu, Port St Johns and Grahamstown). The Foundation for Human Rights provided an amount of R10 000 for the purchase of these books, which were then donated to the three local schools that still do not have ready access to the Internet. A download option was also created for accessing the poetry book to promote international dissemination of the project and a network was established to support phase two of the project. Fifteen lesson plans were created and are soon to be accessible, in both English and isiXhosa, for downloading at http://www.technauriture.com. The lesson plans will be complemented in due course with a facility to download the complete book, thereby expanding the reach of the project. The project team aims to work with local, national and international partners to expand and develop these resources to promote the harnessing of the human rights theme for wider audiences across the world. One of the essential elements of the *imbongi* tradition, indeed of any spoken word today, is to focus on what is happening in a community. This includes a socio-political commentary, which often highlights issues related to human rights.

Through the project team's international links the project has been introduced into various educational forums. Interest has been forthcoming from the United States, Italy and the United Kingdom in terms of developing the model, while partners in Cameroon and Ethiopia are approaching local funding sources to support a pilot exercise. Once the book is available for downloading the project team has negotiated a donation to market the material across the EU through Gestform.[5] This will generate momentum and move the model on to the international stage. The model could then also be replicated for other oral poets across the African continent. Even Microsoft programmes now make use of oral poetry, hence allowing for its absorption into the modern technological arena. A contract was entered into between Microsoft and Sitole in 1999 whereby he sold the rights to some of his orally produced isiXhosa poetry. The recorded snippet was sent to Microsoft on tape (they paid $350 for a 45-second snippet of a praise-poem in honour of Nelson Mandela).

Increasingly, technology is opening up the field of oral literature in terms of commercialisation of the discipline. It is important in these circumstances that the rights of the performers be protected contractually. This is an area that requires further exploration in relation to oral poetry as technauriture. With regard to the sePedi oral tradition of Kiba song and dance, Sello Galane concludes:

> Dance and drum designs are not . . . protected by any copyright law . . . Kiba and other forms of classical art and culture are continually being recorded by various radio stations . . . The royalty accrued on these songs should be paid back to the communities through a foundation or directly to the group that has performed the recorded and broadcast text . . . The institutional memory of South African . . . communities needs to be protected (2003: 147–9).

The proposal of some kind of foundation is commendable and needs further exploration. The real question is how one goes about placing a financial value on the oral, recorded word and, even more, on the oral, recorded, technologised word.

Further comment on selected websites
A poet who has achieved great financial gain and who is able to work closely with technology is Mkiva. This is also true of spoken-word artist Mashile, as well as storyteller Mhlophe. Both Mkiva and Mashile performed at the World Cup Soccer draw in Cape Town (4 December 2009, broadcast on SABC 1). These artists can be booked for functions and Mhlophe plays an active role in television productions related to storytelling and other media forms. The traditional payment of a cow and a bag of maize by the chief to the poet has now been replaced by contractual agreements and agents who represent the performers. Perhaps the commercialisation of this age-old art form is best depicted in the work of Arthur Goldstuck (1994) who shows how urban legends make their way from orality onto the information highway. The legends are then downloaded, published and purchased in written form. This provides a clear illustration of a three-way dialectic: primary orality, literacy and technology.

This commercialisation of oral art is also depicted on performers' websites where one can investigate online performance bookings, purchase books and related published material as well as hire performers such as MCs and compères.[6] This 'genre-crossing' is what Flora Veit-Wild, quoting Susanne Gehrmann and Viola Pruschenck, refers to as 'transciplinary and inter-/transmedial processes' (2009: 4), which are encapsulated in the introduction to Mashile's website where she is referred to as 'the poet, performer, actress, presenter and producer'. This forms part of what Veit-Wild refers to as the new global 'transmediatic' culture (4). The websites all have interesting cross-disciplinary approaches and are technologically innovative, with podcasts, visual performances, examples of poetry, information about publications and performances and so on. The website is the 'window' through which we view the poets, their lives, history, performances and publications. It is through the technological page that poets come to life and offer themselves for critique through the medium of technauriture, whilst allowing for commercial viability.

The global popularity of Mkiva is represented in the awards that he has won and what he lists on his website as milestones in his poetic career. These include performances and awards in Germany, Libya, Ireland, Brazil, Turkey, France and Uzbekistan. In the early 1900s the Xhosa bard S.E.K. Mqhayi became known as *imbongi yesizwe jikelele* (the poet of the whole nation) in South Africa. Mkiva now refers to himself continentally and perhaps over-ambitiously as the 'poet of Africa'. This title is also reflected in the name of his website. Digital performers now have access to a worldwide audience, perhaps through a new code-switched language idiom, 'globalese', as represented in some of Mkiva's poetry, where up to seven languages may be used in a single poem to attract and appeal to global as well as local audiences.

Another group which has done particularly well in South Africa is the spoken-word poetry collective, Botsotso Jesters. Performers include the well-known Lesego Rampolokeng, Siphiwe ka Ngwenya, Ike Muila and Allan Horwitz. The transdisciplinary and transmedial nature of their work as well as their cutting-edge social commentary is encapsulated in this statement on their website, which refers to

> art that is of and about the varied cultures and life experiences of people in South Africa as expressed in the many languages spoken ... Botsotso is committed to a proliferation of styles and a multiplicity of themes ... multidisciplinary art forms and performances are similarly embraced.[7]

It concludes by pointing out that the lesson of apartheid must still be discussed, whilst the 'challenges of the current period throw up ... difficulties ... [and] complexities'. Similarly, Comrade Fatso refers to his poetry as 'Toyi Toyi Poetry, radical street poetry that mixes Shona with English and mbira with hip hop. It's an art form that is an uprising against oppression'.[8] This form of poetry is best illustrated in Rampolokeng's piece 'In Transition', in which the poet critically assesses South African politics and societal structures:

> Wailing around the burning tyre
> we raise a sacrificial pyre
> songs of struggle turn quacks in the quagmire
> in transition we wear our hearts
> on the outside in t-shirt fashion trend and style
> colourful speeches popular talk
> of hypocrisy
> by the graveside
> in transition
> it's an arty farty party
> riding on the back of genocide
> somewhere a head cracks full of lead
> & someone cracks a wise aside
> it's all a fart in the wind
> we leave behind
> & run and hide with pride, at every stride
> in transition
>
> Eating the brains of the dead unborn
> how can we mourn the dead
> wearing the umbilical cords around the neck
> drunk on amniotic fluids
> smiles glittering in the night
> of chandeliers, of mind control
> in transition [. . .]
>
> Thus we rush to the future
> unless the wheel of time
> gets a puncture (Botsotso Jesters 1996: n.p.).

Conclusion

It seems that almost all African countries have their recognised oral artists who are linked with each other and the rest of the world through technology. Whether one is using technauriture to research Mkiva or Comrade Fatso, this can be done at the click of a button from anywhere in the world. In adapting to changing power bases, *izimbongi* such as Sitole have proven the adaptability of culture and traditions in the face of drastic social, political and technological changes in southern Africa. In the midst of these changes the voice of the *imbongi* links the traditions of the past to new directions and visions of the future as represented in the work of Mkiva.

The need to develop and harness indigenous knowledge systems across the developing world is a central aspect of maintaining cultural identity. Widening exposure to the traditions and customs of indigenous societies through technauriture will go a long way towards ensuring that the momentum of globalisation benefits all the world's communities. The Sitole project has allowed the poet's work to be made available to the world, as well as being an exploration of the structures that will support the collection, collation and utilisation of historical treasures. Not only does this project honour the name of a great yet relatively unknown South African poet, but it also helps to bring back to life and to preserve, via technology as well as the written word, his poetry.

No poet or oral performer remains untouched by the influence of radio, television, the Internet and the constant interaction between the oral and written word. In Africa, television and radio remain the driving technological influences promoting the oral word. Increasingly, the Internet plays a pivotal role. The influence of technology on both the oral and written word has reached a point where they are inextricably linked, where each feeds off the other. Performers, through the use of technology, are positioning and repositioning themselves not only as continental performers, but also global performers. This is clearly illustrated by Mkiva, who has won international awards. This implies both continental and global poetic interplay, largely facilitated through technauriture and the embracing of contemporary technology.

Notes

1. See also http://www.poetryinternationalweb.org (accessed 20 May 2011).
2. See http://www.comminit.com/global/spaces-frontpage (accessed 20 May 2011).
3. See http://www.chimurenga.co.za/ and http://kwani.org/ (accessed 20 May 2011).
4. This study guide will soon be downloadable from http://www.technauriture.com, together with the oral poems (both the isiXhosa and English versions).
5. See http://www.gestform.it (accessed 20 May 2011).
6. See http://www.kalavati.org/lebo-mashile.html and http://www.poetofafrica.com (accessed 20 May 2011).

7. See http://www.botsotso.org.za (accessed 20 May 2011).
8. See http://www.myspace.com/comradefatsoandchabvondoka (accessed 20 May 2011).

References

Barber, Karin and P.F. de Moraes Farias (eds). 1989. *Discourse and its Disguises: The Interpretation of African Oral Texts.* Birmingham University African Studies Series 1. University of Birmingham: Centre of West African Studies.

Botsotso Jesters. 1996. *we jive like this.* Johannesburg: Botsotso Publishing.

Coplan, David. 1994. *In the Time of Cannibals: The Word Music of South Africa's Basotho Migrants.* Johannesburg: Wits University Press.

Dhlomo, H.I.E. 1993 [1939]. 'Nature and Variety of Tribal Drama'. In: *Foundations in Southern African Oral Literature*, edited by R.H. Kaschula. Johannesburg: Wits University Press: 187–202.

Feral, Claude (ed.). 2004. *Founding Myths of the New South Africa: Alizes: Revue angliciste de la Reunion.* Reunion: University de la Reunion.

Finnegan, Ruth. 1988. *Orality and Literacy.* Oxford: Basil Blackwell.

Galane, Sello. 2003. 'A Critical Analysis of Kiba (Song-Dance-Drama) Discourse'. Master's thesis. Cape Town: University of Cape Town.

Goldstuck, Arthur. 1994. *Ink in the Porridge.* Johannesburg: Penguin.

Goodnow, Katherine J. and Yngvar Natland. 2002. 'Storytelling and the Web in South African Museums'. In: *Museums and the Web 2002: Selected Papers from an International Conference*, edited by D. Bearman and J. Trant. Toronto: Archive and Museum Informatics.

Hofmeyr, Isabel. 1993. *'We Spend Our Lives as a Tale That Is Told': Oral Historical Narrative in a South African Chiefdom.* Johannesburg: Wits University Press.

Kaschula, Russell H. 1999. 'Imbongi and Griot: Toward a Comparative Analysis of Oral Poetics in Southern and West Africa'. *Journal of African Cultural Studies* 12(1): 55–76.

———. 2002. *The Bones of the Ancestors Are Shaking: Xhosa Oral Poetry in Context.* Cape Town: Juta Press.

———. 2004a. 'Imbongi to Slam: The Emergence of a Technologised Auriture'. *Southern African Journal of Folklore Studies* 14(2): 45–58.

———. 2004b. 'Myth and Reality in the New South Africa: Contemporary Oral Literature'. In: *Founding Myths of the New South Africa: Alizes: Revue angliciste de la Reunion*, edited by C. Feral. Reunion: University de la Reunion: 103–18.

Kaschula, Russell H. (ed.). 1993. *Foundations in Southern African Oral Literature.* Johannesburg: Wits University Press.

———. 2001. *African Oral Literature: Functions in Contemporary Contexts.* Cape Town: New Africa Education.

Kaschula, Russell H. and Christine Anthonissen. 1995. *Communicating across Cultures in South Africa: Toward a Critical Language Awareness.* Johannesburg: Wits University Press.

Kaschula, Russell H., Mandla Matyumza and Bongani Sitole. 2006 [1996]. *Qhiwu-u-u-la!! Return to the Fold!!* Cape Town: Nasou Via Afrika.

Kaschula, Russell H. and André Mostert. 2009. 'Analyzing, Digitizing and Technologizing the Oral Word: The Case of Bongani Sitole'. *Journal of African Cultural Studies* 21(2): 159–76.

Landzelius, Kyra (ed.). 2006. *Going Native on the Net: Indigenous Cyber-Activism and Virtual Diasporas over the World Wide Web*. London: Routledge.

Ong, Walter J. 1982. *Orality and Literacy: The Technologizing of the Word*. London: Methuen.

Opland, Jeff. 1983. *Xhosa Oral Poetry: Aspects of a Black South African Tradition*. Johannesburg: Ravan Press.

———. 2005. *The Dassie and the Hunter: A South African Meeting*. Pietermaritzburg: University of KwaZulu-Natal Press.

Propp, V. 1968. *Morphology of the Folktale*. Austin: University of Texas Press.

Street, B.V. 1995. *Social Literacies: Critical Approaches to Literacy Development, Ethnography and Education*. London: Longman.

Van Dijk, Jan A.G.M. 2005. *The Deepening Divide: Inequality in the Information Society*. New York: Sage.

Van Wynegaard, Annetjie. 2009. 'Scientists Make Their Mark'. *Rhodos* 21(7): 10.

Veit-Wild, Flora. 2009. 'Artistic, Cinematic and Literary Practices in the Digital Age'. Working document.

Yai, Olabiyi. 1989. 'Issues in Oral Poetry: Criticism, Teaching and Translation'. In: *Discourse and its Disguises: The Interpretation of African Oral Texts*, edited by K. Barber and P.F. de Moraes Farias. Birmingham University African Studies Series 1. University of Birmingham: Centre of West African Studies: 59–69.

12

Family Albums and Statements from the Dock of History

Autobiographical Writing 1999–2009

ANNIE GAGIANO

> [T]he first step should be a widening of consciousness ...
> — Chinua Achebe, 'Mapping out Identity'

Discussing James Olney's notion of autobiographies as 'metaphors of self' (1972) with his biographer Chabani Manganyi, Es'kia Mphahlele, author of South Africa's most famous literary autobiography, makes the following comment concerning the form and its function: '[I]n its becoming it's a monument and in its composition it is a metaphor'. He adds: 'It is not a monument in the sense of "Here I am! I have qualities of a hero" ... But rather that here is something built on memory'. He explains further that in *Down Second Avenue* (1971 [1959]),

> I was saying to the reader ... here is the story of my life and it is not unique. It is shared by so many people ... This is a typical story of an African in South Africa. I was saying that this is me, but it is not a singular me (Mphahlele 2010: 496–7).

In *Sources of the Self*, Charles Taylor says: 'One cannot be a self on one's own' (1992: 36). His remark is reminiscent of the South African proverb *motho ke motho ka batho babang* (seSotho) or *umuntu ngumuntu ngabantu* (isiZulu): a person is a person because of other people. All autobiographies either are or contain family portraits and community stories; they exhibit the socially embedded and interconnected nature of the author's life. Family, friends, enemies, strangers and officials feature alongside the author; the autobiography is never only the author's story.

Several of the autobiographies featured in this chapter could not have appeared in South Africa under the apartheid dispensation. The present abundance and variety of such texts is symptomatic of the different psycho-social sphere South Africa has become after the major political adjustments of the early 1990s. Pumla Gobodo-Madikizela writes of the unexpected realisation, upon returning to South Africa in June 1994, that she 'could not have described [her]self as a South African' in her 'past travels', whereas she thinks to herself (as the plane lands): 'This is *my* country, *my* home' (2003: 6–7, emphasis in the original). Significant also is the fact that most autobiographies published during the past decade have appeared in English but also require some degree of local knowledge. Not only do they seem addressed in the first place to a local readership, but they also seem to employ the lingua franca of English to reach across South African cultural differences. Whether all compatriots are addressed in the same way is the issue I seek to signpost in the first part of the title of this chapter.

While there are aspects of familiarity with or shared 'familial' (communal) appeal in these texts, there is also a discernible sense that many authors see themselves as accounting to compatriots for and putting on historical record what they have been and become, and what they have 'done with their lives'. Etienne Mureinik's characterisation of the local jurisprudential shift as 'crossing a bridge from a culture of authority to a culture of accountability' (quoted in Sachs 2009: 204) can be linked with this point. However fissured and non-homogenous South African society remains, the suggestion that local autobiographers are addressing and recognising, in their own life histories, a multifarious collection of compatriots is the impression one gets from exploring the last decade's output in this field. Race, class and gender divisions, hierarchies and enmities are still much in evidence, but some of our 'compartmentalities' (Gagiano 2006: 10) have shifted. There is a discernible sense in the autobiographical material that all kinds of South Africans are now confidently claiming a hearing from one another. Both writing and reading autobiographies of the kind noted in this chapter can be seen as learning activities, as the processes of natural adjustment go on within and around us. In his own most recent autobiographical text, Justice Albie Sachs, formerly of the Constitutional Court, writes: 'You cannot have a country with different memories and expect a sense of common citizenship to grow' (2009: 87). The glimpses into compatriots' lives facilitated by autobiographies will not mould us into national homogeneity, but they can contribute to our retracing the different routes by which we have arrived at a dispensation where we share citizenship in relative peace.

Most of the recent South African autobiographers are as aware of the historical situatedness of their texts as they are of the claims to a shared civil space that they explicitly or implicitly stake. Predictably, in works appearing when much rewriting of history has been required and demanded, and while many younger South Africans seem to reject learning about our past as a formally divided people, many of the autobiographers see their work as being in some sense archival. Undertaken by some as a duty or responsibility, these writings also testify, however modestly, to a sense of pride in making a contribution to this society. Autobiographies from diametrically opposite sides of the struggle have been published, showing how autobiographically focused history is being written and rewritten by both 'victors' and 'vanquished' – with Ronnie Kasrils of the African National Congress (ANC) (2004) and Magnus Malan of the apartheid government (2006) as two examples.

The historical and social embeddedness of each autobiographical self may be incontestable, but a wider social range of authors whose texts are surveyed here can now see themselves as co-authors of our common history, however strongly aware they may be that it is always a group project undertaken in the midst of contending forces. Notably, a number of particularly memorable autobiographies record horrors of cruelty and callousness resulting from the animosities, greed and ignorance that prevailed in our recent past, many of which remain (if transmogrified) or have intensified or become more blatant in the present. Ashwin Desai and Richard Pithouse correctly remind us that '[a]partheid South Africa teemed with struggles, and neoliberal South Africa still teems with struggles' (2004: 874). Several of the texts surveyed testify, for example, to child abuse or gendered violence and may be taken as recording such awful experiences as exhortations that these social ills, which have locally taken on epidemic proportions as destructive as AIDS, be addressed. Terrence Des Pres writes in *The Survivor*:

> Where men and women are forced to endure terrible things at the hands of others – whenever, that is, extremity involves moral issues – the need to remember becomes a general response. Spontaneously, they make it their business to record the evil forced upon them ... survival and bearing witness become reciprocal acts (1976: 31).

While autobiographical texts are obviously acts of recalling an experienced past, they need to be recognised also as intended contributions to a shared future or to the history lessons of those who come after.

Braggadocio is not much in evidence in the autobiographies surveyed here. Many of them begin with declarations of shyness or reluctance, yet of the author being impelled to write these accounts by encouraging friends, or because of the desire to leave a legacy (apparent, for example, in the title of a slightly earlier text, *To My Children's Children* [1990] by Sindiwe Magona). While most of the autobiographers surveyed here give the impression of honouring the implicit 'autobiographical pact' (Lejeune 1989: 4) in recording their lives and pasts as truthfully or accurately as possible, the adjustments of hindsight colour all such accounts – not only in the selection of details, but in the *present* recognition of the direction in which a life was unconsciously leading. To use the most famous available example, Nelson Mandela indeed worked or walked all his life towards that 'freedom' which was eventually attained, but he could not have *known* that this struggle would indeed succeed, or that he would one day be writing the story of the making of the first democratic South African state president.

I have used the term 'autobiography' both flexibly (by not, for instance, distinguishing between memoirs and autobiographies – see, for example, Rak 2004) *and* strictly (by excluding fictionalised autobiography or 'ghosted' writing such as the De Lille-Smith collaboration [2002]). Nevertheless, 'assisted' autobiographies that record an author's own words, as well as texts containing groups of brief individual autobiographical accounts – such as the 'ordinary' Robben Island political prisoners' life writing recorded by Jan Coetzee (2000) – have been included. Excellent articles exploring individual or selected South African autobiographies are plentiful; see, for example, Sarah Nuttall and Cheryl-Ann Michael (2000), Margaret Lenta (2003), Cheryl Stobie (2007), Ashlee Potlatinsky (2008) and Sam Raditlhalo (2009), whilst the compendium *Selves in Question* by Judith Coullie et al. (2006) is impressively thorough, dense and analytically skilful. In addition, *Alternation* 7(1) (2000) and *South Atlantic Quarterly* 103(4) (2004, see Barnard and Farred) are both special journal issues on the topic and the annual listing of publications by genre in the *Journal of Commonwealth Literature* is a useful checklist. Two recent issues of the *Journal of Literary Studies* (25[1] and 25[2] of 2009) focus on southern African autobiographies and have instructive editorial introductions. Larger geographical and theoretical studies of the genre abound: see, for example, Olney (1972, 1998); Nancy K. Miller (1991); Sidonie Smith (1998); Linda Anderson (2001); Chinosole (2001); Paul J. Eakin (2008) and Bart Moore-Gilbert (2009). The reading public seems to have an insatiable appetite for autobiographies, further evidenced by the fact that writing competitions nowadays almost routinely reserve places for this genre and international academic conferences on life writing are on the increase.

In terms of the historical reach in the ten years of the autobiographical output surveyed in this chapter, a few go back fifty years or more. Texts by deceased authors first published within the chosen timeframe have been included because of their particular interest: see Herman Charles Bosman (2003) and Bessie Head, Patrick and Wendy Cullinan (2005). Predictably, the historical-political frame most prominently featured in the selected texts is the apartheid system and resistance against it. There are a number of texts by those whose accounts vividly record the experience of extraordinary people whose contributions were insufficiently known. Greater numbers of political leaders and journalists than members of other professions have had their autobiographies published in this time. Several theatre personalities and stage performers as well as numerous sportspeople continue to write their stories, showing how the local political-racial dispensation affected their lives. South Africans working in medical and religious spheres also share experiences and perceptions with readers, their responsibility for physical or spiritual health having transcended apartheid barriers. Participation in the Truth and Reconciliation Commission (TRC), though of limited duration, influenced the lives of its members and functionaries so strongly that several autobiographies reflect on that process, following Antjie Krog's well-known *Country of my Skull* (1998). Novelists and poets ranging from Tatamkhulu Afrika and J.M. Coetzee to Alf Khumalo and Chris van Wyk have written autobiographies during the period in question. Overcoming disability or traumatic events (particularly sexual and child abuse) is the topic of a number of the autobiographies – works that could be described as inspirational or crusading – adding important dimensions to the portrayal of South African society.

Origins – enriching and sheltering, or deprived and harmful – matter a great deal to most autobiographers, whether their life narratives adopt a *Bildungsroman* or a picaresque shape. Endearing or dreadful family portraits acknowledge the inescapable power and the lifelong effect of our earliest environments. Two revered South African struggle icons, Ray Alexander Simons (2004) and George Bizos (2007), both write beautifully though briefly of their childhoods in Latvia and Greece respectively, indicating how the values learnt in their countries of origin fed into the tasks they set themselves and the ways they integrated themselves into South African society, eschewing white isolationism and moral apathy from their earliest encounters here. These autobiographers indicate the moral roots of their enriching contributions to the working conditions and human rights of South Africans. In one telling passage in Alexander Simons's book, she writes that she named her only son Johan for her local fellow trade-union activist friend: 'Johanna Cornelius, who had no children of her own' (2004: 198). This registers Alexander Simons's practicality as much as her compassion, in addition to giving a glimpse of the contribution made by some early Afrikaner activists to the growth of the non-racial labour movement.

The collective text *Finding Mr Madini* (Morgan 1999) vividly depicts non-South African childhoods shared with other homeless people who have had indigenous childhoods. This quirky, unusual patchwork of autobiographical writing is a notable gain to our autobiographical records as South Africans struggle to deal with xenophobia and with the fierce, even horrific and sometimes fatal competitions for scarce resources among the urban poor. The illustrated collection *We Came for Mandela* (Adams 2001) exhibits the diverse African cultures of some of those who seek acceptance in South Africa, while the semi-autobiographical novel *Going Home* (Kikamba 2005) gives glimpses of the horrifying inhospitality shown by some locals towards Africans from elsewhere. Darryl Accone (2005) gives us a memorable family history, describing how his mostly Chinese ancestry gradually intertwined with South Africa(ns), while restaurateur Emma Chen's delightful *Emperor Can Wait* (2009) regales readers with reminiscences of Taiwan and settlement in South Africa. Sita Gandhi in *In the Shadow of Mahatma* (2005) tells of her Phoenix Settlement upbringing near Durban and her adolescence in India before returning here, and of the enriching and inhibiting effects on her own life of her family heritage. Pregs Govender, too, had a warm yet lively family environment in Durban, which helped to prepare her for the gender, class and racial-political struggles she undertook in later life, recorded in her graceful yet tough-minded autobiography, *Love and Courage*, significantly subtitled *A Story of Insubordination* (2007).

Three theatre celebrities, the late Patrick Mynhardt, Pieter-Dirk Uys and Antony Sher, evoke their families' comfortable circumstances and their own gradual transformations into the assured interpreters of South African circumstances which they gradually became. In *Boy from Bethulie* (2003) Mynhardt evokes his spirited Irish mother who could not overcome her grief at her abandonment (for another woman) by her Afrikaner husband, his adored medical doctor father. Mynhardt moved from a never-forgotten, small-town Free State background to the theatre scene in Britain and then back home again. Uys had an old-school Afrikaner father; his mother's Jewishness was not known to him during her lifetime; his two autobiographies (*Elections and Erections* [2002] and *Between the Devil and the Deep* [2005]) are both delightful yet hard-hitting exhortations against small-mindedness of different kinds. Sher, in his *Beside Myself* (2001), describes how his family lived the uncomplicated life of well-off, politically conservative South African Jews of the mid- to later twentieth century in a pleasant Cape Town suburb. Predictably, these four autobiographies are immensely entertaining without being frivolous, abounding in lively detail. By contrast with Sher's, Denis Hirson's family belonged to the activist tradition of politically radical Jews in South Africa and his childhood was indelibly marked by the apartheid state's incarceration of his father when Hirson was in his early teens. He registers his own coming to political awareness in *White Scars: On Reading and Rites of Passage* (2006). Earlier, Hirson produced two charming autobiographical works listing forgotten features of daily life during his Johannesburg schooldays, *I Remember King Kong (The Boxer)* and *We Walk Straight So You Had Better Get out the Way* (2005a and b); these were preceded by his *The House Next Door to Africa*, published in 1986.

Rrekgetsi Chimeloane's *Whose Laetie Are You?* (2001) evokes his Sowetan boyhood and is almost as delightfully told and titled as Chris van Wyk's beautiful memoir, *Shirley, Goodness and Mercy* (2004), which focuses on childhood in mixed-race Johannesburg townships and pays tender tribute in particular to his charming, humane mother and maternal grandmother. He includes poems that he wrote about and for both these women. Although the main focus of Sibongile Mkhabela's important life record is on her anti-apartheid activism and detention (she was the only schoolgirl leader arrested in her area along with ten schoolboys, all detained in connection with the 1976 uprising), her *Open Earth and Black Roses* (2001) tenderly evokes her strong and spirited mother and the aunt who took her mother's place in the girl's life when her mother died young. The well-known journalist Fred Khumalo's *Touch my Blood* (2006) is a lively childhood retrospective prompted by the recurrence of the fierce defensiveness he learnt to adopt in a challenging, macho township environment. It merits careful attention as an exemplar of the experiences of successful young black professionals whose lives reach back into struggles with poverty, oppression, racist exclusion and the tricky adjustment to middle-class South African circumstances. Jacob Dlamini's meditation on the advantages of his apartheid township upbringing (2009), in which he upbraids those who see only disadvantages in such a childhood, fails to take account of how many autobiographies by black South Africans do indeed write with appreciation of the life-promoting aspects of their township childhood and youth.

Although Zubeida Jaffer, a leading journalist, titles her autobiography *Our Generation* (2003), the book lovingly and centrally recalls her sustaining, close family and the Muslim pieties that strengthened her during the ordeals of her incarceration and torture, including threats to the life of the child she was expecting, by apartheid-era police. Struggle heroes Ismael Meer (2002) and Ahmed Kathrada (2005) both grew up in small country towns; both had much-loved fathers from whom they imbibed uncompromising commitment to an inclusive humanity. It was Meer who later persuaded Oliver Tambo and Mandela (through the more persuadable Walter Sisulu) to move away from their initially more exclusively Africanist position to accept a broader vision for South Africa and the ANC. Meer learnt to speak isiZulu before English, whereas Kathrada, who as a child spoke more Afrikaans than any other language, would use his knowledge of poetry in this medium to get through the tough skins of Afrikaner gaolers and policemen. *Still Grazing*, jazz artist Hugh Masekela's rollicking and wide-ranging memoir, starts with a detailed and wonderfully vivid evocation of his upbringing – first by his grandmother and then by his parents, explaining how, in the Transvaal townships, he early on became a 'music addict' (2004: 9), relishing the rich range of available musical styles around him.

Alex Boraine's Cape Town family was (for whites of this time) relatively poor; he lost both of his older brothers, who fought in the Second World War (2008). In his early life he served as an Anglican priest in poor, isolated rural parishes. Both André Brink (2009) and Max du Preez (2003) had well-off, country-town Afrikaner families and both had dominant, prominent and respected fathers. By contrast, Richard Grant's father, also a man of Afrikaner extraction (surname Esterhuysen), who had a highly respectable position in Swaziland's colonial administration, went to pieces when Richard's mother left him, becoming the baffling, beloved but often vicious and drunk parent portrayed in the autobiographical film, which is described blow by blow as it takes shape in *The Wah-Wah Diaries* (2006). Agnes Lottering describes a pioneer-colonial male presence in portrayals of her swashbuckling half-Irish father and Irish grandfather in the unusual dual autobiography *Winnefred and Agnes* (2002), which tells the stories of a daughter and her mother. In Lottering's text, both race-sex integration and cultural, marital or familial clashes – involving Irish, Swazi, Zulu, Afrikaners and people of mixed race – are portrayed, mostly in the lush, paradisal, rural Natal setting of earlier times. Lottering ends up in an abusive marriage, having had to flee from the detestation of the father she had adored, who first loved and then loathed her mother (Winnefred). Fascinatingly, Lottering depicts her mother's experiences in the first person – the mother's story being more vividly told than the daughter's, so strong are the parallels between these two women's lives and the daughter's identification with her mother.

Harsh and abusive childhood circumstances are portrayed in the autobiographies of Tatamkhulu Afrika (2005), Thandeki Umlilo (2002) – who uses an assumed name to recount a harrowing (white) childhood of sexual abuse – and Helen Brain (2006). The last writer's is another account of incest and the awful struggle to surmount such intimate and perhaps indelible damage – a text which she courageously published using her own name. This remarkable work intertwines a 'children's story' found 'not suitable for children' (as her subtitle indicates) with dreams and actual familial encounters through which the author fights her way back to psychic balance. I found Zinhle Mdakane's *No Way Out* (2001) a weaker text than, for instance, Zazah Khuzwayo's fittingly titled *Never Been at Home* (2004): these two accounts are written by young black women who eventually succeed despite bad parents – a selfish and neglectful mother in Mdakane's case and a horrifically abusive and monstrously selfish father in Khuzwayo's. They are both worth reading. An arduous 'ordinary' township youth (which includes serious assault from a would-be partner) is portrayed in Miriam Mathabane's book *Miriam's Song* (2001). Texts such as these illustrate some of the 'other struggles' (distinct from anti-apartheid strivings and strife) to which Desai and Pithouse (2004: 874) refer in the article mentioned earlier in this chapter – struggles that continue within homes and communities.

Mario D'Offici (2007) and Alex Lovejoy (2005) both write of lives indelibly affected by abusive parents, flawed institutions and unreliable authority figures. D'Offici took the brave step of exposing a leading church figure's sexual predation and the shame and horror it caused him – a work that bears revisiting now that sexual abuse within Catholic congregations is being exposed and punished in high-profile cases. Lovejoy's criminal career (in drug smuggling) links poignantly to the cowering little boy he once was. The contrast between D'Offici's quietly dignified narration and Lovejoy's swagger masks the parallels between these texts. Both authors take emotional risks in undermining 'tough-guy' stereotypes to stress the often overlooked vulnerability of male children in a society where the evidence of the abuse of girls is so overwhelming. The difference is that D'Offici later became a respected career and family man, unlike Lovejoy who continued on his path of social transgressions.

Wife-abuse features in all too many South African autobiographies – often a mother's by her husband or partner, where the responsibility towards her children increases the woman's vulnerability – and this is the main focus of the self-published text *Clinging to Fences* (2008) by Heather Capon. The terrible experience of losing a child at birth is the subject of the poet Malika Ndlovu's vividly titled *Invisible Earthquake* (2009); Sarah Nuttall movingly describes losing her newborn, also a daughter, after a few days because of medical ineptitude during the birth process. This testimony appears in her contribution to *At Risk*, edited, like its companion volume, *Load-Shedding*, by Liz McGregor and Nuttall (2007 and 2009). The connection of both works with WISER (Wits Institute for Social and Economic Research) staff members at the University of the Witwatersrand indicates growing local interest in autobiographical writing by South Africa-based academics whose short, vivid pieces help to measure the social temperature of our uncomfortable, precarious, exciting and rapidly adapting nation.

Probably the majority of texts in the body of writing surveyed here, and certainly the majority of the most noteworthy published in English, come from South Africans who contributed to the eventually successful establishment of a deracialised and democratised political-legal system in South Africa. Male struggle luminaries such as Ismael Meer (2002), Ahmed Kathrada (2005), Raymond Mhlaba (2001), Ronnie Kasrils (2004), Allan Boesak (2009) and Rusty Bernstein (1999) all released (or updated) important and informative memoirs during this decade. The style as much as the political-ideological stance of these authors contrasts with the accounts of previously powerful men such as General Magnus Malan (2006) and Colonel Jan Breytenbach (2002) and with that of undercover agent Riaan Labuschagne's swaggering description of his apartheid-era intelligence-gathering for the previous government (2002). Rick Andrews's *Buried in the Sky* (2001) provides an English-speaking conscript's experience of the 'border war', a genre very productive in Afrikaans fictional renditions. Tim Ramsden's *Border-Line Insanity* (2007) is another critical English-speaker's view of the border war and his participation in it. In her foreword to the significantly titled *A Secret Burden: Memories of the Border War by South African Soldiers Who Fought in It* (Batley 2007), Justice Yvonne Mokgora of the Constitutional Court asserts the need to recognise 'the suffering of the unsung "others"' or the 'perceived "vanquished"' (xi), that is, white conscripts. By contrast, a powerful and important account of life (mainly) in the ANC Umkhonto we Sizwe (MK) training camps in Angola appeared recently: James Ngculu's *The Honour to Serve: Recollections of an Umkhonto Soldier* (2009), with a foreword by former president, Thabo Mbeki. This complex, wide-ranging, if matter-of-fact account indicates the enthusiasm, dedication and courage of those who risked much in crossing the border, while convincingly recording the tedium and frustration experienced by many in the camps. Fascinatingly, this decade of autobiographies includes one memoir of a Second World War veteran – George Stegmann's *The Lights of Freedom* (2007).

Important women leaders such as Ray Alexander Simons (2004) and Fatima Meer (2001) have also published their autobiographies during this time; no equivalent texts in English by leading women on the other side of the apartheid divide seem to have appeared. Although contextualised, Meer's is chiefly a memoir of incarceration for anti-apartheid activities, illustrated by her own drawings. Alexander Simons's is one of the most impressive autobiographical texts of the past decade: a detailed account of this brilliantly practical and large-hearted woman's life. Unfortunately, the rich crop of prominent black women's autobiographies that appeared earlier than the demarcated decade (by Ellen Kuzwayo; Emma Mashinini; Maggie Resha; Phyllis Ntantala and Mamphela Ramphele) seems to have dwindled; it is to be hoped that there will be a resurgence of autobiographical writing by leading black women. Judith Coullie's excellent *The Closest of Strangers: South African Women's Life Writing* (2004) is another example of the 'collective autobiography', featuring many eloquent black women's voices, including Winnie Madikizela-Mandela's.

Raymond Suttner's memoir (2001) is one of a large number of 'prison autobiographies' and focuses on the dreary horrors of imprisonment. It is especially moving in its record of the struggle with melancholia and eventually depression caused by prolonged incarceration. The expanded reissue of Hugh Lewin's famous *Bandiet* (2001) now includes more poems by Lewin and gaol drawings by Harold Strachan. They constitute records of moral steadfastness and endurance, but the outstanding example of struggle imprisonment accounts of this period remains Strachan's stylistically, linguistically and morally complex *Make a Skyf, Man!* (2004), a work still insufficiently recognised, perhaps partly because the author says uncomfortable things about certain struggle leaders. Strachan was sentenced to further imprisonment for his newspaper exposure of the injustices and inhumanity of the South African prison system. In his book, humour and wit are employed to negotiate anger, contempt and bitterness and to cut the upholders of apartheid *and* arrogant struggle leaders down to size.

Older leaders such as 'Fish' Keitseng (1999), Stanley Mogoba (2003) and Njongonkulu Ndungane (2003) suffered imprisonment on Robben Island for their political/moral convictions. The latter two both became bishops in their later lives, but their integrity was first put to the test in that isolated space. Other persons of faith – Archbishop Desmond Tutu (2000); feminist theologian Denise Ackermann (2003); and Chief Rabbi Cyril Harris (2000) – similarly had their beliefs tested by the South African reality. We do not yet seem to have an imam's account of the 'struggle years', but we do have some autobiographies by Muslim South Africans. Noor Ebrahim's *Noor's Story: My Life in District Six* (2001) is an important text: poignant and beautifully told, it evokes the mix of people who inhabited that vibrant community. More recently, novelist and film-maker Rayda Jacobs, after making her pilgrimage and recording her reflections on her journey to the holy city, published *The Mecca Diaries* (2005), as well as *Masquerade* (2008), an interesting account of her life since childhood.

The chosen decade of autobiographies just includes former state president F.W. de Klerk's autobiography, *The Last Trek* (1999): a title perhaps unintentionally indicative of a more backward-looking orientation than Mandela's *Long Walk to Freedom* (1994). Four prominent white opposition leaders, Frederik van Zyl Slabbert (2000), Alex Boraine (2008), Colin Eglin (2007) and Tony Leon (2008) produced autobiographies within the decade, highlighting different perspectives and priorities in apartheid opposition politics – for example, in views on Slabbert's and Boraine's exits from parliamentary politics and on President Mbeki's responses to the Democratic Alliance. A text such as Noël Robb's modest *The Sash and I* (2006) is a necessary reminder of the invaluable advice and resistance work done 'under the radar' by the white women of the Black Sash when few of their white female compatriots were prepared to leave the domestic space of white womanhood. Autobiographies by three legal luminaries, George Bizos (2007), Richard Goldstone (2000) and Albie Sachs (2004, 2009), have also appeared recently. Bizos's warm-heartedness comes through clearly in his monumental text, which records extensive examples of his brilliant court repartee, solidly humanitarian arguments and formidable eloquence in key apartheid court cases. Goldstone's excellent book begins from South Africa, but moves on to describe his international legal role as war crimes investigator in other troubled contexts, such as Bosnia, prefiguring his report on the more recent Israeli-Palestinian conflict. As in his earlier memoirs, Sachs's *Free Diary* is an emotionally rich work; another autobiographically inflected text by Sachs, *The Strange Alchemy of Life and Law*, focuses particularly on his role as a Constitutional Court judge.

A significant number of younger South Africans who might be loosely grouped as anti-apartheid soldiers brought out autobiographies during this time, enriching our knowledge of the day-to-day dimensions of the struggle. One among the five texts is by a schoolgirl activist of the time (Mkhabela 2001) and one by a (periodically) Muslim registers an uneasy relationship with the Pan Africanist Congress (PAC) (Sesanti 2005); one is by a Paarl revolutionary and MK soldier, Jama Matakata (2004); two more are by PAC militants Letlapa Mphahlele (2002) and Mxolisi 'Ace' Mgxashe (2006). I found Mphahlele's an especially arresting and memorable account. All five of these youngsters were imprisoned. Notably, Mkhabela raises the question of why Kroonstad Prison (where, she says, most female political prisoners were kept) is not as famous as Robben Island.

Numerous South African journalists went into the belly of the apartheid beast and have produced lively and informative autobiographical texts: the list includes books by Max du Preez (2003), Jacques Pauw (2006), Donald Woods (2000), Benjamin Pogrund (2000), Gavin Evans (2002) and Gerald Shaw (2007), while Anthony Sampson's recent autobiography evokes his time with *Drum* and subsequent visits to South Africa (2008) (Sampson also wrote the authorised Nelson Mandela biography).

The period 1999 to 2009 is rich in autobiographical works by a number of major South African writers. Published in 2005, a collection of Bessie Head's letters to Patrick and Wendy Cullinan begins just before she left South Africa and eloquently records many of her considered ideas about her life and writing. The 2003 Bosman collection, entitled *My Life and Opinions*, conveys the author's fear and hatred of the death penalty. J.M. Coetzee's *Youth* and Antjie Krog's *A Change of Tongue* both appeared in 2003. Coetzee's book, a sequel to *Boyhood* of 1997, is a sardonically retrospective account of a young man attempting to shake off his South African provincialism in the United Kingdom; Krog's *A Change of Tongue* is the ironically qualified, yet future-orientated text of an adult Afrikaner woman coming to terms with an irrevocably altered South Africa.[1] Both Krog and Coetzee published further autobiographical works in 2009. In my opinion, Krog's *Begging to be Black* lacks the nuanced complexity of her earlier autobiographically orientated prose texts and comes close to racial essentialism in delineating 'blackness' and 'whiteness' as cultural determinants of individual and group moralities and conduct. Coetzee's *Summertime* is a text that simultaneously enacts, undermines, parodies and re-imagines 'autobiography'. Set within the larger national and continental racial struggle of the 1970s, white lives are depicted here as enacting their own pain and pathos. This poignant text interacts ironically with some of Coetzee's remarks recorded in the 'Retrospective' section of *Doubling the Point* (1992), where he declares himself 'in a wavering voice' as one who has, willy-nilly, been '*written* as he is as a white South African into the latter half of the twentieth century, disabled, disqualified . . . writing without authority' (392, emphasis added).

Contrasting with Coetzee's and Krog's meditations on 'whiteness' as racial predestination is Breyten Breytenbach's insistence, as recorded in an auto-biographical essay (2009), that, even though as a matter of 'bureaucratic arbitration, tribal superstitions and ideological genetics, not nature', he was 'born *white*', he soon realised that his 'heart was *black*' (191, emphasis in the original). Chris van Wyk's first, delightful childhood memoir (described earlier in this chapter) appeared in 2004 (a 'complementary' memoir appeared in 2010), while Tatamkhulu Afrika's massive, complex and unusual *Mr Chameleon* came out in 2005. André Brink's recently published *A Fork in the Road* (2009) likewise reflects on the author's choices and changes. Afrika's restless, adventurous, lonely, anguished and gender-conflicted experiences and his chequered working-class life would make a contrasting and complementary study to Brink's academic, culture-centred and more outwardly successful career and many intimate relationships.

Two linocut artists from KwaZulu-Natal had their lively, illustrated auto-biographies published in 2005. William N. Zulu's *Spring Will Come* is a moving life narrative relating the author's struggles to free his talent and his spirit from the handicap of being wheelchair-bound. His warm and lucid prose has its equivalent in the strong designs of his artwork, while his autobiography reflects the social and political tribulations of his region. Zulu ends his narrative by proclaiming his personal praises (312–16), reminding us that such compact, eloquent, rhythmic autobiographies are among the oldest indigenous verbal art forms of our continent and country. Azaria Mbatha, too, inserts his praises into his autobiography (2005: vi–vii). *Within Loving Memory of the Century* is an impressive, though uneven work, profound in vision and social comment, but often playful in style and presented in a non-linear form. The text is down-to-earth, exhilarating and open in recounting personal and communal histories. Mbatha states that his book is 'not so much about [his] family as about South Africa and its history' (16), yet familial and communal Zulu perspectives are highlighted throughout. He declares that 'even fiction can disclose . . . only in part . . . how the people thought, felt and lived who were making history – or did not know that they were – in the vortex of events in which they were caught up' (ix). Like Zulu, Mbatha grew up in rural Zululand and worked at Rorke's Drift Art School; he has lived in Sweden since 1969, returning periodically to South Africa. He tells his readers that his autobiography 'is about the *smaller world* that is [his] home and the *bigger world* outside [his] home', although he has 'mixed them together' (4, emphasis in the original). Our country's history, Mbatha writes, is a 'garment' that is 'tattered and broken'; its scattered pieces need to be woven and sewn together to 'form a morning gown of sorts' (209). Perhaps in that image of a morning gown, one can still hear the echo of the mourning clothes that so many South Africans wore for so long and that many are still wearing.

Some of the crimes of extreme racism that were addressed by the TRC and several TRC figures' autobiographical accounts of their participation in its workings have appeared within the past decade. Desmond Tutu's *No Future without Forgiveness* (2000) is a spiritual meditation, while Wendy Orr's book (2000) focuses wholly and in detail on her TRC participation, as does Zenzile Khoisan's (2001): the latter is a controversial but brilliant interrogation of the inner workings of the apartheid system (as an investigator for the TRC), as well as an exposure of some of the racially tinged tensions among TRC staff members. Boraine's 2008 autobiography also recounts aspects of his work as part of the TRC. Like Khoisan's text, autobiographical accounts by Richard Jurgens (2000) and Helena Dolny (2001) challenge and interrogate, from different perspectives. Jurgens casts a satirical eye as much on apartheid South Africa (especially the South African Defence Force) as on authoritarian tendencies in the ANC organisation in exile, while Dolny makes a case in her own defence as a victim of racial polarisation by the post-apartheid Mbeki government, having headed the (post-apartheid) Land Bank during a period of difficult transformations.

The plague of HIV and AIDS is an inescapable presence in some recent autobiographies. Judge Edwin Cameron's measured approach in his book (2005) differs vastly from the fierce wit displayed in playwright Pieter-Dirk Uys's *Elections and Erections* (2002), but both are urgent and serious works. Charlene Smith's clumsily titled autobiography, *Proud of Me: Speaking Out against Sexual Violence and HIV* (2001), raises a powerful voice against rape and inadequate (or unavailable) AIDS treatment: her work is incandescent, though harrowing. The urgency of her topic demands it. 'Attitude is the father of rape,' she writes 'and the incubator of AIDS' (286). In strange contrast with Smith's intensely responsible work is Johan van Wyk's reissued *Man-Bitch* (2006), with its existential perspective and fascination with cross-racial sexual connections. The compilation *Long Life: Positive HIV Stories* (2003) by the Bambani Women's Writing Group, edited by Jonathan Morgan, should also be mentioned here.

A spectrum of interesting autobiographies by intellectuals makes a notable addition to the decade's output; they include the political lectures and diary of the Marxist scholar Jack Simons (2001); the agri-ecologist James Machobane's *Drive out Hunger* (2003); internationally acclaimed palaeo-anthropologist Philip Tobias's *Into the Past* (2005); urologist Johan Naudé's *Making the Cut* (2007); former Rhodes deputy vice-chancellor and African language and orature expert Peter Mtuze's *An Alternative Struggle* (2007); and architect Alan Lipman's *On the Outside Looking in*, subtitled *Colliding with Apartheid and Other Authorities* (2009).

Three white women autobiographers of this period explore and display expertise of different kinds: they are the painter Jean Campbell (2008); psychic Colleen-Joy Page (2002); and businesswoman and culinary expert Zuretha Roos (2005). These latter texts narrate non-political struggles. An interesting comparison might be drawn between the South African backgrounds, and the United Kingdom lives and returnees' perspectives on their country of origin by juxtaposing *The Morning Light* by Prue Smith (2000) with the more recent *Radical Engagements* by Lorna Levy (2009); the first a more 'private' and the second a distinctly 'political' life.

Two Jewish former South Africans (who are friends) wrote contrasting autobiographies upon revisiting South Africa and reconsidering their wealthy and privileged Jewish upbringing, their dissociation from the country after undergoing military training and their continuing entanglement with it: Larry Schwartz's *The Wild Almond Line* (2000) reviews moral complicity (both his own and his family's), whereas Julian Roup's *Boerejood* (2004) recovers his maternal Afrikaner heritage, reporting his encounters with a range of 'new' Afrikaners. Mandela's presence pervades the autobiographies of this decade, while Bram Fischer, Steve Biko, Chris

Hani and Walter Sisulu (that 'most gentle hero', as his son Max described him) are also felt presences in many of the texts.

'Experience' rather than 'auctoritee' – to abbreviate the Wife of Bath's maxim (Chaucer 1957: 76) – characterises the stance of the autobiographer; the autobiographical mode is anecdotal and existential, rather than ideological and theoretical. Autobiographers share their selves and lives with readers and indeed many of these texts contain family snapshots and photos taken with friends and colleagues. Almost all of the autobiographies surveyed break through South African stereotypes (so often race-coloured). If a group portrait could be compiled from the authors' self-portraits described in this chapter, its ambience would be neither predominantly gloomy nor blandly optimistic. An apt comment comes from one of Bessie Head's letters: 'There may be no miracles but only the hard work of becoming aware of what is wrong and making the conscious choice, slowly and bit by bit, in favour of mental attitudes and principles that do not destroy life' (2005: 176). Head's remark fits in with the other strand in autobiography, that of confronting the judgement of history, or of a later South Africa, that was raised in my opening paragraph.

Much has had to be excluded or omitted from this account of South African life writings. Autobiographies of sports stars (abundant and highly popular) have been omitted; there are still few examples of this type by South Africans of colour. The autobiographies of the decade surveyed here do not fully reflect South African demographics. Publishing, writing and reading remain privileged activities; those who tell us *We Are the Poors* (Desai 2002) are still insufficiently heard in their own voices. From South African Bushmen we have only the numerous testimonial snippets cited in one valuable text, *Voices of the San* (Le Roux and White 2004), lavishly illustrated with art work and photographs. The fascinating, co-authored autobiography of Belinda Kruiper, *Kalahari RainSong* (Bregin and Kruiper 2004), tells the story of how the protagonist grew to know and commit herself to the extended Kruiper family within the larger #Khomani Bushman group, eventually marrying the artist Vetkat Kruiper: her autobiography functions also as a biography of the gifts and woes of these Kalahari dwellers. Also insufficiently present are autobiographies by criminals gaoled for reasons other than opposition to apartheid. Lovejoy's *Acid Alex* (2005) is an exception, illustrating the making of an international drug smuggler.[2] While Helen Parker Lewis's *The Prison Speaks* (2003) and Jonny Steinberg's *The Number* (2004) are not autobiographies, they make a start in conveying prisoners' voices, but much more might be done to enable our society to learn from criminals' own life narratives.

Unisa Press has entitled a publication series 'Hidden Histories'. Two highly readable and worthwhile autobiographies by Ramaphakela Hlalethwa (2008) and

Gaby Magomola (2009) feature in this series: in both texts we encounter lives that span many social, political and geographical spaces. The professional role of both authors, Hlalethwa's being educational and religious and Magomola's in the world of banking and finance, are profoundly affected by the racial aspects of their South African origins. Allan Boesak's 2009 autobiography was withdrawn from publication because aspects of it pertaining to a former struggle ally were legally contested. It was fortunately reissued the same year, but 'cut' as required – still representing much of the fascinating history of the United Democratic Front and Boesak's role in this organisation. Will this 'history' now remain 'hidden' and is its ostensible distortion best handled by a ban on the entire text? A great deal of South Africa's history indeed remains unexcavated, much of it shameful, much of it pitiable, and much of it worthy of recognition.

How reliable as 'evidence', though, are autobiographies? On the topic of self-narrativisation Stuart Hall comments: 'The necessarily fictional nature of the process in no way undermines its discursive, material or political effectivity, even if the belongingness, the "suturing into the story" through which identities arise is, partly, in the imaginary (as well as the symbolic) and therefore always, partly constructed in fantasy' (1996: 4). These words articulate the point that individual life stories, even if to an extent imagined or inevitably reshaped, are not idle fabrications and are read, responded to and assessed by others, becoming significant contributions to the imagining or the imaginative adaptation and enlargement of the social space in which we live.

The artist Azaria Mbatha's justification of his autobiography is applicable to many of the texts addressed here. 'I write these memories,' he states in his preface, 'not because of their historical or political significance, but because they signified for me the expression of what life has meant in moments of actual living' (2005: ix). He says that 'to remember is like starting to see' (15–16). Autobiographers' reminiscences may enable readers to see and hear, or to *imagine* more clearly, the complex and constantly shifting combination of influences that contribute to shaping our shared South African reality; Hlalethwa aptly entitled his autobiography *I Listen, I Learn, I Grow* (2008). Recollection, hindsight, insight, imbibed culture and acquired education combine in autobiographies, building usable stores of social knowledge. They make possible the recognition of our South African diversities and differences as sources of mutual enrichment. It bears mentioning at the end of this chapter that they are continuing to appear, unabated.

Notes

1. See Mary West's fine study of this text in her *White Women Writing White* (2009).
2. Two collections disprove my generalisation: one compiled and edited by Julia Landau (2004); the other by Margie Orford (2008).

References

Accone, Darryl. 2005. *All under Heaven: The Story of a Chinese Family in South Africa*. Cape Town: David Philip.
Achebe, Chinua. 1984. 'Mapping out Identity'. *The Classic* 3(1): 24–5.
Ackermann, Denise M. 2003. *After the Locusts: Letters from a Landscape of Faith*. Grand Rapids: Eerdmans.
Adams, Keith (ed.). 2001. *We Came for Mandela: The Cultural Life of the Refugee Community in South Africa*. Rondebosch: Footprints Publishers.
Afrika, Tatamkhulu. 2005. *Mr Chameleon: An Autobiography*. Johannesburg: Jacana Media.
Alexander Simons, Ray E. 2004. *All My Life and All My Strength*. Edited by R. Suttner. Johannesburg: STE Publishers.
Anderson, Linda. 2001. *Autobiography*. London: Routledge.
Andrews, Rick. 2001. *Buried in the Sky*. Johannesburg: Penguin.
Barnard, Rita and Grant Farred (eds). 2004. *After the Thrill Is Gone: A Post-Apartheid South Africa*. Special issue of *South Atlantic Quarterly* 103(4). Durham: Duke University Press.
Batley, Karen (ed.). 2007. *A Secret Burden: Memories of the Border War by South African Soldiers Who Fought in It*. Johannesburg: Jonathan Ball.
Bernstein, Rusty. 1999. *Memory against Forgetting: Memoirs from a Life in South African Politics 1938–1964*. New York: Viking.
Bizos, George. 2007. *Odyssey to Freedom: A Memoir by the World-Renowned Human Rights Advocate, Friend and Lawyer to Nelson Mandela*. Johannesburg: Random House.
Boesak, Allan. 2009. *Running with the Horses: Reflections of an Accidental Politician*. Cape Town: Joho! Publishers.
Boraine, Alex. 2008. *A Life in Transition*. Cape Town: Zebra Press.
Bosman, Herman Charles. 2003. *My Life and Opinions: Herman Charles Bosman*. Edited by S. Gray. Cape Town: Human & Rousseau.
Brain, Helen. 2006. *Here Be Lions: A Memoir, Not Suitable for Children*. Cape Town: Oshun Books.
Bregin, Elana and Belinda Kruiper. 2004. *Kalahari RainSong*. Pietermaritzburg: University of KwaZulu-Natal Press.
Breytenbach, Breyten. 2009. 'Self-Portrait/Deathwatch: A Note on Autobiotrophy'. In: *Notes from the Middle World*. Chicago: Haymarket Books: 187–205.
Breytenbach, Jan. 2002. *The Buffalo Soldiers: The Story of South Africa's 32-Battalion, 1975–1993*. Alberton: Galago.
Brink, André. 2009. *A Fork in the Road: A Memoir*. London: Harvill Secker.
Cameron, Edwin. 2005. *Witness to AIDS*. Cape Town: Tafelberg.

Campbell, Jean. 2008. *I Adore Red*. Cape Town: Contemporary Art Publishers.
Capon, Heather. 2008. *Clinging to Fences*. Cape Town: Heather Capon.
Chaucer, Geoffrey. 1957. *Complete Works*. Edited by F.N. Robinson. Oxford: Oxford University Press.
Chen, Emma. 2009. *Emperor Can Wait: Memories and Recipes from Taiwan*. Johannesburg: Picador Africa.
Chimeloane, Rrekgetsi. 2001. *Whose Laetie Are You? My Sowetan Boyhood*. Cape Town: Kwela Books.
Chinosole. 2001. *African Diaspora and Autobiographies: Skeins of Self and Skin*. New York: Peter Lang.
Coetzee, Jan K. 2000. *Plain Tales from Robben Island*. Pretoria: Van Schaik.
Coetzee, J.M. 1992. 'Interview'. In: *Doubling the Point: Essays and Interviews*, edited by D. Attwell. Cambridge, Mass.: Harvard University Press: 391–5.
———. 1997. *Boyhood: Scenes from Provincial Life*. Harmondsworth: Penguin.
———. 2003. *Youth*. London: Vintage.
———. 2009. *Summertime*. London: Harvill Secker.
Coullie, Judith L. 2004. *The Closest of Strangers: South African Women's Life Writing*. Johannesburg: Wits University Press.
Coullie, Judith Lutge, Stephan Meyer, Thengani H. Ngwenya and Thomas Olver (eds). 2006. *Selves in Question: Interviews on Southern African Auto/Biography*. Honolulu: University of Hawaii Press.
De Klerk, F.W. 1999. *The Last Trek: A New Beginning: The Autobiography*. London: Macmillan.
De Lille, Patricia with Charlene Smith. 2002. *My Life*. Kenilworth: Spearhead.
Desai, Ashwin (ed.). 2002. *We Are the Poors: Community Struggles in Post-Apartheid South Africa*. New York: Monthly Review Press.
Desai, Ashwin and Richard Pithouse. 2004. ' "What Stank in the Past is the Present's Perfume": Dispossession, Resistance and Repression in Mandela Park'. *South Atlantic Quarterly* 103(4): 841–76.
Des Pres, Terrence. 1976. *The Survivor: An Anatomy of Life in the Death Camps*. New York: Oxford University Press.
Dlamini, Jacob. 2009. *Native Nostalgia*. Johannesburg: Jacana Media.
D'Offici, Mario. 2007. *Bless Me, Father*. Johannesburg: Gekko Publishers.
Dolny, Helena. 2001. *Banking on Change*. London: Viking.
Du Preez, Max. 2003. *Pale Native: Memories of a Renegade Reporter*. Cape Town: Zebra Press.
Eakin, Paul J. 2008. *Living Autobiographically: How We Create Identity in Narrative*. Ithaca: Cornell University Press.
Ebrahim, Noor. 2001. *Noor's Story: My Life in District Six*. Cape Town: District Six Museum.
Eglin, Colin. 2007. *Crossing the Borders of Power: The Memoirs of Colin Eglin*. Johannesburg: Jonathan Ball.
Evans, Gavin. 2002. *Dancing Shoes Is Dead: A Tale of Fighting Men in South Africa*. London: Doubleday.
Gagiano, Annie. 2006. 'Moving beyond Compartmentality: South African English Writing from 1999–2005'. *Literatur in Wissenschaft und Unterricht* 39(2/3): 133–55.
Gandhi, Sita. 2005. *In the Shadow of Mahatma: A Granddaughter Remembers*. Calcutta: Sampark.

Gobodo-Madikizela, Pumla. 2003. *A Human Being Died That Night*. Johannesburg: New Africa Books.

Goldstone, Richard J. 2000. *For Humanity: Reflections of a War Crimes Investigator*. Johannesburg: Wits University Press.

Govender, Pregs. 2007. *Love and Courage: A Story of Insubordination*. Johannesburg: Jacana Media.

Grant, Richard E. 2006. *The Wah-Wah Diaries: The Making of a Film*. London: Picador.

Hall, Stuart. 1996. 'Who Needs "Identity"?' In: *Questions of Cultural Identity*, edited by S. Hall and P. du Gay. London: Sage Publications: 1–17.

Harris, Cyril. 2000. *For Heaven's Sake: The Chief Rabbi's Diary*. Goodwood: NBD.

Head, Bessie, Patrick and Wendy Cullinan. 2005. *Imaginative Trespasser: Letters between Bessie Head, Patrick & Wendy Cullinan 1963–1977*. Compiled by Patrick Cullinan, with a special memoir. Johannesburg: Wits University Press.

Hirson, Denis. 1986. *The House Next Door to Africa*. Cape Town: David Philip.

———. 2005a. *I Remember King Kong (The Boxer)*. Johannesburg: Jacana Media.

———. 2005b. *We Walk Straight So You Had Better Get out the Way*. Johannesburg: Jacana Media.

———. 2006. *White Scars: On Reading and Rites of Passage*. Johannesburg: Jacana Media.

Hlalethwa, Ramaphakela Hans. 2008. *I Listen, I Learn, I Grow: My Autobiography*. Pretoria: Unisa Press.

Jacobs, Rayda. 2005. *The Mecca Diaries*. Cape Town: Double Storey.

———. 2008. *Masquerade: The Story of my Life*. Cape Town: Umuzi.

Jaffer, Zubeida. 2003. *Our Generation*. Cape Town: Kwela Books.

Jurgens, Richard. 2000. *The Many Houses of Exile*. Weltevreden Park: Covos-Day.

Kasrils, Ronald. 2004. *Armed and Dangerous: From Undercover Struggle to Freedom*. Johannesburg: Jonathan Ball.

Kathrada, Ahmed M. 2005. *Memoirs*. Cape Town: Struik.

Keitseng, 'Fish'. 1999. *Comrade Fish: Memories of a Motswana in the ANC Underground*. Compiled by Barry Morton and Jeff Ramsay. Gaborone: Pula Press.

Khoisan, Zenzile. 2001. *Jacaranda Time: An Investigator's View of South Africa's Truth and Reconciliation Commission*. Cape Town: Garib Communications.

Khumalo, Fred. 2006. *Touch my Blood: The Early Years*. Cape Town: Umuzi.

Khuzwayo, Zazah. 2004. *Never Been at Home*. Cape Town: David Philip.

Kikamba, Simão. 2005. *Going Home*. Cape Town: Kwela Books.

Krog, Antjie. 1998. *Country of my Skull*. Johannesburg: Random House.

———. 2003. *A Change of Tongue*. Johannesburg: Random House.

———. 2009. *Begging to be Black*. Cape Town: Random House Struik.

Labuschagne, Riaan. 2002. *On South Africa's Secret Service: An Undercover Agent's Story*. Alberton: Galago.

Landau, Julia (ed.). 2004. *Journey to Myself: Women's Writings from Prison*. Cape Town: Footprints Publications.

Lejeune, Philippe. 1989. *On Autobiography*. Edited by P.J. Eakin. Translated by K. Leary. Minneapolis: University of Minnesota Press.

Lenta, Margaret. 2003. 'Autrebiography: Coetzee's *Boyhood* and *Youth*'. *English in Africa* 30(1): 157–69.

Leon, Tony. 2008. *On the Contrary*. Johannesburg: Jonathan Ball.

Le Roux, Willemien and Allison White (eds). 2004. *Voices of the San Living in Southern Africa Today*. Cape Town: Kwela Books.

Levy, Lorna. 2009. *Radical Engagements: A Life in Exile*. Johannesburg: Jacana Media.

Lewin, Hugh. 2001. *Bandiet: Out of Jail*. Johannesburg: Random House. First published in 1974 as *Bandiet: Seven Years in a South African Prison*. London: Heinemann African Writers.

Lipman, Alan. 2009. *On the Outside Looking in: Colliding with Apartheid and Other Authorities*. Johannesburg: Architect Africa Publications.

Lottering, Agnes. 2002. *Winnefred and Agnes: The True Story of Two Women*. Cape Town: Kwela Books.

Lovejoy, Alex. 2005. *Acid Alex*. Cape Town: Zebra Press.

Machobane, James J. 2003. *Drive out Hunger: The Story of J.J. Machobane of Lesotho*. Compiled from interviews by Robert Berold. Johannesburg: Jacana Media.

Magomola, Gaby. 2009. *Robben Island to Wall Street*. Pretoria: Unisa Press.

Magona, Sindiwe. 1990. *To My Children's Children: An Autobiography*. Cape Town: David Philip.

Malan, Magnus. 2006. *My Life with the South African Defence Force*. Pretoria: Protea Book House.

Mandela, Nelson R. 1994. *Long Walk to Freedom: The Autobiography of Nelson Mandela*. Johannesburg: Macdonald Purnell.

Masekela, Hugh. 2004. *Still Grazing: The Musical Journey of Hugh Masekela*. New York: Crown Publishers.

Matakata, Jama. 2004. *Hills of Hope: The Autobiography of Jama Matakata*. Pietermaritzburg: Nutrend.

Mathabane, Miriam. 2001. *Miriam's Song: A Memoir*. New York: Simon & Schuster.

Mbatha, Azaria J.C. 2005. *Within Loving Memory of the Century: An Autobiography*. Pietermaritzburg: University of KwaZulu-Natal Press.

McGregor, Liz and Sarah Nuttall (eds). 2007. *At Risk: Writing on and over the Edge of South Africa*. Johannesburg: Jonathan Ball.

———. 2009. *Load-Shedding: Writing on and over the Edge of South Africa*. Johannesburg: Jonathan Ball.

Mdakane, Zinhle C. 2001. *No Way Out: Story of an X-Street Kid*. Durban: University of Durban-Westville.

Meer, Fatima. 2001. *Prison Diary*. Cape Town: Kwela Books.

Meer, Ismael C. 2002. *A Fortunate Man*. Cape Town: Zebra Press.

Mgxashe, Mxolisi. 2006. *Are You with Us? The Story of a PAC Activist*. Cape Town: Tafelberg.

Mhlaba, Raymond. 2001. *Raymond Mhlaba's Memoirs: Reminiscing from Rwanda and Uganda*. Pretoria: Human Sciences Research Council.

Miller, Nancy K. 1991. *Getting Personal: Feminist Occasions and Other Autobiographical Acts*. New York and London: Routledge.

Mkhabela, Sibongile. 2001. *Open Earth and Black Roses: Remembering 16 June 1976*. Johannesburg: Skotaville.

Mogoba, Mmutlanyane Stanley. 2003. *Stone, Steel, Sjambok: Faith on Robben Island*. Edited by T. Coggin. Johannesburg: Ziningweni Communications.

Moore-Gilbert, Bart. 2009. *Postcolonial Life-Writing*. London: Routledge.

Morgan, Jonathan and the Great African Spider Writers. 1999. *Finding Mr Madini*. Cape Town: David Philip.

Morgan, Jonathan and the Bambani Women's Writing Group. 2003. *Long Life: Positive HIV Stories*. Cape Town: Double Storey.

Mphahlele, Es'kia. 1971 [1959]. *Down Second Avenue*. London: Faber and Faber.

———. 2010. *Bury Me at the Marketplace: Es'kia Mphahlele and Company, Letters 1943–2006*. Edited by N.C. Manganyi and D. Attwell. Johannesburg: Wits University Press.

Mphahlele, Letlapa. 2002. *Child of the Soil: My Life as a Freedom Fighter*. Cape Town: Kwela Books.

Mtuze, Peter T. 2007. *An Alternative Struggle: An Illustrated Autobiography*. Florida Hills: Vivlia.

Mynhardt, Patrick. 2003. *Boy from Bethulie: An Autobiography*. Johannesburg: Wits University Press.

Naudé, Johan. 2007. *Making the Cut in South Africa: A Medico-Political Journey*. London: Royal Society of Medicine Press.

Ndlovu, Malika. 2009. *Invisible Earthquake: A Woman's Journey through Stillbirth*. Athlone: Modjaji Books.

Ndungane, Njongonkulu. 2003. *A World with a Human Face: A Voice from Africa*. Cape Town: David Philip.

Ngculu, James. 2009. *The Honour to Serve: Recollections of an Umkhonto Soldier*. Cape Town: David Philip.

Nuttall, Sarah and Cheryl-Ann Michael. 2000. 'Autobiographical Acts'. In: *Senses of Culture: South African Culture Studies*, edited by S. Nuttall and C. Michael. Oxford: Oxford University Press: 298–317.

Olney, James. 1972. *Metaphors of Self: The Meaning of Autobiography*. Princeton: Princeton University Press.

———. 1998. *Memory and Narrative: The Weave of Life-Writing*. Chicago: Chicago University Press.

Orford, Margie (ed.). 2008. *Fifteen Men: Images and Words from behind Bars*. Johannesburg: Jonathan Ball.

Orr, Wendy. 2000. *From Biko to Basson: Wendy Orr's Search for the Soul of Africa as a Commissioner of the TRC*. Saxonwold: Contra.

Page, Colleen-Joy. 2002. *My Life as an Apple-Tree*. Johannesburg: Red Nolan.

Parker Lewis, Helen. 2003. *The Prison Speaks: Men's Voices/South African Jails*. Cape Town: ihilihili.

Pauw, Jacques. 2006. *Dances with Devils: A Journalist's Search for Truth*. Cape Town: Zebra Press.

Pogrund, Benjamin. 2000. *War of Words: Memoir of a South African Journalist*. New York: Seven Stones Press.

Potlatinsky, Ashlee. 2008. 'Being Judge and Witness: Edwin Cameron's *Witness to AIDS*'. *English in Africa* 35(2): 53–70.

Raditlhalo, Sam. 2009. 'The Self-Invention of Hugh Masekela'. *Journal of Literary Studies* 25(1): 34–52.

Rak, Julie. 2004. 'Are Memoirs Autobiography? A Consideration of Memoir and Public Identity'. *Genre: Forms of Discourse and Culture* 37 (3/4): 483–504.

Ramsden, Tim. 2007. *Border-Line Insanity: A National Serviceman's Story*. Bloomington: Trafford Publishing.

Robb, Noël. 2006. *The Sash and I*. Cape Town: Noël Robb.

Roos, Zuretha. 2005. *The Saffron Pear Tree and Other Kitchen Memories*. Cape Town: Oshun Books.

Roup, Julian. 2004. *Boerejood*. Johannesburg: Jacana Media.

Sachs, Albie. 2004. *The Free Diary of Albie Sachs*. Johannesburg: Random House.

———. 2009. *The Strange Alchemy of Life and Law*. Oxford: Oxford University Press.

Sampson, Anthony. 2008. *The Anatomist: The Autobiography of Anthony Sampson*. Johannesburg: Jonathan Ball.

Schwartz, Larry. 2000. *The Wild Almond Line*. St Leonards, NSW: Allen and Unwin.

Sesanti, Simphiwe. 2005. *Carry On, African Child*. Durban: Vul'Indlela.

Shaw, Gerald. 2007. *Believe in Miracles: South Africa from Malan to Mandela and the Mbeki Era: A Reporter's Story*. Cape Town: Ampersand Press.

Sher, Antony. 2001. *Beside Myself: An Autobiography*. London: Hutchinson.

Simons, Harold J. 2001. *Comrade Jack: The Political Lectures and Diary of Jack Simons*. Edited by M. Sparg, J. Schreiner and G. Ansell. Johannesburg: STE Publishers.

Slabbert, Frederik van Zyl. 2000. *Tough Choices: Reflections of an Afrikaner African*. Cape Town: Tafelberg.

Smith, Charlene. 2001. *Proud of Me: Speaking Out against Sexual Violence and HIV*. London: Penguin.

Smith, Prue. 2000. *The Morning Light: A South African Childhood Revalued*. Cape Town: David Philip.

Smith, Sidonie. 1998. *Women, Autobiography, Theory: A Reader*. Madison: University of Wisconsin Press.

Stegmann, George. 2007. *The Lights of Freedom*. Durban: Just Done Publications.

Steinberg, Jonny. 2004. *The Number*. Johannesburg: Jonathan Ball.

Stobie, Cheryl. 2007. 'Shedding Skins: Metaphors of Race and Sexuality in the Writing of Tatamkhulu Afrika'. *Journal of Literary Studies* 23(2): 148–65.

Strachan, Harold. 2004. *Make a Skyf, Man!* Johannesburg: Jacana Media.

Suttner, Raymond. 2001. *Inside Apartheid's Prison: Notes and Letters of Struggle*. Melbourne: Ocean.

Taylor, Charles. 1992. *Sources of the Self*. Cambridge: Cambridge University Press.

Tobias, Philip V. 2005. *Into the Past: A Memoir*. Johannesburg: Picador Africa.

Tutu, Desmond. 2000. *No Future without Forgiveness*. London: Rider.

Umlilo, Thandeki. 2002. *Little Girl, Arise! New Life after Incest and Abuse*. Pietermaritzburg: Cluster Publications.

Uys, Pieter-Dirk. 2002. *Elections and Erections: A Memoir of Fear and Fun*. Cape Town: Zebra Press.

———. 2005. *Between the Devil and the Deep: A Memoir of Acting and Reacting*. Cape Town: Zebra Press.

Van Wyk, Chris. 2004. *Shirley, Goodness and Mercy: A Childhood Memoir*. Johannesburg: Picador Africa.
———. 2010. *Eggs to Lay, Chickens to Hatch*. Johannesburg: Picador Africa.
Van Wyk, Johan. 2006. *Man-Bitch*. Durban: Johan van Wyk.
West, Mary. 2009. *White Women Writing White: Identity and Representation in (Post-) Apartheid Literatures of South Africa*. Cape Town: David Philip.
Woods, Donald. 2000. *Rainbow Nation Revisited: South Africa's Decade of Democracy*. London: André Deutsch.
Zulu, William N. 2005. *Spring Will Come*. Pietermaritzburg: University of KwaZulu-Natal Press.

13

Healing the Wounds of History
South African Indian Writing

DEVARAKSHANAM BETTY GOVINDEN

A feature of the post-apartheid literary scene in South Africa is the way in which the history of earlier times and of groups which were previously silent is being recalled and recounted. As part of this 'memory work' the history of Indian indenture in South Africa has emerged as a potent theme for both historians and writers of fiction. This history is being reclaimed and recognised as an intrinsic component of any South African narrative.

A definition of South African 'Indians' – the term has persisted 150 years after the arrival of the first indentured labourers from India in 1860 and will be used in this chapter – may be helpful to non-South Africans and even to South Africans who live outside of KwaZulu-Natal. Like many terms used to designate population groups, it is inexact. A considerable proportion of the slave population brought to South Africa between 1653 and 1808 was of Indian origin and after the final abolition of slavery in 1838 their descendants were absorbed into what is now known as the 'Cape Coloured' group. I am not concerned here with this group (for discussion of this broader designation, see Frenkel 2010).

My focus in this chapter is rather with a later group of Indian immigrants, whose descendants continue to call themselves Indian, though they are at the same time South African and participate in all areas of South African life. The first batch of these immigrants, a total of 341 labourers, predominantly Hindu from Madras, came to the colonial Natal sugar farms on the S.S. *Truro* on 16 November 1860. A few years later, in 1870, 'passenger' Indians – predominantly Muslim – began to arrive: they were entrepreneurs, unattached by any contract to an employer, mainly from Bombay and other parts of the west coast of India. Most of them established themselves as traders and shopkeepers. By 1866 a total of 6 445 indentured immigrants had arrived in Natal; by 1911, 152 184 indentured immigrants from India had arrived, as had an estimated 30 000 passenger Indians. It is necessary to see indentured labourers and passenger Indians as part of the same experience of indentured life. The large majority of the descendants of these people – both Hindu and Muslim – continue to live in KwaZulu-Natal, where their ancestors were labourers or traders, but there are sizeable communities in Gauteng and smaller groups in other South African cities.

The history of this wave of Indian migration from 1860 has been surveyed by several South African historians, including Surendra Bhana and Joy Brain (1990). More recently, Ashwin Desai and Goolam Vahed's *Inside Indenture* (2007) – to which I shall refer later – though it contains numerous biographical sketches produced from archival research, has some of the narrative texture of literary writing. In fact, the literature cannot be studied in isolation from the history. The emphasis on indenture in recent literary and historical works confirms this and the literature of indenture connects South Africa and its literary writing with other lands and cultures. As the narrator in Sumayya Lee's *The Story of Maha* (2007) writes: 'Our ancestors – some came before others, some were indentured, indebted labourers and others were tradespeople and professionals looking for new beginnings. Why not Africa, after all, it was just another piece of the Empire Pie?' (2007: 12).

Given the history of Empire, South African Indian writing inevitably intersects with literatures and writings in the rest of Africa, with India and with postcolonies elsewhere. It may be seen as an inextricable part of the literatures of colonialism and of postcolonialism, both on the African continent and beyond. Ronit Frenkel argues that 'a dualistic logic is unproductive in understanding the intertwinings of a world marked by the aftermaths of slavery, colonialism and globalisation' (2010: 3).

Despite the large numbers of people from India who settled in South Africa in the late nineteenth and early twentieth century, indenture in the apartheid past was neglected in South African literature and critical writings, as well as in historical texts before the late 1980s. In this chapter I focus mainly on fiction by South African Indian writers of the past decade that deals with the theme of indenture or matters allied to it. I shall argue that indenture has been an important influence on economic, social and political life in South Africa. A focus on indenture, paradoxically, allows us to see South African literature beginning to move beyond its somewhat parochial and exclusive concern with events in this country towards current transnational investigations of an Indian Ocean map of South/South interaction, as well as to other Indian diasporic sites. In short, South

African Indian literature, especially the literature that deals with indenture, for too long marginalised in discussions of South African political and literary life, can help to reconfigure literary studies in South Africa in terms of its links with countries other than Europe.

Elsewhere I have pointed out that South Africa is currently attentive to historical memory (Govinden 2008a, 2008b). The work of the Truth and Reconciliation Commission (TRC) in South Africa's reconstruction and development period, from 1996 onwards, has attempted to heal the wounds of the past; there has been a need among South Africans other than those most severely victimised by apartheid to recount their suppressed histories. Indenture may be seen as a template for memory among the descendants of immigrants – a memory of suffering, endurance, struggle and survival – and it figures in their reminiscences as the quintessential subaltern experience. Writing on this theme, largely after 1994 and particularly in the last decade, reveals that South African Indian identity, however problematic its singular designation, is constructed against the 'detritus of indenture', to use Vijay Mishra's phrase (2007: xvii).

In the culture of indenture, *girmit* – derived from the word 'agreement' – is a term not only for the (permit) contract-labour system, but it also 'designates a form of consciousness, a system of imaginary beliefs, and defines "a subalternal knowledge category" that grew out of the collective indenture ethos' (Mishra 2007: 22). Like *kala pani* (black water, i.e., ocean) the words *girmit* and *girmitiyas* are being used more widely now, in formal speech and in literature, whereas previously they were used only orally and informally. The presence of *girmitya* or 'coolie'[1] texts in the literature of the community immediately points to the way in which the history of indenture shapes the psyche of Indians in South Africa. Its use in the recent past epitomises a determination by South African Indian authors to tell the story of indenture as their ancestors, rather than the white colonists, experienced it. A few texts published before the first democratic election of 1994 (which may serve here as a cut-off of the segregationist past and the beginning of democracy) used the derogatory term 'coolie' in the title, albeit ironically. Among them are Jay Naidoo's *Coolie Location* (1990) and Kesaveloo Goonam's *Coolie Doctor* (1991). Such reinterpretation of negative identities is an interesting feature of cultural history. There are numerous examples of this in the texts of the past, with Gandhi himself while in South Africa being referred to as the 'Coolie Barrister' (Brown and Prozesky 1996). *Girmit* belongs to the same category, but because of its linguistic origins it can be seen as a term that the oppressed have transferred from insulting colonial connotation to positive utilisation in the definition of their own identity.

Since 1994 South African Indian writing by the descendants of both indentured and passenger Indians has flourished.[2] (There are also the Cape Indian-Malay voices – see Roos 2005.) Writers who began to publish in the apartheid past are still active, such as the poet Shabbir Banoobhai (of contemporary Islamic vision) (2004) and, of Tamil origin, Ronnie Govender, whose play *The Lahnee's Pleasure* (2008 [1977]) – first performed in 1972 – has accrued landmark significance in capturing in stage-speech a working-class South African Indian accent (for example, the character Mothie says: 'Yes, bhai, thirty years I'm working for my Lahnee. Anything I want my Lahnee gives me.'[12]). Recently revived to packed houses, *The Lahnee's Pleasure* continues to inspire several new 'Indian' comedies of manner, including Geraldine Naidoo's *Chilli Boy* (first performed in 2002).

In addition, a number of auto/biographical works have been published. Among them is *A Fortunate Man* by Ismael C. Meer (2002) and *Memoirs* by Ahmed M. Kathrada (2005). Mac Maharaj's memoir, *Shades of Difference* (2007), was compiled by Padraig O'Malley after extensive interviews with African National Congress (ANC) struggle stalwart Maharaj. Given the political background of many of these activists and their experiences of incarceration, their writings add to the genre of the prison memoir in South Africa. In *Prison Diary* (2001) the late Fatima Meer writes of her detention for 119 days in mid-1976, following the students' revolt in Soweto, when eleven members of the Federation of Black Women were detained under Section 6 of the Terrorism Act and kept in solitary confinement. This was during a spate of detentions, one of which led to the death of Steve Biko.

Describing changes in the literary environment in a changing political climate, J.U. Jacobs comments: 'The country is at present engaged in a process of self-narration – a national recollection of those blanked-out areas of its identity. The current proliferation of South African life stories may be seen as part of the autobiographical impulse of an entire nation finally bringing its past into proper perspective' (1994: 878). One such autobiographical volume is Ronnie Govender's *In the Manure: Memories and Reflections* (2008), which deals with his life in the theatre, while his *Song of the Atman* (2006) is a biographical work, describing the life of his uncle, Chin Govender, who travels across a country experiencing its racial troubles. Pregs Govender's *Love and Courage: A Story of Insubordination* (2007) goes beyond 'struggle autobiography' to offer a critique of the inner workings of the post-democracy government and the ANC. An intensive and inclusive analysis of such texts by Indians in South Africa, however, is beyond the scope of this chapter and I turn now to recent literature that depicts the colonial era, with particular reference to indenture, as one particular instance of the literature of this time of memory.

As I have already suggested, collective and individual memories, both orally transmitted as well as formal history of Indian indenture, have often provided a background for writings by South African Indians. The often distorted nature of previously received South African history is laid bare when local history and memory is brought to the fore; subjugated knowledge is revealed and legitimised through the trope of indenture. In the same way as we have literary sub-genres such as the Afrikaans *plaasroman* (farm novel) or the crime novel, we are acquiring a discernible literature of indenture, which has not yet been classified or considered in any significant way. This reveals a freeing up of our understanding of the past, in which apartheid was seen as the defining element. There is an attempt to look at a variety of nodes of experiences, of which indenture is one. There is also an attempt to posit indenture as an original historical indignity, compounded by segregationist legislation. The apartheid era built on this discrimination, with the Population Registration Act of 1950 classifying people by race. Further legislation defined and legalised inequalities between groups. The Group Areas Act of 1950 confined people from designated racial groups to particular residential areas, which resulted in social and cultural separation.

Aziz Hassim's *The Lotus People* (2002) depicts the Casbah in the Grey Street complex in Durban as a space of separate living (see also Naidoo 2002). He begins his novel during the time of indenture, when passenger Indians came to Natal. We are presented with an experience now fading and forgotten, but excavated by Hassim from the archives of memory:

> And life in the Casbah was about politics too. Children were weaned on it, as children elsewhere were weaned on mother's milk. It was the logical outcome of the policies of repression, the common denominator around which their lives revolved. Spectators watched sport and simultaneously talked politics, diners enjoyed their meals and discussed the latest developments, young couples impressed each other with their awareness and the depth of their knowledge, and street sweepers picked up pamphlets and debated the merits of protest as a force for peaceful change. There was no other area under one square mile that could equal it for the intensity of its emotions and its pursuit of justice (103).

The narrative reminds us that a city is a palimpsest, with layers of history and memory. It presents Durban as a key site in the larger history of Indian indenture, as it chronicles the story of a single family, arriving from India in the 1880s, but set against a larger communal backdrop. The family's history in South Africa spans

100 years, but began centuries before in India. In a discussion with me in 2003, Isabel Hofmeyr drew my attention to the novel's 'epic' proportions:

> The novel's epic reach is announced on the opening page which starts in 325 B.C.E. in the Pathan warrior class in northwest India. And it is indeed an exhilarating experience to read a South African novel that starts in this way . . . The dagger is a repository of legend, memory and wealth. It is not static, but is made and remade as it circulates. Like all traditions, it can only gain value and meaning because it travels and changes.

Beginning by establishing a small-scale hawking business, Yahya Ali Suleiman, the original immigrant, faces many difficulties in the land of his adoption. The author balances generational continuity and difference by telling of the ancestry and life of the old Muslim patriarch as well as that of his son, Dara, and of his grandsons, Sam and Jake, as each responds to the times and circumstances in which he lives. In spite of many handicaps the family manages to set up large emporiums in the Grey Street complex. While Sam, who is practically inclined, has a successful business career, Jake is a brooding, angry young man, choosing a more defiant and aggressive lifestyle than that of his grandfather and father. It is not surprising that he becomes a political activist in the ANC and is forced underground. Sam and Jake, as they grow up, hover on the edge of the gangster groups in their neighbourhood. In different forms the Pathan 'dagger' is passed on from generation to generation.

The next narrative layer in *The Lotus People* is the political history for which Durban's Grey Street is well known. It is as if the pavements speak, telling what they have witnessed, resounding with the rousing speeches of some of Durban's greatest 'freedom fighters', including Mohandas Gandhi, the young lawyer and activist as he was known during his years in South Africa. These Casbah streets have witnessed 'threshold moments' in Durban's history, such as the 1949 riots (Hassim was twelve years old at the time), the Defiance Campaigns of the 1950s, and the Mass Democratic Movement resistance of the 1980s. Hassim shows Durban's Casbah as a multidimensional site. It is home to a range of colourful people such as socialites, activists, sportsmen, actors and gangsters. It is a locus of political resistance. As such it is the Durban equivalent of Johannesburg's Sophiatown or Cape Town's District Six, areas which, at the margins of apartheid racial engineering, assumed literary-symbolic significance. But the Casbah, in addition, had its particular reflection of the macro-history of Indian indenture, mainly passenger Indian entrepreneurship, but also the Indian market and the proletarian class (see Stiebel 2010).

Healing the Wounds of History

Whereas it is the small stories of community (see Brown 2006) that we encounter in Ronnie Govender's *'At the Edge' and Other Cato Manor Stories* (1996), it is the narrative of indenture that propels his novel *Song of the Atman*, to which I have already referred. Here Govender paints 'an evocative portrait of five generations of descendants of former indentured Indian labourers and their struggle to build an identity in an emerging South Africa' (back cover). Himself a second generation descendant of indentured Indians, Govender – in an English influenced by Tamil syntactical structure – evokes the atmosphere of the 'coolie' era and shows how indentured life in South Africa signalled a continuing struggle for 'Indian' recognition and identity. In following the life of Chin Govender, the novel traverses the physical and political landscape of South Africa, beginning in Cato Manor, where some of the indentured labourers settled after their *girmits* had expired. Govender paints portraits of the first days of indenture and captures the lives of the Indian settlers, the forced removals they endured and their struggles to get a social and economic footing in a country where setbacks were experienced at every turn. Of Mr Baijnath, Chin Govender's employer in Durban, he writes:

> The father had come to South Africa from Bihar in India, where he and others like him had been fed stories of gold nuggets being picked up on the streets of Durban. It was a different story, of course, when they arrived, aching to get away from an India impoverished by waves of Arab and British imperialism. The word 'indenture', as he and his fellows were to discover, was a politics word for slavery. Baijnath's father had saved enough to pay a small deposit on a piece of land in Cato Manor, practically mortgaging himself for life. He'd started a market garden and had built up a steady trade selling vegetables to the housewives on the Berea. He'd hoped that his son would follow him. By the time Baijnath was a grown man, the land would be free (2006: 19–20).

The novel charts a trajectory from Durban to Pietermaritzburg, on to Richmond, East London, Port Elizabeth and Cape Town. Chin Govender, 'a different kind of Indian' (134), moves from wine steward to waiter to manager to owner of a hotel, his peripatetic life marked by dangerous liaisons with white women (at a time when the Immorality Act was not only law, but also governed the psyches of many white people). All the time, however, there is his steely determination to succeed. The novel works as a wide-ranging *Bildungsroman* of a life filled with vicissitudes against the landscape of twentieth-century South Africa.

Riason Naidoo's *Indian Ink: The Indian in Drum Magazine in the 1950s* (2008) is a non-fictional work illustrated with photographs and covering similar, mid-twentieth century subject matter. The first section, 'Meet the Indian in South Africa', begins appropriately with images from indentured history:

> In a collage of identity photos of indentured labourers from the nineteenth century, twelve naked torso-length portraits of Indian males, some not yet adults, face the viewer, each holding up his identification number. Rib cages protrude from beneath some of the men's skins and sunken eyes tell of gruelling voyages. The figures are replicated like patterned wallpaper, suggesting a continuity, an infinite number of other labourers beyond the borders of the image, while also underlining their presence in the colony as mere numbers – commodities in the sugar industry (12).

Naidoo then presents successive images of Indians in different roles and capacities, describing, like Hassim in his fictional work, apartheid, liberation histories, gangs and the social and cultural activities that characterised Indian life in South Africa, as represented in *Drum* magazine.

Using the background of indenture, Praba Moodley has produced historical fiction on a similar theme to that of Daphne Rooke's novel *Ratoons* (1953), which, though written by a white woman, gives a vivid picture of Indian settlers. In her novel *The Heart Knows No Colour* (2003) Moodley, who dedicates her book 'to my forefathers', develops a narrative of family life, which includes the familiar theme of inter-racial relationships on a sugarcane plantation in Verulam, Natal, at the turn of the century. The effect of the work is to redefine not only Indianness, but also other South African identity categories. Intimacy, such as it was, is illustrated in the unequal relations between master and servant, as well as in forbidden sexual love across the colour line. As the back cover states, this popular novel is 'packed with period detail': an apt description also of her latest historical romance, *Follow Your Heart* (2009). While there has been negative criticism of this type of literature, which is sometimes seen as reflecting false consciousness (the cover of the book suggests an Orientalist exoticism), more critical work in this sub-genre of popular fiction – which is influential on readers' attitudes – cannot, I think, go amiss.

Pat Poovalingam's novel, *Anand* (2003), another period piece, also merges the colonial and apartheid eras. It depicts a young lawyer, the 'grandson of a coolie indentured immigrant labourer', and the action is set against the background of sugarcane farm relations in Umhlali on Natal's north coast. Anand, the grandson of an Indian woman and a white sugar planter, is being tried for treason against the apartheid government. The theme is similar to that of Zakes Mda's *The Madonna of Excelsior* (2002), which shows a preoccupation with the apartheid past and in particular with transgressions of the Immorality Act. Poovalingam's narrative contrasts the power and privilege of whites with the solidarity among the colonised. Mishra correctly sees *Anand* as an example of 'the master-slave dialectic that has led to writers using plantation narratives to write either about the legacy of apartheid . . . or about liberation struggles in the country' (2006: 123).

An interesting variation on the indenture theme is to be found in Rubendra Govender's *Sugar Cane Boy* (2008). The history of the Murugappas, a family three generations after indenture, who live in the foothills of Inanda on the north coast of Natal, provides the background for a novel that is set in 1972 in the context of apartheid. The sugarcane plantation culture is ubiquitous, with the protagonist taking naturally to working in the fields. As he says, '"I am a Sugar Cane Boy, just like my forefathers"' (51). A juxtaposition of the old diaspora history with that of apartheid is tacitly achieved.

Girrmit [sic] *Tales* (2008) by Neelan Govender is a collection of unusual stories of Indian indentured labourers in Natal. Govender is aware of the vast canvas against which individual stories are experienced and shows how slavery was transmuted into indentured labour. He locates the scheme of immigration to Natal in the wider setting of Indian immigration to different parts of the world, such as Fiji, the Caribbean, Mauritius, Seychelles and East Africa. He shows that indenture was a soulless contract between employer and employee, which stipulated that the labourer receive ten shillings per month as well as rations of dhal and rice. The agreement included details of the period of indenture, the nature of labour required, the number of days the immigrants were required to work and details of the return passage.

A consideration of South African Indian writings on indenture suggests a different trajectory to a modernity that is usually charted together with its high points in the 'Western' Renaissance, Reformation and Enlightenment, in which 'achievement' is a purely European high-culture affair. South African Indian writings emphasise, rather, a world shaped by slavery and indenture. One effect of this is to propel literary scholarship in South Africa horizontally, across spaces, and temporally, across periods, in a history that is characterised by varieties of transculturation, both voluntary and enforced. An example is to be found in Imraan Coovadia's novel, *The Wedding* (2001) which, like Hassim's *The Lotus People*, is set in the Grey Street (Casbah) district of Durban. Here the texts of Empire – *Moby Dick, Clarissa* – that are read in India are sought out by Khateja, the grandmother of the narrator, when she arrives as a young woman in South Africa, as a way of connecting the two postcolonies, of trying to feel at home in an alien space while keeping the idea of India alive. The ubiquitous English classic, similarly to the

Christian hymn in other contexts, acts as a unifying force among the colonised reading it and is not perceived as it might be later, at least by the 'postcolonially' aware, as a form of mimicry, whether negatively or (Bhabha-like) as 'rebellious'. The grandfather in Coovadia's story brings his prayer mat and Qur'an from India. (I am reminded of V.S. Naipaul's Nobel Prize lecture where he states: '[W]e had brought a kind of India with us, which we could, as it were, unroll like a carpet on the flat land' [2006: 80–1].) Coovadia writes:

> Yes, India, multifold, many-fingered, articulated, cloth-covered India, issued from their luggage: a Koran in a soft cream binding ... Once things were a little clear Ismet took his namaaz mat from the bottom of his trunk and rolled it out proudly. It was worn in places to a translucent dot. Now he could pray in a proper and respectful manner in this new land (2001: 148).

Ismet also brings with him his dreams of the Indian cuisine savoured in the homeland as a way of establishing continuity between his Indian past and his South African present. As Mishra points out, this anxiety about loss of land and homeland is typical of the earlier diaspora of indenture, where the imagination was triggered by the 'contents of gunny sacks' (2007: 4).

There is a tendency among colonists to see the new country as a blank slate on which memories may be inscribed and these have often been transported from the place of origin. While the white colonisers gave colonial spaces names that replicated those of their home countries, tacitly reminding everyone of who has the power of naming, there was also unofficial naming by the oppressed. Wilson Harris has rightly pointed out: 'If one has lived in a country without history, one has to discover it or invent it, for Memory is the cornerstone of identity' (quoted in Flockemann 2008: 6). My poem, 'Memory of Snow and Dust' (written after reading Breyten Bretenbach's novel of almost the same title [1989]), relates Africa to India and invokes memory operating co-laterally, as it reflects my own family's inherited memories of indentured experience. The following is an excerpt:

> I too sat at fireplaces
> on my father's lap
> listening to tales of kings and kingdoms
> of wrestlers and gatekeepers
> of lovers beyond their reach
> wily grandmothers
> temples and human snakes

time collapses
dream and reality
stories of Ramayan and Soundiata
words on water

my grandfather held his mother's hand
severing memory
time of lion and tiger
elephant and demons and stars

castaways
tilling in coolie canefields sighing
toiling for tea for empire
stonebodies in compounds.

* * *

Projects in postcolonial literary and cultural criticism are currently pushing elements of South African literature towards a relatively new category of Indian Ocean literatures, where Africa, the Indian Ocean islands of Madagascar, Mauritius and Seychelles, and India are considered, together with South African Indian writings, as an important area of exploration. A key initiative here is led by Hofmeyr, whose research into the 'book history' of circulating texts as influential in bringing new publics into being began by considering the 'travels' of John Bunyan's *The Pilgrim's Progress* in missionary Africa (2003, 2004) and is focused now on the Indian Ocean equivalent of Paul Gilroy's (1993) 'Black Atlantic' (Hofmeyr 2008). In similar vein Stephen Gray, in his anthology *Invitation to a Voyage: French Language Poetry of the Indian Ocean African Islands* (2008), reminds us that the Indian Ocean has been linked to South Africa for the past 400 years, highlighting the slavery of the eighteenth century, the sugar industry of the nineteenth and socialism in the twentieth century. In the past, scholarship has focused on the Middle Passage and the Atlantic slave trade; attention has now been directed to the Indian Ocean, which was a much older focus of trade – and specifically of the slave trade and of later labour migrations. This must be seen as an interrogation of the 'important spaces between terra-centric polities' (MacDonald 2008: 6).

Further scholarship extending to the investigation of overlapping histories is therefore necessary and the work of critics such as Brinda Mehta, whose *Diasporic (Dis)Locations* (2004) shows points of intersection between the Indian and African diasporas globally, is worth mentioning in this regard. Mehta speaks of 'rhizomatic spatiality' across the *kala pani* of not only the Atlantic, but also the Indian Ocean, and draws from Caribbean and Mauritian writers to develop her argument. Similarly, Hershini Bhana Young, against the background of her own experiences as a young Indian woman growing up in South Africa and of her ancestors who came from India to South Africa, widens her literary and critical gaze to the history of slavery in the African diaspora in *Haunting Capital* (2006). A 'South-South' perspective also characterises Desai and Vahed's *Inside Indenture* (2007), which tells the story of Goordeen Bhagoo and his wife Golaba Lalsa, who arrived in Natal in 1890 from Lucknow, but who were listed by colonial authorities as residents of Guadeloupe (49). Khal Torabully, a Mauritian writer whose father was Trinidadian while his mother's family hailed from India and Malaysia, similarly turns to a 'transcultural' canvas when, evoking the sea as 'a coral imaginary', he suggests the flow, the movement, of people across the Indian diaspora:

> And I anchored in Durban, Fiji, the West Indies,
> In the dust of waves.
> To be scattered in the gales of continents,
> In the currents of continents (in Desai and Vahed 2007: 68).

The notion of a 'coral imaginary' is synonymous with that of a mosaic of shared identities that ultimately embraces all humanity. This certainly expands our understanding of South African identities beyond the ethnocentric, or even the national, imperative.

It is in this expanding literary universe that I believe South African Indian writing, especially on indenture, can make a distinct contribution to South African literature and literary criticism. The problem of an approach from a single perspective is that it denies the fact that writing may move both centrifugally and centripetally. The formulation of literatures as exemplifying *roots and routes* shows that the two processes are intertwined, focusing on circulation and flow as well as on origins and ancestral places. Andrew MacDonald points to 'the zones of contact occasioned by the economics of modernity' and suggests that we need to wake up to the fact that 'the identity of our species is shaped by diasporic and transnational imaginaries of long gestation' (2008: 2).

The notion of contact zones – a much cited trope in postcolonial literature – is valuable in consideration of the many different interactions that may be attributed to individuals or groups and these zones may be found in multiple spaces, given the history of Empire. Differing impulses co-exist and critical readings should open up the literature to showing how strands are intertwined and intermeshed. An element of the narratives in Govender's *Girmit Tales*, mentioned earlier, is the close connection in the characters' lives between India and South Africa. We are told of the immigrants' journey in India to the great ghats that were to take them to distant lands. Their arrival in South Africa is carefully described, as are the places where they were held before they were distributed to sugar-farm owners. Sometimes the life of struggle in India continues on foreign soil. For someone such as Govender's character Jura, for example, who is scraping a living by doing odd jobs in Durban, 'little had changed in . . . life or circumstance. It seemed not so long ago that he was a mere starving youth seeking sanctuary at the temples of Kancheepuram' (2008: 100). India is evoked not only in fact, but also in memory and dream, as incidents in the new spaces trigger recollections of similar happenings in the birth places of the immigrants. Some become drudges in the new place of abode, keeping their souls alive by memories of life lived in another place, another time. For Vengetapathy, for example, in Govender's short story, 'Wrought by Prayer':

> [H]is mind seemed to enter a time-top in reverse gear; he seemed oblivious of the present. His mind was reaching back to a long time ago, as if to gain strength from the past. Sirdar Vengetapathy was once more in his native land . . . his mind projected thus to his ancestors, seven generations away. It transcended time (2008: 55).

Recounting the indentured experience entails a responsibility for writer, critic and reader. The value of work of this kind in South African literature, and particularly in the case of South African Indian writing, is that it offers an interrogation of the shifting politics of identity, now based on mythmaking, now on cold reality. The young writer Miriam Akabor may say that after her collection of stories, *Flat 9* (2006) – based on her own experience of growing up in Grey Street – she wishes to move away from an inner city that no longer signifies 'Indianness'. (Grey Street has recently been renamed Dr Yusuf Dadoo Street, a name associated with the Indian contribution to the wider anti-apartheid struggle, but not necessarily familiar to a 'born-free' generation of Durban Indian teenagers: see Mamet 2008.) Coovadia, whose novel subsequent to *The Wedding* is a rollicking transcontinental picaresque (*Green-Eyed Thieves* [2006]), would probably agree that it is time to turn to the *now*, which he does in *High Low In-between* (2009): a suspense narrative which, set within a Durban Indian family, raises current ethical concerns in South Africa involving, among other issues, AIDS denialism.

The point is that South African Indian identity is not homogeneous. Prithiraj Ramkisun Dullay's collection of short stories and opinion pieces, *Salt Water Runs in my Veins* (2010), for example, focuses not so much on 'Indianness' as on the non-racial ideals of the liberation struggle. This notwithstanding, it would be regrettable after the years of political struggle to turn too decisively from the 'memory work' of the past. As a check on amnesia, Hassim's new novel, *The Revenge of Kali* (2009), remains with the story of indenture – the story that, in South Africa, has defined a people's history.

Notes

1. The *Encyclopaedia Britannica* suggests that 'coolie' derives from the Hindi word *quli* (day-labourer) and is related to the Urdu word *quli* (slave). It came into colonial use in the seventeenth century when it was applied to labourers from south Asia.
2. See Chetty (2002) for excerpts from the work of the following writers: Achmat Dangor; Ashwin Desai; Ahmed Essop; Kesavaloo Goonam; Kessie Govender; Krijay Govender; Ronnie Govender; Aziz Hassim; Farida Karodia; Zuleikha Mayat; Fatima Meer; Indres Naidoo; Jay Naidoo; Muthal Naidoo; Nadine Naidoo; Phyllis Naidoo; Deena Padayachee; Kriben Pillay; Jayapraga Reddy; Agnes Sam; Ansuyah Singh; Kogi Singh; Robin Singh; and Reshma Sookrajh. In the same volume, see also interviews with Shabbir Banoobhai; Ahmed Essop; Kessie Govender; Ronnie Govender; Farida Karodia; Essop Patel; and Jayapraga Reddy.

References

Akabor, Miriam. 2006. *Flat 9*. Durban: umSinsi Press.
Banoobhai, Shabbir. 2004. *Book of Songs*. Johannesburg: Wits University Press.
Benson, Eugene and L.W. Connolly (eds). 1994. *Encyclopaedia of Post-Colonial Literatures in English*. Vol.1. London: Routledge.
Bhana, Surendra and Joy Brain. 1990. *Setting down Roots: Indian Migrants in South Africa 1860–1911*. Johannesburg: Wits University Press.
Breytenbach, Breyten. 1989. *Memory of Snow and of Dust*. Johannesburg: Taurus.
Brown, Duncan. 2006. 'Narrative Memory and Mapping: Ronnie Govender's "At the Edge" and Other Cato Manor Stories'. In: *To Speak of This Land: Identity and Belonging in South Africa and Beyond*. Pietermaritzburg: University of KwaZulu-Natal Press: 127–51.
Brown, Judith and Martin Prozesky (eds). 1996. *Gandhi and South Africa: Principles and Politics*. Pietermaritzburg: University of Natal Press.
Chetty, Rajendra (ed.). 2002. *South African Indian Writings in English*. Durban: Madiba Publishers.
Coovadia, Imraan. 2001. *The Wedding*. New York: Picador.
―――. 2006. *Green-Eyed Thieves*. Cape Town: Umuzi.
―――. 2009. *High Low In-between*. Cape Town: Umuzi.

Desai, Ashwin and Goolam Vahed. 2007. *Inside Indenture: A South African Story, 1860–1914*. Durban: Madiba Publishers.
Dullay, Prithiraj Ramkisun. 2010. *Salt Water Runs in my Veins*. Durban: Madiba Press.
Flockemann, Miki. 2008. 'Memory, Madness and Whiteness in Julia Blackburn's *The Book of Colour* and Rachel Zadok's *Gem Squash Tokoloshe*'. *English Academy Review* 25(2): 4–19.
Frenkel, Ronit. 2010. *Reconsiderations: South African Indian Fiction and the Making of Race in Postcolonial Culture*. Pretoria: Unisa Press.
Gilroy, Paul. 1993. *The Black Atlantic: Modernity and Double Consciousness*. London: Verso.
Goonam, Kesaveloo. 1991. *Coolie Doctor: An Autobiography of Dr Goonam*. Durban: Madiba Publishers.
Govender, Neelan. 2008. *Girmit Tales*. Durban: Rebel Rabble.
Govender, Pregs. 2007. *Love and Courage: A Story of Insubordination*. Johannesburg: Jacana Media.
Govender, Ronnie. 1996. *'At the Edge' and Other Cato Manor Stories*. Pretoria: Manx.
———. 2006. *Song of the Atman*. Johannesburg: Jacana Media.
———. 2008 [1977]. *The Lahnee's Pleasure*. Johannesburg: Jacana Media.
———. 2008. *In the Manure: Memories and Reflections*. Cape Town: David Philip.
Govender, Rubendra. 2008. *Sugar Cane Boy*. Durban: Bambata Publishing.
Govinden, Devarakshanam Betty. 2008a. *Sister Outsiders: Representation and Identity in Selected Writings by South African Women*. Pretoria: Unisa Press.
———. 2008b. *A Time of Memory: Reflections on Recent South African Writings*. Durban: Solo Collective.
Gray, Stephen (ed.). 2008. *Invitation to a Voyage: French Language Poetry of the Indian Ocean African Islands*. Pretoria: Protea Book House.
Hassim, Aziz. 2002. *The Lotus People*. Durban: Madiba Publishers.
———. 2009. *The Revenge of Kali*. Johannesburg: STE Publishers.
Hofmeyr, Isabel. 2003. 'Transnational Circulation: Region, Nation, Identity and the Material Practices of Translation'. *Current Writing* 15(2): 1–16.
———. 2004. *The Portable Bunyan: A Transnational History of* The Pilgrim's Progress. Princeton: Princeton University Press.
———. 2008. 'Indian Ocean Lives and Letters'. *English in Africa* 33(1): 11–28.
Jacobs, J.U. 1994. 'Life Writing (South Africa): Autobiography'. In: *Encyclopaedia of Post-Colonial Literatures in English*. Vol.1, edited by E. Benson and L.W. Connolly. London: Routledge: 878–82.
Kathrada, Ahmed M. 2005. *Memoirs*. Cape Town: Struik.
Lal, Brij V. (ed.). 2006. *The Encyclopedia of the Indian Diaspora*. Singapore: Editions Didier Millet.
Lee, Sumayya. 2007. *The Story of Maha*. Cape Town: Kwela Books.
MacDonald, Andrew. 2008. 'In a Littoral Sense'. *Mail and Guardian*, 28 November – 4 December: 6.
Maharaj, Mac. 2007. *Shades of Difference: Mac Maharaj and the Struggle for South Africa*. Compiled by Padraig O'Malley. New York: Viking.
Mamet, Claudia. 2008. 'Re-constructing Grey Street in Imraan Coovadia's *The Wedding*'. *Alternation* 15(2): 71–90.

Mda, Zakes. 2002. *The Madonna of Excelsior*. Cape Town: Oxford University Press.

Mehta, Brinda. 2004. *Diasporic (Dis)Locations: Indo-Caribbean Women Writers Negotiate the 'Kala Pani'*. Kingston: University of West Indies Press.

Meer, Fatima. 2001. *Prison Diary*. Cape Town: Kwela Books.

Meer, Ismael C. 2002. *A Fortunate Man*. Cape Town: Zebra Press.

Mishra, Vijay. 2006. 'Voices from the Diaspora'. In: *The Encyclopedia of the Indian Diaspora*, edited by B.V. Lal. Singapore: Editions Didier Millet.

———. 2007. *The Literature of the Indian Diaspora: Theorising the Diasporic Imaginary*. Oxford: Routledge.

Moodley, Praba. 2003. *The Heart Knows No Colour*. Cape Town: Kwela Books.

———. 2009. *Follow Your Heart*. Cape Town: Kwela Books.

Naidoo, Geraldine. *Chilli Boy* [unpublished script].

Naidoo, Jay. 1990. *Coolie Location*. London: South African Writers.

Naidoo, Phyllis. 2002. *Footprints in Grey Street*. Durban: Far Ocean Jetty.

Naidoo, Riason. 2008. *Indian Ink: The Indian in Drum Magazine in the 1950s*. Cape Town: Bell-Roberts Publishing.

Naipaul, V.S. 2006. 'Two Worlds'. Nobel Prize Lecture. In: *Nobel Lectures: 20 Years of the Nobel Prize for Literature Lectures*, edited by J. Sutherland. Victoria: Melbourne University Press: 74–89.

Poovalingam, Pat. 2003. *Anand*. Durban: Madiba Publishers.

Rooke, Daphne. 1953. *Ratoons*. London: Gollancz.

Roos, Henriette. 2005. 'Torn between Islam and the Other: South African Novels on Cross-Cultural Relationships'. *Journal of Literary Studies* 21(1/2): 48–67.

Stiebel, Lindy. 2010. 'Last Stop "Little Gujarat": Tracking South African Indian Writers on the Grey Street Writers' Trail'. *Current Writing* 22(1): 1–20.

Sutherland, John (ed.). 2006. *Nobel Lectures: 20 Years of the Nobel Prize for Literature Lectures*. Victoria: Melbourne University Press.

Young, Hershini Bhana. 2006. *Haunting Capital: Memory, Text, and the Black Diasporic Body*. Hanover: Dartmouth College Press.

14

Zulu Literature
New Beginnings

NHLANHLA MATHONSI AND GUGU MAZIBUKO

An enormous change has taken place in Zulu literature in the years after 1994, with added momentum at the turn of the century; it is particularly marked in the period under consideration here (1999–2008). Because the apartheid state severely curtailed African-language publishing, Zulu literature, together with other African-language literatures, was necessarily school-orientated: only books suitable for prescription in schools were likely to find a publisher. Because Africans were disenfranchised, strict state control applied to all political discussion. Any questioning of the apartheid laws that controlled the lives of Africans was firmly discouraged. What we are suggesting is that, although this chapter will focus on Zulu literature, our observations will be found to have general applicability also to the response and practice of contemporary writers among the Xhosa, Ndebele, Sotho, Tswana, Pedi and Venda – in short, to the several African-language literatures of South Africa.[1]

Since the first democratic elections of 1994, authors who write in isiZulu have gradually gained the confidence to address themselves to the adult Zulu community, which has meant that they have felt free to deal with political, socio-economic and cultural issues that were previously taboo. They have started to take as their themes, and to embark on critical discussions of issues which propriety previously forbad, such as sexual matters and institutions of marriage and the position of women and homosexual people. Equally, Zulu society, as it has become increasingly urban, has become less conservative and more willing to discuss and read about matters that would have been thought improper twenty years ago.

We intend here to present some new literary works in isiZulu: books published between 1999 and 2008, during which the change in subject matter that characterises post-apartheid writing has speeded up. The new Constitution, promulgated in 1996, has also had immense influence on Zulu literature, especially in dealing with gender and sexuality and the position of women in general. We intend to consider what is innovative about the books of this period in terms of the changes that have taken place in South Africa and in Zulu society in particular. Our focus therefore will be the subject matter of present-day works in isiZulu, rather than the form, since what we are interested in is the transformation of Zulu texts written for publication into a truly adult literature, after a long period when it was artificially held within the narrow limits appropriate to schoolchildren. Zulu literature, as in the past, retains a strong moral emphasis, but the investigations it undertakes are of modern and, for the most part, urban life.

This is not to say that serious issues in Zulu literature are confined absolutely to books published since 2000: AIDS education, for example, as a literary topic, dates back to 1988 in the short story 'Ilanga Elishonayo' (The setting sun) in N.G. Sibiya's edited collection *Ikusasa Eliqhakazile* (The bright future) (14–18). The story, which pre-dates wide public awareness of AIDS, involves two lovers, one of whom is diagnosed HIV-positive, while they are planning their future together. The impact on the relationship is devastating. In 1993, L.F. Mathenjwa published *Ithemba Lami* (My faith), a novel which posits that there is no cure for AIDS, since even traditional healers have no remedy. In 1994 D.B.Z. Ntuli's short story 'Mhleli' (Editor), which was published in the anthology *Isibhakabhaka* (The sky) (23–4), has the female protagonist confront her rapists with the fact that she is HIV-positive. In 1997, M.O. Mbatha published the drama *Ithemba Lingumanqoba* (Faith conquers everything), in which more facts about AIDS are revealed. The work is set at a time when knowledge and technology in doctors' rooms were not sufficiently advanced to prevent the accidental exchange of blood.

In the first years after 1994 authors working in isiZulu also offered candid assessments of life in the apartheid era and subjects such as miscegenation, mixed marriages and previously forbidden subjects such as slavery and the kidnapping of children into bondage became common (see Mngadi 1996 and Zulu 2000). M.V. Bhengu's *Itshwele Lempangele* (The partridge's chicken) (1998) and *Inkunzi Emanqindi* (A bull with cut-off horns) (1999) are further examples. *Itshwele Lempangele*, for instance, examines intercultural love between a Zulu man and a woman of Indian descent; *Inkunzi Emanqindi* deals with the urbanisation of African people after 1994 when at last they were free to settle in cities, rather than only to work there as temporary residents.

In the late 1990s large publishing companies such as Kagiso, Maskew Miller Longman, Heinemann and Naspers established prestigious literary competitions for works in all the indigenous southern African languages. They were most interested in prose and drama because the market at that point was saturated with poetry. Between 1994 and 1998 eighteen novels won prizes, raising hopes that Zulu literature would enter the new millennium with burgeoning strength and power (see Zulu 1999 and 2000). Whether this bright future in Zulu literature has actually materialised is a question this chapter will try to answer.

The changes in Zulu society in the post-1994 period that have resulted in a potential readership for adult works have involved educational programmes, the extension of tertiary education, the growth of libraries in townships and the establishment of 'centres', often in schools and community halls, comprising lending libraries and Internet-access facilities. Even in prisons, educational programmes have become popular. Book launches have also played a major role in this regard. Zulu newspapers (*Isolezwe*, *Ilanga*, *umAfrika*) have columns where newly published books are analysed and assessed and this exposure plays a major role in promoting books written in isiZulu.

Other initiatives have been undertaken by government departments in promoting readership in African languages. In 2007, for example, the KwaZulu-Natal Department of Arts and Culture launched reading and writing clubs in all the eleven district municipalities of the province to promote Zulu literature. Each reading and writing club is made up of no fewer than twenty members of all ages. Similar activities have also been launched in four Correctional Centres (prisons) to encourage the inmates to read Zulu books. Further, the provincial Department of Arts and Culture co-operates with Library Services, arranging that each year 1 000 copies of recently published Zulu books are bought from publishers by Library Services to be read by the public in municipal libraries. The reading and writing clubs also put pressure on libraries to order books that are not available. These attempts have definitely increased readership beyond the school prescription market and hence have had an effect on the subject matter that is now considered acceptable.

In 2006, for the first time in South Africa, a book fair was held in Cape Town and it has taken place every year since then. Publishers promote books written not only in English and Afrikaans (languages that have long had established readerships), but also in indigenous languages. The Publishers' Association of South Africa (PASA) plays a leading role and most publishers, including those of Zulu works, are members of this association. In the same year the Department of Arts and Culture launched its first literature competition in partnership with Nasou Via Afrika. This has resulted in many young people beginning to write for publication because the competition was aimed at the youth, women and first-time authors.

The year 2006 also saw a challenge to publishers from the government, which planned to set up its own publishing houses that would take the risk of publishing imaginative writings by first-time writers, including those dealing with sensitive issues. In 2007 the Department of Arts and Culture, in partnership with publishers Shuter & Shooter, launched a writing competition in which young people and women were encouraged to write in isiZulu. This stimulated other female and first-time writers into submitting their work: B. Ngcobo, for example, won the competition with her novel *Amandla Esambane* (Power to Isambane).[2] In 2008 the Department of Arts and Culture, in partnership with Maskew Miller Longman, launched another literature writing competition, which included isiXhosa, a language which has become 'official' in KwaZulu-Natal province. Umtapo Publishers started in 2000 and Prince Ndabuko Creative Solutions, which focuses mainly on the promotion of traditional Zulu culture and heritage, has recently begun operations. Usiba Writers Guild, through its annual literature competitions, has encouraged both budding and seasoned writers in the field of literature.

The year 2008 saw the publication of books in isiZulu written in Correctional Services Centres. Two books written by inmates have been published by Nutrend. One of them is a poetry book titled *Ziyokwesulwa Izinyembezi* (Tears will be washed away) (Majola et al. 2008), and the other, *Umuntu Akalahlwa* (Do not give up on a person) (Makhambeni, Mazibuko and Shabalala 2008), is an anthology of short stories.

The growth of education, and still more the growth of employment opportunities, has led to the rapid growth of the Zulu professional class, who are determined that their children shall be proficient in English as the language of government and business, but equally determined that they shall not lose touch either with the language of isiZulu or the culture of the Zulu people. Literary descriptions of life under apartheid, which in the years immediately after 1994 were popular with Zulu authors, have become less common from 1999 onwards. Zulu authors are now increasingly concerned with the topical issues and debates of the present day, namely HIV and AIDS, fidelity to a single partner versus promiscuity, unemployment, violence against women and children, homosexuality, gender redress and other types of social transformation.

A change in subject matter, related to the increase and dissemination of medical knowledge, has taken place in the period between 1999 and 2008. The author N.G. Sibiya, who in these years has dominated isiZulu imaginative writing in novels, drama and poetry, has written extensively about issues that in earlier years would have been unacceptable in print. The work of this later period shows a much higher state of information about the nature of HIV and AIDS and the ways in which it is transmitted. After S. Zimema's publication of a novel, *Amasokisi* (Socks), in 2001, in which the protagonist, Sipho, finds out that he is HIV-positive and eventually hangs himself, Sibiya's novel, *Kuxolelwa Abanjani* (Who deserves to be forgiven) (2002), though it briefly touches on unfaithfulness and forgiveness, deals mainly with a wider range of the problems that have arisen in the HIV and AIDS pandemic. His novel reveals how widespread the disease is and emphasises that being unfaithful in marriage can lead to becoming infected with the disease. Sibiya shows that people can also get the disease from drug abuse. The novel poses the question of whether one partner can or should forgive the other if he or she were infected with the disease during a relationship. Over the years Sibiya has continued to write on the subject of HIV and AIDS, looking at it from different angles. In 2003 he wrote a one-act play, 'Kungcono Ngife' (I better die), published in an anthology of one-act plays, *Amadlelo Aluhlaza* (Green pastures) (31–44), edited by D.B.Z. Ntuli. In this play Sibiya questions the ethics of insurance companies that fail to pay out for the burial of a person who has died from AIDS. When Hlengwa is about to die, he decides to hire someone to shoot him so that the insurance company will have to compensate his family.

Looking at the contemporary myth surrounding virginity and AIDS (that an HIV-positive man who has intercourse with a virgin will be cured) and other issues related to the disease in South Africa, Sibiya published *Kwaze Kwalukhuni* (It's very difficult) (2003), a drama that focuses on the abuse of women and children. A released prisoner who arrives home to discover that his brother is dead forces himself on his brother's wife and unknowingly infects her with the virus. When the ex-prisoner realises that he is HIV-positive, he rapes a virgin who is coming from the Reed Dance in his belief that he will be cured of the disease.

In 2004, M.E. Wanda published *Kunjalo-ke* (That's how things are), a novel about five people who contract HIV because of being unfaithful. This was followed by E.D.M. Sibiya's novel *Ngidedele Ngife* (Allow me to die) (2006), in which the author shows that the trend to see HIV and AIDS as a threat to whole communities continues to be an issue of considerable concern. There is a trenchant political dimension to his treatment of this issue when the protagonist, who has a friend who is HIV-positive, composes a song on how people should behave in the AIDS pandemic:

Ningambheki uMongameli ophethe izwe
Nongqongqoshe wezempilo umkhohlwe
Ngeke akufake ikhondomu
Yizinyembezi zami lezo bakithi

Masiziphathe kahle sizwe sakithi
Nant' ulaka silubona luhlasele
Mabavuke bonke abasalele.
Izinyanga nodokotela sebehlulekile
Sekonakele yebo kaniphuphi
Ningabelokhu ningundaza
Hloman' izikhali nivikel' isizwe.

(Don't look at the State President,
Forget even the Health Minister,
S/he won't put a condom on you.
Those are my tears, fellow brothers and sisters,
Let us behave, fellow brothers and sisters.
Here is the outbreak of a fierce war.
Everybody asleep must wake up,
Traditional healers and doctors have failed.
AIDS's spears are scattering them.
Things are bad; you are not dreaming;
Stop gossiping;
Arm yourself and save the nation) (E.D.M. Sibiya 2006: 17–18, translated by Nhlanhla Mathonsi).

In the same work Sibiya addresses the controversy surrounding xenophobia. The relaxation of the South African borders to the north and the abolition of apartheid prohibitions on the entry of citizens from other countries in Africa have led to the rise of xenophobic intolerance. This has been especially strong among people who have reason to fear competition for jobs and accommodation. Zimbabweans especially have responded to the crisis in their own country by flooding across the South African border. Displaced people from the Democratic Republic of Congo, Rwanda, Uganda and other African states have arrived in the country in large numbers. Xenophobia has therefore become another topic featuring in contemporary Zulu writing. One of Sibiya's characters, John, from Nigeria, is wanted by the police because they are suspicious of the source of his wealth. Evading the police, he and his girlfriend, Khona, a young Zulu woman, head for northern KwaZulu-Natal. Sibiya depicts the stereotyping of foreigners: it is popularly believed that they smell because they do not wash; they are drug-dealers and they get involved in armed robberies. Drug-dealing and possession of unlicensed firearms all incur a heavy punishment, which is why John, who has been selling drugs, is running for his life. Finally, John is arrested and Khona is left alone and pregnant: she has refused to heed the advice of her grandmother and others to avoid involvement with foreigners.

A few women were active in Zulu writing before the period under discussion: Joyce J. Gwayi (1973, 1974 and 1976), A.C.T. Mayekiso (1964), Thembi G. Hodie (1979) and Danisile Ntuli (1996). N.M. Makhambeni (1985, 1989 and 1990), also a woman, wrote and published from the 1960s to the 1990s. Since the beginning of the new millennium the publisher Shuter & Shooter in particular has encouraged women to write novels, short stories and poems. Especially since 2005 women writers, who have emerged, write about issues that affect women. In these writings – and this is a new development – women writers are not afraid to talk about the use of condoms and other sex-related matters. They now seem to aspire to unlimited authority, and therefore appear at times no longer to be 'gendered' – as gender was understood in the past – and certainly they are unwilling to be subjected to men's authority.

In 2005, Gugu Zwane's short story '*Isifundo*' (Lesson) in N.G. Sibiya's anthology, *Wathint' Imbokodo* (You strike a woman) (164–9), openly mentions the use of condoms in a relationship as a protection option. In the same year, Maphili Shange published *Uthando Lungumanqoba* (Love conquers everything), a novel about child sexual abuse. She also encourages the use of condoms by prostitutes for protection against HIV and AIDS. Phindile, who is little more than a child, is sexually abused by her uncle. She leaves her late parents' house (which she has inherited) to escape him and is forced to resort to prostitution. One of her clients, Thulani, marries her and loves her unconditionally. Shange's other literary work, *Ithemba Alibulali* (Faith does not kill) (2007), is also about child abuse: an old, married taxi-owner seduces a girl, abandoning his wife and children. When he has spent all his money the girl decides to have an affair with a boy of her own age. The taxi-owner resolves to kill her.

Much has been written in the past about problems in marriage, but new writers, especially women, approach this subject from new angles. Now that more and more spouses are working overseas – as nurses, for example – the number of unfaithful partners may have increased. At any rate, infidelity is being more widely discussed in Zulu literature. L. Zondi in her novel *Enecala Kayiphumuli* (The guilty is forever restless) (2007) addresses this issue: the unfaithful female partner falls pregnant and decides to give her child to someone else.

The theme of marital abuse is also prominent in female writers' work. For many years men have been writing about the attraction they feel for women; now it is women's turn to express their feelings. Hazel Langa's novel *Ngiyabonga* (Thank you) (2006) depicts a series of events around the idea of love. We are made to understand from a woman's perspective how it feels to be loved. Women in the past would have met with disapproval in Zulu society had they written about such matters and would have been labelled women of loose morals. A sensitive issue in *Ngiyabonga* is emotional abuse. Jabu cannot bear children: she is barren and therefore feels that she has to tolerate her husband Menzi's behaviour towards her, however violent it is. When she discovers that he has had a baby with another woman, she accepts this as the best gift she has ever received from him and is ready to adopt the child. That marital infidelity resulting in a child can be accepted with joy is unusual in Zulu literature. It is not presented as an act of desperation, but as an endorsement of the wife's liberation from her abusive husband.

Politics, once strictly forbidden, has also featured in Zulu fiction since the fall of apartheid. A novel of the immediately post-democratic period is M.J. Mngadi's *Asikho Ndawo Bakithi* (We are nowhere, good people) (1996), which is about the anguish of members of the oppressed Zulu society of the 1980s; Mngadi has also published *Iziboshwa Zothando* (Prisoners of love) (2004), which concerns political and social issues that still surround marriages between white and black people. In the earlier novel an African man encounters problems when he is dating a white woman. Of similar political relevance, R.M. Mngadi's drama, *Ababulali Benyathi* (Killers of buffalo) (2005), focuses on changes in the new era. The play is concerned with the conflict between a democratically elected councillor and an *induna* from the traditional leadership. This conflict has occurred as a result of municipal boundaries being extended into the areas formerly under the jurisdiction of traditional leaders.

Since the early 1990s a thorny issue, especially in KwaZulu-Natal, has been the conflict between two political parties, the Inkatha Freedom Party (IFP) and the African National Congress (ANC). At least until after the elections in 1994 it was difficult and perhaps dangerous to write about this subject. Probably the first author to do so was Condy Nxaba, whose novel *Siyogcinaphi Uma Kunje?* (Where will we end up if the situation is so volatile?) (1997) discussed from a neutral position the painful political divisions in the late 1980s in the Zulu community. The ways in which the conflict was damaging the community are rendered through the voice of an old woman, who seems to suggest that black people are entirely responsible for the tragedies afflicting the community. She suggests that there is something innate in black people that causes them to destroy each other and themselves. Only once is there any mention of any external 'third force' (that is, violence orchestrated by the apartheid state) which is inflaming the conflict. And neither the IFP nor the ANC is mentioned. In 2007, however, in a different political climate, when the worst tensions had died down, Nxaba published another novel, *Umdonsiswano*

(Conflict), in which hatred and political clashes between the IFP and the ANC are described within a single family, the members of which fight over their political affiliations. The third force, which had sided with the IFP, is no longer a presence.

Unemployment, which at least since the beginning of the twentieth century has always been a problem for urban Zulu people, has become another legitimate subject for fiction. Nelisile T. Msimang's novel *Umsebenzi Uyindlala* (Employment is scarce) (2005) deals with an educated woman who cannot find a job and ends up vulnerable to sexual predators. She is offered a job by a man in exchange for sexual favours. In S. Nhleko's drama *Kusa Kusa* (The future cannot be predicted) (2008) a man who cannot find work as a result of high rates of unemployment finds himself without a girlfriend because of his being without work. Women, the man believes (and the author seems to agree), choose to associate with the employed who own motor vehicles, rather than with the unemployed who tramp the pavements on foot.

Another issue, previously taboo, is that of homosexuality. N.G. Sibiya demolishes the idea – prevalent at least in traditional African culture – that homosexual behaviour does not exist amongst Africans or, in this case, amongst Zulu people. In 1988, Sibiya published a short story 'Amathe Ezimpukane' (Drizzle) in his anthology *Ikusasa Eliqhakazile* (51–4) in which a wife discovers that her husband is unfaithful to her: when she follows him to what she imagines is his girlfriend's place, she discovers to her horror that he is in love with another man. In 2006, Sibiya published *Bengithi Lizokuna* (I thought it would rain), a novel that deals with a gay man who chooses to undergo a sex-change operation. After the operation the protagonist, Mhlengi, is known as Mahlengi.

In 2007, N.G. Sibiya and N.S. Ntuli collaborated on a short-story anthology, *Izikhukhula* (Floods). Included in this anthology are two short stories addressing the theme of homosexuality. Sibiya's 'Ngeke' (Never) (9–17) tells of a chief in the process of choosing his heir. He discovers that his eldest son, Falakhe, is about to marry an Indian woman and therefore decides to leave the chieftainship to his second son, Sabelo. He is happy to know that his second son is about to get married, but to his great surprise this son is preparing to marry another man. This story was published during the time when same-sex marriages were being legalised. In the other story 'Oqotsheni' (Caught red-handed) (29–35) Sibiya addresses homosexuality from the female perspective. Mandla is unhappily married to Thabile and thinks that she is unfaithful. Finally he catches his wife making love to his sister and kills both of them.

* * *

We do not feel that the poetry of the last decade has measured up to the standard of the new novels and stories. Neither has it reached the standard of poetry in the 1980s and 1990s. Earlier, from the 1930s until the end of the 1980s, Zulu literature had a number of excellent poets; for example, B.W. Vilakazi, J.C. Dlamini, D.B.Z. Ntuli, C.T. Msimang, R.M. (Mazisi) Kunene, O.E.H.M. Nxumalo, E.S.Q. Zulu, N.F. Mbhele and B.K. Mhlongo (see note 1). Their poetry was characterised by memorable diction coupled, in most cases, with meaningful structure. The reader needed to be conversant with the idioms of isiZulu in order to grasp the implications of the words. In the current period there has been a fall-off in the general quality of poetry, though there are, of course, notable exceptions. There is a tendency for poets to write as if they are writing prose. Though we have been disappointed by the low standard of poetry in general, we feel that some poems deserve mention because of their quality or because they deal with topical subjects.

The first of two poems that deserve attention, J.J. Thwala's *'Inkunzi Emnyama'* (The black bull), appears in the anthology *Uphondo Lwemikhosi* (The horns of the festive seasons) (2006: 12), compiled by two accomplished poets, J.J. Thwala and E.J. Mhlanga. The speaker celebrates the fact that South African black people are at last free, empowered and can forget the past. People must be encouraged to look ahead, be reconciled with each other and live in unity. They were 'knee-haltered' (in the idiom of a cattle-keeping people) in the past, but today they wield political power. The politics of the struggle have given way to those of peace:

Kade uthekelezwe ngezisingakazi
Okwendekane ethombeni ulindile,
Liguqubele libalele ulindile,
Kumnyama kukhanya ulindile,
Usapho lwakho lweqisw' izisele
Neziselekazi; ludundubalisw'amadundu,
Namadwalakazi, luklabisw' ezingwadule
Ubusika nehlobo nanini.
Nkunz' emnyama emhlophe ngezinhliziyo,
Namuhla ukhony' esibayeni sakho,
Okwayizolo nokwakuthangi ukufulathele,
Ukhuthaz' okwanamuhla nokwakusasa.
Khonya nkunz' emnyama kwesakho
Kugqam' ukubuyisana nobunye beqiniso.

(You have been tied by big ropes
Like a calf at the back of the hut waiting,
Cloudy, hot but still waiting,
Dark, light still waiting,
Your offspring made to cross valleys
And big valleys made to climb hills,
And big rocks, made to walk desert stretches
Winter and summer or anytime.
Black bull with a white heart,
Today you rule in your own kraal,
You turned your back against yesterday's and the day before yesterday's issues,
Inspiring about today and tomorrow's matters.
Black bull, rule in your own kraal;
Let reconciliation and real unity prevail) (translated by Nhlanhla Mathonsi and Gugu Mazibuko).[3]

B. kaMgiba's 'Qhawe Lamaqhawe' (Hero among heroes), another example of an impressive poem, describes Mandela's unequalled love for his country (KaMgiba and Ntuli 2006: 17). The power of love reconciles the nation:

Ulishumayelile ivangeli loxolo,
Ulifumbathise abakwelamayo
Mabalincele ngothando.
Unwele olude ROLIHLAHLA!

(You have preached the gospel of peace,
You gave it to your siblings,
They must suck it with love.
Long live ROLIHLAHLA!)

N.T.B. Shandu's poem 'Ihabulankezo' (An alcoholic) – in the anthology *Umcakulo* (A ladle), edited by L.F. Mathenjwa (2004: 28) – concerns the excessive use of alcohol, which often results in domestic violence. The poet asks what will motivate a man to stop drinking liquor. Every day he assaults his wife; what does he think his children say about him?

Sidakwa esehlula amathumbu ethendele,
Mshuphuli wezinkukhu zomakhelwane zokuhashuka

Akusenamehluko ubusuku nemini kuyafana,
Ungena kwamama kusa lize liyozilahla kunina
Liphinde liphume libabale liyozilahla
Uyaphoxa, uyaxova uyiphixiphixi.

(Drunkard, defeating partridge's intestines,
Killer of neighbours' chickens because of craving,
Day and night are similar to you,
You enter the tavern from morning till sunset;
When sun again rises and sets you are still there;
You are embarrassing and cause confusion.)

The first line, '*Sidakwa esehlula amathumbu ethendele*' (Drunkard, defeating partridge's intestines), alludes to an old way of making a drunkard stop drinking liquor. The intestines of the bird would be emptied into the person's drink, causing vomiting and the end of the drinking session. This single line illustrates the more traditional reliance in Zulu poetry – indeed, more generally, in African-language poetry – on the metaphorical mode.

As we have suggested, however, the problem of present-day poetry is the failure of many would-be poets to understand the difference between prose narratives and poems. An example of such poetry – despite its linguistic shortcomings it remains thematically interesting, as it deals with a subject new in Zulu literature – is B. kaMgiba's poem on divorce, '*Bengimthanda Ngimethemba*' (I loved and trusted him). Divorce is a common occurrence these days in African communities; the strong marital bond that characterised these communities is a thing of the past. The speaker expresses resentment and sorrow about being divorced by a man whom she loved dearly. She feels the warmth with which he embraced her. Whilst she still had gleams of hope for the future, there was a sudden mysterious change of heart: she was dumped. She is, to this day, still bitter: '*Angihleki ngiyalinganisa*' (I am not laughing, I am pretending) (KaMgiba and Ntuli 2006: 16). This poem as a whole does not succeed: only the page layout and the fact that it appears in an anthology of poetry, *Phezu Komkhono!* (Work has started), supports its claim to be poetry.

Two further poems of merit are Lungile Bengani's '*Ngingowesimame*' (I am a female) and '*Ngivumele Ngiphathe*' (Allow me to be in charge) from her collection *Kwenzekeni Bazali Bami?* (What has happened, my parents?) (2008: 16–17, 22). These poems concern women who compete for men's favours with other women, thus failing to recognise or value their sisterly bond. The plea is for mutual respect among women, while in '*Ngivumele Ngiphathe*' the poet claims that women are unwilling to respect, or even acknowledge, women bosses: women should open their eyes and unite against men instead of being one another's enemies.

Not especially good as poetry, but topical in subject matter are B. Gaza's 'Ungangibandlululi' (Do not discriminate) and B.S.F. Xaba's 'Ngculazi' (AIDS), both of which appear in the anthology *Izingwazi Zanamuhla* (Today's heroes) (2006: 61, 83), edited by S.E. Ngubane. Gaza's poem pursues the subject of xenophobia which, as explained earlier, has become a common phenomenon of the present day; the people of South Africa seem to have forgotten that African states from which refugees have fled harboured South African freedom fighters in the years of struggle.

Ngempela mfowethu uyangichitha,
Nguwe ongivulela amasango?

(Do you indeed cast me away my brother,
Is it you who opens the gates for me?)

In 'Ngculazi' an AIDS sufferer speaks of her infection, while in another impressive poem, F.F. Mbatha's 'Umajuqa' (Killer) – in Thwala and Mhlanga's anthology *Uphondo Lwemikhosi* (2006: 22) – the pandemic is said to stab and kill indiscriminately and repeatedly. Despite its venom, people who are safe are those who heed advice; the promiscuous do not survive. The poem is constructed as an address to the whole nation:

Kusinda abalalela iziyalo,
Umajuqa ujuqa ondlebe kazizwa.
Umajuqa ujuqa abagcogcomi, Ukukhala akusizi,
Zivikele kuyabanda phandle!

(The survivors are those who heed the advice,
AIDS kills those who do not listen.
AIDS kills those who are promiscuous, crying does not help,
Protect yourself; it is cold outside.)

* * *

The society for which the novels and poems discussed above are intended is far from the society envisaged by the apartheid regime: one of subsistence farmers, rooted in the rural areas of this country, from which a minority would emerge only temporarily to occupy the role of labourers in the urban industrial enterprises, all of which were designated as 'white'. In terms of this ideology, Zulu society, including its social and familial institutions and its language, had to be fixed in the past. IsiZulu itself, as it was taught in schools, took as its model the language as it is spoken in rural areas. In the past, editors insisted on 'standard' language and refused to allow people to express themselves in a way that would be understood by their peers: the spoken language of the urban areas diverged increasingly from that of written texts. Nowadays, new books in isiZulu have urban settings in many cases and must therefore take account of the linguistic changes taking place in urban society. New technical terminology is forcing its way into books, as are instances of multilingual borrowings, code switching and code mixing (as opposed to the monolingual borrowings of the early twentieth century). Urban women and younger people can write and have their work accepted for publication in this new isiZulu without being accused of corrupting the language.

It will be clear to readers of this chapter that the subject matter that preoccupies Zulu writers of the present day – AIDS, urban challenges including marital infidelity and homosexuality, for example – necessitates an adaptable language and that new words for new problems, decisions and situations are likely to enrich isiZulu.

Notes

1. Surveys of earlier African-language literatures pertinent to South Africa are to be found in A.S. Gérard's *Four African Literatures: Xhosa, Sotho, Zulu, Amharic* and, more recently, in D.B.Z. Ntuli and C.F. Swanepoel's *Southern African Literature in African Languages: A Concise Historical Perspective.*

    Two key texts, originally written in isiZulu, have recently appeared in English translation. Sibusiso Nyembezi's novel *Inkinsela Yase Mgungundlovu* (1961) has been translated by Sandile Ngidi as *The Rich Man of Pietermaritzburg*. (Nyembezi's novel was adjudged to be one of 'Africa's 100 Best Books of the 20th Century' in the *Mail & Guardian*'s 2002 project that honoured Chinua Achebe's *Things Fall Apart*.) John Langalibalele's *Jeqe, Insila ka Tshaka*, the first novel to be written in isiZulu, was translated in 1951 by J. Boxwell as *Jeqe, the Body-Servant of King Shaka*, and has been republished in 2008 in the Penguin (South Africa) Modern Classics Series.

    The Indigenous Languages Publishing Project, initiated by the Department of Arts and Culture, is an ambitious programme of returning to print significant literary works in South Africa's nine 'official' indigenous African languages. As of the end of 2009, 27 works encompassing novels, plays and non-fiction had been published. For information on the Reprint of South African Classics Project, run by the National Library, contact info@nlsa.ac.za.

2. When translated from isiZulu into English, 'Esambane' becomes 'Isambane'.
3. Unless otherwise indicated, all translations in this chapter are the work of the authors, Nhlanhla Mathonsi and Gugu Mazibuko.

References

Bengani, Lungile. 2008. *Kwenzekeni Bazuli Bami?* Pietermaritzburg: Kgaka Investments.
Bhengu, M.V. 1998. *Itshwele Lempangele*. Johannesburg: Heinemann.
———. 1999. *Inkunzi Emanqindi*. Johannesburg: Heinemann.
Gérard, A.S. 1971. *Four African Literatures: Xhosa, Sotho, Zulu, Amharic*. Berkeley: University of California Press.
Gwayi, Joyce J. 1973. *Bafa Baphela*. Pretoria: Van Schaik.
———. 1974. *Shumpu*. Pretoria: Van Schaik.
———. 1976. *Yekanini*. Pretoria: Van Schaik.
Hodie, Thembi G. 1979. *Zibanjwa Zisemaphuphu*. Pietermaritzburg: Shuter & Shooter.
KaMgiba, B. and D. Ntuli (eds). 2006. *Phezu Komkhono!* Pretoria: Eulitz.
Langa, Hazel. 2006. *Ngiyabonga*. Pretoria: Eulitz.
Langalibalele, John. 2008 [1951]. *Jeqe, the Body-Servant of King Shaka*. Translated by J. Boxwell from isiZulu (*Jeqe, Insila ka Tshaka*). Cape Town: Penguin.
Majola, N., H. Nqcongo and D. Ntuli (eds). 2008. *Ziyokwesulwa Izinyembezi*. Pietermaritzburg: Nutrend.
Makhambeni, N.M. 1985. *Amathunzi Ayewukela*. Pretoria: De Jager-Haum.
———. 1989. *Ihluzo1 & 3*. Pretoria: De Jager-Haum.
———. 1990. *Amaseko*. Pietermaritzburg: Centaur.
Makhambeni, Ncamisile, Gugu Mazibuko and Thokozani Shabalala (eds). 2008. *Umuntu Akalahlwa*. Pietermaritzburg: Nutrend Publishers.
Mathenjwa L.F. 1993. *Ithemba Lami*. Pretoria: Actua Press.
Mathenjwa L.F. (ed.). 2004. *Umcakulo*. Cape Town: KZN Books.
Mayekiso, A.C.T. 1964. *Imidlalo Enkundlanye*. Johannesburg: Vivlia.
Mbatha, M.O. 1997. *Ithemba Lingumanqoba*. Pretoria: Actua Press.
Mngadi, M.J. 1996. *Asikho Ndawo Bakithi*. Pietermaritzburg: Shuter & Shooter.
———. 2004. *Iziboshwa Zothando*. Johannesburg: Heinemann.
Mngadi, R.M. 2005. *Ababulali Benyathi*. Pietermaritzburg: Nutrend.
Msimang, Nelisile T. 2005. *Umsebenzi Uyindlala*. Pretoria: Actua Press.
Ngcobo, B. 2007. *Amandla Esambane*. Cape Town: Nasou Via Afrika.
Ngubane, S.E. (ed.). 2006. *Izingwazi Zanamuhla*. Cape Town: Nasou Via Afrika.
Nhleko, S. 2008. *Kusa Kusa*. Pietermaritzburg: Shuter & Shooter.
Ntuli, D.B.Z. 1994. *Isibhakabhaka*. Pretoria: Actua Press.
Ntuli, D.B.Z. (ed.). 2003. *Amadlelo Aluhlaza*. Pietermaritzburg: Ikhwezi Publications.
Ntuli, D.B.Z. and C.F. Swanepoel. 1993. *Southern African Literature in African Languages: A Concise Historical Perspective*. Pretoria: Acacia Books.
Ntuli, Danisile. 1996. *Induku Ebandla*. Cape Town: Nasou Via Afrika.

Nxaba, Condy. 1997. *Siyogcinaphi Uma Kunje?* Pretoria: Eulitz.

———. 2007. *Umdonsiswano*. Pretoria: Actua Press.

Nyembezi, Sibusiso. 2008. *The Rich Man of Pietermaritzburg*. Translated by S. Ngidi from isiZulu (*Inkinsela Yase Mgungundlovu*). Laverstock: Aflame Books.

Shange, M. 2005. *Uthando Lungumanqoba*. Pietermaritzburg: Shuter & Shooter.

———. 2007. *Ithemba Alibulali*. Cape Town: Nasou Via Afrika.

Sibiya, E.D.M. 2006. *Ngidedele Ngife*. Cape Town: Tafelberg.

Sibiya, N.G. 2002. *Kuxolelwa Abanjani*. Pietermaritzburg: Shuter & Shooter.

———. 2003. *Kwaze Kwalukhuni*. Johannesburg: Vivlia.

———. 2006. *Bengithi Lizokuna*. Pietermaritzburg: Nutrend.

Sibiya, N.G. (ed.). 1988. *Ikusasa Eliqhakazile*. Mabopane: L.Z.S. Publishers.

———. (ed.). 2005. *Wathint' Imbokodo*. Pietermaritzburg: Shuter & Shooter.

Sibiya, N.G. and N.S. Ntuli (eds). 2007. *Izikhukhula*. Pietermaritzburg: Nutrend.

Thwala, J.J and E.J. Mhlanga (eds). 2006. *Uphondo Lwemikhosi*. Pretoria: Eulitz.

Wanda, M.E. 2004. *Kunjalo-ke*. Pietermaritzburg: Shuter & Shooter.

Zondi, L. 2007. *Enecala Kayiphumuli*. Cape Town: Nasou Via Afrika.

Zimema, S.C. 2001. *Amasokisi*. Pietermaritzburg: Shuter & Shooter.

Zulu, N.S. 1999. 'African Literature in the Next Millennium'. *South African Journal of African Languages* 19(4): 290–301.

———. 2000. 'Racial Relations and Intercultural Love in *Itshwele Lempangele*'. *South African Journal of African Languages* 20(3): 277–83.

15

Representing the African Diaspora
Coetzee, Breytenbach, Gordimer, Mda, Pinnock

J.U. JACOBS

Migrant identities in recent South African fiction

At a deep narrative level, J.M. Coetzee's *Disgrace* (1999) engages with the theme of migration that has also been taken up by a number of other South African writers during the past decade to the extent that it has come to signal an important direction in South African fiction. The narrative of Coetzee's novel, which is set in urban Cape Town and rural Salem in the Eastern Cape, may be seen in many ways to rehearse and also to reverse in contemporary contexts the exploitative and violent historical encounters in South Africa between immigrant colonising cultures and migratory indigenous cultures on the Western and Eastern Cape frontiers. This history of migration behind the contemporary cultural collisions in the novel is underscored, for example, by David Lurie's own professional and domestic dislocation from his home and from his academic position in Cape Town and his relocation to temporary abodes, first with his daughter Lucy on her farm outside Salem and afterwards at the animal shelter in Grahamstown where he ends up working. Emigration is also further emphasised by Lurie's advice to Lucy after her rape to leave South Africa for Holland, the home of her Dutch mother. Coetzee – himself a semi-expatriate based in both Cape Town and Chicago at the time of writing the novel – suggests in *Disgrace* that migration, whether enforced or voluntary, has informed cultural identities in South Africa from the beginning.

Coetzee became part of the present-day South African diaspora when he emigrated to Australia in the period between the publication of *Disgrace* in 1999 and *Elizabeth Costello* in 2003. In *Slow Man* (2005), his first fully Australian novel, which is set in Adelaide where he now lives, Coetzee foregrounds the theme of migration more explicitly than in his previous novels. His protagonist, a retired portrait photographer, Paul Rayment, was brought from France to Australia at the age of six by his immigrant French mother and Dutch stepfather. He eventually settles in Australia, after a brief return to France as a young man. '"I am not unfamiliar with the immigrant experience"' (Coetzee 2005: 192), Rayment declares to his novelist visitant, Elizabeth Costello. He has had the experience of being uprooted from his country of birth, of having tried to recover a native French cultural identity and of being forever uncertain about any notion of having a 'true home' (192) and having to settle instead for 'a domicile, a residence' (197) in his adoptive country. Or, as he formulates his sense of cultural dislocation: '"I am not the *we* of anyone"' (193). Although he can pass among Australians in a way that is no longer possible for him among the French, Rayment defines his essential cultural detachment to Costello in terms of his lack of full ownership of the English language:

> 'As for language, English has never been mine in the way it is yours. Nothing to do with fluency. I am perfectly fluent, as you can hear. But English came to me too late. It did not come with my mother's milk. In fact it did not come at all. Privately, I have always felt myself to be a kind of ventriloquist's dummy. It is not I who speak the language, it is the language that is spoken through me. It does not come from my core, *mon coeur.*' He hesitates, checks himself. *I am hollow at the core*, he was about to say – *as I am sure you can hear* (197-8).

It is from the background of his own – although much more accomplished – English-language (in)competence that Rayment describes the English spoken by his nurse, Marijana Jokić, a recent immigrant from Croatia: '[S]he speaks a rapid, approximate Australian English with Slavic liquids and an uncertain command of *a* and *the*, coloured by slang she must pick up from her children, who must pick it up from their classmates' (27). As the child of immigrants, Rayment also understands the double cultural allegiance of the immigrant Jokić family: to the old country whose memories they have brought with them in the form of photographs of 'baptisms, confirmations, weddings, family get-togethers' (64), as well as to the new country with whose cultural icons they strive to identify themselves. Marijana comes to see that in Rayment's collection of old 'photographs and postcards of life in the early mining camps of Victoria and New South Wales' (48) there is a historical record that corrects her European perception that Australia with its colonial settler and immigrant population is a country with 'zero history' (49) and she comes to grasp that her own story forms part of that national history. As

Rayment puts it to her: '"Don't immigrants have a history of their own? Do you cease to have a history when you move from one point on the globe to another?"' (49). At a later stage in the narrative it is given to the metafictional Elizabeth Costello to offer her own version of the migrant identity when she explains to Rayment: '"[T]here are those whom I call the chthonic, the ones who stand with their feet planted in their native earth; and then there are the butterflies, creatures of light and air, temporary residents, alighting here, alighting there"' (198). At least on one narrative level, the traumatic amputation of Rayment's right leg after his cycling accident may also be seen to symbolise the severance of a chthonic identity as a result of migration: 'But in his case the cut seemed to have marked off past from future with such uncommon cleanness that it gives new meaning to the word *new*. By the sign of this cut let a new life commence' (26).

Most recently in *Summertime* (2009), the third volume of his fictionalised autobiography (or autobiographical fiction), Coetzee offers another variation on Elizabeth Costello's distinction between chthonically rooted and uprooted, transient beings. The informant Martin J. describes himself and his friend and former University of Cape Town colleague, John Coetzee, as sharing a colonial migrant identity in South Africa:

> Whatever the opposite is of *native* or *rooted*, that was what we felt ourselves to be. We thought of ourselves as sojourners, temporary residents, and to that extent without a home, without a homeland. I don't think I am misrepresenting John. It was something he and I talked about a great deal. I am certainly not misrepresenting myself (2009: 210).

In *Summertime*, Coetzee sets up an elaborate, fictional diasporic dialogue. In order to write a book about the crucial South African years from 1971/1972 to 1977 in the life of the émigré, Nobel Prize-winning South African novelist J.M. Coetzee, who has since died in his adopted country Australia, the biographer-narrator, Vincent, juxtaposes extracts from Coetzee's notebooks with transcripts of his interviews with four women and a man who featured significantly in the writer's life during this period. The novel opens with Coetzee's account in his notebooks, on the one hand, of his conflicted filial relationship with Afrikanerdom after his return to South Africa from the United States in 1972 and, on the other hand, his affiliation with English and his English teaching credentials being questioned. The subject at the centre of Vincent's scholarly investigations, John Coetzee/J.M. Coetzee, is variously described in migrant terms – as Martin J. sums up the fictional author's career: 'John left South Africa in the 1960s, came back in the 1970s, for decades hovered between South Africa and the United States, then finally decamped to Australia and died there' (209). To the embarrassment of his Afrikaner family, John and his younger brother 'had become just two among thousands of young white men who had run away [from South Africa] to escape military service' (131) and after his expulsion from the United States some years later he was viewed by his family as a '[f]ailed runaway' (120). Martin J. himself emigrated from South Africa in the 1970s to England, where he is interviewed by the narrator in Sheffield in 2007.

Like Martin J., the four women who were significant presences in John Coetzee's life in the 1970s and who are invited three decades later to share their thoughts about him are themselves all presented in terms of uprootedness. The psychologist Dr Julia Frankl (formerly Smith, born Kiš), with whom he had an affair in Cape Town, is the South African-born daughter of a Hungarian Jewish refugee from the Nazis and is interviewed in Canada, in Kingston, Ontario, where she settled after her eventual divorce from her South African husband. The Brazilian dance instructor, Adriana Nascimento, who rejected John Coetzee's overtures to her while he was coaching her daughter in English, had come to South Africa from Angola together with her husband and two daughters after the emergency of 1973, only to find that as Brazilians they could not enjoy the organisational support provided for the 'many Portuguese who came to South Africa in those days, from Moçambique and Angola and even Madeira' (177). *Senhora* Nascimento is interviewed in her native São Paulo to which she returned after the death of her husband in South Africa. Sophie Denoël, the young, married French lecturer with whom John Coetzee shared a course at the University of Cape Town and with whom he had a relationship, had come to Cape Town via Madagascar, together with her husband, as part of the French postcolonial drive to promote *Francophonie* throughout the world. She is interviewed in Paris where she currently lives. And finally, John Coetzee's favourite Afrikaner cousin, Margot Jonker, who is interviewed in Somerset West, South Africa, is similarly presented as being uprooted – in this case, she and her farmer husband were obliged through economic circumstances to work away from their farm in the Roggeveld.

The complex persona of John Coetzee/J.M. Coetzee that emerges from this diasporic narrative design as well as from his notebooks may be understood at least in part in terms of the dislocations, detachments and attachments of the migrant subject. According to Martin J., he and John Coetzee shared 'a certain provisionality' (211) in their feelings toward South Africa, based on a 'reluctance to invest too deeply in the country, since sooner or later [their] ties to it would have to be cut, [their] investment in it annulled' (211). Julia Frankl describes John Coetzee's failure to connect or at best to connect 'only briefly, intermittently' (82), as verging on autism. For Adriana Nascimento, he was 'disembodied [. . .] divorced from his body' (198) in a puppet-like way. Sophie Denoël remembers him as 'not an at-ease person [. . .] never relaxed [. . .] not at ease among people who were at ease' (231), personally or culturally, but 'happiest in the role of outsider' (239). And to his cousin Margot he remained 'the failed emigrant, the poet of melancholy' (141), whose complex relationship with his native Afrikaner culture remained unresolved.

Few major South African writers have elaborated as fully on the nature of what Coetzee's Elizabeth Costello calls migrant 'butterflies' as Breyten Breytenbach has throughout his writing career. His most recent prose work, *A Veil of Footsteps: Memoir of a Nomadic Fictional Character* (2008), provides yet a further chapter of the Breytenbach macrotext. A demanding work, sometimes irritatingly so (and for this Breytenbach asks the reader's indulgence), *A Veil of Footsteps* needs to be read in relation to Breytenbach's earlier works, especially from the late 1980s onwards, such as *Memory of Snow and of Dust, Return to Paradise, Dog Heart* and *Woordwerk*, whose themes and techniques it continues and still further develops and refines (see Jacobs 2004). In its combination of autobiography and fiction, travel narrative and metafiction, poetry and philosophical reflection, it offers a complex and profound disquisition on death, art and the migrant condition.

In *A Veil of Footsteps*, Breytenbach maps the metaphysical dimensions of his exilic state, of his being an inhabitant of the Middle World, as he explains it, 'where the dialectic between *space* and *movement* can be enacted' (2008: 221). A self-described nomad and wanderer, 'a bird blown from one region to the next' (101), he traces his own nomadism back to the residual Khoi blood in his Afrikaner veins, the ethnic and cultural legacy of his South African 'heartland' (139) to which he always returns. Compulsive journeying, points of arrival and departure, nodes of temporary locatedness, belonging everywhere and nowhere, home and homelessness – these and many other themes contribute to the richness of this text about a text in the making and of a life lived and a verbal art practised in increasing awareness of the spectre of death. The narrator and his various personae – here mainly the ironically named Breyten Wordfool – are presented with unflinching honesty and self-knowledge in a narrative world in which biography, history and dream fantasy are consciously merged and paraded before the reader in a 'migration of images' (10).

The fictional memoir offers remarkable, if ambivalent, descriptions of the cities that have featured in Breytenbach's nomadic life: the Mother City, Cape Town, which is both affectionately and critically evoked; Paris, his adoptive home that he has come to know too well not to be disgusted by many of its inhabitants; New York in the immediate aftermath of the destruction of 9/11; the former slave island of Goreé where he spends much of his time; and the Catalan village where he has also established a home. All are homes where he also feels unhomed, together with the other émigrés, refugees, illegal and legal immigrants, nomads and economic migrants of all kinds in this narrative that leads rhizomically from one topic and chapter to another in a fictional nomadism that Breytenbach has made distinctively his own.

All of these migrant figures are contained, however, within the larger framework of Breyenbach's admission of 'how passionately, desperately passionately, frustratingly passionately [he] fights over the same theoretical and experiential and remembered and dreamed African being-scape' (217) and of how regularly he returns specifically to the African diaspora, especially in its contemporary manifestations. African migrants populate this text of memories: in Paris, the many black people on the streets of the thirteenth *arrondissement*, the Cameroonian owner of a favourite restaurant in Montparnasse and the illegal North African immigrants who share a train compartment with Breytenbach; in Barcelona, Spain, the 'black Africans without identity papers or permits hanging out on the Plaça Catalunya with bundles and plastic bags containing all their worldly possessions' (86); the Nigerian and Ghanaian prostitutes on the roads on which Moroccan immigrant families are heading home for the holidays, and in the south the increasing number of illegal immigrants captured as they land on Spanish beaches or whose dead bodies are washed up there. Diasporic dispersals, too, are what characterise contemporary South Africa in Breytenbach's narrative: in Cape Town, he observes 'how much the Coloured population of Mother City carry in them the fused memories of slavery, of displacement, of exile' (133); the inhabitants of the tin and cardboard shack settlements on the Cape Flats are 'mostly migrants from the devastated Eastern Cape' (134); and parts of the central city have been taken over by Nigerians, Congolese and Zaireans. And immigration into South Africa is matched by emigration from the young democracy, as Breytenbach details:

> Twenty-seven percent of people with university education have already left. Thousands of doctors now work abroad. There are Diaspora colonies in New Zealand and Australia and Canada and Britain and in the States. They meet for church services and sing and cry their hearts out. Displaced families work all over Africa. I don't know of a single Afrikaner family who hasn't at least one member living outside the country. The Indians and the Coloureds are following ... (240).

The historical African diaspora and its continuation into the present-day dispersal of Africans into diasporic communities around the world, including South Africa, have also been taken up in a number of recent South African novels. In *The Pickup* (2001) Nadine Gordimer foregrounds geographic and cultural dislocation and relocation as her theme: on the one hand, the present relocation of white South Africans, themselves the descendants of immigrant European settlers, to the United States and Australia and, on the other hand, the flocking of illegal immigrants from other African countries into cities such as Johannesburg (see Jacobs 2006: 124–9). Gordimer's narrative engages with the plight of illegal aliens – from Congo, Senegal, Côte d'Ivoire, Nigeria, Zimbabwe and Mozambique – who form a major but undocumented substratum of South African society, living under constant threat of deportation and forced into visibility by periodic outbreaks of xenophobic violence against them.

Gordimer employs her usual social typification in presenting the figure of the mechanic, Abdu, who belongs to this international underclass of illegal immigrants who have overstayed their visitors' permits and are eventually ferreted out by the Department of Home Affairs. His personal history is a representative one: he comes from a generic Islamic African country that is a construct of colonialism and characterised by government corruption, religious oppression and conflict across its borders. Abdu's home country is presented as a paradigmatic Third World nation: a place of poverty, dismal health standards, patriarchal subjugation of women and political gangsterism. It is the African home to which he has been repatriated from other countries he entered illegally and where, after his return, he spends most of his time haunting the visa sections of various consulates in his attempts officially to immigrate – to Canada, New Zealand, Australia – only to be rejected time and time again.

Gordimer's treatment of the themes of home and of being 'unhomed', which feature in all of her earlier novels, is given a new twist in *The Pickup* when her South African protagonist, Julie Summers, herself of British immigrant descent, marries Abdu, voluntarily leaves South Africa and returns to his native country with him. His home village on the edge of the desert becomes another one of the heterotopias in Gordimer's fictional landscape: a place where contradictory discourses co-exist. Abdu, determined to get away from the wretched village, persists in his applications until he finally obtains a precious permit to enter the United States. Julie, however, is welcomed and becomes integrated into her husband's family home, which provides her with a nexus of family ties that she has not known in South Africa. She has come home in a way that her husband cannot grasp and at the end of the narrative when he leaves to establish a new home in the

United States, she refuses to join him. The trajectories of their respective migrations into and out of Africa are diametrically opposed, probably irreconcilable.

Zakes Mda's novel *Cion* (2007) engages with the African diaspora from the perspective of African-American culture in two different narrative chronotopes. The town of Kilvert in Athens, Ohio, is the setting for a historical narrative that deals with slavery in the United States in the nineteenth century and a contemporary narrative that provides a thinly fictionalised reflection on African-American and Native American as well as South African culture and politics of identity. The African, African-American and South African cultural worlds are mediated through the reappearance in *Cion* of the (meta)fictional Toloki, Mda's professional mourner from his first novel, *Ways of Dying*. Toloki presents himself as a migrant persona: he was 'conjured . . . into existence a decade or so before' (Mda 2007: 2) by Mda in Durham, England and, after his birth as a fictional being in South Africa, was transported back to Durham, only to be 'abandoned' there until his author later brings him along from Durham to Athens, Ohio, where he finds himself in another fictional narrative.

Mda's novel chronicles the diasporic history of Africans in the United States through the stories of the ancestral slave woman, the Abyssinian Queen, and her two sons, the half-brothers Abednego and Nicodemus, and the parallel story of the slave-dealing Irishman Niall Quigley, who is himself tricked into slavery. As a context for all their stories, the narrative provides a comprehensive account of the commercial enterprise of slave-breeding in the United States in the first half of the nineteenth century – the whole obscenity of breeding slaves as a long-term investment, the 'livestock' needing 'many years to mature and be ready for the market' (91), the rotation of 'studs' over the female slaves in the breeding bays with the aim of breeding mulatto children, the dangers of inbreeding, the separation into house slaves and field slaves, as well as the paradoxes of there having been white slaves and black slaveholders. Mda's readers are introduced to the operation of the Underground Railroad with its conductors and stations and supportive abolitionists and all the main roleplayers in the drama around slavery and its fugitives – slave-traders, slave-chasers with their dogs, slave-stealers and bounty-hunters – are encountered in the narrative.

Toloki's narrative probes in detail the consequences of this nineteenth-century racial engineering in North America and also foregrounds the complex ethnic identities formed by intermarriage between fugitive African slaves, Native Americans and Irish immigrants who sought sanctuary in Tabler Town, as Kilvert was formerly known. During the days of oppression these people had suppressed their Africanness and Indianness and celebrated their white ancestry; Toloki realises, however, that their now wanting to reclaim all three heritages as a source of pride and uniqueness has resulted in racial and cultural uncertainty: 'But they no longer remember who they were, on the African and Native American side' (238). The creolisation resulting from the diasporic dispersal of Africans in North America is also pursued in the novel in terms of cultural continuity and discontinuity, especially with regard to African and African-American traditions. Toloki observes that certain African cultural practices have survived only in the African diaspora, whereas others actually have no African roots, but are purely inventions of the diaspora:

> I have observed that people of African descent in America often create African heritages that no one in Africa knows about. There are some who are descendants of kings and queens who existed only in the collective imagination of their oppressed progenitors. I also know there are many rituals and traditions long dead on the mother continent that were preserved and transformed and enriched by the slaves to suit their new lives in America (119).

Among the most important metafictional tropes that Mda's novel provides for its hybrid fictional discussion of cultural mixture, change and innovation is the tradition of quiltmaking in Kilvert and, in particular, the reverence for old quilts that 'embody the life of the family' (30) and are carriers of memories. In the lore of Kilvert, especially the African design, which supposedly originated with the Abyssinian Queen in the 1830s, represented not simply 'beauty for its own sake' (48), but was encoded with secret messages in the patterns, colours, ties and stitches that mnemonically – in the tradition of the tales of 'the storytellers and the griots of the old continent' (109) – provided guidelines for fugitive slaves and 'reminded them of their duty to freedom' (109). According to the quiltmakers of Kilvert, the creation of expressive textiles that spoke secret languages to the initiated can be traced back via the Abyssinian Queen to the 'old continent' (48) and Toloki believes that their quilting is a development in the New World of an ancient African tradition of 'talking fabrics' (143). Mda's narrative 'quilt' in *Cion* may also be seen as a New World development of an artistic tradition that has its origins in Africa.

Theorising the African diaspora
A number of questions arise from the various representations of migrant identity in these novels and the different notions of an African diaspora. Are the Australian

immigrant protagonists in *Slow Man* entitled to be included in the category of diaspora? Does the current wave of emigration of the descendants of colonial settlers from South Africa, featured in *The Pickup* and in *A Veil of Footsteps*, amount to a secondary diasporic dispersal or out-migration? Do the present-day African economic émigrés and political refugees trying to gain a foothold in Europe (*A Veil of Footsteps*) or in South Africa (*The Pickup*) constitute an ongoing African diaspora as an extension of the slave diaspora? How feasible are the attempts of Gordimer in *The Pickup* and Mda in *Cion* to present past and contemporary South African history in relation to an African diaspora? Even allowing for a more relaxed use of the term, how legitimate is it to include all African migrants, often from diverse national backgrounds and historical experiences, in the homogenising/pan-Africanist concept of an African diaspora? Or is it perhaps plausible to conceive of uniformly traumatic, contemporary African experience that would permit such inclusion under the blanket of a generic African diaspora?

In their introduction to *Theorizing Diaspora* (2003), Jana Evans Braziel and Anita Mannur acknowledge that 'diaspora' and 'diasporic' are contested terms and they caution against 'the uncritical, unreflexive application of the term "diaspora" to any and all contexts of global displacement and movement' (2003: 3). What needs to be interrogated, they maintain, is how diaspora is 'historicized and politicized', especially in relation to contemporary 'ideas of nationalism, transnationalism and transmigration'. They point out that diaspora,

> [o]nce conceptualized as an exilic or nostalgic dislocation from homeland [. . .] has attained new epistemological, political, and identitarian resonances as its points of reference proliferate. The term 'diaspora' has been increasingly used by anthropologists, literary theorists, and cultural critics to describe mass migrations and displacements of the second half of the twentieth century, particularly in reference to independence movements in formerly colonized areas, waves of refugees fleeing war-torn states, and fluxes of migration in the post-World War II era (4).

Other contemporary theorists of diaspora studies such as Ato Quayson and Khachig Tölölyan (1996, 2007) also remind us that 'not all dispersals amount to diasporas' (Quayson 2007: 581) and that in the world today social scientists have had to devise various, different ways of talking about the consequences of globalisation, transnationalism and cultural hybridity. Diaspora studies provide a useful lens for doing so; in Quayson's formulation: 'The binary settler and migrant emphases of earlier models of migration studies are now making way for understandings of transnational networks, with diaspora studies providing the scholarly focus through which the social sciences and the humanities elaborate these phenomena' (2007: 588).

Although ideas of what constitutes a diaspora may vary greatly and the term is often used in a casual way, the typology developed by Robin Cohen in *Global Diasporas: An Introduction* (1997), from William Safran's (1991) identification of the key characteristics of diasporas, beginning with the Jewish diaspora, has nevertheless remained an important point of reference for subsequent theorists. According to Cohen, diasporas would normally exhibit several of the following features:

(1) dispersal from an original homeland, often traumatically ['victim' diasporas, such as the African and Armenian]; (2) alternatively, the expansion from a homeland in search of work ['labour' diasporas, such as the Indian], in pursuit of trade ['trade' diasporas, such as the Chinese and Lebanese] or to further colonial ambitions ['imperial' diasporas such as the British]; (3) a collective memory and myth about the homeland; (4) an idealization of the supposed ancestral home; (5) a return movement; (6) a strong ethnic group consciousness sustained over a long time; (7) a troubled relationship with host societies; (8) a sense of solidarity with co-ethnic members in other countries; and (9) the possibility of a distinctive, creative, enriching life in tolerant host societies (1997: 180).

In her introduction to *Diaspora and Multiculturalism: Common Traditions and New Developments* (2003) Monika Fludernik points out that the first two of Cohen's nine criteria for a diaspora to come into existence are mutually exclusive, the second one applying to a wide range of ethnic immigrant and postcolonial communities across the globe. She prefers to open Cohen's second criterion up into three further categories: the 'colonial diaspora' and, adopting Vijay Mishra's terms, the 'old and new diasporas' (1996: 421–2). For Fludernik the really 'new' diaspora consists of '(admittedly free) labour movements across the globe', a type of diaspora 'motivated by professional considerations – the movement of individual professionals and their families to mostly anglophone industrial nations' and now including also 'cultural and political *elites*' (2003: xii–xiii).

In her study, *Diaspora: An Introduction*, Braziel builds on her previous work together with Mannur and outlines, as she phrases it, 'the historical roots and contemporary routes of international migration' (2008: 11) in order to understand the various ways in which human migratory populations have been and are still being dispersed from their homelands. Braziel begins, like other theorists, with the standard models of the Jewish and African diasporas and she also acknowledges the diaspora typologies of Safran and Cohen. She offers an important clarification as regards the imprecise use in contemporary discourse of diaspora as a synonym for terms such as transnationalism and global capitalism:

> While transnationalism as a term aptly describes the movement of capital, finance, trade, cultural forms of production, and even material forms of production across national boundaries that serve to erode the nation-state as the foundation or ground for capitalist economies, diaspora remains a primarily human form of movement across geographical, historical, linguistic, cultural, and national boundaries: as such, it remains a lived, negotiated, and experienced form of transnational migration; it is in this sense that diasporic subjects may be understood to be transnational migrants, or transmigrants (27).

Braziel further contributes a taxonomy of distinct groups of people whose movement from 'a native country across national or state boundaries into a new receiving (or "host") country' (27) qualifies them for inclusion in present-day diasporas: *colonial settlers* 'living outside of their motherlands and dispersed from the continental confines of Europe' (28); *transnational corporate expatriates* who move freely across national borders to do business; *students*, mainly from developing countries, on study visas in developed countries; *postcolonial émigrés* who have relocated themselves to the colonial motherland; *refugees* from political persecution, civil war or state violence in their own country 'who have been granted political asylum within a host country' (29); *political asylees* (or asylum seekers) who are in the limbo between seeking refuge in a host country and not yet having been granted formal asylum; *detainees* 'who are held in detention camps at immigration prisons' (32); *internally displaced persons* who have been uprooted from their homes as a result of 'violence, civil warfare, famine, disease, "ethnic cleansing", political persecution, or religious oppression' (33) and who seek shelter elsewhere within their native countries; *economic migrants* who move from their home countries to work in host countries because of a whole range of economic constraints and opportunities; and *undocumented workers* or 'illegal aliens' who have gained entry into a host country to make a living there, but have not obtained the legal permits needed for them to enjoy the status of economic migrants.

The characters in the South African novels referred to in the first section of this chapter exhibit most of the typological features and fit into the diasporic taxonomies outlined above and may therefore reasonably be approached within the general framework of diaspora. Importantly, what all these fictional subjects share is what Aisha Khan calls a 'diasporic consciousness' (2007: 142), a sensibility 'that both marks the very act of uprooting as shaping their sense of self and that memorializes displacement in everyday discourse and practice' (161). The particular interest of a diasporic consciousness for the literary scholar lies in the ways in which the different stories of dislocation and relocation are narrativised in the individual and group memory and how a diasporic personhood and cultural identity are shaped. Recent theorists have, however, stressed the extent to which diasporic communities, despite their collective memory and strong ethnic group consciousness and solidarity, are equally shaped culturally through continuous interaction with host societies. Sunil Bhatia and Anjali Ram argue that the development of a diasporic identity formation does not follow the standard psychological model of acculturation, but that the conflict within and displacement from a native culture are followed by ongoing engagement and negotiation with host cultures: 'Far from being a linear process that proceeds along a teleological trajectory, immigrants variously experience contradictions, tensions, and a dynamic movement that spirals back and forth' (2009: 146).

It is this dynamic that also underlies Stuart Hall's often-cited argument that cultural identity is based on differences and discontinuities rather than on fixed essences, and that it undergoes constant transformation, is 'a matter of "becoming" as well as of "being"' (1990: 225) and is predicated on the future as much as on the past. The experience of diaspora, he maintains, 'is defined, not by essence or purity, but by the recognition of a necessary heterogeneity and diversity; by a conception of "identity" which lives with and through, not despite, difference; by *hybridity*' (235). Hall's view of diasporic identity in terms of internal division and motility rather than fixed essence is echoed, more specifically in a black context, by Paul Gilroy's thesis that the 'history of the black Atlantic yields a course of lessons as to the instability and mutability of identities which are always unfinished, always being remade' (1993: xi) and that cultural doubleness and intermixture are the legacies of the African diaspora. Or, as more recently formulated by Geneviève Fabre and Klaus Benesch in their critical reassessment of the concept of an African diaspora: '[D]iaspora is less a condition or a state than a search for identity that is constantly contested, re-imagined, and re-invented' (2004: xiv).

Picturing the African diaspora

Patricia Schonstein Pinnock's novel *Skyline* (2000) provides one of the most inventive treatments of the African diaspora and its legacies of cultural doubleness and intermixture in recent South African writing. *Skyline* was published shortly after Coetzee's *Disgrace* and is dedicated to the child victims of the sixteen-year-long civil war in Mozambique. *Skyline* engages directly with the issue of the African diaspora by representing an African diasporic community in central Cape Town. The novel takes its title from the name of a featureless, run-down apartment block at the top of Long Street. The building is occupied largely by illegal immigrants and refugees from the rest of Africa, who share its crowded spaces, renting beds and corners of rooms. In the words of the young South African female narrator, who is also a fledgling writer: 'Not many have the right to be here and most of them carry forged papers or pay bribes to stay in the country. They arrive from all over Africa by taxi, by bus, by train. Some hitch rides on overland transporters. Many just walk' (2000: 8). Zimbabweans, Nigerians, Ghanaians, Somalis, Angolans – some are economic migrants, others are survivors of wars in every part of the continent; all of them, the narrator says, have 'stories written on the parchment of their hearts which they don't recite easily' (11). They survive in Cape Town by selling sweets, South African flags, African curios or drugs, on the sidewalks and at traffic intersections, at the Pan-African Market or from Skyline itself. As a group, they are the objects of the xenophobic distrust of black and white South Africans alike.

The question of whether an immigrant African community in another African country (here South Africa) can technically be regarded as forming part of the African diaspora is answered, in part at least, by Michael A. Gomez, a contemporary historian of the African diaspora, who defines his subject as 'people of African descent who found (and find) themselves living either outside of the African continent *or in parts of Africa that were territorially quite distant from their lands of birth*' (2005: 1, emphasis added). The state of being 'out of Africa' can also be experienced elsewhere *in* Africa. The further question of whether diaspora in Africa can or should be spoken of as a unified experience, considering 'the complex pattern of communities and cultures with differing local and regional histories' (2), Gomez says, has no easy answer. The mostly illegal African immigrants in Pinnock's novel have, for example, gravitated towards Cape Town because of, amongst other factors, civil wars in Angola, Mozambique, Sierra Leone and Congo, genocidal conflict in Rwanda and Sudan, corruption and failed democracy in Nigeria and economic and social collapse in Zimbabwe. What Gomez makes clear, however, is that there can be no essentialist model of the African diaspora. His definition of the term allows for a vast range of different experiences: it 'consists of the connections of people of African descent around the world, who are linked as much by their common experiences as their genetic makeup, if not more so' (2).

Brent Hayes Edwards, in his genealogy of the concept of the African diaspora, similarly argues that diaspora points to internal as well as external differences within and among transnational black groupings. '[I]n appropriating a term so closely associated with Jewish thought,' he says, 'we are forced to think not in terms of some closed or autonomous system of African dispersal but explicitly in terms of a complex past of forced migrations and racialization – what Earl Lewis [1995] has called a history of "overlapping diasporas"' (2001: 64). Although the truth remains, as Fabre and Benesch state, that whether real or imagined, 'Africa is the matrix of the African diaspora, the lost homeland and center' (2004: xv), they remind us that '[t]hough still a land of origin, Africa has shifted conceptually: it has finally become an amibiguous place, a conflict-ridden continent' (xvi). Because of the differences between the various experiences of dispersal, they point out that '[t]he idea of an African diaspora was thus gradually replaced by that of multiple diasporas, unified solely through their lost center and mythic homeland, Africa' (xvii).

The heterogeneity and the cultural displacement and syncretism of the African diasporic experience can perhaps best be conveyed by means of a fictional work that shares this cultural doubleness and hybridity. In *Skyline*, Pinnock has devised a structure whereby the individual and collective stories of the residents of Skyline can be told. *Skyline* provides one of the most self-reflexive and wide-ranging examples of ecphrasis – 'the literary description of a work of art' (Hollander 1998: 86) – in contemporary South African fiction. More precisely, Pinnock's fictional discourse needs to be distinguished from the merely iconic, for, as John Hollander, quoting Jean H. Hagstrum (1958), explains, truly ecphrastic literary works are those 'that purport to give "voice and language to the otherwise mute art object"'. Furthermore, as an ecphrastic fictional construct *Skyline* combines both *actual* ecphrasis, where a literary work incorporates particular works of art that pre-exist it and *notional* ecphrasis, where a literary text incorporates descriptions of purely fictive works of art. It might be still more accurate to describe *Skyline* as an *iconotext*, in terms of Peter Wagner's argument in *Reading Iconotexts* (2007). Wagner goes beyond the word-image opposition and the traditional view of texts and images as 'sister arts', to break down the barriers between literature and visual art. In what he calls an 'iconotext' neither image nor text is free from the other; they are mutually interdependent in the ways they establish meaning. And in the case of *Skyline*, image and text merge to convey what it means individually and collectively to experience the African diaspora, to attempt to depict its overlapping histories of conflict and dislocation and to write about it from a South African perspective.

The novel consists of forty more-or-less symmetrical chapters, in each of which the (sometimes overlapping) main stories are narrated and almost all of which conclude with the description of a painting. As it turns out at the end, the paintings are all by the narrator's self-taught, close friend, Bernard, a traumatised refugee from the war in Mozambique where his wife was killed and his three children abducted; their fates unknown to him. Most of these fictive paintings have titles; some, however, are untitled. In most of the descriptions of the fictive paintings, an actual, well-known work from the history of Western art is explicitly cited as the inspiration for Bernard's painting, the inspiration being based on a particular colour, an element of composition or technique, a figure, a mood, or a theme. In a few cases, there is no actual Western painting given as the source for Bernard's painting. His paintings tend to be stylistically mixed and experimental, but nevertheless have an expressive aesthetic logic of their own and do not simply reproduce either the fictional narrative or their source paintings.

For example: Renoir's richly exotic, reclining *Woman of Algiers* serves as a point of departure for a painting entitled *It is the Woman of Rwanda*, of an equally richly colourful, fat black woman, inspired by the figure of the hairdresser, Princess, who is a refugee from the Rwandan genocide and whose daughters' terrible fates she cannot bring herself to tell anyone. Henri Rousseau's naive fantasy *Sleeping Gypsy* provides a model for Bernard's painting *It is the Woman Travelling*, based on the actual story of the woman who has fled with her small children, silenced by the horrors that they have witnessed, from the war in Sudan and come to South Africa on foot, sleeping in the desert on the way. There is no source painting given, however, for *It is the Treasures Bought from Heaven*, which serves to memorialise the Ghanaian, Kwaku, who has come to Mandela's promised land to find his fortune, only to die there of AIDS.

The narrator and other principal characters in the narrative are also interpreted by Bernard with direct reference to sources in Western art: the narrator's alcoholic mother, represented in Bernard's charcoal drawing *She Has Sorrow in the Kitchen*, bears a resemblance to the gaunt figure of the woman in Picasso's *The Frugal Meal*. The narrator's autistic younger sister Mossie, who has a passion for beads, is depicted with reference to Modigliani's hauntingly vulnerable *Little Girl in Blue*. Bernard's painting of Raphael, the narrator's Jewish friend from school, titled *It is the Fine Young Man*, is based on Chagall's *The Fiddler* and mimics its lightness and spontaneity, although the background architecture has been transposed from Russian to Cape Dutch by Bernard.

Bernard also attempts to come to terms with aspects of his own life in his paintings: his portrait of the lonely Portuguese *Senhora*, on whose husband's estate he worked as a domestic servant in Mozambique and who was brutally murdered by rebels, has its origin in Matisse's *Portrait of Madame Matisse with a Green Stripe*, the expression in the *Senhora*'s eyes alone resembling the gaze of Madame Matisse. In an untitled painting, Bernard can only recall the tender dignity of the figure of his wife working in the tobacco-sorting shed on the *Senhor*'s estate by means of Giotto's *Madonna*. There is no source painting, however, for *It is the Death of the Holy Mother under the Trees*, Bernard's depiction of the stripping naked and massacre of the holy sisters of a religious order by Mozambican rebels.

Bernard, like so many diasporic Africans who live in Skyline, has been permanently damaged by war and can never escape from its spectre. To convey this, he has painted an untitled triptych on the subject of war (Chapter 17). This is his most ambitious work, its three panels consciously modelled respectively on Chagall's *War*, Goya's *The Third of May, 1808* and Picasso's *Guernica*. Bernard's triptych is a work, the narrator says,

> which should have stood on its own, and it should have been executed on a much larger canvas. But the overwhelming despair it transmits, together with the pain and sense of useless slaughter, suggest that the artist would have been overcome by the horror and palpitation of the episode he was capturing, had he dared to express himself as hugely as did Picasso (79).

By means of an elaborate intertextuality, canonical works of a European artistic tradition have been appropriated and pictorially and narratively reinterpreted in a postcolonial, diasporic African context. The individual experiences of each of these Africans and marginalised South Africans have been framed within Bernard's paintings to record and interpret their stories of unspeakable loss and longing and, collectively, the paintings narrativise an African diaspora. Taken together, all the mutually inscribed and depicted stories and paintings are held, in turn, within the larger framework of the narrator's commitment to 'those who have turned their backs on what they left behind and built a new life here at the top of Long Street' (55), to 'try to re-embroider [their] splintered words into the finery they once were – old litanies from Ethiopia; chantings from Sudan; fables from Eritrea . . .'. In her ecphrastic engagement with the theme of the African diaspora, Pinnock has endeavoured textually to link contemporary histories of African dispersal back to an ancestral past and also to bring Western cultural traditions in relation to new African practices, thereby presenting through the artistic syncretism of her novel the ongoing reimagination and cultural transformation of the splintered African diasporic self.

Chapter 39 has no description of a painting to conclude it, describing instead the killing of Bernard by the insanely jealous Giovanni, owner of the delicatessen. The final chapter, Chapter 40, tells of Bernard's paintings being catalogued, exhibited at the National Gallery in Cape Town after his death and then, appropriately, dispersed in an artistic diaspora among his friends and on permanent loan to the National Gallery and the Pan-African Market.

The chapter concludes with a last description of a painting, comparable in a way to Vermeer's self-reflexive *Allegory of Painting* or to Velasquez's *Las Meninas* or to Picasso's paintings of himself in his studio with his models (none of these is mentioned as a source, however, and it is left to the reader to supply the possible intertexts). This is Bernard's largest painting, entitled *It is the Portrait of the Artist with his Good Friends* and it self-reflexively shows him working at his easel, surrounded by those who knew and loved him and who formed his subjects. And in the left corner of the canvas, as a metafictional strategy, is painted a copy of Sister Wendy Beckett's *The Story of Painting: The Essential Guide to Western Art*, which Pinnock also includes in her bibliography at the end and which is the source of most of the paintings she describes in the novel. It is worth noting, in conclusion, that gathered together into this compendium volume on 'Western' art are nineteenth- and twentieth-century European painters who themselves were exiles and émigrés – from revolutionary Russia, from Fascist Spain, from Nazi-occupied France – and who have all found their collective, diasporic identity and artistic home in the larger category of 'Western Art'. The final revelation of Pinnock's novel may be that what we now uncomplicatedly refer to as 'Western art' is itself not an essential, unified concept, but refers rather to the cultural products of long and continuing histories of migration and to works of art that are themselves scattered among art galleries and collections all over the world.

References

Bhatia, Sunil and Anjali Ram. 2009. 'Theorizing Identity in Transnational and Diaspora Cultures: A Critical Approach to Acculturation'. *International Journal of Intercultural Relations* 33(2): 140–9.

Braziel, Jana Evans. 2008. *Diaspora: An Introduction*. Oxford: Blackwell.

Braziel, Jana Evans and Anita Mannur. 2003. 'Nation, Migration, Globalization: Points of Contention in Diaspora Studies' [Introduction]. In: *Theorizing Diaspora*, edited by J.E. Braziel and A. Mannur. Oxford: Blackwell: 1–22.

Braziel, Jana Evans and Anita Mannur (eds). 2003. *Theorizing Diaspora*. Oxford: Blackwell.

Breytenbach, Breyten. 2008. *A Veil of Footsteps: Memoir of a Nomadic Fictional Character*. Cape Town: Human & Rousseau.

Coetzee, J.M. 1999. *Disgrace*. London: Secker & Warburg.

———. 2003. *Elizabeth Costello*. London: Secker & Warburg.

———. 2005. *Slow Man*. London: Secker & Warburg.

———. 2009. *Summertime: Scenes from Provincial Life*. London: Harvill Secker.

Cohen, Robin. 1997. *Global Diasporas: An Introduction*. Seattle: University of Washington Press.

Coullie, Judith Lütge and J.U. Jacobs (eds). 2004. *a.k.a. Breyten Breytenbach: Critical Approaches to his Writings and Paintings*. Amsterdam and New York: Rodopi.

Edwards, Brent Hayes. 2001. 'The Uses of Diaspora'. *Social Text* 19(1): 45–73.

Fabre, Geneviève and Klaus Benesch. 2004. 'The Concept of African Diaspora(s): A Critical Reassessment' [Introduction]. In: *African Diasporas in the New and Old Worlds: Consciousness and Imagination*, edited by G. Fabre and K. Benesch. Cross/Cultures 69. Amsterdam and New York: Rodopi: xiii–xxi.

Fabre, Geneviève and Klaus Benesch (eds). 2004. *African Diasporas in the New and Old Worlds: Consciousness and Imagination*. Cross/Cultures 69. Amsterdam and New York: Rodopi.

Fludernik, Monika. 2003. 'The Diasporic Imaginary: Postcolonial Reconfigurations in the Context of Multiculturalism' [Introduction]. In: *Diaspora and Multiculturalism: Common Traditions and New Developments*, edited by M. Fludernik. Amsterdam and New York: Rodopi: xi–xxxviii.

Fludernik, Monica (ed.). 2003. *Diaspora and Multiculturalism: Common Traditions and New Developments*. Amsterdam and New York: Rodopi.

Gilroy, Paul. 1993. *The Black Atlantic: Modernity and Double Consciousness*. London: Verso.

Gomez, Michael A. 2005. *Reversing Sail: A History of the African Diaspora*. Cambridge: Cambridge University Press.

Gordimer, Nadine. 2001. *The Pickup*. Cape Town: David Philip.

Hagstrum, Jean H. 1958. *The Sister Arts: The Tradition of Literary Pictorialism and English Poetry from Dryden to Gray*. Chicago: University of Chicago Press.

Hall, Stuart. 1990. 'Cultural Identity and Diaspora'. In: *Identity, Community, Culture, Difference*, edited by J. Rutherford. London: Lawrence and Wishart: 222–37.

Hollander, John. 1998. 'Ecphrasis'. In: *Encyclopedia of Aesthetics Vol.2*, edited by M. Kelly. New York: Oxford University Press: 86–9.

Jacobs, J.U. 2004. 'Writing Africa'. In: *a.k.a. Breyten Breytenbach: Critical Approaches to his Writings and Paintings*, edited by J.L. Coullie and J.U. Jacobs. Amsterdam and New York: Rodopi: 151–80.

———. 2006. 'Diasporic Identity in Contemporary South African Fiction'. *English in Africa* 33(2): 113–33.

Kelly, Michael (ed.). 1998. *Encyclopedia of Aesthetics Vol.2*. New York: Oxford University Press.

Khan, Aisha. 2007. 'Rites and Rights of Passage: Seeking a Diasporic Consciousness'. *Cultural Dynamics* 19(2/3): 141–64.

Lewis, Earl. 1995. 'To Turn as on a Pivot: Writing African Americans into a History of Overlapping Diasporas'. *American Historical Review* 100: 765–87.

Mda, Zakes. 2007. *Cion*. Johannesburg: Penguin.

Mishra, Vijay. 1996. 'The Diasporic Imaginary: Theorizing the Indian Diaspora'. *Textual Practice* 10(3): 421–47.

Pinnock, Patricia Schonstein. 2000. *Skyline*. Cape Town: African Sun Press.

Quayson, Ato. 2007. 'Introduction: Area Studies, Diaspora Studies and Critical Pedagogies'. *Comparative Studies of South Asia, Africa and the Middle East* 27(3): 580–90.

Rutherford, Jonathan (ed.). 1990. *Identity, Community, Culture, Difference*. London: Lawrence and Wishart.

Safran, William. 1991. 'Diasporas in Modern Societies: Myths of Homeland and Return'. *Diaspora: A Journal of Transnational Studies* 1(1): 83–99.

Tölölyan, Khachig. 1996. 'Rethinking Diaspora(s): Stateless Power in the Transnational Moment'. *Diaspora: A Journal of Transnational Studies* 5(1): 3–36.

———. 2007. 'The Contemporary Discourse of Diaspora Studies'. *Comparative Studies of South Asia, Africa and the Middle East* 27(3): 647–55.

Wagner, Peter. 2007. *Reading Iconotexts: From Swift to the French Revolution*. Chicago: University of Chicago Press.

16

Postcolonial Pomosexuality
Queer/Alternative Fiction after Disgrace

CHERYL STOBIE

The development of South African queer/alternative writing is illustrated by the shift from William Plomer's oblique reworking of homosexual desire into cross-racial erotics in *Turbott Wolfe* (1925), through occasional explorations of homosexuality under high apartheid by authors such as Stephen Gray (1988) – although such texts were vulnerable to banning by the censors – to increasingly explicit material towards the end of the century by authors such as Ashraf Jamal (1996) and Tatamkhulu Afrika (1996). In addition to authors who are personally invested in queer issues, Nobel laureates Nadine Gordimer and J.M. Coetzee refer to these issues in works such as Gordimer's *The House Gun* (1998) and Coetzee's *Disgrace* (1999). In view of the apartheid-era legislation declaring homosexuality illegal it is understandable that after the shift to democracy and the passing of legal safeguards for lesbian, gay, bisexual and transgendered (LGBT) people a number of authors have explored the painful self-acceptance of gay identities – mainly also white and male – during apartheid. This exploration forms part of the retrospective cartography of the previously occluded queer nation.

An interesting turn in the post-apartheid era is the handling of the trope of bisexuality, which opens up a potentially useful domain for considering sexuality and national identifications beyond the constraints of binary models (see Stobie 2007). Since the publication of *Disgrace* a significant development in queer writing has been the shift to representing a more varied spectrum of sexuality – not necessarily viewed as a prime marker of identity – as well as greater awareness of gender issues, a consciousness of postcolonialism and an exciting experimentation with form in the fictional narration, which also visualises a future that can countenance new forms of gender performance and sexuality. This collective shift, more evident in the writing of women authors focusing on queer/alternative themes, might be called 'postcolonial pomosexuality'. The term 'pomosexuality' refers to expressions of queer beyond separatist or essentialist notions of sexual orientation (Queen and Schimel 1997) and my addition of the adjective 'postcolonial' sites this intimate domain within wider political power structures.

Disgrace offers a useful yardstick for comparison with queer/alternative fiction of the last decade. Developments, however, cannot be understood outside of a global picture. Over the twentieth century there was an increasing representation of queer/alternative sexualities in world fiction, dealing with matters such as homophobia, the normativity of heterosexuality and gender issues. This burgeoning was made possible by the globalisation of LGBT studies. Latterly, representations of alternative sexualities in world fiction have highlighted the effects of colonialism on the construction of sexuality, expanded and nuanced ideas of contemporary sexuality as developed in the West and reconstructed culturally specific sexualities.

The term 'queer/alternative' is a contentious one. The word 'alternative' conjures up a binary between the hegemonic and its other and simultaneously implies a challenge to the mainstream. The word 'queer' was originally used in the early twentieth century to refer pejoratively to people who were or were suspected of being homosexual. This meaning persists to the present. From the 1960s onwards gay and lesbian communities developed in the West, drawing strength and theoretical insights from gay liberation and feminist scholarship. Some members of these communities came to reclaim the word 'queer' to signify positively in two senses: as an umbrella term to refer to non-heterosexual people and as a movement beyond the identity politics of gay and lesbian studies, a shift that focused instead on questioning the notion of fixed sexual identities and the perception of heterosexuality as normative. The ideas of Michel Foucault, Teresa de Lauretis, Gloria Anzaldúa, Eve Kosofsky Sedgwick, Judith Butler and Michael Warner contributed significantly to the development of queer theory from the 1970s to the 1990s. In contrast to an identity politics, which renders central the white, middle-class male, Anzaldúa (1987) highlights issues of race, class, gender and cultural specificity as they intersect with sexuality. Her work is anti-binarist and she perceives the possibility of coalitions between various groupings such as gays and lesbians of colour, bisexuals and transgendered individuals.

While the term 'queer' is a contested one in the West and in the postcolonial world, global queer theory opposes the privileging of heterosexuality and attempts to be sensitive to specific cultural matrices of 'queerness'. Postcolonial queer theorists are aware that 'discourses of sexuality are inextricable from prior and continuing histories of colonialism, nationalism, racism, and migration' (Gopinath

2006: 3). During the colonial encounter a range of indigenous sexual practices and identities were regulated, pathologised and stigmatised by political and legal authorities as well as religious leaders within the Christian and Islamic traditions. In the postcolonial era these modified practices and identities still do not fit neatly into the Western LGBT paradigm. Homophobia is rife and state-sanctioned in many societies; in the case of Africa, for instance, the appellation 'un-African' is used as a means of controlling variant sexualities and punitive behaviour includes beating, rape and even murder, although discretion about sexual difference is usually rewarded with tolerance. The fiction that emanates from postcolonial societies may be less explicit about sexualities than Western fiction; it may include homophobic judgements; and it may contain relatively veiled or coded references to queer sexuality. It may also appear courageous and fresh in its representation of fluid sexualities that do not conform to Western tropes such as the coming-out narrative. Because of prevalent gender inequality, women's contributions to queer literature tend to be small in comparison with their male counterparts' fictional works.

To return, initially, to Coetzee, *Disgrace* reveals various familiar, painful and disgraceful inequalities. Women are coerced into sex and their sexuality is consumed, deplored or humiliated by men. Across the traditional race and class divisions of this world, men of different ages and educational levels '*do* rape' (Coetzee 1999: 158). Female characters are reduced to silence and their embodied suffering and inner motives are elided and unimaginable. Lucy's rape is only rendered through the prejudiced eyes of the unreliable focaliser, her father, who acknowledges that he is able to enter imaginatively into the mind-space of the rapists, but questions of himself: '[D]oes he have it in him to be *the woman*?' (160, emphasis added).

The question that Coetzee implicitly poses to readers of the novel is whether we can imaginatively occupy the subject position of the raped woman who is also a lesbian. Lucy's lesbianism is not dealt with in any depth in the novel, but it is represented through Lurie's focalisation as unalluring, unfathomable, possibly inauthentic and childish. Gender roles and stereotypes shape Lurie's view of his daughter's sexuality. Lucy fatalistically accepts her role as sacrificial victim inheriting the sins of the father/s. Her queer identity is erased and she feels obliged to accept her position in a patriarchal, heterosexist and polygamous setting.

Although lesbianism appears as a possibility, Coetzee's queer interest is more attuned to masculinity, as Elleke Boehmer notes in another context (2005); in fact, he often views female bodies with sexual nausea. Lucy is 'othered' by her femininity, her whiteness, her (paternal) heritage of sin, which she schematically needs to expiate, her lesbianism, which is notionally raised only to be repudiated, her rape and her unwanted pregnancy. As lesbianism is represented through the lens of Lucy's uncomprehending father, the novel assumes the form of an 'inverted' or 'anti-coming out' narrative, in the words of Brenna Munro (2005: 177–8), showing queerness in the adult children of the ageing heterosexual generation, as in Gordimer's *The House Gun*, dating from the same period. Neither of these novels is characterised by stylistic innovation. Thus, although the content of both novels captures the Zeitgeist of their moment of writing, of anxieties about social change partly articulated through obliquely rendered queer issues, the texts are not characterised by the added dimension of freshness of vision or future orientation made possible by appropriate innovative form.

In the post-apartheid national context of flux, however, queer offers new ways of responding to alterity. Post-*Disgrace* texts with a queer theme would be intellectually engaging if they displayed some of the following characteristics, not present in that novel: queer sexuality viewed from a perspective of interior depth; a coming-out trajectory rather than an anti-coming out structure; the normalisation of queer; progressive representations of women's sexuality, pleasure and agency; and technical innovation that enhances such themes. Although a good number of texts published after 2000 include lesbian, gay and bisexual characters, critical attention to the significance of alternative sexualities is less frequent, so there is not much cross-fertilisation of critical ideas.

As I now turn my attention to specific post-*Disgrace* South African queer/alternative texts, it is necessary to mention that I have selected certain texts for scrutiny instead of dealing equally with the full range of possible fiction. Further, I have elected to look initially at texts authored by men and then turn my attention to texts written by women. There are several reasons for this choice. Grouping texts by authorial gender highlights the binary construction of gender in the past and present in South African society, resulting in different experiences and access to power. In addition, South African 1990s-era literary criticism examining the representation of homosexuality, such as Shaun de Waal's 'A Thousand Forms of Love: Representations of Homosexuality in South African Literature' (1995), tended to focus on the work of male authors. Grouping according to gender thus serves to emphasise the previously under-analysed achievements of women authors who thematise queer issues. Making this connection between women authors is not intended to elide differences in race, class, gender and cultural specificity as they intersect with sexuality, in line with Anzaldúa's project of portraying links and distinctions between particular manifestations of queer (or queer-friendly). Of course, such alliances can and do exist across the gender divide, but, as can be seen in the example of Coetzee's depiction of Lucy, gender, both of character and author, heavily inflects sexuality. My purpose is to examine representations of queer in post-2000 South African fiction as illuminating negotiations between past, present and future. The separation of authors according to gender is not intended to reify a binary system, but to act in a supplementary way, observing social differences and implying ways in which these may be changing.

A measure of how far public opinion has moved since the 1970s can be seen in the recent reissuing of Michael Power's novel, *Shadow Game* (2008 [1972]). This work was the first South African depiction of a love affair between a white man and a black man and when it was first published Powers felt constrained to use a pseudonym, Laurence Eben, to avoid social stigma. The apartheid social climate also finds expression in the tragic ending of the novel. While the first edition of the book received positive reviews overseas, it was embargoed and banned in South Africa. The re-publication of *Shadow Game* reveals that although the text is a reminder of the pressures of an oppressive social and legal system, it also has certain features not unfamiliar to readers of contemporary South African novels about gay male experience: the crucial issue is the establishment of a gay male identity and while an imaginative entry can be made into the psyche of the racial other, there is little focus on the gendered other.

The most frequent subcategory in the upwards of 30 post-2000 South African texts dealing with queer/alternative sexualities is the male *Bildungsroman*/coming-out story authored by white males. While poignant and interesting, these novels offer little in the way of a development beyond Mark Behr's *The Smell of Apples*, translated from the Afrikaans in 1995. Behr's *Embrace* (2000), Ian Murray's *For the Wings of a Dove* (2000), Michiel Heyns's *The Children's Day* (2002), Barry Levy's *Burning Bright* (2004) and Craig Higginson's *The Hill* (2005) deal with boys' developing sexuality. Some of these are set in schools with predatory male teachers and vulnerable boys as characters and each bears some hallmarks of autobiographical investment. *The Hill*, for instance, is set in the early 1980s in a junior school that closely mirrors Clifton Preparatory School (in Durban), which Higginson attended at the same time. The central protagonist is a sensitive eleven-year-old boy, Andrew Hughes, who becomes the object of obsessive interest of a male teacher who was himself sexually abused at school as a child. Andrew is coded as sensitive and different from his peers and he has a bond with the natural world and Bushman mystical art. As the teacher intensifies his pursuit, Andrew feels a conflict between desire and fear of what he and his peers view as degeneracy. He repeatedly loses consciousness at critical moments of emotional intimacy between himself and the teacher and the novel suggests that his distress is prompted by previous, repressed sexual abuse. Andrew runs away and enters a hallucinatory realm of Bushman mythology before he is found and the teacher dismissed. Higginson declines to reveal Andrew as accepting a gay identity, but privileges his potential queerness by portraying him as spiritually evolved enough to identify with Bushmen who were killed off, according to the text, by whites and African blacks acting with common purpose. Andrew thus represents a prior, natural state of being, beyond the binaries of black and white, which was exterminated by a cruel system of othering. His place in South Africa is implicitly guaranteed by his exceptionalism and his racial identification beyond his own group. The novel is characterised by a sense of retrospective healing conferred by identification with a fantasised racial other, which contributes to the establishment of masculinity (albeit marginalised) and belonging.

Many of the post-apartheid novels with a queer theme by white South African men attempt to negotiate the characters' and authors' own positions in contemporary society, where white men have lost much of the power that was their birthright under apartheid. Many of these texts look back at the past, offering a retrospective protest at injustice and prejudice. They display a high degree of self-reflexivity and personal anguish and read cathartically in their rewriting of history. There is often a sense of retrieving imperilled masculinity through the coming-out process.

The white male coming-out novel, whether featuring boys, adolescents, young adults or adults, focuses almost entirely on the masculine domain. André Carl van der Merwe's *Moffie* (2006) deals with homosexuality mainly in the context of army conscription in 1980 and it reminds us that laws of the apartheid era were designed to protect the 'purity' not only of the 'master race' minority, but also of the heterosexual majority. Army duty promulgated the ideology of violent white machismo through homosocial bonding, the repudiation of femininity and homosexuality and the establishment of social paranoia directed against a racialised enemy. While the text clearly reveals this form of hypermasculinity to be pathological, the antidote to the alienation felt by the gay characters is found in healing homoeroticism and gay sexuality, in addition to a nauseated revulsion against acts of violence and racism. The world of the text is firmly masculine in its problems and solutions. Primacy is given to the difficulty of performing masculinity as a queer man in many novels written by white male authors, including Guy Willoughby's *Archangels* (2002) and Michiel Heyns's hilarious *The Reluctant Passenger* (2003), both of which concern the experiences of adult white males in surprising or countercultural settings up to the present and depict same-sex relationships or experiences, mainly between men.

Gerald Kraak's award-winning *Ice in the Lungs* (2006) expands this focus somewhat. The novel is interesting for its juxtaposition of two spatio-temporal strands that mirror one another in various ways and for its frank exploration of gay male sexuality as part of the coming-out/*Bildungsroman* narrative. The earlier setting is Greece in the Second World War, where a group of young people is engaged in political activism. Questions of political commitment as opposed to personal affiliations are raised, as well as issues of intolerance, homophobia and humane values. A character from this earlier setting has learned painful lessons from his wartime experiences and he provides support, wisdom and a comparative framework for the characters of the second setting, Cape Town in 1976 at the time of the anti-government political ferment. A small group of white and black young people are portrayed, joined in opposition to the apartheid system and united by their illegal choices of desertion from the army and contraventions of the Immorality Act through cross-racial sex or gay sex. The novel critiques homophobia (including the gays-are-a-decadent-Western-import canard) and the prioritisation of one form of political activism over another, instead perceiving feminism, environmentalism, gay and lesbian rights and progressive politics as being inherently connected in a human rights culture. The novel is ethically and emotionally nuanced and it contains some breathtakingly erotic scenes.

Fewer black (in the broad sense of African, Coloured and Indian) male authors than their white counterparts have written texts that thematise queer issues within the form of the *Bildungsroman*. Those who have include Tatamkhulu Afrika, Achmat Dangor, Fred Khumalo and the late K. Sello Duiker. Afrika's poignant *Bitter Eden* (2002) expands the cartography of queer to the terrain of the Second World War, where men who identify as heterosexual struggle with issues of masculinity, desire for one another and shame. In a manoeuvre used by Kraak and by many queer writers in all categories under scrutiny in this chapter, Afrika employs dual chronotopes; here, the lingering effects of the events of a homophobic past are highlighted against a more progressive contemporary setting. Khumalo's *Seven Steps to Heaven* (2007) is remarkable for its matter-of-fact representation, three-quarters of the way into the novel, of a love relationship developing between a white man who was behaviourally bisexual and a black man, Sizwe, whose previous experiences were all heterosexual. This shift into same-sexuality occasions no guilt or angst, although various characters use the term 'moffie' as an insult. Several kinds of crossings occur in the novel: the white man adopts the mannerisms of a black persona, while his black former girlfriend sounds white; a lesbian delights in wearing ultra-feminine, sexy clothing to confound stereotypes. Some wry humour attends the suggestion by the white man that Sizwe should write an academic article on 'The Politics of Being Gay in the Black South African Community' and Sizwe's crisp rejoinder that this could be published alongside an article by his partner, entitled 'Confessions of a White Male Prostitute in a Changing South Africa'. Overall, however, the lessons learned by the characters are bitter and issues of doubling, rape, drug addiction and failure despite promise are explored.

K. Sello Duiker's *Thirteen Cents* (2000) and *The Quiet Violence of Dreams* (2001) also focus on discomfiting issues. The central protagonist in *Thirteen Cents* is a twelve-year-old boy who confounds notions of ethnic purity by having blue eyes and a dark skin. He makes a living by engaging in sex work. *The Quiet Violence of Dreams* is a groundbreaking work, original in terms of content and style. It is set in the post-apartheid era and is recounted in first-person narration by a cast of ten characters. The central protagonist whose picaresque experiences form the linchpin of the novel is Tshepo, a black man who has suffered shocking trauma. He is hospitalised in a psychiatric institution, then becomes a sex worker in a brothel, and eventually moves from Cape Town to Johannesburg where he receives intimations of his own spiritual destiny, becomes a member of a brotherhood who share wisdom and commune sexually, and cares for abandoned children. Over the course of Tshepo's quest Duiker engages with the intersection of sexuality, particularly male gay sexuality, spirituality, nationalism and human rights. I have noted elsewhere my reservations about Duiker's representation of Tshepo as a messiah and his endorsement of patriarchal, phallocentric and misogynistic attitudes and practices (Stobie 2007: 200–13). Despite these criticisms, however, I find the novel an impressive meditation on sexual identity and national identity. The novel values syncretic national identity and opposes mindless consumerism and xenophobia. Munro provides a thoughtful analysis and suggests that *The Quiet Violence of Dreams* appropriates 'the coming-out novel in order to dream up queer postcolonialities that may yet transform our own notions of sexuality, race and nation' (2005: 231).

Threaded throughout the novel are comments that provide a new take on queer self and nation. Tshepo's friend, a white sex worker, ruminates on sex work, self-confidence and politics: '"[W]ith all the things we have done and seen we could do anything. I could be president one day,"' he says (Duiker 2001: 244). This sense of personal potential, even aspiring as far as the apogee of political power in the nation, reveals a freshly minted notion of queer citizenship. Sex workers, conventionally viewed with social revulsion as a tainted underclass, are viewed in the novel as possessed by luminous new hopes. In a democratic South Africa black men have been president; here, however, Duiker allows for the fantasy of a white gay man becoming president, thus presenting gayness alongside blackness as categories of unjust oppression under apartheid and as equally possible sources of power, pride and accomplishment.

In one of the visionary sequences in the novel Tshepo gains a sense of hybrid passion, expressed in terms of rainbow nation rhetoric:

> I come to a stadium. [. . .] I see a group of bare-chested men playing soccer. But as I get closer they metamorphose into graceful centaurs with long untamed tails. I run towards them and they form a circle around me. They are handsome in a rugged way and are of every colour imaginable. I become aroused as I watch this rainbow of muscular torsos. They drink wine and run riot on the field, kicking the ball, sweating, galloping, the earth thudding with their hooves (416).

South Africa's obsession with sport as a signifier of national pride through vicarious participation in rituals of machismo is evoked here, as is the relevance of the stadium as a setting for political rallies. In this context, which effectively constitutes a national assembly, the description moves far beyond realism in visualising a carnivalesque, Dionysian scene involving hybrid creatures of varied hues. Change and difference are embraced.

Startlingly, Tshepo views the height of a gay man's passion as possessing a lyrical voice of patriotism: '[T]he expression on a man's face when he comes, for me it would be the true expression of a patriot when he serenades his land and his people' (389). However, Duiker balances this validation of gay citizenship in the rainbow nation with trenchant critiques of national shames: the prevalence of rape, HIV and AIDS and xenophobia. His imaginative range includes the outsider and finds mythic inspiration in a variety of sources, including ancient Egypt. His queer vision transcends the merely national to revitalise the continental past and include a common humanity without arbitrary borders; Tshepo's idealistic credo is: '"I believe in people, in humankind, in personhood"' (454). The novel, with its jostling voices and styles, including realism, the dystopian and the utopian, carves out a new queer space that takes seriously issues of sexuality, race, nation and the global community. It can be considered a prime example of what I have termed the postcolonial pomosexual novel.

* * *

In general, narratives by women dealing with queer issues differ from those by their male counterparts in covering same-sex relationships between men and between women, instead of privileging male behaviour. When relationships between women are represented they are not as anguished as relationships between men, as depicted by many male authors, especially in earlier time-settings. And women authors also tend to present gender issues more fully, including problems associated with women's lives. There is not the same emphasis on the discovery of sexual dissidence in school stories. Taken as a group, the texts by women range more extensively in time and place than the texts by men, where the apartheid past is a staple and one text, Lauren Beukes's *Moxyland* (2008), is set in the future, allowing for a projection beyond the constraints of the past and present. In terms of style, there is a higher degree of experimentation amongst the women authors who raise queer issues than among their male peers, as well as a high degree of critical self-reflexivity.

Rayda Jacobs's award-winning *Confessions of a Gambler* (2003), narrated through the viewpoint of a 49-year-old Muslim woman, adopts a positive attitude towards queer issues within a potentially hostile cultural framework. She employs the confessional mode to reveal not only the main protagonist's gambling addiction problem, but also her acceptance that her son is gay and that he is dying of AIDS. Part of her struggle to accept her son's sexuality is rooted in her devout belief in Islam, which portrays homosexuality as sinful. She decides to flout community convention by inviting him and his lover into her home for him to die there. The rightness of her ethical decision is textually validated by her discovery that a charismatic caliph was gay. She reacts with shock before she remembers her hard-won lessons: 'How could this be? A man who loved God and taught Islam? But of course faith has nothing to do with sexual preference, and it wouldn't have made one bit of difference' (199). This popular novel, which was made into a film in 2007, touches on women-centred issues such as breast cancer and miscarriage and explores complicated family relationships, polygamy and supportive networks of female friends.

Another prize-winning novel, which also appeared in a film version in 2007, is Shamim Sarif's *The World Unseen* (2001). This text, set in South Africa, which was the birthplace of the author's parents, although she was born in India, follows the by-now familiar convention of dual chronotopes. The minor one is set in the late nineteenth century and recounts the narrative of the grandmother of one of the main characters of the major chronotope, which is set in the 1950s against the backdrop of resistance to the recently introduced apartheid laws. Transculturality is shown to be hazardous in the earlier chronotope, especially when paired with patriarchal family structures, but it is also revealed to bear unexpected fruit. The later chronotope depicts the personal costs of flouting the well-policed Immorality Act, but it offers hope for the future in the shape of a blossoming relationship between a lesbian and a married woman, who defies her traditional husband by learning to drive, by rediscovering the power of the word and by achieving independence through paid work. Sarif critiques the linked oppressive structures of racism, sexism and homophobia and foregrounds queer women's struggles as emblematic of female agency and, by implication, a test case of the future national imaginary.

Foolish Delusions: A Novel Auto/biography by Anne Schuster (2005) again employs two chronotopes, but it is highly original in its form, as is suggested by the word-play in its subtitle. The earlier time-scheme is an imaginative reconstruction of the life of a nineteenth-century female forebear. She has suffered an unhappy marriage and become involved in the plight of prostitutes and the suffrage movement. She has fallen in love with a woman, been accused of murdering her husband and has been admitted to Valkenberg Asylum, paralysed, mute and certified insane. Her state of imprisoned consciousness is an extreme metaphor for the position of women at the time. The parallels between the two chronotopes are marked, as both central characters, born four generations apart, are concerned with matters that have particular relevance for women, such as sex work, rape and sexual harassment, as well as more general forms of discrimination, such as racism and homophobia. The 2004 Cape Town narrative concerns the imaginatively reshaped auto/biography of Anna Bertrand, who like her great-grandmother feels passion for women and who is involved in a court case during which the murderer of a sex worker is found guilty and sentenced to imprisonment. Anna reconstructs phases of her identity and expresses her belated sense of being comfortable in her own skin and of being able to make a difference in a post-apartheid society, despite the threat of ongoing male violence. Extracts from a creative writing manual are interspersed throughout the text and these highlight the techniques used in excavating a painful female history and privileging the role of writing in remembering and shaping identity. The text obscures the boundaries between fact and fiction, self and other, past and present, and a range of writing styles and quotations, including historical records, poems and letters draw attention both to the constructedness of subjectivity and the nature of creativity, evoking personal and involved responses from the reader.

Barbara Adair's two novels are thoroughly queer in content and postmodernist in style, clear examples of postcolonial pomosexuality. Her debut novel, *In Tangier We Killed the Blue Parrot* (2004), is a hybrid text that splices the writings of the bisexual American couple Paul and Jane Bowles, long-time expatriates in Tangier, with Adair's own creative narrative, using an array of real and fictional characters. The love and competitiveness as creative artists between Paul and Jane is represented and a major focus is the complications resulting from their same-sex love affairs with Moroccans. Adair's novel examines issues of 'post/colonialism', intimate relationships and nation. More attention is devoted to the male characters than the female ones, including in the representation of erotic acts. The main male Moroccan character is presented with considerable sympathy and interiority, but his female equivalent is presented from the outside and in stereotyped terms as a witch. Gender is thus problematised within the text (see Stobie 2007: 235–68 for further discussion). The main narrative unfolds at various stages over some thirty-odd years from the time of the Second World War, but there is also a brief preface that places the primary focaliser/author as a tourist in Tangier in 1993. In his review, Chris Dunton expresses some bemusement about the intentions of the novel. He suggests that one possibility is 'to read it in the context of South African fiction: to see it, in other words, as an exploration of notions of choice, distancing and home that reflects, very obliquely, on patterns of social consciousness in the author's own environment' (2003: 18). These patterns include othering in terms of race, class, gender and sexuality. Significantly, however, Adair moves beyond the confines of the national to seek a queer genealogy transnationally, spanning the extremes of the continent.

Adair's second novel, *End* (2007), bears many similarities to her first novel, being postmodernist, intertextual and highly self-reflexive about the process of writing. These characteristics, reminiscent of the works of William Burroughs, John Fowles and Kathy Acker, are innovative in a South African context. The setting shifts between Johannesburg and Maputo in the 1980s and the entire text is pervaded with nostalgic and ironic references to the 1942 film, *Casablanca*. One of the striking features of *End* is the placing of the narrator, Freddie, as an authorial construct who laconically discusses her plans for her novel with the characters and readers who are at her mercy. The queer linchpin of the text is Freddie's creation of an unnamed but vital character whose gender she alters back and forth in various scenes. This makes for queerly vertiginous reading as the character interacts with his/her lover, X, and X's wife, Y. Freddie toys with categories of gender and sexuality as she addresses X:

> 'You are not a queer boy. You do not think you are, but I can make you into one if I want to. And I have wanted to, and I still want to. I want to make you boy/girl. Is there anything more than that you could possibly still want? Tell me. I'll give it to you' (2007: 140).

In the novel love, sex, relationships, sex work, drug addiction, blood and war are woven together in a disturbing mix designed to shock the bourgeoisie, not least in the graphic sex scenes – again, mainly featuring males. Gender and sexuality are only two among a host of instabilities and indeterminacies in the novel, which is a tricky and rewarding read.

Another innovative queer-themed book that uses postcolonial pomosexuality to good effect is Jane Bennett's luminous collection of short stories, *Porcupine* (2008). The title evokes an image of a creature with the capacity to inflict harm if provoked and also conjures up thoughts of the quill as a means of writing. Bennett examines familiar issues such as rape, including the monstrous rape of babies, insanity, relationships between people, intercultural relations and South Africa in its global context. Her clear feminist vision enables her to hit her targets – both female and male – with deadly accuracy. Generosity, nobility and selflessness are held up as ideals, but the difficulty of attaining these goals is also sympathetically portrayed. Passivity, stereotypically associated with femininity, is textually rebuked, while activity and activism are advocated. Six of the eleven stories include lesbian characters and Bennett's postmodernist take on lesbianism and gender issues provides an effective queer strategy. Her sympathetically portrayed characters are questioning and conscious of their own deviance from restrictive social norms. The text is politically progressive and stylistically inventive. Some of the stories use fabulation to striking effect. The world of *Porcupine* includes angels, visiting spirits, one of whom is a raped baby, and spoken words, which become visibly encased in speech bubbles. In one story a leader issues an edict by which all men have their penises removed, but this is not a real solution as the problem is later seen to lie in people's heads, not merely men's phalluses. Another story imagines Jesus revealing his side-wound to extend to his groin; his sexual organs having been removed, thus feminising him and enabling him to empathise with women. Yet another story imagines a man's feelings of impotence and grief after his wife has an abortion without consulting him.

In the text lesbianism is examined from a variety of perspectives. Same-sex desire is represented, along with misogyny, internalised homophobia and lack of self-respect, living a closeted life, longstanding lesbian partners still delighting in each other's presence and bodies, and relationships where there is a disparity in degrees of interest or commitment. The degree of introspection required to live a life outside the mainstream makes for absorbing reading. Lesbianism is not made tragic, romanticised or idealised, but is seen as being a valid sexuality with particular problems and joys associated with gender and marginality.

Few texts published in the period under discussion examine queer from a black woman's perspective, although Bennett includes a representation of the additional complexities of being a black lesbian, and of relationships across ethnic differences. Lindiwe Nkutha's short story, 'The Glass Pecker' (2005), explores this terrain. The story is focalised through the consciousness of a bisexual South African black woman, Nonceba, who frequents a bar where the clientele live bohemian lifestyles. An Egyptian woman, her 'extraordinary friend', sends her parcels of cinnamon cigarettes from Egypt. The last of these parcels contains a letter conveying her extraordinary friend's (her lover's) decision to commit suicide, along with a promise to see Nonceba in the afterlife. Nonceba follows her lover in suicide and they are indeed united after death, on Nefertiti's tomb. This short story subverts the tragedy of a dual suicide by concluding with a romantic fantasy of transcultural and transcontinental union. Another book of short stories, *Open: An Erotic Anthology by South African Women Writers* (Schimke 2008), contains a significant number of stories about lesbianism or bisexuality across a range of cultural settings. Almost half of the stories are not about heterosexuality and those that are explore a number of attitudes towards it, with a weighting towards the negative end of the scale. By contrast, Lindiwe Nkutha, Suzy Bell, Makhosazana Xaba, Liesl Jobson, Sarah Lotz and Lauren Beukes all visualise the value of same-sex female desire.

Beukes's novel, *Moxyland* (2008), branches out in a highly innovative direction. She uses techniques of the dystopian, with echoes of soulless technology and the terrorising of the individual as portrayed in *1984* and *Brave New World*. *Moxyland* also displays elements of cyberpunk, characterised by a bleakly visualised world, which shows the effects of technological change on society in general and characters alienated from the elite power base in particular, as in William Gibson's *Neuromancer* (1984). Cyberpunk texts also often portray the effects of radical technological modifications of the body. A third stylistic heritage upon which Beukes draws is slipstream, a surreal and dislocating postmodernist style of writing, which blurs the boundary between speculative and literary fiction, as seen in the work of Kathy Acker. These techniques add to the edgy complexity of *Moxyland*.

The novel is set in the near future in Cape Town and delineates a dystopian society that mirrors the structural violence of the present. Affiliation to corporates confers a privileged status, but the bulk of society belongs to the underprivileged class. In this differential of privilege the overdetermination of race disappears. Technology is used to bombard hapless citizens with advertising. Cell phones are the medium of indoctrination, acquisition and social control and cell phone deregistration signals civic obliteration. A brutally efficient police force crushes dissent by mavericks such as the four first-person narrators, who attempt public acts of artistic and political subversion. The repressive security apparatus unleashes biological, psychological and technological power to dispel the threat to the status quo. One of the four central characters is a gay black man, Tendeka. He is one of the most sympathetic characters and his sexuality is treated as incidental. He and his partner, Ashraf, are a committed and caring couple who run a programme to assist streetchildren. Tendeka has married a pregnant refugee to provide her with citizenship, and at one stage he and Ashraf consider caring for the baby if the mother were unable to. Paired with his sense of social responsibility is a passionate zeal to eradicate injustice, by violent means if necessary. Tendeka's and Ashraf's mindful sexuality is contrasted with the cynicism of a minor character, who suggests that his lover have a lesbian affair to enhance her cachet as an artist, although he concludes that lesbian affairs are passé as emblems of celebrity chic. Beukes's representation of the three heterosexual characters' intimate lives as more problematic than Tendeka's serves to validate ethically grounded queer relationships. By contrast, mutually desired but ego-driven acts of heterosexual intercourse are represented as passing on a poisoned chalice of biological corporate branding, according to which the branded individual is a living billboard, addicted to the product, but immune from injury or disease. In typically dystopian or cyberpunk style Beukes shows the difficulty of challenging the politically powerful mainstream, as conveyed by Tendeka's excruciating death; however, as part of her project of subverting mainstream values and critiquing present-day society she normalises queer and problematises heterosexuality and marriage. Tendeka's last words, which he thinks are being broadcast to billboards over the whole city, are intended as a rebuke to his society (and to present trends in our own) and pay tribute to human rights and the future of the individual. His final thoughts are for his lover, his wife and her baby.

This unsettling novel's near-future setting focuses the reader on the interface between present and future, rather than on the all-too-familiar borderland between past and present and contributes to the amplification of South African writing beyond the limits of realism. The queer theme is minor but treated matter-of-factly, sympathetically, and as contributing to the wider themes of the novel and these characteristics may well prove predictive of future trends in depicting postcolonial pomosexuality in South Africa.

The texts under consideration show a range of responses to place, temporality, queer, desire, art and life. The most homogenous group is that authored by white men, rescripting scenes from the apartheid past and in effect attempting a consolidation of white gay male identity. While there are some poignant and striking texts in this grouping, more issues with regard to the intersection of race, class, gender, cultural specificity, sexuality and nationalism are raised by black male authors such as K. Sello Duiker. A few texts continue the representations in *Disgrace* and *The House Gun* of queer through the eyes of parents, suggesting that the new queer generation should be perceived as having been produced by the heterosexual family and that these individuals need to be embraced by the family and its macrocosm, society at large. Alternatively, to change the focus to the individual member of society, these novels would seem to enjoin accepting queer as part of oneself. A number of texts by male and female authors employ dual chronotopes with multiple functions: bearing witness to a split-self in character, focaliser or author, measuring and coming to grips with change, showing the similarities and hence lack of change in both temporalities, and also insisting on a forward directionality which opens up the question of the present and the future. This future orientation is seen most clearly in Beukes's *Moxyland*. Across many authors some degree of wish-fulfilment is seen in such techniques as the use of visions or hallucinations, or the projection into another dimension. Taken together, the novels and short stories examined do indeed, as Boehmer suggests in relation to *Disgrace*, allow for the exploration of ethnicity, class, gender, family, nation and identity (2005: 227). Further, many reveal queer sexuality from a position of interiority and display a coming-out trajectory rather than an anti-coming out structure. A significant number of texts normalise queer. The texts authored by women in particular explore a range of perspectives on sexuality, not merely one that may be similar to that of the author, as is the case in many of the male authors, and the female-authored fictions also tend to include progressive representations of women's sexuality, pleasure and agency. Further, as a group they display a considerable degree of technical innovation. Queer/alternative fiction post-*Disgrace*, then, and especially that representing postcolonial pomosexuality, does not merely come after this landmark text, but significantly expands the cartography of the gender/sexuality matrix within the context of contemporary South Africa.

References

Adair, Barbara. 2004. *In Tangier We Killed the Blue Parrot*. Johannesburg: Jacana Media.
———. 2007. *End*. Johannesburg: Jacana Media.
Afrika, Tatamkhulu. 1996. *Tightrope: Four Novellas*. Cape Town: Mayibuye Books.
———. 2002. *Bitter Eden*. London: Arcadia Books.
Anzaldúa, Gloria. 1987. *Borderlands/La Frontera: The New Mestiza*. San Francisco: Aunt Lute Books.

Behr, Mark. 1995. *The Smell of Apples*. London: Abacus.
———. 2000. *Embrace*. London: Little, Brown & Co.
Bennett, Jane. 2008. *Porcupine*. Cape Town: Kwela Books.
Beukes, Lauren. 2008. *Moxyland*. Johannesburg: Jacana Media.
Boehmer, Elleke. 2005. 'Coetzee's Queer Body'. *Journal of Literary Studies/Tydskrif vir Literatuurwetenskap* 21(3/4): 222–34.
Coetzee, J.M. 1999. *Disgrace*. London: Secker & Warburg.
De Waal, Shaun. 1995. 'A Thousand Forms of Love: Representations of Homosexuality in South African Literature'. In: *Defiant Desire: Gay and Lesbian Lives in South Africa*, edited by M. Gevisser and E. Cameron. New York: Routledge.
Duiker, K. Sello. 2000. *Thirteen Cents*. Cape Town: David Philip.
———. 2001. *The Quiet Violence of Dreams*. Cape Town: Kwela Books.
Dunton, Chris. 2003. 'Vicarious Reconstruction of an Uneasy Existence in the Interzone'. *The Sunday Independent*, 29 August: 18.
Gevisser, Mark and Edwin Cameron (eds). 1995. *Defiant Desire: Gay and Lesbian Lives in South Africa*. New York: Routledge.
Gibson, William. 1984. *Neuromancer*. Ottawa: Ace Science Fiction.
Gopinath, Gayatri. 2006. *Impossible Desires: Queer Diasporas and South Asian Public Cultures*. Durham: Duke University Press.
Gordimer, Nadine. 1998. *The House Gun*. Cape Town: David Philip.
Gray, Stephen. 1988. *Time of Our Darkness*. Johannesburg: Frederick Muller.
Heyns, Michiel. 2002. *The Children's Day*. Johannesburg: Jonathan Ball.
———. 2003. *The Reluctant Passenger*. Johannesburg: Jonathan Ball.
Higginson, Craig. 2005. *The Hill*. Johannesburg: Jacana Media.
Jacobs, Rayda. 2003. *Confessions of a Gambler*. Cape Town: Kwela Books.
Jamal, Ashraf. 1996. *Love Themes for the Wilderness*. Cape Town: Kwela Books.
Khumalo, Fred. 2007. *Seven Steps to Heaven*. Johannesburg: Jacana Media.
Kraak, Gerald. 2006. *Ice in the Lungs*. Johannesburg: Jacana Media.
Levy, Barry. 2004. *Burning Bright*. Cape Town: Kwela Books.
Moffett, Helen and Ceridwen Dovey (eds). 2005. *180°: New Fiction by South African Women Writers*. Cape Town: Oshun Books.
Munro, Brenna. 2005. 'Queer Futures: The New South Africa's Coming out Narratives'. Ph.D. dissertation. Charlottesville: University of Virginia.
Murray, Ian. 2000. *For the Wings of a Dove*. London: Minerva Press.
Nkutha, Lindiwe. 2005. 'The Glass Pecker'. In: *180°: New Fiction by South African Women Writers*, edited by H. Moffett and C. Dovey. Cape Town: Oshun Books.
Plomer, William. 1925. *Turbott Wolfe*. London: Hogarth Press.
Power, Michael. 2008 [1972]. *Shadow Game*. Johannesburg: Penguin.
Queen, Carol and Lawrence Schimel (eds). 1997. *PoMoSexuals: Challenging Assumptions about Gender and Sexuality*. San Francisco: Cleis Press.
Sarif, Shamim. 2001. *The World Unseen*. London: The Women's Press.
Schimke, Karin (ed.). 2008. *Open: An Erotic Anthology by South African Women Writers*. Cape Town: Oshun Books.
Schuster, Anne. 2005. *Foolish Delusions: A Novel Auto/biography*. Johannesburg: Jacana Media.

Stobie, Cheryl. 2007. *Somewhere in the Double Rainbow: Representations of Bisexuality in Post-Apartheid Novels*. Pietermaritzburg: University of KwaZulu-Natal Press.
Van der Merwe, André Carl. 2006. *Moffie: A Novel*. Hermanus: Penstock Publishing.
Willoughby, Guy. 2002. *Archangels*. Howick: Brevitas.

17

Literature and Ecology in Southern Africa

DAN WYLIE

For the last few years I have run a third-year university course entitled 'Literature and Ecology'. In the first seminar I ask the students to assess their own home-ground ecological knowledge. The questionnaire probes, *inter alia*, what they know about the geological bases of that home ground, what local, alien and migrant birds and plants they know, where their water supplies come from and where their rubbish goes. Invariably, they are shocked by their own ignorance. Hence, as the global ecological climacteric grinds away our environmental certainties and our assumptions of human superiority and safety, I regard it as crucial that education in every sector addresses our impoverished literacy about human relationships with and dependency on the natural envelope of water, air and soils.[1]

All other crises and problems – of politics and populations, wars and diseases, genders and races – are affected by, interfused with, and ultimately subordinate to the fact of endemic environmental degradation. It is increasingly obvious that no one, anywhere, can detach from this climacteric, any more than we can detach from the carbon monoxide molecules we breathe in every five or ten seconds. It is not, in my view, sufficient to sit back and 'let the scientists sort it out', to believe complacently that someone, somewhere, will invent a new technology to rescue us all. Environmental dynamics are also a matter of attitude, of communications, of mythologies, of persuasive rhetorics and imageries, of spiritual leanings and of unregistered assumptions conveyed through a myriad channels, the vast bulk of them non-scientific. Both highbrow and popular literatures, from poems to newspaper articles, play critical roles in sustaining both beneficent and malevolent dispositions towards 'Nature' and its non-human denizens. For all its narrowness, the academy does possess powerful interpretative tools with which to examine such literary and communicative dynamics with a view to promoting efficacious environmental awareness.

Sarah Nuttall's provocative book, *Entanglement* (2009), argues for perspectives and methodologies that transcend the stories told 'within the register of difference' (1). She envisages working instead within 'an imaginary structured by circuits, layerings, webs, overlapping fields and transnational networks' (3). She considers entanglements within history, urban geography and, most insistently, concepts of race, but also (most interestingly for my purpose) the 'entanglement of people and things' (7). She cites Bill Brown's arguments that, given new global dynamics, 'cultural theory and literary criticism require a comparably new idiom, beginning with the effort to think with or through the physical object world' (7). Nuttall zeroes in on consumerism and its manufactured objects of desire; it seems to me, though, that this rethinking might as fruitfully be applied to people/'natural-object' relations, such as with quiver-trees or crocodiles. The question is how to transcend, if we can, the entrenched 'register of difference' between 'human' and 'natural', between 'culture' and 'nature'.

Hence, though 'entanglement' is a powerful metaphor, I propose a term of even more subtle contact between people and 'things': *infiltration*. 'Entanglement' presupposes the continuation of still-discernible threads of persistent inheritances. *Infiltration*'s primary mode is of yet more subtle diffusions of influences between formerly separated entities, places, levels and cultures: it envisages a criticism of infinite shadings and shadowings, a mode based on the assumption of inescapable *influenzas*, influxions or osmoses. Things and words, entities and systems, *become* one another; 'otherings' and individualities are real, but they are temporary and contingent. This suggests a way of reading better suited to the operations of infinitely fluid and changing ecosystems. Ecologists often still represent ecosystems as somehow separate from human influence, including the modes of perception by which they are discerned and described in the first place. *Infiltration* goes further, envisaging the capturing of both material and symbolic interconnectivities, the ways they infuse one another as much as the ways in which they diverge. We would follow, for instance, the implicit and complicit infiltrations of how sunlight moves through a grass stem, thence infiltrates a cow, thence enters the economies of global meat markets, finally playing its part in physically illuminating for this writer the pages of Swiss novelist Beat Sterchi's grim story of bovine slaughter, *The Cow* (2000), thereby reinforcing a personal preference for vegetarian diet. Or we would trace the endlessly ironic ways in which the phrase, 'Love Nature', might be imprinted on a sheet of paper that has emerged from the uprooting of natural forests in favour of pines and has been transmuted through sundry interlocking chemical, social and mechanical processes, each stage with ecological import, the message itself then having further unpredictable ramifications on behaviour and textual production.

This is not merely whimsical: it insists on the inescapable interfusion of 'world' and 'word', of mentality and quotidian behaviours, of imagery and physical causalities. It is the task of ecologically aware literary criticism, as I understand it, to explore how such infiltrations have manifested in text, and what the consequences of reading and writing in all spheres might be for our 'natural' future on Earth. This is to offer a counterpoise to at least two common readings of the meaning of the term 'nature'. At one extreme, it counters the notion of 'Nature' as ineffably external to human-ness: a cornucopia endlessly available to humans as a resource, whether for sustenance, profit, study, symbolic capital or spiritual succour. Such an 'externalising' view has, ironically, bred both unthinking destruction and the 'deep ecological' stance that an independent, unified or 'Gaian' Nature possesses 'intrinsic rights'. At the other extreme, the infiltration model counters the most far-reaching postmodernist worldview in which the natural is inevitably and 'only' a cultural construct, a linguistic or literary mirage or simulacrum of itself.

A number of recent critics, including Jim Cheney (1989) and Julia Martin (1999: 52), have made efforts to utilise postmodernism's capacity to destabilise damaging metanarratives and essentialisms, whilst avoiding its perceived tendency to detach from the material world. *Infiltration* follows this mode and recognises that neither extreme is independently viable: ultimately the infiltrations between putatively separable 'nature' and 'culture' are inextricable. The terms are fictions – and it is with the effects of such fictions that literary criticism is concerned. Hereafter in this chapter, 'nature' will be used to designate the view that there *is* a 'natural' world independent of human perceptions, one that forms the context or base of human and cultural affairs and which would presumably continue functioning in some fashion were humans entirely absent; and 'ecological' will be used to designate study which assumes that all world-denizens, material contexts and symbolisations are inextricably bound up in one another.

In the southern African lit-crit context, then, the infiltration model would involve not merely a text-bound examination of verbal aesthetics, but also thorough contextualising in the specifics of local historical (including social, political and economic) developments; imported, indigenous and intermingled symbolic systems; ecological parameters including scientifically detailed observation of place- and species-aware intricacies; and, above all, the multiple infiltrations between them. Though each of these arenas is contingent and culturally loaded, such a resolutely interdisciplinary criticism offers a broad and eclectic methodology that can fruitfully interact with and cross artificial boundaries between other intellectual approaches and philosophies. Indeed, elsewhere this has been done already, as in Marxian ecological approaches, ecofeminist criticism and postmodernist ecology, and there is massive potential to advance such insights in our own sphere.

We might then frame our exploration of the southern African scene with two simple questions: how do we go about studying ecology and literature; and what literary matter might we study?

Answers to the first question – a question of 'ecocritical' methodology – are by no means settled globally and locally remain even less well articulated. Ecologically orientated criticism is in its infancy in this region, lagging well behind environmental history, itself still a new endeavour (see Beinart 2003, Dovers, Edgecombe and Guest 2002 and Steyn 1999). It is striking how the natural, let alone the ecological, is missing from almost all surveys of southern African literatures, with the partial and pioneering exception of Stephen Gray's *Southern African Literature: An Introduction* (1979) and passing mentions in Michael Chapman's *Southern African Literatures* (1996). The keywords 'nature' and 'ecology' – even 'landscape', about which there is a substantial body of southern African criticism (see Darian-Smith and Nuttall 1996) – appear in no indexes in such surveys, though Malvern van Wyk Smith, towards the end of his *Grounds of Contest* (1990), notes that 'the *topos* of the wilderness, the theme of ultimate encounter with self and destiny in an Antonine wasteland, has retained a powerful hold' over white writers (130). This is, typically, to continue to subordinate perceptions of the role of the natural to anthropocentric, particularly political and deeply urban concerns. In Rita Barnard's thorough examination of 'South African writers and the politics of place', *Apartheid and Beyond* (2007), 'nature' scarcely appears as an element of 'place' at all, though Barnard does note in passing that 'ecological issues will long remain of vital importance' (11). The role of nature is a particularly striking omission from Theodore F. Sheckels's 'thematic introduction to contemporary South African Literatures in English', *The Lion on the Freeway* (1996): the titular figure, taken from a short story by Nadine Gordimer, is read by Sheckels in every imaginable symbolic way except the most obvious – as iconic of the displacement of natural ecosystems by urbanisation.

Even studies that have engaged with 'natural imagery' or 'landscape' have tended to remain conceptually narrow and descriptive, engaging neither with 'ecology' as an emergent paradigm, nor with recent debates about how 'Nature' is conceptualised in the first place – how, as Theodor Adorno argued, 'understandings of "nature" are always rooted in determinate social conditions' (quoted in Biro 2005: 125). One task of local ecologically orientated criticism will be to delineate just what these determinate conditions are for us, here, now, without falling into the traps of merely reinscribing the binarisms of the past.

In a number of recent articles, the issue has been couched as a call to develop a 'South African' or 'African' ecocriticism (Slaymaker 2001, Caminero-Santangelo 2007 and Vital 2008). I venture to suggest here that this grail is likely to prove as chimerical as that of 'African philosophy'. While we certainly need 'ecocritics' practising in south(ern) Africa, this does not automatically translate into some definitive or coherent 'south(ern) African ecocriticism'. The effort is founded, particularly post-1994, on an understandable desire to (re)establish a foundational national identity in the world by unshackling south(ern) African critical studies from models beholden to colonial (or Western, or American) paradigms of envisaging, writing about and conserving 'Nature'. As Helen Tiffin has warned, institutionalised Western ecocriticism may even be deemed 'neocolonialist' (2007: xvii).

Most prominently, therefore, the methodological question has been framed through reconceptualising aspects of postcolonialism (Vital 2008, Huggan and Tiffin 2007 and O'Brien 2007). Certain strands of 'postcolonial' criticism seemed for a while to promise some sort of restitution of colonial and neo-colonial power imbalances and some propulsion of the former 'margins' independently into the twenty-first century. Some scholars have been arguing that modern ecocriticism *must* be postcolonial in nature, that the 'subaltern' who must now be permitted to speak is not only the oppressed human 'native', but the possum and the polar bear, the elephant and the emu. This is fruitful as far as it goes: there are clear and fascinating but long suppressed connections between these forms of oppression. Anthony Vital has usefully reminded us, however, of Anne McClintock's warning that many of postcolonial criticism's theoretical formulations have, by assuming that 'colonialism' was somehow monolithic and uniform, led 'to a damaging blindness to differences in regional conditions, present and past' (Vital and Erney 2007: 3). Many theorists, endeavouring to counter former hegemonies, have found themselves trapped by the very formulation of postcolonialism into reconstituting that which they intended to disburse. Vital and others are working, however, to emphasise opposing tendencies within postcolonial theory that revalorise the specificity of the local, to get 'back to the world', in Susie O'Brien's phrase (2007), and to recognise 'different shades of green', in Byron Caminero-Santangelo's phrase (2007). Local specificity of content (butcher-birds or fynbos, say), specificities of post-apartheid politics (judicial shifts in land-use, say), or instantiations of what is widely being termed 'bioregionalism' (the Karoo, the Drakensberg), would certainly in some ways distinguish a south(ern) African practice, but I remain cautious on several methodological counts.

Some primary modalities of *infiltration* will bedevil such localism. Firstly, the past infiltrates the present and vice versa. The very notion of 'post-apartheid' is mythic, symbolic and untenable on many grounds. There is no past or future idyll to attain: continuities are ineradicable. We will always be 'post-apartheid' and 'postcolonial', just as we will always be 'post-Iron Age', 'post-Romantic', or 'post-Industrial Revolution', not because we have left those eras behind, but in the sense that we will forever be living with their consequences. Equally, any view we take of the past is inevitably infiltrated by our current paradigms. One consequence is that there is no pure, recoverable indigeneity, either in 'natural' or 'cultural' terms: there can be, for instance, no unproblematic reconstitution or application of 'Bushman' values. As recent critiques of Van der Post-style romanticisations of the Bushmen indicate, promotions of indigenous values as ecologically more sound, even if retrievable, are as dubious here as elsewhere (see Krech 1999). Hence a metalanguage, a critical vocabulary, derived from indigenous languages, which might provide a radical locality to ecocritical discourse, has not been discovered, let alone elaborated. Marguerite Poland, for example, in valorising the Zulu concept of *isithunzi* or 'freedom of spirit' in ecological contexts, admits that this is partly her 'reinvention' (Martin 1999: 239–44). As Jean-Bernard Ouédraogo's (2005) discussion of the 'African' concept of nature demonstrates – he premises his exploration on the allegedly unifying factor in African experience of having been colonised – African philosophers and critics generally find it impossible to disentangle an indigenous definition from the infiltrations of subsequent history. Nor – as the work of any number of black writers, from S.E.K. Mqhayi through Mazisi Kunene to Musaemura Zimunya (just to mention poets), testifies – is the 'indigenous' treatment of ecology locked in some anthropological time-warp. Evolving infiltrations over time, in sum, are unavoidable.

Secondly, as the innumerable theorists of globalisation tirelessly remind us, local and global co-infiltrate spatially and conceptually in the subtlest of ways and always have. Institutions of literary criticism may even be regarded as vanguards of such infiltration, with some deleterious but many beneficent consequences. Our primary textual material is inevitably born of sundry infiltrations. Hence, as critics have noted, southern African literature is deeply derivative of (amongst many others) British literary traditions and conventions, American jazz, modernist poetics and indigenous folktales. Various works, each in their own way, build on such predecessor modes even as they challenge and subvert them. A locally practised ecologically orientated criticism therefore, at the very least, needs to track these derivations, commonalities and deviations – for instance, the ways in which Thomas Pringle attempted to utilise Romantic poetic rhetoric to capture Eastern

Cape landscapes, even as he incorporated local vocabulary, related the political situation to the Highland clearances and, incidentally, provided evidence for the history and movements of wildlife. The promoter of the local might rightly wish to note that there is no strict Western equivalent of the *izibongo* or praise-poem; and conversely that some of the major literary material on which Western ecocriticism has formed itself – most notably the American 'nature essay', from Henry Thoreau and John Muir through to Barry Lopez and Barbara Kingsolver – has scarcely appeared in southern Africa. There must be *some* impress of the local. Duly noted, but this is again more a question of content than of critical methodology.

And methodologically, we are already infiltrated. Like it or not, American and British 'ecocriticism' exists as a major intellectual force and for all its 'foreignness', it is enviably rich, even inspirational. It also needs to be recognised that 'Western' theorisations of nature and the world are themselves by no means monolithic: Laurens van der Post would have been unable to valorise the world of the Bushmen without drawing on anti-Cartesian, non-rationalistic, anti-imperialistic strands within his own culture's thinking. Nowadays, ecologically orientated critics are finding inspiration in, *inter alia*, Franciscan theology, Arne Naess's 'deep ecology', Adorno's aesthetics, Maurice Merleau-Ponty's phenomenology and Gilles Deleuze and Félix Guattari's 'rhizomes', all critiques of the rationalist mainstream, which are sometimes regarded as encouragingly congruent with certain indigenous conceptualisations. A localised south(ern) African ecological criticism, then, must be founded not so much on a rejection or valorisation of putatively established, indigenous *or* foreign models, as on the very tensions and *im*purities between various philosophies or models and appropriately historicised content. Ecocriticism is now likely to draw better methodological inspiration from emergent schools of 'transcultural', 'transnational' and diasporic studies than from a race-obsessed postcolonialism. Such an approach indeed will subjugate (though not efface) racial or national differences in favour of examining how ecological dynamics affect *all* beings, above and beyond colour or ideology.

My awkward bracketing of south(ern) raises a third reason for resisting the notion of a 'South African ecocriticism'. Partly because I myself am neither 'Zimbabwean' nor 'South African' nor 'African' in any simplistic fashion, but rather because (at least) all three at once, I am suspicious of overdetermining a critical stance of any persuasion on a notionally national boundary. This is markedly, though by no means exclusively, the case in Africa, where our modern, ethnically and ecologically hotchpotch 'nations' remain predicated on and bedevilled by the ignorant posturings at the 1884 Treaty of Berlin or similar European imperial manoeuvrings. Imagine a local ecocritic deciding to study Shona language writings from eastern Zimbabwe. There seems less than compelling validity in her taking the border between Zimbabwe and Mozambique, negotiated in Lisbon between Cecil John Rhodes and the Portuguese government in 1890, as the primary criterion, when that border split down the middle not only a cohesive mountain ecosystem, but also Manyika *families* – never mind larger ethnic, totemic and linguistic entities. This is not to deny that the border has over time generated its own dynamics of separation: commercial forestry and profitable tourism on the Zimbabwean side has had specific ecological and social impacts, while civil strife-induced neglect and impoverishment set in on the other; a tendency towards English-language education and lingua franca on one side differed from Portuguese on the other, and so on. But the fundamental geologies, animal presences and weather conditions of the region would appear to our ecocritic as a more efficacious and potentially more interesting basis from which to reassess literatures of the 'bioregion'. As several commentators have pointed out recently, even the concept of the 'bioregion', certainly a potentially fruitful avenue for further literary study here, has moved rapidly from a traditionalist, container-like entity, to be defended against external incursion, to a more fluid concept which eschews national and similar political borders. This is in no way, however, to discredit the strength and validity of establishing a sense of belonging through intimate knowledges of one's immediate place, whatever culturally inflected modes of knowing one may be using; indeed, such knowledges may be vital not only to countering hegemonic globalisations, but to survival itself. At any rate, in alerting us in unexpected ways to layerings, connectivities and infiltrations masked by conventional theories, taxonomies and boundaries, ecologically motivated criticism possesses a powerful potential for critiquing established structures – including, most importantly in our context, those inculcated by apartheid.

And, briefly, a final reason for caution: a discomfort with the term 'ecocriticism' itself. As every successive primer of ecocriticism reminds us, the term was coined by William Rueckert in 1978 and inserted most effectively into the fields of academic discourse by Cheryll Glotfelty and Harold Fromm's pioneering volume, *Ecocriticism: A Reader*, in 1996. Since then it has gained considerable traction, particularly in America where it is centred on the Association for the Study of Literature and the Environment (ASLE) and its excellent journal, *ISLE*. A substantial number of English departments in American, Canadian, English and Australian universities now offer explicitly ecocritical courses and the number of monographs and collections of essays has mushroomed. This output becomes, if anything, increasingly diverse in both content and method, with vigorous contestation over possibilities of approach, such that it gets more, rather than less, difficult to delineate a coherent school of thought one can term 'ecocriticism'. It is even more diversified than 'feminist literary criticism', a field with which ecocriticism shares some of its social-activist drivenness. The word also tends to obscure the deep divisions of thought over how to use the language of its purview: the crucial term 'ecology', for example, has become so watered down in public discourse that its stricter definition – the study of the interrelations between organisms and their environments – is frequently lost. While conceding that the conveniently shorthand term 'ecocriticism' is probably here to stay, I favour the clumsier but more forgiving formulation, 'ecologically orientated' or 'ecologically informed' literary criticism and attempt to define the scope and purpose of that field no more precisely than Glotfelty did in her introduction to the *Reader*: 'the study of the relationship between literature and the physical environment' (xviii). I take this very looseness as an opportunity rather than a problem: it allows both for locally inflected methodological innovation and topical concentrations.

What ecological literary criticism has been practised in South Africa thus far? The literary presence of the natural world and of landscape has often been noted and occasionally actually studied in south(ern) African letters – already a 'primitive' but valid form of ecological criticism. A high point of such study appeared in 1988 in J.M. Coetzee's essays in *White Writing*. Though remaining useful and cogent, Coetzee's observations can now be amplified by using an ecological lens. The word 'ecology' attained a stronger presence in a now unhappily neglected volume of AUETSA (Association of University English Teachers of Southern Africa) conference papers, edited by Nigel Bell and Meg Cowper-Lewis and published in 1993 as *Literature, Nature and the Land: Ethics and Aesthetics of the Environment*. Of the goodly number of relevant papers in this volume, two deserve particular mention, those by Ivan Rabinowitz and Julia Martin. Rabinowitz eloquently and scathingly attacks perceived 'totalizing pathologies of the Arnoldian consensus' (18), comprising 'orthodox literary interpreters [who] expend their energies on self-congratulatory gestures aimed at the extirpation of intellectual curiosity' (19). Rabinowitz counters this with a call to literary academics to re-engage with the real world through scientific and ecological knowledges. Here he pre-empts Glen Love's parallel appeal in 2003 to American ecocritics in his *Practical Ecocriticism* (a title that alludes exactly to the I.A. Richards-style exegetical orthodoxy drubbed by Rabinowitz). This testifies both to the persistence of that orthodoxy and to the perceived subversive or expansive potential of ecologically inclined criticism. However, few, if any of us, have heeded Rabinowitz's challenge.

Indeed, almost no one who wrote for that AUETSA conference has continued to work consistently or centrally in ecologically informed areas, with one exception: Julia Martin's essay 'New, with Added Ecology? Hippos, Forests and Environmental Literacy' (1994), foreshadowed her pioneering Ph.D. dissertation, 'The Jewelled Net' (1999), in which she proposes highly charged, innovative and socially engaged pedagogical models for promoting a localised 'environmental literacy'. This provides a thorough survey of the then available ecocritical literature – much more has emerged since – and is provocative in its ideas for both critical and pedagogical practice. (Significantly, the thesis was by no means purely South African in focus, including chapters on Buddhism, William Blake and America's eco-guru Gary Snyder.) Since then Martin has, along with colleagues at the University of the Western Cape (UWC), taught a number of ecologically orientated courses within her English department, probably the first in South Africa and still one of the few to do so (see Martin 2009).

Martin has also been a stalwart of the Literature and Ecology Colloquium, founded at Rhodes University, Grahamstown, in 2004. (In his patchy survey of South African ecocriticism, written in 2007, Derek Barker seems unaware of the Colloquium's existence and much of what follows will complicate his perception of a 'dark green' or quasi-deep ecology and a 'light green' or more anthropocentric divide in local ecological approaches.) Since the first tentative gathering of interested folk that year, each annual colloquium has spawned a collection of selected essays, either as a journal special issue or as a book. The 2005 Colloquium focused on animals, a popular choice then and now a major global industry broadly termed 'Animal Studies'. The resulting special issue of *Current Writing* (see Wylie 2006) included provocative and innovative essays such as Laura Pechey's exploration of the political dimensions of baboons in South African works of literature. Wendy Woodward, a colleague of Martin's at UWC and another staunch supporter of the Colloquium, showed ways of branching away from highbrow literature, simultaneously intersecting with feminist perspectives, in her examination of female 'animal' memoirists: Katy Payne's, Gillian van Houten's and Linda Tucker's narratives of encounters with lions. Woodward has since extended this line of enquiry into a groundbreaking book, *The Animal Gaze: Animal Subjectivities in South African Fiction* (2008). As my own work on elephants in southern African literatures has taught me, there is an almost overwhelming amount of study possible, necessary and yet to be done in this area. As it happens, J.M. Coetzee's *The Lives of Animals* (1999b) and *Disgrace* (1999a) have generated extensive global interest in the rights of animals in general and of dogs in particular. Encouragingly, Louise Green, who contributed an excellent essay on dogs to this colloquium, alongside colleagues at the University of Stellenbosch, has recently initiated moves towards forming a more substantial Animal Studies forum in the country.

The 2006 Colloquium focused on issues of identity, resulting in the book, *Toxic Belonging? Identity and Ecology in Southern Africa* (Wylie 2008). This focus was prompted by the observation that '[i]n a region scarified by centuries of pre-colonial migration, colonial invasion, internecine conflicts across every conceivable ethnic, gender, political and geographical frontier, massive industry-fuelled migrancy, apartheid-era removals and dislocations, and accelerated blurring of almost all formerly accepted categorisations through globalisation, the notion of *belonging* becomes ever more fraught' (3). The volume's essays tackled various aspects of identity and belonging in relation to representations of the natural world and ranged satisfyingly across philosophy, archaeology, the history of missionaries and the biology of squirrels, as well as both 'highbrow' and 'popular' literatures. Inevitably, the collection opens up as many questions as it addresses: while pre-colonial autochthons are held up for examination, for example, we have yet to see thorough, ecologically informed explorations of literatures produced by any of South Africa's present-day indigenous peoples. As far as I know, only Zakes Mda's novels, *The Heart of Redness* (2000) and *The Whale Caller* (2005) and Jane Rosenthal's novel *Souvenir* (2004) have attracted any ecocritical commentary (see Vital 2005, Caminero-Santangelo 2007 and Woodward 2009).

The 2007 and 2008 Literature and Ecology Colloquiums were both headed by colleagues at the University of Zululand and thematised 'Nature and Power: Forests' and 'Birds In and Out of Literature' respectively, proceedings appearing as special issues of *Alternation* (Addison and Bob 2007 and Louw and Mason 2009). As the editors of the former volume have reiterated, 'the critical mass for a more official status and a free-standing journal has not yet been achieved' (Addison and Bob 2007: 3). Moreover, in all cases, hopes that scientists and ecologists might become more involved were not fulfilled, with the exception of an unpublished collaborative paper on Douglas Livingstone by Ian Glenn and Ed Rybicki. The co-infiltrations of South African sciences and humanities remain radically under-explored and many bridges need to be built. Moreover, while both colloquiums offered suggestions for more such thematised gatherings – we have yet to see ecocritical analyses of the role in our literatures of travel, coastlines, waters, deserts, mountains, insects – neither our methodological practice nor the primary materials on which to base it are anywhere near being adequately theorised or methodologically mapped out.

The 2009 Colloquium, organised by Martin and Woodward, moved a little way in this direction: it included issues of pedagogy and was attended by more overseas colleagues, notably Scott Slovic, founder of ASLE and editor of its journal *ISLE*, prominent English ecocritic Greg Garrard, author of *Ecocriticism* (2004) and Australian Helen Tiffin. While these welcome and indeed inspirational connections are being forged (provoking discussion about whether or not the Colloquium might recast itself as a branch of ASLE on the British or Japanese model), it is clear that few local scholars are pursuing ecologically focused criticism or teaching it with any regularity. Nevertheless, the many contributions to the colloquiums have illuminated the astonishing richness of material available for ecologically orientated study.

So to what material might we now apply ourselves? I am not equipped to provide here a comprehensive survey of primary material and I certainly do not wish either to predict or overdetermine future directions. The following offers the most tentative of sketches.

All literature is produced within environments of necessary air, water and soil; all characters 'live' somewhere, breathing, eating and travelling, and to that extent *no* literature falls outside the potential purview of the ecologically orientated critic. 'Nature' or 'ecology', however defined, *infiltrates* works of all kinds: from the deeply embedded-in-nature pre-colonial societies, or at least such records of them as we possess; the animal-populated indigenous folktales; the first European poets romanticising strange topographies; the popular novelists, from H. Rider Haggard onwards, repeatedly re-creating the wild adventurousness of a putative raw 'Africa'; the memoirists of the modern 'wildernesses' of game reserves, from James Stevenson-Hamilton's *South African Eden* (1993 [1937]) to the plethora of recent game-ranger memoirs; up to the literary explorers of South Africa's rapidly expanding urban environments, not excluding the economic and ecological impacts of migrant labour and the racialised architectures of space (see the suggestive volume on 'urban ecocriticism', edited by Michael Bennett and David Teague [1999]; also the theme of the 2010 Literature and Ecology Colloquium). An anthology such as Helen Moffett's *Lovely beyond Any Singing* (2006), while still not overtly ecological in the modern sense, alerts us to the abundance of material accessible to ecologically inflected readings. We need many more such comprehensive 'maps' to lay the groundwork for proper study.

One broad approach, then, is to catalogue and re-evaluate older and established literatures through the refreshing lenses of the various available ecologically informed critical models (in the manner in which Jane Austen and Shakespeare have been enlivened recently by 'green' readings). For example, despite all the anthropological, political and archaeological attention showered upon the Bushman or San peoples, very little of their alleged *ecological* value has been examined; such value is nevertheless pervasively offered up in our literatures, from François le Vaillant to Van der Post, from Thomas Pringle's poems to David Donald's recent novel *Blood's Mist* (2009) and the persistent production of poetic 'versions' from the Lloyd-Bleek archive of !Xam testimonies, written by Jack Cope, Stephen Watson, Antjie Krog, Alan James and Harold Farmer, amongst others. Similarly, the wealth of travelogues and hunting accounts from the eighteenth and nineteenth centuries, with their daily confrontation with the region's aggressive landscapes and abundant wildlife and their infiltrations of early scientific method, cry out for further ecological and literary analysis. The genre of the *plaasroman* (the Afrikaans farm novel) and its precursors and reinventions, from Olive Schreiner's *The Story of an African Farm* (1883) to the novels of Karel Schoeman, endlessly visiting the concern with carving agricultural settlement and racialist civilisation out of perceived wilderness, is particularly ripe for ecologically orientated re-readings. Such studies, importantly, would not be of merely antiquarian interest, or merely judgemental of the ecofriendliness or otherwise of these texts: these literatures propound, exemplify and embody the dynamics of aesthetic appreciation, exploitation division and use of natural resources upon which our present situation is based.

A second approach is more contemporary, both in primary material and methodology. Over the last fifteen years or so, southern African literatures have begun to engage explicitly with the global ecological climacteric and its local manifestations, such as the impacts of climate change, loss of biodiversity, pollution, tourism and urban sprawl. This concern is not merely post-apartheid. It is most obviously adumbrated in the poetry of Douglas Livingstone which, after being politically sidelined for some years, is now being recognised for its ecological prescience and insight, especially his 1991 volume, *A Littoral Zone* (see Brown 2006, Everitt 2005 and Stevens 2004). This has been followed up in a number of works, for which a snippet of Brian Walter's 2008 poem 'Weather Eye' must stand as representative: the poet knows that he is 'fashioned / in mind and tongue by a planet-world / that warms and dries', even our metaphors '[s]haped by the slow earth changing climate' (Walter 2008: 23). Another particularly trenchant and prescient work is Menán du Plessis' novel *A State of Fear* (1983), which interleaves racist madness with ever-present pollution, scientific love of the natural and fears of nuclear meltdown at Koeberg (see Springer 2008). The novel alerts us to the ways in which 'nature' persists within urban environments and bears comparison with, say, Ivan Vladislavić's *Portrait with Keys* (2006) or the late K. Sello Duiker's *Thirteen Cents* (2000), on both of which students in my course have recently offered suggestive ecological readings. The vast majority of our writers today are suburb-based, yet no one has comprehensively examined the role of the garden in our literature, for all its socio-cultural, economic and ecological import (but see Balfour 1997 and Murray 2008). Even a superficial riffle through recent journals such as *New Contrast* or *Carapace*, however, will reveal the centrality of the garden to the literary consciousness of many of our poets. Similarly, though they are well treated in the critical literature, more might be gained from explicitly ecological readings of the several works by Nadine Gordimer, ranging from the earlier *The Conservationist* (1974) through to *July's People* (1982), which engage with people's relationships with land and natural presences. An example of a more comprehensively ecological reading of another Gordimer novel, *Get a Life* (2005), by Vital (in Vital and Erney 2007), is one which addresses many of the potentialities and tensions I have in mind here (see also Dimitriu's analysis in Chapter 5 of this volume). Novels like Gordimer's provide illuminating explorations of the ecology of our cities and there is much material to be explored on the infiltrations of local and global capital and technology into our ecosystems: Michael Green's *Sinking* (1997) is the only one that exposes the ways in which the mining industry has destroyed the very ground on which we walk and build.

As already mentioned, animals play what turns out on examination to be a central role in our literatures, whether as incidental presences – evidentially important in the very fact of their marginalisation – or as more centrally moral touchstones. Examples of the latter include the ill-fated captive baboon Piet in Justin Cartwright's ecologically rich novel *White Lightning* (2002), not to mention its whales, bees and ants; the baboons as victims of animal experimentation in Michiel Heyns's *The Reluctant Passenger* (2003); elephants throughout the works of Dalene Matthee; and the whales in Zakes Mda's *The Whale Caller* (2005). Case studies of textual instantiations of individual species of animal or bird – the butcher-bird, the owl, the hadeda – would undoubtedly yield their own gold of insight. As many commentators have noted, our very notion of human-ness is predicated on antinomous definitions of the 'animal' and the literary articulations of animals, racial policies, land-use and environments in southern Africa are pervasive and complex.

Other recent works engage with botanical eco-dynamics as fundamental to plot and character: in her novel *Mountain of Lost Dreams* (2005), Annelie Botes involves a struggle between a son's love of Knysna's indigenous forest, incorporating modern preservationist philosophies, and his father's attachment to commercial pine plantations, a struggle also crystallised in relations with a particular local leopard. This and similar novels (not to mention non-fiction works, such as the 'nature' essays of Don Pinnock [2007] or the eco-historical river-travelogue of William

Dicey, *Borderline*) raise the obvious question of how we define, aestheticise and therefore relate to 'wilderness': we need a comprehensive survey of this notion in our regional thought-patterns analogous to Roderick Nash's classic *Wilderness and the American Mind*.

There is a surprising amount of science-fiction or speculative fiction in South Africa which, like its counterparts elsewhere, often incorporates cutting-edge thinking about present-day ecological problems and possible consequences well in advance of more traditional genres. It also embodies a subversion of the commonly expressed perception that ecocriticism tends to valorise realism, to focus on 'natural' factuality over myth, allegory and the generation of *mentalités*. Such fiction ranges from J.M. Coetzee's *Life & Times of Michael K* (1985) and Karel Schoeman's *Take Leave and Go* (1992) to Nancy Farmer's Zimbabwe-set *The Ear, the Eye and the Arm* (1995) and Eben Venter's eco-parable of Afrikaner collapse, *Horrelpoot* (2006, translated as *Trencherman* [2008]). The southern Cape coast provides the denouement of a speculative novel by Jane Rosenthal, *Souvenir* (2004), in the form of a tsunami (inadvertently prescient of the Pacific tsunami that affected our shores, albeit less dramatically, just a few years later). The eponymous heroine of this novel is a clone whose job it is to service, via dirigible balloon, windmills in the Karoo: in this way, the work incorporates some of the stock material of science-fiction, elements of the farm novel, environmentalist concerns with our very real water-stress and the global effects of climate change. Less explicitly, but discernibly, global climatic and associated techno-economic changes shadow the backgrounds of Tom Eaton's *The Wading* (2008) and Lauren Beukes's manically colourful cyber-novel, *Moxyland* (2008). Add to this a considerable body of ephemeral performance-art, hip-magazine and Web-based eco-stories and cartoons, alongside the international attention paid to the film of *District 9*, and this genre looks set to play a prominent role in future literary eco-speculation.

There is also a substantial body of relevant literature in more marginal genres. The interfusions of pedagogical assumptions, global modernity and indigenous folktales in children's literature, for example, await comprehensive study (but see Jenkins 2004). Nothing, perhaps, is as important to the future of our environmental literacies as this vast literature. Here I single out only Jenny Robson's teen novellas, especially the charmingly sardonic *Savannah 2116 AD* (2004), in which wild animals are permitted to roam free under the care of tyrannical conservationists, whilst humans are confined to the human equivalent of zoos and reserves. Similarly, the substantial body of drama incorporating environmental and animal themes, ranging from the various productions of Nicholas Ellenbogen's

Theatre for Africa and of Grahamstown-based Andrew Buckland, to Piwe Mkhize's *Back to Nature* and the work of Aubrey Silinyana (2002), remains underexposed. So does the ecological dimension of the short story in southern Africa: such stories range from Jack Cope's oft-anthologised parable about love of nature in a landscape of rampant techno-capital, 'Power' (1967), to Henrietta Rose-Innes's speculative story of ecocidal meltdown in the Cape, 'Poison' (2007).

I hope it will be clear from this sketch that not only does an extraordinary amount of material of ecological import exist in our literatures, begging for further study, but also that it is vital that this dimension *is* studied. Ecology and its emphasis on *infiltration* is one avenue by which our thought-patterns really might advance beyond the lingering binarisms of imperialism and apartheid. It cannot be sufficiently stressed, however, that this is not merely in service of recharging the academic industry, which has an omnivorous capacity to defuse important social movements, even those critical of its own norms, by absorbing them solipsistically into its intellectual ruminations. While it is essential that southern African ecological criticism engage with the global philosophical debates about definitions of nature and human being-in-the-world, of literature's articulations with politics, justice, economics, science, and so on, it is far more crucial that our study extend itself beyond mere *awareness* of intellectual complexities to *participation* in active change in the everyday world – even if, as Adorno put it, 'change succeeds only in the smallest things' (quoted in Biro 2005: 156). Our ecological-critical practice needs continually to reassess literature's complicities in and critiques of what sociologist Jacklyn Cock has trenchantly termed *The War against Ourselves*, and above all provide a critical baseplate from which more and better literatures of our climacteric times can be produced.

Note

1. I wish to thank Dirk Klopper, Julia Martin and Elzette Steenkamp for helpful comments on a draft of this chapter.

References

Addison, Catherine and Urmilla Bob (eds). 2007. *Nature and Power: Forests*. Special edition of *Alternation* 14 (2).

Balfour, R.J. 1997. 'Gardening in "Other Countries": Schoeman, Coetzee, Conrad'. *Alternation* 4 (2): 123–35.

Barker, Derek. 2007. 'Green Fields: Ecocriticism in South Africa'. *Journal of the African Literature Association* 1(2): 55–67.

Barnard, Rita. 2007. *Apartheid and Beyond: South African Writers and the Politics of Place*. Oxford: Oxford University Press.

Beinart, William. 2003. *The Rise of Conservation in South Africa: Settlers, Livestock and Their Environment, 1770–1950*. Oxford: Oxford University Press.

Bell, David and J.U. Jacobs (eds). 2009. *Ways of Writing: Critical Essays on Zakes Mda*. Pietermaritzburg: University of KwaZulu-Natal Press.

Bell, Nigel and Meg Cowper-Lewis (eds). 1993. *Literature, Nature and the Land: Ethics and Aesthetics of the Environment*. Collected 1992 AUETSA Papers. University of Zululand.

Bennett, Michael and David W. Teague (eds). 1999. *The Nature of Cities: Ecocriticism and Urban Environments*. Tucson: University of Arizona Press.

Beukes, Lauren. 2008. *Moxyland*. Cape Town: Jacana Media.

Biro, Andrew. 2005. *Denaturalizing Ecological Politics: Alienation from Nature from Rousseau to the Frankfurt School and Beyond*. Toronto: University of Toronto Press.

Botes, Annelie. 2005. *Mountain of Lost Dreams*. Cape Town: Penguin.

Brown, Duncan. 2006. 'Environment and Identity: Douglas Livingstone's *A Littoral Zone*'. In: *To Speak of this Land: Identity and Belonging in South Africa and Beyond*. Pietermaritzburg: University of KwaZulu-Natal Press: 101–26.

Caminero-Santangelo, Byron. 2007. 'Different Shades of Green: Ecocriticism and African Literature'. In: *African Literature: An Anthology of Criticism and Theory*, edited by T. Olaniyan and A. Quayson. London: Blackwell: 698–705.

Cartwright, Justin. 2002. *White Lightning*. London: Hodder & Stoughton.

Chapman, Michael. 1996. *Southern African Literatures*. London: Longman.

Chapman, Michael (ed.). 2008. *Postcolonialism: South/African Perspectives*. Newcastle: Cambridge Scholars Publishing.

Cheney, Jim. 1989. 'Postmodern Environmental Ethics: Ethics as Bioregional Narrative'. *Environmental Ethics* 11: 117–34.

Cock, Jacklyn. 2007. *The War against Ourselves: Nature, Power and Justice*. Johannesburg: Wits University Press.

Coetzee, J.M. 1985. *Life & Times of Michael K*. London: Penguin.

———. 1988. *White Writing: On the Culture of Letters in South Africa*. New Haven: Yale University Press.

———. 1999a. *Disgrace*. London: Secker & Warburg.

———. 1999b. *The Lives of Animals*. New Jersey: Princeton University Press.

Coetzee, J.M. (ed.). 2007. *African Pens: New Writing from Southern Africa*. Johannesburg: Spearhead.

Cope, Jack. 1967. 'Power'. In: *The Man Who Doubted and Other Stories*. London: Heinemann: 107–21.

Darian-Smith, Kate and Sarah Nuttall (eds). 1996. *Text, Theory, Space*. London: Routledge.

Dicey, William. 2004. *Borderline*. Cape Town: Kwela Books.

Donald, David. 2009. *Blood's Mist*. Johannesburg: Jacana Media.

Dovers, Stephen, Ruth Edgecombe and Bill Guest (eds). 2002. *South Africa's Environmental History: Cases and Comparisons*. Cape Town: David Philip.
Duiker, K Sello. 2000. *Thirteen Cents*. Cape Town: David Philip.
Du Plessis, Menán. 1983. *A State of Fear*. Cape Town: David Philip.
Eaton, Tom. 2008. *The Wading*. Johannesburg: Penguin.
Everitt, Mariss. 2005. 'Jack Sprat and his Wife: Symbiosis in Douglas Livingstone's A *Littoral Zone*'. *English in Africa* 32(2): 53–67.
Farmer, Nancy. 1995. *The Ear, the Eye and the Arm*. London: Puffin.
Garrard, Greg. 2004. *Ecocriticism*. London: Routledge.
Glotfelty, Cheryll and Harold Fromm (eds). 1996. *Ecocriticism: A Reader*. Athens: Georgia University Press.
Gordimer, Nadine. 1974. *The Conservationist*. London: Penguin.
———. 1982. *July's People*. London: Penguin.
———. 2005. *Get a Life*. Cape Town: David Philip.
Gray, Stephen. 1979. *Southern African Literature: An Introduction*. Cape Town: David Philip.
Green, Michael Cawood. 1997. *Sinking*. London: Penguin.
Heyns, Michiel. 2003. *The Reluctant Passenger*. Johannesburg: Jonathan Ball.
Huggan, Graham and Helen Tiffin. 2007. 'Green Postcolonialism'. *Interventions* 93(1): 1–11.
Jenkins, Elwyn. 2004. 'English South African Children's Literature and the Environment'. *Literator* 25(3): 107–23.
Krech, Shepard. 1999. *The Ecological Indian: Myth and History*. New York: W.W. Norton.
Livingstone, Douglas. 1991. *A Littoral Zone*. Cape Town: The Carrefour Press.
Louw, Pat and Travis Mason (eds). 2009. 'Birds In and Out of Literature'. Special issue, *Alternation* 16(2).
Love, Glen A. 2003. *Practical Ecocriticism: Literature, Biology and the Environment*. Charlottesville: University of Virginia Press.
Martin, Julia. 1994. 'New, with Added Ecology? Hippos, Forests and Environmental Literacy'. *Interdisciplinary Studies in Literature and Environment* 42(1):1–12.
———. 1999. 'The Jewelled Net: Towards a Southern African Theory/Practice of Environmental Literacy'. Ph.D. dissertation. Cape Town: University of the Western Cape.
———. 2009. 'Situating Place for Environmental Literacy'. *English Studies in Africa* 52(2): 35–49.
Mda, Zakes. 2000. *The Heart of Redness*. Cape Town: Oxford University Press.
———. 2005. *The Whale Caller*. Johannesburg: Penguin.
Moffett, Helen (ed.). 2006. *Lovely beyond Any Singing: Landscapes in South African Writing*. Cape Town: Double Storey.
Murray, Sally-Ann. 2008. 'Indigenous Gardening, Belonging and Bewilderment: On Becoming South African'. In: *Postcolonialism: South/African Perspectives*, edited by M. Chapman. Newcastle: Cambridge Scholars Publishing: 40–60.
Nuttall, Sarah. 2009. *Entanglement: Literary and Cultural Reflections on Post-apartheid*. Johannesburg: Wits University Press.
O'Brien, Susie. 2007. '"Back to the World": Reading Ecocriticism in a Postcolonial Context'. In: *Five Emus to the King of Siam: Environment and Empire*, edited by H. Tiffin. Amsterdam and New York: Rodopi: 177–200.

Olaniyan, Tejumola and Ato Quayson (eds). 2007. *African Literature: An Anthology of Criticism and Theory*. London: Blackwell.

Ouédraogo, Jean-Bernard. 2005. 'Africa: Human Nature as Historical Process'. In: *Keywords: Nature*, edited by N. Tazi. Cape Town: Double Storey.

Pinnock, Don. 2007. *Natural Selections: The African Wanderings of a Bemused Naturalist*. Cape Town: Double Storey.

Robson, Jenny. 2004. *Savannah 2116 AD*. Cape Town: Tafelberg.

Rose-Innes, Henrietta. 2007. 'Poison'. In: *African Pens: New Writing from Southern Africa*, edited by J.M. Coetzee. Johannesburg: Spearhead.

Rosenthal, Jane. 2004. *Souvenir*. Knysna: Brompvilie Press.

Schoeman, Karel. 1992. *Take Leave and Go*. London: Sinclair-Stevenson.

Sheckels, Theodore F. 1996. *The Lion on the Freeway: A Thematic Introduction to Contemporary South African Literatures in English*. New York: Peter Lang.

Silinyana, Aubrey. 2002. *The Celebration of Cape Mammals*. East London: Nation Building Books.

Slaymaker, William. 2001. 'Eco-ing the Other(s): The Call of Global Green and Black African Responses'. *PMLA* 116(1): 129–44.

Springer, Michael. 2008. 'Ecological Sensitivity in Menán du Plessis' *A State of Fear*'. In: *Toxic Belonging? Identity and Ecology in Southern Africa*, edited by D. Wylie. Newcastle: Cambridge Scholars Publishing: 134–42.

Sterchi, Beat. 2000. *The Cow*. Translated by M. Hofmann. London: Faber & Faber.

Stevens, Mariss. 2004. 'Symbiosis or Death: An Ecocritical Examination of Douglas Livingstone's Poetry'. Master's thesis. Grahamstown: Rhodes University.

Stevenson-Hamilton, James. 1993 [1937]. *South African Eden: The Kruger National Park*. Cape Town: Struik.

Steyn, Phia. 1999. 'A Greener Past? An Assessment of South African Environmental Historiography'. *New Contre* 46: 7–27.

Tazi, Nadia (ed.). 2005. *Keywords: Nature*. Cape Town: Double Storey.

Tiffin, Helen (ed.) 2007. *Five Emus to the King of Siam: Environment and Empire*. Amsterdam and New York: Rodopi.

Van Wyk Smith, Malvern. 1990. *Grounds of Contest: A Survey of South African Literature*. Johannesburg: Juta.

Venter, Eben. 2006. *Horrelpoot*. Cape Town: Tafelberg.

Vital, Anthony. 2005. 'Situating Ecology in Recent South African Fiction: J.M. Coetzee's *The Lives of Animals* and Zakes Mda's *The Heart of Redness*'. *Journal of Southern African Studies* 31(2): 297–313.

———. 2008. '"Another Kind of Combat in the Bush": *Get a Life* and Gordimer's Critique of Ecology in a Globalised World'. *English in Africa* 35(2): 89–118.

Vital, Anthony and Hans-Georg Erney. 2007. 'Postcolonial Studies and Ecocriticism'. *Journal of Commonwealth and Postcolonial Studies* 13(2)/14(1): 3–13.

Vladislavić, Ivan. 2006. *Portrait with Keys: Joburg & What-What*. Cape Town: Umuzi.

Walter, Brian. 2008. *Mousebirds*. Port Elizabeth: Seaberg.

Woodward, Wendy. 2008. *The Animal Gaze: Animal Subjectivities in South African Fiction*. Johannesburg: Wits University Press.

———. 2009. 'Whales, Clones and Two Ecological Novels: *The Whale Callers* and Jane Rosenthal's *Souvenir*'. In: *Ways of Writing: Critical Essays on Zakes Mda*, edited by D. Bell and J. Jacobs. Pietermaritzburg: University of KwaZulu-Natal Press: 333–53.
Wylie, Dan (ed.). 2006. 'Animal Presences, Animal Geographies'. *Current Writing* 18(1): 1–5.
———. 2008. *Toxic Belonging? Identity and Ecology in Southern Africa*. Newcastle: Cambridge Scholars Publishing.

Contributors

Marcia Blumberg is an assistant professor of English at York University in Toronto, Canada. She has published widely on contemporary theatre, especially South African theatre.

Michael Chapman is a senior professor of English and research fellow at the University of KwaZulu-Natal in Durban. Among his more recent publications are *Southern African Literatures* and *Art Talk, Politics Talk*. He edited the collection of essays *Postcolonialism: South/African Perspectives*.

Leon de Kock is a professor of English at the University of Stellenbosch. His published books include criticism (*Civilising Barbarians: Missionary Narratives and Textual Response in Nineteenth-Century South Africa*), poetry, literary translation and collections of South African writing.

Ileana Dimitriu is a professor of English at the University of KwaZulu-Natal, Durban. Her publications include book chapters, novels in translation and *Art of Conscience: Rereading Nadine Gordimer after Apartheid*.

Miki Flockemann has published articles on diasporic writings from South Africa, the Americas, the Caribbean and the Indian Ocean World. Her publications on South African theatre and performance focus on shifts in aesthetic trends.

Annie Gagiano is an emeritus professor in the Department of English at the University of Stellenbosch. Her research on African English fiction includes *Achebe, Head, Marechera: On Power and Change in Africa* and *Dealing with Evils: Essays on Writing from Africa*.

Devarakshanam Betty Govinden is a senior research associate of the University of KwaZulu-Natal in Durban. Her recent publications include *Sister Outsiders: Representation and Identity in Selected Writings by South African Women* and *A Time of Memory: Reflections on Recent South African Writings*.

Eva Hunter is currently a research fellow in the English Department at the University of the Western Cape. She has published widely in local and overseas academic journals on South African and African women writers.

J.U. Jacobs is an emeritus professor and research fellow at the University of KwaZulu-Natal in Durban. His most recent publications include *a.k.a. Breyten Breytenbach: Critical Approaches to his Writings and Paintings*, co-edited with Judith Coullie, as well as *Ways of Writing: Critical Essays on Zakes Mda*, co-edited with David Bell.

Siphokazi Jonas is a Masters student at the University of Cape Town. She writes and performs poetry in isiXhosa and English and has an interest in the development of black female writers.

Russell H. Kaschula is a professor of African Language Studies and head of the School of Languages at Rhodes University in Grahamstown. He has published widely in the field of African sociolinguistics and literature, including his book *The Bones of the Ancestors are Shaking: Xhosa Oral Poetry in Context*.

Margaret Lenta is an emeritus professor and senior research associate at the University of KwaZulu-Natal in Durban. Her research interests are at present in the documents remaining from Cape slavery. Her most recent book is *Paradise, the Castle and the Vineyard: Lady Anne Barnard's Cape Diaries*.

Nhlanhla Mathonsi is an associate professor in the School of IsiZulu Studies at the University of KwaZulu-Natal in Durban. He is currently researching issues of transformation in language and gender.

Gugu Mazibuko is a lecturer in the School of IsiZulu Studies at the University of KwaZulu-Natal in Durban. Her research interests cover both literature and language.

Contributors

Sally-Ann Murray is an associate professor of English at the University of KwaZulu-Natal in Durban. Her award-winning novel, *Small Moving Parts*, was published in 2009, and her poetry has received both the Sanlam and the Arthur Nortje awards.

Cheryl Stobie is an associate professor of English at the University of KwaZulu-Natal in Pietermaritzburg. Her book *Somewhere in the Double Rainbow: Representations of Bisexuality in Post-Apartheid Novels* was published in 2007.

Helize van Vuuren is a professor and head of the Department of Language and Literature at the Nelson Mandela Metropolitan University in Port Elizabeth. She is the author of *Tristia in perspektief* and co-editor with Willie Burger of *Sluiswagter by die dam van stemme: Beskouings oor die werk van Karel Schoeman*.

Louise Viljoen is a professor in the Department of Afrikaans and Dutch at the University of Stellenbosch. She compiled an anthology of Afrikaans poetry *Poskaarte: Beelde van die Afrikaanse poësie sedert 1960* with Ronel Foster and a selection of poetry by Barend Toerien, *Om te onthou*. She also published a book on the work of Antjie Krog, *Ons ongehoorde soort*.

Dan Wylie teaches English at Rhodes University in Grahamstown. He has published two books on the Zulu leader Shaka (*Savage Delight* and *Myth of Iron*); a memoir, *Dead Leaves: Two Years in the Rhodesian War*; and several volumes of poetry. He founded the annual Literature and Ecology Colloquium and edited *Toxic Belonging? Identity and Ecology in Southern Africa*.

Index

Abahlali baseMjondolo 164
Abrahams, Lionel 85, 90, 178
Accone, Darryl 264 see also Horwitz, Allan Kolski & Darryl Accone
Achebe, Chinua
  'Mapping out Identity' 259
  Things Fall Apart 61, 312 n.1
Acker, Kathy 346, 348
Ackermann, Denise 269
Adair, Barbara
  End 346–7
  In Tangier We Killed the Blue Parrot 345–6
Adams, Keith (ed.)
  We Came for Mandela 264
Adams, Quanita 141
Addison, Catherine & Urmilla Bob (eds) 363
Adendorff, Elbie 203
Adorno, Theodor W. 225, 356, 359, 368
Aeschylus
  Eumenides 149
  Oresteia 149, 150
Afrika, Tatamkhulu 180, 182, 186, 193–4, 196, 199 n.8, 263, 266, 271, 335, 341
  Bitter Eden 341
  Mr Chameleon 271
  'Pillion' 194
umAfrika 301
Akabor, Miriam
  Flat 9 295
Akademie vir Wetenskap en Kuns 107

Akasegawa, Genpei 92 n.3
Alexander, Jane
  The Butcher Boys 71
Alexander, Ray 263–4, 268
Alternation
  7(1) 2000: [theme issue] 262
  14(2) 2007: [theme issue] 363
  15(2) 2008: [theme issue] 13 n.1
  16(2) 2009: [theme issue] 363
Altieri, Charles 197
Anderson, Benedict 23
Anderson, Linda 262
Andrews, Rick
  Buried in the Sky 268
Anthonissen, Christine see Kaschula, Russell H. & Christine Anthonissen
Anzaldúa, Gloria 336, 338
Appiah, Kwame Anthony 167
Arenschield, Laura 78
Artaud, Antonin 160, 161, 171
  Theatre and the Plague 174 n.8
Association for the Study of Literature and the Environment (ASLE) 360, 364
Association of University English Teachers of Southern Africa (AUETSA) 361, 362
Attree, Lizzy 83, 89
Attridge, Derek 11, 14 n.6, 128
Attridge, Derek & David Attwell (eds) 6
  The Cambridge History of South African Literature 26, 37 n.3

Attridge, Derek & Rosemary Jolly (eds)   51
  Writing South Africa: Literature, Apartheid and Democracy 1870–1995   50
Attwell, David   3, 12–13
  Doubling the Point: Essays and Interviews   271
Attwell, David & Barbara Harlow   2
Attwell, David (jt.ed.)   see Attridge, Derek & David Attwell (eds)
Aucamp, Hennie   211, 213, 214
  Hittegolf   213
  'Wulpse sonnette'   213
Austen, Jane   364
Avusa Media   29

Baartman, Saartjie   54
Badal, Sean   20
Baderoon, Gabeba   20, 115, 142, 191
  'How not to stop'   191
  'Hunger'   191
Badilisha Poetry X-Change (Cape Town)   198–9 n.6
Bafana Bafana   154
Baijnath, Mr   289
Bailey, Brett   4, 5, 162, 170–1, 172, 173
  Ipi Zombi   171–2
  Orfeus   170, 172, 174 n.9
  The Plays of Miracle and Wonder   174 n.8
Balfour, R.J.   366
Bambani Women's Writing Group
  Long Life: Positive HIV Stories   273
Banoobhai, Shabbir   193, 286, 296 n.2
  'Prayer'   193
  'song of peace'   193
Barker, Derek   21, 22, 362
Barnard, Ferdie   49
Barnard, Rita   14 n.13, 21
  Apartheid and Beyond   50–51, 356
Barnard, Rita & Grant Farred (eds)   13 n.1, 262
Barnes, Hazel   174 n.1
Barry, Shelley (jt.ed.)   see Ndlovu, Malika, Shelley Barry & Deela Khan (eds)

Barth, John   44
Barthelme, Donald   44
Barthes, Roland   161, 177, 184
Bartók, Béla   216
Batley, Karen (ed.)
  A Secret Burden: Memories of the Border War by South African Soldiers Who Fought in It   268
Battiss, Walter   213
Beckett, *Sister* Wendy
  The Story of Painting: The Essential Guide to Western Art   332
Behr, Mark   20
  Embrace   339
  Kings of the Water   42
  The Smell of Apples   339
Beinart, William   356
Bekker, Pirow   216
Bell, David and J.U. Jacobs (eds)   14 n.13
Bell, Nigel & Meg Cowper-Lewis (eds)
  Literature, Nature and the Land: Ethics and Aesthetics of the Environment   361
Bell, Suzy   348
Bell, Terry   83
Benesch, Klaus (jt.ed.)   see Fabre, Geneviève & Klaus Benesch (eds)
Bengani, Lungile
  Kwenzekeni Bazali Bami?   310
  'Ngingowesimame'   310
  'Ngivumele Ngiphathe'   310–11
Benjamin, Walter   172
Bennett, Jane
  Porcupine   347–8
Bennett, Michael & David W. Teague (eds)   364
Bennett, Tony (ed.)
  Popular Fiction: Technology, Ideology, Production, Reading   110
Bennum, Neil   14 n.12
Benzien, Jeffrey   149
Bernstein, Rusty   268
Berold, Robert   178–9, 180, 181, 182, 184, 185, 187, 188, 196, 198 n.3 & n.5
  'Botsotso Jesters'   197 n.1

Index

Bethlehem, Louise   11
Bethlehem, Louise (jt.ed.)   *see* De Kock,
    Leon, Louise Bethlehem & Sonja
    Laden (eds)
Beukes, Lauren   20, 112, 348
    Moxyland   113, 114–15, 344, 348–9, 350,
    367
Bezuidenhout, Andries   206
    'Ons'   208
    'Ons ry iewers naby Ottersfontein verby'
    208
    Retoer   208
Bezuidenhout, Zandra
    Dansmusieke   217
    'Die middag van die ooms'   217
Bhabha, Homi   4, 25, 292
Bhagoo, Goordeen   294
Bhana, Surendra & Joy Brain   284
Bhatia, Sunil & Anjali Ram   327
Bhengu, M.V.
    Inkunzi Emanqindi   300
    Itshwele Lempangele   300
Bieber, Jodi
    Soweto   78
Biehl, Amy   105
Biko, Steve   273–4, 286
Bila, Vonani (wa ka)   184, 187, 197 n.1
    Handsome Jita   197–8 n.1
Billie, Ayanda   197 n.1
Binoche, Juliet   225
Bird, W.W.   55
Biro, Andrew   356, 368
Bizos, George   263, 270
BlackBerry   77
Blackburn, Douglas
    Leaven   61
Black Noise   198 n.6
Blake, William   362
Bleek, W.H.I. & Lucy C. Lloyd (eds)   194,
    198 n.4, 212, 236, 237, 365
Bloom, Kevin   20
Bluebeard   216
Blumberg, Henry   155 n.1

Blumberg, Marcia   145, 160
Blumenthal, Roy   197 n.1
Blumenthal, Roy (jt.ed.)   *see* Helmsley,
    Joanna & Roy Blumenthal (eds)
Bob, Urmilla (jt.ed.)   *see* Addison,
    Catherine & Urmilla Bob (eds)
Boehmer, Elleke   27, 106, 337, 350
Boehmer, Elleke & Deborah Gaitskell (eds)
    69
Boerneef
    'Die berggans het 'n veer laat val'   228
Boesak, Allan   268, 275
Book Café (Harare)   246
Boraine, Alex   266, 269–70, 272
Borges, Jorge Luis   218
Bosman, Herman Charles   90, 263
    My Life and Opinions   271
    Mafeking Road   55
Bosman, Martjie   214
    'Kartografie'   215
    Landelik   215
Botes, Annelie
    Mountain of Lost Dreams   366–7
Botman, H. Russel & Robin M. Petersen
    138
Botsotso   197 n.1, 199 n.7
Botsotso Jesters   178, 184, 187, 197 n.1,
    246, 254, 255
    No Free Sleeping   197 n.1
    we jive like this   197 n.1
Boxwell, J.   312 n.1
Braid, Mary   143
Brain, Helen   266–7
Brain, Joy   *see* Bhana, Surendra & Joy Brain
Braziel, Jana Evans
    Diaspora: An Introduction   325–6
Braziel, Jana Evans & Anita Mannur (eds)
    Theorizing Diaspora   324, 325
Brecht, Bertolt   160, 171
Bregin, Elana   66 n.5
Bregin, Elana & Belinda Kruiper
    Kalahari RainSong   274
Bretherton, Inge   174 n.2

Breytenbach, Breyten 2, 27, 75, 92 n.1, 182, 205, 206, 208, 209, 210, 211, 213, 216, 218, 220 n.3, 225, 271, 315, 319
   Dog Heart: A Travel Memoir 319
   'Die hart se dinge' 213
   Memory of Snow and of Dust 292, 319
   Oorblyfsel/Voice Over 206, 207
   Return to Paradise 319
   A Veil of Footsteps: Memoir of a Nomadic Fictional Character 319–20, 324
   Die windvanger 206–7, 209, 213, 216
   Woordwerk 319
Breytenbach, *Colonel* Jan 268
Brink, André (P.) 34, 51, 66, 92 n.1, 121, 238–9, 266, 271
   A Chain of Voices 61
   A Fork in the Road 271
   'Looking on Darkness' 19
Brink, André (P.) (ed.)
   Groot verseboek 219
British Council 92 n.1
Britz, Etienne 220 n.4
Brook, Peter 160, 174 n.1
Brouard, Pierre W. 14 n.10
Brown, Andrew 20
   Refuge 43
Brown, Bill 354
Brown, Duncan 289, 365
Brown, Duncan (ed.) 14 n.12
Brown, Judith & Martin Prozesky (eds) 285
Brown, Mark 161, 174 n.1
Brownlee, Russel 20
Bruno, Giuliana 74
Brutus, Dennis
   'Knuckles Fists Boots' 19
BTA/Anglo-Platinum Short Story Competition 84
Buckland, Andrew 368
Bulbring, Edyth 20
Bunyan, John
   The Pilgrim's Progress 3, 7–8, 293
Burger, Willie 108–9, 115 n.3
Burroughs, William 346

Bush, George W. 193
iBushwomen 198 n.6
Butler, Judith 153, 336
Buys, Anthea 79, 80, 147

Callahan, D. 101
Calvino, Italo 74
Cameron, *Judge* Edwin 273
Caminero-Santangelo, Byron 357, 363
Campbell, Jean 273
Campbell, Roy 10, 22
Cape Town Book Fair 26, 301
Capon, Heather
   Clinging to Fences 267
   Carapace 366
Carnegie, Dale 75
Carthage Festival 140
Cartwright, Justin 27
   To Heaven by Water 42, 48–9
   White Lightning 366
Carver, Raymond 75
Casablanca 346
Castells, Manuel 120
Chagall, Marc
   The Fiddler 330
   War 331
Chapman, Michael 6, 21, 13 n.4, 14 n.5, n.6 & n.13, 120, 178, 182
   Art Talk, Politics Talk 3
   Southern African Literatures 3, 6, 35, 356
Chaucer, Geoffrey 274
Chen, Emma
   Emperor Can Wait 264
Cheney, Jim 355
Chetty, Rajendra 296 n.2
Chimeloane, Rrekgetsi
   Whose Laetie Are You? 265
Chimurenga 246
Chinosole 262
Chinyola, Kennedy 161, 174 n.2
Chipkin, Ivor 5
Christiansë, Yvette 52, 59, 115, 208
   Imprendehora 4
   Unconfessed 54, 55, 61, 64, 65

Index

Clingman, Stephen
  The Novels of Nadine Gordimer: History from the Inside 122
Cloete, T.T. 208, 216
  Heilige nuuskierigheid 209
Cock, Jacklyn
  The War against Ourselves 368
Coetzee, Ampie 37 n.10
Coetzee, Greig
  Johnny Boskak is Feeling Funny 163, 166
Coetzee, Jan 262
Coetzee, J.M. 4, 5, 8, 9, 11, 14 n.6, 21, 64, 81, 92 n.1, 121, 128, 263, 271, 315, 337
  Boyhood 46, 271
  Diary of a Bad Year 26–7
  Disgrace 1, 7, 315, 328, 335, 336, 337–8, 339, 350, 362
  Elizabeth Costello 315
  Inner Workings 11
  In the Heart of the Country 7, 66 n.1
  Life & Times of Michael K 64, 127, 367
  The Lives of Animals 362
  The Master of Petersburg 9–10
  Slow Man 315–17, 323–4
  Summertime 1, 42, 43, 44, 46–48, 271, 317–19
  Waiting for the Barbarians 64
  White Writing 361
  Youth 46, 271
Cohen, Robin
  Global Diasporas: An Introduction 325, 326
Cohen, Shari 154–5
Coleman, Robert see Rodwell, Bobbie with Lesego Rampolokeng & Robert Coleman
Coleridge, Samuel Taylor 183
Combrinck, Lisa 193
  'Masturbation' 193
Commonwealth Writers' Prize 31
Cooper, Brenda 4
Coovadia, Imraan 20, 37 n.5, 51, 53–4
  Green-Eyed Thieves 54, 295
  High Low In-between 2, 13, 28, 36, 42, 43, 48, 54, 295
  The Wedding 53, 54, 64, 291, 292, 295

Cope, Jack 365
  'Power' 368
Coplan, David 244, 247
Cornelius, Johanna 263
Correctional Service Centres 301, 302
Corrigall, Mary 162
Coullie, Judith Lütge (ed.) 14 n.13
  The Closest of Strangers: South African Women's Life Writing 269
Coullie, Judith Lütge et al. (eds) 14 n.11
  Selves in Question 262
Coullie, Judith Lütge & J.U. Jacobs (eds) 14 n.13
Courbet, Gustave
  L'origine du monde 213
Cousins, Colleen Crawford 189
Couzens, Tim 74
Cowper-Lewis, Meg (jt.ed.) see Bell, Nigel & Meg Cowper-Lewis (eds)
Cox, Robert 24
Cronin, Jeremy 178, 181–2, 186, 188
  'Heron's place' 186
  More than a Casual Contact 186
Crous, Marius 210, 213
  Aan 'n beentjie sit en kluif 214, 216
  'Bed 1' 214
  'Bed 2' 214
  Brief uit die kolonies 209
  'Vergifnis' 209
Cullinan, Patrick 182, 263, 270
Cullinan, Wendy 263, 270
cummings, e.e. 218
Current Writing
  15(2) 2003: [theme issue] 13 n.1
  16(2) 2004: [theme issue] 13 n.1
  18(1) 2006: [theme issue] 362
  20(2) 2008: [theme issue] 13 n.1
  21(1–2) 2009: 37 n.9, 198 n.2

Dalai Lama 120
Dalindyebo, *Chief* Sabata 249, 250
Dangor, Achmat 4, 9, 296 n.2, 341
Darian-Smith, Kate & Sarah Nuttall (eds) 356

Darwish, Mahmoud 207
Da Silva, Lavene 198 n.6
Davids, Leila 141
Davids, Nadia 115
   At Her Feet 141–2, 174 n.4
   Cissie 170
Dawes, Nic 235
Daymond, M.J., Dorothy Driver & Sheila Meintjes (eds) 13 n.4, 14 n.13
Deacon, Thomas 211
   Maagmeisie. Griekwastemme 212
Deb, Siddartha 126, 133 n.2
De Certeau, Michel 72, 80, 81
   'Walking in the City' 76
Deep South 198 n.5
De Klerk, F.W. 178
   The Last Trek 269
De Klerk, Marike 143
De Kock, Leon 2, 3, 4, 5, 8, 14 n.8, 25, 33, 37 n.11 & n.12, 43–49, 51, 65, 66, 80
   'Does South African Literature Still Exist?' 1, 7, 19, 63–4, 70, 81, 121–2
   'How to Get into Bed with a Publisher' 37 n.2
   'so, the gloves are off, now' 195
   'Sorry for what, she asked' 195
   'South Africa in the Global Imaginary: An Introduction' 37 n.1
De Kock, Leon, Louise Bethlehem & Sonja Laden (eds) 2, 37 n.1
De Kok, Ingrid 9, 184–5, 186, 187–8
   'At the Commission' 187
   'Bring Back the Statues' 185
   'What Everyone Should Know about Grief' 185
De Lange, Johann 213, 217, 234, 235
   Die algebra van nood 214, 217
   'Pa' 217
   'Petidiendroom' 217
   'Wabi-sabi' 214
De Lauretis, Teresa 336
Deleuze, Gilles and Félix Guattari 9, 359
De Lille, Patricia with Charlene Smith 262

Dendy, Gail 183, 192
   'Dogstar [. . .] Pluto' 192
   'Nipper' 192
Department of Arts and Culture (DAC) 301, 302, 312 n.1
Department of Arts and Culture (KwaZulu-Natal) 301
Derrida, Jacques 122
Desai, Ashwin 296 n.2
   We Are the Poors 274
Desai, Ashwin & Goolam Vahed
   Inside Indenture 284, 294
Desai, Ashwin & Richard Pithouse 261, 267
De Souzenelle, Annick 126
Des Pres, Terrence
   The Survivor 261
De Villiers, I.L. 216
   Jerusalem tot Johannesburg 214
   ' 'n Ou man klim uit die bad' 214
   Vervreemdeling 214
De Villiers, Phillippa Yaa 142, 143, 155 n.1, 198 n.6
   'Connection' 189
   Original Skin 142–3
De Villiers, Willemien
   Kitchen Casualties 113
   The Virgin in the Treehouse 113
De Vries, Fred 72, 73
De Waal, Shaun
   'A Thousand Forms of Love: Representations of Homosexuality in South African Literature' 338
De Wette, Julian 211
   Tussen duine gebore 211
Dhlomo, H.I.E. 246
Dhlomo, R.R.R.
   An African Tragedy 61
Dicey, William
   Borderline 366–7
Dickens, Charles
   Sketches by Boz 75–6
Dickinson, Emily 218

Index

Dikeni, Sandile   197
   Guava Juice   179
Dimitriu, Ileana   125, 366
Distiller, Natasha & Melissa Steyn (eds)
   14 n.11
District 9   79, 367
Dixon, Isobel   74, 194–5
Dlamini, Jacob   20, 265
   Native Nostalgia   42
Dlamini, J.C.   308
D'Offici, Mario   267
Dolny, Helena   272
Donadio, Rachel   70, 71, 77, 80, 83
Donald, David
   Blood's Mist   365
Donaldson, Andrew, Bobby Jordaan & André Jurgens   72
Dönges, Sarina   216
   'Die dood as minnaar'   216
   In die tyd van die uile   216
Doucet, Lyse   154
Dovers, Stephen, Ruth Edgecombe & Bill Guest (eds)   356
Dovey, Ceridwen   64
   Blood Kin   64, 65, 112–13, 115
Dowling, Finuala   20, 191–2
   'Census Man'   192
   'Detoxing'   192
   'Metaphysical uses for worms (apart from death)'   192
   Notes from the Dementia Ward   42
   'Talk, share and listen'   192
Driver, Dorothy   13 n.4, 21
Driver, Dorothy (jt.ed.)   see Daymond, M.J., Dorothy Driver & Sheila Meintjes (eds)
Drum   270, 289, 290
Drum Generation   22
Dub, Sam   147
Dublin International Gay Theatre Festival   143
Dugger, Celia   152
Duiker, K. Sello   9, 20, 59, 82, 341, 349–50
   The Hidden Star   56, 66 n.2

The Quiet Violence of Dreams   56, 66 n.2, 84, 342–3
Thirteen Cents   52, 55, 56, 61, 62, 64, 342, 365
Dullay, Prithiraj Ramkisun
   Salt Water Runs in my Veins   295–6
Dumas, Marlene   213
Dunton, Chris   346
Du Plessis, Clinton V.   208, 209, 210, 211
   gedigte, talk show hosts & reality shows   209
   'die taal'   209
Du Plessis, Hans   211–12, 220 n.4
   Boegoe vannie liefde   211
   Hie neffens my   211
   Innie skylte vannie Jirre   211
Du Plessis, Menán
   A State of Fear   365
Du Plessis, Phil (jt.ed.)   see Hugo, Daniel, Leon Rousseau & Phil du Plessis (eds)
Du Plooy, Heilna
   In die landskap ingelyf   215
   'Landskapsiklus'   215
Du Preez, Max   266, 270

Eagleton, Terry   196
   How to Read a Poem   177
Eakin, Paul J.   262
Eastwood, Clint
   Invictus   153
Eaton, Tom
   The Wading   367
Eben, Laurence   see Power, Michael
Ebrahim, Noor
   Noor's Story: My Life in District Six   269
Edgecombe, Ruth (jt.ed.)   see Dovers, Stephen, Ruth Edgecombe & Bill Guest (eds)
Edinburgh Festival   140
Edwards, Brent Hayes   328–9
Eglin, Colin   269–70
elearning4Africa   251
Eliot, T.S.   192
Ellenbogen, Nicholas   367–8
Elsen, Albert E.   232

Emdon, Erica
   Jelly Dog Days 43
English Academy Review
   24(1) 2007: [theme issue]   13 n.1
   25(1) 2008: [theme issue]   13 n.1
   26(1) 2009: [theme issue]   13 n.1
English in Africa
   33(2) 2006: [theme issue]   13 n.1
   35(1) 2008: [theme issue]   13 n.1
Erney, Hans-Georg *see* Vital, Anthony & Hans-Georg Erney
Ernst-Auga, Ulrike   120–1, 122, 125, 126, 130, 132, 133 n.2
Essop, Ahmed   296 n.2
Esterhuizen, Louis
   'Elegie vir 'n vaderland'   210
   'Langnagvure'   217
   Liefland   210
   Sloper   217
Eugène Marais Prize   226
Evans, Gavin   270
Everitt, Mariss   365
Every Day, Every Year I Am Walking   169
Ewok   184, 185
   'Lend me that machine gun when ye done, Mr Zuma!'   189
   'Yo Mister'   184–5
Eybers, Elisabeth   215, 236
   'Résumé'   216
   Valreep/Stirrup-cup   215–16

Fabre, Geneviève & Klaus Benesch (eds)   327, 329
Facebook   245
Fair Lady   236
Fanon, Franz   163, 182
Farber, Yael   170
   Molora   149–50
Farber, Yael & Thembi Mtshali
   A Woman in Waiting   140–1
Farmer, Harold   365
Farmer, Nancy
   The Ear, the Eye and the Arm   367
Farred, Grant   139–40
Farred, Grant (jt.ed.) *see* Barnard, Rita & Grant Farred (eds)
Farren, Tracey   20
   Whiplash   42
Fatso, Comrade   243, 246, 254–5, 256
Fedler, Joanne   27
   The Dreamcloth   113
Ferguson, Gus   198 n.5, 235
Ferrus, Diana   206, 208
   'Na tien jaar'   207
   Ons komvandaan   207, 208
FIFA World Cup   153, 154–5
Fingo Revolutionaries   246
Finlay, Alan   197 n.1
Finlay, Alan & Siphiwe ka Ngwenya (eds)
   Insight   197 n.1
Finnegan, Ruth   246, 248
Fischer, Bram   273–4
Fisher, Philip   171
Fleishman, Mark   162, 170
Flockemann, M.   169–70, 292
Flockemann, M. (et al.)   174 n.3
Fludernik, Monika   325
Fludernik, Monika (ed.)
   Diasporas and Multiculturalism: Common Traditions and New Developments   325
Fokofpolisiekar   219
Fölscher, Barbara
   Blind Faith   63
Foot Newton, Lara   162, 171, 173
   Karoo Moose   170, 171, 172
   Reach   148, 170
   Tshepang: The Third Testament   150–1
Foster, Hal   161
Foucault, Michel   235–6, 336
Foundation for Human Rights   251, 252
Fourie, Magdel   220 n.3
Fowles, John   346
Fraser, Nancy
   'Transnationalizing the Public Sphere'   23–4
Frenkel, Ronit   3, 283, 284

Index

Freud, Sigmund 216–17, 218
Fromm, Harold (jt.ed.) *see* Glotfelty, Cheryll & Harold Fromm (eds)
Fugard, Athol 5, 27, 121, 160, 169–70
  The Train Driver 151–3, 170
Fugard, Lisa 20

G20 Club 187
Gadamer, Hans-Georg 174 n.2
Gagiano, Annie 51, 62, 260
Gaia 215
Gaitskell, Deborah (jt.ed.) *see* Boehmer, Elleke & Deborah Gaitskell (eds)
Galane, Sello 253
Galgut, Damon 92 n.1
  The Impostor 30, 42
Gandhi, Mohandas Karamchand *Mahatma* 285, 288
Gandhi, Sita
  In the Shadow of Mahatma 264
Gardiner, Michael (ed.)
  Throbbing Ink: Six South African Poets 197 n.1
Garman, Anthea 24, 25
Garrard, Greg
  Ecocriticism 364
Gaza, B.
  'Ungangibandlululi' 311
Geertz, Clifford 170
Gehrmann, Susanne 254
Gérard, A.S.
  Four African Literatures: Xhosa, Sotho, Zulu, Amharic 312 n.1
Gestform 252
Gevisser, Mark 83, 154
Gibbon, Perceval
  The Vrouw Grobelaar's Leading Cases 55
Gibson, Gilbert 205, 218
  Boomplaats 205, 217
  Kaplyn 205, 217, 218
  Oogensiklopedie 205, 218
Gibson, William
  Necromancer 348

Gikandi, Simon 11
Gilroy, Paul 293, 327
Ginsberg, Allen 218
Giotto di Bondone
  Madonna 331
Glenn, Ian & Ed Rybicki 363
Glotfelty, Cheryll & Harold Fromm (eds)
  Ecocriticism: A Reader 360, 361
Gobert, Darren 155 n.1
Gobodo-Madikizela, Pumla 260
Goldblatt, David 214, 231
Goldstone, Richard 270
Goldstuck, Arthur 253
Gomez, Michael A. 328
Goodnow, Katherine J. & Yngvar Natland 244
Goonam, Kesaveloo 296 n.2
  Coolie Doctor 285
Goosen, Jeanne 217
  Elders aan diens 217–18
Gopie, Rajesh
  Out of Bounds 174 n.4
Gopinath, Gayatri 336–7
Gordimer, Nadine 9, 11, 21, 80, 85, 92 n.1, 119–21, 122, 125, 128, 132, 133, 133 n.1 & n.2, 315, 321, 366
  Beethoven Was One-Sixteenth Black 132
  Burger's Daughter 123, 124
  The Conservationist 128, 366
  Get a Life 122, 124–5, 126–32, 133 n.2, 366
  The House Gun 123–4, 335, 338, 350
  July's People 132, 366
  Jump 9
  'Karma' 9, 133 n.2
  'The Lion on the Freeway' 356
  'Living in the Interregnum' 71–2, 76, 83, 119
  Loot 9, 132, 133 n.2
  'My Father Leaves Home' 9
  My Son's Story 124
  None to Accompany Me 122–3, 124, 128
  The Pickup 124, 127, 128, 321–2, 324

Govender, Chin 286, 289
Govender, Kessie 296 n.2
Govender, Krijay 296 n.2
Govender, Neelan
   Girmit Tales 291, 295
   'Wrought by Prayer' 295
Govender, Pregs
   Love and Courage: A Story of Insubordination 264, 286
Govender, Ronnie 296 n.2
   'At the Edge' and Other Cato Manor Stories 289
   In the Manure: Memories and Reflections 286
   The Lahnee's Pleasure 286
   Song of the Atman 286, 289
Govender, Rubendra
   Sugar Cane Boy 291
Govinden, Devarakshanam Betty 14 n.11, 285
   'Memory of Snow and Dust' 292–3
Goya, Francisco de
   The Third of May, 1808 331
Graham, James 14 n.13
Graham, Shane 70, 72
   South African Literature after the Truth Commission 8, 9, 10–11
Gramsci, Antonio
   Prison Notebooks 71, 139
Grant, Richard 266
   The Wah-Wah Diaries 266
Gray, Stephen 90, 121, 220 n.5, 231, 234, 235, 238–9, 335
   Invitation to a Voyage: French Language Poetry of the Indian Ocean African Islands 293
   Southern African Literature: An Introduction 35, 356
Green, Louise 362–3
Green, Michael 37 n.10, 82, 83
Green, Michael Cawood 14 n.12
   For the Sake of Silence 27, 31, 43
   Sinking 366
Greig, Robert 14 n.7

Grootboom, Mpumelelo Paul 162, 170
   Foreplay 161–2
Grotowski, Jerzy 59, 160–1, 165, 174 n.1
   Towards a Poor Theatre 160
Guattari, Félix *see* Deleuze, Gilles and Félix Guattari
Guest, Bill (jt.ed.) *see* Dovers, Stephen, Ruth Edgecombe & Bill Guest (eds)
Gunner, Liz 22 *see also* Hofmeyr, Isabel & Liz Gunner
Gunner, Liz (ed.) 14 n.12
Gunner, Liz (jt.ed.) *see* Stiebel, Lindy & Liz Gunner (eds)
Guthrie, Adrian John 162, 173
Gwayi, Joyce J. 305

Habermas, Jürgen 23
Haggard, H. Rider 364
Hagstrum, Jean H. 329
Hall, Megan 190, 198 n.6
Hall, Stuart 275, 327
Hamber, Brandon & Hugo van der Merwe 138
Hambidge, Joan 218, 219
   Lykdigte 216
   'Toespelings' 219
   Vuurwiel 219
Hammer, Joshua 91
Handspring Trust 145
Hani, Chris 273–4
Harlow, Barbara *see* Attwell, David & Barbara Harlow
Harris, Chief Rabbi Cyril 269
Harris, Peter 92 n.1
   In a Different Time 2, 30, 42
Harris, Wilson 292
Harrison, Robert Pogue 85
Harrison, Sophie 133 n.2
Hassim, Aziz 9, 52, 290, 296 n.2
   The Lotus People 54, 287–8, 291
   The Revenge of Kali 54, 296
Hassim, Shireen, Tawana Kupe & Eric Worby (eds) 167

Index

Havel, Václav 120
Hayes, Peter 155 n.1
   I Am Here 144–5
Hayes, Peter & Pam Ngwabeni
   Ncamisa! The Women 143–4
Head, Bessie 21, 263, 270–1, 274
Head, Dominic 133 n.1
Heaney, Seamus 218
Heinemann 300–1
Heinemann African Writers series 77
Helgesson, Stefan 14 n.6, 70, 73, 81, 83
Helmsley, Joanna & Roy Blumenthal (eds)
   Of Money, Mandarins and Peasants: A Collection of South African Poems about Poverty 198 n.1
Herbstein, Manu 20
Herman Charles Bosman Prize 13 n.3, 28, 35, 42, 43, 58, 86
Hertzog Prize 107, 226
Heyns, Michiel 45–6, 51, 52, 56, 59
   Bodies Politic 1, 13 n.3, 26, 27, 30, 35–6, 37 n.4, 42, 56
   The Children's Day 55–6, 65, 339
   The Reluctant Passenger 340, 366
   The Typewriter's Tale 56
Heywood, Christopher 6
Higginson, Craig 20
   Dream of the Dog 148
   The Hill 339–40
Higgs, Colleen 190
Hilton-Barber, Bridget
   The Garden of my Ancestors 113
Hiroshima Foundation Award for Peace and Culture 225
Hirson, Denis 265
   The House Next Door to Africa 265
   I Remember King Kong (The Boxer) 265
   We Walk Straight So You Had Better Get out the Way 265
   White Scars: On Reading and Rites of Passage 75, 265
Hirson, Denis (ed.)
   The Lava of This Land 198 n.3
Hlalethwa, Ramaphakela 274–5
   I Listen, I Learn, I Grow 275
Hlongwane, Gugu 105
Hobbs, Stephen *see* Machen, Peter & Stephen Hobbs
Hodie, Thembi G. 305
Hofmeyr, Isabel 3, 5, 7, 22, 251, 288, 293
Hofmeyr, Isabel & Liz Gunner 22
Hollander, John 329
Holomisa, Bantu 250
Homan, Greg 139
   At this Stage: Plays from Post-Apartheid South Africa 148
Homer
   The Odyssey 61
Horn, Peter 121, 178, 179–80, 190
Horrell, Georgina 72, 106, 107
Horwitz, Allan Kolski 197 n.1, 199 n.7, 254
Horwitz, Allan Kolski & Darryl Accone 199 n.7
House of Memory 77
Huggan, Graham & Helen Tiffin 357
Hugo, Daniel 208
Hugo, Daniel, Leon Rousseau & Phil du Plessis (eds)
   Nuwe verset 210
Human & Rousseau 21
Hunter, Eva 107, 110, 115 n.1
Hutchinson, Shaun 164
Huxley, Aldous
   Brave New World 348
Hymes, Dell 245–6

Ibsen, Henrik 151
Ilanga 301
Indigenous Languages Publishing Project 312 n.1
Injula Co-operative 198 n.1
In My Country 225
Institute for Justice and Reconciliation 226
International Museums Study Programme 244

Ionesco, Eugène   159
Isaacson, Maureen   14 n.10, 79–80, 121, 127, 133 n.2
Isidingo   67 n.7
ISLE   360, 364
Isolezwe   301
Iziko Museum   244

Jacana Media   21
Jackson, Samuel L.   225
Jacobs, J.U.   286, 319
Jacobs, J.U. (jt.ed.)   *see* Bell, David & J.U. Jacobs (eds)
Jacobs, J.U. (jt.ed.)   *see* Coullie, Judith Lütge & J.U. Jacobs (eds)
Jacobs, Rayda   20, 115, 269
  Confessions of a Gambler   344
  Masquerade   269
  The Mecca Diaries   269
Jaffer, Zubeida
  Our Generation   265
Jamal, Ashraf   4, 5, 20, 335
James, Alan   194, 237, 365
James, Henry   56
Jameson, Fredric   10
Jansen, Emile   198 n.6
Jarry, Alfred
  Ubu Roi   146
Jauss, Hans Robert   8
Jele, Cynthia   84
  Happiness is a Four-Letter Word   84
Jenkins, Elwyn   367
Jenkins, Myesha   197 n.1
Jennings, Humphrey   74
Jobson, Liesl   190, 348
Johnson, Sarah   184
Johnson, Shaun   20
Jolly, Rosemary (jt.ed.)   *see* Attridge, Derek & Rosemary Jolly (eds)
Jonathan Ball   21
Jones, Basil   145–6
Jong, Erica   236
Jooste, Pamela   81

Jordaan, Bobby   *see* Donaldson, Andrew, Bobby Jordaan & André Jurgens
Joubert, Marlise   213
  'bedding'   213
  'Lapis lazuli'   213
  Lyfsange   213
  'oorsprong'   213
Journal of Commonwealth Literature   262
Journal of Literary Studies
  18(1/2) 2002 & 19(3/4) 2002: [theme issue]   13 n.1
  19(3/4) 2003 & 20(1/2) 2004: [theme issue]   13 n.1
  25(1) 2009 & 25(2) 2009: [theme issue]   262
Joyce, James   44, 218
Judin, Hilton   75
Judin, Hilton (jt.ed.)   *see* Vladislavić, Ivan & Hilton Judin (eds)
Jung, Carl Gustav   171
Jurgens, André   *see* Donaldson, Andrew, Bobby Jordaan & André Jurgens
Jurgens, Richard   272

Kabwe, Mwenya (B.)   167, 169, 173, 174 n.5
  Do Not Leave Your Baggage Unattended   169
Kafka, Franz   64
Kaganof, Aryan   20, 193, 195
  'Vileness'   193
Kagiso   300–1
Kambrogi   73
Kamfer, Ronelda   204, 206, 209–10, 217
  'die huisvrou'   205
  'Klein Cardo'   205
  Noudat slapende honde   205, 207, 209, 217
  'Pick 'n Pa'   217
  'vergewe my maar ek is Afrikaans'   207, 210
KaMgiba, B.
  'Bengimthanda Ngimethemba'   310
  'Qhawe Lamaqhawe'   309

Index

KaMgiba, B. & D. Ntuli (eds)   309
   Phezu Komkhono!   310
Kani, John
   Nothing but the Truth   147
Kaplan, Carol   142, 150–1
Karodia, Farida   296 n.2
Kaschula, Russell H.   243, 246, 247–8, 249
Kaschula, Russell H. & Christine Anthonissen   245
Kaschula, Russell H., Mandla Matyumza & Bongani Sitole
   Qhiwu-u-u-la!! Return to the Fold!!   248, 249, 250
Kasrils, Ronnie   2, 61, 268
Kathrada, Ahmed M.   265, 266, 268
   Memoirs   286
Kearney, J.A.   14 n.13
Keitseng, 'Fish'   269
Kellas, Anne   69
Keller, Lynn   220 n.1
Kemp, Jenny   173
Kendal, Rosamund   20
   Karma Suture   111–12, 114
Kentridge, William   145
Kgosidintsi, Mbali   4–5
   Tseleng: The Baggage of Bags   169, 174 n.7
Khan, Aisha   327
Khan, Deela (jt.ed.)   *see* Ndlovu, Malika, Shelley Barry & Deela Khan (eds)
Khoisan, Zenzile   272
Khulumani Support Group   145
Khumalo, Alf   263
Khumalo, Duma   145
Khumalo, Fred   20, 79, 341
   Seven Steps to Heaven   341–2
   Touch My Blood   265
Khumalo, Mbongeni   197 n.1
Khuzwayo, Zazah
   Never Been at Home   267
Kiba song and dance   253
Kikamba, Simmao
   Going Home   264
Kingsolver, Barbara   359

Kirkwood, Mike   29, 74
Kissack, Mike   21
Klatzow, David   153
Kleyn, Leti   203
Klopper, Dirk   368 n.1
Kohler, Adrian   145–6
Kombuis, Koos   27
Konile, Notrose Nobomvu   237–8, 240
Kossew, Sue   124
Kota, Nosipho   197 n.1
Kozain, Rustum
   'Winter 2003'   189
Kraak, Gerald   20
   Ice in the Lungs   341
Krech, Shepard   358
Krige, Uys   237
Krog, Antjie   9, 24–5, 52, 92 n.1, 106, 107, 109, 114, 146, 188, 194, 198 n.4, 199 n.9, 206, 208, 210, 212, 213, 224–7, 233, 234, 236, 237, 239–40, 271, 365
   'aankoms'   229
   'afskeid'   228
   Begging to be Black   107, 226, 240, 271
   Beminde Antarktika   227, 230
   Body Bereft   194, 199 n.9, 213, 230, 231, 232–3, 234, 235, 238, 240
   A Change of Tongue   106, 107, 224, 226, 229–30, 233–4, 235, 238, 271, 276 n.1
   Country of my Skull   24, 106–7, 194, 225, 226, 228, 231, 233, 234, 238, 263
   'dagboeke uit die laaste deel van die twintigste eeu'   228
   Dogter van Jefta   227, 230
   Down to my Last Skin   206, 225
   'Four seasonal observations of Table Mountain'   232, 235
   Gedigte 1989–1995   227, 230–1, 233
   'God, Death, Love'   194, 232
   'how do you say this'   194
   'it is true'   194
   'it might have been a jellytot'   235

Januarie-suite 227, 230
Jerusalemgangers 227, 230
'klaaglied' 228, 239
Kleur kom nooit alleen nie 206, 210, 212, 213, 214, 226, 227–9, 230, 231, 240
Lady Anne 227, 230
'land van genade en verdriet' 206
'Lied van Peter Labase' 230
'manifesto of a grandma' 235
Mannin 227, 230
Met woorde soos met kerse 212, 236
'Narrative of the diamond sorter' 228
'Niks by te voeg' 228
'onthemelde' 232
Otters in bronslaai 227, 230
'ses narratiewe uit die Richtersveld' 212, 227–8, 236
die sterre sê 'tsau'/the stars say 'tsau' 212, 231, 236, 238
'toilet poem' 233
'van litteken tot stad' 206
'verskrikking'/'terror' 233
Verweerskrif 194, 213, 214, 216, 220 n.5, 230, 231, 232–3, 234, 240
'Wondweefsel' 213
Krog, Antjie, Nosisi Mpolweni & Kopano Ratele
    There Was This Goat: Investigating the Truth Commission Testimony of Notrose Nobomvu Konile 107, 226, 237 8, 240
Kruger, Loren 3, 4, 26, 162, 166–7
Kruiper, Belinda 274 *see also* Bregin, Elana & Belinda Kruiper
Kruiper, Vetkat 274
Kunapipi
    24(1&2) 2002: [theme issue] 13 n.1
Kunene, R.M. (Mazisi) 308, 358
Kunstfest (Weimar) 145
Kupe, Tawana (jt.ed.) *see* Hassim, Shireen, Tawana Kupe & Eric Worby (eds)
Kuzwayo, Ellen 99, 268
Kwani? 246

kwani.org/ 256 n.3
Kwela Books 20, 198 n.5

Labuschagne, Riaan 268
Laden, Sonja (jt.ed.) *see* De Kock, Leon, Louise Bethlehem & Sonja Laden (eds)
La Fleur, Madame 54
La Guma, Alex
    A Soviet Journey 10
Lalsa, Golaba 294
Landau, Julia 276 n.2
Landsman, Anne 9, 27
    The Rowing Lesson 1, 12, 13 n.2, 26, 30, 37 n.4, 42, 113
Landzelius, Kyra 245
Langa, Hazel
    Ngiyabonga 305–6
Langa, Mandla 92 n.1
    The Lost Colours of the Chameleon 31, 42
    The Memory of Stones 10
Langalibalele, John
    Jeqe, Insila ka Tshaka 312 n.1
    Jeqe, the Body-Servant of King Shaka 312 n.1
Lanoye, Tom
    Mamma Medea 236
Larssen, Stieg 110
Laurie, Trienkie
    Uitroep 216
Leavis, F.R. 8
Ledwaba, Lucas 77
Lee, Sumayya
    The Story of Maha 284
Le Fleurs 54
Lejeune, Philippe 262
Lenta, Margaret 97, 100, 262
    'Expanding "South Africanness": Debut Novels' 97
Leon, Tony 269–70
Leroux, Etienne
    Magersfontein, o Magersfontein! 66 n.1
Le Roux, Willemien & Allison White (eds)
    Voices of the San 274
Le Vaillant, François 365

Index

Levey, David & Chris Mann   186
Levinas, Emmanuel   14 n.6, 47
Levy, Barry
   Burning Bright   339
Levy, Lorna
   Radical Engagements   273
Lewin, Hugh
   Bandiet   269
Lewis, Earl   329
Lewis, Simon   133 n.1
Library Services (KwaZulu-Natal)   301
Liebenberg, Lauren   20
Lindberg-Wada, G. (ed.)
   Studying Transcultural Literary History   37 n.11
Lipman, Alan
   On the Outside Looking in: Colliding with Apartheid and Other Authorities   273
Literature and Ecology Colloquium   362, 363–4
LitNet   246
Livingstone, Douglas   73, 182, 183, 190, 363, 365
   A Littoral Zone   365
Lloyd, Lucy C. (jt.ed.)   *see* Bleek, W.H.I. & Lucy C. Lloyd (eds)
Lloyd-Bleek archive   365
London Book Fair   92 n.1
London International Festival of Theatre   145
Lopez, Barry   359
Lossgott, Kai & Mbali Vilakazi   198 n.6
Lottering, Agnes
   Winnefred and Agnes   266
Lotz, Sarah   48
Louw, N.P. van Wyk   *see* Van Wyk Louw, N.P.
Louw, Pat & Travis Mason (eds)   63
Love, Glenn A.
   Practical Ecocriticism   361
Lovejoy, Alex   267
   Acid Alex   274
Loxion   92 n.2
Lyotard, Jean-François   162

Maart, Rozena   20
MacDonald, Andrew   293, 294
Machen, Peter & Stephen Hobbs   86
Machika, Phomelelo   197 n.1
Machobane, James
   Drive out Hunger   273
MacKenzie, Craig   13, 32
Mackenzie, Jassie   20
Maclennan, Don   182–3
Madikizela-Mandela, Winnie   59, 269
Madingoane, Ingoapele   184
Madlala, Bhekimpi   *see* Madlala, Ntokozo & Bhekimpi Madlala
Madlala, Ntokozo & Bhekimpi Madlala   199 n.6
Magnet Theatre   170
   Every Day, Every Year I Am Walking   169
Magomola, Gaby   274–5
Magona, Sindiwe   9, 99, 101, 105, 115
   Beauty's Gift   83–4, 102–3, 104, 105–6, 114, 115 n.4
   'It was Easter Sunday the Day I Went to Netreg'   105
   Living, Loving, and Lying Awake at Night   98, 101, 105
   Mother to Mother   105
   To My Children's Children   262
Mahala, Siphiwo   98–9
   When a Man Cries   57, 58, 61
Maharaj, Mac
   Shades of Difference   286
Mahola, Mzi
   'Being Human'   189
   'In Memoriam Sizwe Kondile'   189
Mail & Guardian '100 Best Books of the Twentieth Century'   312 n.1
Maja-Pearce, Adewale   137
Majola, N., H. Nqcongo & D. Ntuli (eds)
   Ziyokwesulwa Izinyembezi   302
Makgoba, Malegapuru William   48
Makhambeni, Ncamisile, Gugu Mazibuko & Thokozani Shabalala (eds)
   Umuntu Akalahlwa   302

Makhambeni, N.M.   305
Makholwa, Angela   99
   Red Ink   102, 103, 111, 115
Malan, Lucas   214
   Afstande   214, 215, 216
   'Bestek: 2009'   214
   'Genepoel'   214
   'Kuslangs: groen gedagtes'   215
   Vermaning   216
Malan, Magnus   261, 268
Malange, Nise   121
Malema, Julius   120
Malepe, Lesego   99
Maluleke, Tinyiko Sam   154
Malusi, Omphile   163
   Itsoseng   163–4, 165, 169
Mam Catherine   145
Mamdani, Mahmood   33
Mamet, Claudia   295
Man-Booker Prize   33
Mandela, Nelson   121, 139, 153, 154, 203, 235, 236, 249, 253, 262, 265–6, 273, 309
   Long Walk to Freedom   235, 269, 270
Mandela, Winnie   *see* Madikizela-Mandela, Winnie
Manganyi, Chabani   259
Mangope, Lucas   163
Mankell, Henning   110
Mann, Chris   186, 193
   'Carpark Oyster-sellers'   183
   Heartlands   183, 193
   'Heraclitan Heresies'   193
Mannur, Anita (jt.ed.)   *see* Braziel, Jana Evans & Anita Mannur (eds)
Marais, Danie   204, 211, 218
   In die buitenste ruimte   204–5, 209
Marais, Eugène   237
   Dwaalstories   237
Marais, Johann Lodewyk   214–15
   Aves   214–15
   Plaaslike kennis   215

Marais, Loftus   198 n.6, 204, 213, 218–19
   'Die anatomie van M'   214
   'Die digter as rockstar'   218
   ' 'n Pleidooi vir vinniger kuns'   218–19
   Staan in die algemeen nader aan vensters   213–14, 218
Markowitz, Arthur   237
   'The Broken String'   237
   With Uplifted Tongue   237
Marnewick, Chris   20
   Shepherds and Butchers   30, 42, 62
Marshall, Christine   199 n.9
Martin, Julia   355, 358, 361, 362, 363, 368 n.1
   'The Jewelled Net'   362
   A Millimetre of Dust   113–14
   'New, with Added Ecology? Hippos, Forests and Environmental Literacy'   362
Marx, Gerhard   146
Marx, Lesley   138
Masambe   170
Masekela, Barbara
   'Culture in the New South Africa'   13
Masekela, Hugh
   Still Grazing   266
Mashile, Lebogang   20, 197, 243, 253, 254
   'I smoked a spliff'   189–90
Mashinini, Emma   268
Maskew Miller Longman   300–1, 302
Mason, Richard   20
Mason, Travis (jt.ed.)   *see* Louw, Pat & Travis Mason (eds)
Matakata, Jama   270
Matanzima, K.D.   249–50
Mathabane, Miriam
   Miriam's Song   267
Mathe, Themba ka   197 n.1
Mathenjwa, L.F.
   Ithemba Lami   300
Mathenjwa, L.F. (ed.)
   Umcakulo   309

Index

Mathonsi, Nhlanhla   304, 309, 313 n.3
Mathuray, Mark   14 n.12
Matisse, Henri
   Portrait of Madame Matisse with a Green Stripe   330
Matlwa, Kopano   20, 51, 81, 99, 101
   Coconut   56–57, 58, 101–12, 114, 115
   Spilt Milk   57, 102
Matthee, Dalene   366
Matthews, James   121
Matyumza, Mandla   249 *see also* Kaschula, Russell H., Mandla Matyumza & Bongani Sitole
Mavundla, Nhlanhla   165, 166
   A Man and a Dog   163, 164–5, 166, 171
Mayat, Zuleikha   296 n.2
Mayekiso, A.C.T.   305
Maziboko, Nokuthula   99
Mazibuko, Gugu   309, 313 n.3
Mazibuko, Gugu (jt.ed.)   *see* Makhambeni, Ncamisile, Gugu Mazibuko & Thokozani Shabalala (eds)
Mbangeni, Jessica   198 n.6
Mbatha, Azaria
   Within Loving Memory of the Century   272, 275
Mbatha, F.F.
   'Umajuqa'   311
Mbatha, M.O.
   Ithemba Lingumanqoba   300
Mbeki, Thabo   120, 180, 249, 268, 270, 272
Mbembe, Achille   3 *see also* Nuttall, Sarah & Achille Mbembe
Mbhele, N.F.   308
Mbothwe, Mandla   162, 170, 173, 174 n.1
   Ingcwaba lendoda lise cankwe ndlela   159, 161, 162, 169, 172–3
McClintock, Anne   357
McDonald, Peter D.   5
McGregor, Liz & Sarah Nuttall (eds)
   At Risk   267
   Load-Shedding   267

Mda, Zakes   9, 27, 82, 92 n.1, 121, 147, 315
   'The Bells of Amersfoort'   170
   Cion   322–3, 324
   The Heart of Redness   363
   The Madonna of Excelsior   290–1
   Ways of Dying   85, 322
   The Whale Caller   363, 366
Mdakane, Zinhle
   No Way Out   267
Medalie, David   32, 51, 52
   The Mistress's Dog   63
   The Shadow Follows   63
Meer, Fatima   268, 296 n.2
   Prison Diary   286
Meer, Ismael C.   265–6, 268
   A Fortunate Man   286
Meeran, Zinaid   20
   Saracen at the Gates   43
Meersman, Brent   160, 162–3, 171
Mehta, Brinda
   Diasporic (Dis)Locations   293–4
Meihuizen, Nick   183, 192
Meintjes, Sheila (jt.ed.)   *see* Daymond, M.J., Dorothy Driver & Sheila Meintjes (eds)
Melville, Herman
   Moby Dick   291
Memela, Sandile
   Flowers of the Nation   61
Mercator, Gerard   215
Merleau-Ponty, Maurice   359
Metaphysical Poets   192
Metelerkamp, Joan   178–80, 182, 186, 188–9, 196
   Requiem   196
Meyer, Deon   34, 92 n.1, 111
Mgiba, B. ka   *see* KaMgiba, B.
Mgqolozana, Thando
   A Man Who Is Not a Man   11–12, 115 n.4, 165–6, 171
Mgwaba, Philani   121
Mgxashe, Mxolisi 'Ace'   270
Mhlaba, Raymond   268

Mhlanga, E.J. (jt.ed.) *see* Thwala, J.J. &
    E.J. Mhlanga (eds)
Mhlongo, B.K. 308
Mhlongo, Niq 20, 69, 76–8, 79–80, 81, 86
    After Tears 77, 78, 79
    Dog Eat Dog 77–8, 79
Mhlophe, Gcina 167, 243, 253
Michael, Cheryl-Ann *see* Nuttall, Sarah &
    Cheryl-Ann Michael
Microsoft 252–3
Milkowski, Tomasz *see* Osterloff, Barbara &
    Tomasz Milkowski
Miller, Andie 70
Miller, Henry 236
Miller, Kirsten 20
    All is Fish 113
Miller, Nancy K. 262
Miller, Philip
    *REwind: A Cantata: for Voice, Tape and
    Testimony* 146–7, 155
Minyeni, Eric 198 n.6
Mishra, Vijay 285, 291, 292, 325
Miya, Eunice Tsepiso 146
Mkhabela, Sibongile 265, 270
    Open Earth and Black Roses 265
Mkhize, Piwe
    Back to Nature 368
Mkiva, Zolani 243, 249, 253, 254, 256
M-Net Literary Award for Afrikaans Fiction
    37 n.4 & n.7, 107
M-Net Literary Award for Fiction in English
    13 n.2, 26–7, 28–9, 29–33, 36, 37 n.4,
    n.7, n.9 & n.12, 42, 43, 58, 107
Mngadi, M.J. 300
    Asikho Ndawo Bakithi 306
    Iziboshwa Zothando 306
Mngadi, R.M.
    Ababulali Benyathi 306
Mngxitama, Andile 163
Modern Fiction Studies
    46(1) 2000: [theme issue] 13 n.1
Modigliani, Amedeo
    Little Girl in Blue 330

Modjaji Books 21
Moele, Kgebetli 20, 69
    The Book of the Dead 43, 89–90
    'Book of the Dead' 9–90
    'Book of the Living' 89
    Room 207 86–9, 92
Moffett, Helen 190
    Lovely beyond Any Singing 364
Mogoba, Stanley 269
Mohlabeng, Alex 197 n.1
Mohlele, Nthikeng 20
Mokgora, *Justice* Yvonne 268
Molope, Lesego Kagiso 99
    Dancing in the Dust 101, 103
    The Mending Season 101, 103
Momoniat, Yunus *see* Zvomuya, Percy &
    Yunus Momoniat
Moodley, Praba 290
    Follow Your Heart 290
    The Heart Knows No Colour 290
Moolman, Kobus 195
Moore-Gilbert, Bart 262
Moran, Shane 14 n.11
Moretti, Franco 34–5, 36, 203
Morgan, Alistair
    Sleeper's Wake 43
Morgan, Jonathan (et al.) 273
    Finding Mr Madini 62, 64–5, 264
Morphet, Tony 69, 74
Morris, Meaghan 81
Morris, Terry 83
Mostert, André 245
Mostert, Noël
    Frontiers 2
Motadinyane, Isabella 197 n.1
Motana, Nape á
    Fanie Fourie's Lobola 61, 63, 65
Mpe, Phaswane 9, 20, 52, 66 n.6, 83
    Welcome to Our Hillbrow 60–2, 82–3, 88
Mphahlele, Es'kia 19, 77, 259
    Down Second Avenue 66 n.4, 259
    'Mrs Plum' 196

Index

Mphahlele, Letlapa 270
Mpolweni, Nosisi *see* Krog, Antjie, Nosisi Mpolweni & Kopano Ratele
Mqhayi, S.E.K. 254, 358
Msimang, C.T. 308
Msimang, Nelisile T.
   Umsebenzi Uyindlala 307
Msimango, Ziphezinhle 77, 79
Mtshali, Thembi 140–1 *see also* Farber, Yael & Thembi Mtshali
Mtshwane
   'Isingxobo' 239
Mtuze, Peter
   An Alternative Struggle 273
Mtwa, Percy, Bongeni Ngema & Barney Simon
   Woza Albert! 67
Mugabe, Robert 120
Muila, Ike Mboni 193, 197 n.1, 254
Muir, John 359
Muishond, Tereska 198 n.6
Müller, Petra
   Die aandag van jou oë 216
Multichoice 29
Munro, Brenna 338, 342
Mureinik, Etienne 260
Murray, Ian
   For the Wings of a Dove 339
Murray, Sally-Ann 13, 20, 190–1, 366
   'After Douglas' 190
   'Mbilo' 191
   Small Moving Parts 2, 28, 36, 42, 43, 44–46, 48, 58
   'Vigour Mortis: an interminable domestic epic of life & death' 191
Mynhardt, Patrick 264
   Boy from Bethulie 264
Myspace 245

Naess, Arne 359
Naidoo, Geraldine
   Chilli Boy 166, 286
   Hoot 166–7
Naidoo, Indres 296 n.2

Naidoo, Jay 296 n.2
   Coolie Location 285
Naidoo, Muthal 296 n.2
Naidoo, Nadine 296 n.2
Naidoo, Phyllis 287, 296 n.2
Naidoo, Riason
   Indian Ink: The Indian in Drum *Magazine in the 1950s* 289–90
   'Meet the Indian in South Africa' 290
Naipaul, V.S. 292
Nandipha, Khuthala 151
Nash, Kate 24
Nash, Roderick
   Wilderness and the American Mind 367
Nasou Via Afrika 249, 301
Naspers 300–1
National Arts Council 184, 198 n.5
National Arts Festival (Grahamstown) 4, 12, 140, 142, 143, 144, 145, 147, 148, 149, 150, 168, 246
National Library Reprint of South African Classics Project 312 n.1
National Lottery 198 n.5
Natland, Yngvar *see* Goodnow, Katherine J. & Yngvar Natland
Naudé, Charl-Pierre 204, 205
   In die geheim van die dag 205
   'Hoe ek my naam gekry het (of: 'n Beknopte relaas van kolonisasie)' 205
Naudé, Johan
   Making the Cut 273
Ndebele, Njabulo S. 4, 5, 52, 59–60, 61, 65, 81, 101, 103–4, 106, 122, 161, 182
   The Cry of Winnie Mandela 58–9, 61, 65, 173
   'The Year of the Dog' 166
Ndletyana, Mcebisi (ed.)
   African Intellectuals in 19th and Early 20th Century South Africa 102
Ndlovu, Lilinda ka 197 n.1
Ndlovu, Malika 195
   A Coloured Place 174 n.4
   Invisible Earthquake 267

Ndlovu, Malika, Shelley Barry & Deela Khan (eds)
  ink@boilingpoint 198 n.1
Ndungane, Njongonkulu 269
Neruda, Pablo 218
New Africa Books 20
New Contrast 366
Newton, Lara Foot *see* Foot Newton, Lara
New York Times 77
Nfah-Abbenyi, Juliana 98, 99, 100
Ngcobo, B.
  Amandla Esambane 302, 313 n.2
Ngcobo, Lauretta 99
Ngculu, James
  The Honour to Serve: Recollections of an Umkhonto Soldier 268
Ngema, Bongeni *see* Mtwa, Percy, Bongeni Ngema & Barney Simon
Nghalaluma, Wisani 197 n.1
Ngidi, Sandile 312 n.1
Ngobeni, Solani 86–7
Ngqoko Cultural Group 149
Ngubane, S.E. (ed.)
  Izingwazi Zanamuhla 311
Ngwabeni, Pam 143–4 *see also* Hayes, Peter & Pam Ngwabeni
Ngwenya, Siphiwe ka 197 n.1, 254
Ngwenya, Siphiwe ka (jt.ed.) *see* Finlay, Alan & Siphiwe ka Ngwenya (eds)
Nhleko, S.
  Kusa Kusa 307
Nicholls, Brendan 69
Nicol, Mike 20, 111
  Out to Score 111
  Payback 111
Nieuwoudt, Stephanie 214
Nkutha, Lindiwe 348
  'The Glass Pecker' 348
Nobel Peace Prize 120
Nobel Prize for Literature 9, 11, 22, 119, 120, 132, 292, 317, 335
Noma Award for Publishing in Africa 85

Nqcongo, H. (jt.ed.) *see* Majola, N., H. Nqcongo & D. Ntuli (eds)
Ntantala, Phyllis 268
Ntshingila, Futhi 20
  Shameless 56, 57
Ntuli, D. (jt.ed.) *see* Majola, N., H. Nqcongo & D. Ntuli (eds)
Ntuli, D. (jt.ed.) *see* KaMgiba, B. & D. Ntuli (eds)
Ntuli, Danisile 305
Ntuli, D.B.Z. 308
  Isibhakabhaka 300
  'Mhleli' 300
Ntuli, D.B.Z. (ed.)
  Amadlelo Aluhlaza 303
Ntuli, D.B.Z. & C.F. Swanepoel
  Southern African Literature in African Languages: A Concise Historical Perspective 312 n.1
Ntuli, N.S. (jt.ed.) *see* Sibiya, N.G. & N.S. Ntuli (eds)
Nutrend 302
Nuttall, Sarah 2, 3, 21, 76, 84, 92 n.2, 267
  Entanglement: Literary and Cultural Reflections on Post-apartheid 3, 37 n.3, 70, 71, 77, 354
Nuttall, Sarah & Achille Mbembe 85–6
Nuttall, Sarah & Cheryl-Ann Michael 262
Nuttall, Sarah (jt.ed.) *see* Darian-Smith, Kate & Sarah Nuttall (eds)
Nuttall, Sarah (jt.ed.) *see* McGregor, Liz & Sarah Nuttall (eds)
Nxaba, Condy
  Siyogcinaphi Uma Kunje? 306
  Umdonsiswano 306–7
Nxumalo, O.E.H.M. 308
Nyembezi, Sibusiso
  Inkinsela Yase Mgungundlovu 312 n.1
  The Rich Man of Pietermaritzburg 312 n.1
Nyezwa, Mxolisi
  'for days I looked for my poems' 189
Nyoka, Mtutulezi
  I Speak to the Silent 51, 57–8, 65, 100

Index

O'Brien, Anthony 133 n.1
O'Brien, Susie 357
Odendaal, Bernard 204, 206, 207–8
   'Gesog' 207
   Onbedoelde land 207, 210, 214, 217
Odendaal, B.J. 203, 212
Oguibe, Olu 81
Olive Schreiner Literary Award 27, 42, 43
Olivier, Fanie 210
Olney, James 259, 262
Olukotun, Deji 91–2
O'Malley, Padraig 286
Ong, Walter J. 246, 248
Opland, Jeff 247, 249
Opperman, D.J. 218, 230
   'Digter' 218–19
Oral Literature Project (OLP) 251, 252
Orford, Margie 110–11, 276 n.2
   Blood Rose 111
   Fifteen Men 110, 276 n.2
   Like Clockwork 111
Orr, Wendy 272
Ortiz, Fernando 3
Orwell, George
   1984 348
Osterloff, Barbara & Tomasz Milkowski 160
Ouédraogo, Jean-Bernard 358
Ozaniec, Naomi 126

Padayachee, Deena 296 n.2
Page, Colleen-Joy 273
Pamberi Trust 246
Pankhurst family 56
Parenzee, Donald 197 n.1
Parker Lewis, Helen
   The Prison Speaks 274
Patel, Essop 296 n.2
Pather, Jay 170
Paton, Alan 21
   Cry, the Beloved Country 61
Pauw, Jacques 270
   Little Ice Cream Boy 42, 49
Payne, Katy 362

Pechey, Laura 362
Peimer, David (ed.)
   Armed Response: Plays from South Africa 148
Penguin South Africa 20
Penguin South Africa Modern Classics Series 312 n.1
Penny, Sarah 20, 106
Perec, Georges
   Species of Spaces and Other Pieces 75
Petersen, Patrick 210
Petersen, Robin M. *see* Botman, H. Russel & Robin M. Petersen
Phewa, Asandi 4–5, 172
   A Face Like Mine 4, 167–9, 174 n.6
Philander, P.J. 216
   Trialoog 211
Picador Africa 20
Picasso, Pablo 213, 332
   The Frugal Meal 330
   Guernica 331
Pienaar, François 153
Pienaar, Hans 109
Pieterse, Henning
   Die burg van Hertog Bloubaard 216
Pillay, Hamish Hoosen 20
Pillay, Kriben 296 n.2
Pillay, Verashini 154
Pinnock, Don 366
Pinnock, Patricia Schonstein 315
   Skyline 327–8, 329–32
Pithouse, Richard *see* Desai, Ashwin & Richard Pithouse
Plomer, William 10, 22
   Turbott Wolfe 335
Poetics Today 2
Poetry Africa Festival (Durban) 198 n.6, 246
Pogrund, Benjamin 270
Poland, Marguerite 358
Poovalingam, Pat
   Anand 290–1
Pope, Alexander 177–8

Popescu, Monica 69
  South African Literature beyond the Cold War
  8–10
Potlatinsky, Ashlee 262
Potts, Donna L. & Amy D. Unsworth (eds)
  14 n.13
Power, Cormac 160, 162
Power, Michael
  Shadow Game 339
Poyner, Jane 14 n.9, 104
Press, Karen 182, 186
  The Little Museum of Working Life 186
  'She came home every night and went
    straight into the kitchen' 186
Prince Ndabuko Creative Solutions 302
Pringle, Thomas 10, 358–9, 365
Prins, Johannes
  Een hart 210–11
prisons see Correctional Service Centres
Propp, V. 245–6
Proust, Marcel 44
Prozesky, Martin (jt.ed.) see Brown, Judith
  & Martin Prozesky (eds)
Pruschenck, Viola 254
Publications Control Board 66 n.1
Publishers' Association of South Africa (PASA)
  301

Quayson, Ato 324–5
Queen, Carol & Lawrence Schimel (eds)
  336

Rabelais, François 234
Rabie, Susan 20
Rabinowitz, Ivan 361
Raditlhalo, Sam 78, 79, 86–7, 88, 262
Rak, Julie 262
Ram, Anjali see Bhatia, Sunil & Anjali Ram
Ramphele, Mamphela 126–7, 181, 268
Rampolokeng, Lesego 180, 184, 186, 254
  'In Transition' 255
  see also Rodwell, Bobby with Lesego
    Rampolokeng & Robert Coleman

Ramsden, Tim
  Border-Line Insanity 268
Rand Afrikaans University (RAU) Prize 226
Randeria, Shalini 24
Random House 198 n.5
Rankin, Ian 110
Rapola, Zachariah 85–6
  Beginnings of a Dream 84–5
  'Street Features' 85
Rapport Prize 226
Ratele, Kopano 86–7 see also Krog, Antjie,
    Nosisi Mpolweni & Kopano Ratele
Ravan Press 66 n.1, 73
Reddy, Jayapraga 296 n.2
Reeves, Ambrose 75
Reina Prinsen-Geerlings Prize 226
Reisenberg, Azila Talit 99–100
Remotewords 77, 79, 80, 81
Renoir, Pierre-Auguste
  Woman of Algiers 330
Resha, Maggie 268
Reznek, Jennie 169
Rhodes, Cecil John 360
Rhodes University 245, 362
  African Language Studies Section 251
  Computer Science Department 245
  School of Languages 251
Ribnick, Matthew 166
Rich, Adrienne 146, 188–9
Richards, I.A. 361
Richards, Jo-Anne 20, 109
  My Brother's Book 109
Richardson, Samuel
  Clarissa 291
Right 2 Speak 4–5, 12
Righteous Common Man 197 n.1
Rilke, Rainer Maria 232
Robb, Noël
  The Sash and I 270
Robben Island 270
Robins, Roy 191
Robinson, Iain Gregory see Ewok

Index

Robson, Jenny
   Savannah 2116 AD   367
Rodin, Auguste
   The Kiss   231
   She who once was the helmet-maker's beautiful wife   231–2
Rodwell, Bobbie *with* Lesego Rampolokeng & Robert Coleman
   The Story I'm about to Tell   145
Rooke, Daphne
   Ratoons   290
Roos, Henriette   286
Roos, Zuretha   273
Roose-Evans, James
   Experimental Theatre: From Stanislavsky to Peter Brook   159, 161
Rorke's Drift Art School   272
Rose, Jacqueline   133 n.2
Rose-Innes, Henrietta   20
   'Poison'   368
   The Rock Alphabet   25–6
Rosenthal, Jane   32–3, 37 n.5, 70–1, 86
   Souvenir   363, 367
Ross, Catriona   97, 106
Roth, Philip   236
Roup, Julian
   Boerejood   273
Rousseau, Henri
   Sleeping Gypsy   330
Rousseau, Leon (jt.ed.)   *see* Hugo, Daniel, Leon Rousseau & Phil du Plessis (eds)
Royal Shakespeare Company   163
Rueckert, William   360
Rugby World Cup   153–4
Rushdie, Salman   5
Russell, Alec   180–1
Rybicki, Ed   *see* Glenn, Ian & Ed Rybicki

Sachs, *Judge* Albie   4, 125, 139, 140, 155, 260, 270
   Free Diary   270
   The Strange Alchemy of Life and Law   43, 270

Safran, William   325, 326
Sam, Agnes   296 n.2
Sampson, Anthony   270
Samuelson, Meg   4, 5, 21, 37 n.3, 112
Sanders, Mark   3, 5
Sarif, Shamim
   The World Unseen   344–5
Scherzinger, Karen   31, 34
Schimel, Lawrence (jt.ed.)   *see* Queen, Carol & Lawrence Schimel (eds)
Schimke, Karin (ed.)
   Open: An Erotic Anthology by South African Women Writers   348
Schnitzler, Arthur
   Der Reigen   162
Schober, Anna   172
Schoeman, Karel   365
   Take Leave and Go   367
Schreffler, Brian   91
Schreiner, Olive   8, 10, 21
   The Story of an African Farm   6, 365
Schuster, Anne
   Foolish Delusions: A Novel Auto/biography   245
Schwartz, Larry
   The Wild Almond Line   273
Scotsman's Fringe First Award (Edinburgh)   164
Scott, Lara   77
Scrutiny2
   10(2) 2005: [theme issue]   13 n.1
Sebald, W.G.   75
Secker & Warburg   66 n.1
Sedgwick, Eve Kosofsky   336
Sepotela, Chuma   171
Serote, Mongane   181, 182
   History Is the Home Address   180
   Third World Express   179, 180
Sesanti, Simphiwe   270
Sestigers   22
Shabala, Thokozani (jt.ed.)   *see* Makhambeni, Ncamisile, Gugu Mazibuko & Thokozani Shabalala (eds)

Shaik, Schabir 184, 185
Shakespeare, William 364
   Macbeth 5
Shandu, N.T.B.
   'Ihabulankezo' 309–10
Shange, Maphili
   Ithemba Alibulali 305
   Uthando Lungumanqoba 305
Shapiro, Jonathan see Zapiro
Sharpeville Six 145
Shaw, Gerald 270
Sheckels, Theodore F.
   The Lion on the Freeway 356
Shell, Robert C-H.
   Children of Bondage 55
Sher, Antony 264
   Beside Myself 264, 265
Shezi, Thandi 145
Shields, David 47
Shukri, Ishtiyaq
   The Silent Minaret 63
Shuter & Shooter 21, 302, 305
Sibiya, E.D.M.
   Ngidedele Ngife 303–5
Sibiya, N.G. 302–3, 307
   'Amathe Ezimpukane' 307
   Bengithi Lizokuna 307
   'Ilanga Elishonayo' 300
   'Kungcono Ngife' 303
   Kuxolelwa Abanjani 303
   Kwaze Kwalukhuni 303
   'Ngeke' 307
   'Oqotsheni' 307
Sibiya, N.G. (ed.)
   Ikusasa Eliqhakazile 300, 307
   Wathint' Imbokodo 305
Sibiya, N.G. & N.S. Ntuli (eds)
   Izikhukhula 307
Sichel, Adrienne 151
Silinyana, Aubrey 368
Simon, Barney 160 see also Mtwa, Percy, Bongeni Ngema & Barney Simon
Simons, Jack 273

Sinclair, Iain 74
   Lights Out for the Territory: 9 Excursions in the Secret History of London 75
Singh, Ansuyah 296 n.2
Singh, Kogi 296 n.2
Singh, Robin 296 n.2
Sisulu, Max 274
Sisulu, Walter 266, 274
Sitas, Ari 4, 186
   The RDP Poems 198 n.1
Sithebe, Angelina (N.) 20, 99
   Holy Hill 58, 101, 103, 105
Sitole, Bongani 247, 248–9, 250, 251, 252, 253, 256 see also Kaschula, Russell H., Mandla Matyumza & Bongani Sitole
Siyakhulu Living Lab 245
Slabbert, Frederik van Zyl 269–70
Slaymaker, William 357
Slovic, Scott 364
Slovo, Gillian 92 n.1, 106
Smit, Johannes, Jean-Philippe Wade & Johan van Wyk (eds) 28
Smith, Alex 99, 100
   'Confidence Within (part 1)' 97
Smith, Charlene
   Proud of Me: Speaking Out against Sexual Violence and HIV 273
   see also De Lille, Patricia with Charlene Smith
Smith, David 78, 79
Smith, Malvern van Wyk see Van Wyk Smith, Malvern
Smith, Pauline 21
Smith, Prue
   The Morning Light 273
Smith, Sidonie 262
Snailpress 198 n.5
Snyder, Gary 362
Snyders, Peter 210, 211
   'Ek is siëker Die Bruinmense' 209
   Tekens van die tye 209, 211
Snyman, Judge Lammie 66 n.1

Index

Sole, Kelwyn 100, 109, 178, 180, 181, 185, 186, 187, 188–9, 196
   'Gardening tips' 186–7
   Land Dreaming 186–7
   'The State of South African Writing' 100
   'This is not a chain letter' 187
Sôls, Loit 211
   Die faraway klanke vanne hadeda 209
   'Goema II' 209
Somniso, Michael 239
Sookrajh, Reshma 296 n.2
SouthAfrica.info 69
South African Defence Force 166
South African NGO Coalition 198 n.1
South Atlantic Quarterly
   103(4) 2004: [theme issue] 13 n.1, 262
Soweto Heritage Trust 77
Soyinka, Wole 5
Spies, Lina 204, 208, 220 n.5
   Duskant die einders 209
Spinoza, Baruch 192
Springer, Michael 365
S.S. *Truro* 283
Staffrider 73, 179
Stalin, Josef 161
Stander, Carina 204, 213
   'Ewenaar' 213
   'Karkaskaal' 213
   Die vloedbos sal weer vlieg 213
Steenkamp, Elzette 368 n.1
Stegmann, George
   The Lights of Freedom 268
Steinberg, Jonny 92 n.1
   The Number 62, 274
   Three-Letter Plague 42
Steiner, George 237
Stevenson-Hamilton, James
   South African Eden 364
Sterchi, Beat
   The Cow 354
Stevens, Mariss 365
Steyn, Johan
   Father Michael's Lottery 62

Steyn, Melissa 14 n.11
Steyn, Melissa (jt.ed.) *see* Distiller, Natasha & Melissa Steyn (eds)
Steyn, Phia 356
Stiebel, Lindy 288
Stiebel, Lindy & Liz Gunner (eds) 14 n.13
Stobie, Cheryl 199 n.8, 262, 335, 342, 346
Stockenström, Wilma 182
Strachan, Harold 269
   Make a Skyf, Man! 269
Strauss, Peter 191
Street, B.V. 246, 248
Sunday Times 29
Sunday Times Alan Paton Prize 2, 42, 43, 72, 75
Sunday Times Fiction Prize 13 n.2 & n.3, 28, 37 n.7, 42, 43, 89, 113
Suttner, Raymond 269
Suzman, Janet 148
Swanepoel, C.F. *see* Ntuli, D.B.Z. & C.F. Swanepoel
Szczurek, Karina 89–90

Tagtigers 22
Taitz, Lawrence 70
Tambo, Oliver 265–6
Taylor, Charles
   Sources of the Self 259
Taylor, Jane
   The Transplant Men 43
   Ubu and the Truth Commission 145–6
Teague, David W. (jt.ed.) *see* Bennett, Michael & David W. Teague (eds)
Telkom Centre for Excellence 245
Thamm, Marianne 152
TheaterFormen Festival (Hanover) 148
Theatre for Africa 368
Themba, Can 77
Third World Bunfight 170
30 Degrees South 21
Thomas, Dylan 194
Thoreau, Henry 359
Thrift, Nigel 81

Thurman, Chris   172
Thwala, J.J.
    'Inkunzi Emnyama'   308–9
Thwala, J.J. & E.J. Mhlanga (eds.)
    Uphondo Lwemikhosi   308, 311
Tiffin, Helen   357, 364
Timbila Poetry Project   178, 184, 187,
    197 n.1, 198 n.1, 246
    Timbila 2001: A Journal of Onion Skin Poetry
    197 n.1
Titlestad, Michael   3, 21, 26–7, 37 n.3 & n.5,
    86
Titus, Marius   210
Tlali, Miriam   99
Tlholwe, Diale   20
Tobias, Philip
    Into the Past   273
Toerien, Barend   210, 211, 216, 230
    'Die egodokument'   217
    Die huisapteek   217
    'Tafereel, met kersieboord'   217
Tölölyan, Khachig   324
Torabully, Khal   294
Trinh Ti Minh-ha   98
Troost, Heinrich   20
Truth and Reconciliation Commission (TRC)
    1, 3, 9, 14 n.9, 100, 107, 137, 138, 139,
    140, 141, 144, 145, 146, 147, 148, 149,
    153, 155, 181, 187–8, 194, 206, 224,
    225, 234, 237–8, 263, 272, 285
Tryhorn, Chris & Richard Wray   83
Tshabangu, Mango   73
Tucker, Linda   362
Turin, Mark   243
Tutu, Archbishop Desmond   138, 139, 153–4,
    269
    No Future without Forgiveness   272

Umez, Uche Peter   79
Umlilo, Thandeki   266
Umtapo Publishers   302
Umuzi   20, 72, 198 n.5
Unisa Press
    'Hidden Histories'   274–5

University of Bergen   244
University of Cambridge   243
University of Johannesburg (UJ)   31, 32
University of Johannesburg (UJ) Literary
    Award   28, 29, 30–3, 35, 37 n.4 & n.7,
    42, 86, 107, 112
University of KwaZulu-Natal   48
University of KwaZulu-Natal Centre for
    Creative Arts   198 n.6
University of KwaZulu-Natal Press   21,
    198 n.1 & n.5
University of Pretoria   32
University of the Witwatersrand Institute for
    Social and Economic Research (WISER)
    267
Unsworth, Amy D. (jt.ed.)   see Potts, Donna
    L. & Amy D. Unsworth (eds)
Updike, John   236
Usiba Writers Guild   302
Uys, Pieter-Dirk   264
    Between the Devil and the Deep   264
    Elections and Erections   264, 273

Vahed, Goolam   see Desai, Ashwin &
    Goolam Vahed
Van Coller, H.P.   37 n.10
Van Coller, H.P. (ed.)   6
Van der Merwe, André Carl
    Moffie   340
Van der Merwe, Chris N. (jt.ed.)   see Viljoen,
    Hein & Chris N. van der Merwe (eds)
Van der Merwe, Hugo   see Hamber, Brandon
    & Hugo van der Merwe
Van der Merwe, J.W.   see Boerneef
Van der Post, Laurens   237, 358, 359, 365
Van der Vlies, Andrew
    South African Textual Cultures: White,
    Black, Read All Over   5–7, 8
Van der Vyver, Marita   27
Van de Werk, Jan Kees
    Karavaan van de verbeelding: Van Gorée
    naar Timboektoe   224
Van Dijk, Jan A.G.M.   245

Index

Van Graan, Mike 170
   Iago's Last Dance 170
Van Heerden, Etienne 34
   30 nagte in Amsterdam 26, 37 n.4
Van Houten, Gillian 362
Van Niekerk, Dolf 216
Van Niekerk, Marlene 34, 52, 81, 106, 109, 204
   Agaat 56, 63–4, 106, 107–9, 112, 115 n.3, 211
   Triomf 108, 115 n.3, 235
Van Rooyen, J. 66 n.1
Van Staden, Ilse 215
   Fluisterklip 215
   Watervlerk 215
Van Vuuren, Helize 37 n.10, 203–4, 230, 237
Van Woerden, Henk
   Domein van glas 236
Van Wyk, Chris 73, 263
   Shirley, Goodness and Mercy 265, 271
Van Wyk, Johan
   Man-Bitch 273
Van Wyk, Johan (jt.ed.) *see* Smit, Johannes, Jean-Philippe Wade & Johan van Wyk (eds)
Van Wyk Louw, N.P. 3, 218, 219
   'Die beiteltjie' 218, 227
   'Groot ode' 227
   'Klipwerk' 227
Van Wyk Smith, Malvern
   Grounds of Contest 356
Van Wynegaard, Annetjie 245
Van Zyl, Wium 220 n.4
Varney, Anna 197 n.1
Veit-Wild, Flora 254
Velasquez, Diego
   Las Meninas 332
Venter, Eben 27, 34
   Horrelpoot 211, 367
   Trencherman 211, 367
Vermeer, Johannes
   Allegory of Painting 332

Versindaba 203
Vilakazi, B.W. 308
Vilakazi, Mbali *see* Lossgott, Kai & Mbali Vilakazi
Viljoen, Hein & Chris N. van der Merwe (eds) 14 n.13
Viljoen, Louise 220 n. 4, 234, 235, 236
Villon, François
   'She who once was the helmet-maker's beautiful wife' 232
Visagie, Andries 203
Vital, Anthony 125, 126, 128, 130, 132, 133 n.2, 357, 363
Vital, Anthony & Hans-Georg Erney 357, 366
Vladislavić, Ivan 9, 20, 69, 72, 81, 83, 85, 92 n.1, 121
   'Author's Note' 74
   'Curiouser' 81
   Flashback Hotel 69–70
   'Itineraries' 74
   Missing Persons 69
   'Notes and Sources' 74
   Portrait with Keys: Joburg & What-What 69, 71, 72–6, 85, 90–2, 92 n.3, 365
   Propaganda by Monuments 10, 69
   'Writers' Book' 74
   'X Marks the Spot' 81
Vladislavić, Ivan & Hilton Judin (eds)
   blank: Architecture, Apartheid and After 75
Volner, Ian 91
Von Klemperer, Margaret 84

Wade, Jean-Philippe (jt.ed.) *see* Smit, Johannes, Jean-Philippe Wade & Johan van Wyk (eds)
Wagner, Peter
   Reading Iconotexts 329
W.A. Hofmeyr Prize 107
Walne, Helen 195–6
Walters, Brian
   'Weather Eye' 365
Walters, M.M. 216

Wanda, M.E.
  Kunjalo-ke 303
Wanner, Zukiswa 84, 99, 101, 104–5
  Behind Every Successful Man 84
  The Madams 84, 102, 104, 105, 115
  Men of the South 84
Warner, Michael 24, 336
Watson, Mary 115
Watson, Stephen 178, 186, 194, 198 n.4, 212, 231, 236, 237, 365
  Return of the Moon 212, 236
WEAVE Collective 178, 198 n.1
Webster, David 49
Weinberg, Paul 228
  'It takes a lot of God to survive here' 236
Weldon, Fay
  Letters to Alice on First Reading Jane Austen 31
Wenzel, Jennifer 14 n.12
Wessels, Andries 235
West, Mary
  White Women Writing White: Identity and Representation in (Post-) Apartheid Literatures of South Africa 115 n.2, 276 n.1
White, Allison (jt.ed.) *see* Le Roux, Willemien & Allison White (eds)
Whitebrook, Maureen 73
Wicomb, Zoë 9, 20, 51, 52, 59
  David's Story 10, 53, 54–5
  The One That Got Away 42, 66 n.3
  Playing in the Light 55
Willemse, Hein 210
Williams, Raymond
  Keywords 75
Willoughby, Guy
  Archangels 340
Winterbach, Ingrid 52
Wittenberg, Hermann 66 n.1
Wittgenstein, Ludwig 197
Wolf, Christa 120
Woodhouse, James 87
Woods, Donald 270

Woodward, Wendy 362, 363
  The Animal Gaze: Animal Subjectivities in South African Fiction 362
  'Sharing the Karma/For Chris' 192
Worby, Eric (jt.ed.) *see* Hassim, Shireen, Tawana Kupe & Eric Worby (eds)
Wordfest (Grahamstown) 246
Wordsworths 99
World Cup *see* FIFA World Cup
World Oral Literature Project 243
Woza Albert! *see* Mtwa, Percy, Bongeni Ngema & Barney Simon
Wray, Richard *see* Tryhorn, Chris & Richard Wray
www.botsotso.org.za 257 n.7
www.chimurenga.co.za 256 n.3
www.comminit.com/global/spaces-frontpage 256 n.2
www.gestform.it 256 n.5
www.kalavati.org/lebo-mashile.html 256 n.6
www.litnet.co.za 246
www.myspace.com/comradefatsoandchabvondoka 257 n.8
www.oralliterature.org 243
www.poetofafrica.com 256 n.6
www.poetryinternationalweb.org 256 n.1
www.technauriture.com 252, 256 n.4
www.technowledgeable.com/fingo/ 251
Wylie, Dan 133 n.2, 362
Wylie, Dan (ed.)
  Toxic Belonging? Ecology and Identity in Southern Africa 363

Xaba, B.S.F.
  'Ngculazi' 311
Xaba, Makhosazana 190, 198 n.1, 348
  'Cotton Socks' 190
  'Tongues of their Mothers' 190

Yai, Olabiyi 252
Yali-Manisi, D.L.P. 247
Y Culture 92 n.2
Yeats, William Butler 177–8, 193

Index

Yiswa, Fanisa 169, 173
Young, Hershini Bhana 294
   Haunting Capital 294
Young, Robert J.C. 12–13
YouTube 245

Zadok, Rachel 20
Zapiro 185
Zerbst, Fiona 190
Zikode, S'bu 174 n.3
   'We are the Third Force' 164
Zimema, S.
   Amasokisi 303
Zimunya, Musaemura 358

Zondi, L.
   Enceulu Kuyiphumuli 305
The Zone 84, 92 n.2
Zulu, E.S.Q. 308
Zulu, N.S. 300, 301
Zulu, William N.
   Spring Will Come 271–2
Zuma, Jacob 36, 120, 181, 184–5
   Umshini Wami 189
Zvomuya, Percy 14 n.10
Zvomuya, Percy & Yunus Momoniat 146, 155
Zwane, Gugu
   '*Isifundo*' 305